GUY WILLIAMS

The Man
Behind
the Mask

GUY WILLIAMS

The Man Behind the Mask

An Unauthorized Biography

by

Antoinette Girgenti Lane

BearManor Media
2005

Guy Williams, The Man Behind the Mask
© 2005 Antoinette Girgenti Lane

For information, address:

BearManor Media
P. O. Box 750
Boalsburg, PA 16827

bearmanormedia.com

Cover design by John Teehan

Typesetting and layout by John Teehan

Published in the USA by BearManor Media

ISBN—1-59393-016-X

Introduction

In Spring of 1988 I happened to catch an episode of *Zorro* on the Disney Channel. As it brought to mind childhood days when my younger brother used to watch this show, I decided to watch it just for the sake of nostalgia. Instead, I fell in love.

Guy Williams' dazzling smile and charm captivated my heart and I became possessed, watching and taping the show everyday until I saw every episode, every year. I wondered, like everyone else who had watched *Zorro* as a child, whatever happened to this wonderful actor who had thrilled children across the nation and obviously still was. After combing through bookstores and libraries to get answers, I discovered there was no authoritative biography written about this magnificent man. A few fluff articles could be found from his years at the Disney Studios and 20th Century Fox, but nothing about him after *Lost in Space*, with the exception of one 1985 article in a Disney magazine informing curious fans that Guy Williams was living in Argentina—a teaser, that opened more questions. I became obsessed with finding out more about him. I hoped to meet him, shake his hand, tell him I liked his work, and maybe ask him to write his autobiography. Then on Sunday, May 7, 1989 at the peak of my fever, I heard on the radio that Guy Williams had died in Buenos Aires. I was devastated. With no other fans to talk to I expressed my grief to the Los Angeles Times, who to my surprise printed my letter, with a picture of Guy Williams, as a final tribute to him.

As I heard myself saying, *"Someone* should write a book about him," an inner voice said, "Why not *me*!?" Guy was Italian. I am Italian. His ancestors came from Palermo, Sicily. Mine did too. His real last name was Catalano. My grandmother's maiden name was Catalanotto, a derivative of the same name. Guy was an actor. My husband is an actor. We shared the same ethic background, same religious upbringing, same roots, same ambitions. I felt these factors best qualified me for the job as they would provide me with insight into Guy's personality, and an inherent understanding of his motivations, his behavior, his wants, needs, hopes, dreams, and disappointments.

When a person sets his sights on a goal, that kind of arrow-straight focus opens doors. People you need to meet cross your path, and information falls into your hands, such as film clips, videos of old TV shows, documents, magazine articles, and pictures. You are guided by instinct, the powers that be, and loyal friends.

One such loyal friend to whom I tip my hat is Kathy Gregory. I had the good fortune of meeting "Kathy G", as she is called, at the Gene Autry Western Heritage Museum in September 1989 when we both went to see a screening of a *Zorro* episode in their Wells Fargo Theatre. Kathy had been a fan of Guy Williams since its TV debut in October 1957 when she was a little girl, and she had been collecting Guy Williams articles and pictures since that time. When Kathy spotted the Guy Williams/Zorro button on my blouse she introduced herself to me, and we have been talking about Guy Williams ever since. The following week at the Autry we were both back for another *Zorro* episode. This time, true to her promise, Kathy brought a trunk load of her collection, all of which she relentlessly made copies for me. With that, Kathy gave me the foundation for this book, and thereafter became my "right hand man". She has been a fountain of information, a force of optimism, and source of motivation. I am extremely grateful to her for her endless generosity and faithful assistance throughout these years of research.

When I started this project in 1990 I went from handwriting notes and outlines to using a used computer my husband bought me. No one had the Internet in their homes yet. Legwork and mailings for research was a tedious and time consuming process. Finding fellow fans, especially in other countries, was almost impossible. My research accelerated in 1995 when the computer became a household fixture in most homes and brought the WholeWideWorld to my fingertips. Rarely was there at that time any *new* groundbreaking information about Guy Williams—for that I still needed face-to-face interviews—but it gave me comfort and encouragement to find out that hundreds of people around the globe loved Guy Williams and wanted to read a full biography about him.

I found this out by way of a gift from my other bona fide friend, Mary Spooner. I first met Mary over the Holy Internet (I say that with tongue in cheek) through Kathy Gregory. In 1996 I met her in person at the Autry Museum at a book signing for Clayton Moore, the Lone Ranger. Mary had a Guy Williams website to which she added a page she called the Guyography Guestbook in 1998 announcing my biography as I was trying to find a publisher. Hundreds of posts from all over the United States and the world accumulated over the years: Brazil, Italy, Belgium, Switzerland, Columbia, Venezuela, Argentina, Chile, Japan, Finland, The Netherlands, Canada, France, Greece, Spain, Portugal, Russia, Antarctica, and more; all expressing their love for Guy Williams and a desire to read his biography. I am extremely grateful to Mary for her extraordinary giving nature, her steadfast devotion to helping me make this book richer and complete, and to both Kathy and Mary for their unwavering friendship. Since I have known her, Mary has created a most extensive and beautiful website on Guy Williams compiled from her own personal collection of magazines and photos, all of which she was willing to share with me for this book.

In summer of 1994, my luck soared when I met Guy Williams' wife and son—again at the Autry Museum—at a reception for a Zorro exhibit. I was very fortunate that Janice Williams was open to my ambition to write Guy's biography, and a few months later, agreed to meet with me in her home. My first interview with Janice Williams was on Guy's birthday, January 14, 1995, a coincidence I suspect Janice might have planned, as it was an appropriate date to begin a project that would celebrate his life and hopefully contribute to his immortality. For the next five and a half years, on many Saturday afternoons well into dusk, we spent hours pouring over pictures of Guy, talking about Guy's life, and reading parts of the manuscript together. I treasure that period in my life, because I was welcomed into their lives, not only as a writer, but as a friend: dinners, teas, trips to Disneyland, holding Guy's grandson for the first time, and seeing his reaction to his first visit to Disneyland. Named after his grandfather, little Armand, or Nando as he is called, went to Disneyland for the first time on April 26, 1998. That date, planned by Destiny, not by Guy's family, happened to be the same date his grandfather first appeared at Disneyland as Zorro, exactly forty years earlier, April 26, 1958.

Like most people who see an actor reach great heights of popularity around the world, I thought Guy Williams was a famous person whose dreams were fulfilled; lucky, with lots of money, and everything he wanted. As I came to know him, I found that while he was lucky to get the coveted role of Zorro, he had more disappointment in life than fulfillment. Learning to overcoming those disappointments gave him character and made him the lovable person he was. His keen sense of humor sustained him and made him a pleasure to be around.

I am most grateful to Janice Williams who gave me countless hours of her time, drawing a verbal portrait of the man who was the love of her life, the father of her children, and her idol. Guy knew this and at the peak of his career as Zorro, while he was signing and handing out pictures, he passed one across the crowd to her, on which he *half* jokingly wrote: *To Jan, my #1 fan. Thanks for being so in love with ME! All the Best, Guy Williams, Z.*

The first questions I put to Janice Williams came from the material Kathy G had given me. From that first interview Guy's life and personality began to mold and take shape until over time it blossomed and branched out into this full volume. That process of development required many people, many hours, and years; years of filling missing time frames, finding dates, finding proof in documents and passports of trips to and from Argentina, finding all the missing pieces of the years after *Lost In Space* when the press stopped writing about him.

One of the reasons this book took so long to finish is that I double checked stories and dates for accuracy. If someone told me a story about Guy and another person denied it, I didn't use it. If a story was backed by one or two other persons, and dates were confirmed, then I used it. If someone told me something that didn't fit his personality, and I could not find proof or hear it from another source, I didn't use it. I did not want to write a book based on rumors or hearsay, but on confirmed facts and data. Everything I wrote in this book I believe to be true according to the information I found or was given by reliable sources.

I pulled up ships' logs, studied official certificates of birth and death, studied photographs, visited where Guy lived and worked in California, where he sailed his boat in the San Pedro Harbor, listened to homemade tapes of his voice in casual situations at home, studied him in home videos interacting with family and friends, watched nearly every known film he made, and read dozens of magazine articles. To get to know Guy's personality without physically meeting him, I had to talk to people who lived with him, worked with him, walked with him, talked with him, ate with him, and knew him for years. I have tried my best to be as thorough in my research and as factual as I could be. After hundreds of interviews with Guy's fellow actors and friends, the final adjectives to describe him were always the same: He was a wonderful man; a gentleman. No one said a disparaging word about Guy Williams. He had his faults and weaknesses like everyone has, but nothing that cost him his friends. He was loved and is missed by all.

My deepest thanks to Janice Williams, the only woman Guy ever married, and to their children, Steve and Toni for so kindly and generously giving their time to tell what it was like growing up with a celebrity father, and sharing their memories of their famous father. Ever polite and gracious, they always accommodated my requests. None of them knew me from Adam when I came into their lives, but their love for this exciting man, loving father and husband, who had been the center of their lives and died much too early, was the driving force that made them want to share him.

That love was also evident in the kind people of Argentina who knew and loved the Guy Williams who worked in Buenos Aires from 1973-1980 and lived there permanently from 1983-1989. I held extensive interviews with those closest to him: Patricia Goodliffe, Fernando Lupiz, Aracelli Lisazo, Carlos Souto; Leon Balter, Juan Carlos Fauvety, and fan/collector, Alejandro Rosso over a period of three and a half years via telephone, emails, faxes, and in a couple of cases met them in person when they came to California for reasons unrelated to the book. *Mil gracias* to these generous people of Argentina, some of whom volunteered to go to TV stations and newspapers and copy articles and dates to confirm information, or contributed photographs, both personal and professional, and videos.

From the bottom of my heart I thank the friendly and generous people in the United States who allowed me to interview them, many of whom welcomed me into their homes: Dennis Weaver, William Shallert, Wright King, Britt Lomond, Tony Russel, Don Diamond, Richard Anderson, the late William Anderson, Buddy Van Horn, Tracy Sheldon, Margaret "Peggy" Sheldon, Suzanne Lloyd, Anna Wehling, Janice Williams, Toni Williams Anderson, Steve Williams, June Lockhart, Marta Kristin, Lawrence Montaigne, Valerie Catalano Fitzgerald, Don Burnet, Peggy Stevenson, Elise Triniol, Tom Waters, Tony Svarla, the late Marie Pezze, the late Fred del Cordoba, Steve Silver, Robert Foster, William Ramage, Ted Dalbatton, Doris Blum, Russell Johnson, Doug Warren, Terry Auzenne Alvarado, Sonny Hudson, Lester Martinson, John Ericson, Laurie Stewart, Kevin Burns, Joe Resoler, Tony Grapes, Donald T. Beard, Rita Ractcliff, Dennis Quaid, Suzzie Parry, Aletha Auzenne, and Lindsey Boggess.

To the following people I am extremely grateful for their assistance and support: Consultants: Dr. Reginald Goldsby, the late Dr. David L. Belzer, Dr. Carmon Cappadano; Geraldine Hecker, for giving me the confidence to make that first call; Photos and research: Kathy Gregory, Mary Spooner, Wendell Vega, Lorman "Augie" Augustowski, Peter Mitchell, Lynn Hodges, Jackie Hunt, Jill Panvini, Paulette Hopkins, Janis Whitcomb, Janet Doctors, Leslie Horne, Sergio Gonzales, Dr. Merry Ovnick; Support and encouragement: John Lane, Sean Lane; Catherine Lane, Michael Lane, Bobby Lane, Frank Thompson, Neil Summers, Kathy Nance; Fencing information and history: Sud De Land; Collaboration: Bill Cotter, Gerry Dooley; Constructive Critique: Dr. Charles Spurgeon; Translators: Beatriz Sandroni, Marc Sandroni, Lincoln Ramirez, T. J. Campbell, Gaela Clairacq, Patricia Gatica, Marie-Jo Machefert, and Cynthia Gonzales.

I don't presume to know Guy Williams like the people I have talked to, but after years of research, I began to feel as though I had met Guy Williams and knew his personality to a degree. One of my objectives in writing this book was to make the reader feel he had met him too. Guy had some predictable traits, but he was also a walking paradox: masculine yet sensitive, firm yet gentle, conservative yet nonconforming, macho yet intellectual, simple yet complicated. Being somewhat of a mystery is what made him so fascinating, and he probably liked it that way. Overall, Guy was determined to be happy, and he wanted to make everyone around him happy. That was his nature. To enjoy life to the fullest was his goal. In the process of doing that, he hoped he could please everyone who loved him. Although he worked at it, Guy knew he could not please all of the people all of the time, and in trying to do so sometimes someone he loved got hurt. Guy never deliberately hurt anyone, especially those he loved.

I feel so fortunate to have had some Power or Force leading me to all the wonderful people I have met while working on this project. Some have become and will remain good friends. All of them have made my life richer for knowing them.

Because I feel Guy Williams gave the world so much joy with his endearing performances, it was my intention from the start of this labor of love to write a Tribute book, one that would help preserve his memory. As his close friend Carlos Souto said, "As long as we talk about him he is alive". I hope this book will be instrumental in keeping Guy Williams memory alive in the hearts and minds of the public forever as the kind, loving, and unique person he was.

AUTHOR'S NOTEs
Curiosities and Coincidences

For the Numerologist, you will notice that in Guy's lifetime the numbers 14 and 4 consistently appear, in events happy and sad, on addresses and important documents. Many important events in his life occurred in April, the *fourth* month.

Guy's only grandson (as of this writing) Armand Anderson, was born on April 28th 1996, the fourth month and the number 14 doubled. It was exactly seven years (a spiritual number) to the day Guy was last reported seen alive, April 28, 1989.

Guy's mother, Clare, came to America from Sicily in 1919, the same year Johnston McCulley's book *The Curse of Capistrano* about Zorro was published with huge success. Guy was born on his mother's birthday, January 14th. The year was 1924, the same year Johnston McCulley changed the title of his book from *The Curse of Capistrano* to *The Mark of Zorro*, which Douglas Fairbanks called his 1920 movie version.

On *Lost In Space* Guy's TV daughter, "Judy", falls in love with a man named "Don." Guy's real life daughter, Toni, married a man named Don (Petrie).

Angela Cartwright who played Guy Williams' daughter on *Lost in Space* played a "Williams" in *Make Room For Daddy*, and Guy Williams played a "Cartwright" on *Bonanza*.

The address on the Hillside mansion Guy bought in 1960 was 7475. If you think of it as years (1974 and 1975), it seems prophetic in that those years marked a pivotal period in Guy's life, during which he sold the house and changed his life's course.

The word Fox comes up time and again throughout Guy's career. Aside from playing Zorro, the Fox, his first film in New York was produced by 20th Century Fox. He found his first apartment in Hollywood through Alexander Korda, director of 20th Century Fox. Guy's son went to Black Fox Military Academy, a happenstance. Guy worked at 20th Century Fox on *Lost In Space*. Years later Guy's *Lost In Space* TV series was distributed on videos by companies called Fox Home Video and *Foxstar*.

Guy Williams starred in only two television series, *Zorro* and *Lost in Space*. Both held high ratings during their runs, yet both were canceled at the peak of their popularity, and both ran for years in reruns in the United States and abroad. Nine years after

Guy Williams died in 1989, both TV shows were remade into feature films with a whole new cast: *The Mask of Zorro*, and *Lost in Space*. Some of the original cast members of TV's *Lost In Space* appeared in the remake. Both movies were being filmed at the same time and were released the same year, 1998. New Line Cinema's *Lost in Space* of 1998 was filmed at Shepperton Studios, where Guy Williams filmed *The Prince and the Pauper* for Disney in 1961.

A special Thanks to the Reader. I hope you enjoy the book.

– Antoinette Girgenti Lane
Los Angles, CA February 2005

Part 1

New York

1924-1951

Prologue

MANHATTAN, WINTER 1944

The pace was quick along Fifth Avenue. Everyone walked with a purpose, and Armand had his. Headed to his modeling agency, his arms swung gracefully at his side. His handsome six-foot, four-inch figure turned heads wherever he went. The clerks in the bookstore and the record store waved as he passed by. He was one of their regulars.

Armand loved walking in the city, especially on cold days like this. "It's good for you," he said. But for him, the benefits just happened to come with the pleasure. He loved Manhattan; the sounds, the people, the culture. He was one of those people who knew how to use the city. He took advantage of the great concert halls, the museums, and libraries. The favorite part of this daily walk was Central Park. He walked through it at every opportunity. Anything outside of Manhattan, he thought, was a foreign country.

Pat Allen's Agency was at 46th Street near 5th Avenue, not a long walk by Armand's standards from his eastside apartment on Lexington. Up the stairs and into the warmth of the room, he took off his coat and gloves, and looked in the mirror to check his hair. Impeccably dressed, he *looked* like a model, with his boyish good looks and dark wavy hair. Most of his friends were there checking the boards when Pat motioned him into her office. He took a seat in the straight-back chair while Pat stayed engrossed in a conversation on the phone.

Patricia Allen was a short, energetic woman in her forties, with short, red, curly hair, heavy-rimmed glasses, and a perpetual cigarette in her mouth. Always on the phone, she was talking to a client who was asking her for an All-American type for a magazine ad.

Pat looked into Armand's hazel eyes as they stared back at her with curiosity, and she said, "I've got the perfect guy for you. I'm sending over Armand Catalano."

The client replied, "No, no. We don't want him. We want an *All-American* type."

Pat rocked back pensively in her chair, then said, "O.K., I'll call back later."

She took a puff on her cigarette and told Armand what the client had said. They decided then and there to beat this system. Clients had a habit of fixing a stereotypical image to a "foreign" name. But Armand and Pat knew that not *every*one with a German name was blond with blue eyes, nor was *every* Italian swarthy with a big nose. They tossed around some "All American" names, and put a "non specific" first name with a bland non-colored-sounding last name, and came up with the best "master-key" name they could think of: Guy Williams.

1

Pat got on the phone. She rocked back in her chair with assurance looking into those hazel eyes, and said, "I have an 'All-American' type for you. Yeah, his name is Guy Williams."

"Fine! Fine!" said the client. "Send him right over!"

A smile crept over Pat's face. Guy Williams got the job for Armand and from that day forward he *was* Guy Williams.

Chapter 1

"I was born bleeding from the pores"
— Guy Williams

Guy Williams was born in a small private hospital called Mt. Hope, in the borough of New York called the Bronx. He was born on his mother's 22nd birthday on January 14, 1924. It was a Monday, and as the nursery rhythm says, he was "fair of face."

It was a cold and cloudy forty degrees, according to the *New York Times*, with fresh winds from the North. No lightning streaked across the sky to foretell of his fame, but the stage was being set for his Destiny.

Calvin Coolidge was President of the United States. Prohibition was in full force. "Pictures" were silent and were being scrutinized for censorship. Radio was the medium of the day. In Hollywood, Metro-Goldwyn-Mayer Studios officially opened, and a young Walt Disney was starting his own small studio in a rented garage. A young writer from the Midwest named Johnston McCulley, who had written a novel in 1919 titled *The Curse of Capistrano* about a fictitious dark hero called Zorro (The Fox), reissued his book in hardback, taking its new title, *The Mark of Zorro*[1], from the silent film Douglas Fairbanks made which created a new wave of popularity to the stories. On January 14, 1924, The *New York Times* announced another birth of sorts. Obscurely placed, next to the obituaries, as though unimportant, the small article read:

> January 14, 1924 — Dateline: Paris, France
> "TELEVISION" PROMISED BY FRENCH INVENTOR
> After Pictures, He Says, He Will Reproduce Human Faces at a Distance.
>
> Edouard Belin, inventor of…the telautograph for transmitting fac-similes of handwriting and pictures, stated today that he would transmit animated surfaces and human faces within a year.
>
> "…I believe it will not be long before the entire scene with numerous persons in the background will be transmitted."[2]

3

Destined to meet, these two infants would play a part in the enduring success of the other.

Guy's parents were Italian immigrants. They came to America separately, met in New York, and married. His mother Clara Jonaith [sic] Arcara Catalano, was born January 14, 1902 in Messina, Sicily. His father, Attilio Catalano, was born January 4, 1894 in Lercara Friddi, in the province of Palermo, Sicily, Italy. The Catalano name originated in Catalonia, a region in Northeastern Spain along the Mediterranean. Families of that name migrated to Bologna, Italy, and in the course of hundreds of years dispersed throughout parts of Italy and Sicily.

Clare (she dropped the *a* to Americanize her name) and Attilio named their son according to Italian tradition, which is to name the first son after his paternal grandfather. Attilio's father was Joseph Armand Catalano. The recorder wrote Joseph A. Catalano, on his birth certificate. His family would call him "Armando," and in school he would be called Armand Joseph Catalano.

Doctors soon noticed that Baby Catalano was not losing the natural redness on his skin that comes with birth. He had red pinhead spots on his body which were of great concern for his parents and the medical staff. The doctors did not know what it was. Clare was afraid of losing her baby, and called for a priest to administer the last sacrament of Extreme Unction to him while she prayed for him to live. The doctors gave the baby Vitamin B complex and in a few days the red spots began to go away. Today this condition is called Petechiae—a localized hemorrhaging, or leaking, of small capillaries just beneath the skin—and is neither uncommon nor serious. It is still treated with Vitamin B complex.

To the amusement of his family, Guy used to dramatize his birth by telling people "I was born bleeding from the pores," usually adding that this was something he and Peter the Great, had in common.

Baby Armando thrived after prayer and treatment, and went home to be nurtured by his parents, his aunts, his uncles, and maternal grandmother. The address on his birth certificate is 3044 Kingsbridge Avenue in the Bronx, very possibly near or with Clare's mother and siblings who could help her with the newborn.

Attilio moved his family a lot, always trying to find a better place. Before Armand was of school age, he had several addresses. Attilio's father owned a house and acres of farmland in Spring Valley, New York, and it was available to Attilio and his family, as long as they would oversee the farm and the raising of horses there. Armando lived there until he was two. Clare liked stability, but Attilio liked change. He was more the adventurer. He moved his family twice when Armand was a toddler into apartments in Washington Heights, an area in upper Manhattan, before finally settling down in a larger apartment at 374 Wadsworth Avenue on 192st Street in Washington Heights. Clare's mother, Maria, moved next door to them. They often made trips to the farm, sometimes spending weeks there at a time.

Armand grew up in an environment of creative people in the arts. His parents had many friends who were writers and musicians. They often came to the house to visit and the lively conversations, accompanied by a lot of laughter, food and wine, were a part of his formative years.

Opera was usually playing on the radio. Italian was the household language, so much so that Armand remembered being taken aback one day when he heard his mother speaking English to someone. Before he went to school, he had learned enough English to get by, and what he had not learned, he learned in school.

Little Armand had a magnetism about him from an early age that drew people to him. Total strangers approached Clare to comment on her beautiful child. His relatives doted on him. Uncle Eugene Catalano and his wife, Josephine, had three daughters, Gilda, Mary, and Ophelia, all older than Armando, who adored him and catered to his every whim. When Clare took him to their house to visit, all three girls made such a fuss over him, he was nicknamed, "The King."

Armand grew up in a very diverse neighborhood which changed from one block to the next, with Irish and Jewish, Italian and German families, and a small mix of Orientals and Armenians. Clare and Attilio were Catholic and when Armand was little, Clare took him to church to give him a foundation in the religion. But as Armand grew older, into adolescence and teens, his mother did not insist that he go. She, herself, did not go every Sunday, but that is not to say she was not religious. Clare kept her prayerbook from her childhood in Sicily by her bed, and had all the prayers committed to memory, in Latin *and* Italian. She lit holy candles in the house, and maintained a deep faith in God. Attilio was not a churchgoer, although he went on occasion.

Clare's love for books transferred to her son. Throughout his life he clearly remembered a book she treasured, a very old copy of Dante's *The Divine Comedy*, written around 1307, in which Dante wrote about a family named Catalano.

Both Clare and Attilio were good cooks. Clare bought fresh vegetables and meats from the neighborhood street vendors, and prepared delicious meals. Even during the Depression they could make anything taste good. Mealtime was a special time in their house and Armando was taught to respect his elders and the food at the table.

Young Armando had an assertive air, and gave Clare cause on more than one occasion to discipline him. One his family never forgot was when Armand, very young at the time, sneaked and took some of his father's shirts, piled them in the bedroom, set them on fire, then ran out the door. (Reason unknown) His mother quickly found them and knew where she could find Armand: upstairs at his friend's apartment. With the smoldered shirts behind her back, Clare went upstairs. The friend's mother answered and told Clare the boys were playing in her son's room. Clare knocked on the boy's door. Armand heard his mother's sweet voice at the door, singing, "*maaan*-dooo, Venuto qui, caro. I have something *fooor* yooou."

Armando thought, 'Is she stupid! I just tried to burn the place down, and she wants to *give* me something!'

She gave him something all right. "I got a beating," he said, "from my mother, and then again from my father."

Over the years, whenever there was a family gathering with Armand there, someone would invariably bring it up. "Remember the time Armando tried to burn the house down?!" they'd say. Everyone would laugh, including Armando, and the story would be told all over again.

Another family story goes: One day little Armand was in the kitchen playing with a live lobster on the table while his grandmother was boiling a big pot of water on the stove. When she reached for the lobster, he suddenly realized what the boiling water was for. Armand began to plead for the poor lobster's life and yelled at her not to do it. Desperate to stop her, he tried to throw hot water on his grandmother.

Armand started school at P.S. 189 at the corner of Audubon Avenue and 189th

Street. He was in the first grade when the stock market crashed in October 1929, marking the beginning of the Great Depression in America. Despite the Depression, Armand had a relatively comfortable life growing up. His school day began with a hearty breakfast, usually of eggs, meat, or hot cereal. On cold wintry mornings his father would make him a Zabaglione to warm him up, a traditional drink many Italian children are used to, made up of egg, sugar, and sherry whipped together. Clare packed delicious lunches for him, sandwiches of Italian meats and cheeses drizzled with olive oil. His lunches smelled so good the other children wanted them. Armand was usually willing to trade, especially for the delicacy of peanut butter and jelly, which he never got at home.

On the first day of school the corner of Audubon and 189th swarmed with hundreds of boys with bags of marbles: aggies, jimmies, and cat's eyes. They shot them into a little wooden box their mothers saved from cream cheese. On the neighborhood streets Armand played kick the can, and Ringalivio—a hide and seek game—and his favorite, stickball, for which all the mothers saved old broomsticks for the kids. For a dime they could buy a soft red rubber ball called a Pennsylvania Pinky. Homeplate was the manhole cover near the center of the street, and base was the sewer drain. If there was a car parked on the curb, the fender was base.

Armand was liked by his teachers. In a group-shot taken on a field trip by his teacher when he was six, many of the children are not smiling, but young Armand is not only beaming, he is hamming it up for the camera in a pompous pose with his small fist across his chest as though he were Julius Caesar. Many years later when Guy became famous his teacher sent him this photo.

A precocious child, Armand showed maturity at an early age, so much so that Clare gave him more freedom than most boys his age, allowing him to go on the bus or train with some friends or even alone to Central Park when he was in grade school. He played with his friends in the park and when he was older he learned to ride a horse there. It was always one of his favorite places to be.

Clare and Attilio wanted to give Armand the best well-rounded education possible. In the fall of 1934 they enrolled him in Peekskill Military Academy for the 6th grade. Only

Peekskill Military Academy founded in 1833, with its famous large oak tree which is still standing. (postcard; from author's personal collection)

The Junior Building (dormitories) where young Armand lived during his years at Peekskill. (photo courtesy of Lorman "Augie" Augustowski '57, Pres. Of PMA Alumni Headquarters)

one hour away by train, Peekskill was a reputable school founded in 1833 with diverse academic classes, gym, and athletics for boys from fourth through twelfth grade. The beautiful campus lined with elm, was meticulously kept with classical style red brick buildings donated by the Ford family. The pride of the campus was a mighty oak that still stands today. A plaque was placed on the oak in 1912 saying, "In honor of this tree upon which was hanged Jan. 27, 1776 an American who was employed as a spy by the British."[3]

From the sixth through ninth grade, Armand donned the formal military uniform at Peekskill, where he learned self reliance, discipline, and to live up to the school motto, "Quit ye like men." In the winter he learned how to ice-skate on Lake Mitchell adjacent to the school. He particularly liked the weekend movies screened for the boys in the school's own Paramount Theater.

In the 1934-35 Peekskill yearbook, Armand is listed as Armand Joseph Catalano, as a sub-freshman under Third Form (or, sixth grade).

His report card, dated January 31, 1935, reads:

Conduct:	A-
Arithmetic:	C
English:	A
Geography:	A+
American History:	A
Penmanship:	B
Reading:	B
Spelling:	B

Armand struggled with math for years, but he loved to read and go to the movies. Clare's way of helping Armand acquire writing skills was by insisting that he write to her *ten* times before his next trip home.

Once again Armand tried to outwit his mother. He sat at his desk one day and

Lance Corporal of Company E (1935-36 yearbook) Armand is believed to be the tallest cadet on the top row. Donald Beard is in the middle row on the left end.
(photo courtesy of Lorman "Augie" Augustowski '57, Pres. Of PMA Alumni Headquarters)

wrote, "Dear Mother and Father, How are you? I am fine. Love, Armando" ten times, on the same page, and mailed it. When he couldn't remember a word in Italian, he wrote it in English.

His mother was not going to put up with that. "Dear Armando," she wrote, "Your father and I were not amused. You know that new radio you've had your eye on in the store window? Well, your father and I have decided that you should wait a little longer for it."

Clare always said "your father and I," but she was the disciplinarian in the family. Attilio was strict, but he was inclined to bend a little. Both, however, insisted that their son live up to certain standards. Clare was a proud and intelligent woman, conscientious

The Library where Armand loved to read.
(photo courtesy of Lorman "Augie" Augustowski '57, Pres. Of PMA Alumni Headquarters)

of social status. She had high standards and her friends did too. One day when she was strolling through Central Park with a friend who lived on Fifth Avenue—both dressed to the nines in hats and gloves—she spotted Armando playing with some friends. His clothes were disheveled and he was dirty from playing. Clare did not want this woman to know that this child who looked like a street urchin was hers, so she ignored him and kept walking.

Peekskill Military Academy had a summer camp called Poko Moonshine in a rural area north of Peekskill. There were lessons in the morning, then an afternoon full of outdoor activities and sports in the afternoon. Tutors were usually upperclassmen from Peekskill. As Guy sometimes made reference to going to camp, it is believed that he probably spent a summer or two at this camp. Every summer Armand spent some time on the beach at Sea Cliff on Long Island, where his parents rented a beach house.

In the PMA 1935 yearbook Armand is pictured in Company E and was one of ten who had earned the rank of Lance Corporal, which put a stripe on each arm of his uniform. This rank was a recognition of achievement and meant that he was experienced in executing all commands correctly for certain positions in military formations.

When Armand came home on holidays, Clare cooked huge delicious dinners and all the relatives got together for a feast. His Uncle Oscar Arcara, Clare's younger brother, was only eighteen when Armand was born, and had taken his nephew under his wing from the time he could walk. He strolled with him, pulled him in a wagon, took him to the neighborhood parks, Inwood, and Fort Tryon, taught him how to skate, ride a bike, play chess, and often took him to the Bronx Zoo, one of Armand's favorite places. Uncle Oscar had a camera and his favorite subject was little Armand, who came to like photography through his young uncle. As Armand grew into manhood, Uncle Oscar was his best friend and mentor.

Chapter 2

"Just a regular guy."

— Tom Waters, Classmate

Armand's parents loved each other, but they argued a lot. Attilio was a handsome man, known to some as a Don Juan, and Clare was sometimes suspicious and jealous. Attilio was a spendthrift and Clare was frugal, so their arguments were usually about money, or women.

Attilio was 5'11" with dark wavy hair, a broad friendly smile, and unusual orange eyes, like that of a tiger. He was very social, very likeable, quick to laugh, and always joking. When he walked, a slight spring in his leg could sometime be detected, a trait Armand inherited. He loved going to the race track and staying out late with his friends smoking, eating, and talking. He drank a dozen espressos a day. He loved life and knew how to enjoy it to the fullest.

Attilio had been an officer in the Italian Army, which he joined when he was eighteen. When he was a boy in Sicily, it was customary for a family of means to choose a respectable vocation for their children. They decided Attilio would be a priest. At sixteen he was sent to Rome to live with Joseph's brother and attend the Vatican School. Joseph dutifully sent Attilio money for his tuition and books, plus living expenses for two years. Priesthood, however, was the farthest thing from Attilio's mind. He was miserable and compensated by playing hard, and squandering his school money on pleasures. The strict rules and regimen of prayers and study gave Attilio an aversion to the Church and its Doctrine. All he saw was hypocrisy among the priests. After two years his grades were so bad he was called in before the superiors, to ask why his grades had fallen. Attilio said, "My father is not doing very well, and cannot afford to buy me books."

Shortly thereafter Joseph received a letter with the great Vatican seal on it, saying, "...sorry to hear about your financial reverses," signed by the Pope.

The fires of Joseph's Italian temper blazed a trail straight to the Army for Attilio. It was an occupation that suited him and soon earned him the rank of officer. He served during World War I (1914-1918) in the infantry and artillery in Europe.

There was a story Attilio loved to tell during his lifetime. After he died, Guy continued to tell it. While the war was raging in Europe, Attilio often rode the train from city to city speaking to the people from the back of the train about the war. When the train stopped in Rome, it was raining. People, most of them poor and without umbrellas, stood in the pouring rain to hear his news of the war. Attilio saw the priests sitting smugly in their dry carriage, in their clean white robes. Memories of the years he endured at the school came back to him and something riled inside him.

As he gave his speech he said, "*Let us all get down on our knees and pray for peace!*" He knew the holy men would have to oblige. As everyone went down on their knees in the puddles, Attilio watched the pristine priests get out of their carriage and kneel in the mud with the rest of the crowd. When the prayer was over, it gave him great satisfaction to see them getting back in the carriage with their robes wet and dripping with mud. Revenge was sweet, and he used to laugh as he recalled the power he had at that moment.

The first sword Guy ever held was the one his father had in the Italian Army. When Armand was six years old, Attilio wanted to teach his son rudiments of an ancient art the Italians had preserved. After guns were invented, sword fighting was starting to become a lost art in Europe. The Italians made it a sport, and for a very long time Italy had the best fencers in the world.

"The sword was too heavy for me to hold," Guy said. But he did absorb the basics during those first lessons, which gave him a foundation in the sport in later years.

Joseph Catalano, Attilio's father, was an enterprising man who owned real estate in Sicily, but like most Italian males from the old country at this time, he looked to America to make his fortune. While his wife stayed in Sicily, Joseph made a trip to New York and bought acres of farmland in New Jersey as an investment for his sons. After the war he brought his sons, Attilio, Eugene, and Salvatore[4] (called Torto), to America with him to oversee the farm. It was stocked with thoroughbred horses, to be bred and trained for racing. The business was lucrative and reinforced Attilio's lifelong love for "playing the ponies." Attilio and Eugene decided to stay in America, but Torto returned to Italy.

Torto was the intriguing rogue of the family with a proclivity toward gambling and women. Always involved in some "business venture" in Chicago, New York, or Italy, he once shipped a champion racehorse from Italy to run in a high stakes race at Jamaica (now Aqueduct Race Track) in Queens. It won!

Torto was one of the last of the real swashbucklers. He fought real duels in Italy, usually over women. A bon vivant, with a lifestyle most men envy, but never dare to try, he was flamboyant, had many friends, and a woman on each side of the ocean. One day his promiscuity caught up with him and he was kicked out of Italy after being caught with the wife of the mayor of a province. He settled in Chicago with his wife on that side.

Torto had no children, and he was not an old man when he died before Armand was born. Although Armand never met his colorful uncle, he knew him well through the "Uncle Torto Stories" that reached his tender young ears at an impressionable age. The adults laughed, so Armand did too. Torto's daring and outrageous, sometimes scandalous, escapades captivated his imagination. As an adult he told these "Uncle Torto Stories" at parties with zest and fervor. Someone else might be reluctant to tell such mischievous tales, but Guy told them with delight and a sense of pride. Men, particularly, liked them.

Attilio landed a job as an insurance and real estate broker at 55 Liberty Street in the Wall Street district of Lower Manhattan, a job he would keep all the rest of his life. Although he was attractive to many women, Attilio gave his heart to Clara Arcara, a beautiful young Italian woman who had come to America with her mother and brother a few years before Attilio.

Clara was the first born of John Arcara and Maria Zumba Maiorana Arcara. (Maiorana being a name from her previous marriage.) About four years after Clara was born, her mother gave birth to her brother, Oscar. Life was good for little Clara in Sicily. She had many friends, a nice place to live, and she was happy. One day her father left and did not return. As months turned into years she could barely remember him. Not much is known about him. One relative of Clare's said, "He was a handsome, flamboyant type who had come into her mother's life. Clare never talked about him."

After several years of raising her children alone, Maria faced the fact that her husband was not coming back. Her older set of children, from a previous marriage, had moved to New York. When they received a distressful letter from her, they talked her into joining them in America. Clara did not want to leave her home. She could not understand why she was being pulled up from her happy childhood, and her friends, to go to some strange land.

With her trunks packed with what she could take, and two children in tow, Maria boarded the San Guglielmo for New York Harbor, never to return to Italy again. Young Clara, 11 years old, pouted and cried the whole way. When they arrived at New York Harbor on April 25, 1913, the discontented Clara made a secret promise to herself that she would return, somehow, someday.

In school she learned English quickly, and like most Italian immigrants she wanted to Americanize her name. She dropped the "a" from Clara and became Clare with an "e." She attended Baptist High School in Manhattan, where she excelled in Math and Literature, and discovered she was very proficient in languages. Aside from English and the pure Italian she learned from her mother, she also learned French, Spanish, Russian, and Latin.

Clare matured into a lovely brown-eyed beauty with an oval-shaped face and fair skin. When she met Attilio, he was someone with the same cultural background, and he had a good job on Wall Street. He was also handsome and charming. He asked for her hand in marriage, and knowing how much she missed her homeland, he promised he would take her back to her beloved Italy one day. Clare accepted.

It is not known why they did not have another child soon after Armand was born. Perhaps the Depression years and the expense of putting Armand into private school had a bearing on it. While Armand was at military school Clare and Attilio had more privacy and time together, and she became pregnant for the second time after fourteen years.

Clare gave birth to a baby girl on August 13, 1938 in Colombian Presbyterian Hospital on 168th Street. They named her Valerie. Armand did not quite know how to react to this new addition.

"I had been king of the house all those years!" he joked years later, "and *now* here comes this screaming kid!"

Valerie remembered, "I know my brother hung around my mother all summer before I was born anticipating a baby brother, so I know I was a disappointment to him, because I wasn't a boy."

Armand might have had to give up some attention in his house now that there was a baby, but to his adoring girl cousins, he was still "the king" and someone they always made a fuss over.

Fall was approaching and after Armand had spent his years of puberty under strict discipline in a private all-boys school, he was now going to be enrolled in George Wash-

George Washington High photo from 1943 Yearbook. (courtesy of Marie Pezze)

ington High, a large co-ed public school in his neighborhood, at 549 Audubon.

"I was an indifferent student," he said. "I flunked English because I spent a good deal of time gazing at J. P. Morgan's yacht, the *Corsair*. I think that's where I fell in love with boats."[5]

He didn't like school, but his favorite place was the New York Public Library, where he spent hours reading, learning more outside of school. He was still having a difficult time with math.

At this point he had no career goal, but he knew he'd like to own a boat one day, and he knew he enjoyed drama when his English class read "Evangeline" by Henry Wadsworth Longfellow, aloud. He loved classical music and the movies, but he had no clue that he would ever want to be an actor.

When Armand was thirteen, Uncle Oscar took him to a museum called The Cloisters. Built by the Rockefellers in 1930 near the banks of the Hudson River in Washington Heights, the Cloisters is an exact replica of a monastery in Italy, replicating even its beautiful meditation gardens. Housing the majority of the Metropolitan Museum's Medieval Art, it quickly became one of Armand's favorite places. Five Gothic and Romanesque arcades from Rome, France, and Spain display tapestry, sculpture, furniture, armor, and swords from as far back as 1000 A.D. The half-dome of the apse from Spain features a painting of the Virgin and Child from a church in Catalonia. Armand would be transported to ancient Europe by its thick walls, vaulted ceilings, and arched walkways that led to outside gardens. Here began his love for antiquity, and history of the old world. He visited the Cloisters often with his uncle.

It was also Uncle Oscar who instilled in Armand a love and appreciation for classical music that would last his lifetime. While other kids his age were listening to Swing, he was listening to Beethoven, Puccini, Vivaldi, Wagner, Mozart, and Bach. He started his own classical 78-rpm record collection when he was a teenager.

Armand was a movie buff from an early age. Gangster films and musicals dominated the film industry in the 1930s. Some of the major screen stars that fed his imagination were Clark Gable, Carole Lombard, Ginger Rogers, Fred Astaire, Loretta Young, Edward G. Robinson, Mae West, the Marx Brothers, W.C. Fields, Laurel and Hardy, and Humphrey Bogart. A few years later he preferred science fiction and European films.

There were as many as seven movie houses within four blocks in Armand's neighborhood. Three on 181st Street alone were the Lane, the Majestic, and the Gem. There was the RKO Coliseum and the Washington Heights on Wadsworth, near 181st Street. "It opened around 10 in the morning, and it cost ten and twenty cents to get in," said Guy. "We would spend all of Saturday watching movies." He used to say they watched movies so long on a Saturday that when they came out their eyes were square.[6]

Armand heard of Walt Disney when he saw his first Mickey Mouse cartoon and *Pinocchio* (1940), but the Disney film that impressed him the most was *Fantasia*, because it combined animation with classical music. "When I was a kid, I saw *Fantasia*, and there has never been anything like it since."[7]

Fourteen year old Armand (left) with a friend in the neighborhood. (Paulette Hopkins collection: Courtesy of Paulette Hopkins)

Walt Disney's *Fantasia* was playing at 53rd and Broadway on March 2, 1941 on exclusive engagement. The ad in the *New York Times* said this movie "cannot be shown in any other theater within 100 miles of New York." Weekend matinees were 35¢, 85¢, $1.10, and $2.20.

Tom Waters, one year older than Armand, grew up in the same neighborhood, went to the same grammar school, and remembers Armand from high school. Tom recalled those Saturday mornings when they were kids at the movies. "In the 1930s and '40s you could see a double feature, then stay and see them over and over again for ten cents. You saved your ticket stub, because at one point on that Saturday afternoon, the stage curtain would open up, and there would be a spread of the biggest array of toys you'd ever seen: bicycles, baseball bats, all kinds of toys. Some kid would be chosen to get up there to dig his hand into a hat and come up with a winning stub. They'd call it out and they'd give the winning kid a baseball. *All* those toys, and it was always one baseball!" He laughed. "Then the curtain would come down, the movie would start again, and they saved it all for the next Saturday."

In high school Armand worked in the neighborhood candy/ice cream store at St. Nicholas and 190th as a soda jerk, so he could afford his movie habit and his records. Tom Waters remembered the popular store. "All the kids hung out there. You would meet your friends there and have a malted or ice cream and listen to the jukebox. I used to see Armand in there sometimes."

Around 1936-1937, when the boys were in their early teens, the all-time favorite screen siren was Jean Harlow, who Tom said, "was the most exciting thing on the screen for young men."

Armand and his school chums would get together and see as many movies as possible in one day. In his teens he and his friends would meet girls there and walk them home after the movies.

Parents were especially strict with their daughters, but they were also strict with their sons. Tom, of strict Irish Catholic background, said, "I couldn't go out on a date with a girl until I was about to graduate from high school."

No one had evening dates. Donald Beard, who went to Peekskill and lived in Washington Heights, remembered when he liked an Italian girl in this small but diverse melting pot of a neighborhood. "They used to have Italian block parties, with streamers hanging and whatnot. This girl's father insisted I come in and eat. They had red wine and I got sick eating so much. The boys in their family ruled and the father ruled the roost with an iron fist. The daughters were well protected."

One such protected Italian girl regrets to this day that she missed out on a date with Armand, because she was too young. Marie Pezze was a pretty blonde, blue-eyed sophomore in high school when she met Armand. "Armand was a junior," remembered Marie, "and my girlfriend, Gloria, and I used to see him in Study Hall, and we talked about how good looking he was. One day in the auditorium, she noticed that he was sitting about eight seats behind us, across the aisle. We turned around to look at him, and just as he saw us looking, he looked down. My girlfriend had been making a big effort to get to know him, and finally one day she started a conversation with him. I just stood on the side and listened. Then one day after that, I was surprised that he came up to *me* and started talking. He didn't flirt the way most guys used to do. He just seemed interested in talking with me. He put his foot up on a chair and bent over to talk to me. I remember that, because he was very tall, and I'm only 5'2". Then, he asked me if I liked sailing, and would I like to go on a boat with him that weekend. Well, I was too embarrassed to tell him that I wasn't allowed on dates until I was eighteen. So I think I made up some excuse, like, I didn't care to go. He was so good looking and charming, I hardly remember *what* was said. I was so flattered. He didn't insist or persist. He was very gentlemanly, soft-spoken, clean-cut, and very handsome. I mostly remember his eyes. They were just sooo…," she swooned, lost for words. "I hope he understood why I didn't go. He must have known how Italian parents were."

Armand's congenial personality put him in good favor with his teachers. His Spanish teacher, Emily Bradford, took a special interest in him, and after meeting Clare, became a friend of the family for many years. She and her sister, Marietta, had a huge mansion in Pelham Manor, an affluent neighborhood near Westchester, and sometimes babysat little Valerie there. Valerie remembers going with her mother and these two ladies to Avon-by-the-Sea to stay at their place as guests when she was eight. It was a long and wonderful friendship that came about through Armand.

There was something about Armand that made older people like him. Clare had a wealthy friend who lived on Fifth Avenue who was so fond of Armand that she offered him a rare and precious gift: an original copy of the Gutenberg Bible. It had been handed down through her family, and knowing Armand's love and appreciation for

Marie Pezze, Seated second from the right, in photo of reps for the yearbook, "Hackett" (courtesy of Marie Pezze)

books, she wanted him to have it. Young Armand was thrilled. He thought it was the best present anyone could give him, but when he got home his mother told him he would have to return it. This rare book, printed in the mid-1450s, was one of only forty-seven existing copies in the world. In 1926 a Gutenberg Bible sold in New York at auction for $106,000 and was presented to Yale University. It was too precious to accept. Armand tried to understand. Disappointed, he took it back to the woman. Years later, he often wished he had kept that famous bible.

Another family friend who was deeply fond of young Armand was John Corliano, the First Violinist in the New York Philharmonic Orchestra. He had been Attilio's friend for years, and knew of Armand's love for music. When Attilio was wondering what to get Armando for his eighteenth birthday, Corliano handed him season tickets for two in box seats at Carnegie Hall. Armand loved those V.I.P. seats. "Right over the piano!" he said. "Instead of giving me a car, my dad gave me that." Armand didn't need a car in New York. His father didn't even have one.

Armand dressed in a tux and took his date to Carnegie Hall. "I was different from the others my age," he said. "Instead of taking a girl to the movies and a coke afterwards, I would take them to the symphony!"

Everyone's mother, grandmother and aunt in this diverse neighborhood were great cooks. The best delicatessens and bakeries were on every street corner. Nevertheless, when Armand was in high school, the favorite of most every kid in the school was Nick's hot dogs. "I always wanted a hot dog or a hamburger," said Guy. "I remember the hot dog man really well—little man who used to come around the school yard with a cart and umbrella. They were about a *foot* long! And very thin. And they were always in this boiling water. You got sauerkraut and mustard, and a two-cent lemonade. Refills were free. And it was really cheap, ice-cold, lemony water with sugar in it. But it was *great*! So, a hot dog ran a nickel, and with the lemonade—for *seven cents* you lunched on a hot dog and a lemonade. For 15 cents, you know, you could eat yourself sick!"[8]

Tom Waters relishes the thought of those hot dogs of his youth. The old man "kept those hot dogs boiling with a little kerosene thing that heated up the water. He had a little pump that pumped out the lemonade. One lemon, *two gallons* of water" he laughed, "and a *lot* of sugar! Five cents for a hot dog with sauerkraut and mustard! And it was great! My friend's mother used to say, 'Don't you know those are not good for you!' Then one day she took the hot dog away from him and tasted it, and she loved it!"

At some point Armand went to Brooklyn Academy. Since his school records were never transferred from George Washington High, it is believed he probably went to the Academy during a summer for extra credit or for tutoring to pull up his math grade. He often talked about a special teacher who at some time during his education turned on the light bulb for him in math. "The only subject I excelled in was math," he used to tell his family. "This teacher opened it up to me and I couldn't get enough of it. Math clicked with me. I was a whiz at it!" After this tutor, he was understanding concepts and problems way beyond his grade level.

Of Math and Music, Guy said, "They are very similar. They both have structure and they are both languages."

A highly accredited school, George Washington High was one of twenty-five academic high schools in New York at that time. It was also one of only three such schools that required their students to pass a Regents Exam in order to graduate. Marie Pezze said, "They gave the test on one day *only*, so you had better be there. If you missed the Regency Exam, you didn't graduate, and you had to wait until the next semester to take it. They would take no excuses. They put the fear of God in everything back then. Our classes were so big we had two graduations, one in January and another in June." Marie graduated in January 1943 and was a representative for the school yearbook called the Hachet. Marie didn't see Armand again after he asked her out, but she never forgot him. Her friend Gloria saw him a few times after he graduated when he would visit his grandmother on Sundays. His grandmother, Arcara, lived in a house that belonged to Gloria's aunt. She never did know him well, but she said she has "a vivid memory of how good looking he was, and that he was a very nice person."

On May 28, 1941, Armand got his first regular full-time job at a thread company called Belding, Heminway & Cortielli at 119 West 42nd Street in the Garment District. "My father said I should look for work," said Guy. "'You just have to do something,' he said to me. So I would find myself going on interviews, but hoping I wouldn't get the job."

Attilio had offered him a job at his firm, but Armand did not want to sell insurance. At Belding he was an office boy doing a variety of general tasks, mostly "a lot of running around," he said, doing errands for them. He hated it and lasted only a few months there. "It would take me three months to catch on to a job and then I'd get canned."[9] Whether or not this statement was made just for a laugh (something Guy would do in interviews), it was a fact that for a few years he did change jobs frequently.

On January 6, 1942, President Roosevelt gave a State of the Union message during World War II, calling for the production of 60,000 planes and 6,000,000 tons of merchant ships to aid the war effort, creating jobs for those on the homefront. Next door to Armand's high school there was a very large WPA (Works Progress Administration) building, a government agency that helped find work for people. Factory jobs became filled by young men and women fresh out of high school.

Armand got a job in an aircraft factory as an inspector. It also was short-lived. Years later he told a friend that inspecting the aircraft for cracks was too heavy a responsibility for an eighteen-year-old. "If I missed a crack or defect, someone could be killed," he said.

He got another job in a shipyard, where he learned welding. The government was building housing for workers in shipyards and large plants at that time because many came from out of state for the work. Armand probably stayed in one in New Jersey, because he used to talk about having to take showers after work, with men much older than he was from all walks of life. He was a kid having to live among grown men from all social and economic levels. This job did not last long either.

When he was eighteen, he and his friends found a place in the German part of Manhattan where they could buy beer. They would walk home late at night sometimes fairly smashed. Clare was more tolerant of this than some of the mothers so if one of his friends had a little too much, Clare would let him sleep over. She never let any of them go home alone if it was not safe, or if they would get in trouble for having too many.

One day Armand found himself answering his call for duty in the Army. He had extremely high arches, and his little toe on each foot was high and grew over the top of his foot, which made it difficult for him to fit into regular shoes. He had to buy extra wide shoes to accommodate his high arches. The end of his shoes often curled upward, because his toes usually didn't reach the end of the shoe. Tom Water, who served in the Army Air Corp., said, "If you couldn't fit into the 'issue,' you were rejected." Armand was 4F because of his foot problems.

It was no disappointment to him that he was rejected. He was not the typical gung-ho type about the war. A liberal from an early age, he opposed the war.

Donald Beard served as a Navy pilot, and Tom Waters served in the Army Air Corp. When Tom came home from the war one of the first persons he ran into was Armand. "I have a vivid recollection in my mind of meeting Armand on the corner of St. Nicholas Avenue and 190th Street right after the war. I was all dressed up in some new clothes my mother had talked me into getting, when she took me shopping after I got home from the war. There I was, in this bright-colored Vicuña overcoat, and a dark-brown homburg hat, and an appropriate shirt with a spud collar. As I came to the corner with my mother, I saw Armand standing there, and he says to me, 'Boy! You look like a lawyer!' I'll never forget that, 'cause it kinda pumped my confidence, you know. I remember him as very tall and very good looking, but very affable. He was handsome, but he didn't have any airs about him. *Just* a regular guy."

Chapter 3

"The apple of my mom's eye"

– Valerie Catalano

"I grew up with Wagner thundering through the house," said Valerie, with her typical New York accent. "When my brother babysat me, he would turn the volume up very loud. One time a neighbor came to the door and said to him, 'Don't you think that's *too loud*?' And he replied, 'No. That's the way it's *supposed* to be!'"

"My brother liked art, culture, and classical music. Me, I'm a Philistine," she laughed. "I must admit though, I did begin to like and appreciate classical music by listening to it so much."

Even Attilio, who preferred opera, was won over. One day he came home and heard Armand's music playing loudly, but instead of complaining he listened. "What is that?" he asked. Armand smiled and thought, "Aaah! I've got him now."

"My brother and I were never close. I spent the first half of my life trying to figure out why he rejected me. I was like an impediment. More than the age and gender difference, we had personality clashes.

"He took after my mother, and I didn't get along with my mother. He was the apple of my mom's eye and I was a daddy's girl.

"My brother was always very judgmental of me when I was growing up, and very bossy. He told me what to do, and what not to do. He was a know-it-all, a smug sonofabitch.

"One time when he was babysitting me, he spanked me. He put me over his knees and spanked me! I became furious, and I thought, 'It wasn't his right to do this. Only my mother could spank me!' So I sank my teeth into his thigh, as deep as I could, and he let out a yell. I think I drew blood! But, he never spanked me again," laughed Valerie.

"He was the type who, if he got mad at you, he'd yell and carry on. Then, when he was finished, he'd *watch* you, just to see if you'd do it again, so he could *really* let you have it.

"My brother had a big ego, and he was very smart. I remember he was written up in the *Brooklyn Eagle* newspaper for excelling in math.

"When my brother was in high school, he made an A on a test. My mother had told him if he made an A, she would make his favorite pie, which was apple. So the next day she baked the pie. After school my brother strolled into the house, and he had all his buddies with him. My mother looked at him and all his friends, and he said to her, 'They made A's, *too*!'"

Valerie speaks sentimentally about the apartment on Wadsworth where she spent the happiest years of her life. "We had a beautiful view to the East of the Hudson River and the Washington Bridge from my bedroom. I had the best room in the apartment. My view overlooked many parks in the area: Inwood Hill Park, Fort Tryon Park, and Fort George. There was a valley between Washington Heights and Fort Tryon and in the fall we could watch the trees turning colors. It was beautiful.

"I loved that apartment. It had two bedrooms, and a large living room and dining room separated by French doors. It was big. We had to walk up five flights of stairs to get to it—then when I was six years old an elevator was put in the building."

The building was fairly new when the Catalanos moved into it. Doric columns gave a Grecian look to the entrance, which led to an impressive lobby with an Italian marble floor, graced with a wide staircase, and supported by ornate Doric columns. Two huge mirrors in decorative gold frames flanked a large fireplace. "There was a terrazzo gazebo on the roof," recalls Valerie. "I used to love to sit up there and dry my hair in the sun. The rooftops were so close I used to jump from roof to roof to visit my friends."

Armand spent a lot of time with his Uncle Oscar, who by this time had matured into a tall, handsome man who resembled Errol Flynn. Armand looked a lot like his uncle. Valerie watched many times as the two sat at a table playing chess, while Uncle Oscar puffed on his pipe.

"When my Uncle Oscar and my brother would be engaged in a game of chess, I would stand next to them and watch. I would ask my uncle over and over, 'Teach me how to play chess. I want to learn too,' but I would be waved away by both of them, 'Oh, you're a girl. Girls don't need to play chess,' they would say. I always resented them not teaching me."

"My brother and my pop were pretty close and got along well. They used to play chess together and a few times they went to the racetrack together." Valerie was never allowed to go to the track. "My pop used to always tell me he was going to Jamaica.[10] I'd say, 'I wanna go! I wanna go!' and he would tell me I couldn't go there. I didn't know it was a horseracing track. My brother went with my pop a few times, but I don't remember him going there a lot, because I think gambling took an opposite effect on him. Instead of getting hooked, it made him more cautious. He didn't like losing, but he liked the fun of playing the odds. So he went occasionally for fun."

Valerie resented the advantages a boy had in an Italian family. Her brother had liberties she never had, simply because she was a girl. "My brother didn't have to go to church, but *I* did," said Valerie. "My parents didn't go to church regularly, but I had to go. If I didn't go with them, I went with friends, or by myself, but I *had* to go to church. I went to church in Washington Heights (St. Elizabeth) and I went to St. Philip Neri in the Bronx. My family did go to mass together a few times, all four of us, after my brother left home. We used to stop at the bakery after for buns."

"My brother moved out of the house when he was nineteen. I was only five, so we didn't grow up together," said Valerie. "He did teach me how to skate at the Fort Tryon playground near our home. He came over a lot, but we had nothing in common, nothing to talk about.

Guy Williams, model on cover of *Exciting Romances* magazine, early 1940s
(courtesy of Mary Spooner, the Mary Spooner personal collection)

"Then when I was nine years old, my brother left a book lying on a table in our house after one of his visits. I picked it up, and saw it was a collection of science fiction stories. I read every one of them, several times. That began for me a lifelong love for science fiction, which I have always attributed to my brother. He loved Science Fiction so we finally had something to talk about!

"I began to buy sci-fi magazines with planet stories in them. My mother didn't like them. She was very controlling and didn't want me to buy them. She called them escapist literature. But I bought them anyway.

"I finally had a connection to my brother through that book he forgot on a table. We finally had something in common."

Valerie went through a rebellious teenage stage. She began to take the liberties her mother had forbidden. Clare would turn to her son for advice. "My mother was always complaining about me. She and my brother argued a lot and I think it was usually about me. Dad and Mom's arguments could have been about me as well. Guy would always say, 'Leave her alone!', which is the advice he took himself."

In her late teens Valerie began to write science fiction stories and won the Promising Young Writer Award for a novel she submitted in a competition. In her early twenties she worked as a writer of pulp fiction stories published in magazines, such as *True Romance* and *True Confessions,* for a few years. "They were nothing to brag about. Just a way to make a living," she said.

Valerie came so late into the family that she missed the talks about family background and relatives. "A lot of my people were a mystery to me. They wouldn't tell me things. I used to wonder why there were so many years between me and my brother, but I never got an answer. Mother was always nervous. She had problems with the vapors, or what she called 'i nervi.' Whenever I would start to ask her things, her excuse for not wanting to talk would be, 'i nervi, i nervi.' I reached a point where I wouldn't ask, because my mother would get agitated and upset with me for asking questions. No one in my family told me much.

"I learned a lullaby from my father once, in a foreign language. When I told my mother about the song she got angry, and I never knew why. She said she thought it was a gypsy song, and didn't like it.

"*Twenty years* later I sang the strange words to a friend, who told me it was Russian. I never knew where my father learned it, and my mother didn't tell me."

Chapter 4

"I didn't know there was such a business!"
– Guy Williams

Armand landed a job in Manhattan as a salesman in the luggage department of Wanamakers, one of the oldest and reputable department stores on the East Side at Lexington. Although he was bored and didn't like the job, he kept it longer than any previous ones. It afforded him a small apartment in Manhattan, and his independence.

"I didn't do a thing there," he said. To pass the time during the day, Armand would often talk to a young attractive woman named Minelda, who was the store photographer. Minelda was the sister of actress Hope Lange. She would later marry Bob Jarris, who was a highly successful make-up artist for stage and screen with innumerable movie credits. It was Minelda who told Armand that his tall, lean frame and good looks could get him work as a model.

The thought had never crossed his mind. "I didn't know there was such a business," said Guy, remembering those early years. "I didn't know it existed."

Minelda offered to help him get started. She took his first head-shots at Wilson Studio. He was nineteen. Then she introduced him to someone named Toni, who knew everything about the business.

He took his pictures to different agencies and got a call from Patricia Allen of the Pat Allen Agency at 2 West 46th Street, who signed him right away. "I brought the pictures over and was sent out on jobs," said Guy. "The pay was better than anything I had been earning up 'til then."

"I ran into a girl who knew everybody in this underworld," he recalled. "It was a super job, not tiring, good money. Toothpaste, cigarettes, I was doing all that, and this was printed in the magazines, *Vogue* or *Harper's Bazaar*. Sometimes they sent you to the Caribbean. You ran into the most beautiful women in the world."[11]

Armand Catalano and his agent changed his name to Guy Williams within a few minutes. "The name Guy Williams was born out of a conversation," he said. "I chose my name because I thought it would fit any part."[12]

Work became steady and after two years Guy was one of the busiest and highly paid professional New York models. He quit his job at Wanamaker's after a year, his longest run at a "regular" job, and supported himself solely as a model. It was just the kind of job he liked. It was easy, didn't require long hours, there was variety, and it paid well. He could work and still have plenty of leisure time to socialize, play chess in the park, and play cards

Guy was the first male model to appear on the cover of Glamour magazine, February 1946
(the author's personal collection)

with his friends he met at the agency. It took him to interesting locations and gave him the
opportunity to date beautiful women.

For ten years Guy's face was printed in ads in the top magazines around the country—*Life, Look, Mademoiselle, Modern Romance, Saturday Evening Post, Collier's*, and all
the major fashion magazines, as well as newspaper ads, catalogs for leading department
stores, and fiction magazines. Guy was the first male model to appear on the cover of
Glamour Magazine, for an article called "All About Men," in February of 1946.

Marie Pezze remembers when she found out that the handsome boy from study hall
had become a supermodel. "A couple of years after graduation, Gloria and I were at 191st
in the subway waiting for a train," remembers Marie. "I looked up and saw this large
poster of a handsome man in a cigarette ad, Chesterfield or Camel, and I said, 'Wow! Isn't
he good-looking!' And Gloria said, 'Oh, Marie! You know him! That's Armand Catalano!'"

In 1946, big money was still being poured into print work and illustrations for
advertising. Very few "television sets" were in homes, so TV was no threat to print
advertising. Models and commercial artists were in big demand into the 1960s.

A prolific colony of gifted commercial artists in New York made a very good living at
this time. Almost every ad for a product was an artist's rendering of the model, rather than a

Guy did many cigarette ads, usually as a soldier, 1945, Life magazine.
(author's personal collection)

Guy modeling as a character in a story for *Amazing Detective* magazine, April 1948.
(author's personal collection)

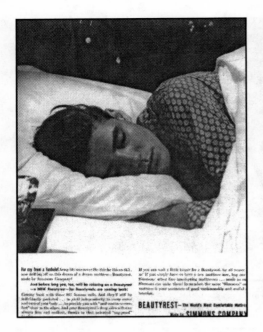

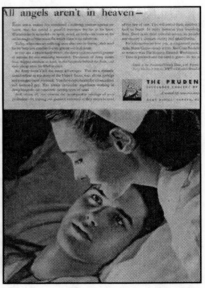

Guy in ads in major magazines in 1945.
(Clockwise: Beauty Rest, Kreml, Prudential, Norge)

Guy in 1946 ad for 7 UP, a product that in his future would sponsor his TV show, *Zorro*. (courtesy of Mary Spooner, from the Mary Spooner Personal Collection)

Pepsi Cola ad, 1946. (author's personal collection)

Guy for Eversharp Pens, 1946 (courtesy of Mary Spooner, from the Mary Spooner
Personal Collection)

photograph. Models were drawn from life, or from photographs taken of them. When Guy
modeled clothes for catalogs for department stores, the pictures were usually photographs.

Models advertised products, and they were also used for pulp fiction stories in magazines such as *Detective Stories, True Confession, True Romance*, to represent characters in the
stories, as though they were actors in a play. Writer Doug Warren,[13] who knew Guy in the
1940s, was a working model and actor at the time. "I remember walking down Fifth Avenue
with a friend," said Doug, "and running into Guy while we were making the rounds in New
York. We were struggling to become actors and would do modeling work when we could.
Guy was so good looking we used to envy him, because he would get all the good jobs," he
laughed. "If we were getting a whopping $25 an hour for a job—which was a lot—Guy
would get the $50 an hour job. He was a very likable and friendly guy." Doug still has a copy
of *Amazing Detective*, April 1948 in which he and Guy are pictured together (page 25) for a
story called "Trailing the Baby Face Cop-Killer." Doug is Baby Face, the outlaw, with his
hands up and Guy is the detective holding the gun on him.

When Guy decided to become a model, his father was not pleased. "Why don't you
get a real job?" Attilio had said. One day Guy took a handful of his paychecks to his
father's house, and placed them on a table in front of Attilio. A big smile slowing spread
across his father's face as he saw the large figures, and that was all Guy needed to see.
He'd made his father proud. The two had a good laugh together.

Chapter 5

"Guess what! I'm going to Hollywood!"

              – Guy Williams

Guy used to say that he sort of "drifted" into acting. He had modeling friends who were actors, but he had no aspirations of being one. Then one fateful day he was literally "picked out of a crowd on Fifth Avenue," so he told a journalist in the 1950s, to be in a *March of Time* film short.

The *March of Time* short subjects were the forerunners of what we know today as the documentary. Thirty million minds a month focused on the *March of Time* films by the mid-1940s.[14] Starting in 1935, they were produced every four weeks by *Time* and *Life* magazines, and distributed by 20th Century-Fox under studio president Spyros Skouras. American moviegoers were no longer content with fictional romance and musicals. They wanted knowledge, about human affairs and events on the homefront and abroad.

Guy played a returning war veteran tormented by visions of the catastrophes of war. With no lines to memorize, he was shown during voice-overs, acting out his visits to the therapists and adjusting to civilian life. This was his first time on film. He was a standout.

A prominent MGM acting coach and talent scout, Lillian Burns, was in New York looking for new talent. Pat Allen showed her photos of Guy and a clip from the film. She signed him with MGM for a term contract, and gave him a train ticket to Hollywood.

Guy went home to tell his parents. His father answered the door. "Guess what!" exclaimed Guy, waving his contract. "I'm going to *Hollywood*!" His family and relatives were excited and happy for him. A *movie star* in the family!

The westbound train pulled out of Penn Station and Guy was headed toward the city of glitz and glamour. Hollywood! A city of hopes and dreams; a city that seemed to exist only in the imagination; home of Gable, Grant, Bogie and Bacall. Idols he'd seen on the screen in the darkness of a movie house would now be all around him.

The train ride seemed endless. Was acting as easy as modeling? Would he become a movie star? Outside, the beautiful "land of the free" spread as far as the eye could see, across the western plains. He was the first of his ancestors to travel the breadth of this vast country they had dreamed of and sacrificed to come to. The red setting sun dropped

In a *March of Time* film Guy played a veteran suffering from traumas of the war.

After treatment he was able to get a job and adjust to civilian life.
(*Courtesy of Mary Spooner*)

behind the mountains far off in the horizon, where his fate awaited him.

From all indication it seems Guy arrived in sunny California in late spring of 1946. He lived at the Hotel Carmel on 2nd and Broadway in Santa Monica. He took the Red Car (Pacific Electric Cable Car) every weekday to the studio in Culver City where he attended Lillian Burns' classes in acting, elocution, dance, and social graces. On weekends he went to the beach to jog, swim, and bike ride.

Post-wartime was a jubilant and exciting time in Hollywood. Many box office giants had returned from the war to resume their movie careers: James Stewart, Henry

Fonda, Clark Gable, Tyrone Power, John Wayne, and Robert Taylor, to name a few.

Each studio was a nucleus with its stars orbiting around it. That nucleus drew young starlets, extras, and stuntmen from every city and state like a magnet. Together the studios made up a small universe called Hollywood, and the studios ruled Hollywood and they ruled their stars. Contract players were properties of the studios. They were told what to wear, what to say in public, and who to date. Dress code was stylish and impeccable. Behavior in public had to be contained and respectable at all times. In return, they would make you a star.

Movie mogul Louis B. Mayer ran MGM like a tight ship. Every major star and ingénue was expected to live up to his strict moral codes if they aspired to become a box office success. In return, newcomers were pampered, provided for, and promoted. They were photographed by the great studio photographers, and given publicity as *the* rising star to watch. Guy was sent out on dates with actresses Beverly Tyler, Marilyn Maxwell and Marie Windsor for the purpose of taking his picture for magazines to expose him to the public.

The popularity of documentary-style films, just after World War II, made Hollywood aware that audiences had a thirst for knowledge and realism, as well as entertain-

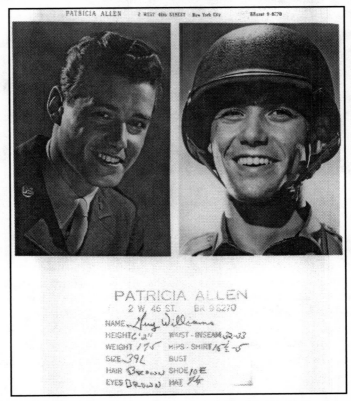

Photos taken for Patricia Allen Agency, early 1940s, along with stats in Guy's own handwriting, selling Guy as the All-American male. These photos got him work for a *March of Time* movie which lead to a contract with MGM. (author's personal collection)

Headshot taken at the MGM studios.
(courtesy of Kathy Gregory, the Kathy Gregory personal collection)

ment,[15] and some producers decided to quench that thirst. After America dropped the atomic bomb over Hiroshima on August 6, 1945, ending the war, there was concern about the power of atomic energy. The American people were confused and wanted to know more about the development of nuclear fission and atomic energy. Producer Samuel Marx wanted to get the atomic bomb story to the American people, and do it before anyone else did. He talked MGM studio boss, Louis B. Mayer to buy off producer Hal Wallis, who had started a similar subject for Paramount. Marx had Frank Wead adapt a story by Robert Considine about the atomic bomb, calling the docudrama *The Beginning or the End* (released February 19, 1947). The title was directly lifted from a phrase used by President Harry S. Truman.[16]

By July 1946 the movie was cast. *Life* magazine, August 5, 1946, plugged the movie and showed a picture of actor Godfrey Tearle, who would be playing President Roosevelt. Newcomer Guy Williams was cast in his first movie. MGM's own in-house newspaper ran an article to introduce him to Hollywood.

From *The Beginning or the End* Guy, center front, in classroom training.
(courtesy of Mary Spooner)

MGM Spot News—July 8, 1946
"Actor in Screen Debut As Bomber of Hiroshima"
HOLLYWOOD—Handsome Guy Williams, new leading man prospect signed recently by Metro-Goldwyn-Mayer this week, was awarded his first film role and found it loaded with dynamite-plus. In *The Beginning or The End*, he will portray the man who dropped the atomic bomb on Hiroshima. Williams is the youthful actor who signed a film contract after appearing in a *March of Time* short subject. Prior to that, he was a photographer's model in New York.

The movie opens with scientists and officials watching the burial of a time capsule to be opened in 2446 AD. The capsule will reveal to the world symbols and products of the first humans in history to use Atomic Energy. The movie reenacts the plans and development of the bomb, to its final use.

During the film Guy can be spotted in a training classroom scene, and in the background of a few other scenes. Near the end of the movie he has considerable screen time in the bubble of the Enola Gay with three other men who have the unnerving assignment to drop the first atomic bomb. As the bombardier, he sites the target and gives the fatal command, *"Bomb Away!"*, he yells. As the disastrous mushroom cloud rises, there is a close-up of his reaction to what they have just done.

The Beginning or the End starred Robert Walker, Tom Drake, Brian Donlevy, Audrey Totter, and Beverly Tyler, and a host of other talented actors, and it was directed by Norman Taurog. Although it did not do as well as expected at the box office, it became, over the years, an important piece of documentation drama because of its historical and controversial content. Today, it is often shown on the History Channel, followed by discussions on the war, and on Turner Classic Movies.

Guy showed promise in his performance, but his anticipation for bigger and better

From *The Beginning or the End* Guy, close up, reacting to the enormity of the devastation of the first atomic bomb. (Courtesy of Wendell Vega)

roles was met with disappointment. This would be his only significant role at MGM. "They put you under contract on a yearly basis," he said in 1985, "and used you in little filler spots, walkthroughs, and such. If the part was of any consequence, they would usually pick someone from outside to play it. The only advantage was to be able to glance at Spencer Tracy, or Clark Gable when they were having lunch at the table nearby."[17]

Guy enjoyed the social element of the experience as well as the acting classes. He met many new faces and familiar faces. He particularly enjoyed talking to the gifted composer/pianist/actor Oscar Levant, whose quick wit and zany sense of humor he greatly admired. Guy became friends with Wally Crocket, and his girlfriend, Vivian, both beginning actors at MGM. They would be part of an important event in his life in a few years.

After a year at MGM, Guy's contract was not renewed. What he thought would be the beginning of a new career, seemed like the end. Years later, when he reflected on his career, he had to laugh at the irony of the title of his first film. Regarding his career, it seemed like both the beginning *and* the end.

Guy reluctantly packed his bags for New York. The long trip home gave him time to think. He had liked the whole experience. He liked acting. He wanted to make more movies. The opportunity had landed in his lap too soon. All he needed was more training. He would save up and enroll in a good acting school. He would make this "the beginning."

The relatives gathered to greet him with a sumptuous dinner and listened attentively to his stories of Hollywood and movie stars. Valerie was proud of her big brother, but felt no reciprocation in her love for him. "I think he said 'Hi' to me, but I don't remember having a conversation with him."

Guy's reputation as a good model still held in New York and he was able to pick up right where he left off. Assignments were rolling in after his stint in Hollywood and he

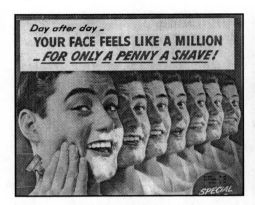

Guy did a number of ads from 1948-1951 including (starting on previous page) Eversharp-Schick, Phillips Milk of Magnesia, Mallory Hat, Eveready Hearing Aid Battery, (continuing this page) Jergens Lotion, Champ Hat – the Gaucho. (courtesy of Mary Spooner, from Mary Spooner's Personal Collection)

worked more than he ever had. For the next five years his image and likeness was seen advertising products in every major magazine: *Post, Life, Ladies Home Companion, National Geographic,* fashion catalogs, and as characters in romance magazines.

One thing had changed: the purpose. Modeling for him now was a means to an acting career. He now had a goal—to be a movie star on the big screen. He would save up and enroll in the prestigious Neighborhood Playhouse.

Guy rented a small apartment on Lexington near Central Park East, where he enjoyed his solitude. Guy was a paradox. He liked people and was social, but he also like being by himself and often preferred it. He would be the first to tell you that he was his own best company, along with his record collection. He was never lonely with himself. He stocked his bookshelves with an eclectic selection—geography, science fiction, astronomy, photography, ancient religions, the Egyptian and Greek civilizations, theology, American history, and politics—and he read them all, and could discuss each subject with anyone. Music and science were his constant and most passionate interests, with politics following close. Guy was very liberal. While he sometimes agreed with the Democrats and sometimes agreed with the Republicans, he never completely agreed with one party. He usually favored the Independent party.

Guy was a nonconformist. He didn't want to do something simply because society dictated it to him. He didn't like to be told what to do in general. If it was Mother's Day, he might not go out and buy a present for his mother simply because someone said he had to. He wanted to get his mother a gift whenever he wanted to—and he did.

Nearly every day he stopped off in Central Park to play chess with a group of older men who were always there passing the time of day enjoying the game. He would always beat them.

January 1946, Guy was on the cover of *True Romance* with then model Grace Kelly.
(from the author's personal collection)

Guy met many beautiful women in his profession, models and aspiring actresses. One young beauty who was modeling while studying at the American Academy of Dramatic Arts was Grace Kelly. In a few months she was to become the hottest new face in the modeling world, then the movies. Guy met her during a photo shoot and dated her briefly. Grace and Guy made a handsome couple when they appeared on the cover of *True Romance*, for the January 1948 issue.

Chapter 6

"In a tiny town called Toone"

– Janice Cooper Williams

TENNESSEE, 1945

In Memphis, a beautiful nineteen-year-old named Ruby Janice Cooper boarded the northbound train for New York City to pursue her dream of becoming a fashion model. Born on March 13, 1925, Ruby was the third of eight children (four girls and four boys), born to Virginia Sylvester Cooper and Utley Thomas Cooper. "U.T," as he was called, was a deputy sheriff in a small town near Memphis, and Virginia, a full-time mother and housewife. Both were old-fashioned southerners, who still addressed each other in public as "Mr. Cooper" and "Mizz Cooper."

The Coopers were devout Baptists, of English and Scottish heritage. Proud of the fact that they could trace their ancestors back to one Thomas Cooper, who came to America on the Mayflower, they were of sturdy stock. The name Thomas was passed on to every generation of Coopers thereafter.

When Ruby was born, her mother couldn't decide what to name her. A close friend named Ruby came over to see the baby and suggested a name she liked a lot: Janice. Virginia thought it was a fine name, but said she would name the baby Ruby Janice, in honor of her friend who named her.

"The Ruby part stuck," said Ruby Janice. "I never really liked that name for myself, so when I went to New York I changed it. But to this day, when I go back home, I am called Ruby by everyone."

"U.T" was close to his little girl and anxious for her as he watched the train take his daughter away. She was going to a city bigger than any she had ever seen, where she knew no one.

"I was born in a tiny town called Toone in Hardeman County, Tennessee," said Janice. "Toone was so tiny that the locals made fun of it with a little jingle:

Toone, Tenn, Toone Tenn-
Two-stores, and a cotton gin.

38

"My earliest remembrances are of this tiny little town. I really have nice memories of it. Jump rope, and jacks. Being barefoot, playing outdoors. We'd make our own toys. I remember whittling for hours." With a natural instinct for homemaking she learned to cook at an early age and made her own clothes. "There was a field by my house and I used to spend hours picking the tall clover and tying them together. I'd make long chains, and then decorate my room with them."

She was only four years old when she started school. "My mother had five children at home by the time I was four, so we were put in school as soon as possible," she said. "There was no kindergarten."

When Ruby was in her first play at school, she found out how important her dad was to the community. "I remember doing a play when I was in the first or second grade. The high school was doing a play and they had me playing the child in it. It was late and dark, and they heard funny noises during rehearsals. Everyone was frightened, and they call my daddy. He came over and saved us all," she laughed. U.T. looked all around the place, checking everything, and made sure everyone was safe. "He was like that. I remember people calling him in the middle of the night to go out looking for bank robbers. During the Depression banks were being robbed right and left, and he and his posse would go out to look for them."

When Ruby was eight years old, her father was asked to be the deputy sheriff in Bolivar, Tennessee. This was a step up because Bolivar was the county seat. She was excited about the move. "It was still a small town, but Toone was so small, Bolivar seemed like a big city to me."

Ruby never feared her father like some children do. "He was always easygoing with me," she said. "I always thought he could do anything, and he practically did. He was involved in so many things. For instance, the Central Telephone in this little town was in our house. Everyone in the family, even the kids, knew how to operate the cords and plugs in this switchboard. People would call my mother and tell her where the robbers were that day, and my daddy and his men would stay out chasing them in their Model A Fords until they caught them. Bonnie and Clyde were around then."

Ruby enrolled in the only school in town. Although it was called Central High, it contained all the grades from one to twelve. She made good grades in all her subjects, but she made straight As in math every year. When she was in high school, she became a star player on the girl's Varsity basketball team.

During the long hot summer days, she played at the swimming hole, which was a spring dammed on one end by the townspeople to make it deep enough to swim in. Ruby never did learn to swim there, but she loved to swing off the rope tied to a branch with all the other kids.

Although she was a beautiful teenager, with blonde hair, fair skin, and mystic blue eyes, no suitors came to call. "My daddy was the traditional Southern, over-protective father, who was so afraid that someone might just look at one of his daughters in the wrong way. And everyone in town *knew* this. So the boys stayed away," she laughed. Years later her brother-in-law tried to make her realize how frightening it was for any boy who wanted to date one of U.T.'s daughters. "Your father was a lethal weapon when you all were teenagers. He was the sheriff, and he carried a *gun!*"

Sports, studies, movies and books filled Ruby's time as well as her share of household duties. Reading was her favorite form of entertainment. "I read everything I could get my hands on: books, magazines," she said. "I liked to read in bed before I went to sleep. When my parents said 'Lights out,' I read under the covers with a flashlight."

"I went to the movies with my friends at the Luez Theatre in town. My favorite actor was Richard Greene. I thought he was so handsome, and I used to think, 'Boy! His wife is *so* lucky!" she smiled.

Ruby graduated when she was only sixteen and left home to attend Union University in Jackson, Tennessee, about 25 miles away. "I took a part-time job there with Sears to defray my expenses," she said. "They started sending me to different little towns to do the accounting. I was good at math so when they had problems with their bookkeeping system they'd send me around to the area and I'd stay a week or so to get their accounts straightened out. One of these little towns was called Paris, and the woman tending the books was incapable. They wanted me to stay on there and take the job as manager of the store. What amazes me now, when I think about it, is that I was only sixteen. I was in my first year of college, and they were offering me this terrific job of running the store. So I quit school, and I ran the store for three years.

"I was getting very bored and one of the clients who came all the time, kept saying to me, 'You ought to be modeling in New York.' One day I said, 'Well, I think I will.' I quit my job, and got on the train, and went to New York. I was *that* bored."

To prepare for her daring adventure, Ruby sent out applications to the Powers, Coniver, and Barbizon modeling schools. Ads in magazines coaxing young girls to apply were easy to find. Powers and Coniver, the two biggest, required interviews and if they liked you they'd take you. But Barbizon replied that she would be great and they would be expecting her. They sent directions to their place from Grand Central Station. Once she got there, they would give her a list of places she could stay.

"I didn't know anyone in New York. I had never left Tennessee and that bothered me. I knew there was a whole world out there that I had never seen. I knew what I wanted, and I was doing it. I got a little nervous on the train because it took about two days and one night. I had a berth, but it took a long time to get there.

"I arrived with about half-a-dozen other girls going to the same place. It was morning and our first stop was the school at 5th Avenue and 47th Street. Each one of them had a letter saying, 'Oh yes, you'll be great! Come,' and, I mean, girls converged from everywhere.

"I remember my first impression of New York. The buildings were *so tall.* I was looking up to find the sky. I kept saying, 'Where's the sky?'

"When I told the people at the school my name, they asked me what name I wanted to use, and I said, 'Janice Cooper.' Anyone who met me after that knew me as Janice.

"Three of us were given some addresses of places to check out to find a place to live. So my first day in New York, we were out on the streets looking for a place to live, but at least they told us how to get the subway and whatnot. By nightfall, I had a bed. It never occurred to me at the time that I might not get a place. I knew I could always get back on the train and go back."

Janice was destined to work with the biggest and the best. Her beauty and talent singled her out one day when she was modeling fur coats for the prestigious furrier, Haddie Carnegie at 42 E. 49th Street. A journalist who was covering the show was ex-supermodel, Robin Chandler, one of John Robert Powers' most successful and famous models. Janice's style impressed her so much, she went to her former agent, John Robert

In this issue *Using Camera Swings and Tilts*

Janice Cooper on the cover of *US Camera*, August 1947. (Author' personal collection)

Powers, the most powerful modeling agent in the country, to recommended her. "This model is better than I ever was!" she told him. Powers called Janice immediately and hired her on the spot. From that time on she remained an elite Powers Girl, known in the business to be the epitome of poise and sophistication.

In 1946, Janice's lovely face was on the cover of *U.S. Camera* in a tight close-up taken by Andre De Dienes at Jones Beach. Like Guy, Janice worked all the time, modeling for products and fashion. She was in biggest demand for swimsuits.[18]

Her room on 75th Street was far too cramped and after a year Janice began to look for a larger place. Housing in New York is hard to find, but after the war it was the worst. Fortunately, through work, Janice had made friends with some newspaper people and they promised to be on the lookout for her. One day someone in public relations at the *Herald Examiner* was moving to Los Angeles, and they called Janice. "It was in the Des Artistes Hotel. A wonderful place to live. I was very lucky to get it. It was just one block from Central Park West near Tavern-on-the-Green."

The Hotel Des Artistes, as the name suggests, housed many of the most important artists and photographers of the 1940s: Howard Chandler Christy, Russell Patterson, Arthur William Brown, to name a few. The walls of the hotel lobby and restaurant were painted with beautiful murals by Howard Chandler Christy. Most of the artists who lived here had studios across the street and Janice had worked for all of them many times over the years. One artist at Rahl Studio across the street was the niece of the great French impressionist, Claude Monet.

It became routine for Janice to go downstairs for breakfast and be invited by the artists to join them and friends. They had their own Algonquin-style clique. "It was a wonderful time. New York was wonderful then," she marveled.

Janice had many suitors now that her father was not around. Most of them were uninteresting to her, so she welcomed the curfews set by the hotel for the young women living there. She had many friends, but "Mr. Right" had yet to come along and sweep her off her feet.

There is a saying in the South about inevitable true love: "Two people's cradles rock together." Hers and Guy's were on a collision course.

She grabbed her coat and ran to her modeling job. Print work for a Mum deodorant ad at Rahl Studio.

Chapter 7

"…the most gorgeous creature I had ever seen."

– Guy Williams

MANHATTAN, 1948

Guy crossed Central Park and headed for Rahl studios for his next photo shoot for Mum deodorant. When he arrived, he was outfitted with ski clothes.

Janice Cooper emerged from her dressing room, a vision of radiance in her ski outfit. When Guy met Janice there was an instant attraction between them. He took one look at those crystal blue eyes, her big, lovely smile, and could hardly keep his eyes off her.

"I thought she was the most gorgeous creature I had ever seen," he said. "I still remember how staggered I was by her beauty. And I still am, right to this day."[19]

Janice felt the same way. "My first impression of Guy was simply that he was the best looking, and nicest, sweetest person I had ever met. Right off, I was swept off my feet; right from the start. He was just perfection."

Janice, in her snug sweater and ski pants, brought to mind the sultriness of Lauren Bacall, the sexiness of Ava Gardner, and the classiness of Grace Kelly. Guy—tall, fit, handsome—was the epitome of the all-American male. They were a photographer's dream.

They went through several modes of action. Guy tied her shoes. Guy helped her with her jacket. "The photographer was a perfectionist and shot this sequence about fifty times, over and over again, which I didn't mind, because it gave us a chance to get to know each other. We were falling in love while we were being photographed."

"Not only was he handsome," continued Janice, "but I was drawn to his attractive inner quality. He was a gentleman, so polite, and so intelligent. It was love at first sight."

After the shoot they each went to change. Guy hurried so he could catch Janice before she left to go out for coffee, but she was quicker. When he came out of his dressing room, she was gone. Janice had rushed off to her next assignment, and Guy did not know how to get in touch with her.

In a 1959 interview, Janice said:

Sweaters a problem?
Not for me...

I'm a **safety-first girl** with Mum

Mum safer for charm

Mum safer for skin

Mum safer for clothes

Guy and Janice in Mum deodorant ad, a drawing from photographs made the day they first met. (from the author's personal collection)

I was afraid we were going to be fired from the first assignment we ever worked together. Guy kept ignoring the photographer's polite directions for us to pose this way or that. He was so busy trying to get me to go out with him afterward for a cup of coffee. But I had two more assignments that afternoon.[20]

Janice hoped she would see him again. A few weeks later she was walking along 45th Street with a friend and spotted him in the crowd. "He and his uncle were walking together at a brisk pace. It was near Sloanes where his uncle worked. I recognized him right away. I waved and he didn't see me, so I raised on my toes above the crowd, waving, and saying, '*Hiiiiii*!!' He looked at me kind of startled," she laughed. "As if to say, 'Well, who are you?' And he kept walking. So, I thought, 'Well, he doesn't even remember me. But I remember him.'"

Guy had not forgotten Janice, and considered himself lucky when he found himself working with her again. This time he was not going to let her get away. Janice, however, had a date after the shoot, but Guy laid on the charm. "The next time we worked together," said Janice, "I was supposed to meet someone after to go somewhere with him and some friends. Instead, Guy came along with me to tell this fellow that I couldn't make it. I never did see that fellow again," she laughed, "nor the other friends we were supposed to meet. Guy and I went out for coffee and that's when he told me how he had tried to catch me the time before and I had gone. During our courtship I saw Guy and only Guy.

"After that we were absolutely inseparable. That evening he saw me home, then the next morning he came to get me for breakfast. Every morning he would walk from Central Park East and I would walk from Central Park West, and we would meet in the Park. Then we'd walked together to Central Park South for breakfast at the St. Moritz. After that we walked as far as we could together before we had to go to our agents, and the first moment we had a chance to meet again, we would. Sometimes we did the same thing for dinner," she smiled, enjoying the memory.

"Guy invited me to his place to see his piano. He had rented a baby grand piano that was jammed into his tiny apartment on Lexington, and he was taking piano lessons! He was always doing something. I had never known anyone as cosmopolitan and intelligent as Guy. He was reading books like *Cybernetics* when I met him! He knew about so many things, and I loved his sense of humor. If I had to describe Guy in one word, it would be 'Exciting!' It was always exciting to be with him, because he was always delving into something interesting."

Guy and Janice worked together a few more times. One job together was for a Sucrets advertisement. Janice and Guy are holding sheet music in front of a microphone offering another man a Sucret while he is coughing.

"I was frightfully busy with photographic jobs at that time," said Janice. "I remember having to trot from New York to Philadelphia to Boston—and curiously enough, Guy always managed to turn up wherever I was. How I ever managed to get to any of those photo appointments on time is a matter of some wonder to me now, but I did."

After two weeks Guy knew he had found the girl of his dreams. He wanted to marry Janice, so he took her home to meet his family. Attilio was thoroughly enchanted by Janice from the moment he met her, and the feeling was mutual. He affectionately called her "Janina." On many occasions he told Guy how lucky he was to have Janice.

"I loved Attilio. He was a sweetheart," said Janice, "a lovable man. We got along famously together.

"Clare was beautiful. Guy looked like both of his parents, but as he got older he looked more and more like his father. Attilio taught me how to make some wonderful Italian dishes. I had always cooked southern, but after I met Guy I never cooked southern again."

Vitalis **LIVE-ACTION** care gives you Handsomer Hair

VITALIS and the "60-Second Workout"

Guy and Janice for Vitalis in one of many ads they did together. 1949. (courtesy of Mary Spooner, The Mary Spooner Personal collection.)

Janice feels more Italian than she does English. "My soul is Italian. I love the architecture, the culture, and the food of the Italians."

Attilio and Clare were both great storytellers, mostly stories about family history. They were more expressive than what Janice was used to. Clare's English was better than Attilio's. He had a strong accent, but Janice loved the way he said certain words, such as ice cream as "eechy creamy." She loved to watch their expressions and their hands move as they talked. "Guy was like that too. He had large hands, beautiful hands, and when he talked those hands were always going."

When Clare told a story she became so animated, her voice was melodic, and her face, full of expression. "I loved to listen to her," said Janice. "She was very smart and she had a great sense of humor."

Clare had a writer's soul. In the 1940s her gift of languages and storytelling earned her a nice salary, as she filled the position of writing the subtitles of foreign movies. Her business card read:

Clare Catalano
Director, Editing and Story Department, IFE
(International Film Editing)
An Italian Company Release Incorporation

"Humor can so easily be lost in translation," noted Janice, "but Clare had the talent to express in English the same humor intended in the Italian version."

Many of the movies by acclaimed director Vittorio De Sica were subtitled by Clare. Some of the well-known Italian films she translated for the viewing audience were: *Ladri di biciclette/ The Bicycle Thief* (1948), *Riso Amaro/ Bitter Rice* (1949), *Le Petit Monde de Don Camillo/ The Little World of Don Camillo* (1952), and *La Romana/Woman of Rome* (1954).

Film censorship made Clare's job of distributing Italian films in America in the 1940s difficult. Most of the movies under fire were mild compared to today's standards, but they were considered too risqué in those days. "Clare was so good at what she did, and they passed them," said Janice.

When *The Bicycle Thief* won at the Cannes Film Festival, Clare was flown to Italy with her company to celebrate with De Sica. *The Bicycle Thief* went on to win an Academy Award in 1948 for Best Foreign-Language Film. The visit to Italy prompted Clare to begin saving for her dream trip to Sicily with her family.

Valerie was ten years old when she met Janice. She was awestruck by Janice's poise and beauty. She remarked, "If Janice had been in the movies, there would have been no Grace Kelly." Janice's kind and sweet disposition endeared her to Valerie forever. "Janice was like a big sister to me. I love my Jan!"

Guy was head over heels in love. He hung around the lobby of the Des Artistes hotel waiting for Janice every day. One night after they had known each other only five weeks Guy asked Janice out for a special evening. He took her to the Red Coach Restaurant at 7 East 58th Street for a romantic dinner. After dessert he popped the question, sort of.

"We had this wonderful dinner. Guy was so sophisticated, he knew how to order in a restaurant. Guy had great *savoir faire*. I was just a little Tennessee gal, not used to the big city. We had a dessert that I had never had before called Indian Pudding. Then he took my hand and said, 'I love you,' and I said, 'I love you, too.' Then he said, 'Well, you know what *that* means, don't you?'

"That was it! After that we spent every waking hour trying to figure how we could get married right away."

Guy's old friends from MGM, Wally and Vivian Crockett, had gotten married and were struggling actors living in New York. Janice and Guy were having dinner with them one night and told them how they wanted to get married without having to wait three whole days. The Crocketts became excited for them, and were willing to help. They had heard that in some states the waiting period was only one day instead of the three days in New York. The Crocketts offered to drive them in their old station wagon to all the neighboring states to find out. They took them up on it.

"We literally drove from state to state to state to try to find a place that would marry

The Bird in the Bottle Inn in Garrison, NY, where Guy and Janice celebrated their marriage.

us over the weekend," remembered Janice. "We found out we had been misinformed and no one would do it. I think we went as far south as Virginia. We drove back up to New York and decided to do it the slow way."

They applied for a license and on the sixth weekend of their courtship, Guy and Janice were married in Harrison, New York, on Saturday, December 4, 1948 in a private civil, double-ring ceremony with Wally and Vivian Crockett standing for them. Judge Harold Menger officiated.

Wally and Vivian drove them to the Bird and Bottle Inn in Garrison, New York, where they celebrated with a candlelight dinner. The rustic charm of the dining room with its warm fire burning in the large hearth was a welcome respite from the freezing cold outside.

"Guy was a very affectionate person," said Janice. "Through all the years we were together, when we were sitting next to each other, for instance, with friends or wherever, he would put his hand on my arm or my leg. He liked to touch." When he talked to a friend, he would put his hand on their arm or shoulder. He was a very expressive person.

"We had a wonderful romantic champagne dinner," said Janice. "Then the Crocketts[21] drove us north to Sleepy Hollow, not far from Peekskill, where we spent our honeymoon weekend at Great Colonial Lodge. We had a beautiful room with a great view of the lake outside. Guy was a very romantic person." She demurely allowed, "It was *veeerrrry* romantic." Pan to window.

Chapter 8

"in the fresh fallen snow...the words 'I LOVE YOU.'"
– Janice Williams, *TV Picture Life*

Janice went to the hotel to tell the manager she was moving. "The manager used to tease me a lot about Guy hanging around the lobby so much. So when I told him we had gotten married, he joked with me and said, 'I'm so glad! You were beginning to give the place a reputation,'" she laughed. Nothing could have been farther from the truth, because all the women in that building were respectable. "Some things just weren't done," she said.

"I called my mother in Tennessee to tell her I had gotten married. When I told her his name she said, in her Tennessee accent, 'Oh, you married an EYE-talyun!!' Janice promised to bring him home to meet the family in the summer.

Guy's apartment was too small for the two of them, but it was still nearly impossible to find an apartment. They liked a place at London Terrace on 24th Street between 8th and 9th Avenue, but were told that nothing was available. The manager liked them so much that after talking to them a while, he said he'd let them have the next available apartment.

"We didn't have to wait too long. Neither of us had furniture, so we rented a furnished apartment. It was the largest space either of us had ever rented."

Guy and Janice were both making good money. Janice worked more than Guy because women were more in demand for products and runway modeling. They were also paid more than men. Thrifty and smart about saving, they studied the stock market with Guy's mother and began to invest. In an interview in 1957, Guy joked about getting married, "We consolidated our finances," he said. Cracking a joke for effect was part of Guy's personality. It was also a way sometimes to distract from his sentimental side. Privately, Guy expressed his love for Janice often, sometimes creatively.

Janice remembers their first New Year's Eve together:

It seemed like everyone we'd ever known was tossing a party that night. We were invited to at least six of them. Over dinner, we decided that a party with its noisy crowd, its smoke, and the heat of some small apartment, was not the sort of atmosphere we wanted for welcoming in a year which, we sensed, would be the most exciting we'd ever spend.

So we spent the evening together, just the two of us. Along toward midnight we went into Central Park for a walk. It had been snowing, and everything was covered with a fresh blanket of white. It was like daylight almost, so bright, with a big full moon. I remember lots of bright light on the snow and the park was deserted on this festive night.

We had the park all to ourselves. And if I live to be 180 years old, I shall never forget the sight of that huge suitor of mine, all bundled up in muffler, mittens and overcoat, with his big goulashes flapping, as he tramped, hopped, and jumped around in the fresh fallen snow. He was tramping out the words 'I LOVE YOU' in letters six feet tall.[22]

Most of their leisure time was spent taking walks. "Guy loved to walk, so we walked everywhere. We loved the Met and went there once a week. From 24th Street where we lived it was about sixty blocks, so there and back was 120 blocks, and we covered that easily."

Guy's favorite section in the Metropolitan Museum was the Ancient Egyptians, filled with statues and sarcophaguses of Egyptian kings, queens, and gods of mythology, the sculpted head of Nephratiti, and Osiris, God of the Nether world and the symbol of Life, Death, and Rebirth. "Guy's favorite painters were the Impressionists, particularly Van Gogh and also El Greco. One time he sneaked a touch of a Van Gogh. I believe it was the Sunflowers," said Janice. "I was so afraid, because you are not supposed to touch them. Many years later that same painting was in Los Angeles and Guy and I went to see the exhibit. All the guards were telling people, 'No touching, please. No touching.' Guy made a point of going over and touching it. He looked over his shoulder, and when no one was looking, he touched it. I was scared to death, but he thought it was funny. He said, "I touched it before, I'll touch it again."

Weekends saw them often with friends who drove them on short trips. An artist friend and his wife took them on fishing trips upstate, and sometimes to Jones Beach.

"We used to play cards all night with Guy's friends he had met at Pat Allen's. Gin and Hearts. Guy could beat me at chess, but he could never beat me at Hearts. He couldn't catch on to it."

In the summer of 1949 Guy and Janice rode the rails together to Tennessee. U.T. and Virginia prepared a big southern dinner for them and family and relatives met the new member of the family with warm southern hospitality.

Janice was used to the local suitors fearing U.T., so Guy's boldness startled her. "Guy was meeting my dad for the first time and he said to him, 'Well, she begged me to marry her, so I had to.' I looked at him," her eyes widened with shock, "I was so scared my father would disapprove of that, but he realized Guy was joking and they hit it off."

Like most newlyweds they only had eyes for each other. When they went to town they did silly things, like play Last Tag, mindless of who saw them. "We bought water pistols one day in Bolivar and chased each other around this little town with water pistols. People thought we were crazy."

"We wanted to cook an Italian meal one night for everyone," said Janice, but she was in for a culture shock she had been unaware of before. "Of course there was no olive oil in the house, so I had to go out and buy some. When I got to the store I found there was no olive oil anywhere on the shelves. None of the grocery stores sold it! I ended up buying a bottle of olive oil at a pharmacy!"

Bolivar was a "dry" town, but people from Hardeman County, where the Coopers lived, would go to Shelby County and bring back liquor. "When my father and brothers wanted to take Guy out for a drink they would say, 'We have to see a man in another county about an insurance policy,'" she laughed, "and they would head out to get some beers."

Guy enjoyed the country, and since he liked fishing and hunting he loved listening to the hunting stories told by U.T and one of Janice's brothers. "I have four brothers, but the one called the black sheep is the one that Guy liked best." Janice laughed because this was so like Guy. "He was a hunter and so was my father. One night they were telling Guy about their hunting trips, and Guy told them he wanted to go on one. So, very early in the morning, while it was still dark, Guy and my brother left for the hunt with flashlights, and dogs running and barking through the hills and valleys. Well, we were to leave that night to go back to New York on the train, and they didn't show. More time past and they still didn't show. At first, I was the only one worried, but then by nightfall everyone was worried. A posse was sent into the woods to look for them. We were so afraid something had happened to them. Finally, about two in the morning, they found them. They were lost! They were so tired from walking round and round in circles trying to get back home."

When they told their tale, Guy said, "When your brother looked at the river and said, 'That river is supposed to be over there,' I knew we were in trouble."

Janice's brother was an experienced hunter and he couldn't figure out what had happened. Knowing how much Guy could talk, Janice figured they were probably talking too much. The event was written up in the local newspaper.

Although relieved to get back home, Guy said he was never afraid. "Guy had no superstitions or fears. For him, everything was an adventure."

When the two returned to New York, Guy decided to buy a car, his first. He wanted to take Janice on trips to places of his youth, like Peekskill and Sea Cliff. "Guy bought a 1949 Hudson," said Janice. "Hudsons had a good reputation at that time. They were very big and long. Not what the average person was buying. It was just like Guy to not get what everyone else was buying. He didn't follow trends or the norm. He was always different, and the car suited him."

"It's really weird who sold Guy his first car, because we became friends years later in Hollywood. It was Jack Lord,"[23] she said still amazed. "He was a young actor at the time putting himself through drama school at The Neighborhood Playhouse by working in the showroom."

"Guy bought the car but he couldn't drive. His father didn't drive either, so his Uncle Oscar taught him how to drive. Every day in the evening, he'd take Guy out to teach him to drive. Attilio and I went along for the ride."

Attilio was color blind, so the signal lights all looked gray to him. Valerie wanted to teach him to drive, and she showed him how the top light was always the red one, but he didn't feel secure about it. Fearing he might make a drastic mistake, he never would drive.

"Guy was not accustomed to having a car in New York so when we'd come out of the movies, he would forget where he parked. He was so funny," said Janice. "He'd put his hand on his hip and look up and down the street, and say, 'Now, where did I park that car?'

"One time we drove to New Jersey to go see a movie called *The Thing*.[24] It was playing at an outdoor theater, and I remember how scary it was. Guy loved science fiction and he loved European movies, especially French films. Sacha Guidry was his favorite actor, so we used to see a lot of his movies. He also loved Italian movies by De Sica."

Every weekend Guy took Janice somewhere. At Peekskill he showed her where he went to school. "Guy had fond memories of going there. It was a beautiful place. We used to run into people who had gone to Peekskill in our work occasionally. There were two brothers, twins, who were photographers that Guy and I sometimes worked with and they had gone to Peekskill. It was always fun for Guy to meet someone else who went there."

Guy drove across the Hudson to Spring Valley to show Janice where his grandfather had settled, and to Sea Cliff where he enjoyed his boyhood summers. They would take the Staten Island Ferry for a jaunt and, both being adventurous spirits, they might spontaneously get in the car and not know where they were going until they got there.

Janice recalled driving in Long Island once, and they saw what was the first tract houses to relieve the nation's housing problem for the returned veterans. "There was a building boom on Long Island and we could see all these new little cookie-cutter houses lined up row after row. There were no people in the houses yet, but there was a TV antenna on every roof."

Guy's ideal society was one with freedom and equality for everyone. He questioned everything from the existence of God to affairs of state. "Guy was an independent thinker," said Janice. "He didn't follow the masses. I think Guy was ahead of his time and knew some things just had to change.

"When I met him, he was a big Wendell Wilke fan, and he was always saying 'One World, One World,' which was the name of the book Wilke wrote. Ever since I knew him, he was interested in politics. But he was an individualist in his thinking and his opinions sounded leftist at times."

The threat of communism was serious. Senator Joseph McCarthy was targeting people in the entertainment field for so-called un-American activities and associations with the Communist party. "Guy was so outspoken about his views when we were around our friends, who were also models, that when they heard him talk and talk so openly on the job, they would say to me, 'Tell Guy not to talk so much. It's dangerous.'"

Guy got into the Neighborhood Playhouse at 340 East 54th Street in the latter part of the 1940s to focus on studying acting. Classes consisted of scene studies, character analysis, walking, movement, and articulation. Guy could juggle his modeling assignments with his classes. At this point in his life Guy had the impression that acting was an easy profession. Janice laughed, "Guy always wanted a job that required only his presence and very little work."

At the Playhouse Guy had the best teachers in the business: the great Sanford ("Sandy") Meisner and the world renown teacher of dance and movement, Martha Graham. Regarding his training, Guy said, "Over there it was not so much the text that was taken into account as the physical moves and diction. And believe me, when we come from a Martha Graham class, we know how to go down the street. We knew how to walk."[25]

After living at London Terrace for a year Guy and Janice moved to 17 West 67th Street near 5th Avenue. "It was a great apartment in a good location," said Janice, "but it was so close to the stables[26] in Central Park we could smell them. Nearly every Sunday

Guy and I would walk across the street and go horseback riding. He had learned to ride when he was young, in the Park and at summer camp, and was very good at it."

They spent a lot of time together in Central Park. "We used to meet each other every chance we got. One of our favorite places was Rumplemayer's restaurant in the St. Moritz Hotel. They were famous for their ice cream. Guy's favorite was vanilla."

At the crest of a small hill there were tables with chess sets under a rotunda for relaxing and playing chess. Guy could never resist stopping to play. "We'd always stop there and I would watch Guy play chess with the old men who were regulars there. Guy always won. I only saw him lose once. It was to someone down in Greenwich Village, and he could never get over that. He kept saying, 'He beat me so *quickly*.' He was always trying to figure how it happened.

"I told Guy I felt sorry for the old men in the park. I said they must be lonely, having nothing to do, but sit in the park and play chess. He laughed at me and said, 'No. They are happy. They feel very lucky to be able to do that all day.'"

Guy took Janice to hear the New York Philharmonic. She knew Guy was a big fan of Toscanini, so when she was able to get tickets for a Toscanini recording session, she surprised him with tickets for the two of them to sit in at Studio B of Radio City Music Hall to see the legendary maestro himself. "It was a big moment for Guy," said Janice. "He never forgot that."

Guy and Janice both liked to cook. "Guy's mother made dishes I had never tasted before and they were delicious. One of our favorites was a sardine casserole, made with sardines, pine nuts, raisons, and bread crumbs. I got many recipes from her and from Attilio. Some of Guy's favorite dishes were risotto Milanese, Viennese calf liver, smothered with onions, and pasta aglio e olio (pasta with garlic and olive oil)."

Guy and Janice used their creativity in making up menus sometimes to amuse their guests. They knew a couple who was struggling to make ends meet. The husband was a writer, the wife was an artist, and neither knew how to cook. Guy and Janice invited them over for dinner one night to play a little joke on them. This was the same couple who had called them over to their place one day to help clean beans off the ceiling. "She put a can of unopened string beans in the oven one time to heat the beans. When she took it out of the oven and opened it, the can exploded and there were beans all over her ceiling. She was known to do strange things with food, so Guy and I decided to play a joke on them. They both had a sense of humor that encouraged people to do wacky things they would appreciate. So one night, to show them we could cook a whole meal on a low budget, we served them a full-course meal, based only on rice. The first course was soup of chicken broth, with rice. Then the main course was Risotta Milanese (Italian rice with cheese), followed by dessert of Rice Pudding. By the time they got to dessert they had caught on."

Guy and Janice took up photography as a hobby. "Guy bought a Roliflex camera and we rigged up a dark room in our bathroom to develop the film ourselves. We picked up a lot from the photographers we met on modeling jobs and we learned by experimenting. We would go to Central Park and take pictures and write down the number of the frame and the setting we used for that picture. Then we'd develop and print them ourselves in the apartment. We'd check our notes with the results and we learned how to make them better."

Janice is gifted in the art of photography, with a natural eye for composition and lighting, and the ability to capture an image at the precise moment.

Chapter 9

"My life changed when my pop died."
    – Valerie Catalano Fitzgerald

In 1950 Guy auditioned for a summer stock company founded by John Kenley, and made it. Actors learned total theater: performing, set construction, stage management, lighting, and clean up. There were no prima donnas in summer stock. Well-known actors played the leads and the rest of the roles went to the stock players. "We had such a good time in summer stock," said Janice. "Guy had a bit part in *Pal Joey* as a soldier and understudied several other roles. The director was Bob Fosse,[27] who was even then a great choreographer. He was [later] married to dancer Gwen Verdon. Fosse played the lead in *Pal Joey* that year. They did about six plays in a summer. If you weren't in the play, you worked it in some aspect."

Located in a wooded rural setting in Lakewood Park, PA the playhouse had an atmosphere of summer camp. Actors would sit outside on the grass or in chaise lounges in comfortable shorts and halter tops learning their lines or playing cards. "We had a grand time that summer. Guy drove us there in the Hudson," said Janice. "Many of his young actor friends from the Neighborhood Playhouse were in the cast, some already known, and some who would become well known later on. Barbara Britton was there that summer."

When summer stock was over, Guy and Janice drove to Tennessee to visit her folks. They were treated as celebrities in Bolivar and their visits always made the local newspapers. "Sometimes we'd decide at the last minute to go to Tennessee and we'd just hop in the car and go. We would stay a couple of weeks at a time. Guy always enjoyed visiting there."

When they got back to New York, Clare was preparing for her long awaited dream trip back to her homeland. She was smart and knew how to invest. She had studied everything about the stock market. Attilio wouldn' touch it. He preferred the short term gamble at the race track. Clare had saved a long time for this trip.

"Clare was very organized and thorough. She had bought new clothes for everyone and they were packed," said Janice. "Shortly before they left, Guy took a whole roll of film of the three of them in their new clothes for their passports. They planned to visit Attilio's brother in Palermo, Sicily, then go to Messina where Clare was from." Clare had finally gotten the tickets and passports in her hand. A few days before they were to leave, Attilio was watching television when he suffered a heart attack and was rushed to the hospital. Clare was torn with grief and disappointment. Valerie was riddled with guilt because she had been arguing with him at the time over what to watch on TV, and she blamed herself.

Attilio stayed in the hospital for a while and when he was released Clare took him to the quiet beach at Sea Cliff to recover, but Attilio never fully recovered. He never worked again after the heart attack, and during the next year he went from a husky, solidly built man to one who was thin and frail looking. Guy went to visit his father regularly during his convalescence.

Valerie remembered how much this trip had meant to her mother. "I really don't believe we would have come back. My mother thought it was a better life in Italy because of her childhood memories and I think she intended to stay and raise me there. My mother had been grooming me to be a nice little Italian girl, not an American-Italian, and I think she would rather have raised me there than here."

In the spring of 1951 Attilio suffered a second heart attack and was hospitalized for a long time. He had to be put in a convalescent home. Guy was attentive to his father while he was sick, but when he was hired for another season of summer stock with the John Kenley Players he had to say his goodbyes.

Guy and Janice reluctantly left for Lakewood Park near Barnesville, PA, where Guy was in a production of Johann Strauss' *Fledermaus*, which ran from June 11-16, 1951. Guy played a Lackey in the chorus of this witty opera. Guy claimed to have no talent for singing at all, so his voice must have been drowned out by those who had.

Janice stayed with Guy until she had to return to New York for a modeling assignment. Models were needed now for television, the popular new medium. Janice did a live commercial for Tinthair, where she actually tinted her hair on camera. The commercial aired on the *Somerset Maugham Theatre.*[28]

While Janice was in New York Attilio took a turn for the worse and on June 14, 1951, in the middle of Guy's production, Attilio passed away from heart failure. He was only 55 years old. Janice called Guy. "I just couldn't tell him over the phone, so I told him his father was very ill and to come home right away."

Guy came home immediately, in time for the funeral. The burial was at the Gate of Heaven Cemetery in Valhalla, New York in the Bronx.

Valerie's grief ran deep when she lost her father, just when she seemed to need him the most. "I was just two months shy of my thirteenth birthday when my pop died. I didn't get along with my mother, and my father used to take up for me when my mother and I had loud arguments. My life changed when my pop died. I lost my best friend.

"My father wasn't home a lot when I was little," remembered Valerie, "because he traveled all over selling insurance. Just before I was born, he had been in New Orleans. He liked it there, but my mother would never want to live there because she and my Uncle Oscar and I all have a phobia of bugs that fly. We're scared to death of any kind of flying roach, moths, things like that.

"I remember my dad gave me my first lesson about the importance of enunciation at supper one night. It was when he almost lost his job because of his accent. A wealthy married couple went out on a boat ride with my father to look at beach front property in New Jersey. The man's wife was very attractive, and as they were looking at the beach from the boat my father put his arm around the man and said, 'Sheza beautifulla beeetch, isn't she?' The man thought he was talking about his wife, and he was furious with him, but he didn't *say* anything to him. My father had no clue why the man turned cold and pulled out of the deal until his boss told him one day why he lost the sale and almost his job! So he came home that day, and I learned my first lesson about enunciation while I ate my soup.

"I remember that my pop and my mother wanted us to use our right hand. If you used your left hand, it was called maldestra, which in Italian means 'bad hand,' you were corrected, which is why we both are ambidextrous. Not only did this stem from superstition that being left-handed was a kind of curse, but it was also inconvenient because desks were not made for the left-handed people, nor was anything else."

Guy fenced with his right, ate with his left, wrote with his right, clapped with his left, pitched a ball with his right, usually pointed with his left, and gestured with both.

After the funeral, Guy returned to PA to finish the summer stock season. From July 16-21,1951 he played the part of "Private Griggs, U.S.M.C." in a play by Somerset Maugham called *Rain*.[29] The star was opera singer Lawrence Tibbett.

The shock of Attilio's death took its toll on the family. Valerie was becoming a rebellious teenager and was falling in with the wrong crowd. "After I lost my father, the rest of my life was hard for me. My mother was always complaining about me.

"My Uncle Oscar was very kind. He understood my situation and said to me after my father died, 'I'm like your father now. You have nobody else.' He was a comfort to me."

The neighborhood was changing and Clare no longer felt safe where she and her daughter lived. She worked during the day. At night she was lonely and afraid. Her dream of going back to Italy was shattered. She never talked about it again. "It's too late," she told Janice.

When Guy returned to New York, Clare asked his advice on how to curb Valerie's irresponsible behavior. Getting her away from the bad influences was one way, so Janice suggested they send Valerie by train to Bolivar to spend the rest of the summer with her family. She and Guy would pick her up at the end of the summer. It would give Clare a break to deal with her grief and take Valerie's mind off her guilt. Everyone agreed, including Valerie. "It was my first time in the South and I had a wonderful time. Everyone there was so nice to me."

Guy and Janice drove down to Tennessee to pick her up. "While we were there," said Janice, "Guy decided to trade in his Hudson for a new one at a dealership just across the Mississippi state line. But first, he had the car painted a blue color, because he thought it would give it better resale value, and he drove it down to the dealership before the paint was dry. The salesman gave Guy a great deal on a trade-in and we drove the new car back to New York. When we got home Guy got a phone call from this irate salesman who was yelling about having blue paint on his hands, 'You knew that car was still wet and you didn't tell us!' Guy thought it was funny."

Valerie left Bolivar happy but was in for a rude awakening when she arrived in New York. She was not taken back to her house on Wadsworth, but a new place on W. 67th Street. While she was away, a vacancy had turned up in Guy's building and he and Janice helped his mother move in. Clare wanted to move. She loved the central location, the security of the building, and she was near Guy and Janice. No one asked or told Valerie.

"I came back and didn't have my house anymore!" said Valerie. "I came back to a strange new place. I was just told I had moved. I missed my house, my bedroom I loved, and my neighborhood."

Clare had always provided Valerie with good books and lessons in dance and piano, in an effort to enrich her life, but she was too controlling. Clare chose Valerie's clothes, her hobbies, her part-time jobs, even filled out the applications for her. Guy would sometimes come to her defense, but not as much as Valerie would have liked. They never had a close relationship.

Clare's children reacted differently to her controlling ways. Guy, by simply doing what he wanted, and Valerie by being mischievous. "When I was a teenager, I loved a comic book by Bob Kane[30] that had a woman in it with beautiful red hair. So I started dyeing my hair red, and I have ever since."

Valerie's anger about the move was directed to her mother and she became more rebellious. Clare sent her to boarding school for discipline. "It was like prison," said Valerie. "I took piano lessons from the nuns there, and if you made a mistake they would hit your hands with a ruler. I had bruised fingers." After a year there, Valerie went to Julia Richmond in Manhattan where she graduated.

In 1951 Guy was nurturing an unspoken goal to go to Hollywood. Janice remembers when she found out where Guy had his sights set. "We had very little furniture of our own and just a little borrowed from Clare. We basically lived out of boxes. So, one day I mentioned something to Guy about buying a piece of furniture, and he said, 'No, no. We're going to California.'"

Near the end of 1951, Hollywood drama coach Sophie Rosenstein, from Universal-International,[31] was scouting for new talent in New York. Guy was singled out at the Pat Allen Agency. He had "the look" of that movie era. A screen test was arranged and Rosenstein was impressed. She called Paul Kohner in Hollywood, an established agent who handled stars from Universal-International (U-I).

Janice recalled, "She asked Paul if he would represent Guy Williams, and he said 'Well, I don't know who he is! I've never seen him!' Sophie said, 'Well, he's another Jeffrey Hunter.' At that, Paul said, 'I'll take as many of those as I can get!' And he signed Guy, sight unseen."

Guy had a year-to-year contract beginning at the first of the year. His acting career was taking bloom. He landed his first TV role on *Studio One*[32] for CBS, playing an American soldier in a drama called "The Paris Feeling." Guy is in several scenes, with a few lines, some of them humorous. His style is already evident in his movement, delivery, and facial expressions. The leading actor was his buddy, Wright King, who had previously played the paperboy in an unforgettable scene with Vivien Leigh in the movie version of Tennessee Williams' *A Streetcar Named Desire*.

The show, sponsored by Westinghouse, was taped, but the commercials on it were live. Everyone's favorite spokeswoman, Betty Furness, demonstrated the newest innovations in some of their appliances: "a television set with a dial that quickly changes your channel and locks in good reception," and a new Westinghouse clothes dryer that "lets you know when your clothes are dry!" Miss Furness closed the program by tearing off the last page of her 1951 calendar, and saying, "1952 is going to be a really big year for our show. And on behalf of Westinghouse, may the new year bring you just *everything* you want!"

Everything Guy wanted was in Hollywood. He and Janice headed West.

Part II

Hollywood

1952-1973

Chapter 10

"We loved California"

– Janice Williams

"We packed boxes with a few incidentals and sent them ahead to California," said Janice. "What little furniture we had, we gave to Guy's mother. We put our precious things in the trunk of the car because we did not want to risk shipping them: Guy's record collection and record player, our silverware, things like that. We put all the clothes we could in the back seat of the car, and we left for California.

"We traveled over the Christmas holidays. It took us a good two weeks to get to California, because we stopped first at my parent's house in Tennessee. Then Guy wanted to stop in a very famous town in Tennessee that makes sour mach liquor, and, when we went through there, our car went on the blink. Someone stopped to help and drove us into town where we called someone to pull the car into a garage. Then, they took us to Aunt Someone's boarding house to stay, and the next morning we had breakfast with all the overnighters. We thought it was funny that we had been so protective of our things in the trunk by taking them with us, and it was in the hands of strangers all weekend. Guy just said, 'Ah, the hell with it,' and we laughed about it."

With the car repaired, Guy and Janice were on there way for their first cross-country trip together. The first of several, but the only one they would make alone, and with such expectations and wonder.

"We arrived in Hollywood around New Year's Day and the town was packed," said Janice. "We were a day early, so Paul Kohner was not expecting us yet. He was not even home. We had no place to stay so Guy called a little motel on Santa Monica Boulevard near La Cienega, and we stayed there for about a week.

"Paul told Guy he would take him around the studio after the New Year's holidays. Guy wanted everything to be perfect, so he insisted on getting a haircut. He didn't know the barbers in Hollywood yet so he went to one Paul recommended. He should never have done it. It was too short and he didn't like it. He had to go to the studio with the worst haircut I'd seen in my life."

Kohner took Guy around the studio. He would join the other contract players in the acting workshops. An appointment was made for Guy's glamour shots and he had caps put on his teeth to fill a gap between his two front teeth, for the pictures.

Some young actors at the studio were already making names for themselves: Rock Hudson, Tony Curtis, Piper Laurie, Jeff Chandler, Jeffrey Hunter and his wife, Barbara Rush, Gig Young, who was married to talent scout and acting coach, Sophie Rosenstein, to name a few. Other contract players in Sophie's acting stable with Guy were James Best, Dennis Weaver, John Smith, Russell Johnson, Stuart Whitman, Jack Kelly, Hugh O'Brian, John Lupton, Richard Long and his wife Suzan Ball, David Jannsen, Anita Ekberg, Kathleen Hughes, Lori Nelson, Julie Adams, and many more glamorous and handsome faces of the early 1950s. A young stuntman named Buddy Van Horn was working steadily on the lot and would cross paths with Guy in a few years.

Guy and Janice moved into an apartment building whose Spanish-style architecture was a direct influence of Douglas Fairbanks, Sr.'s *The Mark of Zorro* silent movie of 1920. When Californians saw this movie, they fell in love with the arched doorways, romantic wrought iron balconies, and stucco walls. The set of this movie was not patterned after the real colonial California, but rather the Spanish architecture that Fairbanks and his wife fell in love with during a trip to Spain. He was reading the *Zorro* script at the time. The walls of the set were stuccoed merely to give them texture so the one-dimensional eye of the camera could see depth. Californians loved the look and began to build stucco houses. The Spanish styles in Fairbanks' *The Mark of Zorro* carried over into most of the architecture during Los Angeles' building boom of the 1920s.

Mary Pickford went before the American Institute of Architecture in December 1926, and brought to their attention that California homes were a hodgepodge of styles built like the homes the settlers had come from all over America. She asked that the style of architecture for California be predominately Spanish, Mexican, or early Californian, reflecting the charm of California's precious heritage. They agreed, and in some sections of California the homes have to be up to that code. Because of the popularity of *The Mark of Zorro*, California homes from Santa Barbara to Rancho Santa Fe[33] and San Diego line the coast with their clay-tiled roofs and textured coatings.

Guy and Janice moved into one such beautiful Spanish-style apartment building in Hollywood, built by actress Norma Talmadge. Some of Hollywood's greatest silent stars lived there such as Nazimova and Shirley Mason. Located at 1330 Harper Street, just one block south of Sunset Boulevard, it was called El Pascadero, and is an historical landmark. He couldn't have been in a more suitable building when he became Zorro than this.

Joan Korda, wife of director/producer Alexander Korda,[34] was the owner of the building, and Guy's agent, Paul Kohner knew her. Janice remembers her first impression when she saw the apartment. "Paul had gotten us an appointment to see a vacancy there, and we loved it. Within days we moved in."

There were four spacious apartments in the building and Guy and Janice were in number 104 on the first floor. "When you entered the apartment there was a wrought iron staircase that curved up to the top level that went to the bedroom and bath. The living room ceiling was two stories high with an indoor balcony overlooking the room. Rooms on the second level were off this indoor balcony. There was a stained glass window that opened from the master bedroom and looked down over the living room and there was a little wrought iron balcony you could stand on. It was absolutely fabulous.

"So we moved into all that space with only what we could put in the trunk of the car! We had no furniture. Just a few inexpensive essentials in boxes.

Guy and Janice moved into this famous complex called El Pascadero, 1330 Harper St in Hollywood, built by movie queen Norma Talmadge in the late 1920s, when they first arrived in Hollywood in 1952.

"We went to Akron and bought a hollow door, some cast-iron legs, and some cushions, and Guy and I fashioned a sofa together. I covered the cushions for it and made drapes for the large window in the living room. Guy had his big speakers in the living room, and we eventually got a small TV. We had what we needed."

In 1952, their first year in Hollywood, Guy and Janice shared that same spirit of adventure they had in New York. "We loved to drive," said Janice. "We traveled around a lot when we first got to California. We went to see the bullfights in Mexico, and went to Las Vegas, San Francisco, all over Los Angeles, and the beach cities. We would drive all around just looking at the city. We loved California. It just looked so different from anything I had been used to, and it *smelled* so good.

"We were driving around Beverly Hills looking at the big houses and Guy said, 'I hate to say this—because it's against my philosophy—but I'd *LOOOOVE* to have one of those,'" she laughed.

Chapter 11

"Eminently Forgettable" Roles

– Guy Williams

Guy's glamour shots were taken by the studio for publicity. The studio wrote his stats on the back of the pictures in pencil: Height: 6'3",[35] Hazel Eyes, 180 lb., Age: 28.

Guy felt much more prepared now for Hollywood than he did when he went to MGM, but for any beginning actor there is always fear and doubt with effort and hope. The acting classes in New York, summer stock, and the TV debut on *Studio One* helped give him confidence for his second chance in Hollywood. He had the talent and the looks, all he needed was that big break.

Sophie Rosenstein, a petite brunette in her 40s, was warm and caring about her actors. She protected them and made them feel safe.

Actor Dennis Weaver met Guy at U-I and they began a friendship that lasted more than twenty years. They were both in small roles at the time, hoping the next role would be bigger. "Guy and I were both in a movie called *The Mississippi Gambler*[36] at U-I in 1953," said Dennis. "We didn't actually work together that much, because I may be in a scene in the first part of the picture, and he'd be in a scene in another location. We had small parts, since we were under contract. Two years later we were both in *Seven Angry Men* for Allied Artists."

Dennis recalled those early days of their career. "At Universal there was a program to groom their up-and-coming stars. There were classes at the studio, because they wanted to make their actors as talented as they could in many different areas. We had dancing lessons, singing lessons, drama lessons. You didn't get a salary cut if you missed, but you were supposed to attend classes. It was semi-voluntary, but they expected you to attend *something*. A lot of times you were working and couldn't attend."

Contract players were taught The Method by Sophie Rosenstein, the acting coach who hailed from Northwestern University, one of the best acting schools in the country. While some described Sophie as petite and homely-looking, Dennis amended that. "She had a wonderful heart, which made her very attractive. She was a wonderful and giving teacher," he said.

A prerequisite of acting in those days was knowing how to ride a horse. "There were wranglers at the stables on the back lot to teach us how to horseback ride. I took advantage of the horses by doing a lot of riding all over those hills where the Universal Tours are now. You

Young Guy, publicity shot taken at Universal-International in 1952.
(The Kathy Gregory Personal Collection; courtesy of Kathy Gregory)

could learn how to ride or polish what you could already do. We got coached in 'running mounts' and 'flying dismounts,' all kinds of stuff most of us didn't know how to do, but would be useful theatrically. Being able to get off and on a horse in a 'flashy' way, gave you a certain status—as far as the audience was concerned anyway. Guy used to be there. That's where Guy learned to ride for *Zorro*."

Guy said of his earliest roles under contract, some credited some not, "I used to play anonymous men leaning in doorways with cigarettes dangling from their lips. There were times when I seriously doubted if I were cut out for this business."[37]

His first credited role at U-I showcased him in a speaking part in a movie called *Bonzo Goes to College*[38] (released September 1952). It was directed by Fred de Cordova, who later directed the Johnny Carson Show. Guy plays Ronald Calkins, a private tutor to young actress Gigi Perreau, who is raising a genius chimp (orangutan) named Bonzo in her house. He's in a scene with Perreau and Irene Ryan, years before she gained international fame as "Granny" on television's *The Beverly Hillbillies* in the sixties. The stars of the movie are Maureen O'Sullivan (Mia Farrow's mother), Charles Drake, Edmund Gwenn, Gene Lockhart (June Lockhart's father), and new-comer David Janssen, who later became famous for TV's long-running *The Fugitive*. When

Scene from *Seven Angry Men*, Left to right: James Best, John Smith, Larry Pennell, Jeffery Hunter, Raymond Massey, Dennis Weaver, and Guy Williams, Universal-International, 1955. (the Kathy Gregory Personal Collection, courtesy of Kathy Gregory)

Seven Angry Men, L to R, Larry Pennell, Jeffery Hunter, Debra Paget, Guy Williams (The Mary Spooner Collection, courtesy of Mary Spooner)

asked in the mid-1980s to remember anything about this movie, Guy said, "Mercifully, I forget." He laughed, adding, "The least known thing about it is the picture itself. It was eminently forgettable." Eminently forgettable was a phrase Guy often used about most of his early pictures.

Guy had a part in a long scene playing an Army inspector in *Willie and Joe: Back at The Front*, an army comedy starring Tom Ewell (released in October 1952), in which he had lines.

"Guy's agent would have us over to his house for dinner," said Janice, "and that is where Guy and I first met Jeff Hunter and his wife Barbara Rush. They were one of the first couples we met in Hollywood. Jeff's real name was Herman Henry McKinnis, but we called him Hank. And we always called Dennis 'Rupe,' just as his wife did. Jeff and Barbara were friends

Guy with Gigi Perreau in *Bonzo Goes To College*.
(photo from the Mary Spooner Personal Collection)

of Estelle Harman, who was there for dinner with her husband Sam Harman. All of us became good friends."

Estelle Harman was a talented acting coach who replaced Sophie Rosenstein, at Universal, after the latter's untimely death in the early 1950's. A few years later Harman taught at UCLA, the other best acting school in the country, then started her own acting workshop, which Guy would later attend.

On July 21, 1952, just six months after Guy and Janice arrived in Los Angeles, they experienced their first earthquake. With the epicenter in Tehachapi, California, at a magnitude of 7.77, it was strongly felt in Hollywood. Twelve people were killed in Tehachapi and many injured. "We were at home when it hit. It was early in the morning and suddenly everything shook," said Janice. "At first we didn't know what it was. When we realized it was an earthquake we were frightened because we had seen the movie with Clark Gable about the 1917 San Francisco earthquake and we expected huge chasms to open up in the earth and swallow us up. Then, there were several aftershocks."

Just before the earthquake hit, Janice had found out she was pregnant. It was not planned. "Guy wanted to wait longer before having children. He liked things the way they were. He'd say, 'Later, later,' wanting to put off having a child. But when I got pregnant, he did a turn around, and was very excited about it."

On December 18, 1952 at Cedars Sinai in Hollywood, Dr. Harold Boris delivered the Williams' first child, a beautiful healthy blue-eyed baby boy, with curly blond hair. When Janice went into the delivery room, Guy was pacing nervously up and down the waiting room. Dr. Boris, who was also a friend, managed to calm Guy when he said to him, "Don't worry. It's just like squeezing the pit out of an olive."

"Guy loved that," laughed Janice. "He thought that was so funny. I didn't think it was that funny, but he told that story every time Steve's birthday came up."

They named the baby Guy Steven Catalano and would call him Steve. Guy was the typical Italian father, proud that his firstborn was a son. The Catalano name was put on his birth certificate, but he would be known publicly as Guy Steven Williams.

When Steve was a baby Guy and Janice took him with them to dinner at Paul Kohner's house. Paul and his wife, the beautiful Latin actress Lupita Tovar, had a lovely teenage daughter, Susan Kohner, who delighted in babysitting little Stevie. Susan was a senior at Hollywood High at the time, and wanted to be an actress. Her mother would tell Janice about Susan's school productions. It would only be a few years before Susan Kohner would become a bright new starlet. She first appeared in *To Hell and Back* in 1955, with Audie Murphy. After making a few more movies, she made a name for herself in 1959 with her performance in *Imitation of Life*, with Lana Turner and Juanita Moore, which won her an Academy Award nomination for Best Supporting Actress.

In January 1953 Guy's contract at U-I was renewed for another year. Eager to play leading roles, Guy worked hard to do his best. He was on time, knew his lines, his cues, and practiced his riding, so he would be ready for any role.

In *The Mississippi Gambler* (released in January 29, 1953), Guy is seen elegantly dressed as Andre, a close friend to the aristocratic Dureau family of 19th-century New Orleans. Piper Laurie was picked among the contract players to star as Angelique Dureau, with handsome star Tyrone Power, as the riverboat owner/gambler, Mark Fallon. Ty Power had played Zorro in the ever-popular version of *The Mark of Zorro* in 1940, the first with sound. *The Mississippi Gambler* was directed by Rudolph Maté, and also featured Julie Adams, John McIntire, John Baer, and Guy's friend, Dennis Weaver. Guy has lines when he has to stop his friend, Laurent Dureau, from fighting Fallon in a bar. In another scene, Guy is introduced to Fallon/Power. They bow to each other and, for a few moments, cinema's two most famous Zorros are face-to-face in the same frame.

In another scene by the famous Dueling Oaks—the giant oak trees that stand today in New Orleans' City Park—Guy is seen wearing an elegant black cape, as he watches the duel. Actor Frank Wilcox in this scene would later work with Guy on *Zorro*, ("Rico" in episode 45), as well would the Belgian fencing master Fred Cavens, and his son, Albert Cavens.

In *Take Me To Town* (released in May 1953), Guy has a few lines playing an actor in a play within the movie. The romantic comedy was directed by Douglas Sirk, and starred Sterling Hayden, Ann Sheridan, Philip Reed, and Lee Patrick. Sheridan is putting on a play for the community, with Guy playing the lead in the play called *The Hero*. He brings humor to the role as a young man overly zealous about his part in the play. Guy shines brightly on screen with the two stars, Hayden and Sheridan, who flank him in a close up. Dressed as a lumberjack, his good looks and strong features dominate the screen in the short time he is on.

In *All I Desire* (released in June 1953), starring Barbara Stanwyck, Richard Carlson, Lyle Bettiger and Maureen O'Sullivan, again directed by Douglas Sirk, Guy appears several times as one of actress Lori Nelson's young school friends with a sprinkle of lines here and there. He appears as the ticket taker for Lori's school play, just outside the theater door. He is also a guest at her birthday party where he has a line with screen legend Barbara Stanwyck. Guy was star struck—one of his idols was Barbara Stanwyck—so it was a high point in his life to make a movie with her.

In *The Man From the Alamo* (released in July 1953), director Budd Boetticher put Guy on a galloping horse for his screen entrance. He had more dialogue than usual and about five

Guy stole the scene in *Take Me To Town (1953)* with Sterling Hayden, left, and Ann Sheridan. (courtesy Mary Spooner)

Barbara Stanwyck (left) *in All I Desire*. Lori Nelson, far right, and Guy, next to her. Guy was so delighted to meet Stanwyck he kissed her hand and loved to tell about it. (Mary Spooner Collection, courtesy of Mary Spooner)

minutes of screen time with closeups. As a Sergeant bringing a message from Sam Houston's army, he has a noteworthy spot in a scene with Hugh O'Brian, Julie Adams, and the inimitable Glenn Ford. The movie also features Victor Jory, Chill Wills, Jeanne Cooper, and Neville Brand.

While filming *The Man from the Alamo* on location in Thousand Oaks, California, a few miles northwest of Los Angeles, Guy asked a wrangler if he could take a horse out for a ride during a break. The wrangler consented and Guy took off alone in the tall grass and high chaparral of a vast area surrounded by huge rocks and mountains. As he rode away from the

Guy, center, played a messenger in *The Man From the Alamo*. Left is Chill Wills, right, is Hugh O'Brien. (1953)

camp, he thought he heard the roar of a lion. Believing he must have imagined it, he ignored it and continued to ride. New Yorkers had heard tales about the mountain lions in California attacking people. Guy stopped and listened, and this time he heard more than one lion, and they sounded closer. Instinctively, he drew his fake sword from his costume. But it was only a wooden handle with a six-inch stem. Defenseless, he pointed his horse toward the set at a fast gallop to warn the others of mountain lions. The set was deserted. For a moment, he feared the worst. Then, he found everyone eating lunch at the tables and he began to warn them that he heard mountain lions. Someone popped up and said, "Oh, you just got near Jungle Land! It's a public park over there where visitors can go see the lions." The roar of the lions echoes and ricochets off the mountains, making them sound louder and twice as many. Guy had a good laugh over this, and laughed about it for years to come as he told the story.[39]

The Golden Blade (released August 12, 1953) starring Rock Hudson, Piper Laurie, George Macready, Gene Evans, Kathleen Hughes, was one of several movies filmed at this time on a soundstage filled with desert sand from Arabia. The cast and crew called them "tits and sand" movies, because of all the beautiful harem girls running around the set in see-through costumes. Guy's role was that of a Town Crier who enters the gates of a village on horseback, pulls open a scroll, and reads an announcement of a forthcoming jousting event.

Guy called his small roles at Universal "eminently forgettable," but one thing was unforgettable: His appearance onscreen. He had star quality. The look of a leading man. He had what it takes to be a movie star. Guy felt certain his contract would be renewed. Universal was promising him better roles. They were grooming him for stardom. It was just a matter of time before the right script came along. As 1954 was approaching, he hoped he would finally get the break he was looking for, that a role in a significant film would launch his career as a leading man in the movies. Instead, it brought his first bad break, literally and figuratively.

Chapter 12

"The bone in his upper left arm had snapped in two."
— Russell Johnson

Between the end of summer to early fall of 1953, Guy went to the stables on the back lot of Universal to practice his riding. He liked the looks of one particular horse he wanted to ride and as he went to put the saddle on him, he decided he would ride him bareback. While galloping the horse, Guy lost the reins. He clung onto the horse's mane, but the horse's back was lathering with sweat and becoming as slippery as a bar of soap. Guy slid right off, with the horse at a fast gallop. As he went down, the horse's hoof kicked him in his left shoulder.

Someone saw it happen and alerted others for help. Guy's friend, actor Russell Johnson, was nearby. "I heard all this commotion and saw people running from all directions, so I ran to see what had happened," said Russell. "When I got to him, I could see he was in extreme pain. They took him to the nearest hospital right away. The bone in his upper left arm had snapped in two, and his shoulder was out of its socket. They kept him in the hospital a long time."

Guy was rushed to St. Joseph's Hospital in Burbank, about a mile away and across the street from the Disney Studios. Jeff Hunter rushed to Guy's house to get Janice. "Jeff drove me to the hospital and dropped me off at the entrance and I went running in to see Guy. They wanted all this information first. Steve was a baby and I was holding him like this," she demonstrates as though he were a feed sack on her hip, facing outward. "I was holding him with one hand, and signing papers frantically, with the other. Finally, I got to see him. He was in terrible pain. His upper arm, the humerous bone, was protruding from under the skin. His arm was completely out of the shoulder socket and he needed surgery immediately. He had to have two steel pins temporarily placed through the humerous to hold it together. When Guy came out of the surgery, he kept telling me to call the nurses at the desk to get him more pain killers. The pins were gruesome looking. They stuck out about an inch or two from his arm. Sometimes he would accidentally hit them on a door jam and he would throw his head back in pain. It took six months to heal. First he was in a cast, then he used a sling while the pins stayed in the remainder of the time. He had a large scar that ran from the front of his shoulder down under his armpit in a sort of 'S' shape," she said running her finger along her shoulder to describe it.

1954 came, and Guy had months to go before the pins were to come out. His contract was not renewed. It was a low blow for Guy. He knew the consequences of being "out of the loop" in Hollywood for six months. It was probably the lowest period in his life; one he never talked about.

Guy knew his chances of getting a role in a prestigious picture were slim without a studio contract. Now with a baby to support, he and Janice had to come up with some creative means to survive in a tough town. "Guy used to always say, 'Life is no bed of roses,'" said Janice. "And Guy would say funny things, like 'Now, if only I had that Gutenberg Bible my mother made me return!'" she laughed.

"We had to really watch our pennies. We called these our 'Rice Days' because we ate a lot of it. I remind our kids about that when they think they are having a hard time. But we liked rice, so we didn't mind."

As for making ends meet, Janice was frugal and versatile. Not only could she cook and sew, but she also did the minor repair work around the house. Most of the time, she was the one with the hammer and screwdriver in hand, not Guy.

Janice was always optimistic, always encouraging, and supportive. "I knew I could still get work modeling in New York, because my friends there had always reminded me of that. I took Steve with me to New York to show him off and he stayed a while. I got a nurse for Steve (Guy's mother was working, and couldn't babysit), and borrowed a perambulator from a photographer friend down the street. Every morning the nurse took Steve to the park in that perambulator, while I'd go off to do the fashion shows. I'd just called the people I knew and got right back into work, because I had only been gone a year. I did that for four weeks, then I was so anxious to get back to Guy. I didn't even go to Tennessee first to see my family like I had planned. I got a nonstop to L.A."

Janice plunged into modeling work in Los Angeles to help make ends meet. "Someone in New York told me to go see Mary Webb Davis, the biggest agent for models in Los Angeles. She signed me on recommendations alone, and I could begin working right away. But I realized I had to get a car, and I didn't know how to drive. Guy took me to get a car. He bought me a green secondhand Pontiac to learn on. This car had literally been owned by a little old lady, so it was like new.

"Jeffrey Hunter taught me to drive, because, you know, they say, 'Your husband can't teach you.' He was so gentle and easygoing. Jeff took me in the green Pontiac to take my driver's test. I took the test, got my license, and the next morning, bright and early, I put Steve in the car, drove over Laurel Canyon to drop him off at the Weaver's (Dennis and Gerry's) on Emelita, in the valley, got on the freeway, went downtown— drove in downtown traffic!—did my job, which took all day, then got in the car and just reversed it." It amazes Janice now that she did that.

By the time she picked up Steve in the valley, it was dusk. She took Laurel Canyon to Sunset Boulevard, then turned South on Harper. "And as I came down the hill from Sunset I saw this silhouette of a figure standing in the middle of the street. It was Guy! He was so worried; he was waiting for us in the street!"

"I was about to call the police!" he said, relieved to see them.

Janice continued to work for a few more years. The majority of her work was for Jantzen Swimsuits. She also worked fashion shows, promotional events for auto shows, advertisements, and other print work.

Guy was capable of babysitting Steve, but he would be anxious for Janice to come home the whole time, so it was easier for her to take Steve along with her.

"Modeling in California was different than in New York. I didn't enjoy it like I did in New York. It was not as much fun," said Janice. "And Guy didn't like for me to work anymore. In New York he didn't mind it, but now he didn't want me to work."

Guy is quoted to have said:

> It [modeling] gives her a feeling that she can do what she wants. She also makes money.
>
> In Egoville (Guy's word for Hollywood), I don't think it's good to have two careers going. The wife goes on location then the husband goes on location and they see each other in passing. That's not good for a marriage. And then there's the ego thing. One career goes up, the other goes down and the other goes sideways—it can get pretty messy.[40]

When the pins came out of his arm and the sling was no longer needed, Guy began an exercise regime of swimming, hitting the speed bag (boxing), and, of course, walking, to rehabilitate himself physically.

Now came the arduous task of jump-starting his career. First, he had to have new pictures taken to submit to agents and casting. An actor friend from Universal, Willard Sage, had taken up photography, and he took pictures of Guy. Some were of the outdoor, rugged Western-type for Westerns and some were in his fencing jacket with gauntlet and foil inside the salle. With no agent, and no studio, he had to freelance. Months and months went by with no roles coming his way. For a short time he thought it was all over and considered going back to New York, but he decided not to give up his dream.

"Walking was something we always did together in New York and Hollywood," said Janice. "On our usual route along little Santa Monica Boulevard in Beverly Hills, Guy used to notice the Aldo Nadi Fencing Studio near Cañon Drive. He thought fencing would not only be good exercise, but a good thing for his career as well, and he stopped in one day and signed up for lessons."

While most actors were spending time playing the trendy sports, golf and tennis, Guy was with the illustrious Italian champion and maestro, Aldo Nadi and his brother, Nedo, enjoying fencing lessons. "Guy never did follow trends or fads," said Janice. "He did what he wanted to do."

In the year Guy took up fencing, he got back into shape. "We were always weight-conscious," said Janice, "so we tried to eat right. But once in a while, we would get so tired of eating healthy we would just binge on jellybeans and popcorn and candy while watching TV in the evening. We'd sit there and laugh at ourselves eating all this junk. Next day, we were back to the diets."

When Guy was not working, he found comfort in the company of other up-starting actors. Every Sunday Gerry and Dennis Weaver had a barbecue in their backyard, or a get-together inside, and invited actors they had befriended from the time Dennis started at Universal-International to *Gunsmoke*. Some regulars were Russell Johnson, Willard Sage, William Shallert, Strother Martin, Lew Brown, Gene Evans (also in *The Golden Blade* as Capt Hadi), Wright King, Mary Carver, and (then) husband director Joe Sargent, Sid Clute, and Guy. Most of them brought their families. The camaraderie in Dennis' backyard gatherings provided these actors, who were all struggling to survive at the time, with the kind of support they needed, while trying to get a foothold in the business in the 1950s. All of them eventually met with very successful acting careers.

Wright King recalled those early days in their careers where he and his wife June met Guy and Janice in 1955. "We were mostly just young eager-to-go supporting performers. The barbecues were the basic simple neighborhood-type affairs. We played boisterous charades games. Amanda Blake who played Miss Kitty (*Gunsmoke*) was at some of the gatherings. All real fun people."

As Dennis said, "We joked around, didn't get serious. Just got together socially."

Janice recalled, "Guy would cook things and bring it for pot luck. Dennis had fruit trees in his back yard and one time Gerry and I picked fresh peaches from the tree and I made a fresh peach pie. We'd talk, play music, sing, and just have fun. For a long time, for us, that was *Sunday.*"

Steve remembers how he loved playing outdoors with the other children on those visits when the valley was like going to the country. "I saw my first big spider there, and I started yelling out, '*Come see what we found!*' It was really hot that day, so everyone was inside and my mom and the others weren't responding quickly. Finally, they came out on the front porch and there was all this excitement when they saw me playing with this black widow spider that could have killed me."

The camaraderie at Dennis' backyard gatherings provided these actors, who were all struggling to survive at the time, with the kind of support they needed, while trying to get a foothold in the business in the mid- to late 1950s.

Russell Johnson remembered happy times with Guy during the 1950s. "Guy was a wonderful person, a very nice man. I used to go to Guy's house with Strother Martin and we'd drink and smoke cigars. We all liked classical music. That's what we had in common and enjoyed most together. Guy would play his record collection."

Russ, as Guy called him, remembered one occasion when he and his wife, Kaye Cousins,[41] invited another guest over to dinner at Guy and Janice's house. It was Michael Dupont, of the famous wealthy Duponts of New York, who at that time wanted to be a playwright. "Michael Dupont came over with a very expensive bottle of wine, which none of us could have afforded, a well-aged Chateau Lafitte Rothschild. We savored every drop," he said with a chuckle.

Janice remembered the occasion and how fortunate they felt to taste such a rare wine. "You know how there are only a few bottles of wines in your entire life that you remember?" she said, "Well, *that* was one of them. It was wonderful. We all sipped very slowly that night."

When Guy met Russell Johnson in 1952 at Universal, Russell had already made several popular westerns. One titled *Law and Order* also featured Dennis Weaver, and starred the future president of the United States, Ronald Reagan in 1953.[42]

One night Russ and Kaye invited Guy and Janice to join them at the home of actor Paul Henreid for a private screening of a movie he was in that Henreid had produced and starred in. Paul Henreid had made many memorable movies in the '40s, but is most remembered as Victor Laszlo in *Casablanca* (1942), and he was often imitated for lighting two cigarettes at once in *Now, Voyager* (1942), one for himself and the other for Bette Davis.

"We went to Henreid's house," said Janice, "where we had dinner with him and his wife and Russ and Kaye. Steve was a baby, and we took him along. It was easy to take him with us almost everywhere when he was a baby. Then we spent *hours* watching movies. Three movies. All Paul Henreid movies."

Estelle Harman invited Guy and Janice to both take acting lessons at her studio. Janice's scene partner was a budding young actor named Michael Landon. "It was very obvious to everyone how talented he was," said Janice. "He came over to the house a few times to practice our scene. Guy didn't like," she smiled. "Michael was just a boy, a teenager, and he was very nice, but Guy was jealous."

In 1954 Guy signed with The Henry Willson Agency at 1046 Carol Drive in West Hollywood, but it was a dry year for him. Of Henry Willson, Guy said, "His specialty was to create names that sound good for his clients: Rock Hudson, Tab Hunter. Me, I chose the most insipid, the most master-key name as possible."[43]

Henry Willson[44] was usually good at getting his clients publicity and recognition. His "gay" lifestyle was well known among Hollywood circles, and did not appeal to Guy. When Willson invited Guy to one of his lavish parties, which he considered mandatory, Guy didn't show up. "He simply did not feel comfortable about going," said Janice.

Willson helped him less after that.

Guy needed a place to act, a place to practice his craft. Russ and Kaye Johnson trained in the Actor's Lab, an offshoot of the Group Theatre in New York. Kaye wrote and directed for the workshop. "Guy did a play or a scene that Kaye directed," recalled Janice. "It was a Tennessee Williams play, *The Glass Menagerie,* in Hollywood on Santa Monica Boulevard, and Guy played the gentleman caller. It was around the time Guy had recovered from his accident in 1954. Jeanne Cooper was another fine actress in the workshop, who was a good friend of ours."

Strother Martin and Dennis Weaver were in a group called The Stage Society, located on Melrose Avenue in West Hollywood. "Russ Johnson and Guy and I hung out a lot together," said Dennis. "Russ was in workshops with the Group Theatre that his wife, Kaye, was involved in as a writer and director. I was in a play she directed called *The Big Knife* by Clifford Odets, but Guy was not in it."

Memory is a strange thing. Russ Johnson thinks Guy *was* in *The Big Knife,* which they performed at The Las Palmas Theater in Hollywood. Jack Palance starred in the movie version.

Guy and Janice went to see Strother Martin in a production by the Stage Society called *The Music-Cure* by Bernard Shaw, directed by Kaye Johnson. "Before the play Strother came over to the house to see Guy," she said. "He had been trying to figure out how to play the role, which was the lead. When the show opened he was wonderful in it, and he told us he had watched little Steve at the house and just imitated some things he was doing for the role."

By 1957 Estelle Harman had established a theatre and workshop at 522 La Brea Avenue in Hollywood where she and her staff also made live broadcasts for KTLA in a small studio behind the playhouse. Her list of students at the workshop reads like the Hollywood Walk of Fame: Rock Hudson, Lisa Gaye, Lee Majors, Bill Bixby, Michael Landon, Victoria Principal, Gregory Harrison, Carol Burnett, Barbara Rush, Sharon Gless, Tony Curtis, Farrah Fawcett, Jack Kelly, Diane Baker, Richard Long, Robert Horton, Russell Johnson, Jeff Hunter, Hugh O'Brian, Audie Murphy, David Janssen, Chuck Norris, Guy Williams, and many, many more.[45] She became one of the most renown and respected acting coaches in Hollywood. Since Estelle Harman's death in April 1995, the establishment has been named West Coast Theatre Ensemble.

Chapter 13

"The Lean Years"

– Guy Williams

Guy's accident was the beginning of what he called "the lean years"; the years he avoided talking about in future interviews. Acting jobs were few and far between, nothing steady, which meant, like it or not, it was necessary for Janice to continue to work.

Guy was happy when he landed a role in a movie with some of his old friends from Universal. It is titled *Seven Angry Men* by Allied Artists, and starred Raymond Massey as John Brown, the obsessed abolitionist of Kansas. (Massey had played the same role earlier in Warner Bros.' *Santa Fe Trail* in 1940.) Guy was reunited with buddies Dennis Weaver, Jeffrey Hunter, John Smith, James Best, Larry Pennell, all who played his brothers in the movie. Guy played Salmon Brown. The beautiful Debra Paget plays Elizabeth, wife of Jeff Hunter/Owen Brown. Although often in the background, Guy had a fairly good role, which gave him a few weeks of work, and enough lines to earn him a movie credit. The movie was first released on March 27, 1955. Today it is shown regularly on cable movie channels, and because of its historical content it is sometimes shown on the History Channel with intermittent commentary about John Brown.

Dennis Weaver recalls how this movie led him and Guy to audition for a new TV show called *Gunsmoke*. "Guy and I had just done a movie together about six months earlier called *Seven Angry Men,* and the director of that movie was Charles Marquis Warren. (We called him 'Bill.') And Bill was also the director of *Gunsmoke*. When he cast the new TV show, he called almost all of us 'brothers' from that movie—John Smith, James Best, Guy, and myself—to test for [the role of] 'Chester.'"

"I'll tell you a funny story about Guy," Dennis laughed as he recalled. "Guy and I had a conversation one day and Guy said, 'You know, I got called in for this thing called *Gunsmoke.'* And I told him I knew about it, and had tested for it too. I said, 'I've got to go back in soon. They're talking to me about the role; about salary, and what-not.' I was freelancing and pretty far down in the hole as far as money was concerned, so I asked Guy, 'Well, what did they offer you?' And he said, 'Four hundred a week.' I said, *'Really!'* They offered me three hundred!' Guy said, 'Well, they offered me four.' So I said, 'Well, thanks a lot, Guy. I appreciate it.' And when they called me back in to talk about doing the role, I said to them, 'I can't do this for less than four hundred.' And *I* got it! So Guy added $100 a week to my salary in 1955, by talking to me that day.

"Guy wasn't upset about not getting the part because he knew he wasn't right for Chester. Guy was *Zorro*. It's a funny thought though, isn't it? *'Zorro'* could have been *'Chester!'*" he laughed. "Guy had that flare for Zorro. He was flashy, flamboyant. It's like he was born to play that role."

The role of Chester Goode on *Gunsmoke* was the big break that made Dennis a famous name. But Dennis did not sit back on his laurels. He kept learning his craft by starting an actor's workshop and invited Guy to learn with him. "I knew after I got the role in *Gunsmoke* that I would be doing this one character for a long time and I wanted another outlet for my creative juices. This workshop was totally separate from the studio. It was a personal project that lasted about four years.[46] Guy was a part of it, along with William 'Bill' Shallert, Mary Carver (who later played the mother of TV's *Simon and Simon*), Betty Harford, a wonderful character actress, and Strother Martin."

Bill Shallert, whose career has the kind of longevity any actor dreams of, remembered the early years when his career was beginning to take off. "In Dennis' workshop we worked with Joe Sargent, now a great director, who studied with Strasberg in New York. We concentrated on Sense Memory. We produced a couple of plays there with Dennis, but Guy was never in one. Guy was a nice guy, good looking, a good leading man, but too mechanical. He never opened up or loosened up."

In the late 1960s, Bill Shallert and Guy had shows on opposing networks, and were opposite each other in the same time slot. Bill said, "Guy's TV show, *Lost in Space*, bumped my show, *The Patty Duke Show*, off the air."

Dennis said, "Strother and Guy were very close. Guy wasn't as serious as some in the workshop, but he wanted to be a good actor and he was. He may not have been the consummate actor, but he was very effective. He was a *great* Zorro. Guy came for a while to my workshop, but he just didn't have the kind of intense interest in it."

Unlike Dennis who felt the need for a workshop after he landed the role of Chester, Guy did not after he landed the role of Zorro.

"Guy, eventually, dropped out," said Dennis. "Guy was much more interested in eating and drinking," he chuckled. "Living the good life, you know. Driving the big cars, and stuff. That was Guy's talent. I was the station wagon type, more practical. Guy liked sports cars. He lived bigger than life. He was flamboyant. Big! He liked to do things in a big way. And he liked to eat in a big way. He liked the biggest leg of the turkey, you know, and ate it like he thought he was Henry the VIII back in medieval days and throw the bone to the dog," he laughed. "I think movies and being an actor with star status was a door-opener for him to enjoy life."

"At that time, when I knew Guy in the mid-1950s, he was not careful about what he ate," said Dennis, who in the 1970s became a Vegan. "Guy liked to live life. He liked his martinis and his wine with dinner.

In 1955, work picked up for Guy, with small roles in a few movies but more in the ever-growing medium of television. It was easier for an unknown actor to get work on television. The movie studios were feeling the impact that television had in the entertainment world. People were staying home to watch TV. Moviemakers had come up with innovations to lure people back to the theaters, such as CinemaScope and "3-D"

Candid shot of Guy taken in 1955 in Hollywood.
(The Kathy Gregory Personal Collection, courtesy of Kathy Gregory)

movies. Cecil B. DeMille produced spectaculars such as *Ben-Hur* and *The Ten Commandments* in the late fifties.

The little screen, that the big studios had waved off earlier, thinking it would not survive, had become fierce competition. Rather than try to beat it, Warner Brothers and Paramount were the first two studios that wisely joined it, and made Westerns for television in the early 1950s. Many established movie stars of the late 1940s would not work on television because they felt it would ruin their movie career. Some who did, like Roy Rogers, Gene Autry, and William Boyd, benefitted tremendously from television. For newcomers in those early days, such as James Dean, Clint Eastwood, Charlton Heston, and Paul Newman, the door was wide open, and many actors such as these got their training and their start in the business on television before going on to movies.

Guy was not impressed with television. He rarely liked the shows it offered. Unlike most families in the 1950s, whose living rooms were dominated by a large console television set, Guy's was dominated by two large speakers for his record player. He bought a small unimposing Philco television and placed it in a corner of his living room. "He never watched it," said Janice. Rather than watch TV, Guy preferred reading, listening to music, or seeing a movie. Occasionally, if a good horror movie came on TV, he enjoyed that, but generally, Guy thought television was at the bottom of the totem pole in quality entertainment.

Little Stevie and his friends would sit on the floor and watched TV. "There was some grill work on a divider between the living room and the kitchen," said Janice, "and when they got afraid of something scary on TV they would get up and go behind the grill work and watch."

Anthology shows were a popular staple of early television. Guy got a day's work on *Four Star Playhouse*, a popular anthology show (1952-1956)produced by four well-known stars: Ida Lupino, Charles Boyer, David Niven and Dick Powell. On occasion, one of these four stars was featured in a half hour show. The shows were filmed much like a live play, in that they usually had only one set, and actors entered and exited as they would do in a stage show. Guy's show was titled "Trudy," which starred Joan Fontaine in the title role. It aired May 26, 1955 on CBS. Guy plays Trudy's fiancé, for whom she is anxiously waiting to marry during the entire show. None of the others waiting with her think he will show up for the wedding. Guy arrives during the last two minutes of the show, has no lines, but his anticipated entrance, and the surprise to the others that he is *blind*, makes it a memorable performance. Hans Conried plays Reverend Tuttle and Steven Geray (also in *The Golden Blade*, 1953) is Mr. Yin.

Another day job in 1955 was on the short-lived (August 28, 1954 to June 4, 1955) *The Mickey Rooney Show*, also known as *Hey, Mulligan* directed by Les Martinson[47] on NBC. The show starred Mickey Rooney as Mulligan, a young man working as a page at a studio in Hollywood while aspiring to be an actor. In a short scene in the episode titled "The Average Man," Guy plays a TV executive, who, with his partner, meets the producer and tries to negotiate a deal. The producer is played by John Hoyt, who had made many movies by this time, and would, in a few years, be a guest on Guy's show, *Zorro*.

Guy landed another role on television as a football player opposite film actress Mona Freeman[48] on *Damon Runyon Theatre*,[49] a dramatic anthology series of which many shows were based on stories by Damon Runyon. Guy's episode, titled "Big Shoulders," aired on June 17, 1955.

Many TV shows were still being filmed live. Janice remembers Guy telling her how quickly he had to sometimes make changes. "One day he came home and said, 'I found myself striped right down to my underwear, changing clothes right in front of people to get from one set to the other in time.'"

Another movie came Guy's way called *Sincerely Yours* (released Nov. 1, 1955) at Warner Brothers, produced by International Artists. This movie, a remake of George Arliss' *The Man Who Played God*, starred the great pianist Liberace, in his only leading role. The film, considered a camp classic today, was universally panned by critics at the time. Guy had a small non-speaking role playing the husband of Lori Nelson. Dressed in a tux at his wedding reception, for which Liberace is playing a lively tune, Guy is seen clapping his hands with the others to the rhythm as they listen, and cheer. This was probably just one day's work.

In the summer of 1955 Guy's mother and sister came to California for a two-week visit.

Clare knew Guy wanted a Cadillac he had his eye on and she fronted the $5,000 to buy it. Guy took the wheel of this large yellow Cadillac with red upholstery, and drove them and his family to the beach, to Marineland of the Pacific on the Palos Verdes Peninsula, and the sights of Hollywood and Beverly Hills. A year later Guy would pay her back in full.

Clare loved the Spanish-style California architecture, the landscape, and the many flowers. With her Kodak 8mm she brought with her, she took home movies capturing the family around Guy's apartment on Harper Street, as well as the homes in the neighborhood and the hills across Sunset Boulevard. Janice still has the footage today, and some of it can be seen on A&E's biography of *Zorro*. In the home movie little Steve is seen wearing his coonskin cap, because of the popularity of Walt Disney's *Davy Crockett* on TV. Guy could never have imagined what Fate had in store for him in a couple of years at the Disney Studios as he would follow Davy's footsteps. Janice is seen holding a tiny kitten. "Kitty Pooh was a tiny Siamese/Burmese kitten that came into our lives when someone gave it to Guy and me, and Steve," said Janice. "Guy named her Nephretiti, after the Egyptian queen. When I met Guy, all he had in his apartment was his chess set, his books, his records, and this well known sculptured head of Nephretiti. But the name 'Kitty Pooh' stuck, and we had her for a long time."

Guy's little sister was sixteen years old, with a cute childlike face, and the full-figure of a young woman. Her wardrobe, however, which was selected by her mother, was modest and conservative. Guy took her swimming at the home of his photographer friend Rick Straus in the Hollywood Hills, and Clare filmed Guy teaching Valerie to dive into the pool while Janice and Steve looked on.

Valerie loved California. "I used to babysit my little nephew, Steve, and I loved to play with him," remembered Valerie. "One time my brother was studying a script for some Western and I had been blowing spit bubbles for Steve, who decided to pop them with his hand and he busted my lip! I went running to my brother, and said, 'Look what your kid did to me!' I showed him my bloody lip. He looked at my lip, and said 'Go put some cold water on it and bring me the kid.'"

Valerie was excited to be in Hollywood, where her favorite movie star lived. "I asked my brother to introduce me to Jack Palance, who I just absolutely adored, and he just looked at me like I was crazy."

"I said to him, 'Do you *know* Jack Palance?'

"Yeah, a *little*.'

"'Do you ever have him over to the house?'

"'Why do you ask that?'

"'Cause I wanna *meet* him,' I said.

"'Why?'

"'Because I friggin' *love* him! That's why!'

"He was *shocked*," she laughed. "That *got* him a little bit, and he walked away. Of course, I never got to meet Jack Palance. I walked around in circles like a dog chasing his tail, thinking, 'What the heck am I doing here!? I'm babysitting his child, who bit me, and almost broke my jaw. He could bring this movie star over for me.' He knew dozens of movie stars, and they all came to the house. But the *one* I was interested in never showed up. He wouldn't do that for me. So, I wrote him off. There was never a relationship between us to start with and it wasn't my fault, because I did try. I kept getting put off. I was bitter about him not calling Jack Palance for me for a long time, but I was very young and that was the way I felt at the time," added Valerie.

"Even though he was always busy, I wanted to live with my brother in California. I found the atmosphere with Jan and the baby very congenial. Since my mother was always complaining about me, I thought it would be good to get away from her and live with them." For whatever reason it never happened.

Guy landed a feature role on the ever-popular *The Lone Ranger* television series, starring Clayton Moore and Jay Silverheels. The episode is titled "Six Gun Artist" and first aired on June 30, 1955. In it Guy plays Sheriff Will Harrison, who unwittingly falls in love with an artist, Elaine Riley, unaware that she is a gun-totin' outlaw. In the last scene, after the artist is arrested, Tonto and the Lone Ranger are with a sad and disappointed Will. Tonto gives Will some words of wisdom, "Woman with pretty face and evil heart always make trouble."

Fans of *Zorro* and *The Lone Ranger* are treated to a rare moment on film when two of the world's best-loved masked men of television are face-to-face. Tonto and the Lone Ranger leave Will's office, then there is that inevitable dialogue between Will (Guy) and Hutch (Emmett Lynn), the old stagecoach driver:

> HUTCH: A masked man, workin' on the side of the law! I *still* don't get it.
> WILL: I didn't understand it either, 'til the Indian told me.
> HUTCH: You mean you know who he *is*?
> WILL: Yes, Hutch. We've been face-to-face with a legend. He's the *Lone Ranger*.

Guy went to Mexico for four weeks for a small role in a film called *The Last Frontier* (a.k.a. *Savage Wilderness*), which was released December 7, 1955. The movie stars Victor Mature, Guy Madison, Robert Preston, and Anne Bancroft. Guy plays Lieutenant Benton

Guy and Clayton Moore, two most famous masked men of television, are face to face in this Lone Ranger episode title "Six Gun Artist" in 1955. (courtesy of Janis Whitcomb)

and did not get credited, but he is easily recognizable throughout, in Calvary charges and scenes at the fort, and has one line. It is the last line in the last scene of the movie, with Victor Mature and Guy Madison.

In this movie fans see two famous *Guys,* in the same frame side by side. Guy Williams, who chose his name when Guy Madison was already an established movie star *(Since You Went Away* [1944] and *Till the End of Time* [1946]) was then, and is now, most often confused with Guy Madison. Madison made the transition from movie star to TV icon when he starred in *The Adventures of Wild Bill Hickok* from 1951-1958. When Guy Williams became a TV icon during that same time, their names were often confused. Since Madison was already a known star, his name dominated, and was always the first to come to mind when someone mentioned Zorro, whether as a slip of the tongue or just not knowing. Bridget Madison, Guy Madison's daughter, said, "I have been asked many times, 'Didn't your father play Zorro?'"

In 1956, Guy signed with the Fred Katz Agency at 9171 Sunset Boulevard, ironically the same building where Paul Kohner was located. Months passed without work. Then, he got a role in four episodes of the popular *Highway Patrol* show which starred Broderick Crawford, playing Crawford's partner, Officer Hanson. He appeared in episodes, "Harbor Story" (1956) with Stuart Whitman; "Plane Crash" (1956); "Runaway Boy" (1956); and "Officer's Wife" (1957). In the latter, he gets shot in the opening scene. He was once again out of work. Each episode was only a few days work, and with few lines, but he was getting exposure, experience, and credits.

Janice continued to get work, most of the time taking her toddler Steve along with her. Steve began to get work too, sometimes by himself, sometimes with his mom. Janice and little Steve posed as mother and son in a print ad for a gas company when he was fifteen months old. Janice is holding Steve in a bath-a-net. There were several ads they did together. When he was two, little Steve was on the cover of *Town Journal* magazine by himself, playing with a bucket and shovel.

"I was a drag-a-long model," Steve joked, "I can remember as far back as two years old, spending a lot of time with my mom in the car, going to shoots. I can still remember the smell of that green Pontiac, with that fuzzy lining on the roof."

Many of the photographs were taken by their friend, Rick Strauss. Later, a British photographer who was new in town, needed a male toddler to pose with his little daughter in a Valentine's Day ad for the May Company, one of Los Angeles' biggest department stores. Three-year-old Steve got the job. The little girl was four-year-old model/actress Angela Cartwright, who would in years to come work with Steve's father as Penny on *Lost in Space* (1965-68). The two tots posed leaning into a kiss while Steve is holding a box of chocolates for her behind his back. The ad ran in all the newspapers in the city.

1956 was rather lean for Guy.[50] Things began to pick up in 1957. Guy filmed a helicopter rescue scene over Griffith Park for an episode of *Code* 3, titled "Bail Out."[51] It was the most dangerous work he'd ever had to do. When he was lifted up into the helicopter, he was accidentally drawn to the door and nearly fell out. Janice remembers him telling her about it. "It really gave him a scare. He came home shaken, and told me it was the closest he had ever come to death."

Early in 1957, Guy bagged another day job on the *DuPont Theater* in an anthology show titled "Decision for a Hero," which aired February 7, 1957. It starred John Ericson and Joan Evans (later on *Zorro*), both of whom had already been in numerous movies in Hollywood. For the small role of "First Player" with one line, Guy was given a screen credit. In an opening scene Guy is a football player entering the locker room after a game. The large number 10 is seen on his back. He takes off his helmet, turns to Ericson, the hero of the game, and says, "Hey! Ya did it again!"

In March Guy's agents were getting his name out to the industry in the trade papers.

Thursday, March 7, 1957 – *The Hollywood Reporter*,
"TV Castings – Guy Williams for *Sergeant Preston of the Yukon.*"

Guy landed a feature role in the popular *Sergeant Preston* show in an episode titled "Generous Hero" (CBS). He plays a courier with a thick (fake) moustache, whose huskies take him by sleigh to the home of a woman and her father who are being held hostage by outlaws. The episode didn't air until January 2, 1958.

Sometime in the first half of 1957 Guy got a role in a movie that has become a classic: *I Was a Teenage Werewolf* (June 19, 1957). It was made by American International Pictures, a company that set out to make low budget movies in the mid-1950s that would appeal strictly to the teenage set. These were black and white movies pumped out in two weeks time in a small studio in Hollywood. The starring role of the boy who turns into a werewolf at night was played by newcomer Michael Landon in his first starring role. Guy got the role of a police officer, Chris Stanley, who helps hunt him down and ultimately shoots the werewolf six times in the last scene of the picture. As a young high school boy Landon is under the psychiatric treatment of Dr. Brandon/Whit Bissell (later on *Zorro),* who plays a mad scientist experimenting with a new drug. In a seething rage as the all-out-transformed-werewolf, Landon attacks the doctor and his assistant just before the detective and Officer Stanley kick down the door and settle the matter. As Guy shoots, he rises on his toes after each shot; the bounce in his left knee and this pounce position he takes in most of his action scenes, is characteristically Guy Williams. Humphrey Bogart's imitated tight upper lip, was not intentional, like most people thought, to give him a tough guy demeanor. He was unsticking his lip from the dry caps on his teeth. James Dean's famous squint considered sexy, was not intentional. He simply couldn't see without his glasses. Likewise, Guy's characteristic pounce was due to his high arches, which threw his balance forward, but it made him look action-packed. One reporter wrote: "Even when he's standing still, he is poised on the balls of his feet, seemingly tensed for action and ready to explode. When he walks, he swaggers, and when he enters a room, he seems to leap in…"[52] This was a natural trait that made him suitable for action films.

Guy's improved acting style is obvious in this movie as he is more relaxed and natural than his first years at Universal. His six scenes throughout the movie, with dialogue and close-ups, merited him a screen credit and some recognition. This movie now has a place among horror film buffs, but at the time it was considered in the low budget B movie category and not something Guy was proud of. After he achieved fame, he never referred to these roles, or talked about them. They were of no significance to him, except to get him to the next job.

Guy made a primetime Pepsi commercial shown during Rodgers and Hammerstein's

I was a Teenage Werewolf. Left to right , Barney Phillips, Robert Griffin,
Guy Williams (Photofest)

Cinderella, starring Julie Andrews and Jon Cypher, one of the first original musicals written for television. It was taped live from New York City, the commercial, however, had been taped earlier. *Cinderella* had been heavily publicized, and on March 31, 1957 a good portion of the nation tuned in to see a Broadway musical (in black and white) right in their own homes. At the intermission Guy had a key role in the lengthy and elaborately-set commercial for Pepsi-Cola. In progressive scenes, a voiceover tells the story about a young woman from the time she is a little girl playing "grown-up" in her mother's high heels, to her married life. Guy, in a tux, plays the groom in one scene, then he is seen coming home in a business suit to the wife. He sits to read the paper, while she serves him Pepsi, which they enjoy together with amorous looks. The tag line: "Pepsi! Not too sweet, and keeps you fit."[53]

Early in April 1957 a television role in *Men of Annapolis* took Guy to Annapolis, Maryland to film. This was an anthology show about the incidences during the training of men at the US Navy Academy at Annapolis, with exteriors filmed there. The episode (#9) is titled "The Crucial Moment,"[54] and aired November 21, 1957. Guy played a football player, Paul Towner, who is rejected from the Navy football team and has to prove himself to the coach, played by Robert (Bob) J. Stevenson. It is believed Guy was in three episodes, one of which may have been "The Sea Wall Adventure" (October 24, 1957). Jeff Richards and Jack Diamond were also in this series.[55]

Bob Stevenson and Guy quickly became friends. They were drawn together by their common interest in sailing as well as their lively discussions of politics. A few years earlier Bob Stevenson had played a dangerous convict escapee in the pilot for *Highway Patrol* in 1955. He continued acting a few more years before he gave it up for a career in politics.

Bob's wife, Peggy Stevenson, remembers meeting Guy shortly after he and her husband returned from Annapolis. "When Bob came back from Maryland, he said to me 'I met this *terrific* guy! I want you to meet him.' A few days later we were invited to Jan and Guy's for dinner. Their apartment on Harper was so beautiful. When we got there—I'll never forget—we walked in, and there was this *gorgeous* guy and this *equally* gorgeous woman, Jan, and this adorable little boy, with all these blond curls, Stevie. He and Jan were doing commercials together. And *Guy*! Well, my husband was tall, but *this* fellow was even taller. Bob was 6'1" and Guy was 6'3" or 6'4". Ab-so-*lute*-ly the most charming man you would ever want to meet! I have to tell you, in Hollywood you see a lot of gorgeous men, so it's not that unusual. But this one was not only gorgeous, he was more than that. He was *so interesting*. When he came into a room, somehow the conversation always evolved with him in the middle of it. He dominated it. Interestingly enough, while the women understandably fell apart for him, men liked him too! He was a good guy, you understand. Some men resent a man who women gush over, but everybody liked Guy.

"Guy and Bob and Jan and I became very good friends. We had so much fun when we went to Guy's house for dinner. Guy would cook and the women would set the table and Guy would give the orders. There was always lots of stimulating conversation. He and Bob used to like to debate about politics, history, music, *anything*. Guy would say he didn't like the way the government was handling a situation and Bob would tease Guy and say 'I'm *not* talking to you about it until you go out and register to vote.' And Guy *did*! He registered that year,[56] just so the debates could go on," she laughed. "Guy was very funny."

Guy liked to tease and joke with his friends in a way that would provoke them into debates. "This was great entertainment for Guy," continued Peggy. "One night he might take Side A, and the next night, if someone agreed A was fine, he would argue Side B just for the sake of a good argument. Much of the time he would be joking and just having fun.

"Jan was, and still is, a very beautiful woman. She's a saint. I see a halo over her head. She is not one of those persons who is good and knows it. She is just a sincere, real, dear, sweet woman. Nobody could be nicer. She has gone through a lot in her life and I have never heard her say a mean word about anybody. I've been very close to her throughout a lot of crises in her life and through it all she has always been an outstanding woman—First Class, in every way. She's a *wonderful* person. She really is.

"Janice is a gourmet cook. She can cook anything, but the Italian cook in her came from Guy. Guy was an Italian born and raised in New York, but he was more Italian than any Italian from Italy. I remember once he came over to the house to pick up Bob to go sailing. Bob was on the phone, so while he waited we talked in the backyard with an Italian fellow who was doing some handy work for me. This man was an Italian *from* Italy. So Guy went over and started chatting with him in Italian. The handyman was doing most of the listening. Guy was speaking to him in such an educated tongue, and he made a big impression on this man. After Guy and Bob left, the handyman said to me, 'Señora, I was embarrassed to talk to him. He spoke so intelligently, and of the upper class dialect. I couldn't keep up with him.'"

Chapter 14

"...A WANTED JOB"

– Guy Williams

Since the beginning of 1957, Hollywood had been buzzing about a new series Walt Disney planned to make for television. *The Hollywood Reporter* mentioned it several times and by the time Guy returned from Annapolis an extensive search for talent was underway for Disney's new show.

Hollywood Reporter, Monday, January 21, 1957
Disney, ABC in new $9 million TV Deal; New pact calls for...a new half-hour live action series, *Zorro* with 39 weekly segments. William Tunberg is doing the teleplays and series bows in October.

Hollywood Reporter, Tuesday, February 5, 1957
Disney soon launches a new telefilm series *Zorro* scheduled to begin showing on ABC the first week in October.

Hollywood Reporter, Thursday, February 14, 1957
"*Zorro* for 7-Up
New York. Half of Walt Disney's new *Zorro* teleseries for ABC-TV has been bought by 7-Up.

Daily Variety, Tuesday, March 19, 1957
"Seek *Zorro* Lead"
Norman Foster has been set to direct the *Zorro* TV series for Walt Disney. He is auditioning actors for the title role.

"Once in a while in Hollywood," said Guy in 1983, "there was a role in town that everybody was talking about. And *this* was one of them. The fact that *Walt Disney*—that's a big start right there—was going to make *Zorro*, everybody immediately thought of Douglas Fairbanks, the original film; the Tyrone Power one,[57] which really made a big splash—so, when you coupled the name Disney and Zorro, it was a *wanted* job! I mean,

84

it was careersville all the way, if you got *that!* So everybody in town who could *possibly* qualify, in *any* way, showed up for that one. And I was one of them."[58]

An agent at the Fred Katz Agency named Stanley Cohen had a young green agent working for him named Lester Kendall. Lester's father had been with the agency for years and had retired, so Lester took his seat, and was trying to get a handle on the business. One day Lester called Guy about an audition at the Walt Disney Studios in Burbank for *Zorro* and made the appointment for him. Guy went to the Nadi studio to brush up on his fencing skills for the audition.

Guy showed up with more than a hundred actors, unknown and well known, to be seen by casting agents Lee Traver and Jack Lavin for this coveted role. After Disney's huge success with Fess Parker in Davy Crockett in 1954, Walt was looking for another "unknown," but an unknown with acting experience and the ability to handle a sword. It was a cattle call, with many people and a long wait, and Guy thought about leaving. As it turned out, he got a call-back.

Disney had been wanting to make a *Zorro* series as early as 1952 when he bought the rights from Mitchell Gertz, the literary agent for author Johnston McCulley, who created Zorro. Then in 1954 he saw an opportunity to make the series when he needed to give ABC a TV show in return for 2.5 million dollars the network put into escrow for him to build Disneyland. The trade papers speculated that *Zorro* would be part of the package presented to ABC, but ABC insisted on seeing a pilot first. Walt was insulted. "Look, I've been in the picture business for thirty years," he exclaimed. "Don't you think I know how to make a film?"[59] Furious, he refused to make a pilot. ABC was the smallest network at the time, behind NBC and CBS, and was struggling. They settled for Walt's anthology series called *Disneyland*, which gave Walt an opportunity to advertise the new park he was building.

In 1955, Walt again tried to make the *Zorro* series. He wanted Richard (Dick) Simmons for the leading role.[60] Simmons, a tall good looking actor, had starred in a Republic serial called *Man with the Steel Whip* in 1954, in which he played a masked crusader dressed in black. But in 1955, Simmons was already committed to his TV show, *Sgt. Preston of the Yukon*, in which he played the title role from September 29, 1955 to September 25, 1958.

Walt didn't pursue it further. Instead, he decided to present ABC with the adventures of Davy Crockett, a popular figure of American folklore. He hired Fess Parker in the starring role and Davy Crockett took the country by storm. The three popular Davy Crockett episodes were directed by Norman Foster, and established Walt Disney as a giant in the television industry, as well as animation and movies. Foster also harbored the ambition to do a *Zorro* series at that time. Foster was a friend of Tyrone Power and had loved the Zorro character since his friend had played him in 1940.

Guy had much admiration for Walt Disney from the first time he saw Mickey Mouse as a child, then *Pinocchio* and *Fantasia*. "Disney was a very creative person," said Guy. "Just look back and remember he made something called *Fantasia*. There hasn't been anything made like that ever again."[61]

Guy had not been impressed with the TV shows he had been on, but he was excited about auditioning for *Zorro*. He wanted it. He knew Walt Disney would do nothing but the best quality television could offer.

"I really did not believe that the worst television show was much different from the best," he said. "I didn't see the differences between a very popular show and one that wasn't very popular in those days. They were all more or less the same. So I thought, well, heck, the Disney shows are as well made as *anything*. Nobody's making it any better, so I was happy with that."[62]

On April 18, 1957, Guy went to the Disney Studios for the audition that would change his life. "I could hardly have gone there with less hope," he said for a *Zorro* newsletter issued by Disney Studios. "They wanted a Latin type. Well, I had just finished some *Annapolis* TV shows for which I had a crew cut. I was a funny looking Latin—but to my surprise, they passed me."[63]

After years of modeling and acting roles as the all-American type, Guy said, "I didn't have a mustache when I met Mr. Disney. I'd played different nationalities, but never anything especially Spanish or Latin. Mr. Disney was the only one who saw me as a Spaniard."[64]

Zorro is a double personality, so whoever was chosen to play Zorro would also play Don Diego de la Vega. Diego is a Spanish aristocrat, while attending college in Spain he was called home by his father to help the dons fight the tyranny and injustices of a corrupt government in the Pueblo de Los Angeles, circa 1820. Instead of fighting, Diego pretends to be a weak coward by day, but at night he disguises himself as the champion, El Zorro. Dressed in black, riding a black horse by moonlight, and brandishing his swift sword, he sets out to right the wrongs of the evil commandant, "Capitan Enrique Sanchez Monastario."

Guy knew what Fairbanks and Power had brought to the screen as Zorro and he wanted to have his own signature for the role. He wanted to bring something of himself to the character. He consulted his closest friends, Dennis Weaver and Strother Martin, about the character, but he didn't tell anyone else he was up for the role. Dennis Weaver recalled Guy's anxiety. "He talked to me about being up for the part. I could tell he was pressed. He wanted the role *real* bad."

Guy's daughter, Toni, remembers her dad telling her how he came about some of the characteristics for his Zorro. "Dad said it was Strother Martin who suggested to him how to play Zorro. Before my dad went to test for *Zorro*, Strother Martin told him not to play it 'serious,' but to smile and move around and have fun with it. So, he fenced with flair, bobbed his head, and smiled, which to the adamant fencer was terrible, but to Norman Foster was the Zorro they were looking for."

After weeks of auditioning actors, the casting agents were down to four actors for the two leads, Zorro/Don Diego and Monastario, Zorro's archenemy. They were Tony Russo, Armando Silvestre, Britt Lomond, and Guy Williams.

Screen tests continued for four days,[65] for the four talented actors working with each other in all aspects.

Hollywood Reporter, April 24, 1957.
Anthony Russo has completed extensive tests for both the lead and permanent heavy in Walt Disney's *Mark of Zorro* TV Series.

Anthony "Tony" Russo was a tall and handsome Italian with wavy brown hair and dark brown eyes. He came to Hollywood from Kenosha, Wisconsin and studied acting at the prestigious Pasadena Playhouse, a hothouse for most of Hollywood's major stars of the 1940s and 1950s, where he learned to fence as well as act. "I played 'Tybalt' in *Romeo and Juliet* at the Pasadena Playhouse to Margaret O'Brien's 'Juliet,' with Gene Raymond in 1955," said Tony. "Someone who saw me in that show came up to me and said, 'They're trying out for the role of Zorro at Disney. You should go. You're perfect for it.' I didn't even have an agent. I just went to the casting director."

Most of Tony's work at this time had been on stage. He wanted to break into television and movies for the money, but at the time he thought *real* actors were in legitimate theatre. Although they were looking at him for either role, Tony wanted the role of Zorro. "I had a good audition," he said. "I felt like I was a better actor and fencer than most. I was Latin and looked Latin, and could do the dialect. I thought it was a shoo-in. Then one day I came out of Schwab's[66] and ran into another actor who asked me, 'How did that audition go for *Zorro*?' I told him I thought it went very well, and I thought I had the part. Then he said to me, 'I don't think so. I just saw Guy Williams and his agent having lunch in Frescotti's[67] with Norman Foster, the director of the show.'"

Tony said, "It was the biggest disappointment of my life. My agent had said to ask for $325, a pre-contract offer you have to adhere to if you get the job. Guy's agent asked for $350 week, minimum was $250. My agent thought I would be more likely to get the part if I asked low." Tony shrugged. "Hollywood goes for a face, not talent."

Tony's talent was not forgotten. He was later cast in three memorable episodes, in two of which he played a Zorro imposter.[68]

Hollywood Reporter, May 12, 1957
"Disney Teeing Off *Zorro* Series With Foster Directing"
Walt Disney will tee off his new *Zorro* telefilm series of 39 episodes with Norman Foster signed to direct. The weekly half-hour will bow on ABC-TV next fall. Foster currently is helping in the studio search for an actor to play the title role as well as interviewing other cast possibilities.

Daily Variety, Thursday, May 16, 1957
Zorro…tentatively starting in June. Meanwhile, production coordinator Lou Debney and director Norman Foster are still testing for the *Zorro* lead.

Britt Lomond was born Glasé Lomond in New York City, of German/Scottish ancestry. His movie idols growing up were Douglas Fairbanks, Sr. and Errol Flynn, who influenced him to take up the sport of fencing. "I was first put *on guarde* at New York University by an Olympic Fencing coach named Costello. After that, I was on the New York Fencing team, under René Pinchard, coach of United States Olympic teams for sixteen years, and also Hungarian saber champion, Meiterkurster."

In the late 1940s Britt moved to Hollywood where he entered the movie industry as a stuntman. While sitting in a room waiting for an audition for a swashbuckler movie, his former fencing coach spotted him and said to the director, "He can do it!" "I didn't know what he was talking about," said Britt. He soon found out he was being recommended as Mel Ferrer's stunt double in George Sidney's now-classic *Scaramouche* (1952). Britt's daring ten-minute nonstop fencing segment with Stewart Granger is the performance that he is most proud of in his career. The climatic sword duel is the longest in swashbuckling history.[69]

Britt recalled when he first heard about the auditions at the Disney studio. "My agent called me and said 'They're going to do *Zorro*. I'm going to send you over there, because you're perfect for it.' I had done many fencing pictures, not with lines, just stunt doubling." Britt was an expert fencer, and he had the medals to prove it. He had also been establishing himself in the business for the last ten years for fencing and other stunts.

Britt walked into the interview with his naturally blond hair and china blue eyes. "The first time I interviewed for the part, the casting director reminded me, 'Britt! This is a *Spaniard*, you know?' So for the screen test, I bought some dark contact lenses to put on my eyes and some washable black hair spray to put in my hair.

"I was up for the role with a few others, and we were given two weeks to prepare for the screen test," said Britt. "I first met Guy at Aldo Nadi' studio where we both used to fence before we knew we were both up for the part."

Guy recalled, "Britt and I used to fence together before we ever heard of *Zorro*. We did sabre work then. We both learned about casting for *Zorro* at the same time and we agreed it would be a great idea to work together. We both said, we could get *paid* then to *fence!*"[70]

Disney was looking for the two leads, Zorro and Monastario, but Britt had his heart set on playing Zorro. Britt remembered, "I went to practice for the screen test at Nadi's studio. I knew they were testing someone else, but I didn't know who it was. So, in walks this *kid*. And we started fencing together and struck up a conversation and he said he was practicing for a role. I said, 'I am *too*.' Then he told me what role it was, and that's when we realized we were practicing for the same role!" he laughed. "We both kept going back to Nadi's to fence. We didn't know who was going to get hired or what, and we would talk and practice together. I offered to help him in any way I could with his fencing, especially fencing for the *camera*, which is much different from strip fencing for competition, because I had lots of experience in that. I think he appreciated that a great deal, so we became very good friends."

Britt and Guy could quote the maestro's principle of fencing, handed down to fencers through the ages: "Hold the weapon as delicately as you would hold a small bird, gently enough that you do not crush it, yet strong enough that it cannot fly away."[71]

Armando Silvestre was a popular Mexican actor, but his strong accent was to his disadvantage. "The director wanted to be able to control the accent," recalled Britt Lomond. Other than trilling "r"s and pronouncing "i"s like "e"s, there was hardly any Spanish accent at all from the actors.

The concept for *Zorro* was Norman Foster's. He had put the *Zorro* package together, and Walt had complete confidence in Norman's judgment. Many of the first thirteen episodes, which established the characters and set the mood of the show, were written by Foster. Norman's son, Robert Foster, who calls his father by his first name, said, "One of the reasons Walt liked Norman was that they had similar childhoods. Both had to work *very* hard. Both were hand-to-mouth when they were growing up. Both came very near financial destruction. Norman was not a 'yes man,'" he points out, "like all these stuffed shirts in the office who say, 'Oh yes, Walt!,' 'Good idea, Walt!,' 'Glad you thought of it!' and, 'You're right! You're right!' Walt was very suspicious of people like that, because Walt was an old-fashioned kind of guy, who I feel went on eye-to-eye contact. He knew Norman was sincere."

Walt's employees feared him when he was angry and were known to agree with him all the time, even if they really disagreed. Guy remembered how Norman was different in that he would stand up to Walt when Walt criticized him. "Norman was one of the old brigade," said Guy. "That's when he would say, 'Walt, you're wrong. You're making

Guy in a screen test for *Zorro,* April 1957 (Author's personal collection)

a mistake.' And Walt didn't hesitate to fire him, but then he would hire him back the following week! I remember one day Norman was on Dopey Drive. (At the studio every street got named according to Disney's characters: Goofy Drive, Snow White, etc.) And here is Norman, loaded like a mule. He had just finished emptying his desk drawers for the *n*th time. Walt sees him walking and says, 'Norman! What are you *doing*?' He had forgotten he fired him the day before!

"Norman was doing everything on *Zorro.* But later on, when Walt saw how much work had to be done he hired three or four other directors on the series in addition to Norman."[72]

Norman Foster had been an actor in the 1930s in New York, when he married famous movie actress, Claudette Colbert, and they came to Hollywood together. After they divorced, he married beautiful actress Sally Blane, one of the four famous Young sisters: Loretta, Polly Ann, and Georgiana and Sally. He had turned to directing movies in the 1940s and, in the early 1950s, it was his sister-in-law, Loretta Young, who gave him his start in television, when she hired him to direct some of her shows for *The*

Loretta Young Show.

Norman Foster had wanderlust. He didn't like staying in one place too long. Whenever his career stalemated in one town, he moved to another. He believed you could stay in one place too long. During the 1940s Norman and his wife, Sally, and their daughter moved to Mexico, before Robert was born. He made several movies there, giving many Hispanics their first big breaks, one of whom was Ricardo Montalban. Norman introduced Ricardo to Sally's sister, Georgiana. They fell deeply in love, got married, raised four children, and have been happily married to each other ever since.

Norman recruited many of the Mexican actors to come work for him on *Zorro*. While there were many Mexican extras, there were also several leads on *Zorro* of Mexican descent, such as George J. Lewis and Romney Brent (Padre Filipe), a gifted Mexican stage actor whose real name was Romulo Larrade,[73] Perry Lopez, Carlos Romero, Ricardo Montalban, Rita Moreno, Cesar Romero, Carlos Rivas, to name a few. "My father hired the same people every chance he could if he knew they were dependable and would work. He was loyal to them," said Robert Foster. "He loved the underdog, the oppressed, the loyal, and he treated everyone equally. He would adopt the underdog, or the oppressed as though they were a child or brother, and took care of them."

Norman Foster had never met Guy Williams before in his life when he auditioned him, but when he saw Guy's audition he knew he wanted him for the role. He said:

> The first day I had him do three different test fencing scenes. From that film, Guy appeared to have been born with a foil in his hand. As far as I was concerned Guy fit Zorro to a 'T,' or should I say 'Z'? From the beginning I knew he was the fellow I wanted to play the part.[74]

Nevertheless, the final decisions had to be Walt's, and it did not come quickly. Finally it was between Guy and Britt for Zorro and Monastario. Both the producer and the director studied their tests for weeks.

Guy felt confident in himself for the role, and was anxiously hoping to get a call. Janice remembers that Guy felt this role fit him like a glove. "You know sometimes something is just so *right* that you just feel it's got to be you who is going to do it," she said. "And he really felt that way about it. We would drive over to Griffith Park, next to the Disney Studio, and stop at the top of a hill where you could see the *Zorro* set being built. Before he knew he was going to do it, he would look down there and say, 'I'm going to get that role. I just know it. I'm gonna get that part.' So when he did hear he was going to do it, I don't think he was that surprised. It was a feeling he kept inside though. He was never complacent about it with others. He didn't go around talking about it to people."

"*Zorro* was Norman's 'baby,'" she continued. "He had written the shows and brought them to Disney. When he met Guy, he told Disney he wanted Guy, and if Guy didn't do it he wouldn't do it. He was the one responsible for Guy getting the role. He drew the line. He said, 'This is the one who's going to do it, or I don't do it.'"

Finally, Guy received a telephone call from Walt, telling him that he had the part of Zorro and Don Diego. "He was certainly happy, but I think he felt it would happen," said Janice. "Guy's background made him right for that part. Zorro and Don Diego were very much like Guy's personality. We knew that role was perfect for him, and he wanted it."

Chapter 15

Guy Williams Draws 'Zorro'

— Daily Variety

Lester Kendall, the agent who sent Guy to Disney, couldn't have been happier. This was also *his* first big break. Both, agent and actor, were on top of the world when Guy got the part. Trade papers published the progress of those weeks of casting.

Daily Variety, Wednesday, June 5, 1957
"Guy Williams Draws 'Zorro' and New Name"
    Guy Williams has been tagged to portray Zorro in new telefilm series to start filming at Walt Disney studios late this month to bow on ABC-TV net in October. Young thesp will be given new *nom de cinema* for series by Disney. Norman Foster will direct.

"The funniest thing," said Guy, "is that Disney would rather my name be Catalano for the role of Zorro." Disney thought Guy Williams was too much like current actors Bill *Williams* and *Guy* Madison and might cause confusion. "Would people remember a Guy Williams?" asked Walt.

The world-renown Hollywood gossip columnist Hedda Hopper wrote about the situation in her column in 1957:

    Walt Disney thinking of new names for Guy Williams then decided to let him keep his own name. Diamond Decorator, the original name of the horse they got for Guy, wasn't so lucky. He's going to be called Tornado.

Daily Variety, Monday, July 1, 1957
    Guy Williams, six-foot-three actor from New York, will have the Zorro role in Walt Disney's new half-hour series. Doug Fairbanks and Ty Power played it in films.

Hollywood Reporter, Thursday, July 11, 1957
"*Lomond for Zorro*"

Britt Lomond has been signed by Walt Disney to play the heavy in the new adventure series *Zorro* for ABC-TV. Guy Williams stars in the title role, with Norman Foster directing.

TV Guide, July 27-August 2, 1957
New York actor GUY WILLIAMS gets the lead in Walt Disney's new half-hour series, *Zorro* set for Thursday nights on ABC starting in the fall.

Guy was signed to a one year contract with Disney, with a seven-year option. The studio was already behind schedule, so Guy's life immediately became hectic. He was busier than he ever had been in his life.

Zorro Newsletter, June 1957
One month before actual filming began, Guy Williams and Norman Foster were both so busy preparing for filming it was said that even Walt Disney had to have an appointment. A typical day for Guy Williams would find him rising at 6 a.m. to go to a recording studio to tape one of Don Diego's songs. Including preparations, retakes, etc., the session would last as long as two hours. Next he would go to wardrobe for fittings on both the 'Zorro' costume and those of the wealthy dandy, Don Diego. Following a quick lunch, Williams was driven to the 'Hess Studios' one of Hollywood's best known still photographers for studio stills.

The role of Don Diego required that Guy play the guitar. The studio hired well-known Spanish guitarist Vicente Gomez[75] to teach him. Guy's son Steve remembers, "Vicente Gomez would come over to our house on Harper Street to give my dad lessons, and my dad loved to hear him play the guitar." Vincente Gomez was a favorite among the major studios for the soundtracks of Spanish-themed movies.

"Guy couldn't sing," said Janice, "but he had to lip-sync all the songs, so he had to learn all the words. He also had to learn the finger positions of the chords so it looked like he was really playing." Most of the songs were sung by Skip Farrell.[76]

Whip experts Dave Keshner and Carl Pitti taught Guy techniques on using the whip. "Dad used to practice using the whip on the front yard," said Steve. "He would show me how he made it pop. Even after *Zorro*, he still liked to practice once in a while. Years later, I might be upstairs in my room, and I'd suddenly hear *pop! pop!* I knew it was Dad practicing the whip outside. I still have that whip."

The type of fencing Guy had learned in the salle was strip fencing or competitive fencing. He had to *relearn* fencing for the camera. Disney hired the most highly respected, most sought after fencing coach in Hollywood. "We had the *best*," said Guy, "Freddie Cavens." Belgian fencing master, Fred Cavens, considered the best for cinema fencing, trained Guy and everyone who came on the show. Fred Cavens' talent became apparent in Hollywood when he was hired by Douglas Fairbanks, Sr. for his *Don Q, Son of Zorro* movie of 1925. Fairbanks' fencing adviser for *The Mark of Zorro*, (1920), Henry Uyttenhove, had expert technical skills for screen duels, but it was Cavens who gave those skills style, flair, strength, and manly grace.[77] Fred Cavens coached Errol Flynn, Basil Rathbone, Tyrone Power, and many others in almost every popular swashbuckler

Guy took guitar lesson from renown movie musician Vincente Gomez for the role of Don Diego (courtesy of Mary Spooner, Mary Spooner Personal collection)

film throughout the 1940s and 1950s. Guy felt fortunate to be in that category. A reporter said, "Of the three actors who have portrayed Zorro before film cameras, Douglas Fairbanks, Tyrone Power, and Williams, dueling expert Fred Cavens, who coached all three, considers the first the most flamboyant, the second the most serious pupil, and Williams the most talented."[78]

Guy went to Fred's house every day before *Zorro* went into production to practice techniques for fencing for film. "I had to *unlearn* a good deal. Orthodox fencing is all in the wrist, but it doesn't look as impressive,"[79] said Guy. "For film, you have to make everything a little more visible, a little bigger."[80]

During May and June 1957 the business of marketing the show and products was underway. Publicity shots of Guy were taken at several locations: Guy and Fred fencing in Cavens' backyard, Guy and his family at his home at 1330 Harper, and Guy in the oldest part of Los Angeles, El Pueblo de la Riena de Los Angeles, where the story of Zorro is set. Known simply as Olvera Street, this historic part of town is a popular tourist attraction with its original adobe homes and old church. Mexican wares, fresh

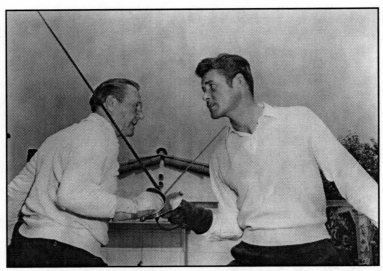

For the role of Zorro Guy was taught to fence for the camera by the best fencing instructor in Hollywood, Fred Cavens. (Kathy Gregory Personal Collection, Courtesy of Kathy Gregory)

Mexican food, and live mariachi music is a major draw. Guy, dressed in a light beige sport coat, a checkered shirt, dark slacks and leather shoes, was photographed walking down the old brick street, feeding the pigeons, playing a guitar, playing maracas in a shop, and with a vendor selling him newspapers with personalized headlines written in bold type.

EXTRA EXTRA
Olvera Street News—
GUY WILLIAMS STARS
IN DISNEY'S "ZORRO"!

The show's two sponsors, 7-Up and AC spark plugs, were creating catchy commercials for their alternating spots at the midpoint of the show. Copyright licenses, and negotiations with sponsors and manufacturers were carefully worked out for advertising and merchandise. Having been unprepared for the great demand of merchandise created from the Davy Crockett craze, Walt Disney had lost millions of dollars on coonskin caps by not protecting his copyrights on products.[81] Anyone could reproduce them and did. Now, with hindsight, Disney had toys and merchandise manufacturers acquire their licenses for *Zorro* products *before Zorro* was even cast. He gave Guy Williams a much smaller percentage of the merchandise than he had given Fess Parker, now that he knew how much it could bring in.

Walt, however, had some reservations about whether the public was ready to embrace a sword wielding Spaniard defending early California at a time when kids were watching gun-totin' cowboys. His doubts transferred to other producers and crew members.

Walt was also casting the lead for a new show called *The Saga of Andy Burnett*, a TV

Vendor, Melone Tanzini, sells Guy a personalized newspaper at his souvenir stand on
Olvera Street (Author' collection)

series about a folk hero. Speculation around the studio was that it would be a bigger hit
than *Zorro* because the studio was using the same formula for *Andy Burnett* as they did
for the popular *Davy Crockett*.

"People at the studio thought Walt Disney was more interested in *Andy Burnett*,"
said Janice, "because he thought it would be another *Davy Crockett*. When Guy went to
audition for *Zorro*, a producer there told him he would be better off auditioning for
Andy Burnett, because they had doubts about *Zorro*. But Guy didn't do it." As it turned
out, *The Saga of Andy Burnett* didn't have much appeal at all, and flopped after six
episodes.

The director and writer of *Zorro*, Norman Foster, had confidence in the well-loved
romantic character. As long as the show was done well, he felt it would be a success.

> *Hollywood Reporter*, Tuesday, July 16, 1957
> Nearing completion is Disney's most pretentious building in several years,
> that of a complete, permanent, Mexican town covering several acres on the
> back lot for the new *Zorro* half-hour series. First of 39 for ABC-TV is now
> shooting with Guy Williams in the title role. Undisclosed price of the series
> is reckoned as the highest for any half-hour on TV to date.

Disney had a large budget and every cent went into production. There were no
stops. The show would be exquisite and in good taste. Pre-production cost $208,000.
The cost of *each* episode was between $50,000 and $100,000, for just under thirty
minutes. The cost of the first season's thirty-nine episodes totaled $3,198,000.[82] Set
construction ran $100,000, furnishings $35,000, and additional props, $30,000. It was
the most expensive half-hour show on TV up to that time.

Guy and his family. (author's personal collection)

The costumes were lavish: Ruffled shirts, laced bodices, and satin skirts covered with Spanish-lace; suits, cravats, and cummerbunds of fine fabrics were sewn with impeccable precision by the studio's wardrobe people. Ornate boleros and pants were embellished with embroidered designs of elaborate Spanish flourishes. The simplicity of Zorro's completely black costume, with a classic poet's-sleeve shirt, made it timeless. The upward slant of the eyeholes for the mask made it the most attractive design of all previous Zorro masks. It resembled the almond-shaped eyes of a fox, and makes it much more appealing than the round eye-holes used in other movies.

The projected date to start filming was in June, but the set was not finished, so filming was delayed until July.

The interiors of the haciendas were furnished with exquisite antiques, richly carved wooden Spanish tables, chairs, and doors that wealthy landowners of that time would own. Silver candelabrums, crystal goblets, walls of tapestry dressed the sets, and patios were tiled and decorated with lacy wrought iron balconies and furniture. A replica of the original church in the Pueblo de Los Angeles was built, surrounded by the entire pueblo consisting of an inn with a tavern, the military's cuartel, the plaza with a well, and vendor huts where the Indians sell their crafts. No other Zorro movie or TV show has matched, or even come close, to the beauty and elaborate designs of Disney's *Zorro* production.

Walt was setting one of his many precedents. It was his studio's first permanent set and most expensive show. From ABC's perspective, the average cost for a one-hour drama

Guy and Janice playing chess at home. (author's collection)

series in the 1950s was $13,840. Walt's average was $82,000 for a half-hour show.

One of the reasons *Zorro* was expensive is the fencing scenes. No other show on TV at the time was offering fencing. Fencing scenes were expensive. A *thirty-second* fencing segment would take two to four *hours* to shoot. Walt would not cut corners by eliminating any of his main ingredient, the *action*. He knew it was necessary to keep the kids interested. Walt's insistence on quality and authenticity rubbed off on everyone working on *Zorro*. Actors, directors, stunt people, crew, everyone involved, strove to make the show perfect. Walt spared no expense.

Before shooting the first episode Walt talked at length with the producers, Bill Walsh and Bill Anderson, and the director, Norman Foster, about filming *Zorro* in color, which was new. Walt's thinking was that if *Zorro's* popularity didn't last more than two years, the show would have more syndication value later if it were in color. Everyone involved with the show wanted it to be in color. Walt asked ABC for the money to film it in color, but the small network, lagging in third place, said it was a "no-go." Color was *too* expensive.[83] They told Walt that if he wanted color he had to cut expenses elsewhere, and Walt refused to do that. Rather than cheapen the show, he filmed it in beautiful black and white.

Guy practiced horseback riding at the studio for hours with wranglers to familiarize himself with the spirited black horse, Diamond Decorator, Zorro's faithful companion, Tornado. "Guy preferred a high-spirited horse to a docile one," said Janice. "He wouldn't have had it any other way. There was a total of seven horses used in the series and Guy had to be familiar with each one."

Determined not to copy Fairbanks or Power, Guy said, "The only time I look at the old *Mark of Zorro* films is when I want to study some particular move in sword-play."[84]

It wasn't the movies—but at 33 years old, Guy had gotten the break of his lifetime.

Chapter 16

"The three of us had a magic between us."
— Britt Lomond (Monastario)

Other principal roles that rounded out the cast of *Zorro* were "Bernardo," Diego's devoted mute servant who would die for him if necessary, played by veteran vaudevillian and Broadway actor, Gene Sheldon; "Don Alejandro," Diego's wealthy and benevolent father played by seasoned veteran actor, George J. Lewis; and "Sgt. Garcia," a kind-hearted, Falstaffian oaf, a friend of Diego, who wants to capture Zorro for the reward, played by opera singer/actor of stage, radio, and television, Henry Calvin. The characters and storyline were based on Johnston McCulley's pulp fiction stories and books.

The first few episodes were essential to the success of the show. The characters had to be clearly defined and the action had to hook the young audience. Director Norman Foster left it up to Guy's creativity to reinvent the character. "With me the problem was one of finding out how to play the character," said Guy. "Don Diego is on three-quarters of the time and one quarter of the time is devoted to Zorro, so you got a three to one mix. Don Diego had been, up to that point [in movies], played very foppish, very effeminate. But I didn't want to do that, and Walt agreed, too. Because even though television was new at the time, we realized then that you couldn't play this kind of character foppish *every* week, and we *hoped*, for *several* years. It was OK for Ty Power to do it in the movie, or Leslie Howard playing the Scarlet Pimpernel, because you're just doing it that way *once*. Fine. There had to be a way to play this part without repeating yourself in what would become unpleasant after a while. So I had to play him neutral, which is difficult, because it's *nothing*. And you have to make *nothing* interesting. That *began* to work. Don Diego began to be accepted as 'OK,' not really peculiar. From time to time, I would even face Monastario and just argue him down in no uncertain terms."[85]

The charm that sustained the Don Diego character for the duration of the television series can be attributed to Guy's projection of his own real personality into it. Traits of Don Diego were actual traits of Guy Williams: his love for books, fine wines, chess, music, art, poetry, philosophy. Guy's personality was so interwoven into the character that when Guy began smoking small cigars, the director let Diego smoke them too.

The hardest thing for Guy to create for Diego was the accent. "Nobody told me

Guy as Diego de la Vega in embellished costume with flourishing embroidery. (Photo fest)

what kind of an accent they wanted," he said. "So when I did the test I was all over the place with a Spanish accent—heavy, heavy accent—because no one would say which way they wanted to go. They didn't know *either* what they wanted. They knew they could always drop it if it was heavy. But, if I were to go too light, that would be worse. For the first couple of weeks, I'd be walking around the set, and somebody would be tapping me on the shoulder. I'd turn around, and it's Walt! And he's just saying one thing: 'Can you bring it down a little, Guy?' He didn't know what he wanted about it yet. It was hard to describe. I'd say 'Sure!' So, I'd bring it down. Then I'd feel this tap-tap on the shoulder and he would motion for me to bring it *up* a little? One day, I had finished a show and he didn't tap me on the shoulder," Guy laughs, "And that's the one I kept."[86]

Britt Lomond's role as Monastario was a key role, a pivotal one, from which the other characters established their purpose. Monastario had to pull it off as a mean and hated dictator, or there would be no purpose for Zorro. Nevertheless, Norman Foster was aware of Britt's disappointment in not getting the role of Zorro.

One night after wrapping at the San Luis Rey Mission for some early episodes, Norman took Britt to dinner and explained the situation. "The reason I wanted you

Set of Diego's bedroom shows expenses antiques of heavily carved bed and Spanish chairs.
(Kathy Gregory Personal Collection, Courtesy of Kathy Gregory)

so bad to play Monastario was because you were a well-accomplished actor with a lot of background. I needed somebody very strong for the first dozen or so episodes to get the thing started, to set the series, because without a strong heavy there is no show. I was behind the 8-ball. If this series didn't sell, I wouldn't work again in this town."

"Norman was a delightful man, very well educated, very well read," said Britt. "And erudite. Very particular in casting, in the things he wanted that show to represent. He was honest with me, and I was always very grateful to him for explaining why I got the role of Monastario and not Zorro. But, it cost me a *million bucks*!"

Britt's wife, Diane Lomond, was a casting agent in Hollywood more than thirty years from the early days of live television in the 1950s to the 1980s. She cast many favorite TV shows. Among them are *Family Affair, Police Woman, Bonanza* and *Bat Masterson*. While Diane is sympathetic to Britt's feelings, she said, "Honestly speaking, physically, Guy was better for Zorro and Britt was better for the commandante. Norman told Britt, 'You *were* the commandante.' He told Britt he had to have an extremely strong fencer for that role for Guy to play off of. Guy would not have made a good Monastario," said Diane. "Guy was exactly like you saw him on screen. He was very flamboyant. He was very 'by the seat of his pants,' unpretentious, a darling, terrific, fun guy, but you would never have believed him as Monastario. Even though it was done tongue-in-cheek, there's a difference between tongue-in-cheek and it not working. The casting was right."

Despite his disappointment, Britt agreed. Then, as images of himself and Guy and Henry Calvin from Zorro came to mind, a smile spread across his face and he said, "We had a *lot* of fun doing that series. Guy was the most wonderful person. God! We had a lot of fun together. The three of us had a magic between us."

Henry Calvin was a 6'3" rotund actor, powerful in voice and presence. A native of Dallas, Texas, he was a journalist-turned-actor when his operatic talent as a baritone won him a role at the Ziegfeld Theatre in New York City in 1953. "Henry was our favorite," said Britt affectionately. "He was a dear, sweet, wonderful man. We used to have so much fun at his house."

"We loved him the most," added Diane, "and spent most of our time with Henry and Edna [his first wife]. Edna was a large woman. Not as large as Henry, but she was a large woman."

Henry Calvin and Britt Lomond had a bond from the moment they met. They had both served in the Korean War. "We were never stationed together, but we were both in the war," said Britt. "I was a paratrooper and served in the South Pacific. Henry served in the artillery, so we had a camaraderie about that.

"By the way, Henry sang on the series. That was *his* voice you hear," Britt said. "Henry would sing at the drop of a hat. What a beautiful voice he had! Henry sang the part of the Grand Wizar in *Kismet* on Broadway. His name is on the record album cover."

Henry played off of Britt also. Some of his most lovable and comedic moments are his reactions to Monastario's abuse. Henry Calvin died in 1975 of cancer. He left his friends with many happy and fond memories, and the characters he played are unforgettable. He had no children.

Gene Sheldon played a mute, Bernardo, who pretended he also could not hear, so that he could spy for Diego/Zorro. Monastario always suspected Bernardo *could* hear, so Bernardo had to be particularly careful not to blow his cover when Monastario was around to test him.

Guy met and collaborated with the creator of the Zorro character, Johnston McCulley, June 1957.(Kathy Gregory Personal Collection, Courtesy of Kathy Gregory)

Veteran vaudeville performer Gene Sheldon played the deaf mute Bernardo, Diego's faithful servant. (courtesy of Anna Wehling)

Gene was sixteen years older than Guy, which lent much credibility to his role as a protective and devoted servant to the young Diego. Brilliantly played by Gene, Bernardo offers tender moments of loyalty to Diego, along with comic relief. Bernardo, the unsung hero of the story, saves Zorro many times from disaster, even death, endearing him ever more to Diego. Gene and Guy had a good chemistry on and off screen, and became very good friends. They kept each other sharp on the set by sparring with each other about their acting. "We argued all the time," says Sheldon, "usually about how we should play a scene together."[87]

In an interview printed in July 12, 1958 for *TV Life* Guy said:

I've been surrounded by a good cast and crew. Gene and Henry, they have a great sense of humor. In the long stretches when there's not much happening on the set, Gene keeps the whole set in good spirits by his jokes and general comments. Henry is the same—in his rotund, good humor. George Lewis, too, is another who makes our *Zorro* set a happy one, and in a series like this if there's not a good feeling on the set between the regulars, it's a rough deal.

Before *Zorro*, Gene Sheldon was often a guest on TV variety shows in the early 1950s such as *The Colgate Comedy Hour*, *The Steve Allen Show*, and Milton Berle's show, performing his hilarious mime act with his banjo. His daughter, Tracy Sheldon, speaks

George J. Lewis, veteran of many Republic pictures, played Diego's distinguished father, Don Alejandro de la Vega.

with pride and affection about her father, whom she often refers to as Gene. "My dad was in show business since 1928," said Tracy. "He performed in Germany during World War II and on the SS Normandie. He also performed for the Royal Family at Buckingham Palace. I have a huge scrapbook of Gene's career, and in it is a telegram sent to him from Buckingham Palace, thanking my dad for his condolences over the death of King George."

When Gene Sheldon met his wife, Peggy, whose real name is Margaret, he was thirty-four years old. He had already worked in London, Berlin, La Scala in Rome, and all over Europe. "Gene was a pantomimist so his act had no language barrier," said Peggy. "He could play any place in the world."

Gene's voice is not heard on *Zorro*, but he had a beautiful speaking voice which can be heard in the often-aired Disney movie, *Toby Tyler*. Although Gene was used to doing pantomime, he told his only daughter that it was very difficult for him not to utter a sound playing Bernardo. The only sound we hear from him is "*swish, swish, swish*" when he makes the sign of the Z with his finger.

Peggy and Gene adopted a son in 1955, and in 1959 they adopted Tracy. Peggy already had her name picked out. "Buddy Van Horn[1] had just had a daughter and they

1. Guy's stunt double on *Zorro*.

Britt Lomond was the handsome villain you love to hate, Capitan Monastario,
with Guy crossing swords (author's personal collection)

named her Tracy," said Peggy. "I liked that name. I had liked it when I saw Katharine
Hepburn in *The Philadelphia Story* and she played Tracy in the movie. So we named our
daughter Tracy, too."

Gene and Peggy's home in Tarzana was a gathering place, not just for the cast and
writers of *Zorro* but many actors in Hollywood at the time. Everyone loved to go there
for drinks and jokes, or swim and relax around the pool. "My dad loved his 'marts,'" said
Tracy, "and he always had friends over to the house for drinks. After my father died [in
1982], I had lunch one day with someone from Disney and he told me, 'The joke was—
if you wanted to *find* someone, go to *Gene's*.'"

Tracy recalled her father's shenanigans and sense of humor. "My father loved to
film things. He used to film on the set using 16mm, color film, no sound. One of the
sponsors of the show was 7-Up, so they would have cases all over the set of 7-Up, and
one day he and Charles Korvin [one of the guest actors on *Zorro*] and some others all
decided they were going to get drunk on 7-Up. Charles Korvin played his sidekick and
they were drinking 7-Up and pretending to be getting drunker and drunker, falling
down on the steps and so forth. They joked and played around like that. I have his old
films, but I wish I could see some outtakes of the show, if there are any."

Guy's and Gene's families used to get cases of 7-Up delivered to their homes by the
sponsor of the show.

Tracy remembers a very memorable party when one of the greatest stuntmen provided the entertainment. "Buddy Van Horn came to my brother's birthday party in our

backyard in the Valley. He did rope tricks for us, twirling the rope, roping things and he demonstrated the bullwhip, cracking it for us. He cracked it so close to one kid we thought he was going to kill him. We had such a good time.

"Gene had fun doing *Zorro* with Guy, and they became friends. Guy and Gene used to like to cook Italian and they were always trying to outdo the other with the most Italian recipe and things Italian. They were always trying to 'one-up' the other. Well, my parents adopted me in 1959, and I am half-Italian and half-Irish. Gene was so proud that I was Italian, he called Guy and said, 'Well, I'm one up on ya, cuz she's *Italian*!' They were always joking with one another like that."

Don Diamond became a regular on the show as Corporal Reyes, after the first thirteen episodes. "I was in the original tryouts in April 1957 where they film you and decide who is going to be in the series. I was supposed to be one of the soldiers, but they didn't call me! I thought I didn't make the show, but weeks later, I got a call to come in, and was cast as one of the Spanish lancers. And episode eight, changed their minds."

In episode #8, "Zorro Rides into Terror," Don, with *no* mustache and very few lines, helps the fat sergeant hold Don Diego hostage in his hacienda. "Consequently, they tested me as a Corporal to be a foil for Sgt. Garcia."

They were looking for freshness after Monastario was arrested in episode thirteen and was no longer on the show. Walt used to stop by to watch rehearsal, then he turned to Norman and said, "Put humor in it." Don was the man Norman needed. A Laurel-and-Hardy-type shtick was created between the large Henry Calvin and the small Don

Director Norman Foster with pipe, Walt Disney, and Guy on the set of the old pueblo on the Disney lot, discussing a scene for the first episode of *Zorro*. (Kathy Gregory Personal Collection, Courtesy of Kathy Gregory)

Henry Calvin added comedy as well as musical numbers as Sgt. Garcia
(Courtesy of Anna Wehling)

Diamond. While the fat sergeant was always being insulted by the mean commandante, he could in turn insult the dim-witted corporal, and they would play off one another. Don and Henry were an act in themselves. Even if the main theme was serious, humor was an ingredient Walt felt necessary for the life of any show.

Don created the character of Corporal Reyes in his audition with Henry. "I downplayed my role so the sergeant could get the big laughs. I let his humor bounce off me. They said 'OK, you've got a run in the part.' And I got about *fifty* episodes after that." As Corporal Reyes for the remainder of the series, Don wore a thick mustache.

Britt Lomond, Henry Calvin, Gene Sheldon, and Guy Williams have been tagged "The Original Four." But fans consider Don Diamond part of the original cast. Don Diamond was born in Brooklyn, New York on June 4, 1921. Realizing his desire to be an actor at an early age, he took acting classes at the University of Michigan in their speech department, because at that time no colleges had a drama department. During WWII he served in the Air Corp. as a ground officer in communications. The years of Spanish classes at the University came in handy when he was stationed in California and other Southwestern states. After the war he decided to live in California, and once again his Spanish came in handy when he met and married a lovely Señorita from Mexico City. They are still married and live in the San Fernando Valley. He keeps fit by playing handball three days a week and takes "a lot of vitamins."

Don Diamond as Corporal Reyes first appeared in Episode 8 as a lancer. He was later given the role of Corporal Reyes and stayed the remainder of the series. (Mary Spooner Personal Collection; courtesy of Mary Spooner)

"When I met Guy on the show," said Don, "he impressed me because he was *so* intelligent and his Italian was perfect. I appreciated his educational background. I enjoyed working with Guy and with Henry Calvin. Henry and I became very close friends, as well as Guy and his wife, Janice, who is a very lovely lady. I went to their house on Harper Street, then to the one on Hillside Drive, and went sailing with Guy on his boat."

His sense of humor is sharp as ever, and similar in real life to that of Corporal Reyes, quiet and subtle. Don said, "Walt wasn't on the set much by the time I joined the cast, but when I did see him, I was in awe of him. I looked up to Mr. Disney. He was the greatest producer. Well, *he owned the studio!*"

Walt was known to put fear in a lot of people just by coming around, because he was known to fire people on the spot if he didn't like something they did. People naturally called him Mr. Disney, and he always told his employees right away to call him Walt, *not* Mr. Disney. "If you call me Mr. Disney," he added, "I'll fire you." While he was congenial, he also sent terror to the core of some who experienced his presence. Don joked about his own intimidation around Walt. "One day Walt said to me, 'Hello Don. How are you?' And I thought to myself, 'I wonder what he *meant* by that?'" his voice quivering, in mock fear.

"That's about all I saw of him, when he said hello to me a few times."[88]

Chapter 17

"We felt we were doing a little ensemble *playing."*
— Guy Williams

On July 15, 1957, the cameras rolled for the first time on *Zorro*. "Presenting Señor Zorro," written by Norman Foster, was the first shooting script. Labeled "Production #5850-014," it had, coincidently, been finished on May 23, 1957, Johnston McCulley's birthday. Weekly TV shows, generally, were filmed three to four months ahead of air time, as these were also.

Regarding those first months of filming, Guy said, "In the beginning, Walt was there all the time. If we were on location, he'd show up occasionally. I would put it this way: As the thing became more secure, more settled, he began having more confidence [in it]. He was doing other things. He was building the park at that time."[89]

A typical work day started at 5:00 a.m. for Guy. "I'm a native New Yorker, used to late hours, and by the time I make it to the breakfast table at dawn," he smiled, "I think I've earned my money!"

"I'd get up and make fresh hot coffee," said Janice. "Guy didn't demand that I do it, I just did it. Sometimes I set the timer. He didn't eat much for breakfast, usually a piece of Italian bread he dunked in his coffee."

When Guy first got the job, he drove his yellow Cadillac to work. A few months later he sported a new red Jaguar through the Disney gates. By 6:30 a.m. he was at the studio ready for make-up. Guy had a white patch of hair over his left ear,[90] and it was covered with mascara for filming, something he was in the habit of doing early in his career. By 7:30 a.m. he was on the set. His work day was usually 12 hours of blocking, rehearsal, learning and re-learning lines, learning fight scenes, waiting for tech, and shooting. *Zorro* and most TV shows at that time required three days of rehearsal and two days for shooting. It was a grueling fast pace.

One of Zorro's sponsors, 7-Up, published the *Zorro* Newsletter. It was a way for fans all over the country to keep up with production notes and news of their favorite actors on the show. One *Zorro* Newsletter, published in 1957, spoke of Guy's workload:

> He wants to be busy, loves a heavy work load. He is up at 6 a.m. for a
> 7 o'clock call at the studio, usually the first person on the set. Guy is good

natured and describes his work as only a half day job...12 hours!

"It's scene, scene, scene, one right after the other, and at home it's learning scene, scene, scene for the next day. Saturday and Sunday's study ahead on the next two shows so that when 16 pages of dialogue comes along I'm ready for them."

In spite of the busy schedule he finds time to play with his 5-year-old, Steven.

The newsletter offered a variety of recipes for "Zorro Floats," made with 7-Up, such as chocolate ice cream, with bittersweet chocolate, whipped cream, and, of course, 7-Up.

In 1958 Guy told reporters for a magazine, "To be honest, I was really frightened at first of all the work that goes into a TV series. When I looked at the first script, I asked myself, 'Can I memorize all that?' Today shooting the series is fun, and the memorizing comes easily."[91]

Television work was new and different to actors who were matriculating from movies. It was not easy to adjust to the quick pace and changes. "We were being very sarcastic, but humorously so,[92] in that we used to call even the acting a *stunt*," laughed Guy, "because sometimes the scripts were coming down with changes at the last minute and none of us were used to that in those days. You prepared stuff, and all of a sudden, you're on the set, and you find out that the scene you were going to do is all changed and re-written! So you're waiting for the new stuff to come down, and well, when it comes down, you've got to chew it, swallow it down and then *do* it. And we used to call that another *stunt*."[93]

"Guy would come home so tired," said Janice. "We had dinner, then he would go over the script for the next day. He was learning lines all the time. If we went somewhere, he took his script with him. He not only had to learn *his* lines, but he had to learn Gene's, too."

Since Gene had to mime all of his dialogue, Guy had learned lines to tell the audience what Bernardo was saying with his hands, such as, "Oh! You mean they are going to hang him!" Or "You want to be someone you are not, too?"

"Guy used to tease Gene about that," said Janice. "He would say to Gene that he should get some of his salary, because he had to learn *his* part too," she laughed. "Guy was a 'quick-study.' Learning lines came easy to him."

In the first episode, "Presenting Señor Zorro," Diego plans his strategy to fight the tyranny and oppression of Captain Monastario, but not as Diego. He will wear a disguise. He reminds Bernardo of an old proverb: "'If you can't clothe yourself in the skin of the lion, put on that of the fox!' From now on, I will be *Zorro*, the *fox*!"

The opening scene of the first show starts with fast-action fencing. Diego is on a ship coming home to the pueblo Los Angeles, from Spain, and for fun and exercise, he and the sea captain are challenging each other with some fancy swordplay. The captain is played by Albert Cavens, son of Fred Cavens, the fencing maestro for the series. "We had just about the greatest there was," said Guy. "Freddie Caven put the fencing together for us. I used to fence with Fred and his son, Albert. They used to double for most of the villains."[94]

These fencing scenes were Guy's favorite part of the show. An assistant from the Walt Disney Archives said: "Our shooting calls indicate that Guy Williams had two doubles while making *Zorro*. Buddy Van Horn doubled in many of the riding sequences, while Carl Pitti doubled in those shots calling for expertise with the whip. Williams

Guy (Diego) interprets what Gene (Bernardo) is miming. He teased Gene
saying he should get his salary because he had to learn "*his* lines" too.
(Kathy Gregory collection, courtesy of Kathy Gregory)

himself was an excellent fencer, and did not need doubling there."[95]

When an interviewer told Guy he thought the show was not as good after Britt Lomond
as Monastario left, Guy replied, "They changed the villains around enough to give it a little
more interest than just one person, but Britt was just as good as he could be. He was *really*
good. We felt we were doing a little *ensemble* playing—you know, Britt, Henry, Gene, and
I—especially if we all had a *scene* together. Oh! We'd *really* go to *town* on it![96]

"During production we'd rehearse our dueling scenes between set-ups—and since
these are grueling chores, it was even more important that we had had all that fencing
before. Britt and I really got to know each other—blade-wise."[97]

"There are two kinds of fencing," explained Britt Lomond, "strip fencing and picture fencing, and I had the finest fencing master of all time to teach me picture fencing—Fred Cavens."

Britt tells why he is so sentimental about the sword he used in *Zorro*. "The sword I
used on the *Zorro* series was the same sword Douglas Fairbanks, Sr. had used! When we
started to do the series, Freddie came to me and said, 'I have the original sabre that
Douglas Fairbanks used in all his pictures. Would you like to use it in the series?' I said,
'My *God*! Would I! I'd *love* it!' Then he held the sword out to me like this," Britt ex-

tended his arms, miming a sword lying horizontally in his hands, being presented formally, "and Freddie said, 'Here it is. I know you won't dishonor it.'

"I was speechless. It was a great honor for me. Then Fred said, 'My only request is that when you finish your part in the series, you return it to me. I don't want anyone else to use it.'

"I remembered every inch of that saber. I loved it. It was plain, and had a very heavy guard. When I finished my thirteen episodes, I carefully handed it back to him. I consider that one of my *greatest* privileges.

"When we filmed our fencing scenes, we couldn't do but about six to eight movements at a time, then we would break," continued Britt. "We had to work up to twelve moves, maximum. They wanted the fencing scenes to be magnificent, some of the finest fencing that had been done on television. It was the first TV series with fencing and we had no time at all. We would shoot the entire show in three to four days, sometimes.

"A fencing routine is a very difficult thing to choreograph and shoot," explained Britt. "It took a lot of time and a lot of trouble. We devoted one whole day each week to our fencing routines. Sometimes Guy would come over to my house in Studio City and we would practice in my backyard. He worked really hard at it." The fencing scenes still hold up as some of the finest fencing ever on TV.

"All the sword fighting stuff we did was done on a Friday," said Guy in an interview in 1983. "That was because, if anything happened, like a twisted finger, some injury of the nature that slows you, you had the whole weekend to get over it, and possibly even Monday. We had people show up for miles to watch those days. That's when we would get all our visitors. I mean, the studio would stop on Friday. Everybody would come on over, sit down, and have coffee, and wait to see what would happen," he laughed.[98]

The foils used were real. Sometimes there was a button tip on the end for protection, but much of the time there were dangerous points on the tip. "It wasn't so dangerous when we had it all worked out," Guy told David Hartman on *Good Morning America* in 1983. "We had real points on them so that when somebody was disarmed and that sword would fly into the wall and go *zing, zing, zing*, it *really* happened."[99]

Britt Lomond carries a mark from Zorro's sword to this day. "See this little scar right under my left brow?" He points above his eye. "That's Guy's sword. *Three* minutes into our *very first* fight scene I get cut over the left eye! Suddenly we saw blood! It scared Guy and it scared me, too. He kept apologizing over and over, and I said, 'Guy, I'm alright. Really! It's OK.' Guy was *so* distraught about it. The make-up people rushed over making a fuss about what to do with this bleeding cut. They were afraid I might get blood poisoning if they put make-up on it, so they didn't know what to do. I said 'Aaawgh. Just throw same make-up on it and let's finish the scene," he laughed. "Guy got very carried away sometimes when he fenced. He tried to put a lot into it. I used to say to him, 'Relax, Guy. Nobody knows how hard you're hitting.'" Britt does not talk about the long scar on his right cheek. He just allows that it is a war wound from his first combat in the Pacific.

In an article from a 7-Up Zorro Newsletter, Fred Cavens raves about the dueling skills of Britt and Guy.

> Why should we use doubles when Williams and Lomond are two of the finest fencers in the country? Williams is considered one of the top fencers of the orthodox school. During one slashing duel, Lomond was

nicked between the eyes by Williams' sword. Even so, neither actor wants a double. When they are not working in a sequence at the Disney Studios in Burbank, Calif., Williams and Lomond generally can be found on the studio back-lot polishing up on their fencing routines. "They are a marvelous pair," says Cavens, with a smile, "I just wish all my fencing pupils were like them."

Michael Forest,[100] who played Lieutenant Santos in episode #42, "A Horse of A Different Color" (first aired October 23, 1958), remembers Fred Cavens for his great strength when he prepared him for his scenes to fence with Zorro/Guy. "Fred Cavens told me he was going to teach me how to disarm someone," said Michael. "Well, Fred Cavens was probably in his late 60s then and stood about 5'7". I was 6'3", in my 20s, young and strong, so I didn't think he could disarm me. I got a firm grip on my sword and, boy! In a blink of an eye, he whipped that sword out of my hand and nearly tore my arm off! I'd pulled a muscle! The man was so *fast* and so *strong*! I said to him, 'How'd you *do* that?' and Fred said, 'It's all in the wrist.'"

Michael Forest as the imposter, Lt Santos in Episode #42 held at point by Zorro.
(The Kathy Gregory Personal Collection; courtesy of Kathy Gregory)

Contrary to what some people told him when he got the job, Guy enjoyed all the people he worked with on *Zorro*. Janice Williams recalled, "Shortly after Guy got the job, someone said to him, '*Norman Foster's* going to direct you?! Oh, I feel sorry for you!' Norman had a reputation of being mean and hard to work with, but he was so *wonderful*. He and Guy just hit it off. Norman was a sweet person, and he and Guy became very close friends."

Norman's only son Robert Foster said, "I think the flack was started by a few actors who had a run-in with him during *Davy Crockett and the River Pirates*. He saw this crew 'gold-bricking' and he didn't hesitate to just fire them on the spot and never hired them again. Norman Foster gave actors a hard time if they weren't absolutely what he wanted. Norman had a reputation of being a task master, but he never had a problem with Guy because he gave 200 percent."

As their friendship grew over the years Guy and Norman found they had a lot in common. For one thing, neither of them were traditionalists about Christmas. The sounds of traditional Christmas music irritated Norman. "Oh is it *that* time of year again!" he'd jest. Norman didn't have a Christmas tree in his house and Guy sometimes didn't either. "We had a tree when the children were little," said Janice, "then eventually we had one every other year."

Oddly, while Norman didn't practice *any* religion, the episodes he wrote and directed contain *more* religious references than any others. The ones he wrote depict Zorro as a quasi-supernatural being, and suggest he is protected and guided by a divine power. In a scene in the church at the mission, Norman has Zorro hide behind the statue of Jesus, which protects him from the searching soldiers. Padre Felipe uses Latin when he says to Don Nacho, "Oremus. Let us Pray." Moreover, at the mission, when Zorro enters the church, he genuflects at the altar and makes the sign of the cross. In other episodes by Foster, there are references to the holy water in the church, the poor box, the angelus, church candles, and so on. Norman Foster was married to a devout Catholic, whose entire family was very religious in the Catholic faith. Perhaps it had some influenced over him.

Walt knew he was taking a chance with a Spanish hero, dressed in black, who rode a black horse at night. Audiences were used to watching the good guy in cowboy films and TV shows who wore a white hat and rode a white horse. His anxiety was evident one evening when he sat down to watch the first dailies. Britt Lomond remembered, "We were all there, Guy, Walt, a whole group of us. It was a day-for-night scene, where filters are used to make it look like nighttime. It was one of our chase sequences and Walt was having trouble seeing the action. Suddenly Walt yells out, 'I CAN'T SEE GUY! ALL I SEE IS BRITT ON THE WHITE HORSE! What stupid ass would put the *heavy* on a white horse? *What* the *hell* have I done?"

The wrath of Walt made everyone nervous. Guy recalled the reaction of people at a meeting with Walt. "Walt could start taping his pencil in a meeting and everybody'd jump into the woodwork! Because, if he didn't *like* something, he'd start to tap his pencil. Everyone would say, 'Oh my God! He's *taping* his pencil!' *That* means somebody's about to get *fired*. Or, *yelled* at."

Buddy Van Horn remembered the apprehension employees felt when Walt came around. "Walt didn't hire you if he didn't like you, but a lot of people who worked for him were afraid of him. When Walt would stop by the set occasionally, a lot of times he'd come talk to me. And what he would talk about was *horses*. Walt loved horses. So we would bull a little bit about that for a while, then he would leave. Some of the production people would come over right away whispering, '*What'd he say? What'd he want!*' A lot of people were scared of him, but he was always very nice to me. In fact, I got letters from Walt thanking me for certain things. I've always kept those."

Norman Foster was open to suggestions from Guy and Britt, and sometimes used their ideas and adlibs. In the first episode "Presenting Señor Zorro," Guy and Britt were blocking their first dueling scene in the cuartel. "Our swords were clashing and we were parrying and lunging, but the scene seemed a little boring," remembered Britt. "Guy said to the director, 'Couldn't we add some balsa wood here, and have Britt's sword go through it?' They did it and it worked!" In the final take Zorro laughs at Monastario with his sword lodged in the wood, "HA! HAAA! *Beauu*-ti-ful!" he says. "Coupé to the wall! You must show me that again sometime. Now will you please get inside the cell."

Another case in point was in episode #2, "Zorro's Secret Passage." A scene between Britt and Guy on the patio under a tree wasn't working, so Guy suggested lowering a branch of the tree so he could get his sword caught up in it. It was much more effective and that is what we see in the final cut.

"One time we had to shoot around this big tree,"[101] recalled Britt, "then they needed *another* big tree. They were going to have to move the company a quarter of a mile away. I said, 'Charlie [addressing the director, Charles Barton], just use the other side of the same tree.' So they moved the camera and shot the scene from the other side of the big tree and saved a lot of money.

"We were rehearsing for the first episode and I was wondering why my character was so mean," said Britt. "I said, 'Norman, I'm beating the women, throwing them in jail, whipping people, and doing all these terrible, horrible things! What am I doing all

Cast and crew of Walt Disney Productions in 1957 filming under the famous old Pepper Tree, gift to the mission from Peru in 1830. It is still standing in all its magnificence. (author's personal collection)

this for?' Norman thought for a while and said, 'You're right. I gotta give you a reason. OK, this scene coming up—the one with the lawyer, at the very end of the scene. Walk down toward the desk, turn into camera, and say, '*Nothing* shall stop me from being the richest man in all of California!'

"So that was my motivation. I gave the line. When the director said, '*Cut,*' a man up in the catwalk said, 'And that's how the Bank of America got started!'

"Everybody broke up!" He laughed. "God, we had a lot of fun on that show."

When Britt got the part of the Capitan, he had a different name at first. "My name was *not* Monastario in the original test script. It was Tolendano. Norman changed it just before we began filming. One day he was telling me about a man in Mexico who was the only man whoever screwed him out of several thousand dollars and his name was *Monastario*. Suddenly he said, 'Goddamn it! I'm going to make you the *worst* heavy in the world! You're gonna be called *Monastario!*'"

Britt, a natural blond, remembers those early make-up calls to make his transformation to a Spaniard. "Early in the series I had to be at the studio a half hour earlier than the others, because the make-up people had to put my beard and moustache on. They dyed my hair and eyebrows black. After about the fourth show I had grown my own beard, and I could sleep in. The call was at *6:30* instead of 6," he quipped.

Britt did not film the series with the thick brown contact lenses he wore for the screen test. They had irritated his eyes so badly he had to take medication for the pain, and the medication hindered his vision. As a result, we see Britt's natural blue eyes in his thirteen episodes.

Two weeks into production, the entire company—more than eighty technicians and extras[102]—checked into hotels in Oceanside and Carlsbad, about 90 miles south of Los Angeles, to film the rest of the scenes in the first three episodes at Mission San Luis Rey. The mission "doubled" as the San Gabriel Mission in Los Angeles, which is near the original Pueblo.

> *Hollywood Reporter*, Friday, July 26, 1957
> Three *Zorro* Segments were shooting at the same time. Setting a TV filming precedent that is proving a 20% time saving innovation, director Norman Foster is currently shooting the first three episodes of Walt Disney's *Zorro* series simultaneously. With each segment calling for location at Iverson's Ranch (the Garden of the Gods), San Luis Rey Mission in Oceanside, Disney stages 2 & 3, and the new Spanish village on the back lot, shifts from one to the other are not being made till takes necessitated by all three episodes are completed. The unit goes to the Oceanside location Monday.

Guy and Gene (Diego and Bernardo) were filmed on horseback at what is now an historic cinema landmark, called The Garden of the Gods, at the Iverson Movie Ranch in Chatsworth, several miles north of the studio. It became stock footage, repeatedly shown when the twosome was traveling somewhere.

To cut production costs, Norman Foster and Walt decided to film segments from as many as four different stories in one day. All scenes that took place at one location, such as the mission at San Luis Rey, or a lake at Bell Ranch in Chatsworth, would be shot while at that location, even though they might be from different episodes.

"[It's] a little confusing at times," said Guy, "*not* remembering the dialogue, but remembering what led up to it. Sometimes I'm real blank and we have to go back and read scenes we've already filmed."[103] Guy added, "I'm only exactly sure of how the film looks in its entirety when I see it in my little black box at home the same time everyone else does."[104]

Episodes 17, 18, and 19 (about The Eagle) are another example of filming three different episodes at the same time. "We're wrapping them all up at once," said Guy. "Most weekly TV series shoot an episode in four or five days, but they generally do one story at a time. I never know from one day to the next what episode I'm in. I'd never bet on its number."[105]

Filming took place at the San Luis Rey from July 29-August 6, 1957. The hand-hewn wooden beams of the old church, murals painted by Native Americans, beautiful brick patios, and artifacts were powerful reminders of life in colonial California days. Of his experience of the mission, Guy commented: "You know, you can't help feeling the history of this place. And the peace of it. I know it sounds overly sentimental and maybe silly, but it's going to be hard to be quite the same after coming here. San Luis Rey rubs off on you."[106]

Chapter 18

"We really had some good people"

– Guy Williams

The second unit was directed by one of the best stuntmen in movie history—Yakima Canutt, with over 178 films to his credit. He is enshrined in the Gene Autry Western Heritage Museum in Los Angeles, as well as other museums, as one of the greatest stuntmen/stunt-coordinators of all time. Best known for his famous stagecoach stunt in John Ford's classic western, *Stagecoach* (1939) starring John Wayne, he started in films in the silent era.

While the actors were filming in the studio, "Yak" was on location at Bell Ranch in Chatsworth, several miles north of the studio, directing his skilled stuntmen, posing as soldiers galloping on long stretches of graded dirt roads chasing Zorro. Zorro was almost always, Buddy Van Horn. He was Guy's double for Zorro and Don Diego. Occasionally, if the whip was required, it was another stuntman in the costume on the horse, but Van Horn is usually the one the audience sees in long shots. Britt and Guy did some of these scenes for the closeup shots, while the second unit was used for the long shots. Among the talented stunt people on the show, was Yak's sons Tap and Joe Canutt, Richard Farnsworth, Jack Lillie, Carl Pitti, Leon Paul, Jerry Brown, Bob Trahune, Lou Roberson, Dean Smith, Bill (Phil) Schumacher, Albert Cavens, Dave Kashner, and Valley Kean, for actresses Jolene Brand and Annette Funicello.

A show done week to week could not be possible without a second unit. Guy said, "The reason we were able to do so much work in that half-hour show and get them done in just three to four days—a ridiculously small number of days to do that much film—was that we used second units. While I'm doing a fencing scene in the studio, or a Don Diego scene, or a Zorro swing through the tavern, Yak was out there in Thousand Oaks with thirty or forty horsemen doing the chasing and all that sort of thing. We'd do that all at the same time, otherwise, there's no way you could do that show in that amount of time."[107]

Guy's admiration and respect for Buddy is evident in his interviews. Any time he talks about the stunts, he mentions Buddy, giving him full credit and praise for his work. In 1986 Guy said, "I had a 'regular' for those high falls and jumps to the horse from rooftops. For anything where you could break your foot, Buddy Van Horn was my

Buddy Van Horn doubling for Guy as Zorro, galloping across the plains on location while Guy was filming on the set at the studio. (The Kathy Gregory Personal Collection; courtesy of Kathy Gregory)

double on that. He would do all the running, jumps, and falls. He was a terrific athlete, and later on, he became a *very* good fencer on the show. So, I was usually fencing with Buddy."[108]

Guy was an excellent rider and could rear a horse, but if there was danger involved or they needed to save time, Buddy would do it. "In *Zorro,* I do all the fencing myself," says Guy, "but I don't jump on fast-moving horses from slanted rooftops. For that, I do have a double. Otherwise, the falls that are taken are all mine.[109]

"I didn't do any of those great big falls where, you know, if I came down wrong on the ankle I don't work for a week. That meant the show would *stop*. So [for] anything like that, we really had some good [stunt] people."[110]

Buddy Van Horn did Zorro's flying mounts, transfers from horse to horse, leaps on and off of horses. "Guy would never run up to a horse and jump on him," said Buddy, "not on the set or on a personal appearance. Not that he couldn't do it. It was just too risky for the show."

Horses are unpredictable and often skittish around crowds. Gene Sheldon's wife, Peggy, used to go to all the public appearances her husband made with Guy at Disneyland. They always rode horses in a parade through the park to Frontierland. "It was always a risk with the horses," she said. "It's dangerous with all the people around, especially kids on the side of the parade route. The first time they did the fencing on top the Riverboat, Guy had to run back and get on his horse, but the horse was either spooked by the crowd or not walked enough by the handlers before the parade, because it kept moving away from Guy and wouldn't let him get on. It was funny and Guy made the most of it, but after that the handlers took the horses away right after the actors dismounted. They were all *good* riders, but let's face it! They were *not* cowboys. They were *actors* on horses!".

Buddy and Guy, look-alikes, with nonspecific names, became good friends. "The first time I met Guy was on the very first day we started shooting," said Buddy, who is five years younger than Guy, and just a tad taller. "Guy was very professional, and he was serious about doing a good job. He didn't feel like he was just collecting a paycheck. He wanted to do a good job because he was serious about his career. He was very nice, very congenial, and as time went on, we just kind of built up a friendship.

"Guy liked *three* things!" he paused. "Italian food, the stock market, and his boat. I made a few trips to Catalina with him on the boat, the *Oceana*. Some on good days, some *not* so good. I've gone through some pretty rough seas with Guy a couple of times, and the *Oceana* used to just plow right through that stuff. It was always an adventure. Guy was confident in himself and the boat.

"Guy was very proud of his Italian heritage and talked a lot about his grandfather and uncle, who he said, 'worked both sides of the ocean.'" His smile implied there was a secret meaning in that statement, but Buddy would say no more.

Buddy's real name, sometimes seen in credits, is Wayne Van Horn.[111] He was sort of "born in a trunk," to use an old show business term. From the time he was two years old, his home was the back lot of Universal studios. "My dad was a veterinarian for large animals, and he was in charge of doctoring all the livestock for Universal. My home,

Guy was an excellent rider and rode for close ups. Here he is riding the white horse, Phantom, used in the second season. The horses name is a favorite Zorro trivia question.
(The Kathy Gregory Personal Collection; courtesy of Kathy Gregory)

when I was growing up, was just down below the town and the stable, where the Universal Tour tram goes now. Before the lake went in, and the Riverboat[112] was there, our house was there—a two-story house. My parents lived there since I was about two years old. There were a lot of animals back then on the lot, so I grew up around livestock."

Buddy learned to ride horses when he was a little boy. Because he lived within a studio, it seemed a given that he would work in the movies when he grew up. In 1950 Buddy got his Guild card and worked for about six months in Montana on a Navaho picture called *Warpath* with Edmond O'Brien. During the Korean War, Uncle Sam called. "I got my draft notice while up there. Couple of months later, I was in the Army. I was lucky, because I was sent from Fort Benning, Georgia, and to Europe on the border of Czechoslovakia and Russia, rather than Korea where the other half of my company was sent."

When he returned home in late 1953, he began to work a lot. His skill as a horseman, and his ingenious methods of achieving stunts, soon got him regular work and

Buddy van Horn, right, and Guy, left with young Robert Foster, the director's son, on location at Bell Ranch for episode 23, *"The Secret of the Sierras"*, the avalanche scene, sometime in December 1957. The show aired March 13, 1958. (courtesy of Robert Foster)

recognition as one of the best stuntmen in Hollywood. In 1957 Buddy Van Horn got the role of Guy's double on the recommendation of George Gesford, with whom he had already worked in pictures. "Gesford was in charge of the livestock for *Zorro*. Norman asked George if he knew anybody who could double Guy for the stunt work. George thought for a minute and came up with my name and I went over for the interview."

A *Zorro* Newsletter by 7-Up erroneously described Buddy's job when it said: "Stand-in Buddy Van Horn…" Pointedly, Buddy said, "*Not* stand-in! 'Stand-in' is a *different* profession."

A *stand-in* fills a space for an actor while the technical crew makes technical changes such as lighting and camera angles. A *stand-in* is rarely used in a shot unless the actor is to be seen from behind. A *stunt double* wears the clothes and persona of the person they double, for any action considered a stunt and is filmed doing that action.

Buddy was not in the Zorro costume from day one, however. "I think Norman Foster actually wanted someone else he had worked with before for the job. At the beginning of filming, Yak Canutt took a second unit out on location and had his son, Tap, wear the Zorro costume. But, Norman didn't like the way things were going, so then I had to get in the costume. After the first few shows, they liked what I was doing."

Buddy remained Guy's double for the duration of the show. Tap Canutt occasionally doubled for Zorro, as well did Carl Pitti, and Dale van Sickle, but it is almost always Buddy in the costume.

From an interview in April 1958, Guy talked about the problems he had getting used to the costume. "The cape is a nuisance. To mount a horse, while putting the sword into the scabbard and throwing that cape over the shoulder is the toughest trick I've ever learned. I still get the cape and my feet and the stirrups all tangled up."[113]

His double agreed. "That *cape!* We had more wrecks because of that cape than anything. Running, and climbing and jumping, getting on the horse—it was always under foot," said Buddy. "If you got in a squatting position, the cape was around your feet and you'd step on it or something."

Janice Williams said, "The cape gave Guy problems because it kept getting in the way when he had to draw his sword. Then he found a way to solve the problem by grabbing the side of it and throwing it over his arm just before he fenced. When he was on public appearances, such as Disneyland, he usually took it off to fence."

In Episode #6, "Zorro Saves a Friend," Guy and Britt had a scene in which they fence each other on ten feet high scaffolds around the church. The director wanted the stuntmen to do it. Britt recalls, "They were preparing part of a building and we fenced on the scaffolding. Originally we were going to be doubled up there, because it was dangerous. I looked at Guy and said, "What the hell is so tough about *that*!' Guy says, 'Awww, come on Britt. Lets do it!' Both of us climbed up there. They rolled the cameras, and we did the fencing scene. Then Buddy came up for the jump onto the horse below."

This was an extremely high jump Buddy had to make onto a trotting horse, who comes at Zorro's whistle. "I had to jump onto a moving horse while standing on a narrow board on the scaffolding," recalls Buddy. "We were throwing bricks at the soldiers before that scene. They were Styrofoam with a rock in them to give it a little bit of weight. We had to do that jump several times. The horse we used was trained by Corky Randall at Liberty Stables. It was a sorrel, so, to make it look like Zorro's horse, he was painted black for the scene with a non-allergenic water-based paint that easily washed off. That shot was so *high*. Corky was down below to call the horse to him, and as the horse trotted to Corky I was to make the jump onto his back and ride out of there.[114] The first time that I jumped, I hit the horse right on the rear. I got a hold of the horn, but it bucked me off. Scared him so bad that on the next try, when I jumped, I was in the air and the horse was *gone*. He wasn't anywhere near there! It was tough timing it, because I was way up on a little pole. I couldn't run along the pole. I had to stand on a peg and I look at him, and just go. We finally just stopped the horse right on the mark, and I jumped and got him. Then I jump over a cart and leave town." The two takes were spliced, so you see Buddy making a perfect landing on the horse.

The jump to horse looked painful, but Buddy assures that he was never injured, even without protective padding. "No," he dead-panned, "but, I used to talk with a high voice sometimes."

"Usually I'd get one shot at a horse and if the scene didn't work, they'd bring in another one, because after the first try the horse would be expecting it. They'd get another black horse and put it in there."

When asked how he rides so gracefully, Buddy said, "I just *aim* him, *point* him, and *ride* him!"

"The studio bought the main horse,"[115] said Buddy. "He was a reining horse. He was very sensitive. Very quick. Guy would ride him in for close-ups and do dialogue. You had to be very quiet on him, 'cause any little movement and he wanted to work."

Buddy is in every episode, as a lancer, a hidalgo at a party, as background in the tavern, driving horse-drawn wagons, doubling villains, doubling Zorro and Don Diego in fight scenes. "Sometimes I'd even ride in and give the line," said Buddy. An example of this is in a stagecoach chase in Episode 14, "Shadow of a Doubt." Buddy—as Zorro—rides along side the coach and yells: "Pull up your horses!" The audience hears Guy's voice, later looped in. Another time was in Episode #16, "Slaves of the Eagle," when Buddy, on Tornado, yells out, "You pay a small price for twenty good men. Zorro is worth twice as much—Dead or Alive!," but it is Guy we hear. Scenes like this saved hours of production time.

When Buddy Van Horn had to rear a horse at nearly ninety degrees to the ground, he had to be sure he would stay in the saddle. "I used to pour water on the leather to grip. You couldn't use Coca-Cola because it would get sticky and draw flies. That saddle had a cover that went over it, too. When it dried out, I'd wet it some more."

Lindsey Boggess, who leased his land in Chatsworth to Disney for *Zorro* location sites, remembered watching them filming one day. "They had the horse up on top of the hill with Zorro on him. It reared up, over and over, many times. Then they would take the saddle off, put it on another horse, and do it again, until they got what they wanted. They had *three* horses they were using that day."

Buddy had a variety of commands he used to make a horse rear. "I had some mouth cues, and some you touch on the side of the neck. I didn't like that one though, because you had to use the other hand. Most rear when you lift the reins up."

"I don't recall us ever hurting a horse, but one of the best horses I ever had as far as doing chases and transfers on, was sent on another picture when we had a hiatus. The man was trotting off the side of a hill and the horse cut his fetlock. Injured him. And we never used him again." Regret still felt, he said, "With all the tough stuff I had done with him, this had never happened."

In episode #8, "Zorro Rides into Terror," Zorro (Buddy) is being chased by Monastario and his men. He gets away by jumping his horse over an extremely wide crevice, then turns, rears up, waves to the soldiers, and rides away. Buddy remembers how he rigged that jump. "I jumped an expanse—two rows of boards expanded—set up on top of orange crates. Then they put in the matte painting of the canyon by Peter Ellenshaw." In the final cut, the TV audience sees Tornado leaping like a winged Pegasus over a bottomless canyon dutifully carrying Zorro to safety.

A stuntman had a big responsibility, and very little time to do it. "There was no school for this. They just say, 'Do this!' and I figure how I'm going to do it," said Buddy. For the scene where he swings on the chandelier to an overhead balcony, he said, "We had it rigged up above, with pulleys. There were guys on four corners with ropes and they would pull me. That's the way all that stuff was done. They could lower me and raise me."

When Zorro ran across those tiled rooftops, it was Buddy in the long shots. "Sometimes those roof tiles were slippery," said Buddy. "I had my feet slip out from under me once, so after that I always wore my stunt shoes. I had to figure a way to wear my stunt shoes and look like I had boots on. I made a boot topping and put a stunt shoe underneath my boot top so that I could do some of the action I did. I wore black stunt shoes that had a good grip on the bottom. The boot top I made fit over it and folded down so it looked like I was wearing boots. A lot of the stunts I did, like those high jumps down to the ground and stuff like that, made wearing boots with a big heel too easy to injure myself."

Some people who worked with Guy in the early episodes described him as awkward. Buddy gave his opinion as to why they might think that. "Guy had problems with his feet. He had high arches and problems with his toes. Certain pieces of action were awkward for him at first because I think it had something to do with the boots he was

Britt and Guy did their own stunt on this scaffolding for Episode # 6, "Zorro Saves A Friend" (author's personal collection)

Buddy Van Horn makes his leap to horse from the scaffolding, but the horse moved too soon from fright.

wearing. The wardrobe people gave him a proper fit, then all of a sudden it came together and he became very good."

When Monastario left, the variety of new villains did not know how to fence. Freddie's son, Al Cavens, began to double most of the villains. When Al accidentally was injured, they realized they needed more fencers for backup.

During "Slaves of Eagle"[116] episode, blood was spilled during Zorro's duel—not Guy's but that of his opponent and fencing instructor, Al Cavens.

As Guy disarmed Al, playing the role of a villainous soldier, the sword hit the floor handle first, and bounced up to inflict a 2-inch gash on Cavens' cheek. The accident was the first such unlucky break and one which the company claim as a freak likely to happen only once in a long while. Cavens was on the job the next day.[117]

By the end of the first season, Buddy was not only a horseman but a good fencer. "I was doing all the stunts on horseback and after a while Fred Cavens came to me and asked me if I'd like to learn how to fence. Guy did his fencing, but as the show went along they had trouble, because a lot of the heavies they would cast didn't know how to fence and you just don't learn fencing overnight. It was hard doubling them all the time. So what they tried to do toward the last of those shows was hire a heavy somewhat similar to my size and I would double him and fence with Guy."

In the second season, Buddy[118] doubled many of the guest stars. Movie star, Cesar Romero played Diego's Uncle Esteban in episodes 55-58. Buddy remembers the extra long make-up calls. "I doubled Cesar and I had to have gray put in my hair, then have my hair waved, and sit under a hair dryer!" he laughed. "I had doubled for Romero before this at MGM." Buddy also doubled Tony Russo in "Affair of Honor" (episode #70), Richard Anderson in "Zorro Fights a Duel" (episode #51), George Neise in "Long Live the Governor" (#75), and many more, including Gilbert Roland in "El Cuchillo" and "Adios, El Cuchillo."

"Boy, was he a *character*," Van Horn laughed remembering Roland. "I remember this ladder fell on my head, and had me on the ground. He came over to me and said, 'Buddy, you O.K.?' I said, 'Yeah.' Then he leaned over and whispered, 'I have some tequila and lemon in my bag. Ya want some?'"

Chapter 19

"I was losing vision in my right eye"
                                    – Tony Russo a.k.a. Tony Russel

Tony Russo's talent as an actor and experience as a fencer at the Pasadena Playhouse had been remembered by the director. He was called back for two consecutive episodes in the first season, then as another character in the second season, episode 70, "An Affair of Honor." He brought excitement and humor to the screen when he played a Zorro imposter in episodes 11 & 12. In episode #11, "Double Trouble for Zorro," Monastario arrests Martinez (Tony), and then, bribes him to turn the people against Zorro in exchange for his freedom. He agrees to dress as Zorro and rob the good people in the tavern during a dinner party where most of the dons have gathered. The imposter pushes a sack toward the innkeeper, and commands him at gunpoint to collect money and jewels from everyone. When the innkeeper moves toward the guitarists, Martinez gives one of the funniest lines on the show: *"Not the musicians*! They never have any money!" According to Guy, it was an ad-lib.

In episode #12, "The Luckiest Swordsman Alive," a continuum to Episode 11, Monastario tells Martinez of one more scheme to win his freedom. He has to put the townspeople up in arms against Zorro, and to do this he must be seen dressed as Zorro stealing the crown of jewels from the head of the Virgin statue in the church. Martinez retorts to the hardcore Monastario: "I have done many things in my life, but I have never robbed the *church*." The callous Monastario comes back with: "Nor have you ever been hanged from the neck until dead! Which do you prefer?!"

The fencing bout between Guy Williams and Britt Lomond at the end of episode 11 is, according to Fred Cavens, "one of the best fencing duels on film." Cavens is quoted in one of 7-Up's *Zorro* Newsletters as saying, "It is the finest fencing on television."

A couple of days into rehearsal, Tony was wondering when they would get to the scene where he steals the crown off the statue. "I asked the A.D., 'When are we going to do the scene in the church,'" said Tony, "and someone on the crew said, 'Oh, we did that six weeks ago down at San Luis Rey. Van Horn did it.'

"I thought, 'Well, OK, that's just less I have to do.' Then an old-timer in the business who overheard the conversation came up to me and said, 'They can't do that.'

Gilbert Roland starred in two one hour *Zorro* shows.
(The Kathy Gregory Personal Collection; courtesy of Kathy Gregory)

I looked at him curiously, and asked, 'What do you mean?' And this oldtimer said, 'There is a clause in SAG[119] called 'Right of Role' which says no one can play your role but yourself, unless it's a stunt.' If there was no stunt involved, which there wasn't, then according to my contract, I have to be paid to play that role.

"Well, I reminded Disney of this, and he said I was right, and he had to pay me for the work Van Horn did. And I was paid retroactively from the time Van Horn did my scene until the day I started. I had a weekly contract for two weeks, with a salary of $350 a week, a lot of money in 1957. But Disney had to pay me for the time lapsed. Later, when *The Sign of Zorro* showed in theaters across the country, I was paid again for my role *plus* that six weeks in residuals. I made more money on that scene I *didn't* do, than I did on the ones I actually did shoot!"

A close-up of Tony was filmed at the studio and inserted into the scene Van Horn played, giving the impression it was Tony who goes into the church and steals the crown.

Tony worked with Buddy Van Horn and has great admiration for him. "Van Horn is a wonderful, lovable man; a talented, *great* guy," he said. When "The Luckiest Swordsman Alive" was being shot among the hills and rocks of Bell Ranch in Chatsworth, California, the cast and crew were there early in the morning with trailers for costumes, grips, makeup, actors, wranglers, and horses. Van Horn and the 2nd unit were always on hand, because work on location usually called for stunts.

A particular scene out there, however, called for Guy and Tony to fence on the top of a flat rock with about an eleven-foot area to work in. It was at the end of this scene that Tony and Guy experienced the risks of fencing for film when they had a serious accident. "It was getting late," said Tony, "which meant we were losing light, so Norman [the director] was worried about finishing the scene. The budget was about $78,000 per half-hour show, which was *twice* as much as any other half-hour black-and-white action TV show at that time, so we had to hurry along, learn the dialogue, and learn the fencing quickly. And it's hard enough to remember dialogue *and* a fencing routine at the same time, but we had to do that on boulders on a mountain, looking to see where we were stepping and so forth. To add to the problem, the scene had not been choreographed. Fred Cavens was not there, but Norman wanted us to fence. I said to the director, 'Well, what are we going to do up here on the side of this mountain if you don't choreograph it?' Norman gave a vague reply, 'Just go out there and do this and this,'" said Tony, suggesting that Guy just slash away while Tony gets out of the way. "Guy and I decided to simply parry high, parry low, parry high, until Guy disarms me. Guy's sword went *pa-ting*! And I felt a blow to my nose. I thought he broke my nose, because that was where I felt the pain. The little button tip on the end of the foil—which is there so you *can't* get hurt!—is what hit the pupil of my eye. It lifted the lens and paralyzed the muscle underneath the lens, which causes the pupil to contract. I immediately touched my nose, to feel what had happened. Norman was not

Tony Russo and Guy fencing on top of a large rock at Bell Ranch in Chatsworth, CA. Guy's sword touched Tony's left eye at the end of the scene and Tony nearly lost his sight permanently. (Mary Spooner Collection, courtesy of Mary Spooner)

careful about the safety of his actors. He didn't seem to care. When my eye was hit, he yelled out, 'Christ! What the hell happened now?!,' irritated because he was losing time.

"I opened my eyes and I was losing vision in my right eye because it was hemorrhaging. Guy looked at me and he must have seen the blood coming into it, because he shouted, 'Rush him to the hospital!' They put me in a car immediately and took me to St. Joseph's hospital where a wonderful doctor, a Dr. Fields, knew immediately how to treat me. They had to bandage both eyes, because your eyes are 'sympathetic.' If you move one, the other moves and any movement could cause a second hemorrhage, which could do extensive damage. So I had to be very careful not to move a fraction of an inch. With my eyes bandaged, I laid so still for five days, the nurses thought I was dead! I don't even know if anyone came to see me or called. I just laid there traumatized because I was preparing myself mentally, in case I was blind."

When the bandages came off, Tony could barely see. Then after four days he began to see his hand in front of his face, like a shadow. Soon his sight came back completely. "The doctor said it was a miracle I could still see. One-millionth of an inch more, and that would have been the end of the eye."

Tony didn't like working for Norman Foster. "Foster should have been more concerned for our safety. When you're not wearing a face guard, it's *dangerous*!"

Buddy Van Horn was nearby when it happened, but had little recollection of the actual event. He suspected that Norman Foster felt confident in that he had a couple of good fencers who could work something out for themselves.

Janice remembered how deeply Guy was affected by this. "Guy was *very* upset about the accident," she said. "He never forgot it. He regretted it happening and it worried him then and for years to come. He used to wonder many times over the years if Tony's vision was still OK."

"The strange thing is," said Tony, almost forty years after the accident, "that my right eye, which is the injured eye, became my healthy eye. I've had a cataract and a lens implant on my left eye, which was not injured." The dilating muscle in Tony's injured eye, however, did remain partially paralyzed. It hardly dilates when he goes from bright light to darkness, so the pupil is always larger than the one in his left eye.

A trophy winning golfer in his retirement, Tony was on the golf course one day when a young woman, who was talking to him, curiously said, "Did you know one of your eyes is bigger than the other?" Memories flashed at blade-swift speed, and Tony just smiled and said, "Yes, I know. I know."[120]

Chapter 20

"The first thirteen..."

– Bill Anderson, producer

The first thirteen episodes of *Zorro* made the series a success. They laid the foundation for the story and characters and are so outstanding they are given the title by *Zorro* aficionados of "The First Thirteen," as an entity that separates them from the rest of the series. They remain the favorites of many fans of the show, as well as those who worked on the show, because they best define who Zorro is and what he stands for. Producer Bill Anderson agreed. "Oh, surely! No question about it. Out of all the episodes, the first thirteen had the best pace, the best writing, and established the characters. It was good slam-bang action and adventure, and the casting was good and it worked!"

In an interview in 1958, Guy, who studied acting with Sandy Meisner, was asked about his use of "the method." He replied with a smile, "Mostly, undisciplined actors are called method actors. In TV, you have to do it quickly, there's no time!" Guy said if he had had more time (as in legitimate theatre), he would do it differently.[121]

"Guy was a quick study," said producer Bill Anderson. "He did the scene and he didn't have any trouble working with the camera. He knew where it was all the time. Guy was wonderful to work with, very cooperative with the cast and the rest of the players. He was very controlled. Always a gentleman and polite.

"He never tried to rewrite the scripts or anything like that. If it bothered him, why, he would talk to the director about it and say what bothered him and they would just find a way to say the same thing in a different way.

"He played it with tongue-in-cheek, but he didn't play down to his audience. He played straight out to them. Certain people in those kinds of parts feel they have to let everybody know they know more than what's going on, you know. But he didn't.

"Guy was perfect for the part, with his background. He was a very warm fellow, and he could play that kind of character. He was plenty sophisticated, but he didn't come off that way. The small fry audience was fabulously struck with him and liked him. He was a very happy guy."

According to Bill Anderson, Walt loved working with Guy and Britt, Henry and Gene, but he was afraid repetition would breed boredom. He wanted to change the villains to keep the show fresh, a pattern he continued periodically. Walt himself explained to Britt why he would be written out of the script and let go. "I had a lot of respect for him for telling me himself," said Britt. "Walt said he planned to bring me back in another season as the Governor of California, but by then, they had a big falling out with ABC."

There was never any doubt that Britt was brilliant and unmatched in his role as Capitan Monastario. Walt just knew when to not overdo a good thing.

"They took away the nemesis," said Diane Lomond. "Once the nemesis left, the show went down." The show remained popular without Britt, but it was never as rich in content or in character relationships as when Britt was on it.

A call sheet from Britt's memorabilia shows the filming date of his last episode as Tuesday, September 24, 1957, about two and a half weeks before *Zorro* first hit the air waves. Britt, however, was still under a three-year contract with Disney and was working on various other Disney TV shows. His popularity among *Zorro* fans as the villain-you-love-to-hate was obvious by his fan mail, so Disney sent Britt on personal appearances with Guy for two years, satisfying fans who loved seeing the duo battle it out in their famous sword fights.

Chapter 21

"Be careful or I'll have you holding horse."

— Bob Wehling, writer

There were several directors and many different writers who worked on the *Zorro* series. There were only two who had a hand in writing all seventy-eight of the scripts that made up the series, plus the four one-hour specials after the series ended: Robert Wehling and Lowell Hawley.

Hollywood Reporter, Tuesday, March 19, 1957
Robert Wehling has been signed to Walt Disney Studios to script the *Mark of Zorro* TV series.

Norman Foster hand-picked Robert (Bob) Wehling for the *Zorro* series. Some of the fan's favorite episodes were written by Wehling. "The Practical Joker" with Richard Anderson is one. Bob Wehling penned this memorable episode with wit, dignity, and lyrical dialogue. He had that enviable ability to choose words with a beat and rhythmic sounds, pleasant to the ear and easy on the tongue. He could spice up the dialogue with sarcastic humor. Another favorite, "Amnesty for Zorro," with Jolene Brand, was penned by Wehling with some of the series most poignant moments. Good writers for *Zorro* are one of the primary reasons *Zorro* has withstood the test of time, and Bob Wehling was a primary writer for the run of the show.

Born in 1919, in Sioux Falls, South Dakota, Bob Wehling was an aspiring actor at the University of South Dakota. He preformed in plays at the Black Hills Playhouse, then later served with the Signal Corps Counter-Intelligence during World War II. After the war he went to Hollywood, and from 1951-1958 Bob was director of the Hollywood School of Drama. His talent as a writer prevailed over acting, however, and he made a career of it in movies and for Disney.

Lowell Hawley, the other primary talent for the show, also penned some memorable lines in *Zorro*. One in particular, recited by George Neise playing Capitan Briana, in episode #73, "The Captain Regrets,"[122] curiously sounds like a speech yet to be made by President John F. Kennedy in 1960! Written in 1959, the Capitan's line is in reference to the people's allegiance to Spain. He addresses his country: "Is this the time for us to be asking, 'What have you done for *us?* We should be asking, 'What can we do for *you?!*" *(applause, applause, from the townspeople)*.

A few months after this aired on May 28, 1959, John F. Kennedy said to America, "Ask not what your country can do for you. Ask what you can do for your country!"

After the first thirteen episodes Walt felt *Zorro* was off to a good start and turned production over to William (Bill) Anderson. After that, Anderson couldn't get Walt interested in reading the scripts for approval. He was too preoccupied with adding attractions to Disneyland, but Bill Anderson would have welcomed some advice or comments from his boss. "It was very difficult after we had done those first thirteen. Zorro was such a stylized character. It was *very* difficult to get a story that was different," said Bill. Lowell Hawley & Bob Stevenson[123] came up with the California takeover plot of "The Eagle" from their research of California history. They told Walt about it visually by acting it out. He liked it. Walt thought up the feather used in the episodes and the shadow on the wall made with Zorro's hands and the feather forming a *Z*.

Bill Anderson soon practiced more and more authority, reading the scripts and making decisions, so that by the time the 20th episode, "Agent of the Eagle," aired February 20, 1958, he was a full producer with his name in the credits. Other talented writers besides Norman Foster, Wehling, and Hawley, were John Meredyth Lucas, Lewis R. Foster (not related to Norman Foster), N. B. Stone, Jr., Robert Bloomfield, Anthony Ellis, Jackson Gillis, Maury Hill, and Robert J. Shaw. Their rare writing talents, along with Walt's demand for authenticity and attention to historical detail, and the right casting of good actors, stuntmen, and crew working together, made *Zorro* a lasting television classic.

Storylines were based on actual early California history such as the attempt to take over California by foreign countries, and real names from aristocratic Spanish families such as Verdugo, Cabrillo, Avila, Gregorio, were used. This blend of fact and fantasy added richness to the content, and gave a fictional character believability.

Anna Chiodo Wehling, wife of writer Bob Wehling, remembers those golden years when *Zorro* was riding high. "I met Bob when he used to play chess with my brother, Fred," said Anna. "He was working for Disney writing *Zorro* at the time. When we started dating, Bob invited me to the *Zorro* set to show me around, and that's when I met Guy for the first time. Bob introduced me to Guy, and said, 'Well, here's another Italian!' I really didn't know that Guy was Italian, and Guy's reaction was so funny. The first thing he asked me was, '*Oh!* Did your mother cook spaghetti with oil and garlic!?' I said, 'Yes! As a matter of fact, my mother and my grandmother cooked that all the time. I *love* it.' He told me that was his favorite dish. So that gave us something in common right away. He was *so* nice. He and Bob got along real well. Guy was perfect for the role of Zorro. He just looked like you would imagine Zorro to look!

"Bob enjoyed working on the show. He didn't talk much of Walt. He didn't know him intimately, but he never said he feared Walt. Bob talked about Bill Anderson more than any person, because he was Bob's supervisor on the show. They worked together on rewrites and so forth. The directors he worked with were Charles Barton, Hollingsworth Morse, whom Bob talked about frequently, and Lewis Foster, who Bob wrote a script with. Writer Lowell Hawley was Bob's dearest friend. I had lunch in the executive dining room one time with Bob and Lowell Hawley, but never Walt. Bob and Lowell were such good friends we named our son after him—Fred Lowell Wehling, who was born in 1963. Fred is a professor of Political Science and International Languages, but he inherited his father's and his namesake's talent, and is a published writer. Bob and Lowell continued to keep in touch many years after they left Disney.

Guy with Disney executive looking at a display case full of Zorro merchandise being sold.
(The Kathy Gregory Personal Collection; courtesy of Kathy Gregory)

"Gene [Sheldon] was Bob's best friend. We went to their house almost every weekend. Bob and Gene would swim and Peggy and I would sit around the pool. The three of them would sip Martini's—their 'marts,' they called them. Gene knew I hated martini's, so one day he said to me, 'I have something you would like,' and he gave me some Harvey's Bristol Creme. To this day, I love it and I think of him every time I drink it. He was such a dear man—so kind and so talented, and he had a *lovely* voice.

"My husband and Gene used to have this funny joke going between them. If Gene teased or played a trick on Bob, something like that, Bob would say, 'You'd better be careful, or I'll have you holding horse.' And Gene would laugh."

Bob Wehling left Disney because he refused to cross the picket line during the writers' strike in 1962. He became an Associate Professor of Drama at California Lutheran College in Thousand Oaks, California. In 1965 he moved to Carson City, Nevada and taught drama at Tahoe-Paradise College at Lake Tahoe. Before he passed away in 1983, the Disney Channel began showing *Zorro* that same year. "People began calling us to tell us they saw Bob's name in the credits," said Anna, "and he really enjoyed that. We didn't get the Disney Channel, but Bob was happy to know about the show's comeback. He was proud of the *Zorro* scripts he wrote. For his birthday one year, I surprised him with all his scripts bound in leather books. They will be handed down to our son."

Among Anna's keepsakes of that special time is a framed photo of the entire cast and crew taken on the set of *Zorro* in the tavern. "It's a long shot," she said, "but you can tell who everyone is. There's Charles Barton, Buddy, Walt's son-in-law Ron Miller, Henry, George Lewis, Guy, and many others. Another picture of Guy inscribed to Bob, says, *To Bob, Whose words never fail me, Best Wishes, Guy, Z."*

Chapter 22

"I'm gonna see if you score it."

– Guy Williams

The music for *Zorro* was scored by the talented William "Bill" Lava, a seasoned veteran of numerous Republic Pictures, years before *Zorro*. Lava scored a theme or motif for each principal character in the show—Diego, Bernardo, Sgt. Garcia—played whenever one entered a scene. Even Tornado had one, a noble brassy tune, when he appeared.

Reminiscing on the fun he had doing the show, Guy talked about Lava's remarkable talent in an interview. "We had Bill Lava doing the music cues. Bill was terrific with the music! One of the things we liked about that show is all of the private stuff that had nothing to do with audiences. We never talked about this. We just—among ourselves—did things like move a certain way just to see if Bill would score it."

Bill Lava could catch the slightest move and could put music or sound to it to emphasize the move or convey humor. Lava's attention to detail so amazed Guy that he decided to have some fun testing him one day. "I told Bill once, 'Bill, I'm gonna *drop* you one. I'm not gonna tell you what it is, I'm just gonna *drop* you one, and I'm gonna see if you score it.' Bill said 'OK. I don't care. I'll score it.'

"So I had a scene where I had to leave the living room, one of those Diego scenes, and as I walked across the room to get to the door I had to pass this long refectory table there and it just occurred to me to take my two fingers and walk myself with them. I just ran the fingers down, just a casual—if you look at it you'd never see it. Well, I waited and waited until the show came on the air and as soon as that scene came up and I'm looking at it and Bill Lava did a whole series of pizzicato violins as I moved my hand down there. I called him I say, '*Bill!*' He says, 'You *saw* it didn't you?' I said, 'You son-of-a-gun! You *really* did it, didn't you!' He put about four strings pizzicato-style, while I'm moving my hand through a table. Nobody's gonna notice that except the guy that's doing it. Over all, it sounded fine. We used to *live* on things like that. So the series was really a lot of fun to do."[124]

Chapter 23

"…preview of Zorro*"*

– On the Air

With twelve episodes in the can, Disney began giving preview screenings of *Zorro* to the press in September 1957. Disney had signed with the ABC network in March 1954, an enterprise to financially help him build his theme park. In the following October, his new show *The Disneyland Story* aired. The huge success of his Davy Crockett shows, written by Norman Foster for his first season on television, skyrocketed Walt Disney and Fess Parker into television history. By the fall of 1957 Disney was so pleased to be renewed for a *fourth* season he produced a special called "The Disney Fourth Anniversary Show" for *Walt Disney Presents*. It aired September 15, 1957[125] and introduced Disney's fall lineup featuring *The Saga of Andy Burnett* and a new mysterious character called El Zorro.

> *Daily Variety,* Friday, September 13, 1957
> Telepix Review—"Disneyland (Fantasyland) Fourth Anniversary Show."
> Cast: The Mouseketeers, Fess Parker, Jerome Courtland, Guy Williams, Walt Disney.
> …there was also a trailer on Disney's new series, *Zorro*, to insure that nothing at the Burbank plant was overlooked…Fess Parker, Guy Williams (who plays the title role in *Zorro*). Teenagers Annette Funicello and Darlene Gillespie of the Mouseketeers, all took part in the trailer.

On the *Fourth Anniversary Show,* Walt Disney is sitting in a chair with the Mouseketeers around him. After touting *The Saga of Andy Burnett*, Moochie keeps asking Walt, "What about *Zorro?*"

Walt tells Moochie and the Mouseketeers, "Zorro is a different type of character of old California. He is a myth." Suddenly, Zorro appears, dressed in black—his face covered with a mask. The kids are enthralled while Zorro speaks to them and the viewers about his mysterious character:

"Some would smile and say 'Zorro! *Pouf!*—He's a ghost—a dream—a

Guy as Zorro on horse in Disneyland Parade waving to crowd.
(Mary Spooner Collection, courtesy of Mary Spooner)

myth—a something of the imagination.'"

(Just then, the kids see a menacing shadow behind him and scream: "Look out!" *Zorro fights and disarms the opponent, then confidently laughs his devious laugh.)*

"Ha-ha-ha-ha-ha-ha-haaaaaaaa!

"So you see, my friend. It is entirely a matter of opinion. This is a personal thing between *you*—and *me*. Whether I am real or not is for *you* to decide. Each of you. In your own mind and heart. Meantime—til we meet again!"

The Zorro act on top of the Horseshow Saloon in Frontierland shows Zorro (Buddy Van Horn) leaping off the roof while stuntmen dressed as soldiers try to catch him. The crowd at Disneyland was spellbound. (courtesy of Gerry Dooley)

He makes the sign of the *Z* to the camera with a loud "HAH! HAH! HAH!" as he cuts the three slashes. The smoky *Z* remains onscreen until it dissipates. Zorro slips away into the shadows.

The boys on the set begin imitating him, saying "Hah! Hah! Hah!," slashing Z's in the air everywhere as they feign sword play. Before *Zorro* aired that fall, Walt decided to change the "HAH! HAH! HAH!" sound made by Guy, to the "swish-swish-swish" sound made by special effects. On the show, Bernardo was always making the swish-swish-swish sound when referring to Zorro. It remains on the lips of fans around the world today.

The trade papers heralded in the new show and announced the hoopla:

Hollywood Reporter, Friday, September 13, 1957
"TV Review" Disneyland, Sept 11.
"We saw good action clips from Disney's new series *Zorro*, with Guy Williams in the title role."

Hollywood Reporter, Friday, September 27, 1957
A screening *Zorro* Preview Party

Walt Disney is giving a cocktail party and entertainment in the studio the-atre next Wednesday starting at 6:30 p.m. to mark the Oct. 10 debut of his new TV series *Zorro*. A screening of the program will be held.

Hollywood Reporter, Tuesday, October 1, 1957
"TV-Radio Briefs"
...members of the press attending Walt Disney's party and screening of his new TV series *Zorro* at 6 p.m. Thursday will have a chance to see Disney's new $500,000 Mexican village set on the back lot if they arrive no later than 5:30 p.m.

October 3, 1957
"On the Air"
Disney is partying tonight for a preview of *Zorro*.

Chapter 24

"...out of the night..."

– Bruns and Foster

On October 10, 1957, *Zorro* hit the airwaves and Guy Williams became Zorro forever to kids across America. They were hooked every Thursday evening and sometimes the little tykes were willing to put up a fight to get to see their favorite show. It wasn't long before newspapers and TV guides were putting a Z in ThurZday and calling it Z-night. Parents began watching it too. At eight o'clock, a thunder bolt flashed onto the TV screen, across a dark moonlit sky, and took the shape of a large Z. A quartet, The Mellomen, sang the rousing theme song that became etched in the minds of millions of young fans forever:

> Out of the night
> When the full moon is bright
> Comes a horseman known as Zorro.
> This bold renegade carves a Z with his blade
> A Z that stands for Zorro.
>
> Zorro, the fox so cunning and free.
> Zorro, who makes the sign of the Z.
> Zorro, Zorro, Zorrooooooooo

These memorable lyrics were penned by Norman Foster. The music was written by George Bruns. Over a million copies were sold within two years. The Chordettes' version of the theme song reached number one on the popular *Hit Parade* show, topping out Henry Calvin's recording of the theme song. Not sung in the TV version, but sung on the recordings, was the second verse:

> He is polite
> But the wicked take flight
> When they catch the sight of Zorro.
> He's friend of the weak

And the poor and the meek
This very unique Señor Zorro

Daily Variety, Monday, October 14, 1957
"Presenting Señor Zorro"
　　　Williams is excellent in the dual role of Diego and Zorro. He displays a flair for the flamboyance called for in this 19th century version of Robin Hood.

In only two weeks *Zorro* rose to number three in the top twenty new shows.[126] Thirty-five-million Americans now owned that great invention called television and about one third of them were watching *Zorro* on ThurZday nights. El Zorro (the fox) rode to defend his people of Spanish Colonial California against tyranny of a corrupt government. He dressed in black with a cape and mask, rode a black horse in the night and skillfully used his sword, his whip, or his musket to punish the unjust. Hero to the meek, protector of the poor, every kid wanted to be him.
　　　He could be cocky: "I am known by many names, but *you*—can call me *Zorro*."
　　　He could be threatening: "Let me *never* again hear of you putting a man to do a mule's work, or it will be the last order you *ever* give."
　　　Or caring: "Here is your *four months* pay!"
　　　Or loving: "I will never be far away from you."
　　　He was funny, laughing while he carves a large *Z* in the seat of Sgt. Garcia's pants. He was ever courteous, as he graciously bowed or saluted friend and foe alike, before he disappeared into the night.

Guy during a personal appearance at Disneyland's Magnolia park in Frontierland, interacting with children as they are selected to swordfight with Zorro. John Ormond, at the mike.
(author's personal collection)

When Guy Williams hit the small screen in 1957, he gave the world an unforgettable Zorro. For him, and those who knew him, Guy had grown into the role, as though it had been waiting for him. He was tailor-made for it. No other actor has reached so many people around the globe and remained in their hearts as "the ONLY Zorro."

When it aired October 10, 1957, the critics gave favorable reviews.

Hollywood Reporter, Monday, October 14, 1957
"Zorro"—ABC-TV October 10, 8:00—8:30 p.m.
...The setting is in early Spanish California and Guy Williams plays the foppish Don Diego by day and the dashing, bemasked Zorro, liberator of the oppressed by night...Producers at Walt Disney have given this series important mounting with sumptuous settings and scripting that nicely mixes humor with the dashing swordplay.

Under the scrutiny of the press, because this was his first leading role, Guy fared well: "Guy Williams shows good thesping, as well as athletic ability in his key role and should have no trouble catching on fast."[127]

Another writer saw the humorous and fun side of the first episode:

New York Times, Friday, October 11, 1957
"TV: New Disney Series"
"*Zorro,* Presented on Channel 7, Will Appeal to Juveniles, Young and Old"
by Richard F. Shepard
Zorro, the new Walt Disney film series on Channel 7, started life last night as a chip off the old Hollywood block of the same name.
Youngsters and adults who crave dashing heroes, leering villains, the usual comic sidekicks and lots of flashy sword play will enjoy this polished production about life in Spanish-ruled California. Others will merely recall sentimentally that they saw it all on bygone Saturday afternoons at the local movie house.
Guy Williams played Douglas Fairbanks, Gene Sheldon played Harpo Marx, Henry Calvin played Oliver Hardy and Britt Lomond was very good as Carl Reiner in a Sid Caesar takeoff on the same theme. William Lava's musical arrangements were pleasantly rhythmic, and at moments, amusingly tongue in cheek.
The show has the virtue of being honestly juvenile and does well at it; some of the adult Westerns with suspiciously squeaky voices should take note.

One article in a 7-Up Newsletter reported that: "Veteran fencing master Fred Cavens calls Guy Williams 'the fastest study I have ever worked with.'"

Of that time, Guy said to Mike Clark in 1986, "No one was doing any better fencing anywhere than we were doing, so I was happy with that."

After only three months *Zorro* was sweeping the ratings. The *Hollywood Reporter,* January 3, 1958, stated that *Zorro* "has topped Groucho Marx in the share-of-audience ratings for the first time this season. For the week ending November 30, the Guy Williams series scored a 46.8."

Guy signing autographs for children in Frontierland after a live performance on stage.
(The Kathy Gregory Personal Collection; courtesy of Kathy Gregory)

Although it was billed at first as a kids' show, with particular appeal to young boys, it soon became obvious that teenage girls and their mothers made up a large percentage of the television audience. The writers were not practiced in writing for children. They had been writing adult movies, consequently, the show appealed to "children" of all ages, as it still does. Looking back on the success of the show, in terms of its longevity, Guy said, "The success of *that* one is funny. Well, I don't think it was as successful as *Gunsmoke*, which was an hour show which was—someone thought of the word 'Adult' and stuck it in front of *Western*, and you got the 'Adult Western.' If you say that word today you'd have to smile, but *Zorro* was a half-hour show and had all the panache of Disney."

Moms across American bought black fabric to make little capes for their little Zorros. Plastic swords were sold with white chalk tips to fashion washable Zs on almost anything. Still, there were Zs carved into furniture, etched into walls, scratched into school desks, sidewalks, and drawn everywhere! Kids were risking life and limb jumping from balconies imitating their hero.

David Lidia, of Hawaii, is just one example of millions of kids who wanted to be Zorro when they watched him on TV. David remembers with sweet nostalgia his passion for Zorro when he was a young boy growing up in Dallas, Texas:

> I regret I have lost my Zorro lunch box...I remember taking it to school, and I was really 'cool' in the cafeteria when I opened it and took out the food mom had prepared for me. Mom and Dad also bought me a mask and she made me a cape out of some black material. Dad took a piece of heavy piano wire and made me an excellent sword with a wooden guard and at the sharp end, he glued on a piece of cork. That, of course, lasted

about 15 minutes, and I had "Zs" all over the dog house and the back fence.

I had my own horse. It was a tall bay with a gentle nature. I would toss a blanket onto her back, climb on with my Zorro outfit, and for a few hours I would careen through about five acres fighting imaginary villains. There was a broken, low wooden fence I would jump when the imaginary Sergeant Garcia was after me. One day while I was being chased by Sgt. Garcia, and he was in a particularly bad mood, I spurred my horse to a fast gallop. My hat flew from my head and rested on my back with the string around my neck. My horse flew like the wind, and my cape billowed out from behind me. I attacked the mesquite bushes as they flew by with my sword while yelling, "I am El Zorro...the fox!"

As I was bent over the neck of my horse striking at the brush, I didn't notice we were quickly approaching the barbed wire fence which marked the end of the pasturage. At the last possible moment my bay realized she couldn't jump the high fence and made an abrupt left turn. I was thrown across the fence and landed on some rocks, breaking my right arm at the wrist.

Although that ended my career as Zorro, I still thought of him affectionately through the remainder of that summer and throughout the rest of my life.

I now live in Honolulu where I own a computer consultancy. My two sons are in their 20's and have begun their lives. Still I find myself occasionally watching "The Fox" when he comes on the Disney Channel at midnight. [*July 1998*]

Guy was not prepared for the throngs of children that would quickly surround him.

Just after the series started on the air kids began to come up to me and ask where my horse was. The first couple of times, I answered, 'At the studio,' and they'd look at me with a blank expression. Then I wised up. Now I say, 'In the cave. Bernardo is taking care of him.'

I hear plenty of zip-zip-zip, too. Every once in a while a car will pull beside me and a youngster will lean out the window and whistle at me three times.

I've been getting quite a few requests for autographs, and I've reached the point where I automatically put a Z under my signature.[128]

In the November 1, 1957 issue of *TV-Radio Life*, featuring an interview with Guy, the writer describes Guy.

...he is an easy conversationalist, and jumps at any opportunity to discuss his favorite subjects: astronomy, hi-fi, chess, and children.

To further their interest in astronomy they have the telescope set up in the bedroom. Guy proudly describes it, "It's a 6-inch reflector. It works on the same principle as the 200-inch telescope at Mt. Palomar, the equatorial mounts weigh 65 lbs. It's not portable—and has great resolving power. The reflector makes the moon this big," he says enthusiastically spreading his arms as wide as they can go. "In the bedroom a moon that large can be very romantic. It's really out of this world. Recently Jan and I saw the planet Mars when it had come closer to the earth than it will again for 17 years. We even tried to catch a glimpse of the satellites, but no luck."

Guy's favorite records out of his 300 LP's are the last 5 quartets of Beethoven, he explains "as a composer Beethoven was constantly curious about music and constantly exploring new areas of awareness, new areas of sensation."

On the weekends to relax, Guy enjoyed watching science fiction movies on TV with Stevie, who had turned five shortly after the series aired. When *Zorro* first aired, Guy watched some of the beginning episodes on Thursday nights with Janice and Steve to see how the show looked, telling Janice things about the scene or behind the scenes. Other than that, he hardly watched television.

In an January 1958 interview, Guy joked about his son's growing interest in his dad's show.

> Steve never paid too much attention to me on TV, until some of the kids in his school found out that his father is Zorro. Now he makes all kinds of deals…getting candy, permission to raise the flag and assorted other privileges…in exchange for autographed fotos of me.
>
> He gets a kick out of watching the show and always roots for me. He laughs because 'They can't catch Daddy.' No, he doesn't worry about my being hurt or punished. He's sure nothing can happen to me.
>
> He's already got a Zorro hat and mask, and now he wants swords. I've given him a few fencing lessons, but he's a little young. His hand drops under the weight. The foils are bigger than he is.
>
> One thing I warned him about, though. If he cuts any Z's into things around the house—leaving the kind of mark I do with my sword on the show—I'm going to put the Z on him! I like peace and quiet around the house.[129]

Sometimes Steve's resemblance to Attilio got in the way of Guy's disciplining him. "Guy once said, 'I feel very strange reprimanding Steve. It's like reprimanding my father,'" said Janice.

Robert Foster remembers Guy as a non-egotistical person. "He didn't have pictures of himself on the walls of his house or even a large TV screen where his image was seen every week. He had a very small screen for years and years. He was never hooked on watching TV and very seldom watched himself."

Zorro products such as Zorro costumes, wallets, lunchboxes, watches, puzzles, playsets, games, flashlights, sunglasses, bolas, fencing sets, pajamas, roller skates, and much, much more, were selling like hotcakes.

Hollywood Reporter, April 29, 1958
Disney is cleaning up on *Zorro* merchandising.

Guy's agent was able to arrange for Guy to get 2.5% of the gross made on *Zorro* merchandise. Guy said he had to fight even for that, because Disney learned a lesson during the popularity of *Davy Crockett*. No one had any idea how much money could be made on sales of merchandise relating to a show in those early days of television. So when Fess Parker's agent asked for some small salary raise for Fess, Disney decided instead to give him something in the range of 10 percent of all *Davy Crockett* merchandise. Walt lost hundreds of thousands dollars to Parker, who was able to retire on investments made with that money. Disney would never again be so generous with benefits from merchandise, so the most Guy and Britt could squeeze out of Disney for a share of the merchandise was 2.5 percent and 2 percent, respectively.

Photos of Britt and Guy were taken for merchandise agreements before filming began, so those early products—comic books, puzzles, and lunchboxes—carrying Britt and Guy's images were titled "Zorro and Capitan Tolendano," before Norman Foster changed his name to Capitan Monastario.

> *Hollywood Reporter,* Wednesday, December 18, 1957
> "Disney Christmas Party"
> A Christmas party featuring Jimmie Dodd and the Mouseketeers from the Mickey Mouse Club TV show will be held for employees and their children at the Walt Disney Studios on Saturday. Besides all 14 Mouseketeers, Jimmie Dodd, Marvin Ash, Guy Williams, Henry Calvin, Gene Sheldon, David Stollery, Tim Considine, Kevin Corcoran, Tommy Kirk, and Fess Parker are slated to perform, with shows at 9:30 and 11:00 a.m.

Guy's son, Steve, remembers attending the Christmas party in the commissary at the studio and being excited about meeting Jimmie Dodd and the Mouseketeers. "It was a wonderful time. We were like one big family in those days," he said.

Chapter 25

"Zorro...In person!"

– Press releases

Guy kicked off the new year by riding atop his black steed, Tornado, in the world famous Pasadena Tournament of Roses Parade. Magnificent in his black Zorro costume, Guy saluted the crowds with his sword along the five-mile trek, and waved to countless youngsters who watched him faithfully every Thursday night.

Among the crowd that day was Tony Russo and his five-year-old son, Dell. "My son was so impressed with Zorro on TV. Of course, when I was on the show, he was not impressed. I was just his dad, and *besides* I was the bad guy!" said Tony, with a shrug. "So, I took him to the parade to see Zorro and I'm holding him on my shoulders and I see Guy coming on the horse in the costume! Everyone started screaming and waving! I have to admit, he *did* look terrific—I could have fallen for him myself!," he joked. "So I shouted 'Hey *Guy!*' And Guy comes over on his horse to us and —to the envy of all the crowd—he patted Dell on the head and shook our hands. My son loved Zorro, so it was a big thrill for him, and I was proud and happy to be able to do that for him."

Fans went wild for Zorro in person. At the end of the parade some eager young boys managed to break through barriers and follow Guy. He had so little privacy that even when he tried to use the portable toilet after the parade, the boys were climbing up the sides.

Only two and a half months after *Zorro* first aired Guy was getting more than 2,000 fan letters a month, increasing to 4,000 into the second season. They were mostly from teenage girls expressing their wishes to marry him one day. The studio mailed out signed pictures of Diego on postcards with a typed note on the back thanking fans who wrote in.

The Hollywood Reporter, Friday, January 3, 1958
Zorro scores in Nielson S-O-A [share of audience] ratings.

By the end of the first season, *Zorro* was enjoying 35.7 percent of the viewing audience, which meant an estimated 35 million viewers saw the show each week. *Zorro* was bumping competition off the other two major networks, NBC and CBS. *Harbormaster* and *Richard Diamond* folded, as did *December Bride*, and Groucho Marx's *You Bet Your Life* had to change its time slot to get its viewers back.

On April 23, 1958, the *Anaheim (Cal) Bulletin* ran a picture of Guy as Zorro with an announcement that he would be making his first appearance at Disneyland on the weekend of April 26 & 27, 1958.

> For the occasion, Disneyland has created special performances for "Zorro" in which the popular television hero will fight it out in duels with the laughable Sgt. Garcia (Henry Calvin) and the "villain" Capt. Monastario (Britt Lomond). Aiding the daredevil "Zorro" will be his devoted friend, Bernardo (Gene Sheldon). Williams will also be in attendance Saturday night, when Disneyland stays open until 12 Midnight for a special evening of Fiesta dancing. In addition, the star of the early California adventure series will ride his black stallion Tornado, and portray Don Diego, meek resident of one of the Los Angeles Spanish haciendas. There will also be a Fiesta parade featuring the Gonzales Trio, Spanish dancing highlighting the Corina Valdez Dancers, and autographed pictures of Zorro, Sgt. Garcia and Bernardo for all Disneyland visitors.

A personal appearance at Walt's theme park would not only promote the TV show, but boost attendance at Disneyland, now in its third year. Unprecedented crowds passed through the turnstiles that day at "The Park" to see the masked hero in black who had taken the country by storm. For these appearances the studio would send a limousine to Guy's house to pick him up and take him home, as they did for the Rose Parade. Backstage at Disneyland he mounted Tornado and rode his horse down "Main Street, USA" in the Disneyland Parade with Bernardo right behind him. They made their way to Frontierland, where they performed several shows a day.

After the exciting weekend of Zorro's first park appearance, the *Anaheim Bulletin* of April 28, 1958, printed a picture of Guy in his Don Diego costume talking to children as he meandered his way through Frontierland:

> The genial "don" thrilled fans of all ages with demonstrations of swordsmanship and dashing maneuvers but took time out to talk to hundreds of children of all ages who plied him with questions about the early days of California, its history and customs, which have become the heritage of modern day California.

A chase scene was staged on the roof and balcony of the Golden Horseshoe saloon in Frontierland. Under a picture of Sgt. Garcia running along the balcony, in the *Anaheim Bulletin*, it said:

> Sgt. Garcia on the balcony, futilely chases the elusive Zorro as he drops from the scene of a sword crossing incident at Disneyland. The swashbuckling action took place atop the Golden Horseshoe to the delight of hundreds of Zorro's front-room fans and to the dismay of Sgt. Garcia who let another chance at the minion of the old days slip by. The rotund Garcia, puffing and blowing, chased the fleet footed Zorro who had been toying with his long-time adversary in television scenes of the early days of

California's history. Garcia could not negotiate the athletic maneuver so Zorro was free to mingle with the admiring throngs of youngsters who eagerly awaited his inevitable escape.

Buddy Van Horn recalled the routine, as he appeared as Zorro for the stunts. "I used to appear on top of the roof of the saloon, jump down onto another roof (the balcony level), grab a rope, come down to the ground on the rope, and go inside the saloon. And if Guy was there at the time, he would run out and do a little fencing routine, and if he wasn't there, then I'd go do the whole thing."

There were a few occasions when Guy was so tired he asked Buddy to fill in for him, in the mask, perhaps in a parade, or where he was not required to do anything but stand and be seen. "I remember," said Buddy, in his slow soft-spoken speech, "going to Disneyland one of the times Guy didn't want to go down, and I had to sing with the Mickey Mouse Club! There I was standing with them singing M-I-*CEE*, K-Eee—*WHYYYY*—and went through that with the mask on," he laughed.

Attendance was so high when Guy and the cast of *Zorro* appeared at Disneyland, that Disney had them back after only four weeks.

Daily Variety, Tuesday, May 27, 1958
"Zorro Stars Slated Again at Disneyland"
Stars of Disney's *Zorro* teleseries will reprise their April appearance at Disneyland Park Friday, Saturday and Sunday. Guy Williams, who plays the title role in the series, will be on hand with others in the cast—Henry Calvin, Gene Sheldon, and Britt Lomond performing in three shows a day.

A big ad, accompanied by a photo of Zorro, Sgt. Garcia and Bernardo in the *Anaheim Bulletin*, dated May 29, 1958, announced Guy's Memorial Day weekend at Disneyland.

BY POPULAR DEMAND
ZORRO RETURNS,
IN PERSON
To DISNEYLAND!
This big Holiday Weekend! Fri.—Sat.—Sun.
May 30, 31, June 1
These 3 days only
Park opens at 9:00 A.M.
1st Zorro Parade 11 A.M.

Direct from Walt Disney Studio's exciting TV Series!
Here they come again! All your Zorro Favorites are at Disneyland
in person again this weekend—because you asked for them!
ZORRO and his black stallion Tornado, Sgt. Garcia, and Bernardo will be
there to meet you. Be sure to come this big three-day holiday weekend, and
bring the whole family.[130]

Another newspaper article[131] said Guy Williams would be featured in three special performances each day, along with Henry Calvin and Britt Lomond.

> In his three shows each day Williams will portray the dashing swords-
> man role he has popularized as "Zorro"…He'll fight duels, outwit the sol-
> diers, chase his adversaries overboard from the Disneyland riverboat, and
> match his skill with the sword against a variety of opponents.

The shows began with a parade up Disneyland's Main Street and into Frontierland. An action performance was held on top of the paddle wheel boat, a replica of the *Mark Twain*, on the Rivers of America, where Monastario awaited Zorro for a breathtaking duel. With the exception of leaps, jumps, swings on ropes, and fighting on rooftops, it was always Guy in the parades, and meeting the people. Fencing on top of the *Mark Twain* steamboat was dangerous, but it was really Guy and Britt up there. When Britt was disarmed and thrown overboard, it was a double who made the splash in the river. Moments later the crowd saw a soaked Britt Lomond walking past the jeering kids, thinking it was he who had taken the plunge.

The shows were set up on a stage in Frontierland's Magnolia Park,[132] an area in front of the dock for the *Mark Twain*, near the Silver Banjo Barbecue Restaurant owned by actor Don DeFore, one of Walt's favorite places to eat. The *Anaheim Bulletin* taunted by saying, "Zorro, Sgt. Garcia and Bernardo, will exhibit their 'unpublicized' talents in the shows and picture cards will be given to Disneyland visitors." Gene Sheldon would come out on stage with Henry Calvin and they would do a skit which would showcase Gene's talent in performing magic tricks. Then Guy was introduced and he would come out in his black pants and shirt, but no cape, no hat and no mask, waving to the waiting crowds as he approached the microphone and gave a short talk addressing the children and about filming *Zorro*. Kids dressed as Zorro in masks, some with little mustaches drawn on their small faces, waited in line to go on stage and fence with Zorro. Their parents held cameras up to their faces ready to shoot. Monastario made an entrance and he and Zorro had a rousing flashy fencing bout, ending with Zorro disarming Monastario, of course.

On this Memorial Day weekend, a photographer from *Life* took pictures documenting Guy's performance and his interaction with the children for a five-page spread for the August 1958 issue,[133] now a collector's item.

Sandra Curtis, author of *Zorro Unmasked, The Official History* (1998), and wife of John Gertz, owner of Zorro Productions, was there on that Memorial Day weekend with her parents and wrote about an accidental meeting with her idol, which she associates with fate; a bright moment she never will forget.

> One of the biggest thrills of my childhood was a chance encounter
> with Guy Williams at Disneyland…we took a little-used shortcut past the
> old burro ride in the Painted Desert to avoid the crowds.
> Our shortcut was the very one Guy Williams took to reach the
> paddle wheel boat after the parade. He strode past us, his long legs
> propelling him easily across the distance that my short legs took several
> steps to cover. As he swept by, cape draped over his arm, I looked up
> and smiled. I was too surprised to speak but that didn't seem to matter.

He'd probably seen the same look of astonishment and awe in the faces of thousands of kids before me. He reached out to tousle the hair on the top of my head, flashed his fabulous smile, and said "Hi!" A simple word and gesture, but they lifted me as if I'd been touched by an angel. Zorro hadn't reached out to anyone else in my family, just me. I felt wondrously special.

Years later, when I met John Gertz, we joked that Williams' gesture had been a sign that I was destined to marry the owner of Zorro.[134]

Randy Quade ("not the actor" he says) of Minnesota tells a story about seeing his hero in the flesh when he went to Disneyland during that Memorial Day weekend in 1958.

My family was visiting my mom's sister and her husband in San Pablo, California. My uncle had obtained tickets to Disneyland through his work at Standard Oil, and since it was a long weekend we drove down to go to Disneyland. We had no idea at the time that Zorro would be appearing at the park. I think it was just "the luck of the draw." I do remember it being very hot at Disneyland that day. It seems to me that we were waiting in line for a lemonade from a Frontierland vendor when my uncle yells out, "Hey, look at this!" The next thing I see is Guy and what I assume now to be Britt Lomond (or a pretty good lookalike), lunging and riposting their way across the roofs of Frontierland. My uncle started his 8mm camera and caught most of it, as I recall. We watched the swordplay—I think Britt ended up in the drink—and Guy and most of the principals took a bow to a cheering crowd and disappeared. We moved slowly with the dense crowd in the direction of where Guy disappeared. I think we then sat down and waited for the crowd to disburse, finishing our drinks before moving off to the next "Land."

All of a sudden, from behind a fence, near the end of the building, out pops Zorro! I don't remember exactly where it was, but I remember that he just popped out from nowhere from around the corner of a building and was wearing the mask! And *tall!* My God, he was tall! All in all, a very striking and intimidating figure to a 5-year-old! I had to be only 10 feet from him! He looked at my mom and said something about the hot weather and my mom damn near swallowed her false teeth! (She was a BIG fan and was nervously filming all this with an 8mm home movie camera.) I grabbed my autograph book and a pen from my pocket and held it out for him to sign. We were immediately rushed by about 100 or so kids—all with autograph books & pens.

Guy was standing behind a fence, one of those three-rail, split-rail, ranch-style affairs that you see in all the Republic Studio oaters. The top of it came to just over my head. Guy reached over the fence and I thought he was going to take my book, but instead he reached over and picked ME up, sitting me on a buckboard wagon. HOLY COW! For a 5-year-old kid in the '50s this is hog heaven. I was so scared. I think the lemonade passed

Cast of *Zorro* board the plane for St. Louis, MS, October 10, 1958, for a personal appearance sponsored by 7 UP to promote the second season, which promised romance. L-r, Britt Lomond, (clean shaven and blond), Henry Calvin, Jolene Brand, Gene Sheldon, and Guy Williams. (Photo by Williams Eccles, airport photographer; From Guy's own collection, courtesy of Aracelli Lisazo)

right through me! He was the tallest man I'd ever met and had the most piercing eyes! I couldn't get a word out! I remember him talking about the dangers of swordplay and something about how fat Sergeant Garcia was getting. He then signed my book and lifted me back over the fence. In retrospect, I can think of a million and one questions I would like to have asked him, but that day I don't think I even got my name out right. I think he called me "Ronnie."

Actor Tony Russo recalled this same spellbound effect on his son, Dell, the first time he met his idol. "I took Dell to the Disney studio one day to meet Annette (of the Mouseketeers) when she was filming *Zorro*. So I introduced him to Annette and he was very happy about that, but then Guy came out. Dell just stood there speechless, his eyes popping out. I said to Dell, 'This is Guy!' Dell was just looking up at him, and said, 'Hiiiieeee.' So Guy said, 'Hi! What's your name?' Dell said, as though hypnotized, 'Guyyyyee.' Guy smiled, and said, 'No, that's *my* name. What's *yours?*'" Tony laughed.

Guy was invited to be the Grand Marshall of a Rose Festival parade in Portland, Oregon in mid-June, but when he appeared waving from a Corvette convertible instead of his horse, it was Guy's first unpleasant experience with negative press.

> *Daily Variety*, Tuesday, June 17, 1958, Portland Oregon, June 16
> *"Portland Fans Ired as Zorro Mounts Car But Not Horse"*
> Thesp Guy Williams, star of Disney's teleseries *Zorro*, stirred a storm of controversy here with his appearance over the weekend as Grand Marshall of Portland's annual Rose Festival. Local fans complained that Williams did not ride a horse in the two parades, one Friday and one Saturday, and they were disappointed that he signed no autographs. The *Portland Oregonian*, the leading local newspaper, however, explained that Williams declined to ride a horse because he was unfamiliar with the animal and afraid of what might happen if he were swamped with kids getting underfoot. Further, said the paper, the horse was not shod for pavements. Regarding the autographs, the newspaper said it was a studio rule against signing autographs that kept Williams from obliging. In answer to queries from some of the disillusioned, the *Oregonian* said "Zorro can really ride" and "he can really brandish a sword" and made clear any complaints against Williams were occasioned by his efforts to play safe and cooperate.

In an attempt to embarrass Guy, the Portland newspaper printed a picture of a five-year-old boy riding the horse they proposed to give Guy for the parade. Guy explained in a public statement that he had refused to ride the horse because he was concerned about how the horse would react to the crowd, not over fear for his own personal safety.[135]

Just before Guy went back to Disneyland for performances during the Memorial Day weekend, he attended one of several special appearances for a children's charity. Guy had become a close friend to Norman Foster and his wife, Sally Blane, and Sally was involved with the John Tracy Clinic, for deaf and autistic children. Guy and Henry were allowed by Disney to appear at a charity function for the Clinic. Guy was happy to oblige his friends and the children and on May 18, 1958 he was there in person, posing in costume with five-year-old Stevie Longo at the John Tracy Clinic. The little children there were thrilled at the chance to hold Zorro's sword. Newspaper photographers took their picture with Zorro and Sgt. Garcia, who was snapped with the little girls of the Whistling Blue Birds of Encino, and toured the Clinic that day. This publicity was to kick off a benefit open to the public the coming Saturday, May 24, 1958,[136] where he also appeared. The fund-raising Bazaar was held the at 806 W. Adams in Los Angeles, with special appearances by The Mouseketeers, with Jimmie Dodd, and Guy Williams, and Clarence "Donald Duck" Nash. There were four shows throughout the afternoon and admission was free.

On August 1, 1958, a huge event called "Family Night" was staged at the magnificent outdoor Hollywood Bowl featuring a cast of Disney characters and Zorro in full force. The huge proscenium stage is covered by a round half-dome rising from the back of the stage. There is amphitheater seating for 18,000 people with box seats in front. Traditionally, since

Guy and Henry Calvin meeting a young fan on arrival in Flint, Michigan for a personal appearance in the parade celebrating the 50th Anniversary of General Motors, makers of AC Spark Plugs, one of the two sponsors for *Zorro;* 1958. (The Mary Spooner Collection, courtesy of Mary Spooner)

1922, people have attended concerts here, bringing picnic baskets for a relaxed and romantic evening beneath the star-studded sky and natural surroundings of trees and beautiful hills.

This particular night saw a huge audience because of Zorro. With anticipation for the new second season at a peak, Zorro's fans were anxious to see him appear with their favorite villain, Monastario. Principal members of the *Zorro* cast participated in the show as well as some stuntmen to assist Guy's stunt double, Buddy Van Horn.

Janice remembers the excitement of that memorable night. "Zorro came down this long rope and the crowd went *wild*," she said. "I remember how his cape billowed and he spun down the rope."

Buddy Van Horn thought for moment. "Family Night at the Hollywood Bowl," he pondered. "Yes, I do remember the Zorro segment. I was at the *top* of the Bowl and Sergeant Garcia was down at the bottom [on stage] and he was telling the audience what he was going to do to that Zorro if Zorro ever showed up."

Buddy had to climb up the back of the cement half-dome behind the stage, about fifty feet high, in costume, to reach his place of entrance at the top of the Bowl. He stood at the very top and waited for his cue.

"They put the spotlight on me. I'm standing on top of the Bowl and the crowd just went *bananas*! Then, all I did was *this,*" Buddy put his finger to lips. "And they just shut up," he said, amazed at the power Zorro had over the crowd. "Sgt. Garcia goes on and on, and I throw a rope down, and come *all* the way down the Hollywood Bowl on the rope to the stage. That was before repelling," recalled Buddy, "and your hands get very hot from the friction. So, I used to put something like sheepskin inside my glove to protect my hands. When I came down, because of the way a rope is made in a twisted pattern, I was *spinning* all the way down."

The loyal audience remained completely silent, so they wouldn't give their hero away. Zorro's cape billowed in the silence of his spinning decent. "I take my sword out and walk behind Garcia," continued Buddy, "and as he's saying, 'I'll *get* that Zorro,' I poke him with the sword. He goes 'Uhhgggh!,' turns around, runs off stage, and I go after him. Then it's Guy and Britt who come back out on stage. They do a fencing routine, then they go off-stage. Meanwhile, up on the side of the hill off-stage, in the Zorro costume is [stuntman] Dean Smith on horseback. They put a spotlight on him as he rears up and waves to the crowd and rides off out of the spotlight. So we had *three* Zorros that night. Me, Guy and Dean."

The act was sensational and unforgettable. Walt couldn't have been more pleased. "I got a nice letter from Walt for that night," said Buddy. "He said it was exciting and he thanked me and blah blah blah." Buddy didn't elaborate on Walt's praises, but he saved it along with others like it from his illustrious boss.

On October 10, 1958, Guy and Henry Calvin, Jolene Brand and Britt Lomond boarded a private American airliner at LAX for St. Louis, Missouri for a personal appearance sponsored by 7-Up to promote the second season of *Zorro*. Britt remembers, "I arrived in St Louis, Missouri with my natural hair color, which was blond because my role in *Zorro* had been finished. The woman who did my makeup was disappointed when she saw me. She said to me, 'Oh, You don't *really* have that *nice* beard?'" he laughed. "She put a beard on me and a black wig for the p.a."

Britt Lomond was still under contract to Disney with the possibility of returning to *Zorro* for the next three years, making public appearances with Guy, and filming numerous TV shows. "Walt was wonderful, he put me in three or four shows after *Zorro*. I was in *The Swamp Fox, Texas John Slaughter, The Mountain Men, The Nine Lives of Elfago Baca* (with Annette, and playing the same role of a commandante), *Young Jesse James,* and I played General Custer in a movie called *Tonka,*[137] in which I was a blond, so I didn't have to dye my hair. That was my own hair in that movie."

By mid-1958, Britt was informed of trouble with the network about airing *Zorro*, which resulted in its cancellation, and Britt never had the chance to return to the show. Just two weeks before shooting *Tonka,* Britt fell down a rain-soaked cliff in Palos Verdes, CA while leaving on a boating excursion with his wife[138] and friends, and broke his left wrist. It was a holiday and the nearest doctor was a veterinarian who wrapped his wrist and gave him pain killers. Hours later in a Santa Monica hospital it was reset and put in a cast. "For *Tonka,* I had gloves made with long cuffs that went all the way up the sleeve of my jacket to hide the cast from the production people. I always made sure I had his gloves on.

Nobody knew I had a broken arm. I concealed it, and it wasn't until the end of the picture that they realized I had a broken arm. I took a lot of pain pills, because the galloping on the horse and the fight scenes were very painful."

On November 15, 1958, while Guy's television version of *Zorro* was in its peak season, another famous Zorro died in another country. Tyrone Power died of a heart attack at the young age of 44, while filming a fencing scene for a movie he was making in Madrid, Spain.

Only one week later, Johnston McCulley, the creator of the character, died on November 23, 1958 at the age of 75. Six years previous he was so down-and-out financially, he had sold the rights to his Zorro creation to Mitchell Gertz, his literary agent.[139] McCulley lived to see his beloved character ride another giant wave of popularity with Guy Williams.

1958 was the biggest year for Guy in terms of notoriety, demands, public appearances, interviews and popularity. He was learning by experience how to deal with his public and his lack of privacy. His schedule was strenuous and unrelenting.

> Sure I get tired, but this is the biggest thing that has ever happened to me and I'm not going to complain about anything. I must admit, though, that I get a bit concerned when *Zorro* has a higher rating than President Eisenhower's important missile speech. This is really an odd reflection of the American public's interest.[140]

In another interview, he said he was

> ...nonplused by large groups of children. On a recent visit to long-time friend Dennis Weaver (who plays lame Chester in *Gunsmoke*) he was swarmed by neighborhood children who demanded his autograph and bits of his clothing as souvenirs. "I didn't know what to say or do. They had me coming and going."

In April 1958 he told *TV Guide:*

> Success is nebulous. I've been really too busy to think much about it. Of course, some things have changed. When I go to my gas station five guys jump to take care of the car. Before *Zorro,* I had to honk my horn to get any attention.
>
> Sometimes, that mark of Zorro can become a real headache. Like the time I had to repaint my Cadillac convertible because some junior joker etched the sign of the Z all over my fenders with a pocket knife. Then, I get hundreds of letters from teachers throughout the British Empire; they complain Zorro is murdering the Queen's English, because he makes the sign of the "Zee" instead of the sign of the "Zed."
>
> However, I shame-facedly admit I've never really made the sign of the Z myself. Seems ridiculous when you realize I've probably made it the most popular letter in the alphabet with small fry and their pocket knives. But, whenever there's a Z to be carved on a tree trunk or wall during a show, I step aside. A Disney prop man does it with a small hand axe.[141]

Generally there was no trouble, no threats or challenges made to him in public. "The Zorro character was well-liked," said Guy. "I never had any trouble. The only thing bad was when a parent told me his kid broke his leg jumping from a roof or broke his arm. All I could say was 'I'm sorry.'"[142]

From the November 25, 1958 *Anaheim (Cal.) Bulletin*:

In Person, at Disneyland!
Zorro
with Sgt. Garcia and Bernardo
EVERYDAY OF THE THANKSGIVING WEEK-END
Thurs.- Fri.-Sat.-Sun.
Nov. 27 thru Nov. 30 [1958]

DON'T MISS this special added holiday treat! See Zorro and cast in person and enjoy all the exciting, wonderful attractions of Walt Disney's Magic Kingdom.

Thanksgiving Week-End hours;
10 AM—9 PM
Santa Ana Freeway at Harbor Blvd.
ANAHEIM

This was Guy's third appearance at Disneyland in 1958. For this huge Thanksgiving weekend celebration of November 27-30, 1958, Guy rode in parades and performed for four days. This time he took his family with him and their close friends Peggy and Bob Stevenson and their toddler, Bruce. All were guests in Disney's hotel.

For young Steve it was a most happy time in his life. "I remember a time at Disneyland when there was a big tent set up in the parking lot for all the cast when they were doing the parades," said Steve, trying to remember details. "The Mouseketeers were there and it seems to have been a party of some kind, but then," he added, "*every day* at Disneyland was a party."

The four days that Guy and his family stayed at the hotel were packed with fun for young Steve. Just shy of six years old, it was a dream come true to have Disneyland as his playground all day *every* day. His favorite land was Frontierland. He explored Tom Sawyer Island for hours and spent all afternoon watching the real Native American Indians in their Indian Village with teepees, making crafts and having pow-wows. He drove cars at the Autopia attraction. Dressed in his military school uniform he was given the honor of leading the Official Disneyland Band on Main Street, USA. Bandleader, Tommy Walker, handed little Steve his baton, and he waved the stick with confidence and expertise.

Before the parade, Lou Debney, publicity manager for the studio, positioned himself on top of the balcony of the Golden Horseshoe Saloon with five-year-old Steve at his side and took a Super 8 home movie[143] of Guy entering Frontierland in the parade with this *Zorro* cast of characters following. The Disneyland Band, led by Tommy Walker, can be seen entering Frontierland between the gates of the Fort entrance as the guests eagerly await El Zorro.

In the video Gene Sheldon, as Bernardo, rides in on his horse, goes to the Horseshoe Saloon entrance, and dismounts. A wrangler dressed as a Spanish vaquero takes the reins, mounts and takes the horse away. Henry Calvin arrives in a buggy driven by a soldier, as

Guy Williams as Zorro made the cover of TV Guide for the week of April 26-May 2, 1958.
(The Jill Panvini Collection: courtesy of Jill Panvini)

well as the lovely Señorita Verdugo (Jolene Brand), Zorro's love interest, on the series. The envy of all the women, Jolene is dressed in a beautiful Spanish gown of satin and lace and a black Spanish mantilla. She and Henry wave to the crowd and exit, to await their entrance later. Britt Lomond arrives to cheers and jeers from the kids, and dismounts his beautiful white horse, which in turn is mounted by a wrangler and ridden away from the crowd. Britt waves and heads for the *Mark Twain* Riverboat, taking the stairs to the very top level, where he awaits to challenge his most formidable enemy. Zorro enters the gates on his famous black horse. The crowd cheers and waves and calls his name. Zorro dismounts and, as he runs to the steps of the *Mark Twain* to challenge Monastario, he takes off his cape in preparation for the duel, leaving it at the foot of the boat's staircase. A band positioned on the landing in front of the boat plays the theme song of *Zorro*. Climbing the stairs by twos, turning through the wheel house to the top deck, Zorro meets the waiting Monastario. On some occasions he would vanquish a soldier on guard and topple him overboard on his way up the stairs.

When the thrilling fencing act on top of the Mark Twain ends, Zorro throws his arms up in victory, the crowd cheers, and the music swells. On his way down the stairs he grabs his cape, and twirls it around his head with flair as he runs through the crowd. A sea of cameras click, and hands reach out to touch him before he exits through the Saloon to the brief sanctuary of backstage. Shortly afterwards, he returns to walk through the crowd to meet the public, have his picture taken, and sign autographs. Guy would appear as Diego in the fourth show daily.[144]

After hours of working it was difficult for Guy to find solace in his relaxation. "Dad was always recognized when we went somewhere," Steve said. "I remember times having to find back doors to get out of places. He could never walk around Disneyland to enjoy himself."

Janice was amazed at how consistently patient Guy was with fans, always patient and gracious. She could recall only one time when Guy lost his demeanor. It was at the hotel at Disneyland, and Guy was exhausted from doing four shows and meeting people all day. "We were having dinner and someone walked over to us after many, many, people had already approached him for autographs and whatnot," said Janice. "He said to Guy, 'Sorry to bother you, but ...' And Guy interrupted him and said, 'Then why are you?' It surprised me and I was embarrassed, but, *really*, he *couldn't* eat his dinner!"

The huge success of the Thanksgiving weekend was lauded in the trades:

Daily Variety, Monday, December 1, 1958 (Just for *Variety*)
"Live TV"
    The personal appearance of "Zorro" (Guy Williams) and his air waves troupe brought out record-busting crowds to Disneyland over the weekend. Included in the mob Sunday was Williams' own six-year-old son, Steve. His p.a. at the park also included a battle atop Frontierland roofs, and on the top deck of the *Mark Twain*—battles which top anything seen on the filmed Disney show!

"Yep," said Steve, "those were the good ol' days."

Chapter 26

"The family slavered over him"
— Valerie Catalano Fitzgerald

In 1958 Guy was at the peak of his fame. On top of the mountain. He didn' know it yet, but it would not get any better than this for him in Hollywood. It was the busiest and most prosperous year of his career and his life. Photos and interviews of him were everywhere, in newspapers, TV guides, and almost every show business magazine you could buy. His income increased, and so did his family. A new baby was due in May.

After *Zorro* wrapped its first season on March 27, 1958, Guy welcomed the hiatus to do what he did best—enjoy life. At the pinnacle of his fame, he was happy in mind, body, and spirit. His suits were tailor-made at Tartaglia of Beverly Hills. He enjoyed gourmet foods, fine wines—Bordeaux and cognac—and cigars, preferring Dunhill-23. He had his own personalized humidor at Dunhill's on Rodeo Drive in Beverly Hills, engraved in gold among those owned by George Burns and Milton Berle. He enjoyed his state-of-the-art telescope for gazing at the stars, a collection of tropical fish, a new red jaguar sports coup, his extensive record collection, his pipe, classical music, opera, his books, and his beautiful family.

Unlike the rest of the cast and crew who were enjoying a work-free three-month hiatus, Guy had to include interviews, photo shoots, and public appearances. In April of 1958 Guy went back to New York for business and pleasure. He made a guest appearance at a luncheon given by 7-Up, the sponsors of the show, and a personal appearance in a department store, in connection with *Zorro* merchandise, then he visited his relatives.

His mother, aunts, uncles, and cousins were excited to see their famous relative. Everyone gathered at the home of Uncle Eugene and Aunt Josephine where a sumptuous Italian feast was prepared to welcome their nephew home. His Aunt KiKi (a nickname for Katherine) was there, Clare's oldest stepsister, Guy's favorite Uncle Oscar and Aunt Anne and their children, Nancy and Roger, his older cousins, Gilda, Mary, and Ophelia, who now doted on him more than ever. If Attilio could have been there, he would have been proud of his son.

Valerie can't recall her brother having any personal conversation with her of any consequence that day. "He didn't say nothing to me so I didn't say nothing to him," she said. "See, my brother was used to having people fawn over him, and I never did that. I'd say 'Hi' and wait for him to say 'Hi,' then wait for the conversation to continue and it usually didn't. But it wasn't his fault. It was the family's fault, because of the way they treated him. The family slavered over him. And I never understood that. It's great to be adored, but it would be terrific if they treated him like a human being instead of this demigod, which he definitely was not.

"My brother had a big ego. He was self-centered. I think he was alone too much. He was very smart, but he was not down-to-earth enough. He couldn't read people. He should have driven a cab to get to know people. I think he needed to mix with people more, to be in touch with the public, instead of being *adored*."

Valerie considered the root of her animosity. "I told myself, 'Now Valerie, you mustn't be jealous.' Then I thought it over and I said, 'No, I'm not jealous because I want no part of that life for myself. People were always saying to me, 'Why don't you go to Hollywood and get on a show?' because they would see my brother on TV and in the TV guide and movie magazines. I got sick of hearing it."

Valerie knew she wasn't cut out to be an actress. "When I visited him in Hollywood in 1955 I asked him if he would take me to the studio and get me into the movies." Guy explained to her that it wasn't done that way. "He told me I had to do summer stock first. 'What?!' I said. 'Summer stock?! I don't want *that!*' The only thing I wanted was to meet Jack Palance, and he never did take me to Universal."

Valerie has that rare ability to laugh at herself. Very intelligent, with a wonderful quick sense of humor, she touches on the truth with humor to mask a deep hurt and disappointment. It is difficult for her to talk about her "relationship" with Guy because she said, "There was never a *relationship* to start with. There was only that one connection with our love for science fiction. That was all. We had no relationship. I did try, but I kept getting put-off."

Guy loved Valerie, but her behavior seemed to bewilder him. He always had her best interest at heart, but the two didn't know how to reach each other.

Valerie often visited her girlfriend Connie Tampone in the Bronx in the early 1960s. That was when Connie's little son John experienced his first crush. "Valerie was my mother's girlfriend and she used to come over to the house sometimes. I had a big crush on her," he said. "She was a voluptuous woman to me, similar in looks to say, Jayne Mansfield only with red hair." At first he was not aware that she was the sister of his television hero. "When I was five, I loved Zorro so much I had a lot of Zorro toys and a Zorro guitar I loved to play. That's how I got the nickname Johnny Zorro. When I found out Valerie was Zorro's sister, I thought I might get to meet him, but I never did."

John is a well-known vocalist/musician on the New York City blues scene, known by his stage name Sonny Hudson. His little girl, Gabby, is a chip off the old block watching *Zorro* on TV every night.

Valerie married a man much older than herself, whom her mother thought would be her prince and savior. She had three little daughters in the 1960s, but the marriage would prove to be a disaster.

Chapter 27

"Life with Zorro"

— *TV Picture Life*

Guy returned to Los Angeles with a few weeks to spare before Janice had the baby. A daughter was born on Wednesday, May 14, 1958 at Cedars of Lebanon Hospital. Guy was the proud father, grateful for being blessed now with both a healthy and beautiful girl and boy. "We thought about naming her Zora," said Janice. "It's a pretty name, but it was just too close to the show, so we decided against it. Both of us agreed to name her Antoinette. Steve had a little girlfriend in school named Lisa who he had promised if he had a baby sister, he would name her Lisa, after her. So, we named her Lisa Antoinette and called her Toni." Then Janice recalled a curious thing. "Guy's paternal grandmother was named Antoinette, but he didn't know at the time. He found out later that his grandmother Catalano was named Antoinette." Janice was still amazed at the coincidences. "And she sang opera. Toni has a wonderful singing voice, so that must be where she gets it from, because neither Guy nor I could sing a note."

Guy's new "bambina" was showered with baby gifts, many of them were *Zorro*-related. Someone gave her a baby undershirt with a **Z** sewn on the front. There were cards and well wishes from an array of illustrious well-wishers. Walt Disney sent a telegram with her name in reverse: "To little Toni Lisa." A card from George J. Lewis, who played Alejandro de la Vega, Zorro's father, was humorously signed, "Your *Grandfather*," and there was a card from the writer and creator of *Zorro*, himself, Johnston McCulley, with best wishes.

On the night Toni was born Guy was overcome with emotions. "Guy was so happy when Toni was born," remembered Peggy Stevenson. "He came over to our house and we opened a bottle of champagne, and he and Bob drank and drank and talked and talked for hours. Guy was the typical proud parent telling us how beautiful and smart she *already* was, and she was doing *this* and doing *that*. 'You should *see* her!' he would say to Bob and me. 'She's a tough little girl. A real spitfire!'"

Tears welled in his eyes. It was a time in his life when he seemed to have everything he ever wanted or needed. The hour was late. "Guy was smashed, and I offered him our house to spend the night. He lived just five minutes away, but I could see he was in no shape to drive home. We were worried about him getting home safely, so I begged him

Guy and Janice with baby Toni, born May 14, 1958 at the height of Guy's career.

to sleep over at our house," she said. "But, he insisted on driving home. I made him *promise* to call when he got home. Then, Bob and I watched him make his way down the stairs and the path, tromping through the flower bed as he went to his car. I was worried until the phone rang. And he did call! He let us know he got home all right."

Little Steve spent a week with the Weavers while his mother was in the hospital. "I have a lot of happy memories there playing with Dennis' sons. Robby, who was my age, and Rick, his older brother, and I built our own museum. It was a 'just for kids' museum in that you had to 'crawl-through.' We put frames up and covered pictures that were already in them with pictures of airplanes and baseball cards and such.

"One time we set up a candy stand to sell candy on the side of the road. Dennis would end up buying most of the candy from us for himself," he laughed, "and we'd eat the rest. That's funny to think about now because Dennis is a vegan into Self-Realization and eats only *healthy* food.

"I spent a lot of time at their house. In fact, that was where I rode my first two-wheeler—on the sidewalk of Dennis' house. My dad and Dennis taught me."

Steve went to kindergarten at Laurel Avenue Elementary School in Hollywood near his home on Harper. His birthday was at the end of the year, so he was always one of the youngest in his class. In September 1958, when Steve was almost six, Guy wanted him to go to a military school. He and Janice felt it would provide him with the kind of educational foundation that would be good for him. There was only one military school near their home, so they didn't have the task of choosing which one. It was called Black Foxe Military Institute in Beverly Hills, a fitting name for the son of Zorro. "The irony of the name never occurred to us at the time," said Janice. Guy told the teacher, "Just teach him how to *read*. As long as he can do that, he can learn anything."

Most of the students were children of celebrities. "Young Dino Martin, Dean Martin's son, was at Black Foxe when I was there," said Steve. "He was the upperclassman assigned to me. When I first arrived, he was the guy who brought me my Brasso for my belt and steered me around."

Guy was always proudly talking about his family in interviews. Consequently, Janice and their children became objects of curiosity to the press and fans. They, too, began to be sought after for appearances. "I remember my mother picking me up from school one day and driving straight to a studio in my uniform to be on a TV show about celebrity kids," said Steve. "I can't remember the title of the show, but I remember it started with a rocket taking off as the introduction. We had to answer questions for a panel to guess who each child's famous parent was. Dean Martin's daughter was on, and Anthony Quinn's son or daughter," said Steve. "None of the dads were there. Someone guessed Guy *Madison* for my father," laughed Steve, aware of the never-ending confusion.

Janice said, "Steve was *so* little. He was the youngest on the show, but he did the most talking. When he was asked a question, he went on saying lots of things, really enjoying it. He wasn't shy at all. The panel couldn't guess it, so he was on a good amount of time. When the time was up, the emcee talked to Steve about his dad and Zorro. 'Can you make a Z for us?' he asked, and Steve, quite ready to oblige him, said, 'You want a *fast* one or a *slow* one?' It got a big laugh from the audience."

Janice was on a similar show for celebrity wives, with master of ceremonies, Dennis James. The panel was given the name of a famous celebrity, Guy Williams, in this case, and had to guess which woman was really his wife. Janice and two other women gave answers to the panelists, then someone guessed Janice. The winner said she chose Janice "because she *reacted* like a wife would to the questions."

TV Picture Life magazine sought out Janice Williams in 1959 to find out what it was like to be married to El Zorro, one of the most handsome men on film to date. Here is her extensive and revealing account about her guy.

"IN LOVE WITH A WONDERFUL GUY"[145]
by Janice Williams
as told to Maurine Myers Reminih

People often come up to me at parties, with a teasing grin, and ask, "Well, how does it feel to be Mrs. Zorro?" I answer with some absolutely brilliant remark, like, "Oh, it's very exciting!" or "Well, there's never a dull moment!" I manage somehow, to keep control of myself, and even make it a point not to tell them what it's really like. THAT recital would keep them glued to my side all evening—and they weren't really asking for information, they were just making social conversation.

Of course I'm telling them the truth, in capsule form, when I say that the life of Mrs. Zorro is exciting, with never a dull moment. But the full truth, and nothing but the truth, is that the life of Mrs. Guy Williams has always been like that—long before the black cape of Zorro was tossed over Guy's broad shoulders.

Maybe all actors make exciting husbands. I wouldn't know. But I do know that *my* actor makes the common, garden-variety husband look pretty pale by comparison. Guy is a non-conformist from way back, so if it's something "everybody does" -then chances are he's just not interested. Which can make for some pretty wild and wonderful situations.

It's been the same since the very first time we met, while we were both doing photographic modeling, back in New York about ten years ago.

It was a courting done as only a romantic Latin could do it and with a special Catalano flair, at that.

Loads of people have wonderful, wacky courtship's—and then, a few years after they've been married, they start to "settle down," some of the zing goes out of their lives. This is inevitable, I suppose, but, after ten years of being married to Guy, I'm beginning to believe that he's the exception. He's still doing crazy things to court me, still brings home wonderful, impulsive gifts, still is a master at the adept compliment—and as full of bounce as he ever was.

He rebels completely at giving gifts on man-made type occasions— Mother's Day, for instance. Nobody can tell him he must send his mother a gift on one certain Sunday each year. Of course two weeks before, a week after, or some Thursday in October, he'll send her something—just because he thought of her at the moment, and wanted to remind her of his love, or because he saw something in a shop window which seemed particularly appropriate for her. So far as he's concerned, there are probably umpteen Mother's Days a year. And Mrs. Catalano, being of the same turn of mind, would know he was slipping if he ever sent a gift on Mother's Day just because it was Mother's Day.

As you might guess, with a gourmet for a father, Guy has more than the average man's interest in food. That was probably one of the things which flipped me so thoroughly when he was courting me—the wonderful little out-of-the-way restaurants he knew. The food was always divine, the atmosphere so thick you could carry home a chunk in your pocket, and the service made you feel like visiting royalty. And he could order a dinner in a way I'd only read about in books. He was making good money modeling at the time, and the Catalanos had always been comfortably fixed—so it was none of the hamburger and malted routine for him. And he's still that way. And in spite of my Scotch-Irish ancestry and Tennessee rearing, I find I've gone the Roman route, myself.

Just recently Guy has gone overboard, but really overboard. We eat late—Guy is fairly late getting home from the studio, and likes to change and relax a little before settling down to dinner—so it's often 9 o'clock before we eat. So, I feed Steve and Toni their dinner early, and though I'm no nutrition expert, I try to see that they get the meat-vegetables-milk menu which is best for them. And then, after they're settled down for the night, Guy and I can have our dinner in peace, quiet, and serenity. And, of late, in an opulence I'd never ever have dreamed up all by myself.

If Guy isn't ravenously hungry by the time our dinner hour arrives—and this sometimes happens—he'll say "let's just have caviar." That means that we turn on the hi-fi to some nice, soft, dreamy music, and the lights get turned low in the living room. I set out a big jar of caviar, and a tray of Euphrates crackers, while Guy is chilling a bottle of champagne. And that is our dinner. Caviar, crackers, and champagne. It may lack in nourishment for the body, it certainly provides plenty of nourishment for the soul. It's a menu I'd heartily recommend to any "old married" couple, as a sure-fire way to recapture the mood of the days before diapers, installment payments, and that old can-we-afford-a new-furnace-this-year.

Guy is so much of the extrovert that it's just a good thing that I'm a healthy, wiry type, so I can keep up with him. You might think that, after working all week in the middle of a seething mob of people at the studio, a man might want to sort of crawl in a hole over the weekend, do nothing but rest, and see no one.

Publicity shots at home of Guy with his young son Steve, looking at Guy's tropical fish collection (author's personal collection)

Not my husband. Bright and early Saturday morning he's up, claiming that the just-after-dawn hours are the best part of the day (an enthusiasm I must say I've never shared fully, being one who loves to sleep late). Before Saturday is very old, he's promoted some sort of trip or other. Maybe he'll take Steve to the beach for the day, or we'll all drive up to Mt. Baldy, where there is a trout pond he and Steve are fond of. And it's a rare weekend that we don't either go to a party, or give one ourselves.

These parties are never big affairs—generally five or six couples at most. We think it's most fun when the group is small enough to stay together as one unit. Let a party get any bigger, and it breaks into small groups. Then, no matter how interesting the chatter is in your group, you feel you might be missing something even more interesting going on in another group.

When the party's at our house, Guy is generally chef. He has a streak of the medieval in him...He always chooses main dishes which are delicious, but have a very showman-like flair about them and often it's something which can be eaten with the hands—like his Gambas a la plancha—a special way he cooks shrimp.

There are several departments in which Guy does a sort of switch from his customary non-conformist tactics. His clothes, for instance, are really quite conservative. He is fond of fine fabrics, loves the feel of good woolens, excellent leather. But the colors are muted, the cut is conservative, and he rarely goes in for the mad things many California men seem to love. Maybe that's because in costume for Zorro and Don Diego all day, he has all the zip he needs in his costumes.

Guy is one of those annoying characters who is able to maintain a schedule without any visible effort at doing so. If he says he'll be somewhere at 7:30 p.m. he is always ready to leave the house in plenty of time to make the trip at a leisurely rate.

But the non-conformist comes back into focus when you take up the handyman-around-the house role most husbands play. Not Guy. Nothing could move him less than a defective lamp cord or a doorbell with a broken connection. Happily, I'm good at puttering and prone to pull out a screwdriver and get to work on any and all minor repairs. Once in a while, however, I do get in a little beyond my depth. I'll struggle over whatever project I'm working on, trying to solve it first this way and then that. Finally, I give up, and call Guy. "Look," I say, using my Grade A diplomacy, "I'm not asking you to fix this. Just give a quick look and tell me what in heck I'm doing wrong!" He obligingly surveys the situation, and 88% of the time he'll say, "Here, give me that screwdriver!" whereupon, in an infuriating (to me) interval of five minutes, he's fixed whatever it was that I'd been puzzling over for an hour. Oh, he has the know-how all right—he just hasn't the inclination to fuss with such mundane things, until he's challenged into it.

Guy would protest bitterly if anyone ever suggested that he is predictable. But I maintain that by using a sort of reverse logic, he can be predicted as easily as any man. You see, all I have to do is figure out what an average man would do, given a certain set of circumstances. Having arrived at that answer, I just figure that Guy would do the exact opposite.

It's little keys like that which keep this Mrs. Zorro from jumping off rooftops herself, rooftops which aren't in the script. And they keep Life with Zorro the exciting thing it is.

In the late 1950s to early 1960s, Mt. Baldy was a big occasion for Steve, making the long rural trek toward the mountain. "It was a place we went to often and we always liked. The ride along the 10 freeway was long, with nothing then but citrus orchards. There were orange groves for miles with smudge pots burning. None of that is there now. We would go just for a day, mostly for hiking, when there was no snow. Dad also liked to fish for trout in the fish ponds. We'd cook the fish over an open fire and he would put a bottle of white wine in the stream to let it get cool. A funny thing is that years later in the 1970s when I learned to fly sail planes, I had to fly back and forth over Baldy, and one of my favorite things was looking down over where we used to hike. I'd kind of linger there a bit, flying around it."

Guy adjusted well to family life, despite the fact that he had wanted to wait before having children. He liked pal-ing with his son. "Even though I was little, I can remember Dad taking me with him sometimes to his agent's office on Sunset Boulevard."[146]

In 1957 the Disney Studio and sponsors of *Zorro* capitalized on Guy's "family man" image, and took publicity shots of Guy with his five-year-old son surrounded by an

Publicity shot of Guy with son Steve for new merchandise, toy sword and whip like Zorro's real ones. (Personal collection of Kathy Gregory, courtesy of Kathy Gregory)

array of *Zorro* merchandise. There were individual shots showing Steve wearing a Zorro watch, or wearing Zorro gloves, or in the mask and costume, with a chalk-tipped sword. There were "at-home" shots of father and son: little Stevie riding on his dad's back, the two playing chess, playing with his train, looking at the tropical fish. Steve had every Zorro toy made at one time. He had his own Zorro costume by Cooper, but his favorite was the real thing, when Dad let him put *his* costume on.

From as early as Steve could remember Guy took his family to the world famous Farmer's Market at Fairfax and Third, to get pizza at Patty's Pizza. "The donut place," said Steve, "was right next door and it was a big deal to get hot fresh donuts, or fruit drinks, or ice cream, all that stuff. We spent a lot of time there." Steve still enjoys a slice of pizza at Patty's. "Another big occasion for me was when the family went to the Gilmore Drive-In, just behind the parking lot of the Farmer's Market. That was always a treat for us," said Steve. "I remember seeing movies there like H.G. Wells' *The Time Machine*, which had its first-run there. We'd all go in the family car, which was Mom's green Pontiac. Toni and I would fight over who got to sleep in the backseat," he chuckled.

Guy's love for horror movies was inflicted on Steve at a tender age. "One of my dad's all-time favorite horror movies was *The Beast with Five Fingers*. He had me watch it with him on TV one night. The part in the movie when 'the hand' plays the piano by itself scared me and my dad knew it. So, he had the recording of the piece that was played by the hand in the movie and when Mom took me upstairs to bed, he put that piece on and hid out at the top of the stairs. When we got upstairs, this hand came around the corner and scared me," Steve laughed. "He loved to practical joke like that."

Guy and Janice often invited Bob and Peggy Stevenson over to their home for dinner. "I always looked forward to going to their house to eat," said Peggy. "They were both such good cooks. Jan made the *best* lasagna, and the *greatest* Caesar salad, so one time Bob and I went to Jan and Guy's house for dinner and I said, 'Oh, I can't *wait* to have that lasagna!' and Guy said, 'We're not having Lasagna. We're having *Aglio e olio*.' I said, 'What? I'm not eating it 'til you tell me *what it is*.'

"Well, it is pasta with olive oil and garlic and to this day it is my favorite Italian dish! Guy always made that dish himself. Jan would make the salad. He had his own way of making it in a pot, and large thick cloves of garlic in it. That night he made it for us and it was wonderful.

"When Guy first got the role of Zorro, he'd bring out his whips to show us and it was fun to watch him pop and crack them for us. He was quite adept with them. He could make them crack *really loud*. Even though Guy was the center of attention, he made his guests feel important. He could talk about anything," said Peggy. "We loved going to Guy and Jan's."

Guy kept the same friends he had made when he first arrived in California, and enjoyed being lavish with them when he entertained. Sam and Estelle Harman, Peggy and Bob Stevenson, Russ and Kaye Johnson, Norman and Sally Foster, were all frequent dinner guests at his house. There were still many Sundays spent at the Weavers. "The Weavers had great barbecues on weekends for years," said Steve. "Everyone hung out there."

Near the end of the 1950s Janice and Guy met Jack Lord again in Hollywood. They hadn't seen him since New York when Jack sold Guy his car. Guy invited Jack and his wife over for dinner. "Jack didn't have children of his own," Janice recalled. "He told

Guy seeing the children made him wish he had some of his own."

A reporter asked Guy if *Zorro* has changed him. Guy said replied:

> The only thing that Zorro has really changed is my income. I'm just not used to always working all the time. But friends and talks with friends work for you whether you're rich or poor. Zorro adds to my income, but it doesn't change my basic human values.[147]

By July 1958 Guy was back at the studio filming the second season. To crank up interest for the new season Disney had Guy give interviews of a more personal nature about himself. From a fan magazine, dated September 1958:

> "I don't see my family as much as I used to but I've got a great line for my wife now; it ends all arguments because it makes her laugh. I say to her, 'Honey, don't mess around with Zorro.' Whatever we're arguing about goes right out the window."

> Guy continues with a mock scenario, when asked what he and Janice might argue about. "'Honey, where did you hide my military brush set?' I never say to her, 'Where did you put it?' It's always, 'Where did you hide it?' I start looking in the oven and in the refrigerator. She says, 'I didn't hide it. You left it on the table and I put it away.' I say, 'I don't mind your hiding it, but just tell me.' When she starts to get mad, I pull the Zorro line and she breaks up. Or, I might say to her, 'Why is this toast burned?' She'll say, 'Because you haven't bought me a new toaster.' But aside from all that, we also get along."

> "Jan and I both have a sense of humor," said Guy. "If she were a square, it would be pretty boring. She's a sweet, little darling. Write that down," he said to the reporter. "And I would be lost without her."

> Guy jokes so much in interviews, it comes as a surprise when he gets serious.

> Guy's face suddenly changed when he said, "When things are grim, we go into Grimsville." The phrase was amusing, but the hard set of Guy's jaw denied the funniness of what he said. Watching him, you knew that Guy and Jan had had a taste of "Grimsville" and it wasn't as funny as it sounded. But he didn't seem to want to talk about the hard times, the years of struggling for recognition, so we talked more about Zorro.

> "It's a two-edged sword," said Guy. "It's a mark of recognition; but, on the other hand, the area of my private living is becoming smaller and smaller. I personally prefer privacy. Now when I walk down the street, I'm aware of myself more than I ever was and I'm not sure I like this."[148]

> Guy was amazed by his widespread popularity.

> "A few months ago I returned for a visit to New York, my home town. It was my first visit since becoming ZORRO.

> "I had so looked forward to walking through Central Park as I used to. I soon discovered that wasn't so easy. It was OK as long as I kept walking,

but once I stopped it seemed kids came charging from all over, asking for autographs. The same was true of the Bronx Zoo, another New York spot I loved to visit.

"Yes, I do miss the privacy I used to have. But, I'd be crazy—and the most ungrateful person on earth—if I objected to the attention the fans give me. Without them where would I be?"[149]

As for how Zorro has affected his ego, Guy laughed. "My ego shrank when I got married. My wife is a head shrinker." He added more seriously, "You think about somebody else all the time and it does something to you. Before it was me, me, me, all the time. Now it's us, us, us."

Guy and his life seemed to be as carefree and romantic as the adventures he portrays on TV each week as a Spanish Robin Hood. He himself seemed to be more of a legend than an everyday, dollars-and-cents person.[150]

From a 1958/1959 *Zorro* Newsletter, titled "TV Hero Tells: 'What I Like About Zorro'":

How is it to be Zorro? I can't think of a better way to make a living. Getting paid for having fun is one of the best occupations I know of.

Lest you think it's all pure fun, I suppose I should tell you that it's hard work, too.

We work a five-day week on the set and it's not nine to five either. My weekends aren't entirely my own either. I usually have about three scripts to memorize. There are frequent publicity projects or personal appearances in connection with the show. Then there are guitar lessons, fencing, and even brushing up on my songs. Yes, I do get tired, but I can hardly complain even when the 'idol of the younger generation' label begins to wear heavily.

One of the roughest things I've tried to do since becoming Zorro has been to be clever when people ask me questions about our show. I'm expected to have sharp, funny answers when people say, "How did you get started in show business?" "How did you land the *Zorro* role?" and "How does it feel to be the idol of the younger generation?"

Maybe you won't be disappointed when I say I've given up trying to be clever. I just tell the truth and let it go at that.

I enjoy the whole *Zorro* show, the people I work with, the Disney Studio, my sponsors—everybody.

Zorro is easily the most important thing in my career. But the trouble with that statement is that it doesn't mean much. Not a lot of things had happened up to the point that Mr. Disney hired me.

Guy enjoyed his weekends on family outings and visiting friends. Gene Sheldon, Henry Calvin and Norman Foster, all were considered "extended family." "I remember evenings at the Calvins with my parents," said Steve, "Edna, Henry's wife, would sit me in front of the TV and give me a little bell. She said, 'If you want something just *ring*. That's what Henry does," he laughed. "She would give me a fly-swatter when I got there because she knew I liked to swat flies at his house. Henry was a rough-and-tumble guy.

He liked roughhousing. He used to swing me around and hold me upside down. I remember him being very strong. He was like a huge jolly giant."

Gene Sheldon's backyard in Tarzana was a young boy's dream backyard—one and a half acres with a pool, a cabana, a guest house, and a miniature Western town for the kids, and lots of open ground. In the same area lived Bill Walsh, producer for Walt Disney and creator of the Mickey Mouse Club, and his young wife, Noley. "They had a big ranch too that I liked a lot," said Steve. "But Gene had the greatest with the Western town he had built himself, with little houses and barns, and a little jail." Steve played with Gene's children, David, a little younger than himself, and Tracy, a year younger than Toni, both adopted. Tracy, always laughing, has her father's sense of humor. "I remember being locked up in the little jailhouse by Steve and my brother when I was only three. Steve was older—around ten. He had on his leather jacket with fringe, you know, so he didn't want any little kids around. I had to beg them to let me out!" she laughed.

"I spent the night at Guy's house when I was little and he made spaghetti for us. He asked me 'Is it as good as your dad's?' I was afraid to answer so I just said shyly, 'I don't know.' I remember he had all the Zorro swords and Zorro stuff by the fireplace."

Gene Sheldon always had magic tricks for the kids. He made a big impression on Steve. "It was Gene who introduced me to magic. He taught me my first magic trick. It was a disappearing quarter trick, where you pull the coin out of someone's ear. Magic is still a hobby of mine to this day."

Steve had one memory of Walt. "I remember riding on the train with Walt in his backyard, when he took all the kids around the hills at his home. My Dad took me to a party there. I remember lots of kids there. Uncle Walt was on the engine with his engineer's cap and all the kids were sitting on top of the cars behind him."

Steve and Toni agree that they have wonderful childhood memories.

Chapter 28

"The Navigator"

– Bob Stevenson

During the summer of 1958, Guy asked his friend, Bob Stevenson, to help him pick out a boat, to fulfill his fantasy. At that time he told an interviewer: "When I was a kid, I used to load up on the *National Geographic*. I used to dream about owning a 30' sloop and traveling in it. I read about a guy who went to Tahiti all by himself. That was my dream. Generally, the older generation laughs you out of those things. But now I'm an adult and it's legitimate. At this point, you don't laugh about it; you do it. I'm in the process of buying a boat right now. Had I known in the fifth grade that this would happen, I would have skipped school right then. I'm going to travel to Acapulco and Honolulu. Pushing a sloop across 8,000 miles of water is one of the most creative things I can think of at this moment.[151]

"I've wanted a yacht ever since my public school days, when my New York classroom window overlooked the dock where millionaire financier, J. P. Morgan's yacht was moored."[152]

Bob was an experienced sailor and knowledgeable about boats. They chose a steel hull 47-foot ketch built from World War II submarine scrap metal in Holland by a famous ship builder. The owner, a man named Oldenburg, had sailed it from the Netherlands across the Atlantic through the Panama Canal, and up the West Coast to San Pedro, California, to sell it. It was called the *Oceana*.

"When we first saw the *Oceana* it was a greenish-gray color," said Janice. "We couldn't describe it so we just called it 'Oldenberg Green.' Guy loved that boat. He was happiest when he was sailing it."

The *Oceana* was a two-masted vessel, with a Genoa jib, accommodating sleeping quarters and galley. Guy had it painted black with two thin stripes of burgundy and white on each side. A friend gave him a black flag with a large white Z sewn on it to fly at the top of the main, and whenever he sailed with his family and friends, he and Stevie hoisted the "Z flag" to wave in the breeze of the Pacific. An artist at the Disney studio gave him a painting of it.

During the latter part of 1958, and throughout 1959, Guy was intense about sailing his boat. The *Oceana* was docked at Fleitz Landing in San Pedro at 22nd Street and

The *Oceana* as it looks today. (Internet)

Miner Street, about a 40-minute drive from Guy's apartment. The Marina del Rey, which would have been closer, was only someone's dream at that time and not yet developed. Guy sailed almost every weekend when he first got the *Oceana*. Bob taught him what he needed to know and he also learned to navigate from the actor, Don Diamond (Corporal Reyes on *Zorro*), also an experienced sailor. Guy sailed with the vim, vigor, and daring of the character he portrayed. Almost every trip included his wife and son. Janice had a nanny to stay with baby Toni when they went to Guy p.a.'s and sailing. Among his guests and fellow mates were Bob and Peggy Stevenson, Don Diamond, Britt and Diane Lomond, writer Hal Smith, and Buddy Van Horn. All have fond memories either from a wonderful trip or the fact that they returned *alive*.

Peggy Stevenson was impressed by the engine. "It was a diesel engine, a Mercedes, and so stinky it made me sick, but that engine just wouldn't quit. Half the time it didn't have any gas in it. It was *incredible*. I used to say, 'You know Guy, you could sink this boat, and go down to the bottom of the channel and that engine wouldn't quit.' It was *that* good. In the immortal words of my father, 'They don't make 'em like they used to.' It was a wonderful boat built to be sturdy rather than for comfort," said Peggy, who added, "It was the most *uncomfortable* boat, especially to sleep on."

Peggy never considered herself a sailor like the rest. "Guy never told me to do anything because I told him from the start 'I'm not working on this boat. I'm just here, I'm different from Jan.' Jan worked hard on the boat, helping Guy. Guy was the captain and you *had* to follow captain's orders. Guy made that clear. Bob was the first mate, or sometimes Jan was."

Peggy loved to hate the misery on the boat. It was part of the fun of sailing with Guy, and her complaining added much humor to her stories. She recalled a trip she and Bob made with Jan and Guy and Stevie. "I was with Guy once when we went out—and suddenly it is *pea soup*. I didn't take my little Bruce with us, because I didn't trust this guy. He was daring. I mean, *he…was…daring!*" Bruce was Peggy and Bob's only child, only a one-year-old at the time.

"I left my kid with my mother-in-law, who lived with us, and I knew if anything happened to me, she could contact my parents and my kid was in good hands.

"The fog rolled in and I'll never forget that. You couldn't see five feet in front of you. There was no wind, so we couldn't put the sail up. We didn't know where we were going. Basically we were lost. So, we just stayed there," said Peggy. "Guy had no radio on the boat, nothing to communicate to shore.

"It was patchy fog, like a cloud that came up and settled right on *us*. *No one* came to help. Little Stevie was looking out and trying hard to see. Finally, a little spot opened up and Stevie shouted, 'There's shore!' So Guy headed the boat toward shore, and, of course, there was no wind, so he used the smelly engine."

Despite his fearless sailing, Peggy said, "Guy was such fun to be around and he was *so* charming. You couldn't help but love him."

Janice remembered the fear that day. "When there is fog, you just stay in one place," she commented, "and wait and *hope* no one *else* is moving around—*especially* a *big ship*. After that incident, Guy wanted Bob and Jan to take a navigation course offered in the harbor to learn to navigate by the compass in the event of fog."

"Guy didn't have time to take the course," said Janice. "Besides, he felt he didn't need it," she laughed, "so Bob and I took the class."

Guy's first trips to sea were with Bob, who taught Guy how to sail. One time while they were out, Guy and Bob answered a call for help from a very large boat trying to enter the harbor. The call was for more hands needed to bring this boat into port, so they and several other men went out to help. Meanwhile a fog came in and the Coast Guard ended up having to find *them* and bring *them* in. "I'll never forget that," said Janice. "We were waiting and waiting and so worried. It was on the news that night that the Coast Guard was looking for them. I tell you, we had a sleepless night until they found them."

The worst of Peggy's experiences on the *Oceana* came one cold and rainy morning when Guy and Bob were determined to take Janice and Peggy with them to Catalina, despite the bad weather.

"The weather was terrible," recalled Peggy. "I was afraid from the time I walked out on that old landing. Those planks and pilings look old now, but they looked old and rundown even *then*![153] We got to the boat early in the morning and it was *POURING* Rain! I said to my husband and to Guy, '*YOU* mean *YOU'RE* going to take this boat to Catalina, in *THIS RAIN* STORM?' And Guy answered, 'Course! Why *not*?'

"Jan didn't say anything, as I remember, but I went on ranting, because this was *torrential* rain! There was *NO* wind and *NO* one else in the harbor," said Peggy. "Guy was charming and lovable and Jan was such a sweet person that she let him kind of be *IT*, and *rule the roost* like an Italian from the old country. I'm Greek, so I understand Italians, because we are very similar in nature. I never saw Jan get angry, even if she didn't like a situation. She wasn't saying much, but I was doing a lot of talking, and still I couldn't talk him out of it.

"'I'm the Captain,' he would say, very upper crust, very charming. 'And you have to do what the captain says.' You loved him even though you could *kill* him," she laughed. "Now I was mad at myself for getting on this thing, but my consolation was I knew Bob wouldn't let Guy go out if it was really dangerous. So we headed for the breakwater. And it's *pouring* rain, and *freezing*, and *no*body else was sailing but us. The water was smooth as glass. A lake! Which meant Guy had to turn on that stinky engine. Jan and I had no slickers to wear and we were freezing. The men were wearing the slickers, so we went below to try to keep warm. The fumes were worse down there and I became queasy. If Jan was too, I didn't hear her complain. By now, I was so mad at the two of them I was fuming. I wondered what could those two possibly be doing on deck in such cold. I opened the hatch and yelled up, 'What are you idiots doing up there?!' I peeked out, and saw those two sitting in the rear, by the wheel, in slickers, with a bottle of scotch between them having a good time. They thought this was *Wonnn-der-ful!*" she said emphatically.

The trip to Catalina Island was long, cold, and miserable, for Peggy and Janice, by stinky motor, all the way. When they sailed out of the rain, they were finally able to go on deck. Glad to be away from the fumes of the engine, but cold and angry, Peggy suddenly spotted a fin along the side of the boat. "We have company," she told Janice. "This shark went with us all the way to Catalina, right along the side of the boat.

"We finally get to Avalon. By now we are frozen, and starving. *THEY* decided they couldn't eat on the boat. I was so pissed off, but I wasn't talking, because when I was talking I was mad." She laughs now, just thinking about it. "They tied the boat, and we got into a cab. We get out and walk into this kind of a country club. Someone said it's still there. And we looked scruffy as heck, but sailors always look scruffy. We walked in and I remember so clearly there was a big fireplace over there and we all went straight to this big fireplace. We sit down at the table by the fire and I remember, to this day, what we had for dinner: a *great* salad, steak and baked potatoes, and they had martinis. I wasn't a drinker. I drank wine at Guy's house, but I don't remember what I drank. It was the *best* meal we ever sank our teeth in. In those days, steak, baked potato and salad was the most popular thing anybody could eat. I grew up in Los Angeles and as I was growing up, it wasn't like today. The only seafood you could find in a restaurant was shrimp and filet of sole. That was it—and only on Fridays. So that was a great meal! Now we go back to the *Oceana* and try to get some sleep on these *tiny* little bunks. I mean it was miserable.

"Next morning, I expected the shark to be waiting for us, you know, to get the meal he didn't yet yesterday. But the sun was shining brightly. There were big clouds, but they were dissipating. It was windy as hell, and Guy says, 'We're going to have a wonderful sail back!'" Skeptical, but hopeful, Peggy said, "I felt better because we all had a good breakfast and because the wind dropped and that engine could be turned off.

"We started to leave. Guy is at the wheel and I was sitting on the side near him at the back of the boat, with my back to the water talking to him, because, as I said when I went on the boat, I didn't do anything, I lounged it. So I'm watching the captain giving the orders, and the First Mate and the poor scrubwoman, Jan, are back there going, 'yes sir, yes sir.' Guy and Bob were communicating with each other and it was decided it was time to put up the Genoa, which is the big and most important sail for this boat. Bob was forward and Guy back, so Bob says 'Come on, Jan! I need you to help me.' And Jan—she's such a good sport—she goes forward and helps him. And they pull the thing up *by hand*. This boat didn't have any wenches. It didn't have anything. It was all done by hand. Guy didn't believe in using anything. Bob was always saying, 'Put in some wenches on this boat, Guy!,' but he wanted things done by hand. Well, we got a lot of wind and cleared Avalon Harbor and you could tell—Guy was *right*—it *was* going to be a nice sail."

"As soon as the sail went up and in place, it caught a strong wind and made the front of the boat go up like this," she turns her hand up almost at a 90-degree angle, "and that's the way we sailed all the way home, like a *racing boat*. It went over to one side and leaned to the side and I clung to the side for my life all the way to San Pedro. Now Guy is just delirious with joy! Bob is feeling pretty good, too. Bob and Jan stayed forward and Guy and I were chatting. Now I'm braced and it's colder than hell and Guy kept saying to me. 'Isn't it wonderful! Vibrant! See that boat over there? If we pass that boat, I'm gonna jump in the water.' We passed it and I waited for him to jump, but he didn't. I just thought 'Oh well.' At one time, Guy said, 'Peggy would you give me a cigarette?' in the bag or something next to him. My hands were SO frozen I wasn't sure I could get them around the damn cigarette."

Peggy recalled how good-looking Guy was, "I adored him. I was freezing but it was fun just to watch him, with that handsome face." She pressed her cheek where Guy had a dimple. "Anyway, after a while I figured, we're not going to sink after all! The boat was *really* going. We were passing boats all around us, and Guy was waving at them, going, '*Hellooo!, Hiiii!,*' as he passed them, so proud that his was faster.

"When we did get near the harbor, I heard Bob say, 'this will be interesting.' We were coming in right at feeding time about 4:30 p.m., and the seagulls were flying around and in the water you see porpoises and all kinds of fish. I had a Dagwood sandwich I was eating and I was flipping off crust for the fish. It was nice, because I could see land and the birds were flying. I said 'Fine.' And I forgave him. You couldn't stay mad at Guy. It was easy to forgive him *anything*."

"I said to him afterward, 'You know, Guy, I adore you. *I adore you!* But if you were married to me, I'd either throw you overboard the first five minutes or I'd kill you, one of the two,' Bob said, 'And she *means* it,'" Peggy laughed.

Then, becoming serious and sentimental, Peggy said, "Guy enriched my life, because, first of all, I had a chance to meet Jan, who is the finest and most patient person I have ever met. I mean it. Guy was entertaining to be with, and I actually really liked him a lot," she said, waving off any criticism she may have implied. "He and Bob were good together. They had a lot of fun together. It's understandable that women fell apart for Guy. He was a ladies man because he was gorgeous, and a lot of men hate a man like that just because the women gush over him. But not Guy. He was a man's man, because he was intelligent, and he related well to men. *Everybody* liked Guy, men and women.

"It was a very interesting time in our lives. Bob and Guy were both in the same business. They were very close and it was a nice relationship. Guy was down to earth, very giving, and interested in others. Bob nicknamed him 'The Navigator.'"

Remembering his dad's lust for adventure at sea, Steve had to laugh remembering how his dad would get right into the role of a salty old sea captain. "Dad was 'Lord of the Sea,' 'King of the Ocean!'" said Steve. "That was his attitude when he sailed. He

would say 'Remember! On this ship, *I-I-I'm* Master.' He thought he was King Nep-
tune," he smiled. "You could tell he really enjoyed it. It was the whole scene, the cap and
the pipe. He was just in his element there. He wheeled the boat. I loved it too. It was
great. Fantastic! I *always* enjoyed going out on the boat. Sometimes Dad would let me
steer and he and Bob taught him to coil ropes. I was always the lookout. I searched for
submarines, sharks, and whales," he laughed, remembering how seriously he took his
duties.

"My first outing away from Mom was when I went to Catalina with Bob and Dad.
I loved it because they let me be one of the guys and I was learning to be a good sailor.
I felt so grown up. We were stocked with cold-cuts and these *big* rolls and I got to make
my own sandwiches."

But, back home, Janice was worried sick. The men were hours late returning. "They
had left and had taken Stevie with them," tells Peggy. "He must have been seven or
eight. Bruce and I had gone to Jan's on Hillside Drive[154] because we were to have dinner
there together when they got back. So, Jan's trying to cook dinner and they didn't come
and didn't come. She was beside herself with worry. She was sure they had gone down.
She said she could see Steve at the bottom of the channel. That happened to me two
years later. Bruce was out with Bob and Jacques Cousteau's son, Philippe. They went
out and they were late, and I had visions of Bruce at the bottom of the channel. You just
do it as a mother. That channel is not an easy channel. It's a big choppy sea. Jan was so
angry with Guy for taking him she didn't seem to be worried about *him* at the moment,"
laughed Peggy. "Just her son. Bruce went out on the top balcony where he could look
out and watch the street. Finally, after hours of waiting, Bruce says, 'I see them, I see
them!' They came in and Jan ran straight to Stevie. 'His hands are *so* dirty,' she said. She
cleaned him up and we all had a real nice dinner."

On several occasions Buddy Van Horn sailed with Guy to Catalina Island. The two
look-alikes topped off a day of spotting sharks and talking to one another over cocktails,
with a good steak dinner at the country club after they tied in. Recalling a particular day
when they had a very pleasant trip, Buddy said, "We saw sharks quite a few times. We
had good sailing that day. Guy loved that boat. Yes, it *was* authentic, all right. I knew
why he invited me most of the time," he said with a chuckle. "He needed someone to
pull that anchor. He never would get a wench on it."

The Lomonds had a boating adventure with Guy they will never forget. They can
laugh about it now because they survived, but at the time it was nothing to laugh about.
There were gale warnings and the flags were up, but Guy was going out anyway. Britt
and Diane Lomond, Hal Smith (Harold Jacob Smith), who had just won an Academy
Award for his screenplay, *The Defiant Ones* (1958), his wife, and Janice were on board as
Guy proceeded to take the challenge.

"We saw all these boats coming in as we were going out," said Janice. "The women
were begging him to go back."

"Hal had never steered a boat before," continues Diane, "and Guy asked him if he
would like to take the wheel of this large ketch, in a *storm*. And he *did*. Hal's wife became
so afraid, she panicked and started to jump overboard. 'I'm getting out of here!' she said.
'Where are you going?' someone asked, as she had one leg over the rail. 'I'm getting off this
thing!' she said. 'You can't do that,' everyone said, and we pulled her back in. Guy took
over the wheel and Jan and I went into the galley to prepare pasta, which was impossible

Guy sailing with his son, Steve, looking out over the side of the *Oceana*. (1959)
(Kathy Gregory's Personal collection; courtesy of Kathy Gregory)

because the bow was going up and down. Suddenly, out of nowhere, we looked up and a wave was coming—like a 20-ft wave—and hit us broadside. The boat leaned over until the sails touched the water, then it came up and righted itself. It took a lot of water in."

Janice recalled, "Water was on the deck and filling the cockpit. When we suggested going back, Guy reminded us that HE was the captain and we had to do what he says. He didn't say it in a mean way, but in a fun way, only he meant it. *He* was having a good time. Finally, a sail ripped and that is what it took for Guy to turn back." Even then he was unrelenting. "At that point, instead of lowering the sails and using the motor to manipulate the boat through the hairpin turns of the channel like everyone else does, Guy lowered the main sail, when he got past the breakwater, and he *sailed* in, with the one remaining back sail."

Steve added, "That engine was so strong they called it the 'iron sail,' but Dad didn't use it much, only when there wasn't a wind." Steve laughed, "He probably *should* have used it sometimes and didn't. He just wanted to show he could do it."

"All these people on shore, who had been worried about us in the storm," continued Janice, "were lined up on the dock waiting and watching. They couldn't *believe* Guy was *daring* to do this. When he got the boat into the slip, they applauded!"

Cold and exhausted, everyone walked quietly off the boat. "We went into a little café at the landing to get something hot to drink," said Janice. "After we got in, the water was like glass again," she laughed.

Diane remembers the long silent ride home in the car. "Everybody just sat very quiet going home. We were all grateful to be alive, but we were cold and numb and hungry, because we never got to have the meal Jan was preparing. When Britt and I got home, we got a call from Guy. 'We're gonna cook it over here,' he said. 'Come on over.' So everyone went to Guy's house. Britt brought a bottle of wine and we had the spaghetti dinner we were supposed to have on board."

The storm had been nothing to shrug at. The next morning on the news they were saying it was one of California's worst storms. "It was *more* dangerous than we knew," said Janice. "The paper said the waves had been of *record-breaking* proportions. Guy heard me say I had never been so frightened, and Guy said, 'Yes, but aren't you glad you did it?'"

Chapter 29

"feminine lead(s)"

— *Hollywood Reporter*

The trade papers kept readers abreast of the progress of the new show.

Hollywood Reporter, Friday, July 19, 1957
"Eugenia Paul in Zorro"
Eugenia Paul has been chosen by the Walt Disney Studios for a feminine
lead in the new TV adventure series, *Zorro,* starring Guy Williams.

The first female on the show was Eugenia Paul, introduced in the series to "suggest"
a romantic interest for Diego, which was never developed. Since the show was primarily
for kids, the writers were very careful not to turn the small fry away with what they
called "mush" by having Zorro fall in love. Eugenia Paul first appeared in Episode #2,
"Zorro Secret Passage" on October 17, 1957, as the lovely Elena, daughter of Don
Nacho Torres. A song was written about her which Diego serenades to her. Even though
the song was dubbed, Guy still had to learn every note, so it would look like he was
singing it.

Episode #17, "Sweet Face of Danger," co-starred beautiful Julie Van Zandt as
Magdelena Montez, another love interest for Diego. An article from *TV Guide* said:

> Julie van Zandt, the female lead in one of the episodes, readily admits
> that she fell victim to Guy's wavy-haired flashing smiled charm: "I've never
> had so much help from an actor. He's cooperative, gracious and unselfish.
> He's also a big tease. He kept telling me how great I was—but I couldn't
> decide whether or not he was serious."[155]

Suzanne Lloyd, who played Raquel Teledano in six episodes beginning with #24,
first tested for Rosarita in Episode 20, "Agent of the Eagle." Hers is a storybook tale of
being discovered, and making it on raw talent.
Born in Toronto, Canada, Suzanne was a fledgling actress living in Los Angeles

Suzanne Lloyd as Raquel Teledano with Guy as Diego in a scene from one of the six *Zorro* episodes in which she was featured. Suzanne was brought back two years later for the role of Isabella in a one hour *Zorro* Special, *Auld Acquaintances*. (author's personal collection)

when she tested for *Zorro*. She was acting in her first play, *Stage Door* by Moss Hart, playing the lead, Terry Randall, when the head of talent at the Walt Disney Studios saw the production at the Glendale Group Theater. He came backstage and left his card for her. She wasn't sure what to do with it, but her friends urged her to act upon it. "But I don't even have an agent," she said.

New in the business, and having had no acting lessons, Suzanne remembered what other actors she knew did. Call agents. One of the agents she called agreed to come see a few scenes from the play. "He thought I did a pretty good job, but I know I couldn't have even gotten into his office if a possible job had not been waiting. He signed me and set the appointment for the screen test for *Zorro*."

Rosarita is a character in the story who grew up with Diego. She has an essential scene in which she is very angry with Diego for appearing to be a coward and tells him he is not half the man he was when he was ten years old.

Suzanne recalled: "I read the test scene as a confrontation between Diego and her character. I believed he had behaved very badly and she was giving him a piece of her mind, and was very upset at Diego. I watched two actresses test before me and they had chosen to play the scene in a calmer way. The shot for the test was over Guy's shoulder onto the girl. It was night. There was hush over the crew that had worked hard all day. The lights felt warm on my face. I faced Guy and looked into his eyes for the first time as the director said, 'Let's go for a take.'

"What can I say, I went for it and *lit into* Diego. Guy's eyes widened suddenly with surprise, then a slow smile first tugged then pulled at the corners of his mouth. Then I was looking at a full set of white teeth. I turned up the heat a notch and then it was over. The director yelled 'Cut. Print. That's a wrap.'

"I looked at Guy, puzzled. 'What's so funny?' He told me the other two women had been so nice about the confrontation that I had surprised him, and he *liked* it! Actually, thinking back on it, Guy was in character. Diego would have charmed the woman out of her fit of pique.

"Waiting to hear was difficult. I felt as if my life was on hold. When the call came, it was not good news. I was heartbroken."

The role of Rosalita went to ingénue Sandy Livingston, but Suzanne was one of those natural talents that Disney didn't forget.

"But miracles of miracles, Disney called back and booked me for two shows playing

Guy collaborating with director Charles "Charlie" Barton during a rehearsal.
(Kathy Gregory's Personal collection; courtesy of Kathy Gregory)

Raquel Teledano. That day and the days that followed were some of the happiest of my life. I arrived at the studio at 6 a.m., reported to the set at 8 a.m. It takes longer in hair and wardrobe for period pieces.

"To my delight, I found Guy very easy to work with. He was neither caught up in his own celebrity nor in his exceptionally handsome face. He was easy to be around. He knew I was young and he was very kind to me. A gentleman—the likes of which you don't see much today. The greatest gift he gave me was to treat me like a peer and not a novice."

Norman Foster directed Suzanne in her first two episodes. "Norman was fabulous," she said. "First of all, he did not know he had been lumbered with a female that had never been in front of a camera before. He became my teacher. He was patient and taught me what a key light was and to keep my movement to a minimum in a close up, and many things about being in front of a camera. Charles Barton was the other director, but I think my best work was with Norman. He explained everything to me, every shot to me and how I would be able to move. 'You're in a long shot here, so you can move more normally. And over the shoulder you don't move your head, otherwise, you're going to be blocking Guy's light or his shot.' I was learning on the spot. You can't have better training than that. He was wonderful."

After episodes 24, "The New Commandante," and 25, "The Fox and the Coyote," four more episodes were written for Suzanne. A year later she was called back for one of the one-hour *Zorro* shows, as Isabella in "Auld Acquaintance."

When Suzanne recalled her last day of shooting the sixth episode, she said: "It broke my heart to have to say goodbye to everyone. We had become friends."

Suzanne got to see her friends again when she was invited to the wrap party at the end of the season. "I was delighted to be asked back for the party and also for the one-hour *Zorro* episode, where I got to dance with Ricardo Montalban."

The women on the show who brought romance to Zorro's life created a new audience for the show, females in their teens and 20s. Guy's popularity was reaching unprecedented proportions by appealing to a wider audience.

> The reaction of the fair sex is partly due to the fact that *Zorro* is the first TV show to combine romance and action in the dashing fiery tradition of the old Douglas Fairbanks films. Williams regards the role as a real challenge, particularly since he is following in the footsteps of Fairbanks, who starred in *The Mark of Zorro* (1920)…and Tyrone Power, who played the title role in a 1940 remake of the first Zorro movie…Walt feels he has discovered one of the great new personalities of the entertainment world, who may well become one of the big heart-throbs of modern-day Hollywood. And director Norman Foster, who handled the Crockett films and is now directing *Zorro*, declares he is amazed that other studios failed to grab Guy before Disney did.
>
> "It has opened up a whole new life for me," Williams reveals. "It's the most wonderful thing that could happen to anybody. I don't have time these days to do much but live, eat, and sleep Zorro, but I'm not complaining. One of the most important things about it is that I've convinced my five-year-old son, Stevie, that his father's worth watching. Since the series

went on the air I've been a bit bigger in his eyes, perhaps because I've been big in the eyes of the neighborhood kids. The hardest thing to get used to, though, has been the prose teenage girls pen in praise of my moustache. Then, too, I got a bit concerned when *Zorro* hit a higher rating than President Eisenhower's important missiles speech. This is really an odd reflection of the public's taste."

More than anything else, Williams recognized Walt Disney's amazing ability to know what audiences want…Considering his uncertain career as an actor prior to being picked for the part, he has made more progress than any other newcomer in television's history. Or, as he puts it, he has gone "from zero to *Zorro*."[156]

By the second season, producer Bill Anderson was getting hundreds of letters from frustrated *Zorro* fans who wanted a love interest for Zorro added to the show. Writers had to try to bridge the gap between the teenage audience and that of the younger children by introducing a love interest, without repulsing the younger set. The problem was resolved when Disney signed the twenty-three-year-old beauty, Jolene Brand, on June 11, 1958, to be the first and only woman with whom Zorro falls in love.

Jolene Brand played Anna Maria Verdugo, Zorro's love interest in the second season. (The Mary Spooner Collection, courtesy of Mary Spooner)

Jolene Brand changed her name in 1955. She was born Jolene Marie Christina Bufkin, in Los Angeles, of Spanish decent on her mother's side. She had won three beauty contests between high school and her sophomore year at Mt. San Antonio Junior College.

Jolene quit college to become a model and actress. Agent Sid Gold put her in several TV shows before she landed the enviable role in *Zorro*. Five days after she signed her contract she began filming what would be nine unforgettable episodes in the second season.

The second season started on October 9, 1958 with Zorro going to Monterrey, California where he meets the beautiful daughter of a wealthy landowner, Anna Maria Verdugo, played by Jolene Brand. In keeping with McCulley's original story and the Douglas Fairbanks movie, she falls in love with Zorro, but *not* the wimpy Diego, whom she likes only as a brother.

In Episode 42, "A Horse of Another Color," which aired October 23, 1958, Zorro rescues Anna Maria and her father from highway robbers. Anna Maria is captivated by his charm. Fearing she may never see him again, she is reassured by Zorro as he looks

Guy with Barbara Luna, Theresa, the vendor who gets into trouble for selling tamales in the pueblo. Her hot tamales song is one of fans memorable moments.
(Kathy Gregory collection; courtesy of Kathy Gregory)

right into her eyes, "I promise you this. I will never be far away from *you*." According to the *first* script, which is vaulted in the Disney archives, this is what happens next:

> (With a sweeping bow, Zorro turns to leave. Anna Maria puts out her hand, as if to keep him there.)
> ANNA MARIA: How can I thank you?
> (Zorro halts, then impulsively takes her in his arms. Anna Maria starts to resist, then surrenders to his kiss. He holds her close a moment longer.)
> ZORRO (*softly*): Querida. We will meet again.
> (He releases her and slips away into the darkness.)

The producer, Bill Anderson and Walt, were nervous. They had to be careful not to offend the audience or the network, lest Disney be reprimanded by the network, the sponsors, parents, even the kids themselves, especially young boys who don' like seeing their hero stoop to such passions.

The scene was rewritten with a less serious mood.

RETAKE:

Director's note: *This is not* Romeo and Juliet; *it's more in the mood of "Spin the Bottle."*

Final Take:

ZORRO: I promise you this. I will never be far away from *you*.
(He turns and walks away.)

ANNA MARIA frantically calls out: But, how can I *thank* you?

(Zorro stops in his tracks, looks over his shoulder, turns toward camera with a "sly smile of delight, and a twinkle of amusement" that speaks volumes, walks to Anna Maria, takes her in his arms and kisses her. A discreet camera cuts away and shows her father grinning. The television audience sees the last second of the kiss.)

ZORRO: "We will meet again."
(He quickly takes leave.)

It is one of Guy's best executed scenes. Jolene Brand remembers that the "five-second kiss" took *two hours* to film from *eight* different angles while nervous executives looked on. There were codes to follow for children's shows and for TV shows in general, or else the show would be scraped. Zorro was asked to appear somewhat *restrained* and Anna Maria *not too* zealous. Often asked about that famous kiss, Jolene Brand reiterates that she was married to producer George Schlatter—and Guy was married. It "was my most nerve-wracking experience," said Jolene. Young and inexperienced at filming love scenes, she added, "Guy was a very sweet man. He made me feel comfortable."[157]

Annette appeared on the cover of a Zorro comic book with Guy in 1959.
Dell comic No. 1037. (Author' personal collection)

The test of time proves that the limitations forced upon Jolene and Guy reinforces that old adage that "less is more." More than four decades later, the scene remains a romantic favorite among women from one generation to the next.

Jolene Brand was in a total of nine episodes—the first four were consecutive, the others recurring. Between her appearances were four episodes in which Barbara Luna and Perry Lopez were featured in the Monterrey sequence of the second season. The writers gave teenage girls and moms in the audience a thrill when Barbara Luna as Teresa, flirts with Diego and steals more than just one kiss.

It was no secret at the Disney studio that Annette Funicello, the most famous Mouseketeer, had a big crush on Guy Williams. She wrote his name repeatedly on her school notebook and hung pictures of him around her dressing room mirror. A story about her crush ran in *TV Life* magazine in 1958 titled "The Guy Who Broke My Heart." The *Zorro* set was closed to young girls at the studio, but she and a girlfriend from the Mouse Club would sneak over to watch Guy. Annette calls her crush "all-consuming" in her biography, *A Dream Is a Wish Your Heart Makes*. Annette was very dear to Walt and she was also a huge box office draw, just beginning to make movies. Walt asked her what she wanted for her sixteenth birthday and she said a script for *Zorro*.

Guy Williams was the biggest star on the lot, but Annette was a big star in her own right. Walt called Guy into his office and told him Annette wanted to be on *Zorro* as a present for her 16th birthday, and asked how he felt about it. Guy said it was fine with him and was happy about it.

Walt had some scripts written for Annette (three episodes) and before her 16th birthday—October 22, 1958—presented her with them. Annette was ecstatic and forever grateful. It was a fantasy come true.

Annette as Anita Cabrillo, in a scene from *Zorro* when he rescues her. Episode 61, 1959 filmed at Vasquez Rocks, Aqua Dolce, CA (The Mary Spooner Collection; courtesy of Mary Spooner)

The "Annette Episodes" began filming just before her birthday and aired in late February and early March 1959. She played Anita Cabrillo, a Spanish girl who arrives in Los Angeles in search of her father and stays at the De la Vega hacienda. Annette lived out the fantasy of thousands of young woman who longed to be rescued by Zorro and have a good friend in Don Diego. Also, to be envied, was her surprise "Sweet Sixteen" birthday party on the *Zorro* set which Zorro attended. Her mother had arranged it, bringing delicious Italian food spread across a long table and a large birthday cake. Guy carved a *Z* on the cake with his sword, then Annette cut the first slice with Zorro's sword.

"My weeks with Guy Williams were perfect in every way," said Annette in her book, "except that no kiss was written into the script."

Guy would give her an affectionate pat on the head, and called her "Zorina." "I blushed like a beet and my knees quaked every time Guy looked my way," she said. "Guy never embarrassed me about my crush on him, and for that I am grateful to him."[158]

Beautiful Joan Evans starred in three episodes (#71-75), in which she played the daughter of the Governor (John Litel) of California, Leonore. Joan Evans was coming from many memorable western movies, and enjoyed working for Disney and with Guy. Bob Wehling spoke highly of Miss Evans and said she was such a lady and a nice person. In the storyline, Leonore and her father are forced to stay at the de la Vega hacienda until her father's injury has healed. This is when she begins to fall for Don Diego. With fond memories and affection for Guy, Joan said, "Guy was such a flirt."[159]

Chapter 30

"Well, we're doing a South *Western"*

– Guy Williams

THE SECOND SEASON
OCTOBER 9, 1958—JULY 2, 1959

Just before filming began for the second season, the studio and ABC were beginning to have differences in their concept over who owned the Disney shows on the
network. No one except a few studio executives knew that the studio was at odds with
the network. The ABC network kept *The Mickey Mouse Club* for a fifth season, but
because of budget problems, they told Walt he would have to show reruns from the
three previous seasons. *No new* shows.

To promote *Zorro,* a new product was created to sell. The studio had Guy cut a
331/3 record of dialogue from *Zorro* episodes. Reminiscent of radio shows of the
1930s and '40s, the recordings were very similar to the first four televised episodes, in
dialogue, sound effects and music. The album is titled *The Four Adventures of Zorro,*
and, besides Guy as Zorro and Don Diego, it features Henry Calvin as Sgt. Garcia,
Jimmie Dodd(of *The Mickey Mouse Club*) as Padre Felipe, Phil Ross as Capitan
Monastario, Jan Arvan as Nacho Torres, and other voices by Dallas McKennon. Sound
effects were by Disney's inimitable Jim MacDonald and Eddie Forrest. Titles of the
four episodes are: "Presenting Señor Zorro," "Zorro Frees the Indian," "Zorro and
The Ghost," and "Zorro's Daring Rescue." Today this record album is a sought-after
item by collectors.

Well into the second season, on December 11, 1958, a whimsical episode aired
called "The Practical Joker." It featured the talented and prolific actor of movies and
television, Richard Anderson, as an old friend of Diego's named Ricardo del Amo, a
chronic practical joker. By the time he filmed *Zorro,* he had been in several movies
including, the classic fencing favorite, *Scaramouche* (1952) and the sci-fi classic, *Forbidden Planet* (1956). A few years later, Richard Anderson was most recognized from
his role as Oscar Goldman, "the Washington man," in the popular television shows
The Six Million Dollar Man and *The Bionic Woman.* Anderson, a consistently gracious

and friendly gentleman, conjured up some memories of his four consecutive episodes (49-52). "Guy was a very likable, amiable fellow," said Richard. "But I didn't have a chance to socialize with him because there wasn't *time*. We were *always* working. As Myrna Loy used to say about MGM, 'It was a sweat factory.' But I was proud and happy to be a part of it."

Richard concedes that the pace of the show was grueling. "It looked easy," he said, "but it was hard work, with a tough schedule. Everyone was tired. I loved Henry Calvin, a gentle and funny man. One day I passed him as he was taking a little break. I said, 'Hello. How ya doing?,' and he said, looking tired, 'I'm just trying to pay the mortgage.' That was all he ever said to me," laughed Richard. "The work was strenuous—jumping over walls and things, all that fencing—and the hours were long, beginning very early in the morning."

"Walt wasn't on the set," said Richard, "but I used to see Walt taking his daily constitutional around the studio. Guy was wonderful to work with. He was a very good-natured person, fun to be around, and very friendly. I used to see him driving around Beverly Hills in his Cadillac and he was always smiling. Guy was very handsome. And what a subject for him—Zorro! That role opened him up. Like Gary Cooper said, 'It's all right to be typecast, if you are typecast in the right role.' Cooper didn't mind and I didn't mind. And this was a great role that sustained Guy."

Richard's character, Ricardo del Amo, is hopelessly in love with Jolene Brand's character, Anna Maria, who is in love with Zorro.

"Jolene Brand was beautiful, a joy to work with and today she looks very much the same as she did in 1958." Jolene lives in Beverly Hills and Palm Springs and is still married to the successful film director/ producer George Schlatter, known for many award-winning shows like the very popular, influential comedy of the 1960's, *Laugh-In*.

In contrast to the first season, romance was the order of the second season, due to letters from teenage girls requesting it. Aside from Zorro's restricted romance, other characters on the show were allowed to fall in love, but the director had to very careful not to upset the young boys who were turned off by kissing and romance. In "The Runaways,"[160] Diego's servant girl wants to get married and Diego protects her from a lecherous pursuer, so she can find happiness with the one she loves. In "The Gay Caballero" (#55), handsome movie star Cesar Romero plays Diego's Uncle Estevan from Spain. In four consecutive episodes he romances the beautiful Patricia Medina,[161] playing Marguerita, daughter of a prominent don. Although these aired from January 22 to February 12, 1959, some scenes were shot on location as early as September 16, 26, and 29, 1958 at Albertson Ranch in Chatsworth.[162]

A typical "Call Sheet" for an episode:

Actors:

Guy Williams	6:00 a.m. to 6:45 p.m.
Gene Sheldon	6:00 a.m. to 10:30 a.m.
Cesar Romero	6:00 a.m. to 6:45 p.m.
George J. Lewis	6:00 a.m. to 2:20 p.m.
Patricia Medina	6:00 a.m. to 2:20 p.m.

On hand were:
  2 megaphones, 7 Tornando horses, Diego's horse, Bernardo's horse, Marguerita's horse, 3 stretch outs and one 37-passenger bus.

Stunt Doubles:
Buddy Van Horn, Phil Schumaker, Carl Pitti, Dean Smith, Lou Roberson.

Daily Variety, Friday, January 2, 1959
Williams gets 2,000 fan letters a month, with quite a few including proposals from teenagers. To these the Disney people politely reply that the actor is busy, at the same time sending a biography, which discloses that he's a married man.

Walt had plans to make *Zorro* into a full-length motion picture before the second season even began. He would make it the same way he made the full-length movie of Davy Crockett, simply and economically by splicing together segments of the TV episodes, and release it in theaters everywhere. The studio edited the first thirteen half-hour *Zorro* episodes and made a Zorro movie titled *The Sign of Zorro* for theatrical distribution here and abroad. Disney planned to use the same method with other consecutive storylines and make a total of six features.

Daily Variety, Tuesday, November 25, 1958
Disney is planning to telescope four of the telepix in which Cesar Romero guested for theatrical release abroad where the series isn't shown. Disney [who] has already done this with three other telefilms, calls them, *Sign of Zorro*, and is giving them the same theatrical release. Williams believes that in TV-pix, "You have to hit a pace between hectic and dull, pace yourself so that you don't step into a routine, because then it comes out that way."

It became evident to Disney that the TV audience was accepting the addition of women on the show. The ratings increased for the second season, taking 38.9 percent of the TV audience ThurZday evening. As a result, NBC's *Ed Wynn Show* and *Steve Canyon* were cancelled, and ratings for *December Bride* (CBS) dropped.
    Annette's episodes—"The Missing Father," "Please Believe Me," and "The Brooch"—all had scenes shot at the picturesque Vasquez Rocks,[163] now a state park. A call sheet for her first episode, #60, "The Missing Father," has Guy at Vasquez Rocks in Aqua Dulce State Park, on Wednesday, Oct 29, 1958, from 6:00 a.m. to 6:00 p.m. On Thursday, October 30, the same; and Friday, October 31, 1958, from 5:30 a.m. – 6:00 p.m. Cast and crew were back on Monday, November 3, from 5:30 a.m. to 5:45 p.m.; with stuntman, whip-expert—Carl Pitti; Stock shots with Buddy Van Horn as stuntman.[164] This first of Annette's episodes aired on February 26, 1959 and the others followed throughout March.
    Overall the episodes were filmed on the average of three to four months in advance of airtime. Some scenes were shot even more in advance depending on the location. An example of this is when a scene for "Señor China Boy" (#71), which features the highly recognized and seasoned actor, James Hong. It aired on June 25, 1959 but was filmed as

Many notables and actors including Guy can be seen in this gathering of cast and crew and executives of *Zorro* for a 1958 Christmas party on the set. (courtesy of Anna Wehling)

early as Tuesday, September 9, 1958 at the Iverson Movie Ranch. Episodes were shot out of order, and scenes out of sequence, Guy said, "If a set is in three or four pix, they do all of the shooting there, then go on to the next set. It's not too hard, once you get used to it."[165]

Episodes #63 through #65, about a crude mountain man, features Jeff York and the secondary role of a pompous and proud Spanish aristocrat was played by Jonathan Harris.[166] In the second week of January 1959, Guy was filming the sequence about the *robatos* plotting against the Governor.

The popularity of *Zorro* remained high, but Walt was losing interest, mainly because of the growing demands ABC was making. They badgered Walt for more Frontierland shows on his *Disneyland* TV show. Westerns were filling prime-time slots on all the networks. It seemed the American public couldn't get enough of them. Fed up with ABC's request for more and more and *more* Westerns, Disney and everyone involved with *Zorro* sarcastically joked, "Well, we're doing a *South*western!"

During the 1957-58 season, when Westerns were extremely popular on television, Walt's *Disneyland* show still had 39 percent of the share of the audience in its first season. Still, ABC pressured Walt for a new series. He met one day with ABC executives and program manager and offered them a new series called *The Shaggy Dog*. ABC rejected it. For Walt Disney, who had owned his own studio for years, had won Academy Awards, was known and loved around the world for his creative work, it was unbearable for him to operate under the kind of restrictions made by ABC. Their deaf ear was bad enough, but when their program manager walked out of the meeting before Walt had finished presenting his spiel, he was infuriated. He complained to his top producers and directors that ABC would reject *any* ideas for a show *other* than the "blankety-blank *westerns*." He was so angry we went straight to his storyboard and created a *movie* out of his idea of the shaggy dog, which became one of the studio's highest grossing films *ever*. The next time Walt saw ABC's program manager, he said with underlying sarcasm, "Thank you for making me *millions* of dollars." When he saw the blank look he expected, Walt enjoyed rubbing it in that they turned down the shaggy dog series, which enabled him to make a million-dollar *movie* out of it.

Walt felt ABC's control and demands for Westerns blocked the flow of his creativity. He wanted to move onto other things. He liked variety. However, he obliged the network by pumping out *The Nine Lives of Elfago Baca* (Robert Loggia), *Swamp Fox* (Leslie Neilson), *Texas John Slaughter* (Tom Tryon), and *Daniel Boone* (Fess Parker).

By 1959, there was an over-saturation of Westerns on television. Guy said, "...it's not too good for the public to be served up six westerns in one evening...But when they say you've got to worry about the quality of the Westerns, I say you've got to worry about the quality of *all* the stories on TV."[167]

Another peeve Walt had was that ABC wouldn't give him more money to film *Zorro* in color. ABC told Walt they simply could not afford to increase the budget for color. A monster of a conflict between Walt and ABC was beginning to show its head, but Guy had no idea that the mountain he was standing on was to crumble too soon.

Starting on December 23, 1958, *Zorro* cast and crew, got a 12-day vacation over Christmas and New Year's. They had been working since June, without a break.[168]

From Guy's vantage point, things still looked rosy, with no reason to feel his job was in jeopardy. He was kept busy with p.a.'s, where he *always* drew a huge crowd. "Every waking moment was filled with obligations and appearances and work," said Janice.

Chapter 31

"I'd just as soon quit it."

– Walt Disney

Walt Disney told Guy he was to once again be in the Pasadena Rose Parade by popular demand. For some reason—perhaps exhaustion from a grueling schedule, perhaps for more money—Guy asked Disney to let Buddy do the Rose Parade for him. Buddy said, "I never doubled Guy in a parade but I came close that year. Guy didn't want to do the New Year's Day Parade. He wasn't gonna do it. So they hauled me in and said, 'Would you do it?' I said 'Sure.' So they called Guy and said, 'Don't worry, Buddy will do it.' Guy said '*Really?*' Well, a little later, Guy called them back and said, 'No. I'll do it.'" Buddy chuckled softly. "I don't know. He was doing a little 'bit' with them, I guess. If I had known, if he had called me and told me not to accept it I wouldn't, but I didn't know. They just said Guy doesn't want to do it."

Guy once again was up before dawn to ride in the 1959 Rose Parade in Pasadena with other popular Western heroes of the day: Roy Rogers and Dale Evans, Hopalong Cassidy, Richard Boone (Paladin), Tom Tryon (Texas John Slaughter) and Leslie Neilsen (The Swamp Fox). Guy looked bigger than life atop a tall majestic black horse named Rex, owned by Corky Randall. Rex was used for big parades like this, because he was well behaved around crowds. His black leather tack was impressive, studded with decorative silver conchos and a silver saddle horn. The morning sun gave silver highlights to Zorro's black cape, spread over the horse's rump like a king's train. His sword flashed as he saluted the crowd, all the while giving them that incandescent smile only he had.

Asked in an interview in 1986 if he was paid extra for doing parades and personal appearances at Disneyland and elsewhere, Guy smiled and chose his words carefully. "No, uuuh," he paused. "That was *all* for Walt," he said with a little laugh. "I stopped doing the Rose Parade because I just couldn't get up at four o'clock in the morning anymore."

In January 1959 Guy went to visit his family and relatives in New York. Everyone turned out to see him including his mother's oldest half-sister, Kiki, a witty and entertaining personality. It is said that Kiki was once married to a Marquesa—who disappeared one day. "Kiki was into health foods when I met her. She was the only one in the family who ate wheat germ," said Janice. "She was the first person I knew who was into health foods and she began eating that way in the early 1930s."

Back in Hollywood after his break, Guy resumed filming. No one among the cast, crew, and directors knew Walt and ABC were disputing. It was business as usual with Guy and Britt still making some p.a.'s together.

> *Hollywood Reporter*, January 15, 1959
> *"Rambling Reporter"*
> Guy Williams and Britt Lomond will stage a *Zorro* fencing act between bouts at the Thalians Legion Stadium Paddy's Day benefit...

Meanwhile, Walt was talking to NBC, the pioneers of color television, about filming *Zorro* in color for the network. NBC told Walt they would gladly give him the extra thousands needed to film in color. Naturally, he wanted to move *Zorro* to NBC, but ABC would not let him go. If Walt could be granted ownership of his own shows, he would take *Zorro* to NBC and film it in color. But, much to his dismay, ABC held Walt to his original contract, a contract that was spawned in connection with building "The Park"—Disneyland.

Back in 1952 when Walt needed backing for his dream park, banks would not lend him money for such a risky project. They thought he was crazy, so he turned to television for financing. At that time NBC and CBS were healthy, but ABC was a lagging third so they were willing to invest $500,000 in Disneyland with a guaranteed $4.5 million loan so they could have Disney shows on their network.

Walt's first show on television, called *Disneyland*, pushed ABC's ratings to an all-time high. This investment in Disneyland gave ABC the "right of first refusal" to any other product (shows) Disney might produce for television. When Disneyland opened on July 17, 1955, ABC owned 34.5 percent of it. ABC's 1956-57 season boasted that their *Disneyland* TV show had 32% of the Share of Audience (SOA). Disneyland Park was a smashing success from the time its gates opened, so the money in escrow from ABC was never needed. The contract, however, was still in effect. Even though Walt no longer needed the money, ABC owned all of Walt's products which included *Zorro, The Mickey Mouse Club*, and the *Anthology* series. While both Walt and ABC benefited from the deal, Walt felt ABC got the most out of it. In his fourth year with ABC, Walt was slowly losing the freedom of action and control of his shows he had enjoyed during the first three years. Walt said he was now "in a straitjacket." His patience was wearing thin with the limitations put upon him.

Only Walt, a few executives who were in contact with the sponsors, and *Zorro*'s producer Bill Anderson, knew of the sparring going on that could either kill *Zorro* or revitalize it in "living" color.

As early as January 1959, Walt had an alternative plan for *Zorro* and Guy Williams. Walt had been talking for months about making a movie called *Gold*, written by Lowell Hawley, that he could put Guy Williams in, and now it was made public in the trades.

> *Hollywood Reporter*, Monday, January 12, 1959
> "Three Strike 'Gold' at Disney's"
> Guy Williams, Tom Tryon, and Robert Loggia, all under contract to the producer, have been set for lead roles in Walt Disney's *Gold* which Harry

Keller will direct for producer James Pratt. Borden Chase is scripting.

Daily Variety, Monday, January 12, 1959
"Three Disney Video Stars Go Into Film"
Three of Walt Disney's telestars—Guy (Zorro) Williams, Tom (John Slaughter) Tryon, and Robert (Elfego Baca) Loggia—will be teamed in a high-budget feature production, *Gold*. Borden Chase is screenplaying the feature from three novels by Stewart Edward White. The story of the 1849 Gold Rush, James Pratt is producing and Harry Keller will direct. It will be filmed on actual locations in California gold country and in Mexico.

Walt was losing interest in *Zorro* since he could not film it in color. It was not the subject matter, but rather the fact that it was a series. Making a TV series had never been to Walt's liking. In 1955 he had likened it to crawling into a hole.[169]

Meanwhile, ABC was planning its new fall line up with *Zorro* in it, *if* they could find a new sponsor—7-Up had pulled out because their sales weren't high enough. Walt didn't want *Zorro* back on ABC and threatened, "I'd just as soon quit it. I'd like to use Guy Williams in some features, anyway."

Walt figured since *he* did the hiring for the show, and *he* made the sets, and *he* paid the cast, and *he* created it, then he should be allowed to do what he wanted with it. He kept hoping that he could talk ABC into letting him take the show to NBC. Then he would gladly give the good news to his cast and crew about a colorful third season and everyone would be happy. Lest anyone believe the rumors or become suspicious about *Zorro* not continuing, Disney continued to book Guy for appearances and magazine interviews. One of his television appearances was on Tennessee Ernie Ford's very popular show.

Hollywood Reporter, February 5, 1959
"Ernie Sets Four Guests"
Set to appear on future Ford Shows are Guy ("Zorro") Williams on March 5, and Liberace on March 12 . . .

Hollywood Reporter, February 11, 1959
"Add Talent For Telethon"
Milton Berle, George Murphy, Gene Autry, Ward Bond, Billie Burke, Ray Bolger, Müko Tala, Rosalind Russell, Guy Williams, and Col. Dean Hess have joined the talent roster for the Stop Arthritis Telethon, Feb. 14-15 on KTTV.

On February 13, 1959,[170] Disney was filming scenes for *Zorro* episode #70, "An Affair of Honor" (airdate was May 7, 1959). Tony Russo was called back to play a highly skilled fencer named Señor Avila, who makes a living dueling for "sport." Even though Tony had spoken up to Disney about his "right-of-role" previously so he could rightfully be paid for work he should have done, they re-hired him. "I didn't sue them about my eye, so they called me back," he said, matter-of-factly. Tony Russo returned to the show with a new nose, and a new name—Tony Russel, with one L. His agent advised him to have the long tip of his nose removed to enhance his looks and get more work in Hollywood. It did both.

Production notes for the last action scene in this episode, behind the tavern, mention the doubles and stand-ins for that day:

Ramon Martinez	Stand-in for Diego
Tap Canutt	fight double – Diego
Buddy Van Horn	Dueling Double – Avila
Tap Canutt	Zorro double

Filming wrapped for *Zorro* on February 18, 1959, but no one knew it would be forever. The trades reported the completion of the season's filming of *Zorro* and a new project for Guy Williams.

> *Daily Variety*, Wednesday, February 18, 1959
> "Zorro in Hiatus"
> Seasonal lensing cycle of Walt Disney's *Zorro* teleseries winds today, to resume in July. Guy Williams, who stars in the title role, reports back to the studio next month to commence filming of *Gold*, feature in which he will star.

> *Hollywood Reporter*, Friday, February 27, 1959
> "Pictures in Preparation"
> *Gold*, March 23.

First, there was a rush to put *Zorro* on the big screen in movie theaters. The movie had been planned months before the hiatus so Gene Sheldon and Guy had already filmed the short scenes to segue one episode into the other. Now there was nothing to do, but wait.

Two movies were prepared. Clips from the first thirteen episodes with Britt Lomond made up one movie titled *The Sign of Zorro*, and the remaining twenty-six episodes of the first season about The Eagle, (Charles Korvin), made up another movie called *Zorro, The Avenger*.

With relations between Walt and ABC so unpleasant, there was surely the possibility that *Zorro* would not return for a third season. But Walt hoped to get his way and have *Zorro* return *in color* in October. To hold that audience, he would release the full-length feature in movie theaters in the summer. Also, to keep *Zorro* going, Walt had Bob Wehling script some one-hour *Zorro* shows as Specials to be aired on his anthology series, which was called *Walt Disney Presents*. Because the one-hour *Zorro* specials were in a different format from the series, he could legally show them on his anthology show, which stayed on ABC a few more years before finally moving to NBC. The scripts for two of these one-hour *Zorro* specials were finished as early as March 1959, and put aside.

Zorro, the Avenger, the movie, was scheduled as a "double-billed distribution" abroad in Japan, Holland, Denmark, France, Italy, Finland, Brazil, and Portugal and the United Kingdom—countries that had not seen the *Zorro* series on television. It was a sensation, particularly in Japan in September 1959. The United States would see this movie only on television many, many months later. Meanwhile, *The Sign of Zorro*, the movie, lay in waiting.

For a while Guy thought he might be starring in *several* movies.

Hollywood Reporter, Tuesday, February 24, 1959
"20th Near Sale to Disney of Remake Rights to Blood*"*
Twentieth Fox is close to negotiating an outright sale of remake rights to *Blood and Sand* to Walt Disney, who plans feature-filming the Blasco Ibanez classic with Guy Williams starred. Williams, of course, stars in *Zorro* TV series for Disney.

Blood and Sand, which starred Tyrone Power as a handsome Spanish bullfighter in the 1941 film version, seemed a good vehicle for Guy Williams who had followed Tyrone Power as Zorro, also for 20th Century- Fox. But, for whatever reasons, this deal never did materialize.

There was still a lot of hype about Guy Williams making some feature films for Disney and for other major studios, an option Disney had agreed to. There could not have been a better time in Guy's career to make a movie than now. He was in the place every actor dreams of: A box office draw, at the peak of his popularity. An offer came from MGM:

Hollywood Reporter, Thursday, March 5, 1959
"Rambling Reporter"
Metrogling at Disney, contractee Guy Williams is for *The Four Horsemen...*

This did not materialize either. Disney kept Guy on ice. He thought he could settle with ABC, and resume *Zorro*, but talks went into weeks and months. During this time the three highly-anticipated "Annette episodes" began airing on television: "The Missing Father" (Feb. 26, 1959), "Please Believe Me" (March 5, 1959), and "The Brooch" (March 12, 1959). Fan mail poured into Disney studios. While producers worried that the show would not return for a third season, ironically, the second season basked in its peak rating of 38.9% each evening![171]

Guy's hopes were high to star in a role on the big screen. This had been his primary goal in coming to Hollywood. A lead in a movie at the height of his popularity could establish him as a major Hollywood star and it would relieve his concern about being stereotyped. He might finally be a name and his career could be set.

Guy was quoted as saying, "As Zorro, I'm the top TV hero of millions of moppets across three continents, but just mention the name 'Guy Williams' and people immediately assume a blank, inquiring expression. Their astonished lips form the inevitable query: 'Who's Guy Williams?' I'm not complaining...Zorro, has done a lot for me." However, he continued, "...no one has been writing the name of Guy Williams with the same fervor of those making the mark of Zorro—a slashing Z -everywhere from school desk carvings to cement sidewalks."[172]

By the end of March, Guy was still not working on any of the proposed movies as Disney had said. What had looked like the beginning of new opportunities for Guy, was actually the beginning of a string of disappointments.

Hollywood Reporter, Wednesday, March 11, 1959
"Disney Cancels *Gold*"
Walt Disney yesterday canceled plans to field *Gold* following various pro-

duction problems which popped up. Film was to have rolled March 23. Announced to topline *Gold* have been Robert Loggia, Tom Tryon, and Guy Williams, a trio of Disney actors.

Months later, a writers' strike that lasted nine months, from October 1959-June 1960, is said to have shelved *Gold* indefinitely.

On Thursday, March 19, 1959, *The Hollywood Reporter* wrote an article, which reported that a "Z" was scratched on the back of Guy's yellow Cadillac. Guy had to have his car repainted. In the same paper, a week later on March 25, Guy spoke out about his current idle situation.

Playing it cool, Guy "Zorro" Williams estimates he's passed up between $25,000 and $50,000 of easy money during his current production hiatus on the Disney series. "I probably could have done from 8 to 10 guest shots. I could be making a mistake by not taking this dough, but I don't think so. I don't figure I must take everything on the basis that tomorrow may never come." Williams particularly objects to the kind of guest shots he's been offered. "Unless you stick to the things you do well, a guest shot can be harmful. If you're not a comic and you tell jokes, you're crazy. If you're Gene Sheldon, on the other hand, you can put on a funny hat and play the banjo, or if you're Henry Calvin, you can sing. The point is that you have to be a credit to the show you're on. You can't just get up and say 'here I am.' The program may be willing to pay you for this, but it isn't entertainment."

Williams was slated for Disney feature *Gold*—since canceled—during the shooting hiatus. He does feel that a good picture can help his career. "I just as soon play light comedy or drama. But to dance and tell jokes, that's not for me."

Word was trickling down to cast and crew through rumors. There was an overall assumption that there *would* be a third season, but with negotiations dragging on, no one knew if *Zorro* would see a third season or not, and there was always the risk of losing their audience if they missed one season. Hearsay about negotiations between Walt and ABC had the trade papers and the press guessing:

Daily Variety, Wednesday, March 28, 1959
Network now asserts that Disney will produce a third year of the half-hour Thursday night *Zorro* kid adventure, although it appeared as though Disney would not do the show again.

Even though Guy was on hiatus, the TV audience was watching *Zorro* every Thursday at 8 p.m., "Z night" to the fans, and fans wanted to read about their hero. Photographers from a movie/TV magazine were sent to cover Guy Williams and other macho "Heroes of TV" at a family Easter egg hunt at the home of actor Peter Graves for a April 1959 issue.[173] The celebrity heroes included John Smith *(Cimarron City)*; Jeffrey Hunter (numerous Westerns in the 1950s), his wife, Dusty, and their two sons; Peter Graves ("Pa" on *Fury*), his wife and two daughters, Kelly and Claudia; and Guy "Zorro" Williams, his wife and son, Steve. Pictured were Guy Williams and John Smith looking happy as they painted large Easter decorations from a kit equipped with a color palette, little Steve hunting for eggs by the dog house, and the little Graves' girls holding beautiful Easter baskets and stuffed Easter bunnies. A group shot was taken of everyone at a long picnic table.

While the rest of cast and crew were on hiatus for three months, Guy was making guest appearances on TV, giving interviews and doing three weeks of p.a.'s in May.[174] The studio heads kept quiet about the pending battle. The cast and crew thought they would be working again soon. Fans watched three more months of *Zorro* on TV, while Guy met many of them at personal appearances.

He was flown to Cincinnati, Ohio for the weekend of May 9 & 10, 1959 to make a personal appearance for a horse show. Many of these p.a.'s were by request from rodeos, which paid him $2,500 to ride around the area in costume. He made the circuit: Fort Smith, Arkansas; the Calgary Stampede; Madison Square Garden. Disney Productions printed ads saying that Guy "Zorro" Williams was "Available" for p.a.'s such as these, along with a picture of him in costume. Even though a small cut of this went to Walt, Guy said, "I was making more than he was *paying me* when I went on the road to do these shows." Walt Disney generously allowed Guy to get bookings on his own. Guy told friends this was where he made the most money. He said in three days doing a rodeo or a concert he made more money than he made in a year filming *Zorro*. Although this was consolation, he had to wonder, with so many movie opportunities passing him by, if this marking of time would put him out of step forever in the progression of his acting career.

By May 1959 Walt's discontent with ABC was peaking. He wanted to take his shows, *The Mickey Mouse Club* and *Zorro* off the air, and put on new ones. Roy Disney, Walt's brother and financial advisor, suggested selling their anthology series to NBC or CBS, but ABC claimed Disney had given them a seven-year exclusive commitment to the anthology series, *The Mickey Mouse Club, and Zorro*. One solution for Walt was to buy out ABC's share of Disneyland, but ABC would have none of it. ABC flaunted their claim of ownership by threatening to cancel *Zorro* if Walt persisted, but they didn't really want to let *Zorro* go. In truth, they were having sponsor problems. In a further effort to scoff at Walt, ABC said since they owned the show, they could produce it themselves without Walt.[175]

Walt countered by reminding ABC that the sets were on *his* lot and owned *by him*, not ABC, and the *cast* was under contract to *Disney*, not ABC, and they could *not* have them. Roy Disney was furious with ABC especially because they had started out as happy partners. Roy called their conduct a "breach of faith" from which he felt Walt was protected by the federal antitrust laws. They were at an impasse. Who owned *Zorro*? Walt Disney or ABC? Walt took *Zorro* away from ABC.

Daily Variety, Wednesday, May 20, 1959
"ABC Says, 'Tag Too High' So Disney Kills *Zorro*"
Walt Disney will discontinue production of his *Zorro* Series, following inability of the studio and ABC to get together on a price for the show. Disney had submitted a final price of $49,500 per episode on the series. ABC felt the tag too high, arguing that it is essentially a fringe time property, with audience potential not large enough to justify the costs. Web has had diffi-

culty in selling it and had scheduled it only on a tentative basis.

An interview with Guy in the June 1959 issue of *Liberty* magazine indicates that Guy was still given hope of making the movie *Gold* for Disney.

> Next year, Walt Disney plans to star me in a full-length movie with a gold rush background.
> So I hired a publicity agent recently, just to make sure Disney won't have to bill me as Zorro for that movie. I'm worried, like most heroes of weekly TV shows, that a starring role can submerge an individual and even block the progress of his career.

Guy tried to keep up a front for the public, but he knew litigation was coming. These eye-opening realities about the business of show business affected Guy's attitude about Hollywood. In May 1959, with no filming in sight, Guy was asked what he would do if he owned an hour of primetime on a major network. He said: "A hypothetical question, eh?" Then after two seconds he said, "I would sell the primetime and invest the money in a sure thing. My family."[176]

Chapter 32

"He took it away from the network, took it away from himself,
and certainly took it away from me!*"*

                                    – Guy Williams

Guy was told about the coming litigation when his contract with Disney was re-newed in May 1959. Scripts for the show's third season were already written and waiting on the shelf. In the meantime, Walt planned to make six one-hour *Zorro* shows and put them on the air on *Walt Disney Presents*. Even though the two companies were battling, ABC did agree to make a separate contract for *Walt Disney Presents*, which kept that show on the air, while the other shows, *Zorro* and *The Mickey Mouse Club*, could not be shown, until the court settled the case.

Guy's contract was renewed, with a salary increase, and the stipulation that he would be free to do work outside the studio—but he never did. Litigation dragged on and on, and no studio picked him up. Guy found himself on an emotional roller coaster. Walt had given him his big break and now he was taking it away. He was in limbo. In a tedious waiting game.

A New York newspaper article during this time stated that ABC was planning its fall line up and was "bouncing *You Asked For It*, and putting *Zorro* on at 7:00 p.m. *Sunday* night, a pre-*Maverick* time slot," and at the same time mentioned their lack of sponsorship.

> Shift of the Disney half-hour into the Sabbath time slot is not firm yet. It may depend on sponsor commitments, of which there are none at the moment, but if ABC-TV doesn't turn 7:00 p.m. over to *Zorro*, the Disney show may not be back for another season after all. Donna Reed, recently renewed for next season, is taking *Zorro's* present Thursday at 8 anchorage.[177]

Zorro didn't return in the fall of '59. *You Asked For It* was replaced with *Colt.45* in the 7:00 p.m. Sunday slot. Some argue today whether *Zorro* was canceled by ABC or pulled off the air by Walt, but reliable sources claim it was Walt himself who killed *Zorro*.

Bill Cotter, author of *The Wonderful World of Disney Television*, said in his book regarding the dispute, "Unable to come to terms, Disney decided to pull *Zorro* off the air, despite the high ratings the series was sure to receive if it were to return for a third season."[178] Cotter, who did extensive research in the Disney Archives, found memos between Walt Disney and ABC, and documents to back up his statement that Disney did indeed pull *Zorro* off the air.

Guy politely revealed some resentment in a statement on radio in 1983 when Ken Mayer said it was a shame that the show only lasted two years. He replied: "Well, Walt got into a little fracas with the network and, well, that's the way Walt did things—he pulled the show off the air. He took it away from the network, also took it away from *himself,* and certainly took it away *from me!*"

In a 1997 interview with producer Bill Anderson,[179] he stuck to the first version, implying that ABC could not get a sponsor. "Walt was very upset with ABC when they canceled the series," said Anderson. "It was doing so well. 7-Up, one of the sponsors, told Walt and ABC they were looking for a show with a broader audience."

Guy kept making personal appearances to maintain his popularity among the fans until there was a settlement. On June 17, 1959,[180] Guy and Britt Lomond, under contract with Disney for a total of three years, made a personal appearance in Salt Lake City, Utah at Terrace Gardens, Lagoon. *Zorro* fan Suzzie Parry was one of the lucky young fans there who saw the performance, then waited in line to get close to her handsome hero for a photo. On the 40th anniversary of what she called her "encounter" with Guy and Britt, Suzzie shared her feelings with fellow fans on the Internet.

> Lagoon is an amusement park located in Kaysville, Utah, a few miles north of Salt Lake City. Each week they brought in performers like Johnny Cash, the Everly Brothers, the Beach Boys. Zorro and the Commandante mesmerized us with their sword fights. I was 13 years old and I believe this was the first time my heart skipped a beat or two or three. After the performance, Guy sat at a small table [on stage] handing out 8x10 pictures like the one you see on the ticket. No autographs because they wanted the line to keep moving—just like today. Guy kept the Zorro costume on the entire time. At the table he had the cape off, also the hat and mask. It was hot! He smiled the whole time.
>
> I was near the end of the line on stage when I approached him. I was so nervous when he handed mine. By then, he was pretty worn out and didn't look up. But he smiled.

Suzzie Parry saved her ticket stub from 1959 that admitted her to see Zorro in person at Terrace Gardens, Lagoon in Salt Lake City Utah. (courtesy of Suzzie Parry)

I don't remember much after that. It was a three-second bliss I will never forget. This experience made me a fan forever.

I wish Britt would have stayed with Guy at the table so I could see his eyes. They were both so handsome and kind to us young terrors of the neighborhood.

Sigh of the Z, Suzzie Parry

Daily Variety, Wednesday, June 24, 1959
Guy Williams says he's amazed to find that since it was announced that *Zorro* goes off the air, letters of protest from femmes top those from small fry fans.

On Thursday, July 2, 1959, the same day the *last Zorro* episode aired on TV, Walt Disney filed suit against ABC, asking the court to invalidate his contract with the network. Walt wanted to move to NBC, which had more color-equipped stations than any other network. NBC wanted Walt Disney. Walt hoped the lawsuit would be settled soon, and *Zorro* would continue in color on NBC.

Filming did not resume for a third season. Word went out to cast and crew that *Zorro* was "canceled." Everyone at the studio was told that ABC canceled *Zorro*, but most figured Walt had pulled the plug on the show himself. It was no secret that Walt was headstrong and inclined to do something, like take the show away from ABC out of spite, to get his way. It was Guy's belief that Disney thought he could hurt ABC financially by doing this, but pulling *Zorro* off the air didn't seem to phase the network at all.

In 1986 Guy opined, "It was a question of his moving to another network. So he pulls *Zorro* off the air. He figured that'll wipe 'em out, because it's the only hit they have. But, in the meantime they were working with Warner Brothers with all those shows they came up with at that time, but nobody knew about that. So when the new season started and they were going to be without anything and without *Zorro* they came out with about *four* new shows. And that was, *I believe*, a blow to Disney. So, I sat there about three years doing nothing."[181]

Gene Sheldon and Henry Calvin remained under contract while *Zorro* was put on hold and afterward; both made two movies for Disney, *Toby Tyler* (1960) and *Babes in Toyland* (1961). Tracy Sheldon, Gene Sheldon's daughter, was told by her father that the show was pulled by Walt. She had never heard otherwise. "Gene and Henry were at the studio long enough to have heard the true story come out," said Tracy. "Studios used to cover up things more in those days. The cancellation story was probably told so many times that some people believed it themselves."

The problem was simple, related Tracy, "Disney wanted to do color. ABC said it was too much money. Disney wanted to take it to NBC, but couldn't, so he pulled it. The show was too good to be canceled. The ratings were too high."

Buddy Van Horn remembered when Walt called him to his office. "I kinda knew what it was about. We had heard that all the shows were going to go off the air except one, *The Wonderful World of Color*. He just wanted to thank me for the terrific job I'd done. He said that even though *Zorro* was the hottest show at that particular time we're going to lose it, along with *Elfago Baca*, *Swamp Fox*, and *Texas John Slaughter*. He said he was changing networks and the litigation was going to take some time so that's why he let me go.

"Disney Studio, at that time, was a great era. To me, it was like a big family. I knew so many people on the lot, and they were all so nice."

For the one-hour *Zorro* shows filmed the following year, Buddy was called back for day work for stunts, but it did not take long. Most of the long shot riding scenes and jumps used in the shows were taken from stock footage.

By July 1959 the editing of the two full feature *Zorro* movies was completed, and it was announced in the *Hollywood Reporter* (Friday, July 3, 1959) that Disney planned to begin a third movie and eventually make a total of six.[182]

On August 5, 1959, *Daily Variety* stated that 20th Century-Fox wanted Guy for a top role in the movie, *The King Must Die*.

> Even though Williams is under pact to Disney, 20th figures it may be able to buy up the actor's contract so that he could play in *King* plus being contracted by the Westwood lot. Samuel Engel will produce *King* scheduled to roll early next year and Henry Koster will direct. Production of *King* has been postponed a year because of casting difficulties.

Just when it looked like the gates of all the major Hollywood studios would open for him, Disney would not sell Guy's contract or lend him out. Each day Walt hoped the litigation would be over soon and *Zorro* could resume filming for NBC. To compensate for the waiting, Disney raised Guy's salary—again. Disney told him to just enjoy himself, sail his boat, or take a trip with his family. His wife remembered, "Guy was extremely frustrated, because of the *waiting*. It was really terrible, career-wise. He said it was the time in his career when he *should* be working. He felt it hurt his career."

The writers' strike that shelved *Gold* in October 1959, also shelved *The King Must Die* for 20th Century-Fox, forever. Reruns of *Zorro* were shown in the summer of 1959 from July to September, so fan mail was still pouring into the studio for a show that had been canceled.

For the Make-a-Wish Foundation Guy visited a dying boy with cystic fibrosis, whose wish was to meet Zorro. Here are some excerpts from a newspaper article (name unknown) about their meeting, some time in 1959. There is a picture of little David sitting on Guy's lap. Guy, wearing a suit, with white shirt and tie, holding a toy Zorro whip, is looking at the boy and smiling. Little David is wearing his Zorro costume, holding the plastic sword toy.

"Big Day in A Short Life—David Meets Hero Zorro"
By Ben Cunningham

Caption under the photo reads:
Zorro meets a fan: Admiration shines in the eyes of David Arthur Sayer, 7, as he sits in the lap of his hero, actor Guy Williams, the Zorro of television fame. David brandishes a toy sword—Zorro's trademark—in…[illegible]…of the actors visit to the boy's home Thursday. Staff photos by Chuck Sundquist

David Arthur Sayers is 7 years old, weighs 27 pounds and almost lived a lifetime. A lifetime for David will be about 10-12 years because he has cystic fibrosis, mystery killer of children. David has a hero. That hero is Zorro (actor Guy Williams) and Zorro came to his home at 821 Daisy Ave. Thursday.

The frail child who stands three feet tall was on his front porch waiting for the man he admired. His usual sad gaze now sparkled with anticipation. Only the deep, hacking cough that constantly bothers him would cause his eyes to cloud with sadness.

The sadness is shared with his 5-year-old sister, Carol, also a victim of cystic fibrosis. The studio limousine stopped in front of the white bungalow in the quiet neighborhood. Guy Williams, tall and tanned, walked slowly up the porch steps.

Little David struggled out of his chair. Their eyes met. "Hello David, I'm Zorro and I've come to visit with you and Carol," said Williams, softly.

"Hello," replied David, "won't you come inside?"

A few bystanders, many men, turned their heads. There was something in the air that caused their eyes to water.

David asked Zorro as he moved closer to him on the couch,

"Where's your costume?" asked David.

"It's in my secret room behind the door in the bedroom," said Zorro. David frowned. "Besides you wouldn't want Sgt. Garcia to arrest me, would you?"

(Sgt. Garcia is the rotund, bumbling sergeant of the guards in the television series who can't seem to capture David's hero.)

As Williams helped David into the Zorro costume he had brought from the studio, he said, "Don't put too many Z's on the furniture or we'll be in the doghouse with Mommy."

"Swish, swish, swish," said David as he made the sign of the Z on Zorro's chest with his new plastic sword. His laughter filled the room, but it was interrupted by the deep, hacking cough that always interferes with David's fun. In a few minutes the coughing stopped and David and Zorro went into the kitchen to play with the toys Zorro had brought him.

Soon it was time for David's hero to leave.

"Thank you Zorro," said little David, as he placed his thin little hand in Zorro's suntanned hand.

"Thank you, David, for calling me," said Williams, who has two children of his own.

David stood on the front porch and waved goodbye to the man he lived to meet. David, who has already lived almost a lifetime, this day had the time of his life.

Guy was occasionally sent on p.a.'s to stay in the public eye.

Daily Variety, October 8, 1959
"Who's Where"
Guy Williams to Birmingham and Charlotte for p.a.'s.

Daily Variety, October 28, 1959
"Zorro Feature in Offing as 3 Segs Sliced Together"
Walt Disney Productions reportedly is planning theatrical release of a *Zorro*

feature in the domestic market next March. The feature would consist of three half-hour *Zorro* episodes edited together to form an overall story. Disney has been following this procedure with foreign theatrical releases, but this marks the first domestic attempt. Series stars Guy Williams and is no longer on the air.

As it turned out, the full feature was not released until June 1960, and it was a compilation of primarily *five* episodes inclusive of the first thirteen. Filming segues had long ago been finished. The first of the one-hour *Zorro* specials had been scripted since March 1959, but would not begin filming for another year.

At the end of 1959 Guy said, "I would rather quit show business than spend another year like the one that just past. The fact that I could be doing another series at much more money than I'm getting doesn't bother me as much as the fact that I'm *not* working. My biggest concern is getting back to *work*."[183]

Chapter 33

"Guy Williams and family moved into a 14-room home..."
– Daily Variety

Guy bought a mansion in the Hollywood Hills, and moved his family into it on November 1, 1959. The three-story, Spanish-style mansion at 7475 Hillside Avenue became "home" for Guy and his family for the next fifteen years. Built on four levels of land cut into the hill, it had a swimming pool, maid and butlers' quarters, a sauna, a front patio used for recreation, a back patio with a fish pond and an outdoor fireplace, and a total of fifteen rooms.

The trade papers picked up on this latest happening as they closely watched for updates on the status of *Zorro*.

Daily Variety, Monday, November 2, 1959
"Just for Variety"
After seven years of apartment dwelling, Guy Williams and family moved
into a 14-room home, their first, over the weekend.

"Some friends of ours at Harper knew the owners, and had invited us to a couple of parties there, so we knew we liked the house when we heard it was for sale," said Janice.

"We *loved* the house. When we had gone there, before Guy was Zorro, we never *dreamed* we would ever own it. When the Englishman who owned it decided to move back to England, Guy heard the house was going up for sale. He had the money, so they discussed it, and he just bought it, without going through a broker."

When Guy bought the house the owner threw a big party for him and Janice in the mansion. "There were people from all over Hollywood there: Peter Lawford's mother, Lady Lawford, actress Jean Arthur, many actors and actresses, and famous writers. Aldous Huxley, author of *Brave New World*, was there and Guy was so fascinated by him. It was the first time I ever saw Guy in awe of someone. Guy let *him* talk that night. It was an evening I won't forget. Guy was a listener," she laughed.

Great thinkers, writers, and musicians were his idols. "There was a very old man who lived down the street from us on Harper Street who had either been a student of, or

The fifteen room mansion Guy bought in 1959 at 7475 Hillside Avenue,
in the Hollywood Hills. (author's photograph)

friend of, Brahms, and even though Guy was much younger, they became friends and
had a few long conversations together. Age didn't mean a lot to Guy. It was what the
person was, and had to say," said Janice.

The mansion was a dream house, comfortable and beautiful, big, yet intimate. Four
levels made up the Mediterranean-style tile roof house, with steps on the side, like those of
Diego's hacienda on the *Zorro* set, that ran up from the garage on the street level to the front
yard and patio on the second level. On the street level, a wrought iron gate led to another set
of steps that led to the front yard.

A cupola over the entranceway let light into the house. Hand painted Italian frescos
were painted in the ceiling of the dome and on walls throughout the house. Italian
marble floors in the entranceway led to a large living room, which was dominated by a
grand Steinway piano surrounded by plush sofas beside a large fireplace. Most of the
antiques came with the house. Janice bought a few more pieces after they bought it.
Standing in each corner of the living room were Guy' large speakers, and *no* TV.

Off the main hub of the entrance was the kitchen, equipped with a Sub-Zero
stainless steel refrigerator, a butler's panty between the entrance and kitchen, and a large
restaurant-style stove. When guests came, Guy liked to open the pantry and show them
his full supply of DeCecco pastas on the shelves. Outside was a brick oven for breads
and pizza, and a herb garden planted by Janice. Guy had his own wine cellar and dark
room for his photography.

The dining room was Janice's favorite room. Romantically set with a medieval flavor, it was furnished with a long banquet-style table of distressed wood, Spanish-style
chairs, and candelabrums. A painting by Stuart, who painted the famous portrait of
George Washington, graced the room. It was a grand place where family and friends
came together for unforgettable dinners.

Tall French doors on this level led to the much-lived-in patio where the family had
parties and barbeques, and spent most of their afternoons in the summertime. The pool

was behind the patio on a fourth level of the property, accessible by steps. Guy's old friend, Strother Martin, taught Steve to swim in that pool, and Guy taught Toni and Janice. Janice remembered how natural Toni took to the water. "She loved to stay underwater all the time. Then she would tug on someone to pull her up for a breath."

"I remember those squiggly lines at the bottom of the pool," said Toni. Her favorite sport was what the family called The Toni Toss. Guy would pick her up high in the air, and tossed her into the pool.

An enclosed staircase led to the bedrooms. A small chapel alcove was at the top of the staircase. The original owner, who had the house built in 1928, had a sister-in-law who was a nun and came to visit often, so he had a personal chapel built for her. An intimate place to pray, it had a kneeling rail in front of a small altar flanked by two large floor-standing candlesticks which held tall candles four inches thick.

The front bedroom on the second floor was Toni's, which she said had the best view of the city. Steve's room was across the hall, facing the back toward the pool. Guy and Janice had the master bedroom in the front, with a view of the city from French doors that opened onto a wrought iron balcony.

Buddy Van Horn and Guy practiced in Guy's front yard for their 1960 premiere of *The Sign of Zorro*. (Photos courtesy of Mr. Buddy Van Horn; photos by Jim Sullivan, Galaxy Pictures)

The butler's quarters were beside the pool area nestled in the hill among the trees and shrubs. The spa where Guy liked to take a sauna was near the pool, and next to the spa hung Guy's speed bag, which he liked to hit for exercise.

The house seemed tailor-made for Guy and Janice. "The house was beautiful and big, and it fit Guy perfectly," said Peggy Stevenson. "It was *special* to go there. Guy and Janice were perfect hosts. We had such fun over there. Guy always played music. He had classical music, but he also had some favorite LPs—like the one he liked to play from the original stage show of *My Fair Lady*, with Julie Andrews and Rex Harrison. Guy had known the young man who sang 'On the Street Where You Live' from his days in New York. So we would be talking and the music was playing -loud as always—and when that song came on Guy would yell out, 'Sing it, Michael!,'" she laughed.

Shortly after Guy moved into his house he made his fourth personal appearance at Disneyland for the Thanksgiving weekend of November 26-29, 1959, Thursday through Sunday, three parades and three stage shows daily.

> *Daily Variety*, Monday, November 30, 1959
> "Guy Williams Part Renewed at Disney"
> Guy Williams, under exclusive pact to Walt Disney for the past two years, during which he starred in the *Zorro* TV series, has been renewed for an additional one-year stanza. New terms allows Williams outside pix right, which marks one of few times Disney has allowed a contractee to work outside deals.

Litigation between Disney and ABC was dragging on with ABC trying to hold on to Disney.

> *Daily Variety*, Friday, January 29, 1960
> Tom Moore…program veepee, is also in negotiation with Disney for a return to the network next season of *Zorro*.

To Guy's great disappointment he was never lent out for a picture. Stymied by Disney's litigation, the momentum of his career was broken. Had he been able to do a lead role in a movie at a major studio, at this time, he would have become a bigger name. Instead, he landed in a category of obscure actor, because while people remembered his character, they usually did not remember his name, something Guy had always worried about.

Guy made the most of his time off enjoying his new house and sailing his boat. He entertained friends at his house for dinner, swam in his pool, read a lot, took short trips with his family; living each day doing what made him happy was the best way to bury his disappointments. But the idleness affected Guy and eventually caused his family some pain.

Guy had a paradoxical personality. He was predictable, yet unpredictable. He was daring, yet cautious. He was frugal with some things yet extravagant for others. Politically, he was a Democrat, but often-times thought like a Republican. He was very sociable, yet he enjoyed being by himself. The constants in his life were his sense of humor, his love of music, and his privacy. He didn't talk to anyone about his personal relationships, or his finances.

Janice had told the reporters what they wanted to hear when she was interviewed about her life with Zorro, but the reality of it was that it wasn't always fun and easy. A man with Guy's good looks has more temptation in one day than the average man has in a lifetime, and Guy enjoyed the attention.

One particularly upsetting time was at a dinner party Peggy Stevenson gave. A woman, dress in a fabulously expensive designer dress, danced and flirted with Guy openly, using no discretion in front of everyone, including Janice. "This woman—whom I knew," said Janice, "was determined to have Guy before the night was through. Her husband was out of town on a business trip, so she came alone, and was seducing Guy throughout dinner. Guy was loving it!"

After dinner, Peggy noticed Janice was missing. "I had seen how upset she was getting. So I started checking every room and couldn't find her. Finally I opened the front door to look outside and there was Janice, sitting on the front steps. And she said to me, 'I couldn't take it any longer.'

"I began to talk her into coming back to the party. I assured her that neither of them, this woman nor Guy, meant anything by it. I told her, 'Guy just *loves* when women *love* him. So he just *responds*! That's all! *He's going to go home with YOU!* So, just forget it.'

"Anyway, I talked her into coming back in. I'll never forget that. I'm sure that he's always had women attracted to him, and he was attracted to them. So she was always concerned about these women who would throw themselves at Guy."

Janice had poise and patience beyond most women. She graciously stepped aside into the shadows whenever Guy was in the spotlight, with no reservations. "Guy was 'the star,' and I liked it like that. That's the way it *should* be," she said.

Janice knew the swooning and gushing over Guy came with the program, and she could accept that, but it was the open flirting and seduction that took her to her limits. "*That part* was hard to deal with." she said, "*especially* when Guy enjoyed it so. I was *shocked* at how some women—and more than you would think—would throw themselves at him right in *front of me*."

A gnawing fear of losing him was always near the surface. All Hollywood wives went through it. Peggy Sheldon, Gene's wife, said, "We were all so busy trying to keep our own husbands we didn't have time to notice what was happening between other couples."[184]

Chapter 34

"Television's inactive 'Zorro' threatens to resign the business."
— *Daily Variety*

A new year rolled around, and still, no filming for Guy.

Daily Variety, Wednesday, February 3, 1960
"Out of the Tube"

The worst form of payola: That's roughly the way Guy Williams sums up his current relationship with Walt Disney Studios. With four years to go on his exclusive 7-year contract with Disney, Williams has been warming the bench for the past year or so, and is anxious to get back in the starting line up. In fact, television's inactive 'Zorro' threatens to "resign the business altogether if the option for his services for another year is picked up (in May) with nothing in view in the way of work."

"I wouldn't want to attempt to survive another year like this," Williams avers. The actor, who starred for two seasons as Disney's 'Zorro' on ABC-TV, prior to the year of lay-off-with-payoff he's currently observing, sees his predicament as a new and devastating kind of a problem for actors—where, for reasons that have nothing to do with their acting abilities, their careers are short-circuited.

There is talk of *Zorro* returning to a network niche this fall, but as of now the series is off the air altogether, neither a first-run nor re-run attraction—with the result that Williams is in temporary professional limbo.

Frequently, such predicaments as that faced by Williams arouse anything but compassion from the populace. Many see it as a simple matter where, since the party involved is handsomely paid for sitting around and twiddling his thumbs, he has no legitimate kick. This point of view has some practical merit, but it is not a very lofty thought stance. It hardly takes into consideration that almost forgotten element of artistic integrity, where pride of work becomes more important than rate of reward.

Guy used to jest about why he chose to be an actor. Before *Zorro* he thought

215

acting didn't require much work. "You hear Hollywood people say, 'I always wanted to be an actor.' But I *didn't* always want to be an actor. I got into it by the process of elimination, by avoiding the things I *didn't* want to do," he said, poking fun at himself. "Acting seemed a pleasant compromise between considerable laziness and a comfortable income."

After being in the business many years, he made a discovery about himself. "When the series ended, I went on layoff for two years. That should have been ideal. I was getting my salary and doing nothing. Only I discovered after that one encounter with the camera, that I liked acting. I wanted to be in another film, regardless of the salary. And I wanted to freelance."[185]

The next several months ahead were like a paid vacation he had never asked for. Though tied to a contract with no work, he didn't blame Disney, but he was beginning to see the inner workings of the business. Acting was fine, but the red tape in the business was the rub.

The one-hour *Zorro* scripts were being revised and by early Spring of 1960 Guy was in rehearsals. The first one, titled "El Bandido," started filming in late April and the second, "Adios El Cuchillo," in May 1960.

By the first of June, Guy was preparing for an extensive tour of as many as eleven cities in only two weeks with Buddy Van Horn for the premiere of the full feature film *The Sign of Zorro*. Buddy came over to the house on Hillside to practice the fencing routines they choreographed together, for the stage shows they would perform.

Their first stop was the world premiere on June 11, 1960 in El Paso, Texas. They boarded a plane in Los Angeles and when they arrived in Texas, throngs of fans and dignitaries were there to meet them with much fanfare. Waving from the steps of the plane on Friday, June 10 at 5:50 p.m., the handsome hero and his handsome double charmed the excited crowd.

From the *El Paso* newspaper:

"Hundreds Greet Star On Arrival: Zorro, The Fox, is Here!"

by Marjorie Graham

Early California's swashbuckling hero rode an airplane, not a horse, into International Airport Friday for the world premiere of Walt Disney's *The Sign of Zorro*, opening Saturday at the Plaza Theater.

In person, the masked raider is actor Guy Williams, who was greeted by hundreds of cheering children and fans, wearing the 1,000 "Zorro" masks distributed as the plane touched down—between rain showers.

Williams was accompanied by John Ormond of Walt Disney Studios and Buddy Van Horn, his partner in the fencing exhibitions they will give on the Plaza Theater stage Saturday.

On hand to greet them were Major Raymond Telles, who presented the handsome, six-foot actor with a certificate of honorary citizenship; Major Humberto Escobar of Juarez; W.E. Mitchell, president of Texas Consolidated Theaters, from Dallas; Rosa Valdiviez, last year's LULAC

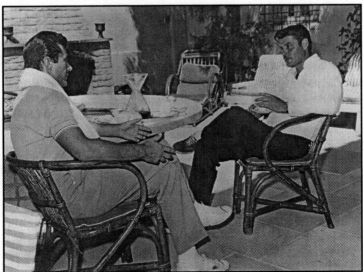

Buddy and Guy sealed off a delicious lunch served by Janice on Guy's patio after choreographing their fencing routine and discussed plans for their national tour for the 1960 premiere of *The Sign Of Zorro* (Photos courtesy of Mr. Buddy Van Horn; photos by Jim Sullivan, Galaxy Pictures)

Fiesta Queen; El Paso model, Josia Johns; and officials of local LULAC councils.

An eight-car cavalcade, arranged by A.B. Poe Motor Co., brought the Hollywood party down Montana Avenue to Hilton Hotel, where Williams met members of the press, radio and television at dinner.

Genial, easy-going Guy, who flashed across TV screens in the weekly *Zorro* series for two years, then made the movie, fits the picture of Don Diego riding in defense of this neighbors and damsels in distress.

His sword fighting will be demonstrated at 2:45 p.m., 4:50 and 8:40 p.m. Saturday only when he and Van Horn exhibited [sic] the technique of staging a duel without getting their ears sliced off.

"Actually, we plan every motion of a fight, going as far as putting it on paper," Williams said. "We'll show how it's done."

"Doing this has been a great experience, but Zorro is a role I both love and hate,"[186] he admitted. "It isn't what I prepared for as an actor and yet it goes on and on. We're making six one-hour shows for TV this fall, and no telling where that will lead.[187]

"Maybe they'll send us to Moscow. I don't know whether it'll be in a DC-7 or a U-2," he grinned.

By now, playing the flamboyant champion of wronged early Californians comes as second nature.

The witty Williams said the popular conception that an actor's life is easy led him to become one.

"I'm getting my retribution—I've never worked so hard in my life!"

"We are very pleased. El Paso was chosen for the premiere because the Plaza is the second largest theater in Texas and because we know how strong Latin Americans feel about the figure of Zorro," he said.

Posters around the city billed Guy Williams as "The Fabulous Zorro," and announced that the first 200 persons attending Saturday's world premiere would receive free personally autographed pictures of Guy Williams. Guy's performances were between screenings of *The Sign of Zorro*, at 1:15 p.m., 3:20 p.m., 5:25 p.m., 7:10 p.m., and 9:15 p.m., Saturday only. Doors opened at 12:45 p.m. Admission was 75c for Adults, and 35c for Children.

Zorro Appears Here in World Premiere Movie, *El Paso*, June 1960

by Barbara Causey

In real life, Zorro is Guy Williams, a tall, handsome fellow with a debonair personality. Last night he and Buddy Van Horn, his rival in a duel on the Plaza stage were guests at a dinner for press, TV and radio people. Children who didn't make it to the airport also came to the Hilton Hotel to get a special Zorro handshake. He greeted them with a big smile and displayed his versatility by discussing baseball as well as fencing with the young fry.

> Mr. Williams is charming to youngsters and ladies alike. While the kids are getting an autographed photo, ladies get their hands kissed.

One newspaper article that featured Buddy Van Horn, along with a photo of him, said:

> Whenever the feared Zorro crosses swords with the "enemy" on motion picture and television screens, his skillful opponent invariable is a tall, dark, and handsome Hollywood actor named Buddy Van Horn.

During their promotional tour, Guy and Buddy sometimes shared the bill with other TV celebrities also making personal appearances to promote their shows. Buddy remembers following Jock Mahoney, who was playing Yancy Dehringer on TV at the time. Mahoney had a magnetic personality that fascinated Buddy. "They loved Jock," he said. "He had a gift for gab and he would smother them with his cleverness and dialogue.

"When Guy appeared, the crowd went *wild*, with cheers and yells. Guy would go out on stage in his costume without his mask and hat, and tell them about Zorro and the studio, and how we choreographed the fencing routines for the show. Then after he talked for a while he would call me out and we'd show them how we'd put a fencing routine together. We'd block the fight step-by-step. Guy did most of the dialogue. After we did that, Guy asked the audience, 'Would you like to see how it looks when we're *really* doing it for the show?' And, of course, they would all shout 'YES!' Then we'd do the routine—non-stop, and Guy would at the end disarm me. When the show was over, we were mobbed."

There was total hysteria. Excitement and noise. Women, teens, and children rushed the stage for their autograph or to try to touch them. Guy and Buddy handed out pictures and gave autographs. Although Buddy had been in movies, and is in every episode on *Zorro* (as a stuntman, an extra, and *featured* extra), he was not accustomed to the limelight. His name never appeared in the credits of *Zorro*. Now, he too, was being swamped by fans.

"There were some *strange* autographs," he said, as he imitated women pulling their blouse off the shoulder. Some offered their arm or back or exposed their chest. "*'Sign this! Put a Z here!* they yelled. *Weird, Crazy* stuff!" he laughed, shaking his head. "Wild women of *all* ages. *Zorro* was *not* just a kid's show. It was *everything*."

Rita Ractliffe was one of the thousands of young teens at the Plaza Theatre in El Paso that day with her mother to see her hero perform in person, and to see the movie. She brought with her a bola tie she had made herself out of a beautiful polished rock from her collection to give to Guy personally after the performance. She held her gift with nervous anticipation. Rita shares her memories of that unforgettable day:

> The day that Mr. Williams was to appear, I finished making for him a bola tie out of agate (being a rock hound at the time). I was thirteen and madly in love with Zorro since 1958. I went to the theatre and saw the stunt performance by Buddy Van Horn and Mr. Williams, then the movie. Unfortunately, after the show, the press and bigwigs whisked him off to some func-

tion and those of us who had so patiently waited to see him were given the short shrift. I left the gift at the box office to be given to Mr. Williams and went home with my mom, sad that I had missed my one great chance to meet him. When I got home, my father told me that some man had called for me while I was out. "Somebody named... ummmm...Guy...Guy...Williams?"

At first, I thought my father was teasing me, making fun of my "crush," which hurt even more, but he did convince me that Mr. Williams had indeed called and that he told Guy that I would be home later and to call back.

By now, I was devastated—to have been so close and missed out *twice!* I went to my room in a bleak state of mind.

Later that evening, around 10 p.m., the phone rang. My mom called me to the phone and it was Guy! I couldn't believe it! The man actually took the time out of his busy schedule to call me back. He thanked me for the tie. He said he really enjoyed it and appreciated the effort that went into it. We chatted for about 15 minutes and I was in *outer space.* I know that for me, the man gained incredible stature for his simple kindness to a small-town star-struck kid. I've never forgotten it, nor him. My only regret was that in moving to Los Angeles and becoming involved in the movie/TV industry, that I was never able to see him again and let him know how much it was appreciated.

In Hollywood, after the El Paso premiere, several Los Angeles newspapers announced the release. About the film, the *Hollywood Citizen News*, dated June 23, 1960, wrote:

The Sign of Zorro, flying the Walt Disney banner, and screening as of yesterday at the Hawaii, Warner Downtown, and several other houses, and Pacific Drive-ins.

The story comes to an exciting climax with all "hands" happy over the final results of Zorro's daring escapades. Henry Calvin, Gene Sheldon, Romney Brent, and Britt Lomond are prominent in support of Williams. The film is attractively mounted, and some contributions, such as the music, costumes and set designs, are outstanding. Norman and Lewis Foster[188] co-directed this film under William Anderson's supervision as producer, with four writers contributing to the screenplay.

One of the eleven-city stops for Guy and Buddy was Memphis, Tennessee, not far from Janice's small hometown of Bolivar. The Memphis papers ran promotions for the movie and articles on Guy. Since Janice was not in town with her famous husband, the Memphis journalists interviewed Janice's sister, Mrs. Stewart.

"Guy Williams Became Zorro By Falling off A Horse."

Zorro: He will appear on stage at the Malco [Theatre] Friday in connection with the opening of *The Sign of Zorro.* He is married to the former Ruby Janice Cooper of Bolivar, Tenn.

"...they call her Jan out there, but we always called her Ruby," said Mrs. Stewart.

Ruby won't be along when Zorro dashes into Memphis Friday but she and the children, Stevie, 7, and, Toni, 2, are expected for a visit later this summer and Jan's mother and father, Mr. and Mrs. U. T. Cooper of Bolivar, will be in town to see their famous son-in-law. "Mother gets so excited in watching *Zorro* she can hardly stand it," Mrs. Stewart says, "and Daddy won't look at anything else."

Mrs. Stewart's children are as yet, however, unimpressed with their Uncle Guy. They are both girls ages 3 and 18 mos.

All the locals in Bolivar anticipated the coming public appearance of Ruby Cooper's famous husband. Whenever Janice was in Bolivar, the local newspapers came out to the house to interview her. Sheriff Cooper and his wife were somewhat celebrities, often approached by friendly neighbors to talk *Zorro*.

Buddy and Guy were traveling with publicity man John Ormond during the two weeks of hopping from one city to the other. Guy knew *Zorro* was over and he wanted to go out in style, on Walt' account. Guy was having a good time on the plane between cities, and ordered drinks for everyone on the plane, "compliments of Walt Disney!"

"It gave him some satisfaction to do things like that," said Buddy. Guy ordered caviar, shrimp and champagne every day. When they got to Florida Guy rented the largest hotel suite. Buddy and Guy went out on a fishing boat and Buddy caught a large fish. Because Walt was tight, Guy got a kick out of making Walt spend money. "He ordered the kitchen staff to cook this huge fish and serve it to us in our suite. It cost several hundred dollars. We ate mahi-mahi into the night."

When Guy returned from his tour for rest and relaxation, the writers' strike was over, but there was no further talk of producing the movie *Gold*, which Guy had so hoped for.

Guy had so little privacy now he began to avoid going out in public as much as possible. Slowly over the next ten years he would hardly ever go to the supermarket or clothing stores. He went to school functions for the children when he wasn't working. "We didn't go to movies much," said Janice, "because Guy didn't like lines. If we could arrange to go in early, he'd go, but he would not wait in a line. He didn't go to restaurants much, but that was because he knew we could cook the dishes he wanted better at home."

Guy's idleness and despair over not working made him desperate for diversion. Janice had no clue it was coming when Guy told her he needed a break from family life. Their relationship had been good and Guy gave no signs of wanting to be with anyone else. "One day," said Janice, "he just packed a suitcase of clothes and said he needed to get away. He said he wanted his independence, and he moved out when Toni was two years old. I used to try not to cry in front of the children, but sometimes I couldn't help it, and later I often worried about the effect that might have on Toni."

Janice had worried that it was only a matter of time for him to fall victim to his fame. By late June 1960 there was a buzz around Hollywood that the Williamses had separated. "It was very strange," said Janice. "He was like a little boy, wanting to be naughty, but not wanting to totally leave home. He'd spend nights out, but he came home during the day. He was still home a lot even though we were separated."

Guy and Janice had a way of life that never let outsiders have an inkling that something was wrong on the homefront. Guy seemed to be most comfortable and happy at home with his family, so he succeeded in giving no indication that he was seeing someone else. "When he was home every day, he was heavily romancing me," said Janice, "so, I just thought he wanted to get away for a while. In those days I wouldn't have wanted to know if there was someone else, so I would avoid knowing. It could have been looking me in the face and I would not have looked at it."

But there *was* someone else and some of their friends knew it. "It was a terribly awkward time for me and Bob," recalled Peggy Stevenson, "because *both* of them were our friends. What do you do when two of your best friends split up? It's uncomfortable and confusing. I was so angry at Guy. He was acting ridiculous. I used to say, 'He needs a *harem!*' He wanted to have his family, because he had a lot of love for them, but he also wanted to have his little fling. My attitude to that is, 'You know, that isn't the real world, bub!'"

During the months that Guy and Janice were separated—but usually living together—Bob Stevenson hung out with Guy, and Peggy hung out with Janice. "I was Guy's friend, too, but I was so mad at him, I decided I would not get near him for fear I would punch his lights out. One day I told Bob, 'You go see Guy and keep him company, because I have something to take care of with Jan'.

"I couldn't punch him so I decided to hurt him where it hurts the most—the pocketbook. I called Jan and said, 'Let's go shopping!' She needed some new clothes anyway. 'Get your credit cards and lets go!' I said. She said, 'I don't have any credit cards.'"

"Well," said Peggy, "Do you have a check book?!"

"Yes."

"Well, *Bring it!*" commanded Peggy.

"I asked Jan to meet me at my house, because, even though, *technically*, Guy was out of the house, he was over there every day. He would have seen me picking her up and would have gotten suspicious.

"I took her to Beverly Hills. Our first stop was Saks. Then we went to Magnin's. Then she bought some shoes from Delmans, which is where Neiman is now. She spent one whole day of *buying*. And we didn't go to the bargain places either," she said pointedly. "I took her to the areas of the couturier shops. Jan spent over $3,000 that day! And in those days, $3,000 bought a *whole lot*. I mean, it was a lot of money. She bought a gorgeous suit with a big fur collar, and we ended up in the lingerie department for a gorgeous negligee and ensemble. I guess the salesgirl had heard us talking, because she said something to the effect of: 'You're buying this? I don't think you're through with him yet.'

"When we got home, I said to Jan, 'Now, if he asks you about these checks you made out for all these clothes, you just blame it on Peggy. Tell him not to yell at you, because *you* had *nothing* to say about this. You just tell him *Peggy* did it, and I'll take care of him!' Well, he n*ever* said a word to me about it," she laughed.

Janice remembered Guy's curious timing. "Guy had leased an apartment somewhere for six months, and six months to the day, he was back!"

"We were all relieved when they got back together," said Peggy.

Daily Variety, November 11, 1960
Happy to report the Guy Williamses have patched it up, reconciled.

"Jan would have taken him back under any condition," said Peggy.

Janice found out some time later that for Guy, it was a fling. Bob Stevenson had met the woman. Peggy only knew she was a flight attendant. Her name was never mentioned, and Janice didn't want to know any more than that. "I was just glad he was back," said Janice.

During these six months of Guy's semi-separation, he filmed the remainder of the one-hour *Zorro* specials, "The Postponed Wedding," in late summer, and "Auld Acquaintance," completed in November 1960. There were to be six, but no more were filmed after these. On October 30, 1960, the first of these one-hour *Zorro* shows, "El Bandido," aired on the *Walt Disney Presents* anthology series. It featured Gilbert Roland and Rita Moreno, with Vito Scotti. Walt introduced the special at the beginning of the show, telling about the legend of Zorro and some Spanish California history. Then, taking Zorro's sword in hand, he playfully cuts a Z to the camera—unable to suppress a childlike gleeful grin.

The second one-hour *Zorro*, "Adios, El Cuchillo" (a continuum of the first), followed on November 6, 1960. All of the one-hour specials included Henry Calvin, Gene Sheldon and George J. Lewis. Guy's desire to resign himself from the role, and move on, shows through to his character at some points in these shows, where he hardly seems to be giving Diego or Zorro anything other than a relaxed Guy Williams.

The third one-hour *Zorro*, "The Postponed Wedding," featured a mature looking Annette Funicello and Mark Damon (previously in "The Iron Box," Ep. #54), and Carlos Romero (previously in the Monterey series, Episode #40-44, as Anna Maria's boyfriend). It aired January 1, 1961.

The fourth one-hour *Zorro* was "Auld Acquaintance," which featured Ricardo Montalban, Ross Martin, and Suzanne Lloyd (previously in a string of episodes, #24-30, as the new commandante's wife). It aired April 2, 1961.

On November 11-13, 1960 Guy made another appearance as Zorro at Disneyland. With *The Sign of Zorro* playing in theaters across the nation, the original cast was in demand again for personal appearances. Anna Wehlings, wife of prolific writer Bob Wehling, remembers the fun. "I remember going to Disneyland with Bob when they had the whole cast of *Zorro* come back to perform little skits and things. We all stayed at the Disneyland Hotel and in the evening we would get together and party. They were all so fun and wonderful. I used to see Guy there. I loved Guy, and I loved Britt Lomond. Oh! The one I really loved was Buddy Van Horn. He was fantastic. Gene, Bob's best friend, was an absolute doll. Henry Calvin was a dear, and George Lewis and his wife were such lovely people. Every year until George died, I got a Christmas card from them from Rancho Santa Fe. He was a gorgeous man, so down to earth and nice."

This was Guy's fifth and final public appearance at Disneyland, so he and Henry intervened in taking charge of the party at The Disneyland Hotel for the *Zorro* cast members, Disney staff, and their spouses. Disneyland's public relations man, Card Walker, was accustomed to planning these parties, but always on a minimal budget. He looked a little worried when he saw the caviar and champagne and grandiose spread of food. Walker's mother came up to him, and said, "Now *this* is the way to throw a party!"

Bob Wehling wrote most of the *Zorro* scripts along with his best friend Lowell Hawley.

Toward the end of 1960 Walt and ABC finally reached a settlement. Leonard Goldenson, in his autobiography, *Beating the Odds*, tells what happened after seven years of partnership with the Disneys:

> At the end of the seventh year, Walt and Roy came to me and said they'd had an offer from NBC—really from RCA[189]—to go into color with *Walt Disney's Wonderful World of Color*. RCA was willing to pay a phenomenal sum. For RCA it was a way to sell color television sets. They owned all the patents and got a royalty on every color set sold in the world. The Disneys offered us the opportunity to match RCA's deal.
>
> I said that we couldn't afford to do that. We just didn't have the kind of money that would allow us to bid against RCA. Furthermore, I thought it was time we reevaluated our whole relationship with Disney. The only reason we'd taken a position in Disneyland was to get them into television, but the Disneys had turned out to be terrible business partners. Disneyland had become enormously successful, but Disney kept plowing his profits back into park expansion. I feared that it would be a very long time before we started seeing any return on our original $500,000 investment.

Since ABC needed cash to finance its own growth, we made a $17 million deal to sell back our share of Disneyland, and we parted company. We took 7.5 million in cash and Disneyland's concession profits for five more years. I felt they would bring in about 2.5 million a year and I wasn't far from wrong.[190]

Now that Disney had full ownership of Disneyland and his TV products, he immediately went to NBC where he began *Walt Disney's Wonderful World of Color* in the 1961-62 season, Sunday nights at 7:30 p.m. But *Zorro* did not return. Bill Cotter explains, "The plan was to bring *Zorro* back as a weekly series once the ownership of the series was clear, but by the time the legal dust had settled, Walt had realized that the time for Zorro had passed." Furthermore, "Walt decided that the public had moved onto other fads and there would be no point in resurrecting *Zorro*."[191]

Now that Walt had no restrictions on what he could produce for TV, he wanted to move onto new shows and ideas. It was the end of a golden era for those involved with *Zorro*.

Guy had more than six months remaining before his contract expired and Walt made good his word to star Guy in a feature film. Walt had some money tied up in England so he decided to make a movie (for TV) there in order to get his money out. He chose to do a remake of Mark Twain's classic, *The Prince and The Pauper*, in color, with Guy as the swashbuckling Sir Miles Hendon, the same role Errol Flynn played in the 1937 black-and-white version for Warner Brothers.

Guy masks his true feelings with a little humor in an article by Bob Thomas, titled "He Is Zorro No More."

> We made two seasons of the series then Walt Disney got mad over his treatment at the hands of ABC. The suit was in court for 2 years and, meanwhile, I wasn't allowed to do anything. I felt like a kept man; all I did was collect my ever increasing salary.
>
> During that time I hadn't a chance to prove I could do anything else besides *Zorro*, but I was fortunate in being able to make *The Prince and the Pauper* for Disney.[192]

From *TV Guide:*
> May 6-12, 1961: *The Prince & The Pauper* is now being shot in England as a 3-part TV show to be televised next season on the NBC series *Walt Disney's Wonderful World of Color*, Guy (Zorro) Williams stars.

Sir Miles Hendon befriends young Prince Edward of England after he has traded places with a pauper boy. Directed by Don Chaffey, it was filmed at Shepperton Studios outside of London. Guy fit solidly into the role of a swashbuckler and protector as he, Sir Miles, unwittingly becomes the Prince/Pauper boy's "champion," defending him from adversities. Coached for fencing by England's Rupert Evans, Guy did his fencing scenes himself and his own riding, except for long shots. The beard and mustache were applied each day to a clean-shaven Guy, who embraced the opportunity to untap his acting abilities in a role other than Zorro and proved he could do it well.

Anna and Bob Wehling had a wonderful reunion with Guy while they were vacationing in London at the time of shooting. "Disney sent a car from Shepperton Studio

Guy as Sir Miles Hendon in Disney's remake of *The Prince and the Pauper*, 1962.
Errol Flynn played the role in Warner Brother's 1937 version.
(Kathy Gregory personal collection, courtesy of Kathy Gregory)

to our hotel in London to pick us up," recalled Anna. "It was quite a drive and they took us to the set to see Guy. All our friends had warned us that it would rain, but the threat of rain was nowhere. It was a beautiful, sunshiny day. We got there as the entire production had shut down for tea, and we had tea with Guy. When he was finished working, Guy insisted on taking us to get a drink, but we found out the pubs were not opened yet, so Guy went to his trailer and found a bottle of Campari that we shared. He and Bob talked and laughed, reminiscing about *Zorro*, and we had a wonderful visit. They got along really well, just as Bob did with Gene and Henry."

Janice and the children stayed in Hollywood during the six weeks Guy was in England filming. Little Toni had a very special Disney-themed birthday party given for her at the home of Noley Walsh, the wife of Disney's producer, Bill Walsh. "I can remember that birthday so well," Toni reminisced. "It was my third, and this big cake had all my favorite Disney characters on it! I can still smell the sugar! I remember blowing the candles out, and the blue dress I had on. My mom painted a picture of me at the cake that day." Peggy Sheldon and her children, Tracy and David, were there, among the many guests.

Meanwhile, Guy did some sightseeing in England, while also doing publicity shots. He found Hyde Park stimulating, because people could get on their "soap box" there,

Guy and Australian actor, Sean Scully, the Prince, chat while waiting for filming to resume. (author's collection)

and give political speeches or express their opinions and radical beliefs. He shopped for gifts to bring home and bought a beautiful set of Wedgewood China edged with a black and gold Grecian motif for Janice.

The Prince and the Pauper was first seen on television in three parts on *The Wonderful World of Disney* on March 11, 1962, March 18, 1962, and March 25, 1962.[193] It received the *TV Guide* award for "The Best Dramatic Series of 1962." That same year it was released theatrically overseas.

Guy enjoyed the departure from Zorro and was looking forward to more of the same. Lou Debney, production coordinator for *Zorro*, said, "Guy was happy to get in and happy to get out."[194]

Describing his final days at Disney, Guy said simply: "I went over to do *The Prince and the Pauper* in London for him, and that was the end of it."

Before filming *The Prince and the Pauper*, Guy did research, visited Hampton Court where
much of the movie is filmed, and other famous sites. (Left, author's personal collection;
Right top and bottom, the Mary Spooner collection; courtesy of Mary Spooner)

Chapter 35

"Here we are doing what we like best."
– Guy Williams

As soon as his contract with Disney expired in May 1961, Guy signed with MGM, who had been waiting months for him to be available to make a movie called *Damon and Pythias* in Italy. Samuel Marx, the associate producer of the film, coincidentally had been at MGM when Guy was there in 1946, but it was during the making of *Damon and Pythias* that they became friends. Production notices about the movie had been in the trades for months.

> *Daily Variety*, November 11, 1960
> "Marx, Jaffe co-producing *Damon—Pythias* for MGM"
>   Writer-producer Samuel Marx and Sam Jaffe will co-produce *Damon and Pythias*, original screen treatment by Marx and novelist Barry Oringer, in Italy, next spring, with MGM releasing, it is announced following Marx's return from New York meetings with MGM president Joe Vogel. Jaffe now is in London to set up headquarters and goes to Italy next week to arrange studio space. Marx says high-salaried stars will be bypassed in casting title roles.

Then there were the inevitable re-writes:

> *Variety*, February 27, 1961
> "MacDougal To Revise Script…"
>   Sam Jaffe, producer of *Damon and Pythias*, MGM release, has set British scribe Roger MacDougal to make revisions on script. Two leads are yet to be set and a director will be inked from Hollywood. Picture is to be shot in Rome, starting not later than July.[195]

In the summer of 1961, Guy was given the script to read with the option of playing either role. He chose Damon, a street-smart rogue and ruffian, a man of action who lives among thieves in Syracuse. Pythias, a Pythagorean nobleman from the Olympian Hall of Athens, is a nonviolent religious intellectual, married with a child on the way.

Guy Williams as Damon in *Damon and Pythias*, 1963
(Kathy Gregory Personal collection, courtesy of Kathy Gregory)

He sets out to find Arcanus, one of their philosophers in hiding in Syracuse, where their religion was forbidden.

By June the producers had found their director.

> *Hollywood Reporter*, June 15, 1961
> "Curtis Bernhardt to Direct MGM *Damon and Pythias*—Rome."
> Producer Sam Jaffe has signed Curtis Bernhardt to direct *Damon and Pythias*, to be filmed here for MGM release. Shooting gets underway at Cinecitta Studios August 22.

Guy put the *Oceana* up for sale when he realized he did not have the time to sail and maintain her. Janice remembers when the neglect became apparent. "My sister and her husband had flown into Los Angeles to visit me while Guy was filming in England. I picked them up at the airport and they wanted to go see the boat. It was a good thing I took them because water was leaking into the ballast." When Guy knew he would be making two movies in Europe, he sold her. His good friend and fellow sailor Bob Stevenson handled the sale for him.

By September of 1961, Guy and his family prepared to fly to Italy. Steve remembers, "I had just enrolled in the fourth grade at St. Ambrose Elementary School on Fairfax Avenue in Hollywood when I was pulled out of school to make the trip.

"All of us loved Italy. I liked going to breakfast by myself sometimes. That was a big deal for me. I felt grown up. I didn't know much Italian, but enough to get my *caffe latte* in the coffee shop," he laughed. "I didn't learn as much Italian in Italy as I did from my grandmother when she would come to visit us. She'd speak nothing but Italian to me so I would learn it. She taught me Latin on a blackboard and it was enough to give me the foundations that helped me later in high school."

During filming Guy and his family stayed at the Residence Palace hotel in Rome, a favorite among the Hollywood set, for four months. "We had a fabulous view of the ancient city," said Janice. "It was an exciting time to be in Rome because Twentieth Century-Fox was there filming *Cleopatra* with Elizabeth Taylor and Richard Burton. Hollywood actors and production crews filled the major hotels. Italy loved American movie stars, so the red carpet was always out."

Academy Award winner Martin Balsam stayed at the Residence Palace[196] and Guy liked to talk to him for hours at a time. Guy also met Art Silver of Warner Brothers Studios at the Residence. Art's son, Steve Silver, recalls the chance meeting that was the beginning of a lifelong friendship. "I met Guy in Italy when I was 19 in 1962, and he was doing a movie Curt Bernhardt was directing called *Damon and Pythias*. My father was a producer at Warner Brothers for 35 years, but he was not in Rome on business. My family was just vacationing at the time and we stepped onto the elevator at the Residence Palace with Guy and Janice and struck up a conversation. I knew who Guy was because I had seen *Zorro*, but I was older than the kids who watched it so I wasn't impressed by him simply because he was Zorro. I had grown up around famous movie stars all the time—at the studio and at my home. I liked Guy because he was fun and because he was so nice."

Janice recalled an embarrassing moment for Guy when he first arrived on the set in the cold of winter. He was a bit nervous and the producer had been introducing him to everyone. "He turned to Curtis Bernhardt, and said, 'And who are you? I didn't get your name.' There was laughter and someone said, "You'd *better* know him. He's your *director!* Curt teased, and said, 'Well, I got *yours.*'"

L.A. Mirror, November 8, 1961
"Lens Views Rome Grotto"
ROME— The Grotte di Salone, the huge underground caves just outside Rome which provided stone to build the coliseum 80 years after the birth of Christ, are featured in MGM's *Damon and Pythias* now being directed by Curtis Bernhardt with Guy Williams and Don Burnett starred. Centuries of quarrying have turned the caves into a vast natural studio. Bernhardt has built four sets there to film the underground dens of the beggars and robbers who are an integral part of the story.

It was during this film that Guy met Lawrence Montaigne, an actor who played a flutist and friend to Damon. Lawrence had been living in Europe a few years making movies there, so he was called upon to cast the locals for the film. "Marx and Jaffe handpicked Guy for the part," said Lawrence, who has a major scene with Guy in the catacombs. The two men wore tunics throughout the movie in the extreme cold. "We froze our asses off in those caves," said Lawrence. "Guy and I had a good rapport. We always kidded around when we were in rehearsal. He would always screw around, you know, he'd try and throw you. But when it came to actually shooting, he *didn't* fool around. In rehearsal, he would upstage me. He would always upstage me! He had a way of moving so he would leave me with the back of my head to the camera," he laughed. "So then I would go upstage and he'd go upstage and then I would go upstage. You know, we'd try to get a better camera position. We kidded around, but when it came to shooting there was no screwing around. I mean, once the scene was set, Guy was a professional at it. My God! Look at the television shows he did, and everything. There's no doubt about it. The guy knew what he was doing at all times.

"Guy absolutely was happy to be making a movie rather than doing TV. I think it was unfortunate that he was cast in the type of roles he was cast in. I don't think he was happy about that. We didn't talk about it, but I mean you've got to realize that *Damon and Pythias* and *Captain Sindbad*[197]—well, he'd much rather be doing a film like *The Great Escape*[198] or one that had some substance to it, but he had been typecast because of *Zorro* and the type of television background he came from. I think that was a little disappointing to him.

"We would talk about a number of things. I wouldn't say he was talkative, but he wasn't a shy person in any sense of the word. I mean, if you got into a conversation with him, he had intelligence. He was an interesting guy to talk to. Very erudite person. The only thing about *Zorro* he talked about was when he was doing a fencing scene and he caught Tony Russel in the eye. He worried about that, but it was just one of those things on the set, you know, where you just made a wrong move and it happened."

Guy would never rock the boat by commenting on the script. "No," said Lawrence, "because, you see, again this shows his professionalism. Once you accept a role, you don't sit around and bitch about it. I mean, if you are a professional you accept it, and that's the way it's gonna be. If you sit there and bemoan the fact that you took the role, I mean, that's the kiss of death. Guy was too much of a professional to do anything like that."

Guy met his co-star, Don Burnett, for the first time on the set of *Damon and Pythias*. He had been in the television show *Northwest Passage*, and was married to beautiful Italian-born Hollywood starlet, Gia Scala.[199] "When we arrived in Italy," said Don, "studios were doing what they called 'Cape e Spada,' cape and sword movies, like *Damon and Pythias,* and other movies about Roman times with swords and capes, maidens and all that stuff. Then when those ran their course, they found *Westerns*. Clint Eastwood and Lee Van Cleef came a few years later. Italian film companies found a place called Zaragosa in the south of Spain to be the ideal location for what Americans would call Spaghetti Westerns. They also filmed a lot in Yugoslavia."

Hollywood was very slow from the late 1950s to the mid-1960s. The Hollywood movie industry had virtually moved to Europe to make movies at this time, and American actors went there if they wanted to work. "A lot of movies were being made in Europe, primarily because of frozen funds," explained Don. "Currency didn't flow then from one country to the next. If someone had money in Europe, he could not get his money out. If an American had a company in Spain, his profits had to stay in Spain. One way to get his money out of the country was to invest it in a film that is shown all over the world, such as

In an action scene from *Damon and Pythias*, Damon cuts the bridge down so the Roman soldiers cannot catch up with Pythias. (Kathy Gregory Personal collection, courtesy of Kathy Gregory)

Battle of the Bulge [1965] or these Westerns. He might invest two million dollars in Spain, and it would make fifty million worldwide and he's got his money out."

Steve McQueen, Alan Ladd, and numerous American actors were living in Europe during the 1960s and early 1970s making movies. It was not unusual to walk into a restaurant in Italy and see someone from home. "We ran into Howard Duff and his wife, Ida Lupino, when we were there," said Janice. "We had met them years before through Chris Dark. Toni had a big crush on Howard and one time we were taking him somewhere in the car and Toni slipped her little hand between the front seats to hold his hand during the entire ride."

Buddy Van Horn was there at the time. "I ran into Ricardo Montalban while I was there. A wonderful gentlemen," he said. "I had worked with him on *Zorro*. I'll never forget, I hadn't seen him in many years and when I was in Italy doing a picture with Stewart Granger, I walked into a restaurant and I heard someone say '*Buddy!*' I looked over, and it was Ricardo—sitting with a bunch of people. He came over and shook my hand, said, '*How ya doing?*,' which you don't expect sometimes. He's a very warm man. A *terrific* guy."

Tony Russel lived in Rome from 1961 to 1967 with his wife and son, Dell. Along with acting, he operated a lucrative dubbing company in Rome. Tony had become a major star in Spain, where he played gladiator-type heroes and had a large following of young fans. Tony got his chance to play Zorro in 1965's *Il Guiramento di Zorro* [*Behind the Mask of Zorro*], in Spain. In 1961, his son, Dell, then nine, played Cleopatra's young son in the movie, *Cleopatra*.[200]

Tony Russel remembers with good humor his chance to star in a Spaghetti Western. "I met Sergio Leone," recalled Tony, "when he was an unknown. He had no movie credits to show me. He told me he had a part for me. He gave me a script to read for a movie called *Fistful of Dollars*. I thought the script was *awful.* There was *no* dialogue! My agent thought it was awful. Even *Clint* thought it was bad! At the same time I was offered a movie up on the Nile in Egypt, called *Secret of the Sphinx*, which sounded exciting, with a reputable director, and I thought it was better so I turned down Leone and took the other one. Clint Eastwood got the part and got paid $27,000 and, of course, it made him a big star. Later he got *$150,000* for *The Good, the Bad, and the Ugly*. Life is full of decisions like that, especially in acting."

From the time they met on the set, Don Burnett and Guy were compatible. Don talks of happy memories with his old friend with great admiration and exuberance. "Guy was a Renaissance Man. Very attractive. With *panache.* Loved cars. Had great taste. *Loved* to read. He loved books and music, and he was a great conversationalist. He had a great curiosity and interest in everything! He had energy. He liked to walk. He liked to fence. I first fenced with Guy in Italy, then later we fenced at his house on Hillside, or in my backyard on Mullholland Drive. We used sabers, and we took off our shirts to make it more daring. Then we'd jump in the pool to cool off."

The setting for *Damon and Pythias* is the city state of Syracuse in Sicily, four hundred years before Christ, but it was not filmed in Sicily. The 1962 MGM pressbook stated the locations at the Roman baths, Caracalla (the prison set), Grotti di *Salone* (caves), Seaside Gaeta and Terracina near Naples.

"*Damon and Pythias* was filmed at the Cinecitte and some locations outside of Rome," tells Don Burnett. "We shot in the Catacombes of Rome, and some of my scenes were shot down by Naples, but Guy wasn't in those. Guy and I filmed outside of Rome, near Castel Gandolfo, the town where the Pope has his summer home. There was a little lake there, very few homes, and *great* pastures of sheep. In the distance from where we filmed was one farmhouse where the shepherds lived and they were always happy to see American actors. We'd start filming very early in the cold wintry mornings in these pastures, and the shepherds would invite us in for breakfast. There would be a warm fire burning in the hearth, and we'd feast on sausages, fresh baked bread, and white wine. *Wonderful!*"

Don found working with Guy easy. "Guy was trustworthy. I mean, if you were dangling on one end of a rope you *knew* he'd be holding the other end."

Don even trusted Guy's driving, which could be hair-raising. Guy bought a bright red Maserati convertible sports car from the factory in Modena, Italy. "When we were on location sometimes Guy would say, 'I found this *great* place for lunch.' So we'd jump in his sports car and go to lunch in a town which normally took about an hour and a half to get to, but we'd be there in a *flash,* enjoying fine foods and wine, then *zip* back to work."

Guy admitted going more than a hundred mph in Italy, but he felt that the roads and cars in Italy were built for speed. He said he would never drive that fast in the States.[201]

"It was fun doing films in Europe because the lifestyle was very good then," continued Don. "It was a great time, a wonderful time. Guy and I would share a bottle of wine

In the last scene, Damon is chained to the sacrificial post trusting his friend will return so he will not be killed. Guy gave an interview for an MGM press release while waiting in the cold to shoot this scene. (Kathy Gregory Personal collection, courtesy of Kathy Gregory)

at lunch in the commissary and go back to work. Well, we could never do that in Hollywood. No drinks were allowed in the commissary then, or on the set, or the *lot*. Guess they were afraid everybody would get drunk. They treated actors like children, but in Italy, we *could*. That was important to Guy and to me. We both liked the lifestyle there."

In the last scene of the movie, Damon is chained to a wall in an arena where he will be executed, unless his friend, Pythias, returns by sundown as he promised. While setting up the scene for this dramatic climax, Guy gave an interview to the people of MGM for their 1962 pressbook release. With his arms outstretched in shackles, Guy expressed his sentiments about making a movie in Italy:

> "We're a lucky lot, this generation of movie actors," he said, squirming.
> "Everyone dreams of wandering around the world at one time or another but few of us really make it. People save for years for just one little trip. Yet here we are doing what we like best, working at our craft while

other people pay the airline tickets."

He squirmed a little more and added, "I wish they'd fire those arrows, and get it over with. It's cold up here."

Despite his Welsh name and New York birth, Williams felt entirely at home in Italy. Both of his parents were Italian and they spoke only their native tongue to their son until he was old enough to go to school. When he went to Rome for the location filming, he found he could remember the language of his childhood without difficulty.

The interview ended when the cameras had to roll again. Pythias enters the arena in the nick of time as he promised his friend he would, before sunset. The Emperor keeps his word to release Damon. But he is so impressed with "this philosophy of brotherhood," that he also lets Pythias live and go free. Triumphant cheers rise from the people in the arena, music swells, and Damon and Pythias are happily reunited in the handshake of brotherhood.

Life imitated art and Don and Guy continued to have a strong friendship throughout Guy's lifetime.

During the months Guy was filming, Toni and Steve were enrolled in schools. Steve was placed in Notre Dame, ironically in the same ancient city where his grandfather Attilio had attended school. The classes were as rigorous and unpleasant to young Steve as they were to his illustrious grandfather. "The classes were *far* more advanced than those in the United States," said Steve. "They were taught by the no-nonsense Jesuits. They don't fool around," he laughed.

Toni went to an Italian preschool taught by nuns, and learned to speak Italian. One particular Sister was devoted to Toni, and attended her closely during the day. Toni still remembers her with fond sentiment. "She wanted me to put on weight so she was always trying to make me eat more pasta," said Toni. "*Mangia, mangia*, she'd say, in this sweet high voice."

On his days off, Guy enjoyed excursions with his family. Janice recalled a funny moment in the Masarati. "The kids were just three and nine years old so they fit in the tiny bucket seats in the back. Guy was driving us around one day to see the sights, and we were about to go through a narrow tunnel when this policeman came screaming up to us shouting in Italian, 'Stop! Stop!,' and speaking in Italian. Guy could understand him so he stopped. The policeman was shouting, 'What are you *doing*?' Are you *crazy*?! This is a one-way tunnel! You're going the *wrong way!* I just saved your *life!*'

"Guy loved antiquity and history. He loved the old buildings and churches of Europe and we visited many. He also *loved* zoos so wherever we went, we almost *always* visited the zoo, and we did in Italy too. He pulled up by the ruins of the Coliseum of Rome and we got out to take some pictures. It was dusk when we got there and the Coliseum was beautiful against a golden evening sky. It seemed still and quiet. We walked through some tall grass, and suddenly we heard this rustle. We had frightened a litter of wild little kittens and they went running into holes and crevices in the stone."

"We spent Christmas in Venice that year [1961]," said Janice. "We *loved* Venice. We stayed in a beautiful suite at the Ambassador Hotel. It had a gorgeous view of Venice and we loved it. The people in Italy were warm, and friendly. Venice was safe then. Toni and Steve could hold hands and walk across the bridge together in the morning to a little bakery nearby and get breakfast together. People were caring and protective of the children. Some sailors from Yugoslavia were in there one day and gave them gifts from their country of Santas riding camels."

Toni said she never missed a traditional Christmas at home with presents under the tree and Santa coming down the chimney, rather than a hotel room. It had never occurred to her, because, she said, "*EVERY DAY* was Christmas!"

Guy and Janice took lots of pictures of the family in Rome by its famous fountains, and statues. In one, they captured the pigeons of San Marcus around their car just as one lit on Toni's little head. Although Toni was very young, she holds some fond remembrances of the trip. "When we went driving around with Dad, we loved the coconut stands. We used to stop at every one we saw and get coconut on a stick. I loved to walk over this little bridge in the morning with Steve to get breakfast. You could smell the breads and cakes and the café latte. I can remember taking a powerboat ride to a little island where glassblowers made little horses for us. We went on Gondola rides, explored the countryside together when Dad had time off." All of the family agrees. Some of their happiest memories were in Italy.

"After *Damon and Pythias,* Guy and I both made another movie in Europe," said Don. "They stayed in Italy for Christmas, while I went to Yugoslavia to make an Italian production of *Robin Hood.* This time I had the swashbuckling role. Yeah. I played the Guy Williams part, and with a mustache," he laughed. "I fenced all these Italians and killed thousands of them. All that fencing with Guy helped me get that part, I guess. It was shown here [the U.S.] and it was a terrible piece of crap, but I had a lot of fun. That was the last thing I did." Don co-starred with his wife, Gia Scala, in the movie.

After spending Christmas in Venice, Guy and his family went back to the States for a few weeks before going to Germany to film *Captain Sindbad.* Janice described their trip back to the United States. "It was fun getting home to the States, because we took so *many* modes of transportation. When we left Rome, we drove the car up to Modena, where they crated it to be shipped home. Then we took the little *motascafa* on the water to get to the train station, where we took a train to Milano. We were snowed in there and stayed overnight. Next day, we got on a plane to the States. *That's* the way to travel!" she said, recalling the excitement. "The kids were never a problem, easy to travel with."

There was one scare though, while flying home from Italy. "The flight got rough when we were flying through some turbulence," remembered Janice. "Guy was behind me with one child and I was in front with the other. Guy told the attendant to give him a drink and he pointed to me and said, 'And give her one too.' We had to make an emergency landing in Iceland, which was dangerous because there was ice on the runway. I looked out the window and saw what I call "my three stars." They were lined up in the sky and I was reassured that everything would be all right. They have always made me feel safe, like a guardian angel. The tires popped when we landed, but everyone was all right."

Safely home, with a few weeks to spare before returning to Europe, Guy and Bob Stevenson drove to the Port of Los Angeles in San Pedro to pick up his Masaratti at the shipyard. After a few weeks home, Guy and Janice leased their mansion on Hillside for six months, because Guy planned to tour Europe after filming *Sindbad* and spend more time in Italy. Janice packed up the family and they flew to Munich in February 1962.

Chapter 36

"It was a big part of my existence."

– Guy Williams

It had been announced in *Daily Variety* and the *L.A. Mirror* as early as December 7, 1961, while they were in Italy, that Guy Williams was signed to play the title role in a $3 million CinemaScope spectacle and Technicolor fantasy called *Captain Sindbad*, directed by Byron Haskin.

> *The Hollywood Reporter*, December 15, 1961
> Director Byron Haskin and assistant Leon Chooluck are remaining abroad to continue preparations for *Sindbad*, with building of sets in Munich due to start right after January 2 and principal photography in early February. A top European art director, Art Schling, also has been assigned to the production. Guy Williams and Pedro Armendáriz are set thus far as cast leads.

Lawrence Montaigne was also cast in *Captain Sindbad*, and was in Germany before Guy arrived. "The director said to me 'Guy Williams is going to be in the film.' I said 'Great! I just finished a picture with Guy. Lets go to the airport together when Guy comes in.' And I knew Guy was going to do *something* when he saw me, because we had a relaxed friendship and could joke with each other. When Guy arrived at the airport in Munich, Byron Haskin, who we called Bunny, and I were there to meet him. Passengers walked down steps onto the tarmac in those days and as Guy came down the stairs he spotted me. He had that 'oh no, not again look' on his face, and he turned around as though he was going back. I laughed, and then he teased and said, 'I have to work with HIM again!'" Lawrence laughed, "That was the kind of friendship we had. To be able to tease each other like that."

Guy and his family checked into the Munich Hotel. He met the director, the producer, and other members of the cast—Heidi Brühl(Princess Jana), Pedro Armendáriz (El Kerim) and Abraham Sofaer[202] (Galgo, the magician)—for the first time.

Steve was enrolled in the American Army School on the Military Base. "I caught the *German* measles while I was in *Germany*," said Steve. "I was delirious for a while and missed a lot of school and a lot of sightseeing, so I don't remember the first part of the

Lawrence Montaigne, far left, with another member of the cast, Geoffrey Toone, and Guy listen to the humor of director, Byron Haskin, on set of *Captain Sindbad (1962)*. (Kathy Gregory Personal Collection; courtesy of Kathy Gregory)

trip. My sister was in an Italian nursery school or kindergarten-type atmosphere with nuns in Italy and a Catholic Nursery school in Germany too. She learned to speak German. She doesn't remember it today but the nuns spoke German to her."

Toni doesn't remember much about Germany. "I just remember the school and the nuns. I remember more about Italy—Venice and the Gondolas. Once again they put lots of food in front of me, because they thought I was too thin. I've heard that all my life," said Toni.

Hollywood Reporter, February 14, 1962
"*Captain Sindbad* Rolls"
MUNICH— The King Brothers production of *Captain Sindbad* for MGM release rolls here tomorrow with Guy Williams in the title role and Bryon Haskin directing. Three huge sound stages of the Bavaria Film Studios are being used to film the adventure fantasy from *A Thousand and One Nights*.

Byron Haskin[203] was, from 1935 to 1944, head of Warner Brothers' Special Effects Department, before becoming a full-fledged director. By the end of his career, he had worked on more than one hundred and seven pictures, yet in an interview in 1984, shortly before he died, Haskin was modest about his achievements. He never mentioned that he won an Academy Award (an honorary one in 1938 for the development of the triple head background projector) and had four nominations for special effects. He had directed Walt Disney's first live-action movie, *Treasure Island*, in 1953.

"*Captain Sindbad* was filmed in the winter of 1962," said Haskin. "It was extremely cold in Germany. Even in June, when our contract was to be up, there was snow two feet high on the curbstones in Munich. I was assured that there were all kinds of facilities in the Bavaria Studios, everything we wanted. I got there and it was absolutely 'Mack Sennett, 1917.' Nothing there. Background all over blue."[204]

Haskin worked against adverse conditions during the entire production. He said he could have enjoyed making it more were it not for the King Brothers (Frank and Herman) who were notoriously tight with budget and lived up to their reputation of being difficult to work for.

"The King Bros. and I ran afoul of each other," said Haskin. "Leon Chooluck was with them as production manager and I knew Leon. He suggested me for the job. Frank King started to give me a per-diem which wouldn't even keep me in a *tent* over there. I said, 'Forget it. I'll just go home.'"

Haskin had lived in Germany before and knew what it cost to live there. "They were trying to chop me in half." When the King Bros. realized Bryon Haskin really meant it, Frank King said to Leon, "Give him what he wants." So Haskin stayed.

There was not much regard for the actors' safety and well being in those days. "The magician's cat in the movie, was a small ocelot. It was wild," said Haskin. "They were taking a chance with it." There were other dangers and one day, reportedly, one worker tragically died on the set. King wanted to dock his pay for that day, much to his widow's chagrin.

Haskin talked about a beautiful water spout for a cyclone he created in a tank, which didn't make the final cut. After a few seconds of filming the glass broke, but fortunately no one was injured.

Guy talked about the danger and discomfort in the storm scenes when tons of water was dumped on him. "They had *BOX CARS* full of water coming at us on the ship. *Real* Box Cars. You could hear that damn thing open on the side," Guy said, "and you'd say, 'oh gosh—*here* it comes,' and *whaaaam!* Then *that* box car would be moved out, and in came *another* one: The *ultimate* deluge! There it was. Noah's Ark! On a *studio* set. One of the lamp fixtures on the tail of Sindbad's boat broke from the force of the water and slammed into my arm. I thought I'd lost an arm!"

"We never saw the ocean," said Lawrence. "It was all shot in a sound stage. They would trip these huge dumpsters and water would come down a shoot and when it hit the bottom it would make these tremendous waves. We were shooting in February and the water was ice water and we were holding on for dear life. The water would literally pick us up and sweep us across the deck of the ship! Everything went flying. Water just came down like a rocket! One on one side, one on another, so water was coming from every direction all on a sound stage!"

Lawrence recalled a scene in the castle when an elephant was supposed to crush the head of Princess Jena as her punishment for loving Sindbad. Guy was not there for this scene. "An elephant on the set went berserk! Something spooked it and it went through the set. Knocked down part of the set inside the castle. Everyone was running in every direction, not knowing what that elephant was going to do. Poor baby was scared to death. But here we are with this runaway elephant and the sets coming down and everybody's running for their lives, trying to get this elephant under control. As for the head-crushing scene we see on film," Lawrence informed, "that was done with Byron's special effects. The elephant didn't get near Heidi."

Sindbad threatens Galgo, the magician, (Abraham Sofaer) to reverse a spell on his beloved Jana. (Kathy Gregory Personal Collection; courtesy of Kathy Gregory)

With no special equipment available, Haskin had to devise his own means of fooling the eye with his camera, with some basic techniques. "The optical machine was not much," said Haskin. "No modern facilities for special effects at all. I had to make all the effects in the camera." He made the girl shrink and become a bird, by putting her on a dolly and projecting her mirror image. Then they pulled the dolly away very fast and it looked like she was shrinking.

"Lee Zavitts[205] is tops," continued Haskin, "and he made the miniature dragon with nine heads that barked like a dog. It was on wires to shoot the miniatures of Sindbad's ship. In June the tank was still eleven inches deep in ice.[206] The contract was running out. Still, the tank was half frozen."

Haskin was happy with the cast he was given. "'Pete' Armendáriz was enjoyable," he said, "and Abe Sofaer was a consummate actor." But he was bewildered by the methods of the King Brothers as many other directors in Hollywood were. Some of their decisions were illogical—such as when they refused to compensate Guy for fencing. "A big influence in casting Guy was that he is an excellent fencer," tells Haskin. "He expected an adjustment, a fee, to do the fencing himself. He did it on all the *Zorro* series. 'No, no,' Frank King said, 'that goes with the fee for the part.' Guy said, 'It's *stunts*. Hell, I might lose my eye. I'm going to get paid or I won't do it.' King wouldn't budge. Guy said, 'All right then, I won't do it. Get a stuntman.' They said 'All right. You don't do it.' So, they sent over to London for Mark Evans' brother, a fencing expert, and he did the fencing. Well, this delayed production a lot."

Haskin wondered what that cost them extra in production, rather than giving Guy what he wanted. "It doesn't make *sense*. It inhibited the continuity I wanted in the

Guy and Byron Haskin exchanged stories and artistic ideas. They struck up a friendship that lasted beyond *Captain Sindbad*. (Kathy Gregory Personal Collection; courtesy of Kathy Gregory)

fencing, from close-ups to action and all, without cuts. With a double, you've got to make cuts to closeups of the principal."

Lawrence had a different understanding about Guy not doing his own fencing. "When Guy starts a film, he's insured by an insurance company. There are certain things they won't permit him to do, like they wouldn't permit Steve [McQueen] to ride a motorcycle. Well, likewise, they wouldn't permit Guy to do the fencing. If anything happens to Guy accidentally..."

When the picture was completed, it went to MGM and into the hands of the King Brothers, who Haskin says were known to be the "weirdest outfit that ever tried to make movies." They did things like, "recut the whole beginning of the movie, swapped the ending reels with beginning reels, such as that," said Haskin. "Anyone who worked with them has a scar that lasts the rest of his life."

Despite the fact that Haskin said the film was "a Persian fairy tale" and an "ad lib all the way," *Captain Sindbad* became tops of the MGM summer season. "That film later came within a half-inch of setting as a TV series called the *Adventures of Sindbad*. It was to be done in Munich. I made a pilot at MGM for the King Brothers using some of the movie footage. It went from CBS to NBC to ABC. They hassled eight or nine months then finally they cancelled out."

Making *Captain Sindbad* was not as fun for Guy as making *Damon and Pythias*, but there *were* some fun and memorable times, like the time he and Pedro Armendáriz took over the kitchen in the Munich Hotel. "Guy and Pete were given permission to go into the kitchen off the main dining room so they could cook their own *aglio e olio*—Guy's favorite pasta dish with olive oil and garlic—since it was not on the menu," tells Janice. "The story goes, literally, 'Garlic was coming off the *ceiling*!' he told me."[207]

Guy had not expected much from *Captain Sindbad*, artistically or career-wise, but he wanted to take his family back to Europe and the money was good. He bought a brand-new Mercedes, black, just off the assembly line there and when his work was done he fulfilled a dream and drove his family on a sightseeing venture through parts of Europe. "Dad took a slow southern route through Europe, back to Italy," said Steve. "We drove through France, stayed in Canne and Nice for a while on the way down from Germany to Naples. My dad was linguistically inclined so he picked up French really quick when we were in France. He said it was easy with the Latin stem. We went through the Alps, the edge of the French Riviera to the Italian Riviera to Naples. I loved it. To this day I remember walking on four-thousand-year-old bridges. Wow! We saw Venice when it was snowing and when it was sunny and warm. We saw the best of it. All of us agreed that Venice was most beautiful in the winter."

Janice and Guy were happy to be back in Venice. "We left the Mercedes just outside of Venice and took a train to the Ambassador Hotel where we had stayed before," she said. "The porter put all our things in a big open wheel cart and we took a picture of Toni sitting on all those bags on the cart. We had not made reservations, but the people there were so accommodating. They remembered us!" she said with surprise, "and they said, 'We'll give you your same suite.' We loved that suite. We had such a beautiful view.

"Guy loved to play in the casinos in Europe. He had a system that worked really well there. Roulette was his favorite. We went to Venice and stayed three weeks with all our expenses paid by Guy's winnings at roulette. In Europe they would catch onto your system and protect you. They don't do that here. If you made a mistake, they'd say, 'Are you sure you want to play that?' In Germany they did that too."

Guy seriously considered staying to live in Italy. "Guy felt at home in Italy. In fact he loved Venice so much we looked at real estate there. He thought the children would have a richer education and richer lifestyle there. I would have loved it and the children were young enough to adapt, but whatever he decided was fine with me."

Steve recalled, "Dad felt Europe was number one because of the education system. The school in Rome was hard to keep up. We had thought there were very good schools here in California, but when we got to Europe, we found out how deficient they were. Dad thought in terms of what was best for the kids. He felt we should have been brought up over there."

Guy was at his crossroads. Should he stay or go back to Hollywood? It was not an easy decision to make. He decided to go home.

From an actor's point of view, Lawrence Montaigne thought about Guy's decision. "It was like going back to your roots for Guy, with his Italian background and everything. But

Guy was a pragmatist, too. After all, they did have a home in Hollywood, and he had made a career in Hollywood. Even though he was doing some films in Italy and Germany, they weren't the type of films that you would build a career on. He was hoping, I imagine, to get into something more substantial. And he did. He got the science fiction show with Irwin Allen."

After nearly six months abroad, Guy knew he had been away from Hollywood long enough to set his career back. Still, he was not in a hurry to get back to the rat race. To extend the vacation, he decided to take a ship home. "First we drove to Naples," recalled Janice, "where we boarded the ship. We had the Mercedes loaded onto the same ship. So the whole family came back with the Mercedes below and when we got to New York, it was unloaded, we got in it, and drove across country!"

Among Janice's keepsakes is the ship's list, which reads like an Italian phone book with passengers from Italy and New York: Balsamo, Dittori, Luigi Salvatore, Spinsosa, Tamalini, Viggiani, and one *Williams* from Hollywood, California.

"Guy had so much fun talking in Italian to all the passengers. We took pictures coming into New York past the Statue of Liberty where both his parents had sailed. That really was an emotional moment for Guy. That was a *great* trip," said Janice.

Steve recalls, "First we visited relatives in New York. We stayed with my dad's mom for a few days then drove to Tennessee and stayed with my mom's family for a few days. Then, we drove the rest of the way across the U.S. to LA-LA Land."

In the 1986 interview with Mike Clark for *Starlog* magazine, Guy said, "I took *six* months to get home from that European trip. And six months is like *two pilot* seasons for contracts! So I was blowin' 'em right and left on the trip. So I come back here, and I'd *really* been out of sight. That's been a steady thing with me. I just—if I get enough ahead of the game, I tend to *leave* the business," he laughed. "I don't know *why*. But it seems to be the *right* thing to do. In the meantime, my agent didn't know where the hell I was, and that kind of thing was getting to be steady. I had missed so many opportunities. Well, they tell me it was like a good *two* seasons. But the trip was *worth it!* So my career has sort of had this kind of *checkering* all throughout it. I've been *leaving* the business all the *time!*" he quipped.[208]

"The trip was worth it. I took the roles in the two movies primarily for the trips. I had my family with me and the kids had a marvelous time. I know there was a lot of good done in that area, especially with the two children and traveling all over Europe—Christmas in Venice—snow, ice, everything—Germany. They were beginning to pick up language. It was a *big* part of my existence, you know. And on a *familial* basis. Had nothing to do with *show business!* As a matter of fact, I just overlooked show business the entire time, to the point that we took the *boat home!* We *sailed* home. Right through the Statue of Liberty, everything. We took the Christoforo Columbo. Wow! Great boat. And we sailed from Naples. We did the traditional European trip right through, and when we got to New York, well, that's my home, so we stayed in New York awhile."

Guy had thought long and hard about staying in Italy and discussed his feelings with Janice, but the final decision was Guy's to make. "He was really torn between the two places. He probably *could* have had a career there," Janice reflected, "but he got nervous about his career in the States, and thought he should get back where things were happening. He felt he was missing out at home and felt he needed to return or else he may not have a career. So, we came back. Years later, though, he said he regretted it."

Chapter 37

"I'd Really Been Out of Sight"

– Guy Williams

Guy and Janice told Peggy Stevenson about their trip to Italy. "Guy *loved* Italy," she said, "and he spoke Italian beautifully. When they got back Guy said to me—and Jan was with him when he told me this—he told me they'd stopped at this little bakery and got nice hot bread and Italian pastry and people would stare at Janice. These two would be motoring through little villages in their convertible—here's Guy and this gorgeous lady, and you know how Italians are. They admire beautiful ladies. Guy liked to brag about Jan and how the people there would tell him, in the gestures Italians make, that she was beautiful. He was really proud of her."

Howard Duff and his wife, Ida Lupino, knew the lease on Guy's house would not be up when they returned home, so they invited Guy and his family to stay in their house while they remained in Europe. When the Duff's returned, Guy and his family checked into the private and sedate Chateau Marmont off Sunset Boulevard. Don and Gia joined them there when they got back from Europe.

"It was a grand time to be at the Chateau Marmont," said Don, recalling some wonderful memories. "Film people would come in from New York and stay there, such as Franchot Tone, with whom we became friends."

Guy and Don were both good cooks. They had adjoining suites with a kitchen in each, and for Guy, an extra bedroom for the children. "One of the dishes we enjoyed making was Gambas a la Plancha. Grilled Shrimp," said Don. "Guy and I would put these large prawns on rock salt, then under the broiler and cook them til they're done. The broiler cooks the top, the rock salt gets hot and cooks the bottom. With white wine it's *wonnnderful.* We'd finished off our meals with a great Cuban cigar."

Gia loved white wine, but often would drink too much for her own good. Janice remembered the evening at the hotel when Don was angry with her and was giving her the silent treatment. "One night after drinking, Gia started singing 'To-night, To-night' from *West Side Story* and would not stop. She was determined to get Don's attention. Finally, Guy and Don said, 'We can't stand any more of this. We're going for a swim,' which got Gia so angry she threatened to do something drastic if they left to go to the pool. The men left and Gia took off all her clothes and headed for the pool—running past people in lobbies, to the elevator, through a garage and out to the pool, where fortunately most of the guests had left. I grabbed a towel and covered her in the elevator. Then she got away and ran around the pool—naked. Guy and Don totally ignored her, acted like they didn't even see her, but she was satisfied because she *knew* they saw her. I was just glad she didn't jump in. We walked all the way back to the room with me holding the towel around her. The best part is, I thought Gia would not remember *any* of this later, but she used to tell this story remembering *every* bit and said she thought the funniest part was *me* trying to keep her covered!" laughed Janice.

Gia Scala was born in Rome, and moved to England to escape the devastating horrors of World War II. Then she moved to the United States with her mother and sister when she was in her late teens. She was a sensation as a starlet in Hollywood in the 1950s, known for her beauty on the screen, and her famous sapphire eyes.

When Guy and Janice moved back into their house on Hillside Drive late into the summer of 1962, they invited Gia and Don to stay with them until they bought their house on Mullholland Drive in the San Fernando Valley. Gia loved children and doted on Toni and Steve. She would babysit for Guy and Janice when they went out, and Toni grew to love her very much. "Gia was so beautiful," said Toni. "After dinner at our house, when Steve and I had gone to bed, the adults would wind up in some sort of debate or loud conversation and Gia would escape and come upstairs to be with us. 'Everybody up! We're gonna have a party,' she would say in that pretty accent she had. She'd talk and play games with us. Even if we were already in bed, she would play. She was so much fun.

"Don and Gia were like family. Don would always ask me, 'What's your *favorite* pasta?' He knew it was Rigatoni, but he liked to hear me say, 'Riga-*ME!!*'"

Don got a kick out of Guy's obsession with raising saltwater tropical fish. "The fish were very expensive and very *delicate*. One day Guy and I were ready to leave for somewhere, when Guy said, 'Wait. I have to feed the fish.' He had some cologne on his hands and when he returned a couple of the fish had died—from the cologne. A couple of *expensive* fish. He was so mad. He said, 'That *fish* cost me $100!'" Don laughed. "Eventually he gave it up."

"We started with a small aquarium on Harper Street," said Janice, "then Guy had someone build a large tank in the house on Hillside that covered an entire wall. The tank had to be sealed a certain way because of the saltwater in there. We could write a book about those fish. It was an ongoing thing the entire time we lived in that house. In those days it was a brand-new hobby. No one knew how to take care of them. We'd get all kinds of different advice. One time we put aspirin in the water because one of them didn't look so well. It killed all of them."

Toni remembered, "I was around six years old and Mom and Dad had been tending to an ailing angel fish one evening before going out to dinner. Finally they had to leave, so they left Steve and I to look after this ailing angelfish. We were staring into this tank as the angelfish stripes were disappearing, getting paler and paler. Finally, it died and floated to the top. We were going to take care of this, so Steve got the scooper and scooped out the fish and flushed it down the toilet. Next day, the toilet backed up and we had to confess to Dad about the fish. He just laughed."

Soon after Don and Gia bought their house, Don made a major decision about his acting career. "I had taken a trip to England and I saw Peter O'Toole in Stratford-on-

Avon and realized that I was in the wrong business. Didn't know *what* I was doing. Those English actors are *so* good. So I went back to school at UCLA, and went to work on Wall Street."

Classes were hard and at one point Don wanted to quit his studies. Gia begged him not to give up and helped pay for it. "She would ask us to encourage Don to stay in school and we did," said Janice. "She was smart about that. She knew it would be security for him and she was right. He stuck with it and made more money as a broker than he'd have ever made in show business, and was able to retire young."

Don became a partner and Vice President of the major investment banking firm, White, Weld, and Company. When it was sold, he became Vice President of another major firm, Kidder-Peabody in Los Angeles. Besides being a good business man, Don is also a fine artist. "I drew and painted all my life. My father was an artist," said Don. "I continued painting all the time I was working and when I was in Europe. I would sketch and paint, while others were playing golf." Don's landscape oil paintings are shown and sold in galleries from Sante Fe, NM to Carmel, CA.

Damon and Pythias was released in the United States in the summer of 1962 with favorable critiques.

> *Daily News*, August 30, 1962
> Guy Williams leans toward comedy as the rascally Damon.

> *Variety*, September 10, 1962
> The dialog maintains a relatively intelligent and persuasive level, the acting
> is good or better…As Damon, a sort of rascally bohemian in ancient Syra-
> cuse, Guy Williams etches a simpatico performance…

There was an Italian version of *Damon and Pythias*[209] with Guy and Don's voices dubbed in Italian, but there was never a premiere of any kind. Liana Orfei, played Adriana, Damon's girlfriend, and Ilaria Occhini played Nerissa, wife of Pythias. When Janice and Gia watched the love scenes, they played a game with each other to pacify their jealousies. "We would nudge each other during the love scenes. When Don was onscreen with Ilaria Occhini, Gia would say, '*She* can't act.' When Guy was on with Liana Orfei, I'd say, 'Now, *she's* the one who *can't* act.'"

Gia and Don owned two sailboats, one for him and a smaller one for her. "Guy would sail with me all the time," said Don. "Guy had sold his boat, but we used to see it! She was moored for a while in a slip right by my yacht club in Marina del Rey, so we would sail by it often. We never met the new owner. He just looked at her as we sailed by."

Gia had heard that Guy had a fantasy of sailing around the world with his family. He had heard about the actor Sterling Hayden doing this and thought it was a wonder-ful idea. Gia wanted to make it a reality. She was always trying to talk Don and Guy and his family into sailing their boat to some exotic place together. No one seriously took her up on it, much to the relief of Guy's family.

Captain Sindbad played in Los Angeles on June 19, 1963 and once again Guy was well received:

Greater Amusements, July 19, 1963
Guy Williams plays the title role with effective romantic and swashbuckler portrayal.

Hollywood Reporter, June 24, 1963
Williams is properly fearless as Sindbad.

LA. Times, June 29, 1963
TV's popular Zorro seems an ideal choice for the kids. He has the muscles to dodge all kinds of death-dealing traps, outwitting a fiendish dictator and a sly magician who is under the tyrant's spell.

Chapter 38

"Sony...has not gotten back to us"

– Guy Williams

Guy finished out the remainder of 1962 leisurely enjoying himself with whatever he liked to do. In the fall, Steve was enrolled in the fifth grade at St. Victor's Catholic School on Holloway Drive in West Hollywood, and Toni in the preschool there. Guy chose the school. "Even though Guy was not a practicing Catholic or any religion," said Janice, "he said if they are going to have any kind of religion it should be Catholic."

Steve entered fifth grade but he had missed too much of the fourth grade while traveling in Europe to be adequately prepared for it. He repeated it the following year, which was to his advantage because he had always been the youngest in his class since his birthday is at the end of the year.

"They were going to a Catholic School and they had never been baptized," said Janice. "We went in to talk to the priest about getting them baptized and the priest said, 'You know, if you tell them one thing and we tell them another, we're still going to tell them we're right and you're wrong.' I looked at Guy. And he said, 'That's all right. You just go right ahead if you think that'll work,'" she laughed. "We discussed this later and Guy said, 'You know, I kinda *liked* that priest.'"

Janice made most of the children's school clothes. Whatever style they liked, she made it. Toni remembered, "When I was six or seven, I wanted to be Alice in Wonderland. I *loved* Alice. So my mom made me a blue Alice in Wonderland dress with the white pinafore and the blue headband." Guy wanted a Nehru jacket for a costume party once and Jan made it. She made them wonderful lunches, usually with delicious Italian meats and cheeses like Guy's mother had done for him.

In 1963 Guy signed with the influential Ashley Famous Agency, Inc., at 9255 Sunset Boulevard in Beverly Hills, but things were slow. While he waited for roles to come his way, Guy's active mind kept busy with new ideas and projects. One that had developed on his return from Germany was a joint effort with Bryon Haskin, the director of *Captain Sindbad*, Leon Chooluck, of special effects, and Abraham Sofaer ("Galgo" in *Sindbad*), to manufacture machines that would play movies for the general public in their homes.

The idea was conceived to help producers turn a profit by getting more product (movies) to more people. Until now a person would have to rent a large heavy projector

Headshot of Guy around 1963 as he had to get back into the loop in Hollywood after
dropping out to stay in Europe. (author's collection)

and reels of film to watch a movie. They wanted to invent a machine that used a *special*
film that would hook up to a TV and play movies in the home. They had perceived the
concept of the yet-to-come video tape player, the VCR, and VHS tapes. They discussed
"making movies just for this system."

During several meeting over the summer, they discussed every aspect and answered
all questions they could think of: financing, franchising, patents, type of film. Would
there be a delivery service for the movies or some type of "library" where the public
could rent them? Would it be a pay for view? Should they buy the parts from Sony and
build the machine themselves or have Sony build the machines? They estimated the
price of each movie was to be $89.95.

They needed financing, so they put their heads together and wrote a proposal to
Sony Corporation. Everyone involved in the project made the trip to San Francisco that
summer to present the proposal to Sony. Guy took his family with him. They met with
Sony, who told them they would get back to them.

A portion of the minutes Guy typed up from a meeting on August 1, 1963 follows:

WILLIAMS: Sony, as of now, has not gotten back to us. They haven't
indicated any response. Without any commitment
from Sony we don't have too much except some good ideas.

HASKIN: We need some legal council.

WILLIAMS: Disney is one of the best examples of a man willing to gamble
on new concepts, new sales ideas, on his own initiative.

ABRAMS: I suggest that we four take on a fifth partner with a million
dollars!

They continued to try to find a way to finance the machines.

HASKIN: If Sony doesn't come in, then do we move with Ampex?[210]

Guy's family enjoyed San Francisco, sightseeing and stopping along the way home when they wanted. Then suddenly Steve got sick. "I was coming back with my folks from San Francisco and by the time we got back I had terrible cramps. As soon as we got home, I was in the operating room for appendicitis. Toni had gotten hers out first when she was only about three years old. Both of us had our appendix taken out at the same hospital we were born in, Cedar's Sinai. Mine had burst and for a while my prognosis was pretty bleak. My mother had had hers taken out when she was very young too, so it ran in the family," he joked.

"Guy was always attentive and caring of the children and willing to take time with them as long as he wasn't working," said Janice. "When Toni had her appendix out, Guy and I *both* got up every morning and went to the hospital—not just me. We'd spend the day with her and go home. He did the same thing when Steve had his appendectomy. He was between jobs each time, so he would spend the day with them."

"Dad sometimes had a kind of 'sick' sense of humor," laughed Steve, "He used to come in with his *camera* and crack jokes and it hurt when I laughed. I'd say, 'Don't make me laugh. Don't make me laugh,' but he'd make me laugh and take pictures of me in pain. He would take a whole roll of film of me like this. That was his kind of sense of humor. Like when I was a kid he used to tickle me until I'd almost pee in my pants. He'd get you right to the edge until you couldn't breathe," he said, shaking his head.

Janice was the nursemaid in the family, but she didn't always have the stomach for it. "Once I just had a sty on my eye," said Steve, "and mom took me to the doctor to have it taken off. She was holding one arm and the nurse was holding the other, and the doctor was working on my eye. My legs were kicking and going all around, and Mom got queasy. When Toni got her ears pierced, Mom *fainted*. Passed out right in the office. And she fainted when I broke my thumb in soccer at school, too. But moms are like that though," he laughed.

There was one particular time, among many, when Janice held her own. Toni re-members, "Mom has psychic dreams and when Steve was in Junior High, she had a dream that Steve was choking, and the next night he *was.*" Steve had asthma and sinus problems and during his sleep, complicated by a cold, the passage in his throat became obstructed. Toni jumped out of bed to watch the drama unfold. "I remember there was all this excitement. Dad had Steve in the shower and I could see the red light of the ambulance flashing outside. I ran to the window to watch. Steve didn't have to go to a hospital, but it was scary."

"I woke up coughing and choking," said Steve. "Mom called the Fire Department, while Dad threw me in the shower. I couldn't breathe! He turned on all these jets, getting the steam going and was holding me up, saying, *'Breathe! Breathe!'* Mom kept talking to the paramedics and by the time they got there I had gotten up the phlegm in my throat and was breathing. It scared the *heck* out of me."

Another day they never forgot was on November 22, 1963. Janice and Guy were driving down from Hillside at midday and saw a big sign at Sunset and Gardner: PRESI-DENT ASSASSINATED. "We couldn't believe it," said Janice. "Guy was not working at the time so we watched it on TV for three *long* days. Guy and I were watching when Jack Ruby shot Oswald. Guy was upset, but not visibly mourning as many people were because he was not in awe or admiration of Kennedy like most Americans were. His political views didn't always coincide with Kennedy's, but, still, we watched a lot of TV just like everyone else."

Steve remembers when he heard the news. "I was on the playground at St. Victor's when the somber announcement came over the school's PA system. It was a big shock to everybody. Everybody was upset. The nuns thought Kennedy could walk on water."

The Sony project faded away. From all accounts, it seemed the men involved became discouraged when they never heard from Sony, and eventually gave it up.

Chapter 39

"That's the trouble with traps. The bait always gets hurt."
— Kathy Brown as Laura in *Bonanza*

Guy had not worked in eighteen months when his agent sent him to Paramount to be on the popular TV western *Bonanza*[211] permanently. "I needed a job, and nothing at the time seemed more visible and 'up front' than *Bonanza*. I didn't like the show, but I didn't like *a lot* of shows. I was never a TV lover. But I couldn't keep using that as a reason for not shooting. I said, 'I'll take it.'"

Bonanza was the second most watched TV Western at the time, next to *Gunsmoke*. The show was in its fifth season, and two years later was the number one TV show. In January 1964, it was announced in the trade papers that Guy Williams would be a "regular" on *Bonanza* as Ben Cartwright's nephew, the son of his seafaring brother, John Cartwright, who never could attain the kind of success Ben had. A few months later, TV magazines and *TV Guide* had articles, with photos, of Guy to promote the oncoming episodes, telling the viewing audience that Guy Williams would be the new addition to the show.

The studio sent the illustrious actor/stuntman Rod Redwing to Guy's house to teach him how to use the six-shooter. Redwing (1904-71) was an American Indian, who dressed in a fringed buckskin outfit, moccasins, and braided hair, and for years he was Hollywood's prominent coach for handling firearms, arrows, and the bullwhip for film. His eccentricity made a lasting impression on young Steve. "I remember Rod Redwing well. He was sent by Paramount to the house and drove up in his 'Cadi,' which was decked out with *steer horns* and *Winchesters* mounted on it as ornaments! I watched 'em practice in the yard. They didn't fire the 45s but worked on handling them—drawing, dry-firing, twirls, etc. The intent was to have Dad be natural and comfortable with the old tool of the West."

Bonanza was usually a tough show for a guest artist to work on because the four principal actors were a clique, a family. They were so used to each other that they hardly needed a rehearsal. Anyone who came in felt like an outsider and was often treated as such. Actor John Wheeler played a barber on a *Bonanza* episode in the early 1970s and expressed his feeling of alienation from the tight-knit principals. "No one says much to you. And you have to find your way with your role. The Cartwrights have worked so

Guy was to be a regular on *Bonanza* in Season 5, 1964, according to TV Guide, but did not return after playing Will Cartwright in five episodes. (courtesy of Jill Panvini)

long with one another they know what each one is thinking and what they are going to do before they do it. One day after a scene with Michael Landon he said to me, 'My hat goes off to you. I don't know how you do it—coming in like that to a set like this, where we all know each other. It must be hard.'"

When Guy signed on, he did not know that the tight-knit ensemble he walked into was having inner conflicts behind the scenes. Pernell Roberts, who played Adam Cartwright, was extremely unhappy, and was giving the producer and writers a hard time because he wanted to get out of his contract to do legitimate theatre. He didn't like the storylines, he didn't like his role, he didn't really like the Cartwrights. He wanted more salary and was telling the writers they should write about political and ethnic issues pertinent to the 1960s. In an attempt to keep him from abruptly walking off the set on any given day, the studio had threatened to blacklist him. If he did walk out, they would have Guy Williams to take his place.

Producer David Dortort and the network wanted to keep Pernell Roberts on the show, so they tried to please him in every way. The writers thought he would be happy if it were written for Adam to get married to Laura Dayton, played by Kathie Browne, then he could leave with his bride to start his own ranch, but periodically return now and then. Guy Williams would be the added Cartwright. But before finalizing the script, Dortort found out from loads of fan mail that female fans wanted all the Cartwrights to remain on the show and they wanted them *all* to remain *single*.[212] In reality the other Cartwright actors resented the addition of *another* Cartwright, because they thought he was unnecessary. Even if Pernell walked out, they didn't need a replacement.

Guy's character, Will Cartwright, was introduced in *Bonanza* Episode #159, "Return to Honor,"[213] on March 22, 1964. Ben Cartwright (Lorne Greene) hears that his long lost nephew has been shot and killed in town, and already buried, so he rides to the sheriff's office to claim his nephew's possessions. He finds out it was a case of mistaken identity and Will is alive, but wounded and hiding from the law from a crime he did not commit. Ben smuggles him to the Ponderosa, nurses him back to health, exonerates him, and asks him to stay on at the Ranch as part of the family. Will is undecided, of course, because the writers didn't know yet which way it would go with Roberts.

The scripts began to reflect what was happening in real life. In the closing scene of "Return to Honor," Adam tells the indecisive Will, "Give it a little time. You'll get used to us." Will, a free spirit merchant seaman, not a rancher, replies, "I kinda think it's gonna take some gettin' used to."

Tensions were so thick between Guy, the cast members, and the writers it didn't take long for him to sense something negative going on and it made him very uncomfortable. The off-camera drama seemed to parallel the on-camera dialogue. In episode #161, "The Roper" (April 5, 1964), Little Joe Cartwright (Michael Landon) tries to push Will into a quick decision to either "stay or leave" the Ponderosa, because the longer he stays, he tells him, the more it will hurt Pa if he decides to leave.

Episode #163, "Los Campaneros" (April 19, 1964), was Guy's third appearance. In the closing scene of this episode, Will is beginning to feel at home on the Ponderosa, but is still on an emotional seesaw about whether to stay or leave. Writers still had no guar-

Guy with Michael Landon and Pernell Roberts in a scene from episode # 161, "The Roper," aired April 5, 1964 (Courtesy of Jackie Hunt).

antee Roberts would stay. He wanted out of the show so badly that he had to seek psychiatric help to cope with the idea of staying. The producer accommodated him with a raise and Roberts finally made the statement: "I'm resigned to staying another year and a half. I'll go to rehearsal and give an intelligent reading, but that's all. No more suggestions for script changes. I'll wait it out. And after all, the money isn't bad." The four leads were earning around $10,000 per episode.

Now the marriage script had to be re-written so that Laura would marry Will instead of Adam. In Guy's fourth episode, #166, "The Pressure Game" (airdate, May 10, 1964), Will meets Adam's girl, Laura, and is attracted to her immediately. The feeling is mutual. Adam is not sure he loves Laura out of pity from being widowed or if he really wants to marry her. Seeing her niece's disappointment, Aunt Lil (Joan Blondell) devises a plan to make Adam jealous, by using Will. She invites both men over for a dinner party. Will gets the picture so he plays it to the hilt, sitting close to Laura and holding her hand. Adam is obviously jealous. The next day finds Will, Laura, and Adam in town at the same time and just as Laura comes out of the bank she is run down by the drunken Bonner brothers. Will and Adam both see the accident. Will picks up Laura and takes her to the hotel and Will pulls the Bonner brothers off their horses and cracks each on the jaw. He threatens them and runs into the hotel to see if Laura is all right. Aunt Lil is there with Adam and the doctor is examining Laura who is lying limp on a chaise longue. She's going to be all right, but the accident makes Adam realize he loves her and he proposes to a gleeful Laura. It is a painful scene for Will to witness. While Adam goes to fetch the carriage to take Laura home, Will manages to fake a cheerful goodbye with well wishes to Laura, while his heart is breaking. He leaves the room with the two women in it.

AUNT LIL: It worked!

LAURA: What worked?

AUNT LIL: Using Will to make Adam jealous. That's what did the
              trick. All you have to do is get the right bait in the trap.

(While Aunt Lil is talking, Laura is looking out the window watching a saddened Will slowly riding out of town. Aunt Lil sees how Laura is watching Will.)

LAURA: Well, that's the trouble with traps. The bait always gets hurt.

(Aunt Lil realizes Laura feels deeply for Will. After Laura leaves the room with Adam, AUNT LIL says to herself): We set the trap all right, but I wonder if we caught the *right man!*

Off stage Guy *was* the bait and Pernell Roberts agreed to stay on the show. David Dortort wanted to also keep both Will (Guy) and Laura (Kathie) on the show, but to keep the main cast happy, he had to let them go. The rest of the cast felt Guy was not needed. Some years later David Dortort told a friend of Guy's that Michael Landon and Dan Blocker had come into his office one day and said, "Get rid of that guy." They thought he was getting too much screen time and they wanted Pernell to stay.

In Guy's last show, Episode #167, "The Triangle"[214] (May 17, 1964), Adam seriously injures his back while building a house for him and Laura and cannot walk. He finds out that Laura and Will are passionately in love, but Laura is going to stay with Adam out of loyalty and guilt while Will decides to leave for San Francisco. Just before Will leaves, Adam sees the pain in Laura's face so he shows her he doesn't need her by standing up from his wheelchair. He tells her to go to Will with his blessings. Will and Laura ride off in the buckboard to be married—never to return to the show.

Guy never liked to talk about his experience on *Bonanza,* not to the press or even to friends. In a rare moment in a 1983 interview, Ken Mayer asked Guy if he was supposed to replace Pernell Roberts in *Bonanza.* Guy evaded the subject by merely saying, "It just didn't work out. [pause] It just didn't click."[215]

Guy talked openly about his stint on *Bonanza* for the first time in 1986 with Mike Clark. "I didn't like that whole session. It was very negative for me in every department because I realized I was being used. I realized that they were threatening Pernell Roberts. They were just trying to keep him there. That's all they were trying to do. I didn't get any co-operation from the other guys because anybody there, well…, it was kinda like if one of the members dies, everybody inherits what he has. And somebody coming in, new? Well, *who* the hell is *that*? There were a lot of negatives on that whole thing."[216]

Oddly, these *Bonanza* episodes are considered by many fans and critics to be Guy's best work outside of *Zorro.*

Chapter 40

"A space show…not too far from my house."
— Guy Williams

Life was good at the mansion on Hillside. For Toni and Steve it was the happiest of times. Guy's financial gains from his movies in Europe gave him some security for a while and made life at the beautiful Mediterranean-style home even more splendid. Guy was enjoying the fruits of his labor and the satisfaction of knowing he had enriched the lives of each member of his family.

Toni's sixth birthday was a memorable one. She had a lavish party outside on the back patio. Ben, the butler, and his wife, Bea, the cook, who lived in the servants' quarters during the 1960s, served the guests. "I had about ten of my classmates there from St. Victor's School and their parents. Ben cut the cake. I *loved* Ben. That was a great party," said Toni, remembering those happy times.

Toni and Steve made their First Communion at St. Victor's Church. Janice made Toni's traditional white dress and veil and took a picture of her wearing it in their chapel in the house. The family attended with friend Sally Foster and her teenage son, Robert, who served as Godmother and Godfather. "Toni was so cute when she went to the altar," said Janice. "They are all supposed to walk back but Toni just stayed there with her hands together, and wouldn't leave the altar. We thought she'd never go back to her seat," she laughed.

Between May 1964 and the end of the year, Toni remembers a time she cherishes when she bonded with her dad. Guy had a small Ferrari and he and Toni would drive to the stables together at the Griffith Park. "Dad used to take me riding at Pickwick Stables by the Equestrian Center in Burbank. We went the whole nine yards: boots, jodhpurs, gloves, the whole bit, then we'd go to the stables, rent the horses and ride English together. My dad taught me to ride. Afterwards, we would always have *a Mounds* candy bar together. Dad thought it was appropriate with all the horse droppings everywhere," she giggled. "Those times at Pickwick were so emotional for me. I still have feelings of excitement and joy whenever I go there. I loved going riding with Dad because I had him all to myself.

"Dad used to talk to Steve differently from me and I envied that. They were '*pals.*' I mean, they could talk about '*women,*' and talk to each other in a more intimate way. He never talked to me that way. Dad didn't say he loved me until he was older, when he became more expressive verbally about how he felt. Now that I'm older, I *know* how much he loved us, and I realize how much he did for us. I am grateful that before he died I was able to tell him that."

Steve enjoyed this time with his dad, spending much time together at Guy's high-powered eight-inch telescope studying the stars. "Dad started teaching me from a smaller telescope when I was little on Harper Street, but when I was older I understood it better. It is so intriguing." Guy mounted his camera to the telescope and the two of them took many pictures of the planets and the moon, then developed the film themselves in Guy's darkroom.

"Dad called us '*Men of Science*,'" he chuckled. "Before we went outside at night to stargaze, he would say to my mom, 'We are *men of science*, and we're going out now. So don't expect us back 'til 3 or 4 in the morning.'

"Sometimes we'd stay up all night long. We could see best at night, right on the front lawn at Hillside. We saw a UFO together! My *first*. We were looking through the big telescope—about 2 a.m. My dad saw it first and said, '*Look, look, quick!*' I looked up and caught the tail-end of two red parallel streaks of light that just went *schwoot* across the sky. I saw a pale disc come back from the path over the house. No noise. It just quietly disappeared. There is nothing to measure by in the night sky so you can't tell if something is a mile away or 100 miles away. So we didn't know. It was very fast. It impressed me so much I literally couldn't talk. I was so flabbergasted. Once in a while we would take the telescope to Palm Springs to a friend's house and look at the stars out there in the desert.

"Dad didn't talk about UFOs much. We talked more on the scientific side of things: planets, nebulas, galaxies, and how they work, but he thought that the possibility for other life in the universe was phenomenal. He thought it was silly to believe we were the only people in the universe. We talked about how incredible it was to see how many stars are in one galaxy and how many galaxies are out there and how many potential light sources or environments just like Earth there are. The possibilities are endless. In 1969 after Neil Armstrong walked on the moon, Dad joked with me and told me he thought he saw footprints on the moon," Steve laughed. "Dad never did think the space program was a waste of money. He was all for it and very excited about it. Dad loved space exploration. He was all for any advancements that the country could achieve in space.

"When we did things together, Dad called it 'Father and Sonning it.' We *father and sonned it,* fencing on the front lawn, or with the catcher's mitts throwing balls, or with photography, bike riding, and astronomy. He was a great father," said Steve. "I always felt he had our interests at heart. He thought of the kids first, where we went to school, what we did, how we behaved, if we were polite, and was very much involved in making sure we were going to turn out OK."

Reflecting on times when his parents separated for a while, he said, "Through some rough times we kids, on the peripheral, knew when there were arguments going on, but through everything, Toni and I never felt he didn't have us in mind. We never felt he didn't care for us, or that he didn't make us his primary concern. I never got a sense that he wasn't a family man, by any means."

"I don't think Guy was the marrying kind," said Janice, "but he made the most of it. He really tried hard at it and raising a family, and he always seemed to be most *comfortable* with his family."

Guy taught his son Steve to study the stars through his high powered telescope. Steve saw his
first UFO with his dad through this telescope. Photo taken in 1969.
(Kathy Gregory Personal Collection; courtesy of Kathy Gregory)

As the end of 1964 was approaching, Guy was hoping to get work. The five shows
on *Bonanza* had been his only work since his return from Europe two years before. Guy
knew how to invest wisely, but they had to be careful.

One day Guy got a call to audition for a "space show" for television at Twentieth
Century-Fox. It was a pilot about a family whose mission was to colonize a new planet in
the year 1997, but their course is averted and they become lost in space. Going from a
Western (*Bonanza*), and what he jokingly called a *South*western (*Zorro*), to a space show
made no difference to Guy as an actor. "The material was all rather similar," he said. "It
was standard TV subject matter. When they said we have a space show out at 20th Century, I knew that the lot wasn't too far from my house—but, I wasn't *taken* with the script
or anything like that."

Guy went in for the screen test, and it seemed that Irwin Allen had already made up
his mind for Guy to play the part of the father on the show. Irwin and his associates
rolled the camera and told Guy that while they made conversation with him they wanted
him to look to the left and to the right, do some business, and show some emotion.
During the takes, Guy lit a cigarette and told them his son keeps him abreast of happenings in science and space. Guy was forty, but he looked younger and John Robinson has
an eighteen-year-old daughter, Judy, so he added some gray at his temples for the test to
look older. In the first take Irwin Allen is heard off camera asking Guy how old his
children are. Guy said Steve was 12. The same questions were asked in each take and
each time Steve became older and older until, finally, in the last take everyone off-
camera laughed when Guy said, "eighteen."

"Have you ever worked with June Lockhart?" Allen asked, and, without skipping a beat, Guy said, "Not *yet!*" and smiled. Everyone laughed.

The next step was waiting for the call. "Guy really needed a job," said Janice. "But even when he needed money he took risks and did scary things. I remember we were painting the dining room ourselves, because we didn't want to pay someone to do it and the phone kept ringing. They were negotiating to hire Guy. Someone would call and say Irwin has made an offer for such and such amount, and Guy would answer, 'No, I won't do it for that. I'll only do the role for x amount.' Then the agent would call the production people back and tell them what Guy said, then he'd call back and tell Guy what the producers said. I was *so* scared. But finally they agreed to Guy's *terms*. And he said, 'I'll *do* it.'" The room was finished, and everything looked brighter.

In 1964, America was enthusiastic about the race into space. This was a year before *Star Trek* hit the airwaves, and there was no primetime cliffhanger show about space on TV. President Kennedy's promise to the nation to put an American on the moon by the end of the 1960s had inspired Irwin Allen to do a modern day *Swiss Family Robinson* and call it *Swiss Family Robinson in Space*. But just before production his legal advisors informed him that Walt Disney wanted to make a movie with that same title, so Irwin changed the title of his prospective series to *Lost in Space*. He began pre-production for a pilot called "No Place to Hide." The Walt Disney film was never filmed. (Disney had made a conventional version of *Swiss Family Robinson* in 1960.)

The concept of the proposed series was a family on a government mission to get to another solar system to colonize a new planet because Earth was becoming overcrowded and her resources were running out. While frozen in suspended animation, the Robinsons lift off in the Gemini XII[217] spacecraft on October 16, 1997. "Irwin chose that year randomly, because it sounded *so far away* it wouldn't matter," said his wife, Shelia Allen.[218] They hoped the show would not be forgotten, but they thought of it as temporary.

Funding came from CBS and Irwin started his search for well-known stars to bring the Robinson family to life. He liked to work with "established stars," as his principals and his choice for the two leads were Guy Williams (of *Zorro*) and June Lockhart (of *Lassie).*

Guy was cast as Professor John Robinson, an astrophysicist; June Lockhart, as his wife, Maureen, a biochemist; Mark Goddard (*Johnny Ringo, The Detectives*) as Major Don West, the pilot of the spacecraft. The three Robinson children each had ample acting experience as well. Marta Kristin, twenty, as the eldest Judy, had done theater and two movies; Angela Cartwright, thirteen, as Penny, had already made four movies and the *Make Room for Daddy* TV series; Bill Mumy, eleven, as Will, was already a veteran of numerous movies and TV shows since he was six years old.

The sets were elaborate and built on a huge sound stage at 20th Century-Fox. There was the spacecraft with its different levels and control panels, and elevator, the lunar-looking rock formations and sandy terrain, caves that appeared as underground ruins of ancient cities, and a land-roving enclosed army tank called the chariot. It was the most expensive one-hour show for television of its time, topping out at $700,000.

The costumes were designed by award-winner Paul Zastupnevich, who chose a popular fabric of the 1960s called velour. In the pilot he gave each character a different color to help identify them, despite the fact that the show was in black and white. CBS did not want to pay the extra $30,000 to film it in color. The silver space flight suits

Guy Williams as John Robinson on *Lost in Space*, a modern day space age Swiss Family Robinson. (Kathy Gregory Personal Collection; courtesy of Kathy Gregory)

were made of a fireproof aluminum fabric used for race car drivers. June Lockhart describes the silver suits of the first and second season: "The spacesuits were unbearably hot, and they were so tight we couldn't sit down in them. We had to rest by leaning against a covered slantboard that looked much like ironing boards with armrests. Underneath we wore leotards and tights, so we could drop the tops down between takes to cool off and be comfortable at least from the waist up. Finally, in the third season, we wore silver jumpsuits made of a more comfortable mylar, which had not been invented when the first two seasons were filmed."

The cinematography was some of the best in television to that day. The stunning visual effects and the special lighting of black and white gave this show a dramatically serious overtone. Music by Bernard Hermann had a creepy, eerie sound of mystery and suspense. Writers were Irwin Allen and Shimon Wincelberg, director, Irwin Allen.

Shortly after the Gemini XII lifts off in the beginning of the show, a meteorite storm causes a fire and the controls to blow out. The Robinsons are awakened from their suspended animation when the craft makes a crash landing on an unknown planet. They are lost, and their sole purpose now becomes simply one of survival. They domesticate strange animals, such as the Bloop, which Penny takes in for a pet and names her Debbie. They survive sub-zero weather by heading south. They encounter and survive an attack of a cyclops, endure the agony of Penny getting lost and found just in the nick of time, survive a lightning storm, an earthquake, and while the chariot takes them across a raging sea they nearly drown after being caught in a whirlpool. All this happens in one hour.

June Lockhart recalled the discomfort of filming the water scene. "We were supposed to be in a whirlpool. We were all just sitting in the chariot and these huge drums of water were dumped on us. It was like being in a big bathtub with the water rising up around us. So, by the time the scene was over, we were all absolutely *drenched*. I jokingly walked over to the assistant director and asked, 'Who do I have to be nice to get off this show?'" she laughed.

Marta remembers that it was so hard to keep from laughing. "They kept throwing buckets of water on us. We would all be trying to talk and the water would be coming into our mouths. We were soaked to the skin. We would also crack up about the dialogue, because we would have to say the most inane things. The problem was the way they wrote the scripts."[219]

"Billy and I were just *kids* so we thought it was *great* fun," said Angela. "We even tried to see who could get the *wettest*. I remember in the earthquake scene in the temple Guy accidentally shot us all with the laser gun," she giggled, "and we had to re-shoot the whole thing again. Billy and I loved the adventure of all that."[220]

In a cyber-room chat during the cast reunion on October 16, 1997, at the Museum of Radio and Television, Los Angeles, Angela said about Guy: "He was gorgeous. He was a wonderful person and a very sweet man. He was really, really nice to work with. He was bigger than life, and really something. It is sad that he's not here with us tonight. He was somebody very special."

Guy's own recollection of the chariot in the sea with buckets of water dumped on them was that it was a "piece of cake" compared to the *box cars* of water in Germany. Besides, he quipped, "Nothing is uncomfortable if you're doing it for *that* kind of dough. It's part of *showbiz*."

"We had problems with the Bloop," said June, at a Star-Con in Pasadena, California, where she sat on a panel with other members of the cast. Debbie, the Bloop, was really a monkey with a head piece on that was supposed to make her look like an alien with long ears. Angela commented, "Working with Debbie, the Bloop, was fun. She was a trained monkey. However, the Bloop bit me once, which wasn't very nice, but, she was pretty sweet."[221]

Billy Mumy (pronounced *Moo*-mee) was a seasoned child actor who knew he wanted to be an actor when he was five years old. Working with Guy Williams was a thrill for him because it was Guy who was his early inspiration. "I became an actor by watching *Zorro* on TV," he said. "I broke my leg and while it was in a cast I watched a lot of TV, but my favorite was *Zorro*. I wanted to be a part of those scenes and action I saw on TV and I begged my mother to let me be an actor." Mumy played a variety of roles, from a demon child on *Twilight Zone* to sweet child roles for Walt Disney. Then he landed this exciting role in his favorite category, science fiction, with his favorite hero, Guy Williams, Zorro. "Guy Williams taught me how to fence so I had a real good time with Guy," said Mumy. "I used to tease him about combing his hair all the time.[222] I dubbed him 'The Comb.'"

"Guy was a day trader long before it was fashionable to be one. Guy would be on the phone with his stockbroker buying and selling stocks within hours in the day. Back then he advised my mother on some stocks to invest in and they are still paying off today. I wish I could tell Guy how forever grateful I am to him for that advice," he said to an audience at a collector's convention.

Twenty years after *Lost in Space*, Guy was asked by someone in Argentina if Bill Mumy was a brat and hard to work with. Guy replied, "Not at all. He was a very bright boy, and delightful to work with."

The original cast of *Lost in Space*. L to R, Mark Goddard, Marta Kristin, Bill Mumy, Angela Cartwright, June Lockhart, and Guy Williams, in their costumes from the first season which was shot in black and white. (Kathy Gregory Collection; courtesy of Kathy Gregory)

The cast of *Lost in Space* in their uncomfortable silver jumpsuits, along with cast additions, Jonathan Harris, (Dr. Smith) and the Robot. (author's personal collection)

Irwin Allen was a master of special effects and that is what he loved the most about production. Everyone who worked for him knew he was more concerned about the special effects than he was for the actors. June explains, "In the pilot when we were doing that scene in the temple and things were falling down on us, Irwin was directing us. We had to move from side to side. When Irwin wanted us to lurch in one direction, he would beat, with a *hammer*, on the bottom on a tin *garbage pail*. He would hit the pail and everyone would move right and he'd hit it again and shout, *'Left!'* I'm not making this stuff up. This particular day the prop men were up there dumping rocks and dirt on us. Finally he yells *'Cut.'* Now, mind you, Guy and I have been *screaming*, *'Will! Penny!'*—calling out and acting our hearts out. After Irwin shouted cut, he yelled out, 'The *debris* was *beauuu–ti–ful!'* I looked at Guy and he looked at me, and I said, 'WE'RE in *trouble.'"*

When the pilot was finished, the story editor Tony Wilson, showed it to CBS. They liked it, but they wanted it only if an antagonist was added to create conflict. They also felt there should be a robot to assist the family and to be able to compute whether or not a planet was suitable for life. Tony Wilson agreed and immediately thought of his friend Jonathan Harris, a veteran of Broadway and television, for the role. Jonathan Harris was hired, as a villain. In the words of Tony Wilson, his character was "an irritant, sort of a charming scoundrel."[223] Writer Shimon Wincelberg created the name Dr. Smith for him because it was simple to remember. Since the cast was already given billing, Jonathan Harris was added as "special guest star," a title he himself thought of.

Shortly after CBS accepted *Lost in Space* it was offered another pilot for another space show called *Star Trek*. They said, "We already *have* a space show," and turned it down. They felt sure their show was better because of the human element of a *family* experiencing life in space together, which they felt was something everyone could identify with.

Since the network felt the original pilot lacked the necessary elements of a robot and an antagonist, it was never aired.[224] However, after all the *Lost in Space* episodes were done, many of the producers and writers—including Irwin Allen himself—considered the pilot, "No Place to Hide," to be the best show. Of the three seasons, he was most proud of that and the first season.

Production for the first season began immediately. Many writers and directors were hired. Art director, Robert Kinoshita began designing The Robot and Bob May was hired to operate the robot from inside while Dick Tufeld,[225] the narrator of the show, was hired to be the robot's voice. The cast and crew worked through the summer for the fall premiere.

In the original one-hour pilot the Robinsons had encountered and overcome *several* different dangerous obstacles in one hour. Now, to save time and money—and since the pilot was never seen on television—the writers went to the original pilot for the subject of the first *five* episodes of the first season.

Music composer Johnny Williams was in the early stage of his career. He wrote the theme song and background music. Early into production, Guy and June liked going to the music room to pass the time listening to the orchestra. In time, Johnny Williams would rise to tremendous popularity and fame for his numerous Oscar-winning soundtracks for movies such as *Star Wars* (and its sequels), *Jaws, Superman, Indiana Jones* (and sequels), *E.T. The Extra-Terrestrial*, the theme for the 1984 Olympics, *Harry Potter*, and many, many more. He became the conductor for the Los Angeles Philharmonic Orchestra. June remembered, "Guy and I would walk to the recording studio to hear the orchestra and John Williams showed us how he listed his music cues for the soundtrack. He would write a short description of what was happening on the screen where the music had to go. We were chatting and he said, 'Here's something that might amuse you.' For the scene when Guy kisses me before I enter the freezing tube, the copy read, 'Zorro kisses Lassie's mother.'" Guy later jokingly signed a picture for June with "To Lassie's Mother From Zorro."

Johnny Williams wrote a lovely movement that was played whenever there was a tender moment between the parents or one of the parents and their children. "I had some nice moments with Guy in father-son scenes," recalled Bill Mumy, "and I loved the sweet theme song that John Williams played during those scenes." He hummed a few bars. "The blue costume in the first season was my favorite of all the seasons. I loved doing the show. I loved comic books and sci-fi and superheroes so this seemed a perfect venture for me. I felt like a superhero," he said. "I cried when it was canceled."

Weekly salaries for the cast for the first season were:

Guy:	$2,000
June Lockhart:	$1,500
Mark Goddard:	$1,250
Marta Kristin:	$850
Angela Cartwright:	$850
Billy Mumy:	$1,000
Jonathan Harris:	$1,750
Bob May:	$350
Dick Tufeld:	$200 (as the voice of the robot) and $200 (as narrator)

Everyone in the cast got along very well, but production people sometimes made working on the show unpleasant. For instance, a lack of communication was eminent. When Jonathan Harris joined the cast, none of the other cast members knew about it. They were not told. They found out when they read the scripts. This lack of communication between the producers/directors and the actors destroys the morale of the talent.

Chapter 41

"Jonathan Harris with Billy and the Robot became the show"
— Shimon Wincelberg, writer

In 1986 Guy said, "I didn't hear anything about adding a robot and Jonathan Harris, I just happened to see it." The idea, however, set well with him. "Well, it solved one of my problems. The creation of the Dr. Smith character and him going with the little boy solved one of my personal mental problems about the show, and that was, 'What are we going to *do* up there? With a teenage girl, an older girl, Marta, a little boy, me and June, and a boyfriend? *What* is that combination of people going to *do* in a space show *week* after *week*?' That used to bother me. I knew that the scripts could be nothing. You have to satisfy the boy, the robot, the teenage girl, the little older than a teenage girl, the boyfriend. That was hard. But when they put Smith and the boy together they could write a million stories about that. And eventually our hours got shorter.[226] So the Jonathan Harris and Billy Mumy relationship solved a lot of problems. It just kept me from a lot of scenes that would have been just unutterably boring."[227]

Even though the pilot had serious overtones, CBS wanted *Lost in Space* to be a "children's show." The networks had strict codes about what was considered harmful or disturbing for children to watch. They had to be careful. Most parents watched primetime TV with their children. If they disapproved, the network could be in trouble. In the 1992 book, *Lost in Space Forever*, June Lockhart says, "In the pilot Guy and I were developing a father-mother/husband-wife, relationship. Then for the series the edict came down from CBS that Guy Williams was not to touch me in any way, not even to take my hand to help me down out of the chariot. Someone at CBS thought that any demonstration of affection between the parents would embarrass the children." At a Sci-Fi convention, where she retold the story, June added, laughing, "So, after that, we had to show our affection with *'longing looks.'*"

Marta Kristin feels this edict of no touching is the reason why her romance with Major West was never developed. "I think it would have been fun if a romance had developed, maybe even a spin-off of Don and me and our own family in space, but even the *suggestion* of a romance was suddenly dropped."

Writers were also careful with certain words. For instance, instead of having the robot give the command "Kill!," it was "Destroy!"

In the summer of 1965, before the show aired, there was a lot of publicity about the new space show. The stars of the show had to make personal appearances to promote the show for the network. Guy and June attended the Affiliates Banquets in New York and San Francisco to represent CBS. Janice went with Guy and June's husband, John Lindsey, accompanied her. There were autograph seekers everywhere. Guy was still signing his name with his trademark "Z" below his name. Representatives from TV stations all over the nation attended and each table of actors from a network TV show had a representative of a station at their table. For the San Francisco trip, Guy took his entire family. For the New York trip, it was sort of a sentimental journey for him and Janice alone.

Guy's old friend Russ Johnson, had landed the role of The Professor on CBS's *Gilligan's Island* the previous year. He and his wife attended the banquet in New York, and Guy and Janice were delighted to see them again. They planned an evening together, as it had been a long time since the two couples been together. "It was fun to see them again," said Janice. "We took them to our favorite place, Rumplemayers in the St. Moritz, and after dinner we got ice cream like we always did when Guy and I lived in New York. Guy got vanilla, but Russ couldn't decide whether to get strawberry, vanilla, or chocolate. So Guy said, '*Get 'em all!*' And he *did!*"

When Guy got back to Hollywood there were more bookings for personal appearances to promote the new show.

> *Daily Variety*, Friday, August 6, 1965
> *14 CBSeries Stars on Promo Safari—a two-*day junket of promo-publicity activities by 14 personalities on CBS-TV's fall sked gets underway this weekend, and the thesps leave tomorrow to begin their p.a.'s in Dallas and Atlanta, on first leg of web's fifth annual weekend star treks…the following weekend to Washington and Chicago. Taking off from here tomorrow…Kathie Brown, Bob Crane…and Guy Williams (*Lost in Space*). Half the group will sky to Dallas for interviews and promo filming tomorrow, the other half to Atlanta.

Coincidentally, that same week, on August 2, 1965, *Zorro* returned in reruns, and in many states, Guy was playing opposite himself on TV. On Wednesday, September 15, 1965, 7:30-8:30 p.m., *Lost in Space* first aired on CBS. It captured the imagination of young kids immediately. *Lost in Space* was a unique show in that an *entire family* was out in space. It was tough competition for two half-hour shows that aired at the same time on ABC: *The Adventures of Ozzie and Harriet* and *The Patty Duke Show*, which starred, Academy Award winner, Patty Duke and Guy's old friend, Bill Shallert, who played Patty's father. NBC at the time had *The Virginian*, a one-hour Western viewed by an older audience.

June and Guy appeared together on the cover of the nationwide *TV Guide* for November 6-12, 1965 in a picture of them *floating* in space in the silver spacesuits worn on the show. "The day of that photo shoot was unforgettable," said Janice. "I got a call from someone I didn't know from 20th who said, 'Don't get alarmed, but…' Well, when someone says that you naturally get alarmed. Then they said, 'Guy has had a fall, but he's all right.' They explained that the cable wires that were holding him up broke and Guy fell several feet to the floor. He was sore, but not badly hurt, so they were able to finish the shoot."

June Lockhart and Guy on the cover of TV Guide for November 1965 "floating in space"
to promote *Lost In Space*. During this shoot, Guy fell when his wire broke.
(author's personal collection)

June Lockhart remembers it vividly. "Guy and I were swinging together and then his wire broke. He fell twelve feet onto a cement floor! But Guy was very athletic and he had learned how to fall from stuntmen. When he landed on his shoulder, he remembered to *roll*. And that's why he was not badly injured. But I thought he had broken his *neck*. I yelled '*GET—ME—DOWN from herrrre!*'

"When we did the flying sequences in the show, they were very complicated and uncomfortable. I had to wear a special flying suit with a harness around my pelvis. It's very hard to get your legs up and moving and keep your balance. The harness is very tight around the femoral artery and shuts off circulation, so you can only stay in them a short time. After that accident, we didn't use the flying suits anymore."

The show's popularity grew rapidly. Shimon Wincelberg said, "Jonathan Harris, with Billy and the Robot, became the show, while the two main leads somehow got themselves pushed into the background. They were playing these solid, square parents and it was hard to make them very interesting as characters. I think the actors were excellent. Guy Williams was a pleasure. He was such a nice, cooperative, helpful guy although the show didn't do much for him professionally."

At one point Wincelberg said, "the two main leads got them*selves* pushed into the background." Later, Wincelberg admitted that the writers *overlooked* "what two wonderful actors like Guy and June could do." He conceded that it was more *fun* to write about Smith and the boy,[228] so the writers kept it up.

Dr. Smith's character changed radically with each episode from a dark and fearless saboteur of the first episode, to a cowardly ninny who hid behind the boy when danger occurred and sometimes persuaded him to do his evil deeds for him. By episode #18, "The Sky Pirate," writer Carey Wilber changed Dr. Smith from the sinister *straight* villain to a *comedic* cad. It is sometimes speculated that this change may have saved the show.

Shimon Wincelberg said, "In the first few episodes, Smith was an evil character, who would do horrendous things. Then Irwin Allen changed him to a more comedic type villain. Harris added a great deal of the character by himself."[229]

From *Lost in Space Forever*, Marta Kristin said,

> Jonathan knew how to write the scenes for himself. He would take the script and rewrite it, so he would always have the last word in the scene.

When the great Mercedes McCambridge was a guest in Episode #25, "The Space Croppers," she had many scenes with Jonathan. "Jonathan certainly rules the roost,"[230] she noted.

Marta Kristin, Mark Goddard (Don West) and Guy passing the time while waiting for the special effects to be set up between takes. (author's personal collection)

It wasn't long into the first season that everyone *other* than Dr. Smith, Will, and the Robot, became *bit players*. None of them were happy about it. What amazed Guy was that "the bad guy" was turning out to be the key role of the show. He had thought that the "*good* guy" was always the key figure.

There was one way of saving a bad guy from being hated, though, and that was to make him comedic. It worked. "The two main leads," as time went by, were no longer the two main leads, and sometimes had to struggle just to be *included* in a scene. Guy knew what he had signed for. It never occurred to him that it would change.

Disney's battle with ABC had been a different type of battle, and now this was another, but in both situations Guy knew he had fallen victim to network edicts. He was unprepared to cope with either. Each was out of his control, and each had hurt his career.

A magazine article in the late 1960s reveals Guy's new state of mind.

> Guy Williams is a rarity in show business. He takes everything nice and easy without getting all involved about the importance of being a star. "I don't consider TV a serious medium," the *Lost in Space* star told me. "And I don't consider myself a dedicated actor. If you get wound up in this acting business, it can lead to personal unhappiness."

Halfway through the season a "formula format" began to play each week. Guy recalled the recurring theme. "The boy would misbehave, and the character that Jonathan played would betray the little boy. Well, that's OK once, twice, but all the time, it sounded like ratings suicide."

Irwin Allen was very serious about the show, the scripts, and the special effects, to the point where people around him felt he was *overly* serious. His attitude left no room for a sense of humor. It was this kind of seriousness and his puzzling idiosyncrasies that left him wide open to teasing. But the teasing only angered him and made him more difficult to talk to.

Actors and their dialogue were Irwin's secondary interest. "The main idea of those shows was the *special effects*,"[231] said Guy. "Irwin was very good at special effects and Irwin loved to do special effects. Our struggle was to stay away from all equipment while we were doing scenes. He would always stick us in front of things that were turning and buzzing and whizzing. Who wants to do a scene that one has *worked on* and *learned*, standing in front of a twirling whirling machine?" said Guy. "No one is going to see you. They're going to listen to and watch the machine. Our struggle was to stay away from all the flashing equipment while we were doing a scene. So we tried to move to the left or right to get away from the machine and hoped the camera would follow us."

"Irwin was different than Disney," added Guy. "I liked him. Not as a personal friend, but I understood many of the things that perplexed people *about* Irwin. I liked Irwin once I got to know what makes Irwin move. But, Irwin was not your average guy."

While Irwin Allen was a good storyteller and wonderful with special effects, he didn't do much directing when he directed. Angela Cartwright described Irwin with merely one word: "Interesting."[232] "He had a lot of faith that things would somehow magically come together while filming a scene," she said. "I guess that's why he always tried to get the big name stars for his projects. I think he felt that something special would just *happen* when all these *stars* came together."

Director Sobey Martin was nice and made them laugh, but didn't help with direction. Marta recalls, "Irwin had a friend, Sobey Martin, who was an elderly man and he would go to sleep in his chair. You could suggest things to Sobey and no matter what it was, I mean, it could have been something really ridiculous, but he'd rustle a bit and say in a deep voice, 'Yeh, yeh, *shoot* it. *Shoot* it,'" Marta laughed. "Irwin used him a lot, so Irwin was just pulling the strings when Sobey was directing. Other times Irwin was *sort of* directing in that he was there just to *sort of* move people around and set up the camera angles."

Irwin had little consideration for actors. Director Don Richardson showed the same lack of respect by referring to the actors as lions. Once when Richardson thought Irwin was being influenced by one of the actors, he discouraged it. He advised Irwin to be like a circus master who does not fight with his lions, but has to crack the whip at them.[233] Marta remembers one cameraman saying, "Bring out the animals now."

"Actors are always considered the low man on the totem pole," she said, "even though we are absolutely necessary. We created what the writers wrote and brought it to life, yet we were considered by some to be talentless and unworthy."

Irwin Allen's attitude of no respect and concern for his actors was passed down to some of his directors and crew members. One cast member said that Don Richardson was particularly mean to Marta and Angela for no reason.

Mark Goddard will never forget the day Irwin shocked him with his belligerent behavior. "One day Guy and I were doing a scene and I guess we upset Irwin about something. He yelled at Guy and said, 'You're a *prick!*' Then he turned and pointed to *me,* and said 'And you're a *double* prick!'"

When Guy complained of having very few lines, the director gave Mark's lines to Guy, only he didn't bother telling Mark. When it came time to give the line, Mark heard his line coming from Guy and wondered what was going on. Mark didn't blame Guy. The people running the show did not have a clue how to create harmony among its actors and crew.

As the show progressed, Don Richardson verbally abused the cast members, saying mean things to and about them. Years later in an interview he admitted to going home and drinking a fifth of vodka every night. The cast has some unpleasant memories about those "morning-afters" they would rather not talk about. Aside from Richardson, most of the other directors were nice, but their direction could have been better had it not been for pressure from Irwin Allen. "Irwin was a *'director killer,'*" said Jonathan Harris. "He stunted their creativity by spying on them and made them nervous by enforcing deadlines on them." A few directors quit after doing *two* episodes, and refused to work for him again.

The work was hard. Call time was 6 a.m. The actors worked 10-12 hours Monday through Thursdays and they were always kept very late on Fridays because there was no "turnaround." Years ago actors were not protected by a law enforced today that says actors have to have twelve hours off between workdays, called "turn around time." Since there was no work on Saturday they were kept very late filming on Fridays. All scenes were shot at the 20th Century-Fox studio. There were hours of rehearsal and long hours of waiting around while lights and explosives were set up. Actors have to keep their energy level up for scenes, and their wits about them, after tiring hours of standing and waiting around mostly for technical problems to be worked out. They have to look good, feel good, and know their lines early the next morning, then relearn them when the script is often rewritten. The explosives were dangerous and sometimes even the most cautious were injured. A crew member was sent to the hospital one day because of a mishap with an explosive, which was one of *many* accidents over the years of filming the show.

Guy would leave home at 5:30 each morning. It became routine for him to check the Market first. Then he had the pleasure of driving his Masaratti to work. "Guy would walk to the top of our property and we could look straight down and see 20th from there," said Janice. "We could see the wide turn Santa Monica Boulevard makes and it looked like a picture of a Paris street from up there. Guy would say, 'That's the way I go to work every day,' and he'd talk about what a pleasure it was for him to drive his sports car early in the morning when there was very little traffic. He looked forward to that."

A traffic cop used to stake himself out for Guy each morning as he streaked by toward the gates of the studio. In all the years Guy worked there, that cop could never catch him.

Chapter 42

"Take the money and shut up."

– Bernie Giler

Critics like to talk about typecasting of TV actors. Since George Reeves had a tough time shaking his Superman image, writers were concerned now if Adam West could shake his image as Batman. Guy Williams was an example that typecasting can be overcome.

Charlotte News, Saturday, July 9, 1966
"Guy Williams Beat the Game—He Is Zorro No More"

by Bob Thomas

To the writers of *Batman* Adam West will not necessarily be permanently identified as Batman. The show had started in January 1966 opposite *Lost in Space*.

"I don't mind the fact that *Zorro* is playing all over the world as reruns. Those residual checks can be mighty comforting," said Guy.

Guy said the pictures he made in Europe, "helped establish me as an actor. By the time I returned from Europe...the Zorro image was getting well dissipated."

Williams beat the game. A few years back it seemed that he would be stuck forever in the image of Zorro.

The ratings for *Lost in Space* climbed and remained so high in the first season that ABC's *Ozzie and Harriet* and *Patty Duke* were canceled. They were replaced in 1966-67 with *Batman* and *The Monroes*. The *Virginian* remained on NBC.

The serious space drama Guy had originally signed for had changed, and with it, his top billing. Guy was concerned about his career and the show. He went to Irwin Allen, as a friend, to talk about it. He asked Irwin to consider better storylines for the sake of the show. Irwin knew Guy felt like he was becoming "background," and he promised Guy there would be some new episodes in which he would be featured.

The second season was in color. The Robinsons repaired their spaceship and left the unknown planet. From the start of the second season Guy was not in much of the action. Sometimes he appeared only a short time at the end of the show. He had less to do than ever.

In the September 24, 1966 issue of *TV Guide,* an article about Guy appeared by Mike Fessier, Jr., one of the writers for the show. During the interview it was not known to Guy that the objective of the article was to show the negative side of the production. "He came to the house at noon and we spent a lovely time," said Janice of Fessier. "I made lunch, and we ate and talked, and he interviewed Guy. We thought he had enjoyed himself, but then he wrote this article and it was *mean.* He made Guy out to be bitter and ugly. We never knew how that happened or why."

Guy later found out that it was the current trend for *TV Guide* to try to get the negative on a lot of series. They wanted to sell their magazine. It was happening to a lot of other actors and they picked Guy, and said he was unhappy with the Jonathan Harris character. It was unfortunate publicity and it offended Guy.

It was soon made known that Guy was not the only cast member who had a complaint to take to Irwin Allen. The press was having a field day with the discontentment of most of the cast.

News reporter Allen Rich, of *Citizen-News,* humorously elaborated about looking into these rumors in an article dated Wednesday, Oct. 12, 1966.

From time to time there have been rumbles of great discontent among the actors on the successful *Lost in Space* series. Pivotal point of the alleged acrimony is our old friend, the villainous hamola, "Dr. Smith," as played by Jonathan Harris. It seems that Dr. Smith-Harris has been getting all the juicy lines—and when he doesn't the robot does. This has supposedly caused "great pain and anguish" to the other cast members, as a lawyer might put it.

There are almost as many regulars on *Lost in Space* as on the first team of the Dodgers, although come to think of it, they hit the ball better. They include, in addition to Jonathan Harris, Guy Williams, Junie Lockhart, Billy Mumy, Angela Cartwright, and Marta Kristen.

It has seeped down the TV grapevine that this group, hereinafter designated as the people, is continually taking its beefs to Producer Irwin Allen in a sort of The-People-Against-Irwin-Allen sort of thing. I even read something in a national magazine in which the writer stated that upon visiting the *Lost in Space* set at 20th Century-Fox he found Guy Williams "stalking about and glaring at Jonathan Harris."

Now, personally I do not like to hear about anyone stalking about and glaring at Jonathan Harris who is a splendid old hamola I am only too happy to regard as a friend. So I arranged to interview Guy Williams, question him sternly and get at the truth of the matter. However, my first look at Williams, the program's leader of the space group, was no end discouraging. He is a young guy whom I would have to spot about 20 years, he is 6 feet 3 inches tall and weighs 190 pounds. Also, as you may recall, he used to be Zorro and dispatched many an actor, if not columnist, to the hereafter on the screen.

In addition, while it is traditionally true that a newsman can protect his source, who will protect the newsman? But the show must go on.

"Did you stalk about and glare at lovable old Jonathan Harris?" I asked timidly.

"No, I did not," said Guy, in a surprisingly amiable manner.

"Well, then what is all the fuss about? You know, concerning discontent on the set?"

"It has been overstressed. Look at it from my point of view. When I signed for this series, I got the top billing. And as far as I know, I'm getting more money than any of the others.

"But my roles have been lean, and I like to earn my money. The way things stack up now I've got to be getting more money per word than even, say, Laurence Olivier. So all I am trying to do is to get them to put more derring-do in my role.

"There is absolutely nothing personal in it, nothing at all against Jonathan, whose comedy expertise has added so much to the series.

"You know, as the series was originally written it was little else but special effects and a continuing sequence of accidents, earthquakes, and monsters.

"Now not only myself, but the others, too, feel that if our characters are strengthened and we have more to do—that, combined with Harris' comedy, will make for a better show. Good scenes for the rest of us would be bound to help," he said.

So, how does producer Irwin Allen feel about it all? You've been bothering him to do something about it, I hear, was my comment.

"I do not think bothering is the proper word. Let us say I am working at it—and I think it is paying off. I have at least three shows coming up in which I'll be the central figure."

I said, well, I do not know what the writers have cooked up for you in those coming scripts, but I have several ideas for you that you may transmit to Mr. Allen, your producer. But don't tell old Doc Smith.

Like this: (a) As the world-famous Zorro you used to be pretty handy with a sword. Use it and slash up the Robot until it just can't compute.

(b) In as much as you are the head of the series' Robinson space family, act like it. Tell 'em to write you in as a father figure—the Lorne Greene of Outer Space.

So far as I am concerned that closes the case of The People vs. Irwin Allen. Except to comment in closing that Junie Lockhart doesn't need any better roles. That tight-fitting space suit does it all.

In the first season Guy *was* making more than anyone on the show. But, Guy didn't know at the time of the interview that Jonathan was actually the highest paid on the show, getting $2,750. Salaries for the rest of the cast—Guy Williams: $2,500; June Lockhart: $1,750; Mark Goddard: $1,500; Marta Kristen: $1,100; Billy Mumy: $1,250; Angela Cartwright: $1,000; Bob May: $420; Dick Tufeld: $400.[234]

It didn't take long for Guy to see that the second season was not going to be what he

278 • Guy Williams: The Man Behind The Mask

was promised. Instead, his situation became worse. Guy began to have fewer and fewer lines and shots. Fed up, at times he found ways to cope. Sometimes a camera shot from behind would shoot over his shoulder and being camera-wise, he always knew where it was, so he would lean into the picture. If Guy thought a line was absolutely awful he'd fluff it at every take. The director would finally say, OK, forget that line just say... blah, blah blah, and Guy wouldn't have to say it.

When Guy and June were doing one of the few scenes written for them, they were shocked when the director placed Jonathan in the foreground. Guy wanted to walk out. June gave Guy some level-headed advice. "I reminded him that breaking a contract in Hollywood leaves a *big* stench that can take as many as twenty-five years to go away," she said. "An actor can't get *near* a production company if he has broken a contract."

Janice remembers when Guy did the next best thing at the time. "The biggest disappointment in his career was the way *Lost in Space* turned the story around," said Janice. "One day Guy was so upset with the script he just called in sick. He was becoming very disenchanted at that point and didn't want to go in. A little later the doorbell rang and they had sent a doctor to the house to see if he was really sick. Guy just smiled and said 'Of *course!* Can't you see how sick I am?'"

June was also not happy about the way the show had changed. "The show was to deal with the problems of a family and their experiences surviving in space. As the show went on I was concerned that the relationships between the parents and their children weren't developed more fully; however, that wasn't my responsibility. It changed into more of a comedy. Maybe we wouldn't have had a show if it weren't for Jonathan. After all, we had a good rating, so it was selling. I never considered quitting the series because I think that's bad form. If you sign a contract, you should stick with it. I simply took it as it came when I realized that was how it was going to be. I knew the other cast members were also concerned about the change. I took it as a time to do more reading and to learn more about classical music."

Guy's pal, Bernie Giler, a TV writer who worked for MGM, would listen to Guy vent his frustrations. In 1966 Giler said, "Guy is a real Sicilian. He has all the polish and temperament of a true Sicilian and the tremendous pride and ego to go with it. I have to beat him over the head...'Take the money and shut up' I tell him."[235]

Norman Foster's son, Robert, was at Guy's house one evening when Guy was on the phone with Irwin Allen. "I was in the same room with Guy and I heard him *begging* the producer to get better storylines, better scripts, for the sake of the production, not just for *him*. He begged them to spend more money on the series, to hire better talent to work on every phase of *Lost in Space*. He wanted the best that he could get."

Rob Foster had his own opinions about Guy's discontent with *Lost in Space*. "I think Guy might have been getting flack from friends who told him they didn't watch *Lost in Space*. Guy was used to a certain kind of respect from *Zorro*. He loved that and in *Lost in Space* he was reduced to—what? Guy probably wanted feedback from me, but I didn't watch *Lost in Space*. I wish now that I had, but I didn't like it."

Costumes of large chickens and recycled costumes from Irwin's other shows such as *Voyage to the Bottom of the Sea* began to cheapen the show, along with silly scripts.

Robert never saw Guy lose his temper. "He was brilliant that way. He had a gentleman's anger, always controlled. Guy had a funny sense of humor when he got mad. He would use humor and cynicism when he got angry."

Some critics accused the second season of becoming "campy" perhaps because it was competing with *Batman*. Guy said, "Everybody was using the word camp for the show, but I don't think 'camp' is the right word. To me, when a show gets 'the cutes' it kills itself. You can get campy and do all kinds of stuff. If it's done in good style, it's amazing what you can get away with and have people love it. Well, look, that's what we did with *Zorro*. We did outrageous things but in good style, I mean, Disney saw to that—that the style and the tone was going to be first class. But the things in it were, you know," he laughed, "*incredible,* some of them.

"I loved *Lost in Space* from the stand point of the *people*. I enjoyed working with them. Well, I had the same experience in *Zorro* too. I always enjoy who I'm working with. The only exception I have to that was when I was on the *Bonanza* episodes. I just didn't feel right about any of that."[236]

As Guy began to be written out of the shows more and more, he became more and more concerned about his career. Guy, a star from *Zorro*, and June, a star from *Lassie*, were signed as the stars of this show, but they were finding themselves on the set doing a scene and not even being on camera for that scene. If they or their agents had not said anything, they would not have been seen as much as they were.

Marta Kristin used to also hear "Take the money and shut up," but she noted it was always from friends who were not actors and they did not understand. An actor has to think of his marketability. The saying is: "You are only as good as your last show." If he allows himself to become background, he may never again be anything else.

Marta and the other actors understood what Guy and June were going through. "I was not given what I was promised, but I was too young to know how to handle it. I was not taken care of during that show, and it caused me a lot of emotional distress. Don Richardson was a very difficult director to work for. When Guy and June were doing a scene and they weren't going to be covered, they felt that was very demeaning. One can understand that. I certainly can. I think it was really unreasonable for Don Richardson to say they would *complain*.[237]

"Having committed to the show, thinking they were going to be stars of the show, finding out they indeed were being upstaged by Jonathan, and that the show was no longer written for them, they were just covering their bases, that's all. They were protecting themselves. Nothing more than that. I wish *I had*."

Chapter 43

"...today's father speaking of tomorrow"
— May Mann, journalist

Lost in Space established Guy Williams as the protective loving father to a generation of TV watchers from the mid- to late 1960s, the paradigm of a family man. Teenagers wrote to him for advice.

America was determined to be number one in space. Its people were divided about the Vietnam war, drugs and sex were overused and abused, women were burning their bras, race riots shocked and saddened the nation, and hippies had love-ins in parks. Guy spoke out on his political views and his desire to go into politics one day in an article by journalist James Gregory for *Silver Screen* magazine, August 1967, titled "Hippies, Get me to the White House."

I can't get involved in it right now because neither the Democratic nor the Republican party seems right for me," he said. "You need a base if you want to get into politics, and I can't see mine in either party. I think the only base for me lies in a whole group of people out there who want none of what's going on within either party. Most people call them hippies.

I *am* associated mentally with these people, because I've been that way all my life in terms of questioning everything, of not accepting everything, an attitude which may appear far out to some people. To me it isn't, because when I see a whole group of people, questioning everything as the hippies do, it's just normal. As a matter of fact, it's damn healthy!

Many hippies are superficially unpalatable to most people. But not all. The ones in college who are working hard at an education and coming out with the withdrawal idea are maybe not the same crowd that runs around with earrings. But earrings are okay too, if people want to wear them. And this isn't the first time in history that people have worn long hair! I think a man has the right to wear long hair if he wants to and dress the way he likes.

If he were in politics, he said:

"I'd fight against baloney!

"I like to think of hippies as the baloney-proof generation. The dissemination of nonsense just has to be stopped! They don't *want* baloney—they want the truth.

"I'm against our government's policy on Vietnam. I'm ashamed of what we're doing in Vietnam—on a personal level, because it's being done in my name.

"Personal freedom is a very touchy thing with me. I feel that's possibly one of the reasons I'm an actor. An actor or anyone else in the arts has a great deal of freedom, compared to someone in a corporate structure. I would try to make more personal freedom available to most people."

Among the laws that Guy would favor in order to increase personal freedom, is a law legalizing abortion "under any circumstances," he told me, "because the person whose body it is should have the right to say what to do.

"I think you should have the right to go to hell in a wheelbarrow if you want. You should have that right...And if you don't choose to abuse yourself or whatever, you don't have to. Abortion should never be compulsory and it should never be outlawed. Similarly, I do think marijuana should be legalized.

"I think gambling should be legal too. When I was in Europe, I did a lot of gambling—a lot of roulette-wheeling. I enjoy the game and I don't feel that I was corrupted in any way.

"All the taboos we brought over on the whaling ships are out, they're just little veils of ignorance that have to be lifted. When that's done, it creates a nice, free society where you can then start to grapple with the real problems that are going to be left.

"When we keep people in office if they'll promise that they won't become Communists, we stop there. We don't go further, asking, 'Well, what

Janice and Guy at a party after the premiere of *Is Paris Burning?*, 1966
(Mary Spooner personal collection; courtesy of Mary Spooner)

will you do? Are you going to take people's freedom away?'

"I think the whole scene will change when the younger generations—the bright young people I've been talking about – come into their own and become voters.

"I feel if I were in politics I could communicate with *them* more easily than with any other group—the bright young people of today."

Although Guy believed in legalizing marijuana, he was not fond of the weed himself and refused it at parties. When he noticed his son watching a weed grow in the yard, he investigated and put a stop to it immediately—with a strong lecture that quickly cured Steve's curiosity.

"When I met Guy, his liberal ideals had to be kept underwraps lest he be labeled a *Leftist*," said Janice. "Now being liberal was *the scene*. The 'times' had caught up with Guy's way of thinking on many political issues and rules for raising children." Regarding censorship of sex and violence in movies and TV, however, Janice said, "Guy would want people to have freedom to do what they wanted, but he was already saying they were going too far."

From a magazine article written in the fall of 1966, by May Mann:

"I don't worry about my little daughter facing life on her own! She's very much with everything. She's well equipped. I'll not worry about her, only the guy she goes out with. I won't be worried about his morality as much as I will be about how he drives a car!" Guy Williams is today's father speaking of tomorrow.

"When my little girl goes out the door on a date, I want her back alive and whole...13,200 young people between the ages of 15 and 24 died in car accidents last year!"

"I'm actually a double father image," Guy said, leaving the space travel world to concentrate on the one he lives in today. "Besides my two television children, I have two of my own brand. Namely Steve, thirteen, and Toni, who I say is an eight-year-old teenager. Kids this age are wide open to impression and suggestion, if you don't just *talk* to them, but *level* with them...

"Here's a letter I received from a fifteen-year-old girl today (who was in trouble). She writes 'I wouldn't dare tell my parents. You're hip with an open mind. I'm not scared of you and I have to tell somebody.'

"This isn't the age of the old melodrama, when the father turns his fallen daughter out in the street...

"Personally, I am not as concerned with morals as I am with reckless drivers!

"Until my little daughter goes out on dates, I am her sole male protector, looking out for her from the day she was born, trying to anticipate and thwart any dangers that might beset her. She is very precious to me. I am not going to hand her over, for some reckless careless boy, who wants to let off steam by driving his car hell-bent, without thought of risking her life, to suit his mood.

"Most young boys are not thinking ahead when they go out for fun. But a girl the same age is born with an intuition that gives her an adult outlook far ahead of a boy. Chemically, she is set up rationally. She seems to know by instinct, whereas a boy has to grow up to be a man. He has to learn everything.

"The idea that sex is a taboo subject not to be discussed is for the birds. If people would be natural and not attempt to steep sex with mystery, there would not be so much made about it.

"When I was a kid, a bunch of us would go to movies, usually four guys and four girls. We'd sit with whom we wanted to see the film. There was no special emphasis made on it. We shared popcorn and had a lot of laughs. To us, a date with a girl meant taking a girl to a restaurant and ordering champagne. You had to be older to afford to do that.

"When I went to high school, kids didn't all have cars."

"All any child or parent can do," he reiterated, "is to keep communication between them open at all times. That is the best insurance. For society's demands change with the constantly changing times.

"Times, customs, morals and principals sweep on in this constant change of viewpoint from one generation to the next. Basic values like honesty, integrity, decency, and sincerity alone remain basic."

In 1965, Toni and Steve were both taking piano lessons. "Steve was getting all the sheet music I wanted to play," resounded Toni, with a note of sibling rivalry. "I told my teacher I wanted to play those pieces, but she wanted me to wait. So, I swiped Steve's Bach and classics and learned them, one note at a time. I was very determined."

Janice and Guy went to see Toni in her recital at the Bel Air Hotel. "I was so nervous I barely remember the recital. I just remember the waiting room before I went on."

Steve took piano lessons for three years from Eva Retick, on Little Santa Monica Boulevard across from the Friars Club. "Toni might have complained that she was getting the 'Bumble Bee' and I was playing Listz, but I had bigger hands, a bigger reach," he reasoned.

Near the end of the show's hiatus in 1967, Guy took his family with him to New York to visit his relatives, combining business with pleasure. He appeared for a week on CBS's special *Family Password* which pitted one family against another, each with a celebrity on their side. The other celebrity was Irene Ryan, who was currently starring as "Granny" on CBS's *The Beverly Hillbillies*, which followed *Lost in Space* for its entire run. Host Allen Ludden mentions that Guy was in a movie with Irene Ryan during his early days of acting at Universal, *Bonzo Goes to College*. Of his early film career as a contract player, Guy said, "It was eminently forgettable."

After the game show taping, he went to Albany to help with a Cerebral Palsy telethon. Kevin Burns, now a producer at 20th Century-Fox, remembers when he was a little boy longing to talk to his hero of *Lost in Space*. "Call in your pledge and you can talk to Guy Williams of *Lost in Space*," they said on TV. Kevin was only eight, but in hopes of speaking to John Robinson of his favorite TV show, he called in to pledge. "Will you pledge?" they asked.

Kevin said, "Yes, yes, but can I talk to Guy Williams?"

"Well, he's busy at the moment."

Thirty years later Kevin Burns still regrets missing the opportunity to talk to Guy. As an employee of 20th he has since worked on the sound stage where *Lost in Space* was filmed. He had purchased the original Robot used on the show and exhibits it with other memorabilia from his collection at nostalgia shows he produces for fans.

While Janice and the family stayed with Guy's mother in New York, Valerie was having martial problems. With two young daughters to support, (soon to be three), she was working hard to make ends meet. She particularly wanted to see Janice, whom she loved dearly, and she had not seen little Toni since they visited after Europe. "I loved seeing the children and Jan. I asked about Guy, but I was told he was busy. He was always busy. I didn't know what he was doing, but he was *busy*. The family did get together at dinner at my uncle's house, but my brother and I didn't say much to each other."

Guy's health food consciousness peaked at this point in his life and the family had to follow suit. "We had what we called our Jack LaLanne salads," said Janice, "which were made of lots and lots of chopped vegetables."

Toni remembers, "We couldn't even have cereal boxes in the house with *sugar* on the label. Mom and Dad were so diet-conscious then, but Mom would get it for us as a little treat now and then. Dad would come along, open the box and dump it out very dramatically into the trash in front of us. I'd stand there and watch all that delicious cereal pouring out. Then he would leave the empty *box* out for all of us to see! When I visited my grandmother in New York, she gave us Cheerios! Even though Mommy Clare called them 'Ghastlies,'" she laughed, "she wanted to give us a treat.

"When Mommy Clare came out here to visit, she wanted me to put on some weight so she started making whole wheat-germ hot cereal with bananas and syrup and told me to '*Mangia.*' I learned some Italian from her and later Marge Silver, Art's wife, gave me a book on Italian to supplement what I'd learned."

"Dad would say a few words in Italian to keep our ear in. All *commands*!" she laughed. "Like 'Basta!,' 'Mangia!,' and '*Vene qui subido*!' (Come here right now!). When we had farfalle pasta for dinner, he would put a Trini Lopez record on and we knew Dad was saying dinner was ready. There was a line in the song where he says farfalle and Dad would play it *real loud* so we would come down to dinner.

"Dad was unpredictable. You never knew if you were supposed to fear him that moment or that day or whether he was in a great mood and you were going to have the *best* day of your life. You never knew. When times were good, they were great."

"Dad was a walking encyclopedia," said Toni. "You could ask him anything. He was very intelligent. I miss his sense of humor most of all. He could see humor when someone else didn't.

"I was never surprised in public when fans chased my dad or thought he was special because he was treated that way at home. Dad was impressive in his personal life. Weren't all fathers like this? It was no surprise to us that everyone else thought that. We treated him like everyone else did. I thought all fathers were like this."

"Life with a celebrity father, the news articles, TV shows, to me was normal," explains Toni. "It was business as usual—*life* as usual, ever since I can remember. It wasn't until I started breaking into the business myself that I knew how diligent he had to have been, how *good* he had to have been, and how all those things had to line up. I realized how hard it was to achieve what he had."

Chapter 44

"Dad was always a mystery to me."

– Toni Williams

Guy's temper was uneven during the frustrating times in *Lost in Space*, especially from fall 1966 to the Spring of 1967. His frustration over the scripts and the change in the show was something he brought home with him. Janice understood it. Steve overlooked it. But Toni was too young to understand it and she took it personally.

Toni's childhood memories are different because she didn't have her formative years with Guy as Steve had. From the day she was born, her dad was working and not home much. She knew he was important because the household evolved around him and her mother made him important.

"As a child I felt he was mean, but as an adult I understood why he did things," she reflected. "I felt I had known Mom a long time, but Dad was a mystery to me, because he wasn't there much. What I loved about him was his humor. He laughed at things that were not funny. It was twisted sometimes, but in a good way. It was unique, and it was part of what made him interesting. He always had a different slant on things."

Guy had his moods just like anyone else. Janice said, "He was quick to anger, and quick to get over it. He had a typical Italian personality. He blew up and got over it and went on. Didn't hold grudges."

"One day when I saw my dad on the set," said Toni, "I felt like I was watching a different person. This quiet, docile, and sweet person sitting around the set was not the person I saw at home."

Guy's disposition changed as conditions at work changed and, because *Lost in Space* was so trying for him, he often brought his frustrations home with him.

"When I was a child a lot of times I was just really scared of him," said Toni. "First of all, he was so much *bigger* than me, and more imposing. And he was *firm*. I never knew where a rule was coming from. Sometimes it just was coming from out of the blue because that day it wasn't right. One day something would be OK, but next day it was not. I would tell him he was being unfair and he would come back with, 'Life is not fair, and I'm going to teach you first hand.'

"Or, his favorite, 'This is not a democracy. No one elected me.' I hated when he said that, especially when I was angry. I got tired of hearing that, and also, 'I am the benevolent ruler.' As an adult I understood why he did things and I appreciated him more as an adult."

"I think Toni and Guy clashed because they were so much alike," said Janice. "Of our family, Toni was the one who would talk back to Guy. From the time she was little she would speak her mind, and she wasn't afraid to get angry at him or show her feelings. When Toni thought he was not being fair, she *told* him so."

There were the contrasting times when he was Super Dad, agreeable and very nice. "Mom used to be the one who took me to Griffith Park when I was little, and I would ride either the train or the ponies," said Toni. "One day *Dad* took me and that was *really* fun! Because—maybe he was feeling guilty or something," she laughed, "but he let me do *both!* I thought, 'This is *really* cool.'"

Traditionally, when Guy took the family to the beach he would always stop to get everyone some ice cream. One particular time Toni never forgot was when Guy wanted to discipline the children and he *didn't* stop. "We'd go a lot to Zuma Beach, and if we were *good*, we could go to Frosty Freeze! On Pacific Coast Highway between Los Angeles and Malibu there is a big giant 'hamburger guy' on a building holding a hamburger. Well, back then, he used to be a big 'Frosty Freeze guy' holding a big ice cream cone with swirly ice cream in it. I only remember one time we were bad enough to not go. Steve and I were doing whatever we were doing in the backseat—I guess misbehaving. Then, about a block before the big Frosty Freeze guy with the big ice cream cone, we got *real* quiet. We folded our hands and stared at that statue coming at us. It got closer and closer—*and we passed it!* I mean, our hearts just went to our feet. *Oh man!* It was just like the worst moment in childhood history."

Janice interjected with a smile, "Yes, but I think he ended up stopping at the 31-flavors ice cream place on Santa Monica Boulevard."

Toni hadn't remembered that part. "Oh well, maybe we learned our lesson between there and Santa Monica Boulevard. Or maybe Dad felt guilty and gave us a second chance," she laughed.

Toni remembered the tender times when Dad came to her rescue. She was around ten years old when she and another girl were invited to spend the night at a friend's house. The other two girls played that cruel childhood game of leaving the third one out and made Toni feel unwanted. Uncomfortable and hurt, she called her parents. "My dad said, 'We'll come get you right now.' I watched for them at the window, then I saw my dad coming in the car with my mom to get me. I was so glad to go home."

She was also grateful to her dad for letting her keep her dog. Janice and Guy saved a lost dog one night when they got home late one Christmas Eve. "We saw something moving in the culvert by the house," said Janice. "Guy put the car lights on it and it was a scared little wet and hungry pup, trembling in the cold. It was the cutest thing. He looked like a lapso apso. We picked him up, took him inside, dried him and put him on Toni's bed to surprise her for Christmas—as though Santa Claus had come and delivered him. Toni *loved* him, and for no apparent reason she immediately called him Sam. He was funny because he was so small and yet he would pick up things too big for him and bring them to you."

After they had the Sam for a while, a man came to the door one day claiming the dog belonged to his little girl. He said the dog had gotten away from her and she wanted it back. Janice stood grief-stricken. Guy knew it would break Toni's heart so he refused to give him the dog. The man said, "What will I tell my little girl when she comes home from school and the dog is not there?"

Guy countered with, "What will I tell *my* little girl when she comes home and the dog is *gone*? Tell your little girl that you tried, but I wouldn't give the dog back." Sam remained a part of the family for years to come.

"Dad loved fast sports cars," said Toni. "Sometimes when he took us for a ride in his sports car he'd go fast because he said he had to 'blow it out'—to clear out the pipes. He'd find a clear stretch of road and blow it out, reaching top speed for just a few seconds. I thought it was exciting fun."

"One time Guy took me for a ride," said Russ Johnson, who shared Guy's interest in sports cars. "He loved his cars. I remember the red Maserati. We got to PCH,[238] and he opened it up to 101. He gave me a few white knuckles in that thing!"

"I have only been most frightened twice in my life," said Janice, "and they were both with Guy: in the storm on the boat and when he opened up his sports car on the freeway at 100 mph. He was always careful when he did it. Always in control, but it was still scary. I told him how scared I was, and he said 'Yes, but wasn't it *exciting*?!'"

"He used to draw a lot of attention when he picked me up at school in the Masaratti," said Steve. "It got to where kids at school would ask 'Is your dad coming to pick you up?,' which I thought was neat. Also, when we'd go places and he'd get recognized and sign autographs, I thought 'WOW, that's cool.' I was always real proud of him. I loved riding with Dad to the studio in that red Maserati with the top down."

In 1968 at the Hollywood Celebrity Showcase, Guy bought another Ferrari that had been Steve McQueen's. A few years later he sold it, because it was always needing repair. Several years later Steve discovered why. "I met McQueen while I was researching his last movie, *The Hunter*, and when I told him my dad bought his car, he said, 'Yeah, I *crashed* that car.'"

"We used to love going to the studio," recalled Toni. "When I visited the set, it seemed *so huge*, maybe because I was little or maybe because it *was* huge. Everything seemed big to me. It was exciting and fun. Jonathan Harris was such a nice man. He loved children and always had cookies or candy in his trailer. He always gave us Tootsie Pops."

"We would occasionally visit Guy on the set," said Janice, "The children always loved going. I took my mother once when she came out for a visit. They said, 'All quiet!' and started to roll—and my mother moved to take a picture. The sand beneath her feet swished and made sounds and then she flashed a picture and the director got so mad. She didn't know any better, and felt so bad."

"I liked *Lost in Space*," said Toni, "better than *Zorro*. When I was old enough to watch *Zorro* during the 1965 reruns I was unimpressed. It was just Dad and it seemed like a boys' show. After I went to the studio, I got a crush on Billy. He was four years older, so he was an older 'man' to me, you know, a big guy. I think my dad knew I had a crush on him (I don't know *how*. I didn't tell anybody), because I remember one time we went to the set and Dad sent Billy and me to the commissary for ice cream. I was in shock. I sat there and I could not say a word! He must have thought I was really stupid. I was eight years old and I just sat there with my ice cream melting. I just couldn't eat. Mom and Dad, and June came in and sat at another table and I was with Billy—just *dying*. Every bite was excruciating. I had *such* a crush, it was painful."

Steve had a crush on Angela Cartwright. They had worked together long before his father worked with her, when they were preschoolers modeling. Before she would be Guy's TV daughter on *Lost in Space,* Angela Cartwright would play a Williams (Linda) on *Make Room for Daddy,* and Guy Williams would play a Cartwright (Will) on *Bonanza.* Now Steve was 14 and he wanted to take 15-year-old Angela out on a date, but he was shy about it.

"It was Dad's coaxing that gave me the courage. He told me, 'If you want to go out with her *just ask her!*' He kept saying, 'Call her up! Call her up!' So I called her up and she accepted. Dad drove us in the Mercedes down to Ships, a popular restaurant on Santa Monica Boulevard, then I took her to a movie. The movie was *The Sound of Music* and I didn't know that *she was in it.* So you can imagine how surprised I was to see her in the movie! We went back to Ships, where my mom picked us up. I figured I'd better take her to see a movie she *wasn't* in and another time after that I took her to see *The Russians Are Coming! The Russians Are Coming!* Dad used to give me tips on dating. He'd say, 'You know how you put your arm around a girl in the movie, don't you? You streeeetch, and then you drop one arm down behind her,'" he laughed.

For the first ten years of her life, Toni didn't see her father during the week, but only for a few hours during supper. "He left very early in the morning before I was up and came home for dinner when it was dark. He was at the studio all day. But Mom was always around. She was a stay-at-home mom, and my dad worked. I always remember Mom being with me for all important events. Sometimes Dad was there. Later, when he was free, he came."

Toni felt safe and secure when her father was home. "When I would go to sleep at night, I could hear my dad's classical music playing downstairs and it would put me to sleep. It meant my parents were home and all was well. To this day I like to go to sleep with classical music on to relax."

Guy had a strong presence. "When he was home," said Toni, "he could be downstairs in the living room reading, but you knew he was there. You were aware of his presence. You could feel it.

"Dad and I watched *George of the Jungle* together. Dad never watched a lot of TV, but I remember he liked *Laugh-In.*"

In 1967 Guy said, "You don't have to watch TV to be in the business. I'd rather read a book or talk to someone. Lately I've taken to the conversation shows, but other than that, I've gotten out of the habit. I used to watch all of the old movies but I got tired of the way they were cut. And the biggest single annoyance was what makes it possible to be on at all—*the interruptions!* If I'm reading or listening to records, I'm the one who decides when the interruptions will come, when I'll put down the book to get a cheese sandwich."

"My dad loved science fiction and horror films ever since I can remember," said Steve. "He got us interested in them. At Halloween our house was known as 'the scary house.' Toni would decorate the bottom floor where the wine cellar was and scare the neighborhood kids. She and Robert Foster and I loved making our own home movies at that time. *Horror* was our *specialty.* Dad and I used to watch the original *Outer Limits* together and anything else that was scary. Dad called scary movies *BOO-kers.* Don't ask. I don't know why, but that's what he called them.

"Along with *The Beast with Five Fingers*, another favorite of ours was *The Attack of the Mushroom People* because it was *so bad*, it was *good*. For instance, crazy things like, the interior sets were *bigger* than the exterior. Sometimes just as the action is about to happen it cuts away and never lets you know what happened," he laughed. "The worse they were, the more Dad liked them. He'd say, 'Let's watch this. It's *really bad*.' But he didn't like to watch *Lost in Space*, because to him they weren't bad, they were 'tacky.' And there's a big difference."

Guy's dancing was a form of amusement for the children. "We'd get in the living room with the kids," said Janice, "turn the music on and dance with them. Guy had his own style. He had his own beat. Steve and Toni would laugh and laugh. Toni can imitate him."

Toni said, "He would dance to Trini Lopez or some such song and had this goofy way of dancing. We called it frog legs. And he'd squinch up his shoulders."

Janice gave him credit, however. "Guy didn't like formal dancing, but he could get on a dance floor and move around and do what he wanted to do."

In 1966 Guy took his family to Marineland, but it was in tremendous contrast to the first time Guy took his family and mother in 1955. No one knew him then and now his family had to learn to adjust to his fame. This visit was for publicity and pleasure as they were escorted and photographed for a magazine spread with seals kissing them and whales being fed by them. After their escort left them free to go to the tanks to see the fish, a mob of fans forced them to leave before they could see the attractions. "Dad was always recognized," said Steve. "I remember many times having to find back doors to get out of places. This time we had barely gotten inside the gates before word got around that he was there. We were on the scissor-ramps going up to see the tanks when we saw a crowd of kids running toward us on the ramp. It was like those scenes we saw when the Beatles were here. I heard my folks say 'Uh-oh! *Let's go*.' We grabbed hands, turned

Guy and his family were given the VIP tour at Marineland, 1966- L to r. Janice, Toni, Steve, and Guy break for refreshments. (author's personal collection)

Guy and his family checking out the fish tanks just before they were mobbed by a crowd who recognized him. (author's personal collection)

around, and headed for the car. We didn't even get to see the museum and by the time we were at the car people were asking for autographs."

"I remember two very disappointed kids that day," added Janice. "Guy was too, but he just took it in stride. He patiently signed some autographs while we waited in the car. Then we left."

Toni had never known a time when her father was not a public figure. Since she could remember, her dad went to work, and she saw him on TV. "There was no big realization that Dad was a public figure because I grew up with it," she said. "Kids in school would ask me, 'What's it like to have a father who is a famous star of a TV show?' And I would answer, 'I don't know what it's *not* like. It's like asking a fish, 'what is it like to live in water?' A fish doesn't know it's wet."

Janice admired Guy's cool reserve and ability to handle crowds or even himself in a crisis. "He was washing his Ferrari one day in his bathing shorts when two policemen

To stay in shape Guy liked to punch the speed bag on his patio, and swim in his pool, which he kept very cold. (Kathy Gregory personal collection, courtesy of Kathy Gregory.)

pulled up in a frightful rush. I could see them from the window and it scared me to death, but Guy was so calm. I went running down to the driveway to see what had happened, and Guy gestured to me that it was all right. They told him they had gotten a call about a stolen red Ferrari in the neighborhood. And Guy in his shorts just joked and said, 'Well, where do you think I'd hide the gun?' They apologized and left."

Home was Guy's castle. He was most comfortable and happy there. He had numerous pastimes and hobbies that kept him there. Writing at this time was a major passion. He wrote anything that came to mind: ideas for TV shows, parodies, and spoofs which he typed out on his typewriter.

Guy's favorite time of day was late afternoon, just before dinner. "If he was home from work before dinner we would take a glass of wine or a cocktail and go out and watch the sunset, or he'd listen to music, read, then come in for dinner," said Janice wistfully. "Guy liked to sip wine while he read. He always said, 'Wine helps you *think*.'"

Chapter 45

"...he was canceled and he didn't say anything!"
— Guy Williams about Irwin Allen

After his visit to New York, Guy returned to Hollywood to begin filming the third season of *Lost In Space*.[239] He was glad he had a job, but his lack of love for *Lost in Space* is evident in this published comment. Guy felt the overall viewing of television at that time had dropped off, but he was not concerned with the "next year, renewals, or ratings." He said, "All I have to worry about is getting up at six in the morning!"[240]

The third season opened with a rousing new theme song by John Williams with many other exciting new features. The opening credits inserted a clip of each character in action. New costumes reflected the psychedelic age of that time in lavenders and orange, and there was talk of a plan to go back to more serious scripts that included all the players. Also, the Robinsons would be doing more space travel, visiting new planets more often.

Salary increases for the third season were: Jonathan Harris: $3,500; Guy Williams: $2,850; June Lockhart: $2,000; Mark Goddard: $1,750; Marta Kristen: $1,534; Billy Mumy: $1,500; Angela Cartwright: $1,250; Bob May: $520; Dick Tufeld: $400. The budget per episode: $164,778.[241]

The third season started with episode #60. The first ten episodes of the third season hold some exciting scenes for Guy, and Episode #74, "The Anti-Matter Man," gave he and Mark Goddard something to sink their teeth into for a change. The episode (#70, "Deadliest of Species") about the army of little mechanical men, about 8 inches high, attacking them, was difficult for most in the cast to keep a straight face.

For a while the third season looked bright with some of the changes promised. The actors bonded and joked with each other between takes and the long hours waiting for tech. Jonathan and Mark used to do "bits" off stage, ad-libbing dialogue that was in character to their roles. Many times on camera it was difficult for Mark not to break up at Jonathan. June and Guy had fun with Jonathan as well. "One time Jonathan had to stay very late for his close-ups and he was upset because he had opera tickets that night and was worried about being late," told June. "Guy and I looked at our watches, and I said, 'Well, he's *missed* curtain.' We went to Jonathan's dressing room and stood there singing the overture of this Wagner opera to him, going *Bah baaam, Mah bah baaah*. He *loved it!*" she laughed.

Guy was always ready to play a joke on his friends to make them laugh, like the time he found out his old friend Wright King was on the Fox lot filming *Planet of the Apes*[242] (1968). One morning after being in Makeup for his three-hour transformation, Wright headed for the set in full ape make up. Guy was waiting. As Wright came walking down the street Guy passed by him and casually said, "Hello, Wright". Wright was set back and turned around to see who could have possibly recognized him. "'*Guy! You* sonofagun!' We both just broke up,' said Wright, laughing. "When you knew Guy, nothing like this would surprise you. He had that sly sense of humor.

"He was a cool cat. And by that I don't mean slick at all, just very easy-going, not pushy, but very firm, and in a good way. He was a wonderful guy, and very bright, extremely bright."

Wright remembered the backyard barbeques at Dennis's house with fond memories of jokes and talks of their careers, and the time he and his wife invited Guy and Jan to their house for a steak dinner. Guy was doing *Zorro* at the time so Wright's young boys were very excited to meet him.

Wright King is retired now after enjoying a long and illustrious career which spanned from the mid 1940s on stage in New York until the late 1980s in film and television in Hollywood. He and June, his loving wife of fifty-six years, have three grown sons. He misses Guy and all his old acting buddies who have either passed on or moved away.

Marta spent time listening to music and fantasizing about Mark. "I was twenty, which made me closer in age to Angela and Billy, so we hung around together. We listened to the same music and had lunch together. But sometimes I went to lunch with Mark. I had a big crush on Mark, even though I was married. I didn't socialize with Guy much, because he didn't hang around the set much; he'd go to his trailer, but mainly because of the age difference." Marta married very young and her marriage was in trouble when she started working on *Lost in Space*. It didn't last long thereafter.

Guy liked talking to Marta. He thought she was intelligent. They used to play Scrabble on the set. "Guy was great at Scrabble," she said. "He taught me how to play to win. To this day, no one can beat me at Scrabble, and it's all because of Guy."

June and Guy loved playing word games. "Each of us would make up our own idea of how idioms got started. It might start with a funny phrase from the script and we would elaborate on its meaning or origin of expression with silly concepts. Guy loved these kind of mind-games with words. He also liked to play Chess and listen to music."

June knew Guy liked wine so she surprised him one day with a mock wine cellar she made for him. "There were different levels of the Jupiter II. When we got on the elevator to go to the next level it looked like we went directly there, but the different levels were actually on different sound stages. So when we went down the elevator, we actually went into a dirt hole dug out for the elevator. We had to wait there for the scene to finish being shot and go up again. Well, I ordered cases of wine from Napa Valley, Chardonnay and Cabernet, with personalized labels that said 'From the Personal Collection of John Robinson,' and put them in the mock 'wine cellar' of the Jupiter II which was this dugout hole—to surprise Guy," she smiled. "He really enjoyed that. It was quite a surprise."

Halfway through the third season the writers fell back into their second season formula scripts and the series continued to fall in the ratings.[243] "The Great Vegetable Rebellion" (Episode #82) is unanimously the most ridiculous episode of the series. The cast had to talk to a living carrot named "Tybo," played by Stanley Adams, dressed in a big orange carrot suit with an orange-painted face. Penny falls asleep and starts to take root in the hot house, becoming a plant. The family sets out to find Dr. Smith. As they hack their way through a jungle of vegetation, they hear faint moans and sighs with each hack of John and Don's machetes. They find Dr. Smith an immobile figure, as he has taken root and is becoming a stalk of celery. June recalls, "The sound of the plants moaning coupled with our reaction and dialogue was just too much. Guy, Angela, Mark, Marta, and I laughed so much through that; it was the most excruciating experience. Mark is seen on camera laughing. Guy and I were written out of the next two episodes for giggling—at full salary! This is the way Irwin Allen thought he should discipline us. That episode, everyone in the cast agreed, is dearest to our hearts as our favorite."

Jonathan Harris recalled his reaction when he got the script: "I was in my dressing room and Peter Packer, the writer of the show, came in and handed me this script. I began to read it and of course I couldn't believe what I was reading. A celery stalk? I looked at him and he looked at me apologetically and said, 'I don't have *another* idea in my head.'"

The third season wrapped and the cast went on vacation. By all accounts, the cast had no reason to think they would not be back for a fourth season. During the summer Guy went to the Beverly Hills Hotel to take publicity pictures. A representative of CBS was present while the press took photos and asked questions.

Guy remembers: "I found out about the cancellation in typical *Lost in Space* fashion. A reporter in the photo session asked me if we were starting the new season. I was about to answer 'Yes' when the network person said, 'Oh. Well. That isn't certain yet.' I said to the reporters, 'You *heard* him. It's not certain yet.' That's how I heard about it." None of the cast knew about it. "We talked on the phone afterward and Irwin said, 'Well, I would have told you, but I was out in New York fighting the good fight and I wanted to present you with a new season already done.' But yeah, he was canceled and he didn't say anything!" said Guy. "He had four shows canceled at once: *Time Tunnel*, *Voyage to the Bottom of the Sea*, *Land of the Giants* and *Lost in Space*. So, I asked him, 'Well, how do you feel?' and he said, 'Well Guy, I am not exactly dancing in the street.' *That* was Irwin."

Some say the real reason *Lost in Space* was canceled was simply because the head of the CBS network, Bill Paley, hated the show.

Chapter 46

"I've written a few scripts, and now a series."
– Guy Williams

Guy had found creative satisfaction in writing around the time he finished his stint on *Bonanza* in 1964. As weeks turned into months before he worked again Guy enjoyed sitting at his typewriter writing comical situations or outlining ideas for a movie or TV show, always with humor. He collaborated with his friend Art Silver on the idea for a show called *Two for the Road* and another with a comical character he made up called Captain Fermin Bartholomeo of Riaga. In June 1965, while working on the first season of *Lost in Space*, Guy and Art Silver put together a treatment for a TV situation comedy about a detective who loved to gamble. MGM was interested. They hired William Peter Blatey[244] to write the script for them.

Bill Blatey was a good writer and also a friend of Art and Marge Silver, who often invited Blatey to their home. When Blatey went to Guy's house to collaborate on the script, Steve noticed how much his dad enjoyed the creative freedom of writing. "I remember seeing Bill Blatey and my dad sitting under the jacaranda tree in the yard at Hillside writing that thing," said Steve. "They'd drink wine and smoke cigars while they wrote the script. Art and my dad were hopeful when Blatey presented it to ABC." From Guy's notes he called it "a comedy with mysterious overtones—*The Adventures of Rex Holmsby and Balasco Watts.*" The title was shortened to the catchy pun *Olms and Watts.*

On onion skin paper in large pica type, Guy sketched out the characters as the ideas came to him:

> Holmsby is one hell of a piano player. When he gets a tough one, it helps clear his mind. OK, it helps clear his mind. So, who the hell is Rex Holmsby? Go over there and look at that picture on the wall. It's not really a picture but look at it anyway. That's right. A glass framed poker hand. Makes you sick to look at it? 10, Jack, Queen, King, FOUR? That sir, is the famous *Holmsby Straight...*
>
> Well, sir, one night Rex Holmsby touted a bank teller from California who held three 9's for six thousand clams with that hand. They were playing in Rio.

This portrait of Guy for the foreign press after *Lost In Space* clearly shows the face of a still handsome leading man. (Gerry Dooley personal collection, courtesy of Gerry Dooley)

A show about a gambler? Well, not really, Rex Holmsby is an EX-gambler…

Wait, an ex-gambler who through his knowledge of odds and probabilities and uncanny memory is much sought after. His services are much sought after by many in other fields of endeavors. People in medicine, politics, crime detection, all kinds of people for his unique talent as a consultant. Why doesn't he just shut up and become King of The Stock Market or something, go to the Riviera and leave everyone alone? Good question. With a mind like that, why work for a living? I mean, why the hell did he give up his gambling? He who could have made a life—the likes of Barnes and Jacoby. His sense of probabilities would have made an Einstein shutter, except for one thing—Rex Holmsby *hated* gambling.

How's that? Well, you see his uncanny mental facilities were far ahead of his nervous system and no point in belaboring the situation when he found himself trying to work out a way to bet on all the horses in the same race. Naturally a guy like that just doesn't pick up and go into the upholstery business. Hence his present endeavor. A bad hombre to mix with if you were plotting something, a very bad hombre indeed.

Is he darkly handsome and debonair? No. He's short, fat and has inclinations to be unconsciously funny. Seen through the eyes of a real citizen he might even seem clownish at times. The guy who works with him (if you want to say his sidekick that's OK, you know the one who mixes all the drinks and says, "Yes, but I thought…" Well, *he's* the darkly handsome and debonair one in this show. He's got everything. He's even got nerve. But, our darkly handsome, debonair and so forth can only bow to the master. Anyway, his ego is so big in other areas none of this really bothers him.

Guy talked about his writing ambitions in an interview printed in April 1967:

> "There are no motion pictures in the immediate future," he said in answer to a question. "But I've written a few scripts, and now a series. It was bought by MGM and one of the networks is interested.
>
> "Sure, I'd like to get into the production end of the business, but *Lost in Space* comes first right now. So even if something should happen with this new series, my partner, Bill Blatey, would do most of the day-to-day work."[245]

ABC liked it but rejected it. Steve Silver, Art and Marge's only son, recounts the chain of disappointing events for his father and for Guy. "The problem of *Olms and Watts*, as I recall, was basically it is Sherlock Holmes and the estate of [Sir Arthur] Conan Doyle still owned the rights to Sherlock Holmes. It was not public domain. The names were changed and everything, but the studios thought it was too close, so they never did it. The script was one of the funniest things I ever read. It was very good. It was well written."

Not long after that rejection Art Silver was watching a movie for television starring Zero Mostel and suddenly he realized he was hearing the dialogue from *their script*, clearly, word for word. He called Guy immediately. "Turn on the TV!" he said. "That's *our show!*"

Consequently, *Olms and Watts* ended up in litigation. Guy and Art believed that Blatey slightly altered the script and sold it to the ABC network. They took action and sued ABC and Blatey for plagiarism.

"They really had bad luck because they lost the case on a technicality," said Janice. "Their lawyer had let an allotted time to file run out, so they lost by default." The plaintiffs and everyone who sympathized with Guy and Art had reason to believe it was no accident.

Steve Silver said, "I know both Guy and my father were very upset about this. My father was probably the most respected person in the business. His integrity was above anything I've ever come across, so he was pretty upset about someone doing this to him. He even made a remark that was very unusual for my father. He said someone had gotten to the judge, because in the transcripts the judge, at one point on the records,

said 'I can see the copying.' So Guy and my father always felt ABC or someone plagia-
rized, but there was no proof. It was just a gut feeling."

"My father retired early and I think he missed the business," continued Silver.
"Had he really wanted to get back into it, he couldn't anyway, because once you are out
of this business for *two years* you are *out*. There were some who wanted him back in an
active position as a producer, but he didn't take it. He liked working independently, and
he liked the type of creative work he did with Guy throughout the remainder of the
1960's, trying to create ideas and shows to produce. They enjoyed each other's company.
They liked to talk about old movies of the 1930s and 40s. There was a good chemistry
between them that brought out creativity. They liked to go sailing, or play chess, or just
talk about movies and the business. Guy always had new ideas."

Chapter 47

"A big enigma "

– John Ericson

In 1969 while Guy was unemployed and wondering what new roles would come his way, if any, Zorro returned in his life—not in the United States, but in other countries around the world. *Zorro* had been airing in countries such as Holland, France, Belgium, Italy, Japan, Korea, South America since 1968 and had begun to gain a huge following of fans. Audiences had fallen in love with Guy Williams as Don Diego and Zorro and wanted to know all about him. Many of these countries invited Guy to visit and be on TV shows there, pictures and interviews were requested. If he didn't go, there were still huge spreads in magazines about him and his family, such as the one in *Katzo* magazine of Finland in September 1969.

"A lot of people know Zorro," Steve said with amazement, realizing how widespread his dad's fame is. "I've been to Europe and Japan, and they know Zorro, my dad's Zorro, everywhere. I remember my dad going to Holland for some kind of public appearance after *Zorro*. But it was for *Zorro, not* for *Lost in Space.*"

Guy and his family did an extension photo shoot at their home some time in 1969 to accommodate requests from international magazines. He grew back his mustache for the pictures.

But no work came. Guy's son, Steve, agreed that there were a lot of TV shows suited for his dad at that time, but he thinks he didn't try very hard. "I think Dad just turned it off. I saw a lack of interest. He didn't go after it. I think he let it go."

After so much disappointment in the business, Guy acquired a degree of cynicism. The letdown of the Sony proposal in 1963 was mild compared to the Bill Blatey case. Disappointment, broken promises, and lies were changing Guy's attitude about Hollywood. Once all-trusting, he was becoming skeptical, and cautious. Hollywood was becoming a place of cold, uncaring people for him.

Don Burnett remembers having lunch with Guy several times while he was filming *Lost in Space*. "He used to talk to me about how disappointed he was in the direction the show was going. It started out as a space adventure of a family and ended up a silly children's comedy, a farce, with him almost written out. He talked to me about the Bill Blatey incident, and I believe all that affected his attitude about Hollywood."

Guy and his family in a publicity shot in 1969 for foreign magazines.
(Kathy Gregory personal collection, courtesy of Kathy Gregory.)

In a magazine article, Guy became nostalgic about his boat and revealed his fantasy to get away.

> He says he sold his ketch when he was in Europe and remembered how he used to gaze out the school window at a sleek schooner docked in the harbor. He had visions of being skipper and sailing far out to sea. His idol is Sterling Hayden, whom he calls "A sailor's sailor. I really envy him, because he took his children sailing around the world, and they learned different things and saw how other people live. They became real people. This is something I'm looking forward to. To leave show business if I want, and take off indefinitely on a sleek, two-masted schooner, just like the one I used to dream about as a child."[246]

It remains unknown if the reason for his not working again in Hollywood was simply that his luck ran out, or he had acquired a reputation of being "difficult." Steve defends the idea that his father might have been passed over for parts because of being labeled difficult. "He battled furiously with Irwin Allen and there were misunderstandings, but when I look back and analyze what was happening I think he was perfectly right to make the stands he was making from a professional standpoint. An actor's career is his professional livelihood, and Irwin's moving Jonathan Harris into the limelight affected my dad's marketability as an actor. He was looking at it totally as a business issue and he was right to be making those points. I don't think it's unreasonable. He didn't like the dishonesty."

Robert Foster remembered that time. "Guy kept a happy-go-lucky attitude despite it all," he said. "When Guy was not working, when he was not being adored by all his fans, I liked the idea that he didn't show it, *wouldn't* show it. You'd never know it. You could see Guy and ask, 'How ya doin'?' and he'd say, 'I'm doing just *great.*' And it was not forced at all. I guess he was philosophical about it. He wasn't like a panicky actor, whining saying 'God! I don't know where the next feature's going to come from,' or 'God! We're gonna lose our house,' and so forth. He never did that. He was a happy-go-lucky person. My father was a little bit like that too."

Guy on the cover of *Katso* magazine in Finland, for an article about Zorro which was airing there in 1969. (courtesy of Jennie Askland and Helena Mela)

Guy kept his picture in the Players Directory until 1977, a reference book of actors used by producers and directors for casting purposes. "If the right thing had come along," said Janice, "Guy would love to have been working."

While Guy was not working, he enjoyed the luxuries and comforts of the mansion he had acquired with his talent and labors as an actor. He had everything he needed: swimming pool, sauna, various hobbies—tropical fish, stock market, astrology, photography, cooking—books to read, ideas to write, and he could sleep late if he wanted to. He found it relaxing and entertaining to sit at the typewriter and make up dialogue for absurd parodies of *film noir* movies of the '40s like *Double Indemnity* (1944) and *The Strange Love of Martha Ivers* (1946).

Another pleasure for him and Janice was having friends over for dinner. Actor John Ericson and his wife at the time, Milly, were often guests at Guy's house for dinner in the late 1960s and early 1970s. Guy and John had done a short scene together on television's *DuPont Theater* in 1957, but their friendship didn't start there. Ericson couldn't recall when their paths had crossed again, but he thought it could have been when they both worked for CBS. John was starring in *Honey West* with Anne Francis from September 1965-September 1966. "We used to go to his house a lot," said John. "Guy and Jan used to cook up a storm and they had *wonnderful* sit-down dinners all the time. Jan set a *beautiful* table. Oooh, just *lovely*! For about three or four couples. They had this long table with Jan sitting at the head of the table and Guy at the other. Oh, Jan was *so* beautiful, and *what* a hostess! And Guy was a wonderful host also, with great charm, great wit. He was really an all-around, nice guy. Guy had this big espresso machine," he

Guy enjoying an glass of wine on the upper level of the patio of his mansion on Hillside (Kathy Gregory personal collection, courtesy of Kathy Gregory)

chuckled. "He got it from Italy and he loved to show it off. He would make cappuccinos and café lattés for his guests.

"We never discussed his career or personal things. We didn't have that kind of relationship where you talk to each other about everything that's going on, you know. Men of that time didn't talk about things like that with each other. Guy talked to me about the astronomical telescope he had out on his balcony. That's what I remember most."

Two years younger than Guy, John Ericson had a career that began much like Guy's. He studied in New York at the American Academy of Dramatic Arts before coming to Hollywood, where each of their careers took shape within the same time period. John's career took off after he starred with Elizabeth Taylor at MGM in *Rhapsody* in 1954. After a few movies in which he had a lead or featured role, he moved into early television. He managed to stay in the business for nearly forty years, until he dropped out in 1989.

John understood having to maintain an image for the public as well as agents. "You always felt you had to kind of live the characters you were playing on screen. Otherwise, if they didn't feel you were that way, they wouldn't cast you as that. So, you know, that used to drive actors crazy, going in to see a producer or director, and wonder, 'God, if they know me as a real person, as me, I'd be totally wrong for this part. I better put on a little act here.' So the actors in those days, were taught to put on a facade. In other words, that was drummed into them, and I think Guy was a part of that school. And I think that's maybe one thing that was going against him, because also you had to adjust to new times. The new times were about the individual's 'truth of the being.' I mean the acting self. You gotta be true to your acting. You gotta be true to yourself. You gotta be true to this and that, you know. You gotta be believable. So all this is going on. If you're used to doing a style of acting where you're making believe all the time, you start thinking, 'What am I really? Which character am I really? Who am I really,' you know? It just goes on and on.

"Actors in the '30s, '40s, and '50's were *acting* more than trying to be more realistic. That was hard to do for some people, especially if they were playing real make-believe heroes like Zorro, you know."

Guy indicated his dislike for a certain kind of Realism when he said in 1983, "I don't believe that people prefer this to the extent that TV shows it to you—but I think when TV shows discovered car chases and pistols held with two hands, the *fun* went out of the whole thing. I mean, I would say, 'If I see one more car chase, I'm gonna throw the TV set out the window!' I mean, *Bullitt* was great, but then they did *Bullitt* to death. And those guys that hold the guns with two hands, you know, there's no need for that, but, anyway, it looks very official and everything. That's where all of the heroes have gone, I guess."[247]

There were so many shows on TV in the five years after *Lost in Space* that Guy could have starred in or guest starred in. John could only speculate why he did not by relating to his own experience.

"That is a big enigma actors face. Always! Some actors keep working all the time, until their old age, others get to a certain point, then all of a sudden they're not getting parts offered to them. I certainly didn't like the parts I was offered in the last few years, so I just stopped even accepting or even asking."

Pondering Guy's lack of work after *Lost in Space* and the fact that he changed agents many times after he returned from Europe, John opined, "He should have had a good PR man to straighten that out. Those things can be overcome if you have some people working for you that are on your team. You collaborate and you have a 'game plan' and you follow that. If someone is willing to do that, then you've got the right person.

"In the beginning of my career I had a very good agent that I liked a lot, then I started going from agency to agency because none of them would take a personal interest in me. Agents would just see dollar signs when they looked at you. By the late 1970s, if you had not made $100,000 last year in this business, they didn't want to even talk to you.

"In the 1950s there was a much different relationship between agent and client. Years later agencies became so big there were too many actors out there that you were up against. Your agent would be busy selling the client who had recently been a success and would make the most money and suddenly you're out of the picture."

As for Guy's disappointment with *Lost in Space* and with Bill Blatey, John said, "I'm sure Guy was a very *trusting* man. He trusted the people who were handling his career to do right by him, and I hate to say this, but you just can't trust *anybody*. Deception goes on a lot in the business of Hollywood. You really don't have any control over that. You just have to be philosophical and accept that as part of the business. You can stay on it and let it eat at you or you can move on. If you love it enough, you will bend with the wind, and realize there is something else out there, and not harp on it."

For actors such as Guy and John, who were used to playing leading roles, it was a difficult decision whether or not to stay in the leading man category as they got older. John was willing to take guest appearances and non-starring roles but after *Lost in Space* Guy did not. He wanted leading roles. To accept a supporting role could mean never being a lead again. Guy wanted to make features. Unfortunately, at this time, it was very difficult for an actor to make the transition from television actor to movie actor. If a good leading role on TV was offered, one he liked, and the pay was good, he would have taken it.

"I took roles that were not the lead," recalled John. "They were called 'guest shots.' Well, it wasn't always a nice role, but you go on as a guest star. A lot of times it was just for the money, because they can offer you such good money, and give you guest star billing. The *billing* was always *so* important. Agents and other actors would say, 'As long as you get the billing, *do it!*'

"I only knew Guy a short time. I don't know why the business does this, but you have short term friendships. You are close friends, then all of a sudden, you don't see each other for years sometimes. You just don't see each other, because everybody's working and doing things."

Guy and Janice managed to keep up some of their old friendships. Dennis Weaver, for instance, left *Gunsmoke* in 1964, and the two families occasionally saw each other until the Weavers moved to Florida in 1967 where Dennis filmed *Gentle Ben*. Guy's son Steve recalled a welcomed reunion. "When the Weavers returned to Los Angeles in 1969, they invited us to their house in Calabasas to watch the show about the bear, Gentle Ben. After that, Dennis got the part of *McCloud.*"

In the 1970s Dennis became a figurehead member of the Self-Realization group in Hollywood, and became a vegan. "We didn't see each other much anymore," noted

Guy on his balcony in front of his house by his much used telescope.
(Gerry Dooley collection; courtesy of Gerry Dooley)

Janice, "because we didn't eat the same *food*."

In the 1980s Dennis and Gerry married each other again and Guy and his family attended. The Weaver children and grandchildren walked down the aisle with them in a lovely small ceremony at the Self-Realization Temple on Sunset Boulevard where they renewed their wedding vows. The reception was at their home in Malibu. In the 1990s they moved to Colorado.

Chapter 48

"He lavished his food and his hospitality on you"
                                        – Robert Foster

After *Lost in Space* Guy was home a lot. He had time now to socialize, and be with his family. He and Janice had many dinner parties at his home. Norman and Sally Foster and their son, Robert, continued to be frequent dinner guests and close friends of the Williamses. "The best thing that I remember about Guy was that whether he was one the *top* or on the bottom he behaved the same way, and he was *always* generous," said Robert, whose affection and admiration for Guy was obvious. "You'd never know if he was depressed or worried. And he lavished his food and his hospitality on you."

"Guy treated his children very well, with a lot of humor, always kidding," tells Robert. In May of 1971 Toni was a tall thirteen-year-old, feeling the pangs of self-consciousness and puberty. Guy was never intentionally hurtful, but sometimes Toni did not know how to take his teasing. Robert, who was nine years older than Toni, often came to her defense. "Guy used to tease Toni at the table and I would change the conversation if I could because I felt sorry for her," he said. "She was smart enough to know what they were up to, if Steve and Guy ganged up on her, joking at her expense. She was a *beautiful* child. Sometimes after we ate, I stayed in the dining room with Toni. We would blow out two of the three candles and with the one left burning, we would practice moving the flame with her mind. We did stuff like that."

Toni took the teasing to heart and Janice was always assuring her that her father loved her dearly and was just joking with her. "Toni couldn't see it because he was always picking on her: silly things like calling her 'the girl with two backs.'" said Janice. "She was tall and thin and it was important to her to develop into a young woman. That really had a bad effect on her.

"When Toni was around twelve, they stood in a picture with her. She's tall and skinny, laughing happily at the camera, but she didn't know Guy and Steve are stooping down behind her, real low, to look shorter, making fun of her, giggling. He was just joking, but she didn't know how to take it. It hurt her."

Like every adolescent going through puberty, Toni was insecure about her looks. "Dad would say I was the only girl who could take a G-rated shower. Your appearance is so important at that age. It hurt, but I know now he didn't mean it. When I tried to throw a ball, it would go the opposite way, and Dad and Steve made fun of me and called me Princess Retard-o. That's how I remember my growing up stage, when I was trying to be accepted."

At the same time, Guy was telling friends how "beautiful and willowy" Toni had become. "She's going to be as beautiful as her mother," he would say. Guy always bragged about his children to friends and to interviewers, a fact Toni was not aware of until she was much older. In a magazine article written during *Lost in Space*, Guy became sentimental when he spoke of his "eight-year-old *teenager.* She's a tiny thing and very thin, but she's got it all. She's going to be a long-stemmed rose someday."

Janice remembered, "Guy used to anticipate Toni's first date and he said, 'When the first guy comes to call I'm not going to ask about education, I'm going to ask if he has any traffic tickets.' He was so worried about reckless driving." More than anything he worried about her getting home alive and well.

Generally after dinner at Guy's house, everyone would get up from the dining room and go into the living room. Robert remembered. "Guy would say, 'I'll give you a concert!' and he'd play this classical music loud. *Loud.* The *floors* would shake! And it's strange, but my mother used to complain about loud music, but she *loved* that. He cranked it up all the way. He could do that, because he lived in a mansion way up in the hills and it didn't disturb anyone.

"In the daytime, Guy and Jan used to religiously take walks after they ate because they were afraid of getting flabby. I walked with them sometime and it was hard to keep up. They were like Olympic runners! And they walked fast for *two hours*. Didn't matter what they ate, because they would walk it off."

Robert's mother, actress Sally Blane, was a devout Catholic, so Guy loved to tease her by starting a controversial conversation about Catholicism. "He would just do it for the sake of the argument," said Janice smiling, "and the fun of seeing her get riled, just as he predicted she would.

"I would tell her, 'Oh, he's just *teasing* you.' Then Guy would laugh, and Sally would look at him and say, 'Oh, *yooouuu!*'"

During this time and throughout the 1970s Guy continued to proudly tell the stories about his favorite Uncle Torto to guests at dinner parties. Daring Uncle Torto and his women "on both sides of the ocean" remained an object of fascination to him, so much so it began to bother Janice. "At first they were funny, but then he told them with such delight, as though he was proud of it, and that's when I began to get a little worried and upset. I wondered why he liked them so much. It got to where I would tell him, I didn't want to hear those stories anymore. It didn't seem like something you'd *want* to tell, but Guy thought it was wonderful."

For years Christmases were spent with either the Silvers or the Fosters. "When Guy wasn't working, he had so much free time. That's when we had some wonderful times," said Robert Foster. "My father and Guy shared the same attitude about Christmas. My father was a 'Bah Humbug' person about Christmas. He hated Christmas music," he smiled with amusement. "And I don't think Guy liked to be told he had to buy a tree and when to buy presents and all that commercialism. They were alike in many ways and enjoyed each other very much. Norman was older than Guy and I think he was somewhat of a father figure to him."

If there were two people who could have influenced him with wanderlust, it was his father and Norman. "Attilio didn't like to stay in one place too long. They moved a lot when Guy was little and Attilio loved to travel," said Janice. "Guy was like that and Norman was like that too, particularly if he wasn't working. When work slowed down for Norman in New York, he went to California to work. When it got slow in California, he worked in Mexico. He warned Guy once about staying in one place too long when there was no work."

Steve Silver remembers those Christmases with Guy and his family. "Guy was very close to my father," said Silver. "He and Janice were over at our house in Beverly Hills all the time, not just for Christmas, but for dinner and other occasions. I remember Guy loved Cockburn Scotch. I used to perform magic tricks for them and I taught some to young Steve [Williams]. He liked magic, too, so I gave those tricks to him."

Steve Williams remembered, "When I outgrew those magic tricks Steve Silver gave me, I passed it back to him for *his* son, Jeremy, to learn. Seeing Gene Sheldon doing his magic tricks when I was a kid left a big impression on me."

Steve Silver's childhood was not like that of the average child. His father was a producer at Warner Brothers, and Steve feels sweet nostalgia for an era of glamour that faded away by the 1960s. "After school I'd go play on the back lot of Warner Brothers," he said. "I had free access to the whole place. I remember playing on old sets, especially the oversized props from the hit movie *Them*. It was a *great* time, a *wonderful* time, that will never happen again. It was actually the beginning of the end of the Golden Age. All of it changed when the movie moguls—like Louis Mayer, the Jack Warners, the Zanucks—no longer owned the studios. When they sold out to corporations, lawyers, accountants, and *'committees'* ran things, that changed it."

Jaded from growing up around the giants of the silver screen—the world's gods and goddesses—Silver was not in awe of Guy Williams when he met him. "To me, when I met him, I didn't think of him as a celebrity or Zorro, he was just a *very nice* guy," he said. "I liked Guy very much and I loved Jan. Still do. I see and visit her often." By 1968 Silver, then in his mid-20s, moved to Florida after he married. He commuted on weekends and holidays to Los Angeles. "When I would come back, I usually saw Guy and his family and over the years Guy never changed. Never changed.

"Guy was funny. He was a person who was always trying to 'beat the system' at this point in this life. You know, he was always trying to think up a way to make money. He always had some angle, some idea," he smiled. "But a lot of people were trying to do that, though. As far as I know, nothing ever worked. Guy liked to play the horses and the stock market. He made some investments. I don't know if he was ever very successful at it. One system he had was kinda wacky. In the early 1970s when hand-held calculators first came out, I clearly remember he bought this little calculator that was supposed to tell him when to buy stocks and when to sell stocks. He thought he was going to make a lot of money in the stock market with this little gadget. From my understanding he lost a lot of money on it.

"I didn't find Guy self-centered. No more self-centered than any other actor. He was *fun* to be around. I thought his sense of humor was *great*."

Silver pondered the fact that Guy never acted again after his successes in *Zorro* and *Lost in Space*. "After *Lost in Space* maybe Guy wasn't interested in acting anymore. He was still trying to produce things with my dad. Maybe it was his own idea to not act anymore."

Les Martinson, director/producer of over one hundred productions, and his wife, Connie, were another couple who enjoyed dinners at Guy's house during the late 1960s and early 1970s, as well as Don Burnett and Gia Scala, Chris and Eleanor Dark, and Peggy and Bob Stevenson.

One night Guy and Janice were guests at the home of Paul Winchell and his wife for a pasta dinner. Winchell was a talented ventriloquist, famous in the 1950s for his comical act with his dummy, Jerry Mahoney, but he was also an important scientist and inventor, having pioneered the artificial heart. Guy must have had stimulating conversations with Winchell, since he had a fascination for science. Also there was Ruth Buzzi, star of *Laugh-In*, and her husband. "They put all the pasta in a huge pile in the center of the table," said Janice, "and everyone pulled pasta from the pile. It was fun. Something different."

Toni and Steve remember visiting Chris and Eleanor Dark at their house for Christmas many times during their youth. Chris and Guy had known each other since the mid-1950s. It was the Darks who introduced Guy and Janice to Ida Lupino and Howard Duff. At this point there was a huge network of people Guy and Janice knew in Hollywood as a result of Guy's peak time at the Disney studios and 20th Century-Fox.

Guy's son, Steve, recalled, "Chris Dark had a large telescope like my dad's in his house, so when we left the Dark's apartment in the La Brea Towers, he and dad would plan to wave to each other through the telescopes when we got home. That was fun, seeing each other waving, while we were miles apart." Guy and Chris remained close friends until Chris' untimely death on October 8, 1971, at the age of fifty-one. His wife, Eleanor, remained a close friend.

Invitations to Guy's house were always fun for Russell Johnson. "Guy had a sauna and a pool, and Jan's Italian cooking was the greatest. She cooked some wonderful meals. I remember one time she had melon slices wrapped in prosciuto. Everything was so elegant. Then they made espresso on a big espresso machine they had ordered from Italy. I loved going to Guy's house."

The coffee machine that made a lasting impression on all of Guy's dinner guests was an Agaggia coffee machine for fresh espresso and lattés. Guy had ordered it from Italy and had it plumbed into the house. Peggy Stevenson remembered, "Guy's espresso and cappuccino machine was huge. It was beautiful. It had all kinds of coils and things. It looked like a boiler. But that was Guy, the way he did things."

Especially memorable was a Fourth of July barbeque in Guy's backyard, during the time Guy was doing *Lost in Space*. "That was the time Steve threw a cherry bomb into the fish pond and all this water came pouring out." The small round pond with goldfish was built up from ground level so that it looked much like a well. Janice recalled, "Russ and his wife, Kaye, were there and Steve was telling us about some firecrackers he had that could blow up *underwater*. Guy wanted to see if they really would. So he said to Steve, 'Try it in the fish pond and let's see!' Steve didn't think it was a good idea, but Guy said, 'Go ahead. I give you permission to do it.' Steve reluctantly said, 'OoooKaay.' Well, the sides buckled out and water *poured* into the patio. Steve felt terrible, but Guy just laughed. He didn't get mad. He had *told* Steve to do it." The next day Janice bought some plaster and cement and repaired the cracks.

Guy's Uncle Oscar and Aunt Anne from New York visited on more than one occasion, while he lived at Hillside. Toni remembers the time Janice took them to Marineland

and Disneyland. Guy was working at the time on *Lost in Space* and didn't go with them. "I was eight and it was my first time at Disneyland. I never forgot the wonderful time I had there," said Toni. "My favorite character was Alice in Wonderland. I loved having relatives over. I always wanted to stay up with the adults and listen to the conversations."

Toni and Steve would be sent to bed just when the adults were ready to relax and talk. Toni would listen to the sound of movement below her room and the soothing hum of conversation. "Toni used to sneak downstairs and listen behind the swing door of the pantry," said Janice. "We'd see the door move a little and I'd whisper to everyone, *'It's Toni!'*" she laughed. "I'd let her stay a while and listen then I'd say, 'Time to get back to bed now.'"

"Steve used to put me up to it," said Toni. "He wanted me to be the spy, and let him know what everyone said and what was going on, so I'd write down all my observations and report it to him," she laughed.

In the latter part of the 1960s Guy's mother, Clare, came to visit. The children called her "Mommy Clare." "She was a riot!" said Toni, recalling happy memories. "When she would stay at our place, I would do anything to sleep with her. She'd sit up in bed and tell stories. Her voice was so expressive, going up and down, and she used her hands when she talked. She was so much fun."

"Mommy Clare was a very strong-willed lady," said Steve, with all fondness and respect. "She taught me Latin and Italian when I was a kid. She was a very regimented, forceful person. Once when she was visiting here we took a walk down the hill to Sunset and Gardner to a little newspaper stand to buy a paper. She put her coins in and the machine wouldn't open. She swore in Italian, 'Disgraticato!,' pretty near disassembled that machine right there on the street," he laughed. "I thought it was going to be thrown out there on the roadway. She was a strong person, but very loving."

By the late 1960s Clare was afraid to live alone in New York City and Guy helped her find a place to relocate. He hoped she would like Los Angeles, but she would have none of it. She was used to walking everywhere. She would sarcastically say, "Where are the people down the street who sell fresh vegetables? Where is the flower vendor? The boot black?" "It made Guy angry," said Janice. "He didn't understand how she couldn't find *something* to like. Guy and his mother were not close. I think it was because they were too much alike. He was closer to his father. It was the same situation with Toni and Guy. They fought a lot, because they were both alike. Steve is very easygoing, never fought with his dad, ever.

"I don't think Guy understood his mother. She was always trying to do what was best for Guy and Valerie, but it came across as too controlling, overbearing, and it alienated them both from her."

Clare found a place she liked in San Michel de Allende, Mexico. Guy visited her there a few times.

Chapter 49

"It was something fun to do…as a family."

— Janice Williams

When Steve was 15, Guy bought him his first car, a 1968 red Volkswagen bug. "Dad bought it a year before I got my license. It was a stick shift and he taught me how to drive in that car. He took me out to the parking lot of the Pan Pacific Auditorium and taught me. Then the drive home was my graduation, because just before we got home there was a hill, and he had me learn to stop on a hill and start again. So he taught me how to work the hand brake and clutch and all that on hills. By the time I took my driving test for my license I could drive that thing really good. Dad really liked that little car.

"My Dad got out of the sports car a few years later and really enjoyed driving the VW Rabbit. He and Hal Fishman got VW rabbits together, and that was the best car on earth to him."

When Steve reached high school, and Toni was in the 4th grade, they were both enrolled in the Buckley School, an exclusive private school in the San Fernando Valley. Steve got his license and drove the two of them to school. Steve was on the upper campus on Woodman Avenue and Toni was on the lower campus on Stansbury Drive.

"I used to take a shuttle bus to my campus with John Gable, Clark Gable's son, and Nat King Cole's youngest daughter," said Toni. "I have fond memories of my school days there from 4th to 8th grade."

Years later grades one through twelve came together on the Stansbury Campus. Other classmates they knew were Richard Crenna's son and Melissa Gilbert of *Little House on the Prairie*. Some of Steve's classmates were Natalie Cole, Nat King Cole's older daughter of recording fame, Barry Van Dyke, son of Dick Van Dyke, Perry Diller, son of Phyllis Diller, and Claudia Graves, daughter of Peter Graves. Both Steve and Toni were happy at Buckley, where they both went for four years. At this school they were known as Toni and Steve Catalano.

"All their lives, to this point," said Janice, "my children had been using the Williams name. But when Steve got to high school, Guy told me he wanted Steve to use the Catalano name. Then he said, 'Well, if *Steve* does, then Toni has to do it too.' We agreed to it and it was done. Legally we were *all* Catalanos—their birth certificates and my marriage license say Catalano—but Guy's passport says *Williams*, and oddly, *my* passport says *Catalano!*" she laughed. "His was Williams because the studio had gotten it for him. I can't tell you how much excitement and confusion that caused when we traveled together," she smiled. "I *always* had to explain my passport. But he *never* did!"

"When I went to Buckley, I remember the words," said Steve. "My dad said, 'I don't want to start a dynasty of Williams.' He said 'You're a Catalano.' I said, 'OK.' It didn't bother me. It was fine with me. Most people called me Steve, anyway, but to this day, when I sign something it's Guy S. Catalano, because my legal first name is Guy. It's kind of a nice mechanism, because I know if somebody doesn't really know me they call me Guy, or if I get a phone call for Guy, I know it's a salesperson or someone who got my name off whatever. So, I use the name Steve Catalano, but I sign everything Guy S. Catalano."

One summer when Guy was no longer working on *Lost in Space*, Janice put into motion an idea for a small family business venture. They made and sold Panforte, which means "strong bread" in Italian, and is traditionally made in Siena, Italy during Christmastime. "It was just something I thought would be fun to do together, as a family," said Janice. "I never really thought we could make a lot of money from it. And it was fun."

The idea started when they would make Panforte at Christmas and their friends, especially Norman Foster, raved about how delicious it was. Janice decided to try their hand at marketing it. "Every Monday the four of us, Guy, Steve, Toni, and I, would go to Melrose and La Brea Avenue to the Via Fettuccine Restaurant. It was closed on Mondays, so the owner would let us use the kitchen," tells Janice. "I would read out the recipe and measure and Toni would help put the ingredients in, and Guy was the mixer because the honey made the ingredients heavy and thick and hard to stir in this big vat. He would mix it with a long wooden ladle and then we'd pour portions over a thin layer of rice paper in a thin pan and baked it in the large ovens. The result was a fruitcake-like large cookie,[248] much like the energy bars sold in health food stores today. Steve was the driver. I rented a panel truck and Steve made the deliveries to the stores that agreed to carry it like Hughes Market, some health food stores, and some Italian groceries. We called it *Guy Williams' Panforte*. I designed the labels with a picture of Guy on it. Guy put his signature on the master copy and Steve made the copies. Toni and I wrapped and put the labels on, then Steve made the deliveries. Most of the profits were eaten up by Norman," laughed Janice. "He *loved* it and would eat two or three of them when he came over." They continued to do this for a few years in the early 1970s.

During this time a friend suggested they write a cookbook. "We practically lived on the patio in the summertime," said Janice. "We cooked and ate on the patio and we enjoyed creating new dishes, so a friend of ours, a writer, Ruth Brown, who was the sister of writer Garson Kanin, suggested we put together a cookbook. There were foods that Guy was curious about and we both loved trying them. Guy had the talent to create main dishes of meat, chicken, or fish and I had the knack of knowing what would go well with it."

Some recipes were new, created by Guy alone or by Janice and Guy, and some were dishes they had enjoyed cooking for their family. Ruth would meet Guy and Janice on their patio and listen to Guy's ideas for unique ways to cook certain foods. Then she wrote as Guy dictated. "After we discussed and planned the recipes," said Janice, "we would go to the kitchen to prepare it. Guy would do the *directing*, and I was the *operator*," she laughed, "and with Guy *right* over my shoulder at all times."

The process of creating a dish was important to Guy. If something had to be added at a certain time, it had to be *precisely* the right time, lest the dish be spoiled. Freshness was their creed. They picked fresh herbs from their yard and bought fresh ground meat. "We would go down to the butcher at Dominick's, the Italian Market, have him cut the fat off the meat, and freshly grind it," said Janice. "Guy loved beef and he liked it *rare*. On the way home in the car, he and Steve would reach over and pinch little pieces of the ground round with their fingers and eat it raw. Later we bought a grinder so we could grind the meat ourselves."

One day when the cookbook was being discussed on the patio with Ruth, Janice recorded Guy talking about some of his favorite foods. In a voice much different from his "stage voice," he sounds relaxed as he tells about his and Janice's favorite way to make grilled hamburger more *interesting*. "You take meat for a burger and divide it in half," he says, "flatten it, and put a piece of Roquefort or Gorgonzola cheese in the middle, then press the ends of the two patties together. Anytime you can grind your own meat, round steak, whatever, it's better. The nice thing about this is the *surprise* of what's in the hamburger. It's a change from the ol' pickles and ketchup. We call them *hamburgers for grownups*." Janice said the two thin patties pressed together makes the patty puff up when they are grilling, making them fun to cook and very flavorful.

On the tape, Ruth is heard asking Guy what he would eat it with. He says: "I don't like hamburger buns. Eat it with bread. Whatever you like. I would eat it with a fork and serve with wine."

Jan said when Guy ate meat on a bone he liked to eat it with his hands. "Guy had an idea once that he would like to open a restaurant where you could eat with your hands," said Janice, "and just bite the meat off the bone. He loved doing that."

The lettuce leaves for a Caesar salad, one of his favorite dishes, are so large, Guy preferred to pick it up with his hands and eat it. On the tape, after he says he makes his own dressing with fresh ingredients, he is heard saying, "I prefer eating a Caesar Salad with my hands, simply because it's *better* that way."

When asked about casseroles, Guy says, "I don't like casseroles."

On making Chinese food, Guy says to Ruth, "Janice and I go to the store and get *three magic cans*: litchi, mandarin and pineapple, and make delicious Chinese dishes."

Looking back, Janice added, "We loved Chinese food and for a while we made it often until we got tired of doing all that chopping."

Guy is heard saying how much he and Janice love to make an Italian dessert called Grenitas: frozen espresso, blended with strawberries, or peaches into a frothy, snowy ice. To complete the cookbook Guy added a Wine List, explaining the characteristics and essence of each wine and what foods they go well with.

The book was typed on white paper and bound with a heavy paper cover. Although Janice had contributed greatly to the book, she insisted her name not be on the cover. She wanted it to be strictly a Guy Williams cookbook. The others conceded and it was titled *Cooking to Score* by Guy Williams and was *dedicated* to Janice. It was never published, but it was used by Guy and his family regularly for years, and was a pleasant reminder of another project they had done together.

One evening when they were preparing dinner together on the patio Guy said, "Do you realize in the years we've been married, we've spent more time together than most married couples do in a lifetime?"

"It was true," said Janice, "because he was an actor, and when they are shooting you never see them, because they work 12-15 hours a day. But when they don't work, they have a lot of free time and he would be around all the time. I felt lucky. There were some long periods of time when he was home."

One night in February 1971, while Guy and his family were asleep, Los Angeles was hit by one of its biggest earthquakes. The city suffered tremendous damage. It was the worst Guy and Janice ever experienced and the first for Steve and Toni. In the cold predawn hours the earth began to shake furiously. All over Los Angeles beds scooted across bedrooms, books flew off their shelves, dishes crashed, and pantries and refrigerators emptied themselves over the floor.

Guy and Janice bolted out of bed and ran straight to the children. Electrical transformers outside lit up the sky as they blew. Everyone was calling out to each other in the dark. Guy reached for his flashlight and calmed everyone, while the earth groaned, and shook, and rolled. The flashes from powerlines lit up the rooms. Water from their pool on the *upper* level of the property poured water into the lower level in the patio.

"Mom and Dad came running down the hall in the dark and it was just like one of those scenes in *Lost in Space*," recalled Toni, "where they are moving from one side of the wall to the other," she giggled. "My dolls and things were falling all over the floor. Mom was trying to get my slippers on and the bed would shake and move and the slipper would come off again."

"I don't know *why,*" said Janice, "but I just had to get these slippers on her. Then we all went downstairs and stood in the archway of the dining room for safety."

"Dad was cool," recalled Toni. "He seemed to have everything under control, so I felt safe. We listened to the radio and Steve and I were mostly concerned about whether or not we had to go to school. I remember we stayed home that day."

"It was terrible. Really scary," said Janice. "In a crisis such as that, Guy was the calmer of the two of us." There was a big mess to clean up, but they were grateful everyone was all right.

After *Lost in Space* in 1969, Guy saw his friend Don Burnett's marriage deteriorate. Gia doted on Don. She called him "mio tesoro," but her drinking made their marriage impossible. Don wanted out of the marriage and filed for a divorce. Gia was heartbroken and never got over him.

Gia's problems ran deep and Guy and Janice felt sorry for her in spite of her wild and reckless ways. Her childhood had been misspent in war-torn Italy where she and her younger sister played in bombed-out houses, dressing up in clothes and high heels they found among the ruins, escaping into a world of make believe. Her father worked for the British government and was away a lot, but she was extremely close to her mother, who brought her to the United States when she was fifteen to begin her acting career in Hollywood. When her mother died at age 42 in the 1960s, Gia was devastated, and would never learn to cope with life. She would smell the inside of her mother's purse to bring back memories and the nearness of her mother. She missed her painfully.

World famous model of the 1960s, William Ramage was a devoted and loving friend to Gia since 1957. "I was the brother Gia never had," he said. William knew of

Gia's depression and suicide attempts and tried with all his being to keep her happy and out of trouble. While he was on a business trip to Italy in 1972, Gia took some prescription pills and too much white wine, and died in her sleep. She was found the next day by a friend. The coroner told William that Gia died of advanced arteriosclerosis, inherent in her medical history. She was only 38.

Guy and Janice never abandoned Gia, like many actors and old friends in Hollywood did. "Janice was so kind to Gia, and Guy, although sometimes he would get a little frustrated with her, always came to her aid, sometimes getting her out of the precinct. He was a very kind man. He had kind eyes," said William Ramage.

Toni loved Gia. Her death came as a blow. "I was in Junior High on my way to school with Steve and heard about Gia's death on the radio. I was too upset to go to school. I called home and said 'Come get me. No way can I go to school today!'"

On May 4, 1972, Guy and his family attended Gia's funeral at St. Victor's Catholic Church on Holloway Drive in West Hollywood, on the campus where Steve and Toni had gone to school. Guy was a pallbearer along with John Ericson, two sons of writer Dorothy Kingsley, a young male ingénue from MGM, and her closest friend, William Ramage. As they positioned themselves outside to carry the casket, only William noticed a yellow cab pull up behind the hearse. Out stepped a slightly overweight Rita Hayworth in a large hat and sunglasses. She leaned over to pay the cab driver, then immediately threw her shoulders back in that movie star posture the studio had taught so well. She sat alone in the last row of the church. When William and Guy took their seats in the church together, William whispered to Guy that Rita Hayworth was in the back of the church and Guy could not resist turning around for a glimpse of "Gilda." Miss Hayworth had been at the studio when she overheard Dore Freeman say Gia Scala died. "I met her once," she told him. "She was so beautiful and such a nice person."

As young as Guy was, he had already lost several of his young friends: Willard Sage, Chris Dark, Jeffrey Hunter, and now Gia.

Right after Steve graduated in 1972,[249] that dreaded call from Uncle Sam came. The Vietnam war was still out of control. The seemingly endless war was a dismal controversial disaster and one that most Americans did not believe in. Guy and Janice had the family doctor write a letter. "I had a high lottery number," he said. "That means, like, 'You're on your way!' I went down to the draft board in my little red VW with a letter from our family doctor in my pocket that told about my medical history when I was a kid. I had had asthma, but I hadn't had a wheeze or an asthma attack since I could remember. The only residue I have of it is the postnasal thing. But, it came back to me that day. I guess it was just destiny, but when I got there, I just happened to have a wheeze. It picked a good day to come back. The doctor said 'It's a *sleezy* wheeze, but I'll buy it. You're outta here.' I guess he was opposed to the war too, because he said, 'I like to get people off, if I can.' So I was 4-F and out the door." It was a great relief to him and his parents.

Shortly after, he got a part-time job delivering film for Hollywood film companies while he went to Valley College with a major in Theater Arts. A few months into his freshman year he moved out of his father's house on Hillside Drive and into his own apartment in the San Fernando Valley. He earned his Associate of Arts Degree, taking acting classes and fencing. In addition, he took an acting workshop from Estelle Harman, who had years before taught both his parents and had become a good friend of the family. After two years of Theater Arts, Steve had a change of heart. "I was just bored to tears in the Theater Arts Department, and after I got my AA in 1974 I went another year to take a few courses just because I was interested in them, such as astronomy and cultural anthropology.

"I remember when I was in high school doing a little student film for a grade, and I went back to Disney to see Cotton Warburton. He did the editing and cutting for *Zorro*. And he helped me with my school project. He pulled out clips for me to teach me how to hot splice and he said, 'I cut your dad's show.' We talked about my dad and the show with some fond memories. One of the things about Disney back then—that it doesn't have now—was that it was like a family.

"While I was in college, I made a Metropolitan Life Insurance commercial that had a good three- to four-year national run. It was the last commercial Met-Life did using real people just before they put Snoopy in as the 'spokesperson.' I lived off that for a long time and managed the apartment building where I lived."

Toni loved the Buckley school and the friends she had made there. She was in for a bitter surprise when her dad made a shocking decision. "I was *pulled out!*" said Toni angrily. "I didn't know *why* I had to leave. I had thought Dad was mad at the administration about something. I didn't understand it and since Steve had graduated from there, I just thought I would too. So I felt it was unfair. I was never given any explanation. It was just because *'Dad said.'* Dad ran the house like a dictatorship."

Toni was enrolled in Immaculate Heart, a private Catholic school, which was closer to home. "I don't think Dad chose a Catholic school so much to provide us with religious training, as it was that he thought Catholic schools offered a higher quality education not found in public schools.

"Dad was the typical Italian father. I was not allowed to date until I was sixteen."

At first it was difficult for Toni, missing her school and old friends, but she soon made new friends. She continued to see her old friends by going to ballgames and events at Buckley for a while. When she was of age to drive, she took a driver's education class in school and got her license. Sometimes she was allowed to take the car to school, which was only about three miles away from home at the corner of Western and Franklin Avenues.

Guy continued to keep his picture, with his mustache, in the Players Directory. He was still in the game. His agent Bob Raison had offered him commercials and guest shots, but Guy refused them. To him, it was a step-down and of no benefit to his career. In 1972 he got a call from Raison to go to CBS for a lead role in a new TV show. Guy thought it was be a feature film for television, but when he got there, he found out it was for the lead in a new daytime soap opera. He was *furious*. Soap operas to Guy, and many stars at that time, were an insult to a star. It's not like that today, but then they were considered the graveyard for has-beens, the all-time low in television. Guy was so upset, he got a new agent, Lew Deuser.

In late November of 1972 Guy and his family was asked to be in the 41st annual Santa Claus Lane Parade, popularly called the Hollywood Christmas Parade. Each year, around Thanksgiving, crowds come out in droves along Hollywood Boulevard to see their favorite TV celebrities riding in the parade in convertibles, vintage cars, and floats. Usually a family is featured near the end of the parade and this year it was the Guy

Williams Family. It was a special and memorable occasion for Toni. "I remember being with my family in a buggy pulled by six Clydesdale horses," she recalled. "And *right* behind us was Mickey Dolenz of The Monkees. All my friends from Immaculate Heart came and cheered us as we went by. It was so fun!"

New Year's Eve was fun too. William Ramage was with Guy and Janice that night. "Janice called me and invited me to go with them to a New Year's Eve party at Sally and Norman Foster's house."

Guy was happy because, he and William and Norman were planning to make a movie. William had done extensive research on Virginia Hill and had gotten backing for the film. Norman was going to direct and Guy was going to star as Bugsy Segal. He was ecstatic. Even Janice had a part. "Guy was so excited about this," said William. "He couldn't wait to get started."

At midnight Guy decided to sing "Auld Lang Syne" for everyone. William recalled one of his funniest memories of Guy. "First of all, it was funny, because Guy *couldn't* sing. We had all had a lot of champagne and Guy got up and sang the first line and couldn't remember anymore! 'I can't remember the words!' he shouted. Then he said, 'I wonder if this ever happened to Judy Garland!' I thought I would die laughing. It was something you would *never* expect him to say. Not Sinatra, or Dean Martin, but Judy Garland!," Williams laughed. "But that was Guy—always surprising you with something unusual and funny."

1973 came and Guy had not worked in nearly five years. "Guy knew how to enjoy his leisure, but I know he wanted to be working," said Janice. "He needed something. Anything. It was just a shame what was happening in his career. He didn't let on, though. He never felt sorry for himself, nor did he ever want anyone to feel sorry for him."

Happy at home in his favorite chair with a glass of Bordeaux and some classical music surrounding him, Guy would open a book, perhaps one of the *Great Books of the Western World*, and read. He continued to write and think up ideas for TV shows to produce. "Guy could entertain himself," said Janice. "He liked being with himself, in fact he used to say that. He really didn't need someone or TV to entertain him because he could happily sit with a book for an evening, or play chess with himself. He loved to listen to music and he loved to conduct while he listened. He knew *every* note in those symphonies. Sometimes when I'd walk by the room, I'd catch him waving his arms around in big sweeping motions to the music like a conductor. He would be *so* wrapped up in the music he wouldn't know I was watching. I think if he could have been anything else other than an actor he'd have wanted to be a conductor.

"Guy read Plato and Socrates, all the philosophers, and he would *literally* read the encyclopedia from A to Z. His appetite for knowledge was insatiable. I'd walk into the living room and find him in a chair with the big book spread across his lap reading about whatever interested him at the moment," continued Janice. "He could converse about anything and he had a *broad* vocabulary. I had a game I'd play where I'd try to catch him on a word. I'd think of the most obscure word I had read or heard and he would *always* know the definition."

When his friends were over Guy loved an argument just for the sake of the argument. He enjoyed the process of logical thinking. He loved a debate. "Guy would deliberately disagree with a statement someone made over dinner—it could be Norman Foster, Bob Stevenson,[250] Don Burnett, Art Silver, or any of our guests—just to argue the point all night. Then the *next* time the same subject came up, Guy would take the *opposite* point of view and argue *that*," she laughed, "just to keep the debate going.

"Food was important to Guy. He loved to eat, but he had to be careful or he could gain weight easily. He stayed at 185-200 pounds for years and years, which for his height of almost 6'3" was good. One time when he felt he was gaining weight he told me he wanted to try this technique of a famous boxer he had heard about who controlled his weight by chewing meat, swallowing the juices, then spitting the meat into a bag. So, the next time we barbecued steaks in the backyard we had these brown paper bags by our sides. And Toni had a friend over and when they passed by the patio, there were her parents spitting into these paper bags!" Janice laughed. "She was so embarrassed. She thought we were *crazy*. We thought it was funny."

Guy enjoyed the preparation of a meal as much as the ceremony of the meal itself. The art of cooking was something he appreciated and when he cooked it was almost scientific. "At one time when we would make tea, we'd buy the leaves and all the apparatus and we would actually read the encyclopedia all about teas and study the different techniques of how to brew the leaves properly for the best flavor. Guy wanted everything to be genuine. The whole *proper* procedure was fun for him. His favorite tea was Oolong.

"We had dandelions growing wild in our yard, and we had always liked dandelion leaves in our salad. Guy liked everything fresh, so we'd just go right in our backyard and pick dandelions for our salad. They were *delicious!,*" said Janice.

"One time when Guy had not been working for a long time, we were picking and we started laughing because we started imagining how we must look to the neighbors. Not many people at that time ate dandelions leaves. Guy started making up funny dialogue of what they would say if they saw us. A helicopter flew over and Guy joked that it was probably the paparazzi taking pictures of us and it would be in the gossip columns in the morning that things must be really bad at the Williams house, because they have to eat *weeds* from their yard for supper. We were both laughing so hard."

Early in 1973 William Ramage found out unexpectedly that he could not get the rights to do his film. He was shocked and couldn't bear the thought of telling Guy. "We were ready to go, ready to start production," he said. "I had sunk a lot of my own money into it. I had the option on it and paid for a treatment on it. But the worst part of all was having to tell Guy. That was the hardest thing for me to do. Guy thought maybe there was something he could do to help, but it was no use. The film could not be done. This was to be the role he thought would make him the Hollywood movie star he wanted to be. He was heartbroken. And that's what hurt me the most, because he was such a sweet man."

Chapter 50

"He was so fun to watch."

— Terry A. Alvarado

Terry Auzenne (Alvarado), one of Toni's girlfriends from Immaculate Heart High School, recalled the fun she had whenever she stayed overnight at Toni's house. "I was fourteen or fifteen years old at the time. I didn't know Toni as Toni *Williams*. She was Toni *Catalano*, when I met her, so I called her parents Mr. and Mrs. Catalano. I had no idea that her father was Guy Williams, the actor. The first time I went to Toni's house her father was not there. Toni said her father was in South America on a business trip, so I did not even know what he looked like.

"Toni's mother, Jan, was a great cook and she did everything with such good taste and care. At lunchtime I could see Jan through the opened French doors on the patio setting up the tables and chairs for our poolside lunch. She had made homemade lentil soup. Well, I had never had lentil soup, and at that age I was not one to try anything new. But when Jan asked me *just to try it*, I had so much respect for her, I did. And I found out I *loved* it. It was also at Toni's house where I was introduced to other foods I had never tried before, such as tabuli and panforte. I think of Jan and Toni to this day when I eat those wonderful foods.

"The house was a very impressive one, large and elegant, but very homey. Each time I spent the night there, I never wanted to leave!" mused Terry. "When you walked into the alcove of the house, the living room was off to the left. There was a grand piano in the room and a big fireplace. The dining room was very long and reminiscent of a banquet hall in medieval Europe, formal but very comfortable. We had delicious pasta dinners there. Guy always liked wine with the meals."

Raymond Burr[251] lived next door and a canyon separated the houses with lots of trees and scrubs. He had bought a tropical island and helped many of the natives by bringing them to America for work and education. "Toni and I used to try to see them working in the yard next door, while we listened to them singing in their native tongue.

"One time Toni showed me lots of Zorro toys and things that were stored in their garage. She told me her dad had played Zorro on TV, but I had never seen it. There were things from the set, children's books, toys, and records from *Zorro* and we were playing with her dad's cape and mask, when Steve came in and caught us. His mother soon came in and said very gently to Toni, 'Now, Toni, you know you shouldn't be playing with those things.' We put everything back the way it was and moved on.

"I don't remember seeing her brother, Steve, much, maybe once. He usually was not at the house, because he had a car and his own apartment at that time.

"Jan was so sweet. I thought 'What a mom!' She was so patient and gentle. One time Toni was upset because her hair wouldn't do what she wanted it to do. Her mother just calmly took her in hand and combed her pageboy neatly under, just the way she had wanted. I thought Jan could do *anything*! She took Toni and me with her to a fabric store in Century City and while she looked at fabric to make curtains or *some*thing,[252] Toni and I played with the feathered boas, dancing around the store," she laughed.

"The next time I went to Toni's house, her father was home. The first time I met him, I was bounding down the enclosed winding staircase, and ran into him as he was coming up. He smiled that big smile and said, 'Hellooo.' I said 'Hi,' and ran back upstairs to Toni with my mouth open and said, '*Your dad is the Dad on Lost in Space!*' Toni just said, 'Oh yeah, he did that too.'

"Mr. Catalano had very politely asked me not to run down the stairs," Terry remembered. "I was so embarrassed and I remember thinking, 'Oh, I hope he's not mad at me.' I wanted him to like me. He was never loud or rude to me, always polite. He was a gentleman even to a young fifteen-year-old kid.

"He had a ritual late in the afternoon. Toni and I would hide and watch him. He would sit in the hot sauna by the pool a while, then he would come out and dive into the ice cold pool. He'd yell and make sounds from the shock of the cold water, and Toni and I would giggle our heads off. Then after he swam a couple of laps he would get out, put on his robe and slippers, and go change. No one ever wanted to swim in their pool because he kept it too cold. He said it was healthier for you that way. Later, we would watch him again, when he came into the living room with a large chilled glass of wine, his pipe or a cigar, and sat in his chair where he listened to opera or classical music close to the speakers. He had a big dark-colored English-style leather chair that he sat in. And it was *his* chair. It was not to be touched or moved. His ritual was to schedule, like clockwork. He was so fun to watch, because he had so much class."

Terry was not aware that her mother, Aletha Auzenne, had been in love with Guy Williams for years since she watched him on *Zorro* when she was a little girl. "Well, my mom came to pick me up one day when Mr. Catalano was home. He answered the door and my mom just *froze*. He turned and called out to me, "Your mother is here to get you! It *has* to be your mother because she looks just like you.'"

Aletha Auzeene recalled the surprise of her life. "When he answered the door and flashed that big smile, I was in *shock!* He said, 'Come on in and we'll talk a while.' He was *gorgeous*. He was more handsome in real life than he was on TV. When I was a little girl growing up in Louisiana, I *adored* Zorro," said Aletha. "I used to race home after school to see it. Then I married and moved to California and one of my three daughters, Terry, became friends with a girl named Toni, whose parents she called Mr. and Mrs. Catalano, so there was never any connection to *Guy Williams*. Never in my *wildest dreams* did I believe I would ever meet him. So, there I sat, not knowing what to say, but I know *I* must have mentioned watching him on *Zorro*. We talked about the nuns at Immaculate Heart because he was concerned about their methods of teaching. The nuns at that time were in a transition, giving up many old traditions, such as no longer wearing the habit. He said, 'What about them anyway? Are they teaching anything? Kinda of frivolous, aren't they?'" she laughed, remembering her effort to make conversation. "I just couldn't believe it! It was like a dream. And I *loved* Jan. She was sweet, a little shy, and very much a lady."

On their way home that day Aletha said to Terry, "Why didn't you tell me he was *Zorro*?!" Terry replied, "Well, I didn't know.*"* Reflecting on the chance meeting, Aletha summed up: "They were wonderful and sweet people, and my life has been all the richer from having known them."

Terry remembered one evening at Toni's house, while waiting for dinner, Guy reprimanded her and Toni, in defense of Sam, the dog. "Toni liked to make Sam chase us to the dining room because when he got to the marble floor he would slide like a missile across the room. And this time he slammed into chairs and into the wall. Her dad heard us laughing and came in and patiently said, 'OK, ladies, don't tease the dog. He's old. It's time to give Sam a break.'"

During one of Terry's stay-overs Janice's mother was there. "We were eating our pasta dinner, when Mrs. Cooper began to choke on some food. Toni's dad jumped up immediately and with Jan at his side they dislodged the food and she was fine. Then, they just sat down and went on with dinner as though nothing had happened.

"Toni was very sweet, fun to be with, and very pretty. The change from one school to another didn't *seem* to bother Toni, but I think Toni missed Buckley a lot. She accepted it good-naturedly, but deep down I think it did affect her. I went with her a few times to events at Buckley after she had left there, and she was always so happy to see her old friends again."

Terry's lasting impression of being at Hillside was a sense of harmony in the house, where Guy was the master. Janice had a compromising disposition that came out of love and respect rather than duty. She and Guy were compatible because they enjoyed so many of the same things and she let him rule the roost. "It was a house of love and happiness," said Terry, "and I'm grateful for the wonderful times I spent there. Mr. Catalano was friendly and nice, not arrogant or smug, and yet he had an air of importance around him. All of his things were always in place -waiting for him. He had a large presence. When he was home, you *knew* he was there. When he was not home, the house seemed still."

Part III

Argentina

1972-1989

Chapter 51

"Is it possible that I'm this famous here?"
— Guy Williams

At this time in his life, Guy thought his career was over. The train had left the station. That was it. He'd never work again. If he dwelled on it, which was rare, it would depress him. He could use a good job as an ego boost. Expenses were becoming harder to meet. *Lost in Space* was continually in reruns, but residuals were dwindling and royalties from *Zorro* were few. He had kept his picture listed in the Players Directory at the Guild under Armstrong-Deuser, but it seemed Hollywood had forgotten him.

Reflecting on Guy's short career, in the sense that he only did two TV series and never had a big box office success, his friend Steve Silver theorized, "Guy could have been Errol Flynn, but the time frame was wrong. Guy was the real swashbuckler type, but he came to Hollywood near the *end* of that popular swashbuckler era. He was *almost* Errol Flynn."

Some thought he could have been a Cary Grant or a Clark Gable, had he been less outspoken, less opinionated, even less complacent at times. Guy knew that dropping out whenever he was a little ahead of the game had not helped. But the reasons for him not getting work was pure speculation. There is no formula for success in Hollywood.

As Guy approached fifty, he probably asked himself some common questions among Hollywood's mature actors: "Where do I fit in now? Am I still the leading man, or am I a character actor now?"

Guy had reached that time in life when transitions are inevitable. Mid-life can be either productive or destructive, depending on a person's state of mind. Soul-searching questions for any man, particularly an actor, come to mind: "Have I reached my goals? Am I a failure or a success? Do I have enough money to retire? Am I still attractive to the opposite sex?"

In spring of 1973, it had been a long stretch of nearly five years since Guy had worked. While keeping the happy façade, Guy was, on the inside, a disappointed man, who felt his career was over before he had made that feature film he dreamed of that would catapult him into the realm of memorable movie stars. He wondered if it was too late now to ever have that opportunity. He was close to giving up all hope of being wanted again.

Suddenly, out of the blue, came a phone call from an Argentine representative in New York. Leo Gleizer was on a mission to find Guy Williams, El Zorro, and bring him back to Canal Trece (Channel 13) in Buenos Aires with him. Disney's *Zorro* series had been airing in Argentina since January 2, 1968, and El Zorro had captivated the hearts

Guy first arrived at Ezeiza Airport in Buenos Aires in April 1973. The huge welcome completely surprised him. His big smile tells how happy he was about the warm and unexpected reception. (author's personal collection)

of the South American people to an obsession. With sweeps week coming, Canal Trece would surely win the ratings if they could get Guy Williams to appear on their children's shows at their TV station. Guy had no idea the series was playing in Argentina or that his popularity there was building to a frenzy.

Canal Trece sent their public relations man, Gleizer, to New York to find Guy Williams and convince him to come to Argentina to appear on television on their station.

Leo Gleizer's said:

> When I arrived in New York, it was quite difficult to find Guy's where-abouts and, then, it occurred to me to look in the phone book. It took me by surprise to find out that Guy Williams was living in California. I called and his wife, Janice, answered, and gave him the phone. I told him I had come from Argentina to find him and he thought it was a joke. I asked him to come to New York to make the specific arrangements and he said I should go to his house. I insisted that I would pay for his airfare and, finally, I convinced him. When I saw him, he was without his mustache—"mostachos" as he called it— and I suggested he let it grow again. In this case, he did. We become good friends, and fifteen days after my first call, we arrived in Buenos Aires.[253]

It couldn't have happened at a better time. Janice remembered, "Guy was hurting for work. He didn't talk about it, but, sure, he wanted work badly. He would have loved it if the right thing had come along. I can't understand why he couldn't get work, but they say in this town, 'It's 10% talent and 90% luck.' I've heard working actors say that, and I really think a lot of it is *timing*."

If Guy had questions, he found answers the moment he set foot on Argentine soil. It didn't take him long to believe his life may have just taken a major turn. Guy could never have anticipated the welcome that was in store for him by the people in a country so far away from home. Canal Trece gave Guy first class round-trip tickets to Buenos Aires with all expenses paid at the Buenos Aires Sheraton Hotel. From the time he arrived at Ezeiza Airport, some 30 miles outside of Buenos Aires, on April 1, 1973, he received the VIP treatment. Argentina was in the midst of political transition and turmoil. Juan Peron was sure to win the upcoming election. Arriving that same day at the airport was Peron's constituent, Hector Campora, who would fill his seat until the election was final. This made the crowd double in size. They could support Peron & Campora and El Zorro at the same time!

The moment he walked out from customs, many kids tried to get his autograph, and touch and kiss him, which he gladly did. He was very cordial with the public, but also somewhat surprised. At a certain moment, while observing a crowd of young "peronistas" shouting, "Zorro and Peron, One heart!," he asked: "But, is it possible that I'm this famous here?"[254]

Argentineans love Hollywood actors, but it had been two decades since Hollywood movie stars, Rita Hayworth and Johnny Weissmuller, had visited here. Very few other actors, such as Broderick Crawford, had come since then, but Guy Williams was the first major Hollywood actor of enormous popularity to come to Argentina in a long time. For them, he was more than a Hollywood actor, he was a national hero.

Guy Williams struck a handsome figure at 49 years old. He wore his black Zorro hat so he would be recognized, but he was told in Argentina they would have known him without it. Guy was not prepared for the huge crowd that awaited him.

Guy could not believe the outpouring of affection from so many. He was an idol. A Superstar! The crowd was jubilant. Children pushed pen and paper in front of him for his autograph. Others reached out just to touch him. Excited reporters scurried around him and hounded him with questions as he walked through the usual customs. TV cameras were on him and news photographers were taking his picture as they tried to talk to him everywhere he went.

Representatives of Channel 13 took him to the Sheraton Hotel. Reporters followed his car from the airport, and continued to follow him even into his room, where they continued to ask him questions. Guy could not believe it! Even as he laid down on the bed to rest, after the fifteen-hour flight, they continued to talk and take pictures.

Some excerpts from Revista Canal TV, Número 770, April 7-13, 1973, told about El Zorro's first arrival to their country.

"Zorro Came to Buenos Aires and Took Off His Mask"

Channel 13 made a dream come true for thousands of kids by bringing "Zorro" to this country in the flesh so they could look at him close up and touch him.

When on Sunday, April 1st, Guy Williams stepped down from the plane at Ezeiza, he was wearing the hat that was part of the Zorro character, for so many years. If it was because he was afraid of not being recognized, he was in for a great surprise when he noticed the numerous groups of kids running toward him to greet him and take a close look at their hero.

Only then did he take off the hat, as if he no longer needed his ID. The first questions fell on the actor as he was waiting for his passport.

Guy speaks a Spanish mixed with Italian. Sometimes an English word would slip in between.

From the airport to the hotel, we managed a long talk with "El Zorro." Guy must be between 6'1" and 6'3" tall. He has green eyes and light brown hair with a little graying. He likes to laugh and as he talks each phrase is accompanied by his enormous hands, moving as though they have a life of their own.

If you had to define Justice, from your character's (Zorro) point of view, how would you do it?

The moment Guy walked out of customs he was swamped for autographs.
(author's personal collection)

Well, I think that here, in Latin America, they like the show, because of the social justice shown in it, but the Zorro character is really an authentic revolutionary who refuses to allow his land to be converted into a colony. But I also believe that the biggest fans are the kids. They love action.

Who are your idols?

I like Douglas Fairbanks, the first Zorro, from whom I learned many things. Later it was performed by Tyrone Power. And I like Carole Lombard, an excellent actress. But, at the present, I have no idols.

Argentina embraced Guy. They smothered him with love and adulation beyond his wildest dreams. He was rejuvenated beyond his expectations. It was 1957 and 1958 all over again, only bigger. In a troubled country where thousands were oppressed, El Zorro was their national hero. People wore buttons with his picture and held up signs saying "Guy Williams for President!"

Ricardo Pollera, from public relations at the Channel 13 (Canal Trece), gave a big welcome barbecue for Guy at his rancho outside of Buenos Aires where he was introduced to their daily routine of asados. Since Guy loved meat, this quickly became one of his favorite rituals. Word got out around the community that El Zorro was there and by the time Guy got back into the car to leave for the city, the local people had lined up along the country roads to see him. Many got in their cars and followed making an unbelievably long caravan for miles, just to show him their love and welcome.

Chapter 52

"Chee, Chee, Hey"

– Fernando Lupiz

Guy's career had gone through Birth, Death, and Rebirth. He was Zorro all over again. There were the same young adoring fans, doing the same things they had done sixteen years ago. The rush lifted him to another level, and revitalized him. Fame at this time in his life felt better than the first time around.

Canal Trece put Guy on a popular children's show called *Porcelandia*, hosted by a famous Argentinean comedian named Jorge Porsel, where he talked about *Zorro* and did some fencing demonstrations. For one of these demonstrations Guy was given a female fencer. Guy liked to use real swords, with no protective tips, and he was not comfortable fencing with a woman. The studio set out to find a well-trained skilled fencer to be his partner. A nineteen-year-old named Fernando Lupiz, who had already won many competitions and had represented Argentina in the 1972 Olympics, came to mind immediately and was tapped for the job. Fernando was the son of the famous maestro of South America and Europe, Enrique Lupiz, a champion in three weapons, who had trained Fernando since he could walk. Fernando had recently won the Pan-American youth contests.[255]

Just two weeks before his twentieth birthday, Fernando received a phone call from Channel 13 that would change his life forever. They asked him to come to the studio and try out for the fencing of El Zorro. "I could not believe it," said Fernando. "I was *thrilled* that they chose me! Guy Williams was my hero from watching him on TV, so it was a great honor for me."

Channel 13 sent a car for Fernando and drove him to the studio, where he met Guy Williams for the first time. With swords drawn and the formal salute, the two began to practice fencing. Guy was very pleased with Fernando's ability to handle a sword, and he liked his style. The producers liked the chemistry they had. Everyone was happy, and Fernando became Guy's partner in all the fencing exhibitions he would do. "It was like something surreal to me, like a *dream*. I couldn't believe it was happening."

The next day, Fernando took Guy to the salle where he trained, The World Gymnastics and Fencing Club in Buenos Aires, one of the largest and best salles in the world. Guy had not seen salles like this since he was in Europe, with extensive displays in the Salle d'Arms of every type of sword, and *two* floors for fencing. Guy was introduced to Fernando's father and teacher, the prominent maestro, Enrique Lupiz. As they talked, they soon discovered that they had both been taught by the same famous Italian maestros, Aldo Nadi and his brother, Nedo. They hit it off immediately. Enrique gave Guy a lesson to "loosen his hand" and instructed him about different saber techniques. Guy was in his element.

At this point Guy did not know much Spanish and the fencing duo had to establish a "language" for the cues. At first, Fernando spoke Italian to Guy because his Italian, although limited, was better than his English. But the two soon formulated their own language for cues. Guy called the positions where the sword should be: *cheek-check-head*, or *leg-leg* - and Fernando memorized them. But in his poor pronunciation the cues came out, "chee, chee, hey." Eventually Guy called the commands as Fernando did, so they were speaking the same "language." To anyone watching them practice this became very funny, but for two fencers with a language barrier, it worked!

Guy wrote their routines down step-by-step on a piece of paper. He would pull the paper out of his pocket and jokingly call it *la receta* (the recipe). Then they would practice it, and memorize it, until Guy would exclaim his typical remark, *"Terrific!"*

Two days later they were on Rafael "Pato" Carat's popular children's show. A large crowd had gathered outside the studio to see El Zorro arrive, and inside everyone was excited. The place was *packed*. Guy and Fernando did a fencing expo, then it was time to introduce the *Zorro* episode of the day. Fernando recalled, "Guy was asked what his

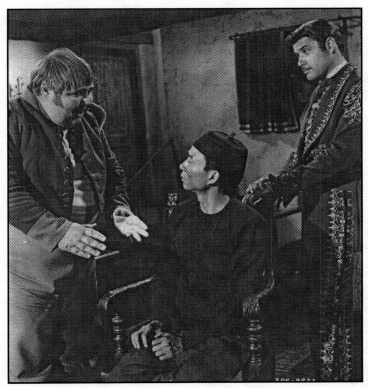

Scene from "Señor China Boy", Episode #77, starring James Hong, center, between Henry Calvin and Guy. (Kathy Gregory Personal Collection, courtesy of Kathy Gregory)

favorite *Zorro* episode was, and he answered, 'Number 77, 'Señor China Boy.' 'Oh!,' Pato said, 'That *just happens* to be the one we are showing today.'"

In Argentina Guy's role was dubbed by Guillermo Romano, a South American actor. Guy was taken aback at first when he heard someone else's voice coming out of his mouth for the first time as Zorro. When the show ended, the network switchboard was jammed for *hours* with excited *Zorro* fans calling in to ask him questions. Many asked about Henry Calvin and Gene Sheldon.

Many more children shows followed for Guy and Fernando on Channel 13. In their skits Guy spoke Spanish, as he memorized the dialogue, but when it was time for a lengthy interview, he was not confident yet in speaking Spanish. Once when he tried, he laughed at himself after a few sentences, and said, "Ah! This is ridiculous," and switched to English and Italian. Most of the time, he relied on an interpreter provided by the TV station.

Outside the studio, among the crowd, was an eight-year-old boy who was well known among the people who worked at the station. Juan Carlos, who walked with a crutch, lived two blocks from the station and played every day with his friends right in the doorway of the station. He loved meeting the celebrities as they went in, and took pride in all the autographs he had acquired. When he heard his hero, El Zorro, was there, Juan Carlos could not have been happier to be given the privilege of sitting at a table with other representatives from the station to talk face to face with his idol. Amazement filled his young eyes when he saw El Zorro enter the room. He told Guy he had no idea he was that tall!

"I watch your show, and I like it. I like the part when Zorro stands up for the good people," he said. "Are you the one who fights with the sword?" he said, pronouncing the Spanish word for sword as a child does.

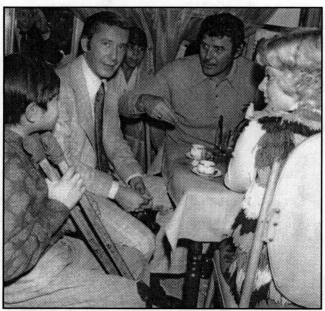

Young Juan Carlos, left, holding his crutches, met his hero at the studio and had the chance of a lifetime to ask him questions. Leo Gleizer is seated between Juan Carlos and Guy, April 1973. (Author's personal collection)

GUY:	Yes, my father taught me when I was very little. He was very good at it. He also taught me how to ride a horse.
JUAN CARLOS:	Are you a friend of Sgt. Garcia?
GUY:	Oh, yes, he is a really charming, good guy. He lives close to my house. We are friends.
JUAN CARLOS:	Do you have horses at home?
GUY:	No, my house is not that big.
JUAN CARLOS:	I would like to be like Zorro.
GUY:	You can be like Zorro. All you have to do is be good and behave yourself.
JUAN CARLOS:	No. What I mean is I'd like to fight with the sword and ride a horse.
GUY (*laughing*):	Well, that you have to learn, but you have a lot of time.
JUAN CARLOS:	Are you going to teach me?
GUY:	I'd be delighted!
JUAN CARLOS:	What is the name of your horse?
GUY:	Tornado. He is very obedient, but if he doesn't know you he can be bad.
JUAN CARLOS:	Did the horse obey you from the beginning?
GUY:	No, I had to work with him, until finally he got accustomed to me.
JUAN CARLOS:	At home, sometimes my mother gets mad at me because I change the channel to see your show, but finally, she gives in.
GUY:	Well, now we have to shake hands, and we are going to be friends forever.
JUAN CARLOS:	When are you leaving?
GUY:	I don't know. I'm going to stay a few days in this wonderful country.
JUAN CARLOS:	How can we be friends if we are leaving?
GUY:	We can continue to be friends. The important thing is that you don't forget me and I don't forget you.
JUAN CARLOS:	When are you coming back?
GUY:	Soon. Pretty soon.

Guy visited the little children in the Hospital de Niños: Ricardo Gutierrez, and orphanage. When he entered the room in his costume (with no mask), and saw their little faces light up, his did too. He held them and kissed them as he went around the room, with that big winning smile radiating the entire time.

Before he left for the United States, Guy shopped for gifts to bring home.

> During the days he was in Buenos Aires, he bought several regional articles at Florida Street, a vicuña poncho, a "charango"[256] and a whip made of "tientos."[257]
>
> He also bought a soft leather jacket for himself and one for his wife. Of course he paid in dollars, and the shop owners were very grateful. The fact is that "El Zorro" came with two pieces of luggage, and returned with four.

Guy told the reporters:

> "Here the people are all beautiful; the women, the children. Also they are much warmer than in California."[258]

Leo Gleizer talked Guy into coming back in just two months. July was the school winter break. Children would be out of school, and parents took them to see shows. There were always lots of children's shows at that time, and the children could stay up late to watch *Zorro* on TV.

Some reporters in Argentina had read that Guy's grandfather had gone to America and bought land in New York, so they suggested he follow his grandfather's trend and buy land in Argentina. Guy promised to think about it.

He loved Argentina so much he wanted his family to see it. He told reporters he would return soon and bring his family.

Guy's face lights up when he meets the children of the orphanage. They watched *Zorro* on TV every night and now he was standing before them in the flesh. (courtesy of Pat Goodliffe)

Chapter 53

"You won't believe it"

– Guy Williams

Guy went home to Janice with stories of the beautiful people and scenery, his unexpected popularity there, and the incredible reception given him. "You have to come with me and see it to believe it," he told her. "It's beautiful country there and I want you to see it with me."

"He called me," said William Ramage, "when he got back and he was *so happy*. He was *so* excited, he sounded like a little boy! He talked for about two hours telling me everything they did for him there and what they were offering him. He was so happy. He *loved* it there."

News that *Zorro* was airing in Argentina, Puerto Rico, Chile, Venezuela, Peru, Brazil, and other countries in South America was getting around the United States. One newspaper article said that Guy Williams was "Zorro Again" in Argentina.

The New York Post[259] said:
> The *Zorro* (TV series) made in 1960 starring Guy Williams is now the No. 1 program in Argentina and will soon be reissued in the U.S. on Spanish-speaking stations.

Zorro had returned to TV in the United States in reruns in 1965, the same year *Lost in Space* began. In several states, *Zorro* and *Lost in Space* were on at the same time, pitting Guy against himself on TV stations across the nation. *Zorro* reruns ended after two seasons in 1967. *Lost in Space* first aired in Argentina in 1967, before *Zorro* ever aired there, but it was never *nearly* as popular as *Zorro*.

"I can't believe it," the handsome 49-year-old actor said when he returned. "I can't walk five yards down there without being mobbed. When I enter a restaurant people leap to their feet and applaud me. Entire families stop me on the street to shake my hand, get an autograph or to steal a kiss."

"I have to admit. It would be nice to be as popular in America as I am in Argentina," Williams said. "But on the other hand, it's nice to have a bit of privacy and not be continually asked for my autograph and mobbed."[260]

"In America I'm as unknown as a doormat," Williams told *the National Inquirer*. "But in Argentina where they're running the old *Zorro* series on TV, I'm a smash. Everybody knows me."

When he recently visited Argentina to go on a nationwide TV talk show, thousands of people lined his route from the airport and hundreds of cars formed a cavalcade behind his.

The fact that he was appealing to a whole new generation of kids pleased Guy, but it also surprised him. It gave him cause to reflect on the merits of the *Zorro* series and also its place in television history. "When you're filming something, you have no idea how important it will be years later," he said, "but *this* seems to go on and on."

If Guy ever had any doubts about the validity of his portrayal of El Zorro, his experience in Buenos Aires must have given him reason to believe he just might have interpreted Zorro with timeless perfection. At a time in his life when he wanted to be on the production end of show business, writing or producing, he was back to playing Zorro again. Surprisingly, he was loving it. It was better than going to the studio every day, memorizing scripts, working sunup to sundown. Performing in front of a live audience was Guy's forte. He liked the freedom and control it gave him, and he thrived on the immediate audience response.

Then, just when things seemed to be going so well, Guy got a phone call that his mother was gravely ill. He and his mother had had their differences, but he loved her. Whenever she needed him, he was attentive and caring. Guy flew to Mexico to get her and brought her back to Los Angeles. He admitted her in Cedars Sinai Hospital in Hollywood, where she would get excellent care and be near him. "Guy never left the hospital," said Janice. "He stayed with his mother all day. I would relieve him for a while then he would be back, every day.

"Guy didn't want you to think he was sentimental. Men of his age were taught not to show their emotions outwardly, but he felt things deeply."

Clare passed away on April 22, 1973 at the age of 71—sixty years almost to the date that she had arrived in America, April 25, 1913. Although she had cancer, her death was attributed to cardiopulmonary complications. Guy took her body back to New York to be buried next to his father in the Gate of Heaven cemetery in Valhalla, New York. It had been many years since he had seen his relatives. Valerie's marriage had ended in divorce and she was struggling to raise her three little daughters alone.

Guy stayed a few days making the rounds, and visiting relatives. He flew back home with many things to think about, now that his life had taken an unexpected turn with new and unexpected offers in South America.

The family mourned Mommy Clare's death and Guy settled her estate. Then he made plans for his second trip to Argentina. He called his old friend and co-star, Gene Sheldon, hoping he would join him on his next visit. He told Gene how often the kids had asked about Bernardo, and Sgt. Garcia.

Gene's daughter, Tracy Sheldon (who calls her father by his first name) remembers. "Guy called and asked Gene to go to Argentina with him to make an appearance. 'You won't believe it!' he said to my dad, trying to make him understand how unbelievably popular *Zorro* was down there. But my dad didn't go, and I'm not sure why. I think it could have been just bad timing. He and my mother separated in 1968 and went through a very bitter divorce that didn't finalize until 1971. I think he just wasn't up to it."

Guy then contacted Henry Calvin, and although he had been seriously ill and had lost a lot of weight, Henry was happy to make the trip and rehash old times. During *Zorro* in the late '50s and early '60s Henry made numerous appearances with Guy, in parades across the nation, and at Disneyland. After Henry's first wife, Edna, died, he remarried. His second wife, Billy, made the trip with him along with Guy and Janice. Janice made arrangement for Toni, then fifteen, to stay with friends.

There was wild anticipation for El Zorro's second visit because this time he was bringing his wife and "Sgt. Garcia." On July 14, 1973, the day Guy and Henry arrived, Channel 13 sent out two camera trucks each with several cameras to cover the arrival from different locations. One truck covered Ezeiza Airport, the other the Sheraton Hotel. Of the four cameras at the airport, one covered Guy et al at the customs entrance, the second at the terrace, the third on the field, and the fourth (on top of the truck) covered the route as El Zorro and Sergeant Garcia rode into the city to the Sheraton Hotel. At the Hotel the other truck took over with three cameras: one on top filmed the arrival, another the activities on the 24th floor, where the Hotel Tea Room was, and the other at the reception. In all, *twenty* buses were deployed from the Channel 13 studio at 1135 Cochabamba Street to the Airport. Channel 13 televised the event from 11:30 a.m. throughout the entire afternoon. The huge reception was comparable to a reception for the Beatles in the 1960s, or Michael Jackson in the '80s.

Guy and Henry rode together in the caravan to the hotel while Janice and Billy rode in a car behind them. Janice saw people lining the streets for miles as they drove into the city. "What are *all* these people *doing* here on the streets?" she asked her interpreter. "Don't you *know*?" she replied, "They are here to see *Guy*!"

It took an hour and a half to go about 25 miles to get to the hotel because of the crowds. Guy had been right. It *was* more than Janice had expected.

Henry Calvin arrives with Guy at Ezeiza Airport in July 1973, thrilling *Zorro* fans. Victor Sueyro, with the mike, eagerly greets them with a warm welcome and questions. (author's collection)

A Buenos Aires TV Guide gave a full account of their first day.

> Over 3,000 people, mostly kids, gathered at Ezeiza Airport waiting for Guy Williams "El Zorro" and Henry Calvin "Sergeant Garcia." Many signs could be seen at the Ezeiza terrace. Some of them said "Welcome to Argentina," others "Welcome Zorro and Sergeant Garcia."
> Exactly at 12:20 p.m., the Pan Am plane landed. The first one to step down was Guy Williams, engaging in a long embrace with Leo Gleizer, after which Sergeant Garcia did the same. Both wives received bouquets of red roses, in each a card that read, "Welcome to Argentina, Channel 13."
> Zorro was wearing a white polo shirt and grey pants. While people at the terrace shouted "Zo-rro, Zooo-rro," he answered waving the classic hat worn on the series. Sergeant Garcia wore a brown overcoat and grey pants, holding a brief case with his right hand. (We learned he was carrying some Spanish Dictionaries). The first words of both were to thank the magnificent welcome offered to them.
> A red sport car was to take Zorro and Sergeant downtown, but due to the amount of people at the airport, they were forced to leave in a black "Ambassador" limousine, covered, of course, and both wives in another car. After lunch they were able to board the red sport car. A lot of people gathered alongside the Ricchieri Drive, to see these legendary characters pass by.
> Many kids welcomed him at the "Hotel Sheraton." At a certain time, they were scheduled to come out to the first floor terrace, to wave at them. Both of them, Guy Williams and Henry Calvin, stayed on the 22nd floor in two adjoining rooms connected by a hallway.

Guy and Henry were asked to do skits reviving their roles from *Zorro* for various TV shows pleasing audiences everywhere to see El Zorro and Sgt. Garcia together again.
(Author's personal collection)

Around 5:00 p.m. they both retired to rest. At night, they dined at "Martin Fierro." They ate roasted baby goat, and afterwards went for a ride around the center of town.

At two in the morning, they arrived back to the Hotel. Sunday 15th, they went to lunch at "Pepe Fechoria," always in Leo Gleizer's company. That afternoon they took a walk along Florida Street, and that night went to Juan Boliche. Monday 16th, they rose early to attend a meeting at Channel 13, lunched at the Hotel, and after noon they did some sketches for VIDEOSHOW.[261]

Videoshow was a news and entertainment report that aired on Channel 13, from Monday through Friday at 2:30 p.m., hosted by Victor Sueiro, Jose de Zer, and Alfredo Garrido. The three hosts did a skit with Guy on the show and talked to him about *Zorro*.

"When we got to the hotel, they took Guy through these throngs of people and up to a balcony on the first floor where the crowd could see him," said Janice. "It was like those scenes you see of Evita, where she would emerge from a balcony to loud cheers. And there was Guy - up there waving to the people," she laughed as she imitated him, amazed at the whole scene. "He got a big kick out of that, as well as the fact that people were trying to get to him *wherever* he went."

Channel 13 included Janice in their TV interviews. The Argentine people were delighted that Guy had brought his wife with him. They were curious to know her and hear what she had to say about living with El Zorro. She soon won their hearts. Reporters were saying she possessed the same charm and friendliness as her husband. They hoped Janice would like Argentina as much as Guy did, because it was everyone's secret desire for Guy Williams to stay and live in their country among them.

Buenos Aires' *TV Guia* published notes called "Zorrerias" about Guy's second visit:

Guy Williams and Henry Calvin in Buenos Aires
"Sgt. Garcia Followed Zorro to Buenos Aires" – July 1973
Every day the kids see how Henry Calvin tries to capture Guy Williams, El Zorro. Last Saturday they saw how Zorro came for the second time to Buenos Aires and this formerly chubby Sgt. was following right behind him. The TV channel was with them through the whole week.
Just a few months ago, Guy Williams left Buenos Aires with a phrase which is today reality, "I will come back to this country because it is *marvelous*."
On Saturday, July 14, he returned on Pan Am Flight 201, but this time he came with none other than Henry Calvin. Both were accompanied by their wives.
We started talking with Guy who responded in Italian.
Are you happy to come back to Argentina?
"I am very happy. Moreover I will say that getting together again with the people here is making me start to think of when I can come back again."
How is it you decided to make this trip?
"Well, I was very impressed with this country in my prior flight, so I already had in mind that I was coming back. Leo Gleizer, a very good

Guy and Henry were on the cover of the Argentina TV Guia, July 21-27, 1973.

friend, invited me to come at this time of the year because the kids are on winter vacation and I also thought my friend Henry could come, since a lot of kids were asking me about him. So we talked it over with Leo and today. I, and even my wife, are very happy to have made this trip."

At the present, what are you doing in the United States?

"We are manufacturing a sweet bread and it has been going very well, but I also love to write novels. I've produced some shows."

What good memories did the Zorro *series leave for you?*

"A lot. There are too many for me to name. But one is the popularity of the show and the good friends I made."

Now we turned to his wife to ask her some questions:

Are you happy to accompany Guy on this trip?

"Very much. He had told me about the customs and the people that live in this sophisticated country. But to see so much show of love and affection, I think we should come back again, and next time with our children."

What is Guy Williams like?

"He is very interesting, very nice, very understanding. He loves to eat spaghetti and he is almost always with a good sense of humor."

What are you planning to take home as a souvenir?

"I plan to buy a lot of regional things. I hear very good things about this country, and the very nice things you have here, primarily articles of leather, shoes, purses."

Henry Calvin was following the conversation attentively, and in English, half of which we could understand, we tried to get to know his real personality.

In the series, El Zorro, you portrayed Sgt. Garcia, a very good-natured man and pretty chubby. Why is it that you are so skinny now?

"Mainly because I am under treatment to lose weight and I have done very well. I lost 176 lbs. in three years. It was said that I was sick but that is incorrect. I am very well and I expect to be that way for a long time."

Henry Calvin is a person who is very happy. He is constantly smiling. Besides, he is constantly imitating Sgt. Garcia. He lives in Dallas, Texas, his height is nearly 6 feet. His hair is all white. His eyes are a deep blue and he has no children.

What do you think of the way the people have received you?

"Really sensational! I could say a lot of things about my life but it's this kind of thing, and the reception here, that make me feel very good, because it means if we acted good in our life, we get back good rewards."

How did you get the part of Sergeant Garcia?

"My career as an actor started around the 1930s. At that time I was a mediocre actor. In 1936, I started as a singer, but the critics were saying I was bad. Consequently, I turned to the theater. One good day some producers saw me working and proposed to me to do *Zorro*. Immediately it was a hit. And well, there I became popular."

We understand that you do very good imitations. And you do "the Fat and the Skinny one." (Laurel and Hardy) Is this true?

"I was a friend of Oliver, and that is why I can imitate him. A lot of people say I do it very well. In fact, on The *Dick Van Dyke Show* I personified the fat one so good that the people were calling constantly by phone to congratulate me."

The sea of humanity that gathered around these characters far surpassed the expectations of our reporters' imaginations. They had crossed the barrier of mere mortals and were as worshipped gods, a true measure of success for a man.

"The Buenos Aires people really outdid themselves," said Janice. "I wasn't expecting to be interviewed, but they asked me many questions. Some, I couldn't understand. Guy was standing a distance from me and when they asked what I thought about Guy, I laughed, and looked over at him before I answered. He saw me and mouthed, '*I'm GREAT!* Say, I'm *great!*' Well, the camera picked it up, and everyone saw him. It got a big laugh."

"Guy picked up the Spanish language quickly," said Janice. "He was able to speak it well enough to do some interviews in the local language." The locals thought Guy's strong accent was charming. Usually he mixed Italian with Spanish and English. Canal

Trece provided each of them with a personal translator: Leo Gleizer for Guy and Patricia Luteral, originally from Canada, for Janice.

Guy and Henry were driven to the TV station for interviews and TV appearances for an entire week. Then they were driven through the city and countryside with their wives to sightsee and shop. "The pampas was just like a picture from my school geography book," said Janice. "They stretched for miles in the beautiful countryside, with gauchos on horseback watching their stock, just like the pictures I had seen."

Pat Luteral's husband, Carlos, manufactured a very expensive automobile called the Luteral, in which he used a very soft plush leather for the upholstery. He gave some of this fine leather to Guy and Janice and they had matching jackets custom-made with it. They wore them while in Argentina and for years to come in the United States on several occasions.

Guy and Janice were learning the culture of the people as they strolled the streets, parks, and the cemetery. "One afternoon we decided to take a shortcut through the famous Recoleta Cemetery on our way to lunch," remembered Janice. "We went to see where Evita Peron was buried. Well, suddenly we see people coming out of the ground! First, we could see a head, then shoulders, then legs. They were all wearing blue smocks, and were coming from everywhere. It was the weirdest looking sight. What was happening was they were coming from the underground tombs where they work. They were attendants who clean the rooms of the underground tombs during the day, and since it was lunchtime, they all were coming up staircases to the ground level to have their 'asada.'" Janice laughed, remembering her and Guy's reaction. "It was so macabre. We were expecting to see Boris Karloff any minute! We were so relieved to find out they were workers just coming to have their lunch. Within minutes you could smell meats of all kind - steaks, ribs, chops, sausages, all cuts - being barbecued. Word got around fast that Guy was there and soon we were being invited to stay and eat, but Guy politely declined. The idea of eating at a cemetery didn't appeal to him."

When Guy was interviewed Janice was interviewed as well and asked what it was like to live with El Zorro.

Carlos Montero, the managing director of Canal Trece, who made all the arrange-ments for Guy and Janice, invited them to his home for dinner. They visited the home of Mrs. Montero's parents, in the northern part of Buenos Aires, where Perón's palace is. "It was a beautiful, opulent home," said Janice. "Guy posed for pictures with Mrs. Montero's sister, her husband, and their little niece. They were all very nice. A few days later, Montero gave us a beautiful custom-made hand-tooled brown leather scrapbook filled with pictures they had taken of us and articles on all the events during our stay. The cover has a large *Z, Guy Williams* tooled on it."

Teleshow, Porcelandia, El Circo Magico de Carlitos Bala, were some of the children's shows Guy and Henry were on during their hectic schedule. Guy did some fencing on these shows, and he and Henry would sometimes do a little *Zorro* skit. Costumes had been made for them for these shows and for a special personal appearance at a Zorro *Fiesta* in Luna Park.

Every day the newspapers and TV guide advertised the TV shows and Fiesta with pictures and promos. The *Zorro Fiesta* was particularly exciting for the kids because Zorro was going to choose a little partner.

EL ZORRO COMES IN SEARCH OF A PARTNER

ATTENTION:
EL ZORRO is coming with a very important mission. He is looking for a "chico" who is very gallant and loves justice, and he will be Channel 13's new partner for El Zorro in our country.
AND
you can participate in the contest. You have to draw a picture of this fa-mous character and bring it to the "Teleshow" at San Juan 1170. The first prize is fabulous: Zorro's very own cape, hat and mask. He will present it to the child himself in person at the grand Festival in the Luna Park. Everyone is invited. Free passes are available at Channel 13.
HURRY!
Zorro is waiting for you and he wants you to be the proud PARTNER of Channel 13 and El Zorro.[262]

Guy and Henry were invited to be on the prestigious television show *Almorzando with Mirtha Legrand* (*Lunch with Mirtha Legrand, July 1973*). Only important dignitar-ies and celebrities were on her show, where she conducted interviews as conversation over an elegant seven-course meal. It would be Guy's first of many appearances on her show.

Another popular show they were on was *The Final Judgment* (July 19, 1973, Thurs-day), with Horangel, a popular astrologer. This show was advertised as the show that would tell viewers what El Zorro and Sgt. Garcia were *really* like in real life through his zodiac signs.

Someone who became a good friend to Guy by way of his taking care of all the red tape for Guy when he was in Argentina, was León Balter. It struck Leon as funny that they had met by chance back in Hollywood, a few years previous. "I met Guy Williams during a brief encounter at Fazzi's Italian Delicatessen in Los Angeles in the late 1960s," said León. "He was purchasing some Gorgonzola and other Italian cheeses. We exchanged some words, but I didn't reveal that I was a member of the Hollywood Foreign Press.

"In 1973 I settled in Buenos Aires for a few years. One day I read in the papers that Guy was in Buenos Aires. He was the center of interest due to the success of his *Zorro* series. I discovered Guy's taste for pickled pork, and I invited him to taste one cooked by Betty (my wife) and he accepted immediately. Our friendship started through *Guy's appetite*! And it was a very good friendship.

"On his next trip he came with his wife Janice, and Betty again prepared the pickled-pork for both of them. The dinner was again another big success. Only a few little bones were left!"

In contrast to the warmth of these friendly people, there were somber and oppressive soldiers of the military government posted everywhere, watching the people all over the city. Juan Perón and his wife, Isabelita, arrived from Spain in June 1973. He won the final presidential election in July, and in September 1973 he took office.

No one could speak out against the government without punishment. People were stopped and questioned anywhere at the will of the soldiers. To those who had very little hope for justice or wealth, El Zorro was their idol, a symbol of the hero they hoped they could have. Argentina was a fearful place at this time for the average visitor, but to a person of celebrity like Guy, the "red carpet" was laid out for him.

"One night just the two of us walked to a restaurant and came across a group of soldiers who were stopping everybody at this point to check them out," said Janice. "I was scared, but Guy wasn't frightened at all. They were asking us all these questions. Then I saw one of the soldiers lean to the officer who was questioning Guy, and he whispered, '*That's El Zorro!*' At that moment, everything changed. They passed us through. Guy said to me, 'I knew they would eventually know who I am,'" she laughed. Guy was not arrogant, or conceited. His boastfulness had an innocent playful quality to it.

"There were some strange and scary happenings there when I first went down," remembered Janice. "People in Buenos Aires were mysteriously disappearing. The military had their hand in everything. I went with Guy for several P. A.'s at Canal Trece and one evening they took us to this great dining room upstairs, and there were all these military people there. Even though the station was run by the same people who ran it before the military government took over, the military occupied the head offices. The soldiers in arms were there to check on everything. It made me a bit uncomfortable.

"Guy fell in love with Buenos Aires. There were many great restaurants, and steaks were in abundance. There were beautiful buildings, and the architecture was very European, which he loved. The city had the same atmosphere as any cosmopolitan city in France, Germany, England, Spain, or Italy. There was a very social atmosphere everywhere, and the people liked to be outside a lot, at little sidewalk cafes and outdoor barbeques. They hugged and kissed everyone. Guy liked all that. It reminded him of Italy and New York rolled into one. And both Italy and New York were home to him."

Chapter 54

"I think Guy had a plan."

– Janice Williams

Guy and Janice returned to their beautiful home in the Hollywood Hills with a standing invitation to return to Argentina. Before Guy left Buenos Aires he was offered a movie deal that sounded very good, and also a plan to tour as a performer to promote the film, which would star him as El Zorro. The idea was tempting. His agent, Lew Deuser, was not getting him work in the United States. At this point in his life, Guy had no desire to work with network people again. But, if a good offer came his way for a *feature*, he would gladly consider. His dream to make a good feature film with substance and longevity had not been fulfilled. He had made the movies in Europe mainly for the opportunity to see Europe with his family.

John Ormond, the P. R. man who had traveled with Guy in his heyday at Disney, remembered the last time he saw Guy in 1973.

It was a daytime meeting on Sunset Boulevard. I was in a music shop, virtually next door to Jerry's Restaurant[263] when Guy walked in. We had a long talk.

Guy had been down to Buenos Aires in Argentina a couple of times, and he said he was going there to live for a while.

He received a royal invitation, thinking he could do well in the film business there.

I didn't even realize at that point they were playing *Zorro* there. I said to him, the film/movie market is very minimal down there, really. Spanish-speaking films are OK, but they could never produce a financial success because their economy is very poor. But he thought he could be a big star down there.

I told him: "You have a good name *here*, why bother going there?" He said "Well, I think I've had my innings here, and it's time to move on."

I recall he told me after he made his European movies, that coming back to Hollywood was a mistake - because he had great success there. So he wanted to try his luck in a foreign market with a new proposed *Zorro* film.

In a serious mood, he then asked me to go with him to Buenos Aires. He said: "We could work together! I'll throw a few things your way, and you could help me." I said, "Guy, I don't speak a damn word of Spanish. I can't even say *yes* in Spanish at this point."

He said, "Oh, you'll learn quick, there's no problem there." Guy suggested I should come back to his house and talk about it, but I had a lot of things happening at that time. I said, "No, Guy. It doesn't appeal to me, and, frankly, I can't understand why you would want to go down there."

But we shook hands and I wished him the best of luck - and that was the last time I ever saw or heard from Guy.[264]

It was obvious to all his friends that Guy wanted to go back to Argentina. Before he made his next trip there, he made a phone call to William Ramage. "I was about to make a career change and move to New York, and I got a call from Guy. I wasn't home, but he left a message. He said he hoped I had found what would make me happy, and wished me success and happiness. It had strange overtones, like he was saying goodbye. I didn't understand it at the time, but after he stayed in Argentina, I realize he had called to say goodbye."

Janice thought maybe Norman Foster's philosophy had influenced Guy's trips to Argentina and his decisions in the next year. "Norman had always said if nothing was happening in Hollywood in a year, *move on*. That's what *he* had done in *his* career.[265] Norman had wanderlust. Maybe some of that rubbed off on Guy. Also, Guy's father, Attilio, liked to be on the move and Guy was like him."

In May 1974 Guy received an invitation from a TV station in Holland to be on the CLUSTER TV show, *Seven Leap*. *Zorro* had become so popular there, they wanted to meet him and have him do some fencing on the show. The warm reception and five-day tour of the country, helped reinforce Guy's belief that *Zorro* was indeed a moving force around the world now that Disney was airing the series in several countries abroad. He began to realize and accept his popularity and the staying power of the show. He was grateful, but still a bit awestruck by it all.

In 1974, two producers from Canal Trece, Carlos Montero and Enrique Garcia Fuertes, contacted Guy with a contract to make a movie in Argentina about an aging Zorro and his son. The working title was *Zorro, Dead or Alive*. There was also talk of making a TV series for kids. They offered to pay Guy a large sum of money, if he would come to Buenos Aires and perform in a tour of the interior with his fencing act to promote the movie. Guy signed the contract.

Juan Perón died in July 1974 and his wife, María Estela (Isabel) Martínez de Perón became President. Mrs. Perón told Guy she would give him *carte blanche* to move around in Argentina and do whatever he wanted in terms of his shows. She would waive the permits, the visas, all the red tape, and make it easy for him to do whatever he wanted.[266] She knew Guy would get continual bookings for shows and it would be a good thing for him. In return, all she asked was that Guy perform for one of her favorite charities. He discussed it with his family and then agreed he would return to Argentina for New Year's Day 1975 to do her show.

That summer of 1974, Guy made a major decision that would be a pivotal point in his life and the lives of everyone in his family. Exclusively, on his own, with no warning at all, Guy told his family he was selling the mansion on Hillside. Those words sent shock waves through the house, with repercussions that would last forever.

Janice remembered how it knocked her on her heels. "We had always discussed things together," she said. "Guy usually made the final decisions, but not *always*, and when he did, I usually *agreed* with him. But, in this case, we had never even discussed it. What hurt the most about leaving that house was that I had nothing to say about it. He hadn't even asked my opinion. So this was different."

The decision affected Toni the most. She had moved to 7475 Hillside when she was still a baby. It was the only home she had known. Leaving it was inconceivable. She asked her father why. "Dad said something vague about the house being too big now that Steve had moved out. As I became an adult, I tried to pacify myself by rationalizing and trying to understand what Dad must have been going through. I *still* don't know why!" she said with old anger rooted deeply. "No one ever explained it to me. It was just that *Dad said so*."

Toni's sadness further upset Janice. "If Guy had discussed it with me first, *before* he made the decision," said Janice, "I might have *accepted* it easier, and maybe I could have been able to console Toni to some degree. I think the reason he didn't ask me and just did it, was he knew the rest of the family would give him a hard time about it. And that would have made it more difficult for him."

Steve wasn't happy about it, but he accepted it with the least opposition since he had already moved out and was living on his own. "I figured it was just that the family was smaller," reflected Steve. "I'd left and it was a big house. There really wasn't any income to speak of, so I figured it was probably financial as well as sizing down." Steve's sentiment for the house is always evident when he speaks about it, however. "If there was a way today to buy it back, I wouldn't hesitate. It holds many good memories."

Toni felt the turmoil in the house, heard her parents arguing, and it frightened her because she didn't understand what was happening. Terry Auzenne remembered the day Toni came to school crying. "We gathered round her to try to tell her it would be all right, but Toni was inconsolable."

Most of her friends assumed her parents were getting a divorce. "Almost every one of us who lived in Hollywood had parents who were divorced, so we told her it was nothing to worry about, and she'd get used to it. 'Not MY parents,' she said. Toni was proud of the fact that her parents had fallen in love at first sight, and still loved each other all these years."

"The house sold quickly," said Janice. "*Too* quickly! No one had time to get used to the idea." On August 5, 1974, Janice reluctantly signed her name on the Grant Deed right under Guy's signature.

Toni refused to pack. "My mother had assigned me the job of taking care of my own items," said Toni, "and I, in protest of the move, had not packed a *single* thing. Steve's girlfriend came into my room and helped me pack my things."

There seemed to be a pattern among the Catalano women. Like her Grandmother Clare and her Aunt Valerie, Toni had also been pulled from her home with no warning and against her will. "Toni left kicking and screaming," said Janice, sadly. "We *loved* that house. It held *so* many happy memories—of Guy, and the children growing up.

"I didn't feel at the time that Guy felt deeply torn about selling the house," she reflected. "I still don't understand it. He must have had an ulterior motive. Looking back, I think Guy had a plan, or he had a *sense* of what was coming. Something made him feel it was time to sell the house."

It's not clear how Guy felt. His behavior sometimes could be as opposite as the seasons of North and South America. As much as he was predictable, he was unpredictable. He could keep his deep feelings to himself, yet about issues or things concerning his children he was outspoken. Toni said, "There was no question as to what was on Dad's mind, because he *told* you! He said what was on his mind. He wore his heart on his sleeve."

Some friends and family members think selling the house didn't bother Guy, while others think it did. Robert Foster, Norman's son, was one who thought Guy was putting up a front while he was being practical. "Don't you know, deep down, he was hurting?" said Robert sincerely. "It couldn't have been easy for him. He just didn't *show* it. When Guy was not working, when he was not being adored by all his fans, I liked the idea that he didn't show it. He *wouldn't* show it. If he was worried or was discontent you'd never know it."

Guy and Janice and Toni moved into a condominium in Santa Monica on 14th Street, just north of Wilshire Boulevard. Toni's friends from Immaculate Heart said goodbye to her and promised to visit. "We used to go see Toni in her new apartment," said Terry. "She was so homesick and we missed her as well. The move was a *big* adjustment for them all. It was a very nice townhouse, but nothing to compare to that big, elegant house. Jan had fit that house so perfectly. It seemed like it was *made* for *her*."

What Janice missed the most about the house was the dining room with its long, romantic, medieval-style dining-table, where family and friends had gathered for years on happy occasions celebrating over good food and wines, spiked with hearty conversation and laughter. It was one of the many pieces they could not keep. "We kept only a few pieces of furniture," she said, "because the new place was small. We sold the Steinway piano to the Steinway people, sold pieces to Abels, the rental store, and donated things to the Screen Smart Set of the Motion Picture and Television Fund, who sold them for their cause."

Toni was miserable. There was not enough space in her tiny new bedroom to put all her personal things. "To make it worse, Dad didn't seem sorry to sell the house. No one ever gave me good reason or told me why we moved. I didn't understand. I'm still mad. *And,* I had to change schools—*again!*"

A few weeks after the move, Toni enrolled in Santa Monica High for her junior year. Concerned with how lonely Toni felt at the new school, Janice used to pick her up at noon sometime, and take her out to lunch to cheer her up.

Ther cat, Kitty Pooh had been sick and frail before Guy sold the house, and Janice worried that she would not be able to make the move. She thrashed about whenever she had to ride in a car, and would injure herself. At the new place she would not be able to go in and out as she was used to doing, and Janice worried that she would not be able to make the adjustment. Kitty Pooh never had to endure the move. She died before they left Hillside. "Everyone grieved over that cat," said Janice. "She'd been with us for twenty-one years."

Steve and Janice recalled how surprised they were to see how Guy grieved over the cat. He had never openly shown affection for it. "Guy didn't pet it or play with it much, and it had almost *died* at Guy's hand—TWICE!"

They laughed as they remembered how funny Guy was when the cat had made him angry. "The first time was when it ate the bird," said Janice. "It was in our first apartment when Guy was doing *Zorro*. We had a little parakeet Steve had named Tinkie that somehow had gotten out of his cage. Guy saw the cat run under the sofa with the bird in its mouth! He ran to get his sword and demanded the cat to *Drop that bird!*" she laughed.

"The cat just stared back at him," continued Steve, "with feathers sticking out of his mouth." He laughed, "We managed to restrain Dad, but he kept saying, 'She *defied* me! She defied me!' That time he almost *ran her through*."

"And the *second* time," tells Janice, "was when Toni was little. She had the cat cornered and it was so frightened it bit her on the forehead. The puncture drew blood. Well, that time Guy got his shotgun! He was so mad at that cat. That was *it!* He was going to *shoot* it. We called the pediatrician and the doctor said to Guy, 'No, no, don't do that. You have to observe the cat and make sure there's nothing wrong with it.' So with that, he put the gun down. But when she was gone, Guy really missed her."

Living a few blocks from the beach, offered Guy his favorite place to bike-ride. He bought everyone in the family a 10-speed bike so they could all go bike-riding together. "I loved those bike rides," said Toni. "Mom, Dad, and I went to the bike shop together and Dad bought my Gitane, and Mom's Gitane, and his Peugeot. His was white, mine was banana yellow, and Mom's maroon red. I remember Mom, and Dad, and I loading our sacks with huge Italian submarine sandwiches from Bay Cities Italian Deli on Lincoln Boulevard, and riding from our Santa Monica townhouse to the Pacific Palisades Park. We'd picnic, and then we were off again on the bike path along the beach. Sometimes Dad and I would ride all the way down to Redondo Beach. Mom would bow out of that one, 'cause it was so long. The funniest thing I remember about riding these bikes is that the leg distance on Dad's bike and mine were exactly the same. When we stood up our legs matched in length, but when we sat down, my head was much lower."

Toni knew her dad was special and she wanted to please him and she wanted him to love her. It was *normal* for her to have a dad who worked at a studio and was on TV, but she was not quite aware yet of his exceptional good looks and his appeal to women. He was just "Dad."

"One time, when Dad and I were riding together, we approached two girls round twenty or so. They were looking at Dad and I heard one of them say, '*Heee's cuuute!*'—and I thought that was *hysterical!*"

Chapter 55

"Guy Williams Is Going To Make a Movie Among Us..."
                                    – Argentina TV Guia May 21 -27, 1975

Not many people knew Guy Williams was in Buenos Aires on January 1, 1975 until he made a surprise personal appearance as Zorro at The Day of Kings extravaganza in the Velódromo[267] Municipal. This annual event is given by the Department of Social Welfare of the Nation, and may well have been Mrs. Peron's charity event. There was an estimated 30,000 children in attendance and for Guy it seemed like every one of them converged on him after the show. His appearance prompted many offers for work in Argentina.

When one reporter heard Guy was in town, he sought him out at his hotel.[268]

> He received us with the kind of nice manners we don't often see, with so much incredible friendliness, and his charm is so natural it seems to come from his pores.

> The reporter asked if the rumors about him filming a series in Argentina were true.

> "The truth is I was not thinking of staying long—but I have so much love for your country—this is the third time I have visited here—and every time I come I am received so well, and they have also offered me some interesting work. I'm so interested in it I called my family and told them I will remain here longer."

> Williams speaks with a mix of Spanish, Italian, and English and comments to us that he has passed all the morning "footing it" around Palermo to stay in shape. He constantly reminds us how amazed he is at the popularity the *Zorro* show still has in Argentina because it was fifteen years ago. It is still giving him a lot of happiness.

> "There is also a little pain to pay," he adds now with a smile. "You should see the bruises on my arms and my legs."

> *Do you know how they happened?*

> "It happened the day of my performance in the Velodromo when hundreds of children came at me like a storm to meet me. They were all talking

350

at the same time. They were asking for my cape, the hat, the mask, my sword. But these little pains are gratifying."

Guy, you spoke of your family. Are they home right now?

"Since in my country it is winter, my children are in school. The older one, Steven, 22, is already in the University and is majoring in Science. And the youngest Toni, 16, is still in high school. For that reason Janice, my wife, could not accompany me and remained with them in Santa Monica."

Lately, have you made any performances in the U.S?

"No, but I will return to TV very soon. What happens is that, constantly, I am being called to make personal presentations outside the country because of the success of *Zorro*. Last year I was Holland, France and other countries in Europe and now I have an invitation to go next to Japan, where they are showing the series with immense popularity and success."

Are you going to make a TV show in your country, Guy?

"If everything goes according to plan we are going to make a "special" about the "Count de Montecristo" which I will act in as the protagonist and will also be the producer.[269] We already have the first scripts and have cast actors for the first two shows. It will be a great investment and a lot of preparation is involved. Very elaborate sets both interior and exterior. In short, it will be made in the same way as the *Zorro* series."

Guy we were informed that you came here to make a new Zorro *series. That is to say, some new chapters. What happened with that?*

"I heard about this too, only nobody asked me anything. So, I suppose it's some person going around speaking for me to get some kind of publicity for himself by using our name, looking for something, but I don't know what. In any case the *Zorro* series is practically impossible to return to for filming. Henry Calvin (Sergeant Garcia) is not in good health and he is already retired from all television. As for me, I am completely dedicated right now to the "Count of Montecristo." I can only hope when it's finished that here in Argentina they will be able to see my new series."

Buenos Aires newspapers had been reporting for some time that Guy would be making a movie in Argentina, and the producers of Channel 13, Montero and Fuertes, were the producers who planned to distribute it wherever *Zorro* had aired on TV. That was, at that time, *sixty-six* countries around the world!

To promote the movie the producers wanted Guy to make personal appearances in shows that also featured circus acts, wrestlers from TV, and Indians performing with whips and knives. In his personal appearances he was always expected to have a swordfight with a villain.

Guy liked fencing with Fernando Lupiz, but Fernando, having turned twenty-one in April 1974, had been drafted and was serving in the military. A fencing partner, Felix Galimi, was selected for one of Guy's acts, possibly the one in the Velodrómo. Galimi was a gold medallist in Individual Foil in the 1951 Pan-American Games, but, unlike Fernando, he had no sense of showmanship or understanding of the act. During the swordfight he had the audacity to disarm El Zorro before a large audience. It was an uncomfortable situation for Guy. Being the showman that he was, he made the most of it at the time, but it made him decide to put the *carte blanche* promised by Mrs. Peron into play and get Fernando back.

Fernando was serving as Assistant of Ceremony and Audience in La Casa Rosada, a position his father helped him get. "My regiment was Grenadiers, the horse section and Presidential guardians," said Fernando. "Then I was moved to a section where permits are given to the public to see the crystal coffins of Juan Domingo Perón and Evita and the Residential House in Olivos."

Despite his preferential position, Fernando was not happy in the military. Then tragedy struck when on July 3, 1974 his father died suddenly. "It was very painful and dark time for me," said Fernando. "My father, Enrique Lupiz, was more teacher to me than father. He was my fencing teacher from the time I could walk. He was one of the best fencers in the history of South America, when it was very, very strong in fencing. Always, he will be better than me."

At this dismal point in Fernando's life, who should come to his rescue but El Zorro. "The military is something you can't get out of anytime you want. Guy went in person to my superiors to ask if I could do a tour with him of the interior—Cordoba, Santa Fe, and

Guy, El Zorro on his horse, making a grand entrance through the gates of La Rural for a performance. (author's personal collection)

other cities in the central part of the country. And that was *it*! They let me out!" Fernando said, astounded. "I never had to go back to the military again. Guy took me from there forever, so he did me a *big* favor."

On his fifty-first birthday, January 14,1975, Guy was given a lavish dinner party at a "carrito" on Costanera Avenue where he celebrated with many friends from Channel 13. Fernando, who couldn't have been happier to be there, was greeted by Guy with a big hug. A large banner hung at the long table with "14 Bienvenidos! 14." A large crowd of children waited outside to meet him and get his autograph.[270]

His producers sent him to TV appearances and a fifteen-day tour, swordfighting with Fernando, and displaying his abilities with the whip. Fernando picked two well-accomplished fencers from his salle to be the villains

Guy was given a lavish birthday party by the producers of Channel 13, during his fourth visit to Buenos Aires. While he was there over New Years, the first baby of 1975 was named Diego in his honor. Guy paid a visit to the mother and child.

and Fernando played Monastario.[271] In the opening of their act, Fernando, as Monastario, has a flourishing swordfight with the two badmen finishing them both in an amazing display of skill to let the audience know what a challenge El Zorro has ahead of him. "When Zorro came out on his black horse," said Fernando, "the crowd went wild! Then, of course, he defeats Monastario in a rousing swordfight. It was a *wonderful* act." They performed at La Rural[272] in Buenos Aires and in soccer stadiums and arenas in surrounding cities, under the management of Carlos Montero, a producer at Channel 13.

Guy's popularity there never ceased to amaze him. His audiences were always overly enthusiastic. Guy had a natural flair for performing in front of a live audience and his presence was powerful and strong. He enjoyed it more than acting, and the money was good. The situation reminded him of the 1960s in the United States when he made the rodeo circuits and made more money than he did at the studio.

It is believed he stayed about a month in Argentina then returned to Santa Monica satisfied with the success of the shows, and looking forward to returning to make the movie. The Argentineans could hardly wait for him to return.

> *TV Guia* Nr. 616; May 21 -27, 1975:
> ZORRO RETURNS TO ARGENTINA
> "Guy Williams Is Going To Make a Movie Among Us About His Classic Character"
>
> This news will surely thrill the legions of little admirers of Guy Williams. "El Zorro," the charming actor, well known by the Argentineans because of his frequent trips, had signed a contract to travel to our country and do a film.
>
> He is supposed to be in Buenos Aires in July, then travel later to Salta to the North's natural scenery, where production will be shot. But the interesting thing, is that Guy Williams will be the leading performer.
>
> A new story about Zorro!!!!!!
>
> As the script goes, Diego de la Vega travels to Argentina, and finds himself deep in exciting adventures, always defending Justice. He will wear again the black hat and the cape, carve the classic "Z," but a young Argentine actor, under his guidance, will use those same implements. This young fellow, a kind of adopted son of Zorro, will undoubtedly share the actions. The names of the director and other actors, have not been disclosed.
>
> For this kind of movie, he (Guy Williams) would have to stay, at least eight weeks.

Argentina's economy at this time was chaotic. Under Perón, the cost of living increased *335 percent*. Hundreds of people were killed by terrorists from right- and left-wing groups. It was a dark and shameful period in Argentine history. Revolutionaries against Peronistas lurked everywhere. Guy did not return to Buenos Aires in July of 1975.

Chapter 56

"I know Norman's death upset my dad"
                                              – Steve Catalano a.ka. Guy Williams, Jr.

Guy came home to hear the shocking news that his good friend, councilmen Bob Stevenson, had died suddenly of a heart attack while he was away. Bob taught Guy about sailing and the two men had a mutual admiration for each other. They were "brothers-of-the-sea." Guy had known Bob since 1957 when they met filming *Men of Annapolis*. His untimely death was a sad loss. Guy had lost another good friend.

A special election held after Bob's death, put his wife Peggy in City Hall to fill his seat. Peggy decided to remain in their big house on Nicolas Canyon after Bob died. Her son was grown and had moved out, but even though she was alone, she welcomed the sanctuary and solitude after being around people all day, every day. "The house became my refuge. But I wanted to redecorate, freshen things up," she said. "I knew Jan was studying interior decorating, so I called her to do it. Jan had studied under the Interior Decorating Guru, Gladys Belzer, the very famous grande dame of decorators in Hollywood.

Mrs. Belzer was the mother of actresses Loretta Young, Sally (Blane) Foster (Norman's wife), and Georgiana Montalban, wife of Ricardo Montalban. Janice met her through Norman Foster, her son-in-law.

"While Jan was learning the business, as a gofer and helper, she learned to do it *right*. Jan did a wonderful job of getting new carpets, drapes, bedspreads, and the loveseats and chairs reupholstered."

Janice has the greatest admiration and respect for her famous teacher. "Gladys Belzer worked until she was eighty-seven years old. She knew everyone in Hollywood and had so many wonderful stories of old Hollywood. When she died in her 90s, she was still a beautiful woman. She was remarkable!" Janice said. "I feel very, very fortunate to have known her, and to have had her for my teacher. Each day she still continues to be an inspiration to me."

Steve went to work for Peggy Stevenson as one of her deputies for her entire term of ten years. On a regular basis, he represented her for a myriad of appointments, events, or problems in the city. "I had specific assignments, like police and fire liaison, planning and zoning, attending homeowner association meetings, delivering a speech somewhere, or go to the Walk of Fame installation on Hollywood Boulevard with Johnny Grant."

When Steve saw the job listed he knew he could do it, but it was not as easy as he had thought to contact his old friend to ask for an interview. Every time he tried to call Peggy, he was told she was out. No one seemed to believed he really knew her. Finally, the chief deputy gave him an interview, saw that he fit the qualifications, and said, "Well, I want you to meet your future boss." Peggy had not seen Steve in years and when he entered her office, she threw out her arms to him and yelled, "*Steeevie*!!" He laughed, "She had always called me that since I was four, and I kid her to this day about that." Everyone watching was surprised and realized Steve really DID know her. At that moment things began to change for him.

Guy enjoyed his leisure at the Santa Monica condo, taking up projects as he always had, writing, developing ideas that he hoped might lead to a television production. He thought of ideas for the movie he would make in Argentina. He rode his bike along the beach and walked.

In June of 1976 Toni graduated from Santa Monica High School and in September of 1976 she enrolled in Santa Monica College as a theatre major. A born entertainer, Toni loved to sing, and write and perform. When she was fourteen she and her mother were in a stage production together of *The Women* at the Woodland Hills Country Home for the Motion Picture and Television Fund. During the two years she was at Santa Monica High she had been outstanding in several plays. In her first year at college, she landed the lead role of Roslyn in Shakespeare's *As You Like It*, and won the Best Actress Award in the Theatre Department. "My dad came to see me," said Toni. "And Dad didn't go out in public much. He didn't even like going to the grocery store, and if he went to a movie, he would not go if he had to wait in a line. So I was surprised when he came to the play. But he said to me, 'I wouldn't have missed it.' He told me I did a great job. I never forgot that. It meant a lot to me."

Guy remained in the United States longer than he might have expected. In Argentina, Isabelita Perón was thrown out of office on March 24, 1976. A military junta, consisting of General Jorge Rafael Videla (army), Admiral Emilio Eduardo Massera (navy), and Brigadier Orlando Ramón Agosti (air force), seized power (1976-1981).[273] Terrorism was rampant. Murders, arrests, and disappearances numbered in the thousands.

Guy didn't go to Argentina at any time during 1976. In July when Guy usually went to Argentina, Fate made it possible for him to be home to tell his old friend goodbye.

Norman Foster's health was failing and he was hospitalized. An illness had been weakening him for the past few years. Guy's family had remained close to Norman and his family since *Zorro*, sharing dinners, and holidays together. His passing was a sad and somber time for everyone.

When the doctors told Norman's family he did not have much time left, they called Guy's family. Guy and Janice were asked to be witnesses for his last will and testament. Toni recalled, "When Norman Foster was dying we were all at the hospital, Sally was there and her sister, Loretta. Robert, was taking it hard. He had to go off by himself for a while and walk around the block. Dad took a walk with Loretta, and she told us Dad reminded her of Clark [Gable].[274] That evening all of us went to dinner at LePetite Moulin nearby. Loretta was so beautiful. She was sitting across the table from me and I told her she had beautiful eyes. She said to me, 'I'll *trade* ya!' That was such a sweet thing for her to say."

Norman died on July 7, 1976, at the age of seventy-five. His son, Robert, wept as he held his father in his arms. Norman Foster, adored by his wife and children, left a legacy as an actor and director and was greatly missed by his friends. "He was a dear, sweet, lovable, and good man," said Janice.

Even though Guy could blanket his feelings, Steve knew what his dad was going through. "He didn't talk about it to me, but I know Norman's death upset my dad. He and Norman got along like two peas in a pod. They used to love to talk about old movies. Norman's family was our family."

Robert Foster was glad his father had such an honest friend in Guy. "My father was not in a position to help Guy because his own career began to do downhill," said Robert. "My father didn't work for many years when his health began to fail him and eventually he just slid. In Hollywood it is a general assumption that actors will naturally try to cultivate a friendship with a director who has already directed them. It's all very practical, but it's also very phony. Now, there's one thing Guy never was, and that's *phony*. *Norman Foster* was never phony. And Guy kept my dad as a close friend even when he *knew* there was nothing my dad could do for him. That *proved* the friendship."

At fifty-two, Guy had lost most of his close friends, many of them at a considerable young ages. It was an eerie reminder of his own mortality.

The shows in Argentina made him feel young and alive. Next time, he would enjoy it to the hilt.

Chapter 57

"I received an invitation…and I will go."

– Guy Williams

Guy and Janice had their eye on an apartment in Marina del Rey, just south of Santa Monica, but for Toni's sake, they waited for her to graduate from high school before making the move. Now that she had graduated, and was going to college, Guy moved his family from the cramped condo in Santa Monica to a beautiful spacious apartment in the Marina, near the yacht club. Don Burnett, with whom Guy had bonded in real life as well as fiction (*Damon and Pythias*), kept a sail boat in the marina, and Guy sailed with him every weekend. It seemed the perfect place for Guy to live. On Marquesa Way, the apartment was right over the water where boats bobbled in their slips and offered a beautiful relaxing view. It was big, comfortable, private, and by the ocean. Don Burnett recalled a poignant moment when they left the marina together in his boat. "One day we saw *The Oceana*. She was moored for a while in a slip by my yacht club, and we had to sail right by her going out," he said. "Guy just stared at her, and didn't say a thing. We never did know who owned her."

"I loved the Marina," said Toni. "The sound of the water lapping against the boats at night lulled me to sleep." The apartment was close to the college and Toni liked the extra space. She felt her dad was very comfortable here. "Dad told me that anything north of Mullholland was foreign to him. He knew *Hollywood*, and *nothing* about the Valley, except how to get to the Disney Studio. He talked about Hollywood like it was home. He knew Santa Monica and how to get to the marina, but he only knew certain routes. He never really learned the whole city. I guess it was too big."

Toni was going steady now with Don Petrie,[275] the first boy she ever dated in high school, both students now at Santa Monica College. "The first time Don came to the door to pick me up for a date,» recalled Toni, "my father answered and said, 'Here! Have some champagne! And, by the way, will ya put her through college?' That was just his way of joking, but I was so embarrassed."

The marina was also ideal for Guy because of the bike trails. "Mom and Dad had always taken walks together, but now each of us would bike-ride with him," said Toni. "We rode our ten-speeds up and down the bike trails along the beach."

Steve would come from the Valley to meet his dad for a bike ride. "Dad and I would load the bikes on the back of the car and drive to Dockweiler State Beach behind the airport and ride up and down the long strip of beach there," he said. Those outings together became cherished moments.

That summer of 1977 Valerie's daughter, Laurie, visited her famous uncle and his family for a week. "I was 17 and it was my first visit to California," said Laurie, who has happy memories of her celebrity uncle. "I had graduated from high school when I was 16 and then worked to save money to go to London. I was still living at home. My mother knew it was going to be either Britain or California, so she helped arrange my visit. One of these days I will get to London," she laughed. Laurie never regretted her trip to California and seeing her relatives. She had a wonderful time. "A few years later, I had a layover in Los Angeles and Uncle Guy met me at the airport and took me out to lunch at the revolving landmark restaurant in the airport. My description of Uncle Guy is a rather old-fashioned word, *raconteur*, but I think it is a good one," she concluded. He was a great story-teller like her grandmother Clare. "He told some funny stories about working at Disney. Unfortunately, I don't remember the tales, just that I laughed a lot, and it was an enjoyable layover."

While Guy enjoyed his home and environment, he seemed to long for the lifestyle of the Argentineans. Robert Foster remembers Guy saying that the people in the United States were too phony and rude. He was beginning to prefer being in South America where he said the people were warmer, more down to earth, and more sincere. Ironically, the Argentineans would have preferred to live in the United States. But, Guy felt that too many people in Hollywood had lied to him and he was happier now in Argentina. Every time he talked about it he raved about it, and said he was looking forward to going back in July 1977 to do more shows for the kids during their winter break.

Diane Lomond was working for Columbia as head of casting for David Gerber Productions, when she thought of Guy for new production. "It must have been Spring of 1977, because that's when pilots were shot," she said. "They were starting a new series, and I was trying hard to get Guy the lead in that particular show. It was something to do with Space. I can't remember the name of it, but it had the word 'Earth' in it. He was going back and forth to Argentina at that time and I remember I was really looking forward to seeing him again. We were going to meet for lunch first, then I was to take him upstairs to meet with David Gerber."

Guy's lack of interest surprised Diane. "He was not the same person, for whatever reason I don't know. I remember telling Britt he was a different Guy than the one I had known. The Guy I knew was very *up*, very fun-loving, and very funny. He had this wonderful kind of innocence about him, those flashing teeth, happy, you know, his whole thing. Instead, he seemed more serious, more controlled—certainly *not* the Guy Williams we knew and loved. He was going thru *something*, but I don't know what. I think they were having marital problems at that time." The two lead roles for the pilot went to Robert Loggia and Michael McCallan.

If the offer had been something different from what Guy had already done, he might have welcomed it, but another space show for television was not what he wanted. Now his hopes were high to film a feature in Argentina.

The invitation he had been waiting for came, and Guy and Janice were once again packing for a visit to Argentina, Guy's fourth. They arrived on Sunday, July 17, 1977 and stayed until Tuesday, August 5, 1977, ensconced in luxury at the magnificent five-star Alvear Palace Hotel. The ornate European-style building stands on the corner of Ave. Libertador and Ayacucho and is one of Argentina's most elaborate and elegant hotels.

The crowds that greeted Guy seemed to grow larger each year. It was phenomenal. This time, fans were hoping he would stay and make the long-awaited movie. "The crowds were always eagerly waiting for him," said Janice, "because whenever Guy was coming to Buenos Aries there were advertisements all over the city announcing his arrival, by radio, television, magazines, and large posters plastered on walls."

Guy made appearances on TV shows for children on Channel 13, *La Tarde del Capitan Piluso* and *Patolandia,* demonstrating with Fernando how he goes about doing a fencing routine. While Guy and Fernando were being interviewed by Pato Carat, the famous comedian host of the show, Carlos Montero, the owner of the studio, was observing them carefully on the monitor. He liked the ease with which Fernando handled himself with Guy and saw a charismatic chemistry between the two men. Montero decided to put Fernando in the movie with Guy to play the son of Zorro.

"After the show they called me to the third floor," said Fernando, "where the executives of the TV channel were. They told me to sit down and they pushed a glass of whiskey in front of me. I told them I don't drink, but the producer said, 'Drink it, you're going to need it.' So I took a sip for him, and then they asked me straight out: 'How would you like to act in the movie with Guy and be the son of Zorro, one of the most important characters?' I couldn't believe it. I told them I had been a model, and I could ride a horse, but I had never acted before. They said, 'We have acting teachers. You will be able to speak and everything. No problem. Trust us.'

"Between the whiskey and the news, I was floating. It was like a dream! Like something out of a movie! Like something you only imagine!"

Guy and Fernando performed in La Rural for a Children's Day event, August 1, and did several shows at La Rural, a huge arena in Buenos Aires where rodeos and

Guy and Janice went on a shopping spree before saying goodbye to Buenos Aires.

livestock shows are held. This show was bigger and better than the last production they had done together.

"Once again I was Capitan Monastario," said Fernando. "I entered on a white horse, fought the two bad guys, who were two good fencers from my salle, then invited Zorro to relinquish his weapon. A great dramatic fight ensued and ended, as usual, with Zorro disarming me. As my sword went flying through the air, Zorro would hit me on the butt until I was off stage and the children would scream with laughter. Guy's arms went up in victory as he remained on stage to a rousing applause and cheers. The crowds were huge and excited. Guy had to be escorted out of the stadium with security at the end of the show because so many people wanted to meet him and touch him after the show. It was a lot of fun and we were all very well paid."

Janice remembered the pandemonium after the show. She was standing near the stage with her interpreter, Pat Luteral, when Guy finished his act. "They were coming to the final bow and the audience started to surge forward and mob the stage. Pat knew what was happening and it scared her to death. She grabbed my arm and said, 'We've got to get out of here!' And *we ran!* The audience stormed the stage. We would have been trampled. But Guy just handled it like 'business-as-usual.' He just smiled and signed autographs."

The Zorro act was the last act of the entire show, and it was fifteen minutes long. "We were promoting the coming movie," said Fernando, "but there was not even a script yet, just the concept of the movie."

Guy and Janice established a lasting friendship on this trip with Carlos Souto, a man who has a great love and affection for Guy to this day. "When I met Guy, he was with Janice in Buenos Aires," said Carlos. "I was working in financial business in the Exchange House in Buenos Aires, where money is changed for individuals and for banks, and I could speak English. So they came to me to exchange money. Janice was a beautiful woman, a very fine lady, and Guy was a great person, a really *good* person. We often went out to dinner together. She and Guy had a beautiful life together."

It was a fruitful trip for Guy, but, once again, he went home not knowing when production would begin for this phantom movie.

Guy, Janice, and Toni at their Marina del Rey apartment, 1977.
(Courtesy of Alejandro Rosso)

The huge success of Guy's shows at La Rural caught the attention of Carlos Patiño, a manager from the Royal Madrid Circus, owned by the Segura brothers. The *Circo Real de Madrid* pitches its huge tent in the Argentina summer in Mar del Plata, the glamorous beach resort for the social elite. Mar del Plata, nicknamed the Pearl of the Atlantic, plays host to prominently upper class vacationers between late December and March. After three months the Circo Real de Madrid, or Royal Circus of Madrid, picks up and travels to other cities in the interior. It was the grandest, most prestigious, circus of them all.

In September 1977, Nino Segura, the owner of Royal Circus Madrid, asked Carlos Patiño to make an offer to Guy Williams and Fernando Lupiz to be the feature act at the end of the circus the following (Argentinean) summer (January 1978) in Mar del Plata. Fernando was thrilled with the offer, but he wondered if Guy Williams would be. "My first thought to Patiño was, 'Are you *loco*?! Guy Williams is a big Hollywood movie star, and you are asking him to be in the circus?!'"

Patiño, who could not speak English, asked Fernando (who could not speak much more English than Patiño) to call Guy and present the offer to him and negotiate the deal. Fernando was a little uneasy about the call. He was so much younger and inexperienced and Guy was a father figure to him. How could he sell this important actor on a circus?

Patiño knew if Fernando saw the circus for himself, it would be easier for him to convince Guy. So he gave VIP seats to Fernando and a guest. The circus, with its elephants, trapeze artists, clowns, and tigers, was much like America's Barnum and Bailey circus, but in Argentina there is always a special feature act at the end, a main attraction, maybe a short playlet, or a special performance by a celebrity. The grand finalé usually determined the size of the audience.

"I took my mother," said Fernando, "and the circus made a big impression on us. We saw that everything was very well done, very high quality. First class. We went backstage and met many nice people in the circus. Then I met with Carlos Patiño and the owner of the circus, Nino Segura. They began to negotiate and told me what to tell Guy. They told me they were offering Guy $2,000 a week. That was a lot of money back in those days, but I thought it was not enough for Guy Williams. They offered me $1,000 a week. I couldn't believe it. A normal salary was $400 a *month*!

"When I talked to Guy, I explained that they wanted him for the whole summer season. He really liked the fact that the act was to promote the movie, *Zorro, Dead or Alive.* There was even talk among the producers to make a new *Zorro* TV series in South America. The act would give the children the opportunity to ask El Zorro questions and get close to him. I told him it was to promote ourselves and, if nothing else, he should come to just take advantage of enjoying the city for a few weeks, and make a vacation of it, in one of the most famous tourist areas in the world. Guy asked me to send him a letter, in English, with all the precise details. I took a chance and told Guy they offered him $2,500 a week, instead of $2,000. I felt the difference in our salaries was not big enough, and if the producers refused, I was going to tell them to take it from my salary because I would be happy with $500 a week.

"After Guy had time to get the letter, I called him again, and he said yes. I think what convinced him was that the act was to promote the movie. They always told us there was a movie but we still had not seen a script. Once I had Guy's commitment, I had another meeting with the producers. I told them Guy wouldn't do it. They were shocked. I was about to say he wanted $2,500, when *they* said they would raise his offer to $2,500!" he laughed. "I got to keep my $1,000, and Guy got a raise.

"I could not believe I was going to be making more money than I ever dreamed of, and for having fun! For fencing! And fencing with *Guy Williams*! One of the most important fencers. It was like a fairy tale. I will forever be grateful to Guy."

As soon as *Radiolandia 2000* heard a rumor that Guy Williams would be returning to Buenos Aires to stay and work, they sent their correspondents, León Balter and photographer José María Urteaga, to interview Guy in his Marina apartment:

Zorro Takes Refuge in His Spectacular Cave[276]

Guy Williams gave an exclusive report to the Radiolandia 2000 from his tranquil residence in Marina del Rey.

He will return to Argentina in October or next January to film a movie and make personal appearances at Mar del Plata. He's afraid for his daughter to see our country.

It was grand for me to be able to go to Los Angeles and fulfill the promise I made to Guy Williams a little more than a month earlier in Buenos Aires, that I would go visit him at his residence in Marina del Rey. The place is like paradise, located near the coast of Los Angeles.

Guy had told us before we arrived that this was his real cave, El Zorro's hideout, a place where he is practically a recluse with his family and friends: a home built up from that kind of love Sicilians have for home and hearth. And Guy didn't exaggerate a bit: His residence is big and comfortable. He told us, while having lunch in a classic "porteZa" the it was ideal for locking himself and friends in, and forgetting about the outside world.

We were greeted by his wife, Janice. "You are in luck," she said. "Guy is here because the sail boat is being repaired and painted, otherwise, he would be sailing on this beautiful day, especially because it's a Sunday."

At that moment a very beautiful 19-yr-old young lady came from inside the house. It's Toni, Guy Williams daughter. She said she is very disappointed because she was not able to accompany her father on his trips to Argentina. She tells Guy that he promised to take her. Guy said, "I don't want to take her, because she will probably like Argentina so much she may never come back to Los Angeles." Then Toni said, "I think we are going to go either in October or January."

Is that true? we asked Guy.

"For the moment I prefer to say nothing about that."

Then Janice said, "Guy is about to sign a contract for a movie in Buenos Aires, but it's his nature not to talk about things like that until they are concrete. Anyway, we know this is a project for October."

And in January, he is to return?

"To Mar del Plata, León, my friend, to Mar del Plata," said Guy. "I'll explain to you: I received an invitation to go there and make some personal appearances in that beautiful city. It's almost certain I will go."

Can you tell us a little more about this appearance that will be such a privilege for us?

"OK,» he said, "I will say nothing more than it is going to be in a big tent. The rest is up to you to find out."

A hint that the trip is somewhat more than a possibility, is made to us unexpectedly by Janice when she told us, "Guy is planning to become a member of a sailing club and have a little fun sailing in the months he works there." To that Guy gestured to Janice to not say any more about what he will be doing. Janice could only laugh.

To change the subject Guy invited us to look around his house. He promised when we finished, he would surprised us with a grand lunch. While walking through the house, Guy and I exchanged some opinions and comments about our two countries. His humor pops up again: "The only complaint I have about this magnificent country," he said, "is that none of our freeways go to San Isidro."[277]

Guy in the kitchen preparing a sumptuous treat for his friend and interviewer, Leon Balter from Argentina.1977 (Courtesy of Alejandro Rosso)

Then he became serious again reflecting on Argentina.

"I have been to many countries. I am a fervent admirer of Italy, but the only country I would leave the United States for is Argentina."

What is it you like so about our country?

"Everything. Everything attracts me. The people are extraordinary. The places to eat are unequalled. The clothing shops are of the same quality as the major cities of Europe."

Before or after you gained 16 lbs.?

"Before, guys. Let me tell you, I already lost those pounds, and the shirts fit me perfectly."

It was really the most inopportune time to make such a statement, because we sat down to an exquisite table with a delicious "picada," as the main dish, and a large Italian Provolone, marinated for a long time in the best of whiskeys. Guy learned the recipe from his Italian ancestors.

"In our house this is almost a ritual," confessed Guy. "We always eat this on special occasions and now we reserve it for grand friends like you. My children inherited this custom, and they always painstakingly prepare it so the friends we love don't get short-changed when they come to dinner at our home."

Guy's words filled us with satisfaction. To be welcomed that way in a foreign country was something to us that says a lot and above all it compromises us to reciprocate the hospitality. From the moment we leave the Williams' home, the photographer Urteago and I began to plan the royal treatment for Guy and his wife when they next visit our country. We are convinced that we'll go and meet with them in October.

Guy left alone for Argentina the last week of December to prepare for his act with Fernando.

Chapter 58

"I'll be working here all the time, as long as the public wants me."[278]
– Guy Williams

Guy's arrival in Buenos Aires this time made bigger headlines than ever, because this time their beloved El Zorro was staying. Word was that he would be working in the circus and making a movie, then possibly a series. Several Zorro costumes were made for him by a movie company, in addition to some parts of the costume Guy had acquired from Disney. Children and adults alike anticipated going to Mar del Plata to see Guy's performance in the mother of all circuses. Those who could not go to the popular beach resort hoped the act would eventually come to them.

Radiolandia 2000, Dec. 31, 1977, Saturday
Holidays with The Children's Idol of the Year
"Zorro Returns! But This Time To Work"
Guy Williams arrives with all his magnetism arousing the excitement and joy of the children.

This coming Sunday he will be at the Royal Madrid Circus at Mar del Plata. As always, his presence generates a lot of anticipation. The show is for children, but it will also capture the attention of adults. Basically, everyone will feel the same happiness and emotions as they celebrate the adventures and daring do's of the character who for many years has become one of the giants of television ratings.

"Last year I was in this wonderful country," he said on his arrival at Ezeiza, "and my only intention was to visit and relax. Now things have changed. I'll be working here all the time—as long as the public wants me. In my act I will count on the accomplished champion fencer, a master, Fernando Lupiz. So I expect everything will turn out O.K."

Without a doubt this will be one of the most splendid events of the season. It is guaranteed to congregate multitudes under the big top of the huge Royal Circus Madrid because Zorro continues to be high on the pedestal here as an Idol.

(Caption under Guy's picture): Summer's *Happiness: for everyone young and old. Starting next Sunday in Mar del Plata the act of Guy Williams "El Zorro" daredevil, hero, swashbuckler, crusader of justice. A spectacular which guarantees mass success. Pictured here (in photo) as he arrived in Argentina is the smile of a man who spreads much happiness.*

The following is an interview with Guy just before he left Buenos Aires for Mar del Plata:

DAILY POPULAR, Saturday, December 31, 1977, No. 8, p. 17

Guy Williams, known worldwide for playing Zorro, will begin the season in Mar del Plata in which he will do fencing and horse riding exhibitions with Tornado. He will make a movie in our country for which the producers have already put up the money. They will be bringing his costumes directly from Disneyland and he plans other ambitious projects.

"I'm very pleased to meet you. My name is Don Diego de la Vega, Guy Williams, etc., but you must know me by my most famous name, Zorro."

Showing off his famous character in his Zorro voice, the popular swordsman and adventurer who played in the famous old television series of action and adventure received the interviewer from *Diario Popular* at the Sheraton Hotel of Buenos Aires to explain the interesting reason for his visit to our country.

"I came here because I have a really good friend, Carlos Patiño,[279] who kept telling me I should come here to perform for Argentinean children, so here I am. It was hard for me to leave my paradise in Marina del Rey, in the United States, but finally friendship won out."

He looks like he's in great shape, you can hardly tell that in 1958 when he made the eighty [sic] original episodes of the famous TV show he was barely in his 30s. Just like Dorian Grey, he doesn't seem to age. He said it's because he likes to play sports to keep in shape, especially fencing and horse riding. Even though he accepts the compliment of looking young he is still reluctant to reveal his age.

Someone brought over some drinks to the table. His promoter, Tito Rivié,[280] said, "Guy has a big surprise for the public. He is going to be in this country for TEN *weeks.*"

A SHOW IN MAR DEL PLATA

As the conversation went on, Guy said he would be starting a new show the first week of the new year in the Circus de Madrid of Mar del Plata, which would include sword fighting with Fernando Lupiz, who was the Argentinean fencing champion, and also includes horseback riding with Tornado (the horse they are using is almost identical to the horse used twenty years ago).

While they were talking Guy decided he wants to get to Mar del Plata by quickest means, by flying with the Argentinean Airlines.

WIFE IS COMING AND MOVIE BEING MADE

"Ah, here's a good note for your article," he said.

It seems like Guy knows what makes a good story. "You know we are planning to make a movie with Fernando Lupiz, *The Son of Zorro*. It's going to start shooting in Mar del Plata in the next few weeks. We don't know the exact date, but we already have all the producers and all the money lined up.

So you are going to be really busy?

"Well, imagine, we're going to be doing two shows a night, one at 7:00 p.m. and one at 10:00 p.m. and then we're going to start shooting - and to top it all off when my wife arrives next week, I will be spending time with her, sightseeing and so forth."

Guy Williams was charming, a very nice guy, full of funny little stories. Then, afterwards they all went outside to walk along Florida Avenue. All the little kids recognized him and came over for autographs. They couldn't pass up the opportunity to approach him, their mythological hero from television.

Fernando carries Guy's bags off the plane as he arrives in Argentina to work, December 1977. (courtesy of Fernando Lupiz)

Guy was given a royal reception. The manager of Channel 13, Ricardo Polera, gave a sumptuous asada at his Quinta in Guy's honor. Guests included Fernando Lupiz, famous TV personality, models, and movie stars. On New Year's Eve, Polera and his wife wined and dined Guy and Fernando in the elegant Salon des Fiestas del Hermitage Hotel in Mar del Plata, a five-star hotel, where they stayed. They were given the largest *camarino*, close to the big tent; a first class trailer with a living room, two bathrooms, and all the comforts they needed.

Guy enjoyed talking to the circus performers and befriended a young couple, a clown named Medio Kilo, and his wife and little daughter, Alejandra.

Opening night of the circus came and the grand finalé of Guy Williams/El Zorro was wildly anticipated and received by a record crowd. The house went dark, and Guy was introduced with much fanfare. Then the theme from *Zorro* was played. Guy was waiting behind a curtain and Fernando watched from the wings. "Guy made a grand entrance. He appeared on Tornado with just a spotlight on him. There was a big ap-

Fans of *Zorro* gather around Guy and Fernando before they leave in a procession. (courtesy of Fernando Lupiz)

plause, and he circled the arena on the black horse with the spotlight following him. He reared the horse, then circled around the arena a few times. It was sensational!"

The announcer presented El Zorro to the cheering audience and Guy got off his horse, took the microphone, and talked to the children. He told them, in Spanish, that he had come to them from the Walt Disney studios. He talked about filming the *Zorro* series, while questions were collected from the kids in the audience. Guy answered them

Guy and Fernando on the Mirtha Legrand to talk about their circus act which is for the purpose of promoting their Zorro movie. December 1977.

Guy and Fernando were wined and dined in the Salon des Fiestas at the finest hotel in Mar del Plata, the Hermitage, on New Year's Eve, 1977 by Ricardo Polera, producer from Channel 13, and his wife.

Guy and Ricardo Polera in deep conversation over an elegant dinner at the
Hermitage Hotel, Mar del Plata.

one by one. There were always questions about Bernardo: "Can he really speak in real
life?» Or about Tornado: "How many horses did you use?"

Sooner or later in the act, the kids would always ask him to remove his mask. Guy
would say "No, no," and they would shout "Yes! Yes!" This would go on for a while, then
Zorro would remove his mask. And for one night *everyone* knew Diego de la Vega was Zorro!

Guy proceeded to tell the audience that he would soon be filming a movie in Argentina
about Zorro and his son. He told them the premise of the movie and then the emcee introduced the new young actor who would play his son, Fernando Lupiz. At that moment
Fernando came running into the ring dressed in black pants and black shirt matching Zorro,
but without a mask. "We had a special handshake we would make when I came out," said

Guy and Fernando practice at the Hermitage Hotel for their much anticipated act at
Mar del Plata.

Fernando. "We grabbed each other' wrist in a Roman handshake, and Guy would lift me and pull me over to the other side of him. This was our trademark handshake."

The premise of their act was based on the concept of the movie: an aging Zorro, looking for a successor, finds a natural candidate in his son. He trains his son to become a great swordsman and is always putting him to a test to prepare him to take over the role of Zorro.

"We made a very beautiful act. Guy would ask me if I remembered the skills of the sword he had taught me. 'If you still have it,' he said, 'and you can beat me, I will give you the suit, my cape, and my mask, and you can be the *next* Zorro.' We began to fence and in a swift twirling motion, Guy would disarmed me. My sword went flying out of my hand, and, of course, I made up an excuse, like, 'OH, my hand slipped.' All the children would laugh and laugh at my excuses. Guy made fun saying, 'Oh, sure, sure.' The kids would laugh some more. Then I turned to the audience and asked, 'Shouldn't he give me another chance?' All the kids screamed '*Yes! Yes!*' So we'd do more flourishing, and in the end with one swift movement, Zorro again disengages the sword from my hand and this time it flies *very* high. Sometimes it flew so high it would almost touch the top of the tent. Sometimes when this happened, the sword would come down in a beautiful swift dive and stick straight up into the ground, with a spotlight only on the sword. It was very spectacular. The audience would say '*ooouuu*' and '*aaah.*' This was always what Guy hoped for, so when it happened he was *very* happy."

When the applause and cheers died down, Guy would tease Fernando, "What's the matter with you? Do you have oil on your hands?" Fernando gave childish excuses, like, "Oh, uh. It's my *glove*! It isn't on properly." The kids laughed and laughed at these antics.

"We got little cuts a few times, nothing serious. Once I got a little cut over my eye. It was small, but it bled a lot. The audience thought it was part of the act and cheered, 'Bravo! Bravo!' Imagine! I am *bleeding* and they are *cheering*," he laughed. "Guy joked to the audience saying with surprise, 'OH, you want me to cut him *again*?!' We adlibbed a lot and had great fun," said Fernando.

Guy made an appearance at little Alejandra's birthday party, daughter of his friend, Medio Kilo, a clown from the Circo Madrid. Some of the children ignored the camera and just stared at El Zorro. January 1978.

Guy relaxing in his trailer, February 1978. (courtesy of Aracelli Lisazo)

"After the show, someone with the circus went up to Guy and asked him to leave it in the act. Guy could not believe it. He would never do such a thing. This had been an accident he hoped would never happen again."

Guy's circus performance was a smashing success. The entire circus lasted an hour and a half, with Guy's act taking the last twenty minutes. "Guy did not like to perform more than fifteen to twenty minutes at a time and this was one of the reasons he took the job with the circus."

When his act was over the kids rushed from their seats to touch him, or grab him, and get his autograph. Guy liked children, they were special to him. Some, however, could be quite unruly. He once admitted, "I don't enjoy ALL the kids, just the well-behaved ones.»

It was a new day for Guy. He felt alive and young again, happy to be working. The performances were every day, twice a day, tiring but exhilarating.

After the last show of the day, Guy and Fernando would go out to dinner. "Guy always wanted me to come along because if he ate alone too many people would come up to him to talk and he could never eat. It helped him if I went with him. Of course, for me, it was always special to be near Guy, but at the same time, I was very young and single, so I wanted to go out to the bars, date girls, and party. Guy would never go with me. After dinner I would go out, but Guy would stay in his hotel room for the night.

"The circus was making a lot of money with Guy so they treated him like royalty," said Fernando. "Nino Segura made a *quarter of a million* dollars in just *three* months that summer! All with the purpose of promoting the film," he added wryly, because after the three months of performance he and Guy still had not seen a script, or heard of a production date.

"We did two shows a day, every day, seven days a week, for thousands of children. It was Segura's most successful summer. There were 243,000 spectators at the circus that summer! We *still* hold the record to this day for the largest audience in the history the circus Real de Madrid at Mar del Plata."

Chapter 59

"The Fox, Caught in Argentina"
           – *Daily Popular*, Thurs. May 11, 1978

To the Argentina people Guy Williams *was* Don Diego and he *was* El Zorro. They loved what he stood for, they loved his character, and so they loved him. The reaction and acceptance of the children, as well as his adult fans, reassured him that he still had what it takes, as a performer, and as a very attractive man. This, along with being able to keep up with a young fencer thirty years younger than himself, was the ego booster Guy had needed. Life's journey was taking him to unexplored waters, and life as he had known it would never be quite the same.

The large crowds at the circus, the promise of starring in a movie, the new friends and attention, gave Guy a rush he had never felt before and he loved it. He was enjoying it even more than he had in the 1950s and '60s.

Guy worked hard and had little time for sailing or any other form of recreation once the circus began its three-month summer run from January through March. Janice was expecting him back home by mid-March,[281] but just before his stint ended, Guy was approached by Nino Segura and asked if he and Fernando would like to travel with the circus for six more months. He and Fernando gladly accepted.

Since he would not be going home, Guy called Janice to ask her to join him in Buenos Aires for an indefinite time. Toni remembered when her mother had to make an important decision to give up the marina apartment and move. "I remember those letters and phone calls to Mom," said Toni. "He kept telling her to come stay with him in Argentina."

"I still have the letters," said Janice, "asking me to join him in Argentina. His letters were full of love and kisses." Guy often used pet names for Janice, like "Pootsie," or "Booby-Doo," or "Cooper."

Every time Guy was interviewed in March and early April of 1978 he made a point of telling the reporters that his wife was coming soon. The newspapers loved it, and anticipated meeting "Mrs. Zorro." Whenever he was in Buenos Aires Guy was given the use of a furnished apartment at 740 Jose Evaristo Uriburu Street owned by Fernando's mother, who preferred to live at her place in the country.

Janice didn't hesitate in her decision to move to Argentina. The timing was right.

Her children were older and independent. Toni was engaged to Don Petrie and had moved out. Steve had been living in the Valley for years, and was working a busy schedule at City Hall. After she made a few necessary arrangements, she would be free to go. First she'd have to give fair notice to Mrs. Belzer, for whom she had been apprenticing as an Interior Decorator for several years. She would have to give the apartment manager notice, and then put things in storage.

Janice felt this move would be a new beginning, a fresh start. Admittedly, she felt their marriage did not have the fire and passion of its early years, but Janice knew that was common in a marriage of nearly thirty years. Perhaps being alone together in a new apartment would be reminiscent of their first years in New York. She and Guy had looked at real estate on their last trip to Argentina, and she was willing to live there as long as he wanted to.

Now there was Sam to consider. Janice called on her friends in Bakersfield who had taken Sam each time she and Guy went to Argentina. For them it was a wish come true to have Sam permanently. They had tried to keep Sam once before. Janice recalled: "We were taking long trips to Argentina and we didn't think it was good for Sam to keep sending him back and forth. He was getting old and needed more care, and the friends in Bakersfield were attached to him. We could see the trips were not going to stop so we called them to come get Sam permanently. They loved Sam, so they made the drive all the way to the marina right away to get him. Everyone appeared happy when they left. Even Sam was wagging his tail. But the next morning as the three of us sat around the breakfast table, no one said a word. It was obvious what we were all thinking. Suddenly Guy looked at us and said, 'If we leave now, we can be in Bakersfield before dark.' Toni and I looked at each other. Then he said, 'I miss seeing his *dish*!' So we all jumped in the car and went to Bakersfield and got the dog back."

Janice had to once again give Sam to her friends. "I knew Sam would be happy in Bakersfield, but that did not make it any easier. I'll never forget that moment. He looked at me with such a forlorn look on his face while I waited for them to pick him up. I think since he had been through it before, he knew what was happening. That was a hard thing for me to do."

"It was difficult in some ways to leave, but I wanted to be with my husband," she said. "Guy had asked me to bring some costume accessories for some of the girls in the circus who do the flying trapeze act, so before left I went downtown to International Silks and Woolens and bought what they requested: some feathers, plumes, sequins, and brought them with me on the plane."

When Janice closed the door to that apartment, she closed the door to life with Guy as she had known it.

When the circus had finished its run in Mar del Plata, some reporters for *TV Guia* tracked Guy down to ask him what he was going to do now that the Circo Real Madrid was over. His reply was so significant, it was the title of the article:

"I STAY IN ARGENTINA" (¡ME QUEDO EN LA ARGENTINA!)
March 1978
There is no doubt that one of the most successful shows of the season of Mar de Plata was the one with the presence of Guy Williams, "El Zorro," in the big tent of the "Real Madrid" circus. The season was from January

1st to March 12 and now that it is the end of the season we have interviewed Guy Williams because we are very interested in knowing his future.

Are you going to return now to the United States?

"No! I'm staying in Argentina." His answer, with that beautiful accent between Spanish and Italian, surprised us. Seeing our surprise, the actor said:

"First of all, I want to tell you there have been very few times in my life when I have felt as happy and as well, as I have in Mar de Plata. The city is marvelous. I've made hundreds of friends and this helps me not to miss my wife and children so much...On the professional level, the performances in the circus have given me enormous satisfaction by working for hundreds of kids who applaud me like an idol. The worse part was trying to escape the hundreds of children who try to hug me after the show. Well, all this contributed to my decision to accept the proposal of my managers and stay in this country."

Are you saying that you will continue to perform in Buenos Aires?

"First we will go for ten days to Tandíl, always with the circus "Real Madrid," and that includes Holy Week.[282] Later we will go for five days to Azul, and immediately after that we are going to raise the tent in Buenos Aires. I believe we are going to be on a very big field, in Liniers. We expect to stay there until the end of June, at least. So I will be able to see some of the World Soccer Cup."

Are you going to spend all those months without your family?

No, my wife will arrive in Buenos Aires the 4th of April.

Like I told you before, our idea is to film a picture in Salta, entitled, *El Zorro and the Son of Zorro*, and Patiño, my friend and manager, will be one of the co-producers. We've been looking for locations in that province. If every-

Guy making his entrance. His shows broke the record of attendance that summer in Circo Madrid at Mar del Plata. (courtesy of Fernando Lupiz.)

MUNDIALMENTE FAMOSO
Circo Español "Real Madrid"
DE LOS HERMANOS SEGURA

EL HIJO DEL ZORRO   EL ZORRO

EL MAS
PODEROSO CIRCO
DE
AMERICA LATINA

One of many ads to publicize Guy's Zorro and Son act with Fernando in the biggest circus of them all. (courtesy of Fernando Lupiz)

thing goes according to schedule we will be finished (touring) between July and August. And at the same time we are working on a way to start episodes for a new [Zorro] series, with the same characters and it's our ambition to distribute it to the entire world. My "son," as you already know, will be played by the Argentine fencing champion, Fernando Lupiz. In September I will travel to the United States where I have to take care of my business, but at the end of the year I will come back to Buenos Aires to continue working on the series.

"It is my plan to spend a long time in this fabulous country, where I think there are so many things I can do. Believe me, I feel like this is home, and if my wife feels the same way, and I'm sure she will, I'm thinking of buying a large apartment and making a second home here."[283]

Guy liked to walk around the cities he visited and see the people, learn their customs, and visit their stores and restaurants. Anyone who was with him could tell you that he would give the homeless children money. His friends would tell him that this only encouraged them to beg and the whole circle would never end. But Guy would say, "What you say is correct, but it's Utopic. Today they can't go home unless they have a certain amount of money. If I give them some, they will go home quicker, and spend less time on the street."

Janice arrived in Buenos Aires on April 10, 1978 instead of April 4, as the article had stated. The Royal Circus was in the Capital city the first week of April. Janice joined Guy at the Buenos Aires Sheraton. Argentineans gave El Zorro's wife a warm welcome. For them, this meant Guy would surely stay in their country permanently. Headlines in one Argentinean periodical boasted how their children had done what no one else could. They had captured El Zorro. Trapped the fox with their love.

"THE FOX-CAUGHT, IN ARGENTINA!" May 11, 1978
With their love and affection, our little kids achieved the impossible.[284]

(Caption under photo of Guy and Fernando Lupiz at table: "*Many great projects for working as an actor, and the affection I am constantly receiving, are what is keeping me in this country,*" his explanation regarding his long stay in the country.)

(Caption under photo with swords: *Guy Williams and Fernando Lupiz on guard, Zorro and son continue to cultivate friendship and affection from the young audience*)

"How can I not fall in love with Argentina if it is the most beautiful country in the world? I fell in love little by little and now, I can honestly say it's my second home."

During the quiet afternoon against the backdrop of the spacious entrance of the luxurious hotel (Buenos Aires Sheraton) where he is staying, Guy Williams, the North American actor who played the legendary Zorro to the amazement and joy of young children all over the world, told us of the profound affection he has for our country and also added that he has made a lot of great friends.

Guy and Fernando on the beach at Mar del Plata.

A fit looking Guy standing with sword in a publicity shot for his upcoming act with Circus Madrid: (courtesy of Aracelli Lisazo)

Guy practicing riding for the show. It was important to him to know the horse he was going to be riding wherever he performed. (courtesy of Fernando Lupiz)

Are you planning on staying here forever?

"Wow!," his charming Spanish switching to this North American expression. "Well, I don't know about staying forever. For the past few years my life has been spread out over different places in the world. The fame of *Zorro*, even though it has been a long time since I filmed those episodes, continues just as strong as ever in any part of the world and that forces me to travel constantly.

"I should tell you that even though I have a residence in California, I spend very little time there because of my travels, but, even so, my stay in Argentina will be a long one."

You have a lot of Projects in the works, right?

"A lot of great projects. The people who manage my business have prepared a lot of projects which are practically reality. Once everything is concrete that will prolong my stay here many months."

CIRCUS, MOVIES, TELEVISION

Can you tell us anything about your plans or projects?

"Well, one of those is already in full swing. That's a show for the circus, *Real Madrid,* which we already presented with great success in Mar del Plata for the summer. Now we're doing it just as successfully in Buenos Aires. The children, who are my best friends, really love Zorro and his adventures which we try to present with the best authenticity possible. The horse, the riding, the roping and duels (all the little details) drive the kids wild. It's during the sword fight that I count on the collaboration of the great fencer Fernando Lupiz, a young man who is great, not only as an athlete, but is also very charming and has talent to go very far as an actor.

"For now he's playing the son of Zorro, a character who has also won the affection of all the kids who come to see the show. Who knows, maybe

Guy poses in one of Polera's antique cars. (courtesy of Aracelli Lisazo)

afterwards I will be leaving you an Argentinean Zorro, which would please me very much."

What other projects are you doing?

"There's a movie. Well, there is a first movie. The reason I say it's a first, because from a *Zorro* movie we hope to do other *Zorro* movies. A series. But—and here comes the most important part—this project is so special, because at the same time we film the movie, we plan to do a TV version in color which would be completely produced in South America. That would be the first time it would be produced in South America and distributed to the rest of the world. So you can see I have a lot of different plans and they should become concrete at any moment."

Then we went outside to take some pictures and that's where we saw the popularity of the idol who has won the affection of adults and kids with his extraordinary charm and permanent smile, which was even wider than usual at the moment because he was joined by his wife, who has accompanied him during his long stay. "Now that my wife is here with me, you will have to kick me out to get me to leave," he said.

The Argentineans soon took Janice to their hearts, finding her *simpatica*, as charming as Guy with her big beautiful smile and her friendliness. In no time, journalists from every newspaper and weekly magazines were following the couple around each day for a week, taking pictures, and interviewing them for numerous magazine spreads showing Guy and Janice shopping, Guy and Janice looking for an apartment, Janice on the arm of her Zorro.

After a short stay at the Sheraton, Guy and Janice took a four-month lease on an apartment owned by Pat Luteral, Janice's interpreter from Canal Trece. The apartment was in a posh, well-secured building in the upscale part of Buenos Aires called Recoleta, on the prominent Avenida Libertador.

Guy earnings were in the six-digit figures and he was ready to invest in land. For advice he consulted Hugo Cortina, a businessman with whom he had enjoyed lively conversations. Hugo had a business called KanMar, located on the corner of Corrientes and Rodriguez Peña. He bought and sold land and convinced Guy to invest in several acres that were to be developed into an upscale resort-like community. The land would be sold in parcels for houses. Guy liked the idea and began talking the idea around to his friends for partnership. Guy held the largest share, the rest was divided among the others. For the first three years, he made a large sum of money. Then when Argentina became plagued with hyperinflation, the payments dried up completely for the smaller investors, and eventually for him, it was merely walking around change. By 1986 it cost him more to do the paperwork than what he was getting, so it came to an end.

One reporter from *TV Guia* seemed surprised that Guy was really staying and sought him out to confirm it.

TV Guia, July 1978, p. 102
"AS I PROMISED…I STAY!" ("COMO LO PROMETI…¡ME QUEDO")
(photo of Guy with foot on step, hand on rail, dark jacket)
"Last summer I told you I was going to stay in Argentina…And here I am!"

Guy and Fernando at one of several asados given by Ricardo Polera the summer he was in Mar del Plata, 1978: L to r: Aracelli Lisazo, longtime friend of Fernando Lupiz, Fernando Lupiz, wife of Polera, Victor LaPlace, television celebrity, Liliana Poggio, actress, Guy, and Ricardo Polera. (courtesy of Fernando Lupiz)

That was the first thing Guy Williams told me, the very famous "El Zorro," when we found him with his wife on one of his customary walks around the neighborhoods of Buenos Aires.

What has happened in your life since the last time we saw each other in Mar del Plata and what are your future projects, because we've heard a lot of rumors on that subject?

Guy, always nice and smiling, said to us: "As you know, at the beginning of January I started my show in Mar del Plata, with the *Real Madrid* circus. Well, since that time, seven months ago, I have never stopped performing. In March we went to Tandíl for Holy Week and after that we went back to Buenos Aires and put up the tent in Liniers, where we performed in April and May. At the same time they were playing for the World Soccer Cup, we put up the tent on a piece of land next to "Ital Park," because they were having the "Expotelga"[285] there. Then in the beginning of July we moved our show to Puente Pueyrredón, because we wanted to present our show to the people in that part of the city and also in Avellaneda. We will stay there until the end of August."

Then you will return to the United States?

"No! I already told you. I stay. What happens is that during September and October we are going to finally film my movie in Salta. We have to solve a lot of problems. We had to ask permission from the Disney Studios and then register here the final title which is to be, *Bravo Zorro de América*! And in the movie just as in the circus, Fernando Lupiz will play my son. I can tell you in advance that after I finish the movie, starting in November, and continuing into 1979, we are going to make personal appearances with the circus in the capitals and major cities of Argentina."

What does Janice Cooper, the lovely wife of Guy, say about all this?

With the same charm and congeniality as her husband, she said to us: "We have rented a big apartment on Avenida Libertador, and I feel very comfortable and very happy in Buenos Aires. I am getting to know the city by walking around and getting the feel of it, and the same things that please Guy please me as well. The only problem is my children. The oldest, Steve, is already an independent adult and works in Los Angeles. But our daughter is still in college and we can't ask her to change schools at this time before she finishes her courses. That's why I have to divide my time between Argentina and California to take care of the whole family. But I know that Guy is very happy here and it is my duty as a wife to follow him wherever he goes."

There is no doubt that Guy Williams' love for Argentina is proof of the power Argentina has, particularly Buenos Aires, to attract foreigners, because it opens its arms to everyone without restrictions or demands of any type.

Janice was alone a lot. Guy was out of town for weeks at a time in April, May, and part of June. In July 1978 he left again with the circus Puente Pueyrredón. The ever-present armed military frightened her, and the language barrier alienated her. She kept busy and saw her English-speaking acquaintances, León Balter and his wife, Carlos Souto, Robert Cox, an American journalist, and Patricia Luteral, her interpreter. But it was not enough to fill the void when Guy was away.

"He never took me to Mar del Plata or any of the places where he performed after I got there," reflected Janice. One evening while Guy was out of town, Janice watched a military parade from the roof of their apartment building. "It was literally a military parade, with only the military in it, on the widest street I'd ever seen. All their military leaders and soldiers were marching and playing military songs. Suddenly, I found myself surrounded by soldiers carrying machine guns, all guarding the parade from the roof. It was *strange* living there then."

It was during this busy year of traveling and performing that Guy received word that his Uncle Oscar had died in New York. Unable to go to the funeral, he called his sister, Valerie, on the phone and inquired about everyone.

Chapter 60

"...My private life is mine"[286]

– Guy Williams

When their lease was up in the Libertador apartment, Guy sent Janice to find another apartment for them. He knew Janice was apprehensive, but reassured her that there was no need for him to go with her. "Guy set up a meeting for me with a real estate lady who took me to look at a place and I ended up in this building with three strangers. We got on an elevator that took us as far as it could, then they took me up some stairs where a man was pacing about. There were people lurking around every corridor and by the elevators. At that point, I must have looked terrified, because one of them said to me in English, 'Don't worry. We're not going to kidnap you.'"

Janice was scared, and with good reason. During the dirty war in Argentina from 1976-1983 up to 30,000 people "disappeared," were kidnapped, tortured, and killed under the dictatorship.

During one of their stays at the Alvear Hotel Guy and Janice found a passport in the drawer of a desk. It belonged to a young man from Italy. There were other papers that belonged to him and a letter from his mother, wondering where he was and asking him to write. "Apparently, he had just disappeared. We were both very concerned about it, but we both knew it was best to keep quiet about it." Janice and Guy had befriended an American journalist on a previous trip, who had to go back to the United States because his two college-age sons were being threatened.

It was not the best time for visitors to be in Argentina.

The new apartment marked a separation between Guy and Janice that she never expected or wanted. "That apartment on Avenida Libertador had a coldness and harshness to it," said Janice. "I think it was something about the furniture or maybe it was because Guy was becoming cold toward me. It was strange because he had called me to come there. He knew I was coming and he seemed to be looking forward to it. But he would leave in the morning after breakfast and walk, and he would not come back until dinnertime."

Guy was distant. Janice feared what every woman fears, but Guy denied there was anyone else. No matter how warmly she was treated by Argentineans, she still felt like an outsider. But this feeling of distance from Guy scared her more than the politics of the country.

By September it was obvious to Janice that this was not going to be a second honeymoon. Rather than their romance rekindling, it was icing over. Guy was not spending much time with her because of his work and travels from city to city in Argentina, and various places throughout South America. Although she was willing to tough it out, Guy requested that she return to the United States to be with their children, their old friends, and people she knew. He was on a high with his newfound career, and friends, on a different plateau mentally and physically from Janice. Even though his heart was with Janice, he was enjoying this so much, he did not want to break the momentum for anything. *Gente* magazine reported that in 1978 Guy was making $20,000 a month on his personal appearances.

Hurt and disappointed, Janice reluctantly packed her bags. Guy gave her half of his earnings from the circus gig, a sizable sum in the six digits, and left for his next tour. On September 4, 1978, Janice left Guy a handwritten note and boarded a plane for Los Angeles.

"It was incomprehensible for me that this was happening, but it was. And I couldn't do anything about it. After thirty years of marriage I just didn't know how to deal with it."

Guy thought his tours were coming to an end and his movie would begin filming in September, and would be finished by February 1979. However, when production was not ready to begin in September, Carlos Patiño wanted Guy and Fernando to continue three more months traveling with the circus. While they were disappointed that the movie was not ready, they were glad to have the opportunity to continue to perform.

Janice's departure went unnoticed by the press, but in record time, word got around that she had left town. As with all people in the limelight there was speculation as to why she left. Rumors began to fly that there were "clouds in his marriage" and that perhaps Guy had fallen in love with an Argentinean woman.

When reporters heard that Guy was back from his tour they flocked to the lobby of his apartment building waiting to talk to him. The doorman kept them outside, where they hung around for three days. Finally Guy appeared. He began talking to the reporters with his usual cheerfulness and good manners, but when they asked him directly if the rumors were true, Guy said, "I don't have anything to say about that. My private life is mine, like anybody else. I won't answer any of your questions. I will give you my time to talk only about my artistic life."

They left it alone, for a while, but always hounded him, and there were often articles about hearsay.

Toni picked up her mother at LAX, and was shocked and saddened by the news her mother brought. Janice stayed at Toni's place, and the very next day the listings came out for the Santa Monica area. An apartment was available just one block from Toni, at 943 19th Street. "I got an apartment so fast," said Janice. "Someone was looking out for me, because Toni got the listings and we walked over to this nice place near her's that same day, and the woman let me have it on the spot. I was so lucky."

About six weeks later, Janice had some time to think. She decided she would not give up that easily. Neither she nor Guy had any clue when he would return to the United States, so, with all the fortitude of her pioneer ancestors she returned to Buenos

Aires to confront him. "I had to be sure this was happening, that it was permanent. And I had to give it one more chance. But I didn't let Guy know I was coming."

On Monday, October 30, 1978 Janice arrived in Buenos Aires and went straight to Guy's apartment. He had just returned from Rosario, where he and Fernando had done three shows a day at the Francés Dugou circus on October 28 and 29, 1978.

Janice's surprise backfired. It was *she* who was surprised when Guy just took it in stride. "Guy, literally, was walking out as I was going in. He looked at me as though it was *no surprise at all* to see me! He very casually said, 'Oh, it's *you*.' Then he took me by the arm and kept walking, saying, 'I'm going to pick up my shoes at the shoe repairman. Come with me,' as though nothing had happened!"

Janice stayed with Guy several weeks, but she found nothing had changed or could be changed. Guy was in another place. Guy had journeyed into a new and exciting world. It was a very different world from the one he had left in California, and it was creating a chasm between him and Janice, too wide to bridge.

On December 15, 1978, Janice bowed to Guy's wishes and left Buenos Aires. She would never return to Argentina again.

While she waited to board the plane at Ezeiza, a magazine reporter happened to be there covering a story unrelated to Guy Williams. He recognized Janice and started to approach her. When Janice saw him coming she quickly left her seat and went straight to the gate. The attendants let her board before anyone else.

His report appeared in the next issue of *Antena*, with a picture of Janice he had managed to snap quickly as she was walking away from her seat. The article also included a picture of Guy with his family at his home on Hillside taken in 1969, "during happier times," it said.

> The marriage of Guy Williams, the popular Zorro, and Janice is going through a difficult time. Does the fact that his wife was seen traveling alone to Los Angeles reassure the rumor that there is a break up? *Antena* reports everything objectively just as it happened.[287]

The reporter referred to the previous time Janice had left in September:

> Some say she is going home to start procedures for a divorce, but others more optimistic, reassured that she was only returning to Los Angeles to spend the holidays with her children, and that Guy could not accompany her because he was in Mendoza at the time doing several shows.
> Guy Williams said it more than once that he would stay in Argentina while Janice would stay in Los Angeles by the children in their beautiful residence in Marina del Rey.

Guy and Fernando were in Catamarca in November 1978, where he gave interviews, performed, and was given an honorary bronze plaque by the governor of the province. He continued to work into 1979.

Back in the United States, Janice had to face life alone and the challenge of making a living for herself in interior decorating. "It was definitely a separation," she said, "but,

Guy with Fernando and Aracelli on the streets in Tandíl where they gave live performances during Holy Week, late March 1978. (courtesy of Aracelli Lisazo)

I just couldn't believe this was happening."

A friend of Janice saw how distraught she was, and recommended that she see a numerologist, a woman, whom she thought was very good. "I had never been to one because I didn't believe in them," she said, "but I went. This numerologist had our birthdays—Guy's and mine—and she predicted to me that I would have a career—which I did—and I would be very successful—which I have been." Janice has never had to advertise. She continually gets new clients and keeps the old ones. She is always busy. "Then, this woman told me something I never forgot. It was eerie. She said that at some point in time, 'Guy will be near death and if he lives, it will be because of something you do.' That stayed so clear in my mind because I couldn't imagine, at that point in our lives, how Guy and I would ever be in a spot together where that could happen. After a while I gave it no more thought."

Chapter 61

"...the year of the movie"

— Fernando Lupiz

While Guy and Fernando continued to tour with their act throughout 1978, they never lost sight of the purpose of the act: to promote a movie they wanted very much to make. From all they were told this would be their year of production. In every city they visited, they scouted for location sites. "1978 was *'the year of the movie,'*" said Fernando, "but the production of the film had been postponed for so long that the original producers from Canal Trece gave up on it and became disassociated with it forever."

The press asked the co-producer Carlos Montero why it had not been produced and he blamed Guy for the delay, but the fact remained that no one came forward with money or a script. It is believed the basic problem was with the politics of the country.

Fernando allowed, "In those days the people of Canal Trece had many limitations and restrictions because they were controlled by the military government. The military was always in the studio monitoring everything. If they didn't like what was on the news they would interrupt the channel."

Near the end of 1978, Carlos Patiño, Guy and Fernando's manager, broke away from Nino Segura's circus to manage Guy and Fernando's act independently. "The owner of the circus and the producer of our show, had a fight and we had to choose, so we left the circus," said Fernando.

Another manager was hired to handle the finances. By the beginning of 1979, Patiño had created Guy's own troupe which included circus acts that preceded his act with Fernando. The act was very similar to what they had done in the big top only this time it included Fernando's old friend and schoolmate, Aracelli Lisazo, an actress and journalist, as the emcee. Aracelli, the same age as Fernando, had gone to Mar del Plata to see him perform with El Zorro. She had just come from a six-month journalism job in Italy, so she was able to converse with Guy in Italian. When the threesome hung out together, Aracelli often served as interpreter, sometimes for interviews.

As emcee, Aracelli would come out to greet the children and stir their anticipation with, "*Why* are you here?" "WHO are you waiting for?" and they would chant "Zorro! Zorro! Zorro!" Soon the *Zorro* theme was heard and she introduced El Zorro. Guy came out in costume on his horse and circled around the arena. He took the microphone and greeted the kids and talked to them a while about his TV show. Aracelli collected questions from the audience and presented them to El Zorro, who answered in Spanish with his strong American accent. Aracelli would say to him, "It's been a long time since I have seen you use your sword." Zorro would then tell the premise of the coming film, how he was training his son so he can pass his sword and costume to him. But, the son had to pass the tests the father taught him.

At that point he introduced Fernando and they would proceed with much of the act they had done in the Circus Madrid, exciting the children with a flourishing fencing routine, and a dramatic finale. Everywhere they went, the kids laughed and screamed with excitement and rushed the stage after the show to meet El Zorro.

The entire show was about forty-five minutes long, with Guy and Fernando performing the last fifteen minutes. "The riding and fencing routines were very similar to those in Nino Segura's Circo Real Madrid," said Fernando. "Guy was very particular about the horse he rode. In the act at Mar del Plata he used only one horse, but when he went on the road Carlos Patiño brought along a horse he owned. If Patiño made arrangements to get a different horse for Guy at the location, Guy always rode it before the performance to make sure he knew the horse." This was very important to him. Fernando heard Guy tell the people in charge of getting the horse that El Zorro could fall while sword fighting, but El Zorro could not fall from his horse.

Patiño hoped to attain the funds for the film. "The movie was the most important thing on Guy's mind," said Fernando. "He was always thinking of new ideas and scouting. In the meantime, we started looking for new producers. One day Nino Udine, a producer and director, came to us and said he was interested in the project. Udine hired a writer named Doris Band, who concocted a first version of the script, but Guy did not like it." A second version was written by Guy, with Doris Band and Aracelli Lisazo. This version was presented to the government-owned Argentine Film Institute for funding.

A synopsis of the plot and some excerpts (translated from Spanish) was written in *Babylonia Gaucha*:[288]

> Don Diego de la Vega, twenty years after his crusade against injustice, lives peacefully in Los Angeles in his spacious "estancia" with his servant Pepe, and his wife. They await the arrival of Fernando, the only son of Zorro, from Spain. The youngster, elegant, full of life, graduated from the same military college Don Diego did. America, with its new colony and the injustices he heard about, opened his interest.
>
> The Colonel Laplacette, sure of himself and his superiority, rehearses different attacks with his sword with the young handsome Captain André, in the room of arms of the ward of the city. Both are French, they have served in the Napoleonic Army and now, at the service of the governor, Anibal Zuloaga, they have arrived in Los Angeles from Monterrey. These recruits of the lunatic Zuloaga are the reason El Zorro has reappeared and the French are in charge to finish him. The Colonel Laplacette shows a personal hate for Zorro. All of Laplacettes victims are saved by Zorro which accounts for Zorro's support and protection in town.

Author Diego Curubeto commented:

Even though the story of an armed fight against a kind of colonial dictatorship could have been classified as subversive in the absurd Argentina in 1979, the National Institute of Cinematography looked very favorably on this project of Williams. They gave him some credit to do the film. They declared the project in the national interest.

El Zorro, Dead or Alive had to be filmed based on Williams' criteria, in the province of Salta. His ideas for the production were very ambitious for our film industry. For example, based on the USA Western movies, he wanted very detailed construction of the fort of Los Angeles, with a desert landscape, which would later be blown up into pieces. In a scene, a wagon full of ammunitions would roll down a ravine and explode spectacularly. He wanted six to seven wagons like this in different positions to choose the best one. Williams wanted the music to be by Felix Mendelssohn, and played by the Colon Theater Orchestra. Even though Williams did not have experience in directing film or TV, the script was full of technical specifications. For example, the description of the climatic final fight:

"Diverse shots and angles, including air shots, of this final fight: from the sea, from a horseman, from the steep coast, and from any other place that was attractive, including the usage of 2 cameras to show better details of the movements of Zorro, Laplacette, and Dupré which constantly go around trying to attack Zorro with success. The horsemen get into the ocean splashing water and foam, which gives more aesthetic beauty and dramatics to the sequence.

"The mechanism that the actors must develop in this scene consists of Laplacette and Dupré trying to get Zorro's attention to just one of them so the other can kill him."

Guy had complete confidence in himself to direct the action scenes, but for dialogue he turned to director Lucas Demare (author of *Laguerre Gaucha*). Guy asked him to also co-direct the film, but Demare never gave a definite commitment to this project.

The Argentine Film Institute offered Guy a grant of around five hundred and fifty thousand dollars. The offer was not even close to what Guy wanted. He knew he'd need at least three *million*. "Guy was used to the quality of work Disney did," said Fernando. "He wanted the best production crew, best directors, great music, good cameras, grips, a full crew, and the best locations - which he had personally selected. He wanted everything about the movie to be first class. Guy asked me to explain to the Institute why he needed three million. I did this and the Institute replied to him that they could go no higher than 1.5 million.

"That is when Ramon 'Palito' Ortega appeared. He was then the most famous Argentine pop singer." Ortega, at the time, was a singer/writer and also producer/director of cinematography. He later moved to Miami, launched a political career in the Peronist Party, then returned to his native province, Tucuman, where by 1993 he was governor.

"Ortega offered the three million dollars, but on condition. He wanted a certain actor, Carlitos Bala, a stone-faced local clown who has been performing the same old

RADIOLANDIA
2000

GUY WILLIAMS
"El zorro"

Guy's fame was once again on the same level in South America as it had been in 1958 in North America and he was enjoying every minute of it. His face was everywhere in periodicals. Here he is on the cover of *Radiolandia 2000* during his stint in Mar del Plata. (Author's personal collection) tricks for children for some forty years, to play the role of Bernardo, and Bernardo was not even in the script. Guy would not accept his conditions, so nothing came of it.

"So, now, the movie was written, but it was not going anywhere. It was just - *stuck*! We could see that we were not going to be filming any time soon, so we decided to keep going with the act. Always to promote the movie," Fernando added wryly.

When Guy had been interviewed in Mendoza late in November 1978, he was so enthusiastic about his movie, he talked more about *it* than his act. He told the reporter he would like Lucas Demare to direct, because he had seen some of Demare's old films

Guy and Fernando in their trailer during the Circo Madrid, showing a funny sign.
(courtesy of Fernando Lupiz)

and liked his work. The location would be in Salta. Guy had discovered location-spots for the movie when he and his entourage were in Salta to perform. The reporter asked how long he would be staying in Argentina. Guy said, "probably until February when we figure we will be finished shooting. Then I will go to my home in Los Angeles, but I will return to this country, because I love it so much."

On May 12, 1979, Guy was in Corrientes for some highly anticipated events for the children. El Zorro was the central attraction for an extraordinary children's festival of dances, comedians and magicians in Club Córdoba for the benefit of the "Eloisa Torrent de Vidal" Children's Hospital in cooperation with the celebration of International Boy's Year.

> One festival will be on May 10 at Club Resistencia in the province in
> Chaco and one on May 12 at Club Córdoba in Corrientes, with two shows
> at 3 and 6 p.m.[289]

A huge crowd attended these events with much enthusiasm and excitement after two weeks of advertising the event in the papers. It was here on Catamarca Street that Guy had one of his grandest finalés. At the end of their fencing routine, when he disarms Fernando, he sent Fernando's sword flying into the air, right into the electrical wires above the street. It dangled there precariously from a wire creating a power outage for blocks, until a rescue unit came out to retrieve Fernando's sword. Electricity was soon restored, and the incident made the front page the next day. Zorro had struck again.

Guy and Fernando were booked continually throughout 1979, with the exception of the time Fernando had to go to Puerto Rico, where he won the silver medal in Individual Foil in the Pan American games. Some of the cities they went to were Tandíl, Salta, Corrientes, Catamarca, St. Martin, Santa Fe, Neuquén, Necodrea, and more, traveling by plane, bus, and car, and staying in the finest hotels. Guy always enjoyed the traditions of the local people in the different cities he visited. In Neuquén, where several

Greeting children on the street of Rosario, October 1978, where he appeared in Circo Dugou. (courtesy of Aracelli Lisazo)

rivers meet across the plains, Guy dug a hole in the riverbed with a spade to build a fire for an asada, an age-old tradition.

"Guy felt very young and very happy at this time," said Fernando. "It was something different for Guy, a change. We had a lot of fun. One night before a show, we were waiting to go on and Guy wanted to know how many people were in the audience. The only way I could find out was to go outside, climb on top of the roof and hang over to look between the vents. Now, I am in the Zorro costume, and I climb slowly and quietly onto the roof, trying not to be seen doing such a crazy thing. I take a look inside the house and go tell Guy about the crowd. Then I told him how I slowly climbed to the roof and I said, 'I actually *felt* like Zorro out there!' Guy looked at me, and said, 'You know, once in a while, I feel that way too.'"

Refusing to give up on the movie, Guy and Fernando would spend hours talking about how they would make the film in English and in Spanish, with good local actors and Argentine capital. "Neither of us ever abandoned the project. Others who were interested in the project came and went, but we continued to think of new ideas for the film. Every morning we would go to the Palermo Lakes in the park and do some fencing practice to be ready for the film, whenever it might happen."

Palermo Park was Guy's favorite place to practice the fencing routines and also to take walks. He often stopped at the statue of Dante Aleghieri in the park, remembering his mother's antique copy of Dante's *Divine Comedy*, and the fact that Catalanos are mentioned in the story.

As 1979 was coming to an end, Guy got a call that brought him back to the United States and his family. His "baby" was getting married.

Chapter 62

"...always close."[290]
— Steve Catalano, a.k.a. Guy Williams, Jr.

Guy wrote affectionate letters home to Janice and the children and made phone calls to them frequently, with well wishes. "There was always a steady communication," recalled his son, Steve, who never felt disconnected from his dad even though he was far away. "When he was in Argentina he called often, sometimes for no particular reason, just, 'How ya doin'?' and small talk. Sometimes he talked about Mar del Plata, or he'd ask how everyone was and say, 'Give my love to your mom and your sister.' Nothing necessarily of any importance. Sometimes it was just because he was thinking of us. Like the time he had just flown over the Andes. He knew I liked to fly, so he called me just after he landed to tell me about it. Even though, physically, he wasn't here, we were always close."

Earlier that year, Toni had told her dad she and Don Petrie wanted to get married. Guy liked Don and he gave Toni and Don his blessings. He said he would pay for the wedding and he would be there for their special day.

Janice was very busy during 1979 with her interior decorating work. During her separation from Guy, there was one particular gentleman whom Janice considered a good friend, but his intentions were stronger. "He finally gave up on me," she said.

"Jan's a beautiful woman," said Peggy Stevenson, remembering the suitors she had. "She could have remarried, but she didn't want to. She loved Guy."

Despite her keeping busy with work and helping Toni with wedding plans, there were constant reminders of Guy everywhere: old friends, a favorite restaurant, their walking route, stores they had shopped, and on and on with seemingly every turn. With Guy returning after two years away from home, she was excited about seeing him again. "I think I really didn't want to know if there was someone else," said Janice, "because that way I could accept Guy back anytime he wanted."

The wedding took place on December 15, 1979 at the Church of the Good Shepherd in Beverly Hills, with a reception following at the Beverly Hills Hotel on Sunset Boulevard. Guy left Argentina two days before the wedding, barely arriving in time to be fitted for his tux and go to the rehearsal. The next day, as guests began to arrive, Janice was in a little room on the side of the church helping Toni get dressed. Guy was standing in front of the church when he spotted the gentleman he knew was infatuated with Janice. It didn't sit well with Guy and he gave Janice a surprise as he headed for the room where she and Toni were. "I saw Guy coming up the walk toward the little room where we were, and I could tell he was furious. He started yelling at me, asking, 'Why is HE here?' So I stepped outside to talk to him, and here we were having this fight right outside the church," she laughed. "I began to explain to him that I felt obliged to invite this fellow because he had been a great help to Toni and Don about some matters. When I told Guy that this fellow would not be coming to the reception, that seemed to ease his mind somewhat."

Guy walked Toni down the aisle and took his place next to Janice in the front row. Contrary to how he had treated her in Argentina, Guy was warm and affectionate toward Janice, as though nothing had happened. "There was no tension or strain between them that I could see," said Toni. "We were a close family."

Guy and Janice rode in the limo together to the reception at the Beverly Hills Hotel. Guy and Janice were ever the handsome couple standing side by side receiving their guests in the grand ballroom along with the Petries. The two families were very compatible and had become good friends. Toni was radiant and Guy was bursting with pride. Willowy, he thought. He remembered how she had literally grown up overnight, and turned into a beautiful woman.

There was dinner and dancing and pictures taken for the album, and by all accounts no evidence of any discord or a separation between Guy and Janice, who stayed together throughout the entire ceremony.

When it came time for Toni to throw the bouquet, one of Janice's close friends, who was angry at Guy for hurting Janice, tried to force Janice onto the dance floor to catch the bouquet. Guy pulled her back. "I would not have done it, anyway," said Janice. "It just was not the thing to do."

Peggy Stevenson observed. "I knew Jan would never cause a scene, or do anything to embarrass Guy. Jan's love for Guy was unconditional. She always loved him. Still does."

In Salta Guy is greeted at the airport by the governor of the province. Left to right, Guy's manager Carlos Patiño in sunglasses, the governor, Patiño's wife, Rilda, Aracelli Lisazo, FernandoLupiz (partially hidden), Guy, and Américo Sosa, a manager, not shown. (courtesy of Aracelli Lisazo)

Photo of Guy in Neuquén near the bank of one of its many rivers.
(courtesy of Aracelli Lisazo)

Later that day, however, under the influence of friends, Janice did do something she would regret in years to come. "That evening the Silvers invited Guy and me to dinner at their house," she recalled, "but I didn't go. A couple of our close friends would not let me. They were so mad at Guy for what he had done, they said to me, 'You're going to stay with us. He doesn't deserve to have you with him for dinner.' So Guy went to dinner at the Silvers' and I went to dinner with them. And I was miserable the whole evening. Guy was really mad at me for that. He thought I should be there with him for something that important. Maybe I should have gone."

Guy stayed with Janice at her apartment part of the time and also spent some time with Don Burnett while his wife was out of town in a play. Don had married actress Barbara Anderson in 1971. In 1968 Anderson received an Emmy Award for her role as Policewoman Eve Whitfield on *Ironside*, with Raymond Burr (1967-71), then went on to the role of Mimi Davis on *Mission: Impossible* (1972-73). She and Janice became good friends. The two old friends and co-stars of *Damon and Pythias* once again cooked pasta dinners together and caught up with each other's lives.

"Guy told me he loved living in Argentina because it was a beautiful country with beautiful woman, wonderful steaks, and nice people," said Don. "And he could live very comfortably there on the money he had. To top it off, he was a big star down there. He was like a king there!"

Don and Guy were close, but they didn't talk about their private affairs. "Men of our generation didn't talk about things like that very much. We didn't open up to each other in those days. Guy was always interested in things like investing, currency, playing the horses - things like that, and that's what we talked about. He would ask my advice on the stock market and nothing else." Don had worked his way up to vice president of Kidder Peabody, and was working long hours a day. Guy kept his money matters and personal finances to himself. He never discussed his money with anyone.

Guy's family was invited to spend Christmas with some close friends in the Malibu

Colony. The owner was Janice's first client, and over the years he and his family became as part of Janice's family. It was a place Guy had enjoyed going to for walks on the beach and watching the sunsets over the Pacific Ocean.

Guy spent time with Toni and Don Petrie, visiting them at their new house in Sun Valley, and with Steve, who was living in one of the apartment buildings he managed in the Valley. Toni and Steve had not seen their father in two years and they didn't know when they would see him again.

Steve had put in a lot of flying time in the last two years and had acquired his pilot's license for glider planes on May 14, 1978 and also a license to fly single-engine planes on March 22, 1979. Guy was proud of him and with all confidence in him, he took the backseat of the glider and let Steve take him up for a thrill ride. "Just as Dad took to the sea, I took to the air," said Steve. "It pleased me to no end that Dad loved to go flying with me, especially in the sailplane. He particularly liked the aerobatics. I was very happy that I was able to return the enjoyment he had given me sailing on the *Oceana*. Indeed, there is something poetic about that."

Chapter 63

"It was the beginning of the end"

— Fernando Lupiz

Guy went back to Buenos Aires in February of 1980. He had given up the apartment on Libertador because he was always on the road. He lived like a tourist, staying in hotels, or the apartment Fernando lent him. Guy told a friend he liked living this way, because he could leave whenever he wanted to. He was hoping to leave for Salta soon to film.

Guy, Fernando, and Aracelli continued to get bookings and travel throughout Argentina. Guy was still drawing big crowds, but he would never again be as busy as he was in the previous two years.

Bad management caused the bookings to dwindle. "Nineteen eighty was the beginning of the end of the tours," said Fernando. "We caught a sack of bad luck. We would go to places to perform, and different men would not pay us after we got there. Patiño was representing us, but it was not his fault. These other people (who we performed for) would not pay what they had promised us. This began to happen a lot.

"Also, Patiño was making deals Guy didn't approve of, making changes at the last minute, usually as a favor to someone, for their little girl or boy, or a friend. This would upset Guy because he would have the act planned out. He liked to be well prepared. Also, at this time, Patiño began to book Guy at shopping centers to have him sign autographs, and Guy did not like that."

Aracelli adds, "Guy and Fernando would go to perform in a province and Guy would ask Patiño beforehand if the act was going to be different, so he could prepare. Patiño would tell him nothing. Then one hour before the show, Patiño would put out something different for the show, and Guy would get upset. Patiño would say, 'Well, someone asked me and I couldn't refuse. Please, do it for me.' When this kept happening over and over, Guy got mad and decided to let Patiño go."

The other manager had been offering *free* sneak previews for the first show. In most of the cities, everyone came to the free show and ticket sales dropped drastically. It was asserted that this manager was swindling the actors.

Guy dismissed both managers and went out on his own, assigning Fernando to manage them. Fernando, however, had no experience in managing, and finally the bookings stopped. One of their last shows was one of their best. "We went to the Hilton in

Caracas, Venezuela, September 25-30, 1980," said Aracelli, "and we did a TV show and a big show called *Fantasico-Omnibu*. It was *grand!* A beautiful show!"

Guy was tired. Tired of performing and tired of waiting for the movie. By the end of 1980, after three years of traveling with the act throughout South America, Guy and Fernando knew it was time to hang up their capes and swords. "We kept waiting for this great film," said Fernando, "but it never came!"

Guy shaved his moustache, something he did when he wanted to relax. He preferred not to have a mustache and only grew it for work.

With no shows to do, and no movie in sight, Guy accepted an offer from producer David Ratto to make a TV commercial for Schick Super II razors. He thought it would be a good thing, and besides, he did not have to grow a mustache for it! In fact, he had to be clean shaven.

The commercial turned out to be a big disappointment. Aracelli remembers seeing the commercial. "In this commercial Guy was dressed in the Zorro costume covering his nose and chin with a white bandanna like the bandits in cowboy movies," she said. "He drew the sword and made an *S* to the screen. Then facing the camera, he said, 'NO, that's no mistake. It's *S!* For Schick Super II.' Then he removed the bandanna and showed his splendid, clean-shaven face, completely hairless.

"He got $15,000 for the commercial and the whole budget for the commercial was $20,000, so they made a very low budget production. That's why Guy didn't like it. It came out very cheap looking."

Topping off the disappointment, the sponsors thought Guy's Spanish was not good for the final cut, so, without telling Guy, they had his voice dubbed by an actor who did not even sound like Guy. When Guy saw it, he called David Ratto and asked him to take it off the air.

Guy did not want this to be another "TTM&R" job (*Take the money and run*) like *Lost in Space* turned out to be. He told a friend it was nothing short of prostitution when an actor does *any* job just for the money. He preferred being proud of his work.

The commercial was supposed to run about thirteen times during the first week, then less times each week for a total of three months. Guy's request to take it off the air was granted, which he knew would mean he had to forfeit several thousand in residuals. The commercial is said to have been lost in a fire at the studio.

When the tours ended, the threesome, who had performed together for nearly two years, went their separate ways, but they remained friends for the rest of Guy's life. Aracelli went to work in Mar del Plata. Fernando took up acting lessons and landed a role in a TV soap opera. He became a popular TV personality in Argentina. "I consider Guy my real teacher, in acting and in life. He said to me, 'use the bright,' the 'angel' within, as we say here, that certain something within great show people. Guy watched some of my soap operas on TV and critiqued my work for me. He said, 'The important thing is to see you alive up there.' He would get very angry when he saw an actor who was 'dead' on camera or on stage."

Guy had run the course. He had a good time, and made a lot of money, but he felt exploited. He had done his job, but the promoters had not come through with their promise. The movie was to be his last hurrah as Zorro, wherein he could pass his legacy on to the next generation. He was ready to give up being Zorro. It had been six years since he was asked to make a movie in Argentina. With no backers, and no production in sight, he went back to the United States for rest and relaxation.

Chapter 64

"I think he was feeling his oats."

— Steve Catalano

During the first quarter of 1981 Guy rented a furnished apartment at 14020 Northwest Passage, #101, in the Marina del Rey area, just a few miles from Janice's apartment in Santa Monica. They still called each other and saw each other on occasion.

Guy wasted no time buying a Raleigh bike and renting a Volkswagen rabbit. "Dad had gotten out of sports cars for some time now, and he really enjoyed driving the VW Rabbit. He and Hal Fishman[291] both got VW rabbits, and that was the best car on earth to him."

Toni and Steve were often visiting their dad for those one-on-one bike-rides along the beach. "I never did feel an estrangement between Dad and myself, because he always kept in touch," said Steve. "We'd meet often, and do things together. I'd drive from the Valley, pick him up, we'd load our bikes on the back of the car, and head for Dockweiler State Beach. We'd ride our bikes, up and down the beach there, behind the airport, like we always had. That was Dad's favorite pastime for exercise. Other times, I would meet him for dinner somewhere, or talk on the phone. We always remained close."

Guy took Toni and Don Petrie to dinner for her birthday and she visited her dad with a present on Father's Day. Toni and Steve were instrumental in keeping Janice and Guy together. They worked at it, because they knew their parents both still loved each other very much.

Steve, as well as many of Guy and Janice's friends, felt sure this was a passing phase. "My take on it is that my dad was back on top of his game and in great demand with the wild popularity of Zorro in Argentina, but it required a degree of separation from life in the U.S. that my mom was not willing to go through. It was easier for Dad to largely exchange one world for another than it would have been for Mom.

"I figured the whole picture was part of the chapter that would pass eventually," continued Steve. "So it was in my mind like a mid-life crisis, a passage in life. I think he was feeling his oats. I think what he wanted to do was start over, be Zorro again. It represented youth again. I think he ultimately realized it was just a mirage. I saw it that way the whole time. I had a feeling that was not going to be a permanent situation. And I knew my parents were always in love. My mom is a one-man girl and I think deep inside my dad was like that too. He was a good man. He just had other stuff going on in

Guy and Janice attend fundraiser at the Hilton, December 18, 1981.
(photo by Allan Callela; Author's personal collection)

his own mind. Deep down, I don't think there was anybody else for him. I think he just indulged himself in the whole scene. Some people in the industry get on drugs, for instance, and indulge themselves. Maybe this was like his drug. I don't know. I think he liked the fame. I think he enjoyed it, but I think in the later years—I'm not him, but what I sensed was—it was more important to him later in life because he had given up acting. He was probably feeling past his big moment on the screen, and fame starts to die out. Then, all of a sudden BOOM! You're a big star again. I think he went back to his 'hang out.' I think the reason he liked Argentina so much was because he was a big star there, but this time he had more privacy than before."

Guy enjoyed his leisure. He went to the thoroughbred racetracks, Santa Anita and Hollywood Park, where he bet on his favorite jockeys, Willie Shoemaker and Lafitte Pincay. Guy was good at winning because he took racing seriously, studying the horses in the paddock for leg bandages, conformation, reading their past performances in the racing form. He went to baseball games, keeping up with the career of his favorite player, Fernando Valenzuela. He took in the musical *Evita* (Patti Lupone/Mandy Patinkin) at the Schubert Theater in Century City, which he didn't think was quite true to real life.

The lifestyle Guy adopted in Argentina carried over to the United States. He ate late, about ten p.m., stayed up until one or two a.m. Still, he rose early, because he thought sleeping took away too much of your life. His breakfast was different from the huevos ranchero he preferred in Argentina. In the United States he liked English muffins with peanut butter, waffles with syrup, or scrambled eggs with bacon, orange juice or grapefruit, and lots of coffee.

He usually cooked dinner himself capping the evening with two or three shots of Strega. He passed the time reading, listening to Bach and Mozart, writing, usually on his script, and watching the stars through his large telescope.

Never one to watch a lot of television, Guy usually limited his viewing to Johnny Carson's late night talk show, and was amused by the silly used-car commercials of Cal

Worthington,[292] where he always featured some exotic animal. He was also amused the few times he saw any of his own TV shows in Japanese, or any foreign language. He would laugh at how marvelous he sounded, because he could not speak a word of that language.

Guy and Janice visited each other from time to time and kept in touch by phone, always concerned for one another. On December 18, 1981, they made a public appearance together. Janice had asked Guy to attend a fund-raiser for The Actor's Motion Picture and Television Fund with her. He was not one to go to functions like this, but he did it for Janice. As they arrived, arm in arm at the Beverly Hilton, Guy looked surprised when paparazzi recognized him and flash bulbs began popping. He signed some autographs and had his picture taken with some fans.

In *North* America, Guy was still able to keep his private life out of the papers. He and Janice were still a Hollywood couple.

Chapter 65

"I don't want to hurt anyone…"

– Guy Williams

Near the end of January 1982, Guy had just hung up the phone in his marina apartment after talking to his stockbroker in Century City when he felt a strange sensation in his head. He called Janice.

"I picked up the phone and all he said was, *'Jan,'* and I knew right away by the way he said my name that something was wrong. I said, 'Are you all right?'

"'No,' he said, 'I'm not.' He asked if he could come over. His voice was strange, and his speech was slow. He sounded so bad I offered to come pick him up, but he insisted he could drive. He managed to drive himself to my apartment and he stretched himself out on my long couch in the living room and refused to go to the doctor. He said he just wanted to rest. He didn't move all day and he slept there that night. But the next morning he wasn't better."

Janice called a doctor who told her it would probably pass, but to watch him. When Guy's speech didn't make sense, she became frightened. She called their friend, Dr. Bob Richter, an orthopedic surgeon at Santa Monica Hospital, for advice. "I described Guy's condition to him and he said, 'Get him to the hospital *immediately* or he won't be alive in the morning. I'll be waiting for you and I'll have everything ready.'

"Guy did not like to go to the doctor. He had never been sick, or had surgery and he hated hospitals. He refused to get up and go. I tried to make him get up," said Janice, "but he kept saying, 'I'm *not* going. I'm *not* going!' Well, this was one of the few times that I got my way over his. I just said to him, 'Yes, you *are*, mister.' And somehow I got him up. So, then he said, 'Well, I'm *not* getting dressed.' So I said, 'OK then, *I'll dress you!*' I literally had to *force* him to go, and I can't even remember *how* I did it, or what he wore, but somehow I put him in my car and drove him to the emergency room. He was uttering sounds in the car, trying to talk, but by then he couldn't form his words, and was not making any sense. When we got to the Santa Monica Hospital, Bob had everyone ready and, boy! They grabbed him *fast*."

An artery was bleeding at the base of his neck and Guy had emergency surgery on January 29, 1982 for an aneurysm. Toni arrived just as her dad was on the gurney being wheeled onto the elevator. The family rallied quickly to pray and wait. The doctors said Guy had a 50/50 chance.

After surgery, Guy was taken to the Critical Care Unit. The family waited at his side for him to wake up. It was a gruesome and weakening sight to see this strong and animated man, so pale and motionless; his head in a turban bandage. The shaved hair from his head was in a plastic bag at the foot of the bed, "just in case," was a grim reminder of what could happen.

Slowly, Guy came around. When he was able to speak, he raised a weakened arm, and pointed to Toni. Barely audible, he said, "I want to have lunch with *you* tomorrow."

Toni was surprised. She felt honored and happy that he had chosen her. "I wanted to make him happy, so the next day I made sandwiches and packed a nice lunch for the two of us, and went to the hospital."

The two began to talk and Guy opened up to her, expressing how sorry he was to have made everyone so unhappy. It was obvious that he was tormented and torn between his love for two worlds, the one in South America and the one in North America. Tears began to stream down his face. Toni was shocked. "I had never seen my father cry before." For his sake she held back her tears and took his hand.

"He said to me, 'I love your mother. She's my *family*. I don't want to hurt her. I don't want to hurt *anyone,* and I'm hurting *everyone.*' I wanted to cry, but I just smiled and stroked his hand, and told him everything would be OK. Then later when I got in my car, I just broke up."

Janice knew Guy would be angry with her for taking him to the hospital because he always felt he could overcome anything and didn't need doctors. She was reassured she had done the right thing when Guy's doctors and nurses commended her for getting Guy to the hospital in time. They told her if she hadn't, he would have been dead by morning.

Suddenly, Janice remembered the prediction of the numerologist a few years ago, that she would save Guy's life. She had put it aside in her mind, and now it was rooted in her memory forever.

Guy would need care, speech therapy, and medication, and Janice would be the one to give it. Janice took Guy to her house to nurse him back to health. She cooked his meals, washed his clothes, drove him to speech therapy in Brentwood every day for weeks, and, all the while, continued to work.

Guy's therapist, Julie Aperson, enjoyed Guy because he had such a positive attitude. He was not like her usual patients in that he was very academic about his own condition. "The nurse would ask Guy to write a word or a sentence," said Janice, "but when she asked him to read it back to her, he *couldn't,* but Guy's mind was so curious that instead of getting frustrated or upset, he was fascinated by that. He would say, 'Isn't that *interesting*?!' And the nurse got a kick out of that, because it was so different from what other people say."

Guy never lost his capacity to speak nor was he paralyzed, but he had to relearn how to process some thoughts to the brain. "Dad had to learn how to say certain words all over again, but the fact that he could not recall commonly used words fascinated him," said Steve. "That was one of his characteristics: to be more intrigued by his condition than scared. He would have these little 'episodes,' he called them. He had been told while he was healing he would have these flashes or strange things occur. For instance, his speech wouldn't work right, but he didn't seem to get upset about it. He would try to analyze it, with great interest. He was always like an amateur scientist about anything."

Guy told his friend, Art Silver he couldn't get over the fact that numbers had no meaning to him after the surgery, but eventually the concept of numbers came back to him. Once when he couldn't remember the word "elephant," he asked, "What's the animal with the long nose?" And when he tried to think of the word "shoe," he said, "the piece of leather that covers your feet." His speech was slightly slower at first, but eventually it was back to normal.

"It was the strangest thing," noted Janice, "but while Guy was home recovering, all of the family was together again. It was so weird how it happened that way, but for a few months we were all living together."

Steve had broken up with his girlfriend, and moved back home. Toni and Don had separated, so Toni came home. Toni's divorce had been traumatic for her so Janice's friend, who ran a private jet service, thought it would be good for Toni to be a flight attendant to millionaire clients and travel. Meeting and being a hostess to sheiks and their sons, and seeing the world was a good diversion for Toni, but one her father did not approve of. He didn't like it and he told her so. "I think Dad would have been happy to get me to a nunnery," she laughed.

In April 1982 when American troops were sent to help the British fight the Argentineans in the Malvinas (a.k.a. Falkland Islands) over ownership of the islands, Guy was very sympathetic toward Argentina, and critical of the Reagan administration. He longed to be able to help Argentina in some way.

It is calculated that somewhere around the end of July or beginning of August Guy surprised his family, especially Janice, when he told them he was returning to Argentina. After all the love and care that surrounded him, it was surprising to her that he would want to leave. Janice had always hoped he'd stay. The repeated disappointment of these continual departures was creating a protective sheath around Janice's emotions.

His family thought it was too soon after his recovery to leave. They watched with apprehension and concern as he boarded the plane, making sure he had his medication, and carrying a gadget given to him to check his blood pressure. No one knew when he'd be back again, not even Guy. He was free to go where the wind took him, and he liked it that way.

Chapter 66

"Disney called..."

– Guy Williams

When Guy arrived in Buenos Aires, he managed to go unnoticed for a while. A reporter from *TV Guia* spotted him having dinner with some old friends a La Scala, a favorite hangout for celebrities. Guy wanted the public to know that, contrary to some rumors, he was not paralyzed, and had fully recovered from his cva[293] or stroke. A picture of him with rock star Nito Mestre appeared.

EL ZORRO VISITS US INCOGNITO[294]
EXCLUSIVE: Guy Williams is in Argentina.

The rumor reached our desk quite unexpectedly that Guy Williams, the American actor who became popular as Zorro for several seasons on television, was in Buenos Aires unnoticed. At first we didn't believe this was true, because news from the U.S. earlier this year indicated that the actor had experienced a light stroke and partial paralysis, from which he was rapidly recovering. But the truth of the rumor was confirmed, however, when we were surprised see Guy Williams dining at the La Scala restaurant, the frequent haunt of show business people.

He was sharing dinner with a group of friends, among them was rock star Nito Mestre. They had met each other because Nito was at the next table so they began to talk. The reporter asked a question to Guy, but because of his limited Spanish he declined to talk to us.

But due to the fact that there are always sources ready to talk, we were able to ascertain that he is here only to rest and recuperate, that he finds our fair city most agreeable, that during his earlier stay here he made numerous friends, and that therefore he wanted to meet his social obligations. As to whether or not he plans any professional activities, we were told that it would be very difficult [for him], unless it were extremely important for him to do so.

Other people speculated that since he was apparently intending to base himself here he might be taking initial steps toward purchasing land in the Los Toldos area in Buenos Aires Province.

What remains a mystery is the status of his personal situation. Time will reveal that, as it always does.

For the present, we can confirm that he is nicely recovered from his illness, looking as handsome as always, and trying to blend in unnoticed. He is among us and our part is to show him what that means to us television-watching Argentines.

Carlos Souto, Fernando, and Ian Stanley, a stockbroker, Hugo Cortina, and all of Guy's friends and acquaintances were happy and relieved to see him looking so well. As usual, Guy stayed in Fernando mother's house.

He enjoyed life, visiting his friends in the business as he walked many, many blocks a day, stopping off for a cup of coffee and talking for hours. He had lunch with friends, and sometimes when a fan stopped to talk he would stay and chat for an hour or two with them. Guy made a strong effort to change his eating habits, primarily watching his salt intake and giving up smoking completely. The most difficult thing for him to do was abstain from alcohol and red meat. He had those in moderation, but Guy had a witty saying about that: "*Moderation* should only be done *in moderation.*" Occasionally he had a cocktail, or a little champagne or red wine, which he thought was healthy. For a while he took his medication correctly, but Guy was afraid of its side effects, so he eventually took it only if his blood pressure was high.

About six months after Guy arrived in Argentina he received a phone call from Kevin Corcoran at the Disney Studios. Guy knew Kevin as a little boy when he played "Moochie" of the Mouseketeers. Kevin had turned his interests to directing and producing, and was producing a new show called *Zorro and Son,* about an aging Zorro who wants to pass the sword on to his son. He wanted Guy for the role and asked him if he would come to the studio to audition, all expenses paid. Guy was interested because the premise was similar to his movie, and because Disney was doing it, or so he thought.

Carlos Souto could hear the excitement in Guy's voice when he came to him to make the arrangements for his trip. "He came to my place where I worked," said Carlos, "and he said to me, 'I have to go to the States because they want to see me about making a film about Zorro.' He seemed happy about it, and I said, 'Well, that's *great!*' And I got the tickets for him and made the arrangements and everything. Disney paid for first-class round-trip tickets." Guy would not accept anything less. His six-foot-four frame needed plenty of leg room for such a long trip. "I want to be mobile when I get there,"[295] he laughed.

Toni recalled her father's jitters before the audition. "It was after his surgery," she said, "and for that reason he wondered if he would be able to remember lines like he used to. So he was a little nervous."

It had been many years since Guy drove through the gates of the Disney Studios in Burbank. A lot had changed since he was there more than twenty years before. Most of the exterior sets from *Zorro* were still on the lot and for Guy it was a sentimental journey. In the mailroom he spoke to Connie, a woman who had been there during *Zorro.* "It was so good to see him again," she said. "He was still very handsome, with that great athletic physique. He told us he didn't care to have any fan mail sent to him. He said all that was behind him, and that he was a business man now." Actors had to pay the expense of forwarding fan mail and Guy didn't want to deal with it.

Guy saw many familiar faces and even visited the Golden Oaks Ranch to see his old companion, Diamond Decorator (Tornado), who had a much longer lifetime than most horses. But the joy and expectation of being back at Disney ended there.

Guy tested with two other actors who were up for the role of the son, and he just didn't think it was going to work. *Zorro and Son* was a parody on his *Zorro* series, making fun of an aging Zorro who couldn't make the jumps and falls anymore. But that did not bother Guy as much as the broad slapstick, which he felt was so extreme it could not be done. When Guy sat in the executive meeting room, reality set in. "I found out that CBS was *really* in charge, not the Disney people. They decided to give *Zorro and Son* the 'cutes,' and in typical network fashion, they 'cuted' the 'cutes,' and it was an abortion. It happened because Walt wasn't there. I've seen Walt throw network people off the lot. If he had seen their script, he would have yelled bloody murder.'"[296] Sorely disappointed, Guy refused the role.

"Guy came home pretty upset about the script," said Janice, "and also from finding out that the network was controlling everything, and making all the decisions about the script. He would love to have done it, if it had been done a certain way, but he knew he couldn't work with them, the way it was written."

Guy's hostility toward the networks was not in the networks themselves, but rather he said, "in the way some people ran their posts in networks."[297] Guy said if he had known the details about the show *before* he left Argentina, he would *not* have made the trip. Being in Hollywood brought back all the memories of disillusionments and deceit over the years by people in this town.

Robert Foster remembered the *Zorro and Son* incident as a reinforcement of Guy's disenchantment with Hollywood. "I can't remember Guy ever being mean to anyone," he said. "Even when he had this big interview with some stuffed shirts, he never named names. He had flown all the way back here for this big part, and he felt the town had changed. He said to me, 'No one in this town has any humor anymore. They can't even laugh at a joke. Everything is so boring.' He talked about the phoniness, and coldness of people in the United States. He said people are so rude here, and that he was glad he had left."

Henry Darrow was cast as the aging Zorro for *Zorro and Son,* and Paul Regina as his son. Just as Guy predicted, the show didn't work. After only five episodes on CBS from April 6, 1983 to June 1, 1983, the show was canceled.

Steve was in Hawaii when his dad arrived for the Disney audition and was not aware that he was in Los Angeles. Guy decided he would surprise Steve and pick him up at the airport. Steve remembers his dad's sense of humor: "I was waiting for my luggage at the baggage claim," tells Steve, "when I heard this rough grumpy voice behind me making sounds and complaining, '*Aaagh!* You know, you gotta *always* wait *so* long for your goddam baggage all the time! These people…,' blah, blah, and he was going on and on, and I thought, 'Oh God, I don't need this. I've been on this long flight and now I've got some *idiot* behind me and he's picked me to sound off to.' So I turned around, looked up, and *it was Dad!*" He laughed.

While Guy was in town, Steve had a scheduled surgery on his back. As much as Guy hated hospitals, he went to see Steve every day in the hospital, just as he had done when he was a little boy.

Guy's old friend and colleague, June Lockhart, got wind of the fact that Guy was in

Guy's last appearance on TV in the United States was on the *Family Feud* with his cast members of *Lost in Space*: l to r: Bob May, Marta Kristin, Angela Cartwright, Guy, and June Lockhart. He went back to Argentina before it aired. (courtesy of Gerry Dooley)

town just at the opportune moment. She was collecting the cast of *Lost in Space* to be on *Family Feud* (ABC) to compete against other TV shows of the 1960s. Her cause was to benefit the Hearing Dogs organization which trains dogs to aid the hearing impaired. At first Guy didn't want to do it, but as June coaxed, "Oh, come on. It'll be *fun*!," Guy relented with, "Well, *why* not!"

Some of the cast of *Lost in Space*—Angela Cartwright, Marta Kristin, and Bobby May, June Lockhart, and Guy—competed with the cast of *Gilligan's Island, Hawaii Five-O,* and *Batman.* When the show's host Richard Dawson asked June to make the introductions of the cast members, June patted Guy on the back and said, "This was my husband on the show, Mr. Numero Uno—*Guy Williams*!!" After the applause, Guy chuckled and said, "I like the billing."

The show was filmed in front of a live audience on February 3, 1983 and aired April 15, 1983. Janice did not attend. Their relationship was at its worst at this point. Guy enjoyed seeing his old friends such as Russ Johnson and Adam West again. His TV family had not seen him in years, but they had heard that he had suffered a stroke. Believing it had only been six months since it happened, they wondered if he was ready to be in front of the cameras.

"We were all worried," said Marta, "because we thought six months wasn't that long of a time for him to be better. We were waiting for him to not remember things, or to miss out on certain things, or have difficulty with speech, but he was like, wonderful. He talked just a little bit slower, but that's all, and even that was not noticeable. He had come back perfectly. He was great!"

Guy was his old charming, humorous, and flirty self. As he approached the podium to compete with the beautiful Lee Merriweather, he stared her down with a sexy look, and planted a kiss on her lips. Fans were thrilled to see Guy in this rare TV appearance as he had not been on TV since the end of *Lost in Space*.

It would be the last time he would appear on TV in the United States.

Chapter 67

"I had been wanting to interview Guy Williams for a long time."
– Ken Mayer

A business trip to the United States brought Carlos Souto to Los Angeles and he visited Guy for a few days. "He was living in Marina del Rey, a beautiful place. I met his children, Toni and Steve, and we all went out for dinner. I asked him, 'Why don't we have Janice with us for dinner?'

"'No, no,' he said. 'We are having problems.' So, I didn't see Janice at all that time."

Carlos was anxious to hear if Guy got the part at Disney. "When I first saw Guy, I asked, 'What happened? Did you get the part?,' and Guy said to me, 'Nawgh. They wanted to make a *comedy*. I told them, if you want comedy, go call Woody Allen.'" Carlos laughed.

Guy returned to his happy carefree social life in Argentina before the *Family Feud* show aired. The Robinson reunion on the show created quite a stir among *Lost in Space* fans. Guy was not aware of the overwhelming amount of mail sent to Irwin Allen after that show, requesting that he make a movie reuniting the cast in a back-to-Earth theme. Irwin was mute about it, but the idea snowballed, and Bill Mumy began to write a complete movie script to present to him. Irwin would later say that the timing for it was not right.

Years later, Mike Clark, for *Starlog*, asked Guy if he would be willing to do a *Lost in Space* movie with the same cast members.

> I loved *Lost in Space* from the standpoint of the people, just like I enjoyed working on *Zorro*. If the pay was right, I would think about it. It might be fun to do.[298]

Haplessly, the project never developed in Guy's lifetime.

Still drop-dead handsome at fifty-nine, Guy used to stop traffic and women in their tracks all the time. Carlos observed this whenever he went to dinner with his friend. "Guy was a very good-looking man, you know, *really*! You'd walk with him through the street and the girls would come around and look at him," he laughed. "It's true. I went many times to dinner with him, and I saw this, but he was very respectful about that. I

409

mean, he kept it private. He never went around, telling about the women he had. He was the way a man must be. You don't talk too much about that." Guy talked about woman and money all the time, but not *his* money or *his* women.

Carlos liked Janice from the first time he met her. "I would say Guy had a great respect for Janice, and a great love for her. I don't know what happened. Janice is a beautiful woman. Even though they were separated he loved her, as the mother of his children, and as a companion. They had a very strong link between them, a great love. Sometimes certain things happen inside ourselves that we can't explain, you know."

Guy took his daily walks and whenever Fernando was available the famous duo would go to Palermo Park to fence. Fernando often took Guy to dinner and they'd talk with hope that they would one day be able to make the movie. Still with no mustache, Guy was not looking for work. He was just riding the waves, enjoying himself while he regained his health.

Early in September Guy found out he was not forgotten in the United States. He got a call from ABC in New York inviting him to be on *Good Morning America* for a 25-year anniversary celebration of popular TV heroes. Along with Guy as *Zorro*, they were interviewing Kirby Grant (*Sky King*), Adam West (*Batman*) and Van Williams (*The Green Hornet*).

In roughly six months he found himself flying back, first-class, to the United States, this time excited to have an all-expense-paid trip to his hometown. On September 8, 1983, the four famous heroes were given a short segment on *Good Morning America* with host David Hartman, in which they each made a few comments about their shows. During those few minutes, Ken Meyer of WBZ in Boston just happened to catch it. Ken was a big fan of *Zorro* and, thus, Guy Williams.

"I had been wanting to interview Guy Williams for a *long* time, but no one knew how to find him," said Ken. "About once a year someone would tell me he was dead!"

Ken explained how he finally got his long-awaited interview:

> I was watching *Good Morning America* just casually, and I heard David Hartman say, 'We're going to continue our series of ABC heroes in the next half hour, and if you remember the sign of the Z, Zorro will be here.' And I said WOW!, because I had heard that Guy Williams hadn't been doing any interviews, and I had never heard him interviewed, so I had never gone after him...the only question that Hartman asked Williams was: Did the swords have points on them? I was really disgusted. I said "Geez, they brought the guy in—all the way from Argentina—and asked him *that* question?!"
>
> A friend of mine was the talent coordinator for GMA and had told me where they put up most of the guests. So I called and said, "Do you have a phone for Guy Williams?" They said, "Yeah," and I said, "Well, start ringing." He wasn't there and I kept calling and finally about 11:30 he was there. I told him who I was and that I wanted to interview him. And he said, "Oh, geez, I don't know." I said, "I would really love to talk to you, and I would ask you more than just 'did the swords have points on them?'" He was kind of reluctant, but, yet, he would start talking about how in the early episodes Disney was always on the set overseeing everything...And I said, "Well, Guy, this is the kind of stuff people want to hear about!"
>
> He says, "Yeah, but...can't you just paraphrase it and tell everybody

what I said? I won't deny it or anything." I said, "No, I can't do that. They want to hear YOU; they don't want to hear me say, 'Well, I talked to Guy Williams and Guy Williams said this…'"

So, he said, "All right, let me think about it and call me back tonight." So I called him that night around eight and he was still reluctant; he didn't want to do it. So, I played him one of the early *Zorro*'s, with Dick Tufeld narrating the highlights for the next week's show, with the original commercial for 7-Up. And I said, "Look, that's how big a fan of the show I am." I said, "You know, there have been two people in my life that I would love to interview to consider myself a real success in the business. They were both my heroes. Joe DiMaggio was one—and you're the other one."

And I said, "I already got DiMaggio. You do this for me and I'll consider myself a success." So he said, "Well, I don't want to get into who I had dinner with on Tuesday and what I did on Wednesday…" I said, "Look, I'll make you a deal. I'll call you tomorrow morning at 9:30 with a tape ready to roll; we'll start the interview. If at any time during the interview I ask you anything that you don't want to answer, you can hang up, I'll scrap the interview and forget the whole thing." He said, "Okay, I'll do it."

I never had to work so hard to get an interview in my life.[299]

Ken called Guy as planned and taped a twenty-minute phone conversation with him. The interview was advertised and fans tuned in from thirty-eight states and Canada to hear it. Guy had not done an interview in the United States in over fifteen years and curious fans were wondering what had happened to him. Guy talked about the fun he had making *Zorro* and the quality of the show. The interview was a success and copies of that tape remain in big demand by collectors.

Guy had some time to spend in New York and he wanted to share it with Janice. "He kept calling me and begged me to come join him in New York," said Janice, "but I wouldn't go."

Janice had learned to brace herself against Guy's affections because she knew he would leave again. "I couldn't get over the hurt and I couldn't comprehend things being the same again. I was just too mad at him. Looking back, I think I should have gone. We just do strange things, sometimes. We don't live our lives as well as we could."

Guy's round-trip ticket was good for a year. So, instead of returning to Argentina right away, he decided to take a detour through Los Angeles, where he might possibly mend some fences. He knocked on Jan's door and would end up staying nearly a whole year.

Chapter 68

"...he was living a double life."

                          – Janice Williams

"Dad would just pop in sometimes after being gone for *months*," said Toni. "One day I knocked on the door at my mom's place, and Dad answered! He deadpanned, 'I just stopped in to do my laundry. It was building up,'" she laughed.

"I think Dad was wanting very much to relax a bit with life at this point, and Mom was working very hard at her business."

Guy had given up his Marina apartment. Janice tried to describe their unusual relationship, which she didn't fully understand. "Guy and I were separated," she said, "yet he would come back here and stay with me. He'd say, 'Well, it's silly not to.' But, when the time would come, he'd go back. It was weird. It was as though he were two different people; like he was living a double life."

Toni was still a flight attendant, and when she was home, she went bike-riding with her dad. "I was flying about the planet at that time, or as Dad once put it, 'going to places you'd only imagine, wearing watches you can't pronounce.'

"As we were riding our bikes, I told him about a walkman and headset I had purchased for my long flights to Saudi Arabia, and I suggested that he buy one so he could listen to his favorite classical music while he rode his bike. He said he didn't need that. 'I've got it alllll in here,' he said, tapping his head."

"Smart aleck!" she joked. "A few years later I heard he walked all around Buenos Aires with a *Walkman* listening to his favorite classical music! Now, why couldn't he just have told me it was a good idea?"

But that was Guy, never giving Toni much credit to her face, but bragging about her endlessly to friends when she was not around.

Guy's behavior with Janice suggested he wanted to reconcile. From the time he called her from New York, he kept trying to express his love, smooth over the rough edges, make up. With his children present Guy told Janice she was the most important person in his life, but Janice tried to leave the room before he finished. "I was too hurt to listen," she said. Guy insisted, patting the chair beside him at the dining room table. "Now, sit down and listen," he demanded, and he proceeded to finish what he had to say.

"I just thought it was too late for anything. Too late for things to ever be right again. I always wanted it to be the way it had been. It was impossible. I couldn't forgive

412

him, which was too bad. I really wish now that I had handled it differently. Guy was still the most important person in my life. Still is."

Janice wanted Guy to stay, but she knew he was holding a return ticket for Buenos Aires. Living on separate continents suited Guy, but it was not Janice' definition of marriage.

It was during this visit that Toni dared to raise her voice at her father. Guy just got louder and put her in her place for talking to him that way. "He did the 'Italian standoff' routine, saying he wasn't going to speak to me ever again, and blah, blah."

The next day Toni had to fly to Ireland. "I called Dad from an Irish pub to apologize to him, and I sang Irish songs to him over the phone. He really liked that. He bragged about it for years. I brought back some nice cologne for him as a peace offering. He accepted and we made-up."

"Toni was so like Guy," said Janice. "He and Steve never had words, but she and Guy always did. Guy liked to argue. He *adored* Toni, and she didn't know it."

Janice hardly ever raised her voice or expressed her anger. She was easygoing. The few times she did fire up, and it was rare, Guy enjoyed it. "My friends used to tell me I should do that more often. Like the time he made me mad about something, and I said, 'I'll put *starch* in your *underwear*!' He thought that was really funny, but I was really mad. When you got mad at him, he enjoyed it.

"Guy stayed with me a year. We'd go shopping and do things together, but we had a weird relationship. We were like old friends. I wasn't really trying to get him back. If I had tried, I could have. And that's where I think I was wrong. I just wasn't forgiving enough.

"If there was a way at that time to 'fix' our marriage, we just were not smart enough to know how," said Janice. "Many marriages go through what we did, but neither of us knew how to fix it."

Chapter 69

"This is the good life."

– Guy Williams

Guy returned to Buenos Aires in August 1984. His friends and associates were wondering when he'd return. When he left for New York he had told his friends he'd be back in a month, but instead it was a year. Fans on the streets greeted him with warmth and love. Buenos Aires was his. The sidewalk cafes, the opera house, the beautiful parks, his walking routes, the restaurants, the gym where he still kept his membership to fence, the people, the culture, were all things he had missed, and felt at home with now. Argentina was still watching *Zorro,* and Guy Williams was still treated with all respect and honor in their country so he would stay.

With his marriage virtually over, Guy did not foresee any more long visits back to the United States. He stopped living as a tourist in Argentina and rented a furnished apartment on the top (ninth) floor at Juncal 1771 with a one-year lease. His friends felt he now had "the blue and the white" deep in his heart, because he planned to stay. Rent and utility bills would have to be paid on time. He could pay the utility bill conveniently at the bank, but if it was not paid on time—due to him being out of the country, for instance—there would be a big hassle. He would have to stand in a long line at the company, and then have to fill out long tedious forms, all of which Guy could not tolerate. He did not anticipate going back to the United States any time soon.

Women never ceased to pursue Guy, and he was as much a flirt as he had always been. Patricia Goodliffe worked at Guy's bank, Alpe on Sarmiente Street[300]—where he had been cashing his checks for the last few years. Everyone in the bank noticed when El Zorro walked into the bank. Guy would see Carlos Souto for his transactions, but if Carlos was not there, he saw Pat, as he called her, because she too spoke fluent English. Guy didn't seem to remember her, but she remembered her first encounter with El Zorro on an elevator in July 1977 in the Alvear Hotel. Pat had been working out in the gym on the top floor of the hotel to prepare for a ski trip in August. She was the only person on the elevator when Guy stepped in. "He looked at me, and I felt self-conscious, so I turned away. He was very handsome, so I thought he must be conceited, and I wouldn't look at him. When the elevator stopped in the lobby, we walked our separate ways."

Pat remembered the time she and her cousin took their boys to the circus in 1978 when it came to Buenos Aires so they could meet their TV idol. "When the show was

Guy took this picture for his ID at the Fencing Club and Gym, where he exercised and practiced fencing. (courtesy of Patricia Goodliffe)

over, all the kids ran to touch El Zorro," recalled Pat. "My son, Lucas wrapped his arms around Guy's leg in a bear hug, and Guy patted his head."

By September 1984 Guy was coming to Pat's window more often, and one day he asked her to join him for dinner at a favorite restaurant of the stars, La Fecchoria. A roving reporter spotted them at their table and asked Guy if he could take their picture. Guy consented.

The picture appeared in *Antena* headlined, "Guy Tiene Novia." "They printed that I was a very intimate friend," said Pat. "My friends teased me about that and I was embarrassed, because we didn't know each other that well yet. The magazine also said Guy had farms up north. It was a lot of bull like that, and we laughed about it. He owned some property, but never any big ranches like the papers were always saying."

Pat was twenty years younger than Guy, a pretty divorcee with a twelve-year-old son, Lucas. Sophisticated, humorous, and intelligent, Pat was from a prominent family of English and Argentine origins. Her paternal grandfather was sent to Argentina by the British government to oversee the laying of the railroads in the early 1900s. Her father married an Argentinean woman, and Pat grew up in a bilingual household, the youngest of five children (one sister, a brother who is a doctor in the United States, and two brothers in Argentina). Her parents prospered and maintained property in southern Argentina and Uruguay. A flight attendant in the 1960s, she met and married Lucas' father, whom she divorced when Lucas was very young.

Guy enjoyed Pat's company. They saw movies together and took walks together on weekends, dined together. One day Guy was waiting for Pat outside the Metro Theater, near the Obelisk on the 9 de Julio Avenue, when he was approached by young Juan Carlos Fauvety, who recognized Guy easily, even without his trademark moustache. Juan Carlos[301] had been nine years old in 1973 when he stood on the edge of the street waiting for El Zorro to pass by in the procession from the airport. "Guy was saluting the people like a Roman Emperor," said Juan Carlos. "The whole scene was incredible."

Juan Carlos was an ardent and tenacious fan since boyhood, having watched every episode of *Zorro*. He couldn't have been happier to finally run into his idol. After a spontaneous greeting to someone he felt he had known all his life, Juan had a pleasant conversation with Guy before Pat arrived. Juan Carlos was also a friend of Fernando Lupiz, and a distant cousin to Pat. It would not be the last time they would talk.

"Another time about a year or two later I met Guy again, and we talked for two hours, mostly about *Zorro*. During that time, you would not believe how many people waved to him and smile and say hello. In Guy's lifetime, that never stopped.

"Guy told me he had been watching *Zorro* on TV, and he said it was very strange for him. 'I feel like I'm watching my younger brother,' he said. 'And, I see Gene and Henry, and I know they are gone, but I see them alive in front of me on the screen and

I don't know what to do with that.'"

Guy was at a time in his life when he could finally sit down and watch some of the *Zorro* episodes he had never seen before, and there were a lot of them. The show was on every night and sometimes Pat was with him when he watched. Guy would slap his knee and laugh at Gene's antics or Henry's comedy bits. "Sometimes he would start to tell me something about the scene, then he'd stop in mid-sentence, because he didn't want to miss the dialogue.[302] So I never heard some of the stories he could have told. I wish now I had asked him more about it," said Pat.

"He did tell me how beautiful the suits of Diego de la Vega and his father were. He regretted that the show was not shot in color, because it was a pity that the magnificent embroideries could not be completely appreciated in black and white. He said his brown velvet suit had gold embroidery on it. Guy was always looking for a nice Zorro sombrero, but he could never find one equal to the beauty of the one made for him on the show.

"Guy liked the *Zorro* theme, the opening music and song. I remember many times while walking with him, people would whistle or hum the tune, as though they were saying I know who you are. He enjoyed that."

When Pat first saw *Zorro* on TV in Argentina, Don Diego/Zorro was speaking Spanish, which was really not Guy's voice at all. Years later, and after she knew Guy for some time, she saw a video tape of *Zorro* in English with Guy speaking in a subtle Spanish accent. Her reaction was quite different from those in the United States. "I started laughing. It was so ridiculous to hear him speaking English with a Spanish accent, because Guy had trouble speaking Spanish. He had a very strong English accent and in the beginning of the series he speaks in English with a very strong Spanish accent. It was the last thing I ever expected."

Zorro had been on the air continually in Argentina since 1968. In 1983 Disney started airing *Zorro* again on its own new Disney Channel. By now, it was airing all over the world. *Zorro* had become more popular than Guy could ever have dreamed. Now in 1985, it was going to leave the air for a while in Argentina, but in the United States, adults who watched as children, relived their childhood aspirations and adventures as they watched it on the Disney Channel. Some watched with their children, and a new generation became interested in the irresistible masked crusader of the poor.

The Disney Channel began getting so many inquiries about Guy Williams from fans, new and old, wanting to know what happened to him. They contacted his family and people who knew him and ran an article in the September 1985 issue of *The Disney Channel Magazine* titled, "A Far Away Zorro," telling about Guy living in Argentina. It came as a surprise and a

A reporter spotted Guy and Pat Goodliffe in a restaurant on their first date and Guy consented to letting him take their picture. Word was then out that Guy Williams had a new girlfriend. (courtesy of Pat Goodliffe)

Guy and Pat, leaning against her Citroën, at Retiro Station seeing Lucas off to school on a Sunday, around June 1985. Taken by Lucas with Guy's Nikon. (courtesy of Pat Goodliffe)

curiosity to many. Nothing had been written about Guy in the United States in years, which was such a contrast to the continuous publicity he was getting in Argentina.

By Argentina's spring season, our fall, 1985, Guy had gained too much weight and began to get serious again about exercising and losing weight. With *Zorro* off the air, there was no pressure to grow his mustache, work, or do interviews, or so he thought.

France was airing the *Zorro* series for the first time and the frenzy of Zorro had hit like it had in 1957 in the U.S. Philippe Garnier, France's correspondent in Los Angeles, was desperately trying to find Guy to interview him for a two-part article for France's TV Guide, *Télé 7 Jours*:

> Everyone in Los Angeles was leading me to believe that Guy Williams had thrown in the towel on his career definitively. He was unknown in every agency. He no longer subscribed to the Actors Guild. Even in Disney's Studio, nobody knew where he was.
>
> …Finally, after a lot of phone calls and a real stroke of luck, a kindly secretary at an old agent's office[303] agreed to give me Guy's confidential phone number at Buenos Aires.[304]

Guy was amazed at the great lengths this man had gone to find him.

He was also floored when Garnier told him *Zorro* was extremely popular on cable TV in France, that kids in Paris were jumping off roofs and carving Z's everywhere like they had done in America in the 1950s. It did not matter that the show was in black and white. They loved it and they loved *him*. Guy was the definitive Zorro.

"If longevity is *anything*, that's what longevity is,"[305] Guy said later. He had come to realize that *Zorro* was now among those rare shows listed as "TV classics"; those timeless shows that have universal appeal to audiences of all ages and generations.

Guy was flattered and eager to talk about his career and *Zorro*. He agreed to meet

Garnier at a well-known hotel. Guy didn't drive in Buenos Aires. Traffic was fast and chaotic. He thought all drivers in Buenos Aires were potential murderers, besides he enjoyed the buses and subways just like he had in New York. Today, however, he took the wheel of Pat's little Citroën, and with Pat holding on in the passenger's seat, he zipped his way to the hotel lobby where Garnier anxiously awaited. They would spend the next two days talking, lunching, and taking pictures.

Garnier wrote:

> He [Guy] had warned me on the phone that he would be picking me up at my hotel, but nevertheless, it came as a bit of a shock to see Zorro arrive in a 2 CV, then turn the corner of Ave. Cordoba, and finally come to a hard stop on Viamonte Street in the heart of Buenos Aires. It was a little bit too much. Especially after all this research. But, it was really him! Guy Williams, alias Guido (Armando for the Civil State) Catalano, alias Don Diego, alias Zorro.[306]
>
> To gain his goodness, I arrived with gifts for the exiled: an armful of Vitamin E and tubes of Krazy Glue, the miracle glue that they cannot find anywhere in Buenos Aires. To see the joyful look on his face, you would think I had brought a magnum of champagne.

OBLIGATED TO SHAVE HIS MOUSTACHE

In Buenos Aires it did not take me a long time to notice that if in the United States Zorro and Guy Williams had been forgotten a little (he is almost known more for his other role in *Lost in Space*), our man is incredibly famous in Argentina, his country of adoption, and he even has to periodically shave his moustache because of the autograph hunters!

Late in Argentina's winter of 1985 Guy was interviewed by Phillipe Garnier of France. The two spent two days together talking and taking pictures around the city. Here Guy shows off a little piece of Americana in front of a new Kentucky Fried Chicken restaurant.

I experienced this fame first hand myself: Williams' telephone messages had alerted the personnel of my hotel. I see myself as a kindly person, but constantly I was being harassed by the elevator guy and receptionist: "You'll bring him to the hotel, won't you?" they begged. "When will you bring Zorro here? Just for an autograph!" To my great shame, I admit that I signed two postcards with a big Z just to get peace, and to avoid people going through my luggage.

ACCLAIMED BY MILLIONS OF ARGENTINES

The most amazing thing perhaps is that Guy Williams, at 62 years old, did not lose an inch of his stature. His famous 1.83 meters was even more imposing in the thick yellow leather jacket he is wearing tonight. He only thickened out in his neck and waist a bit, but he still has his brown hair. Still seductive. After all, he came with Pat, his friend, "and chauffeur," she corrected with good humor. The 2 CV is hers.

Seated in his favorite restaurant, Il Vero Fecchoria, zestfully eating roasted goat and cheerfully drinking bottles of local Sauvignon, Guy explained to me how he ended up in Buenos Aires.

"First I got invited by Channel 13, the channel which broadcasted *Zorro* at the time in 1973. The frenzied welcome had me really surprised, but then, Argentine people know how to welcome! They put us up in the Alvear Hotel, a very grand hotel. Another time, it was Isabel Peron who asked me to come for one of her charity galas. Another time, I went back with Henry Calvin (the one who plays Sergeant Garcia). From the airport to the Sheraton, thousands of Argentines were following us with cars, only to see Zorro and Sgt. Garcia. What delirium! We made a few TV guest appearances. A little bit later, I started to produce my own tour. In summer, to Mar Del Plata, or to Santa Fe, to a lost hole in Patagonia. I was riding horse a little bit, and doing fencing exhibitions with a man named Lupiz, the sharpest blade in Argentina. All of that is bizarre, because for me, Zorro has never been really very important. But this character keeps on coming back in my life, again and again, and I am happy that in France he is still popular. Mark me well, I am far from complaining, because this is the good life."

To explain Guy Williams' so called disappearance or semi-retirement you have to understand that he is the kind of man who has always put life (particularly, "the good life") before every other imperatives, either about his career or other personal ambitions.

"…the idea of playing something like Zorro didn't exactly thrill me. Like all kids, I loved Errol Flynn and Robin Hood; but at thirty years old, it was difficult.

"What pleased me, on the other hand, was the certainty that this show would be produced in the best conditions possible, only with professionals, because everything produced by Disney at the time was highest quality. They were not skimping on anything. I have to say I loved the idea of working for Walt Disney, who had been my hero in my youth."

Coming from a well-to-do family in New York Guy quickly discovered that he did not like school or any kind of routine. Unable to keep a regular job, he becomes a model for advertising photographers...

"It was at that time that I changed my name so I would not see myself limited to Italian types or Latins. It's even more stupid because I was not dark or swarthy at that time. But in the '40s or '50s nobody in this occupation could afford names like Al Pacino. In Hollywood there was a manager, Henry Wilson, his specialty was to create names that sound good for his clients: Rock Hudson, Tab Hunter. Me, I chose the most master-key, all-purpose name possible. The funniest thing is that Disney, years later, would have rather my name to be Catalano for the role of Zorro.

Caption under a photo of Guy pointing to new Kentucky Fried Chicken restaurant:
"More than 30 years later Guy Williams does not look his age, in the streets of Buenos Aires, he reminisces about *Zorro*.

Caption under photo on second page:
Guy Williams in a grand restaurant of Buenos Aires where the gauchos are preparing grilled meat.

(Subtext under title)
He was not really surprised when we told him he has bewitched and enchanted young and old each Saturday night on the Disney Channel on FR3 and caused a rush on outfits and records bearing his picture. In Argentina, where he has chosen to live, he is very famous and the autograph hounds never ceased to chase him.

PART II, October 1985

"I HAD A YACHT AND A 15 ROOM MANSION"

(Guy is pictured by his computer)

We are at the terrace of one of those many cafes in Buenos Aires called *confiteria* enjoying our cocktails, batidos de Gancia con limon, the fashionable aperitif of the country, and lots of appetizers.

"Disney's doubt (about *Zorro*) was without foundation, because the show became successful right from the beginning. The reason is because at that time they only had Westerns on TV, like the action movies, and *Zorro* was different. It was also superior in the way it was made. Also, we were selling everything that could be worn or held, with a Z on it: shirts, hats, gloves, flashlights, key rings. By contract, I received some of the profits, but the great benefit was the personal appearances everywhere. It was the beginning of Disneyland and we went there to promote the show and also as entertainment at the park. But my contract was only for 40 weeks, the rest of the time I was being paid 800 instead of 1200 a week and most interesting I was allowed to do other things on my own for myself, and it was really then, between seasons, when we were stuck, that I was collecting lots

Guy loved to play games on his computer and learn Word Processor. He wrote letters and his script on it. Photo for publicity in 1985 when Philippe Garnier interviewed him for *Télé 7 Jours*, Paris, France. (author's personal collection.)

of money and other TV actors were doing the same thing. For instance, rodeos and concerts were getting you more money in three days than a year at Disney."

Of all the roles he played he's still most proud of *Zorro* than any other, mainly because of the fencing which for him was first-rate.

"We used regular swords with modified pommels to look like sabers for more protection. Of course, the blades were dulled for safety, but it looked like they were very sharp. It looked like they were cutting candles in half, but they were pre-cut. Still, you had to be able to hit the candle at the right spot for it to look like it was being sliced. Sometimes it would take up to half an hour to do this, just for *one* candle. That's when Gene Sheldon, who played my faithful deaf mute servant, Bernardo, was not so mute. He would joke and say: 'And he wants to be Zorro.'

"Fred Cavens, who was supervising all of the fights, was really the best and very imaginative. He was already a mature man, so it was his son Albert who was the stunt double for the young actors, he and Buddy Van Horn, who was often my enemy on the set. Fred had two mottos: always aim straight, and always have at least one person, one actor, who really knows how to handle the sword.

"Fred who was very good at fencing had also an extremely good sense of what the effect was going to be on the screen. So if on the set, he'll do some figure which looks small, then it *had* to be exaggerated, so it showed up very clearly on the screen, and the other precept was (and very useful) was to always hit your target. The beginner will hold back and try to hit his adversary in the side, for fear of hurting him. This doesn't sound so bad, but it is very dangerous. If I know Freddy is aiming for my face or my torso,

I know where his point goes and therefore his blade. If on the other hand, he pretends, I have no indication, no idea of where his blade will go.

"With Disney we were within the rules. We never rushed on Friday. The fights were shot on Fridays, that way, if there were an injury, I had a few days to recover. I was injured twice, once on the chin another time on the hip. But the only time there was a serious accident was when an actor named Anthony Caruso [sic][307] insisted to do the part himself. I don't know why Norman let him do it. The conditions were extremely bad, on slippery rocks with boots on and everything. We were on a ranch in Calabasas in the valley. I nearly put his eye out. I injured him at the corner of his eye. Nothing serious fortunately, but we really learned a good lesson there."

Guy Williams lives in a studio apartment on the top floor of a wealthy building in Recoleta, the most desirable part of Buenos Aires. He has a terrace, a few good books and his computer. To use it, as with anything else, he has to use glasses; some incredibly pink and patched up glasses with a missing side piece.[308]

The only *memento* he kept from *Zorro* is a leather book cover in which he had carried his script on the set. Now inside it he has a cookbook, but not any kind of cookbook. This is one of his numerous projects that did not come off, which he wrote in collaboration with a woman. This recipe book is guaranteed to seduce women. In short, it is a seducer's guide. He also has in it some recipes selected from his trips to Italy and also a short article on "How to read bottle labels when you don't know anything about wine."

Guy Williams also tried to put together another *Zorro* in Argentina, this time, for the big screen. He spent all last year writing the script and he wanted to play the part and also direct.

"The challenge for me was to offer a version of Zorro for people who were older than 12 years old and I wanted to play an older Zorro. The Cinema Institute here was supposed to support my project. But they imagined that only 20,000 dollars would be enough for me to start, when actually I needed one or two million dollars."

Guy Williams is thinking of moving to another apartment soon, but one within the same area, Recoleta, in which he enjoys a luxurious lifestyle of ease. He is very comfortable here, speaking a sort of Anglo-Italo-Spanish, which he himself calls "papamiento," like a Spanglish, so to speak, based on Spanish. He ordered breakfast at the terrace of his favorite café, facing the famous cemetery of Recoleta, where Eva Peron, the wife of the old dictator, is buried.

"They serve the richest breakfast you can imagine here, with ham this thick!" he says. With that, Guy Williams demands to know if I am just a little hungry? "One of these? Or how about a little bit of roasted goat before you go?"

Well, why not. After all, it is rather difficult to leave El Zorro.[309]

Fame during his retirement was much more pleasant for Guy than the days when he had a grueling filming schedule and had no control over his career. Here in his retirement, he had the luxury of fame and control, and enough privacy to suit him.

On September 14, 1985, back in the United States, Toni remarried. She met singer/songwriter/musician Michael Anderson at a religion study group. After knowing him for only two weeks, she married him in a small informal ceremony. Guy called her on her wedding day to give his blessings and best wishes.

The following month, October 1985, Guy's own marriage came to an end after thirty-eight years, more out of necessity than desire. Only a few close friends knew. Neither intended to remarry. In Hollywood they remained Mr. & Mrs. Guy Williams.

Pat and Guy's friendship grew and they began to see each other more often. On weekends and some evenings they took long walks together, always through Palermo Park, which Guy loved, then ending up getting ice cream at Heladeria Freddo in Recoleta at Ayacucho and Quintana, or Heladeria Cadorealso at Avenida Corrientes and Rodriquez Pena.

"Guy had a great imagination," said Pat. "On our walks we used to often see this fat priest driving a very small car. Guy would joke and say it was probably the *Auto*-da-Fé! (a clever pun referring to the Inquisition). He'd go on to say it was probably running on the burning bodies. 'That's the way they get rid of sinners. We'd better get as far away as we can from him,' he'd say. Every time we saw that priest and the 'auto-da-fé,' we'd laugh like crazy.

"We would see an older couple shopping, or eating at a restaurant, and he would start imagining who they were and what they were saying to each other, and it would be hilarious. He could think of some clever things.

"People recognized Guy everywhere we went," said Pat. "It would start something like: 'It's HIM! It's Zooorrrrroo!'"

The public never stopped acknowledging him, always waving to him, with "El Zorro!" or sometimes addressing him as "Don Diego." Guy was always gracious even if he got tired of it. He often felt like the character, because the people made him feel that way.

"He didn't refer to himself as Zorro to me," Pat points out, "but if we were with somebody else or in some public place and people came up to him and said, 'Are you El *Zorro*?' Afterwards, he'd say to me, 'You see, I AM ZZZORRROOO.' He knew that to them he WAS Zorro, and he felt a moral obligation to live up to that image."

Guy coped with the interruptions graciously, or with his own sense of humor, depending on his mood. "One time someone came to him wide-eyed and gushing, '*Are YOU Guy WILLIAMS*???' And he said, 'Well, sometimes.' He was full of that kind of answer. Another one he liked was, 'No. That's my *brother*,' or '*Who* wants to know?' Sometimes he pretended he couldn't speak Spanish and couldn't understand a word they were saying," she laughed. "That was when he simply didn't want to talk to them, but that was rare.

"Guy loved to ride the subways in Buenos Aires, but sometimes he didn't want to talk to people on the train when he was alone. That was when he made his 'stupid face.' He told me about a time he was sitting on the subway and he saw two women staring at him, and talking back and forth, wondering if it was him. 'So I made my stupid face,' he said. You know, changing his face, looking all around at everything, then he heard them say, 'Do you think that's him?,' then, 'No. I don't think so. It's not him.' And they would leave him alone. Guy was so funny like that."

Guy had his own way of doing things which was often very different from most people. For instance, rather than reading the *Financial Times*, he had his own quick way of checking inflation. "Guy used to check the price of a pair of leather skin moccasin shoes, (gamuza) to see if they went up or down. They were kid skin, very expensive—on sale around the corner of his Juncal apartment. He would say to me, 'You know the

Guy and Pat, and Braulio, her Cocker Spaniel, chat with Andy Curtiss, left, and Peter Ashton, right, while enjoying a "scotch" on the ground of St. George's College in Quilmes. 1987. (courtesy of Patricia Goodliffe)

moccasins have kept the same price for almost two weeks now!' It's true it was accurate, but it was funny, because he would very seriously discuss inflation rates with me, because of his system, the *Money Moccasin Market price*!

"Things got higher in cost for people who earned their salary in Pesos. For Guy it was better in a way, because he kept his money in dollars which meant he had more Pesos."

Pat had a black cocker spaniel named Braulio which Guy became fond of. "Guy used to take Braulio to the park and throw a ball or a stick to him for hours. A few times he even cooked meat for Braulio. Guy set the dish down and Braulio ate it up in seconds. Guy said, 'I took all that time, and he didn't even taste it!'"

Pat and Guy used to take Braulio along with them on picnics at St. George's College when they went to pick up Lucas on weekends. St. George's College, in Quilmes, is a private school where young Lucas was the third generation in Pat's family to attend. Lucas' father and Pat's father had both attended and a classroom was named after Pat's father. Lucas spent summers[310] in Comodoro with his father.

Reminiscent of his days at Peekskill when his parents came to see him, Guy sat on the campus lawn on their folding chairs, sharing cocktails and conversation with the school masters while soccer games and other events were going on. Lucas was the envy of every school boy because El Zorro was his friend. Everyone became excited when Guy came to campus.

Guy brought along his Nikon, and when he saw Lucas's interest in the camera, he explained to him how to use it, and let him take some pictures. It was Guy's enthusiasm about photography and those first lessons that inspired Lucas to fall in love with the art and discover an innate talent with the lens. Today, Lucas is a successful professional photographer in Argentina and Mexico City. His love for Guy is evident, speaking with warm sentiment and gratitude for how Guy enriched his life in those early years.

Over Christmas and New Year's while Lucas was in Comodoro, Guy and Pat went to Le Cumbre in the province of Córdoba to spend Christmas and New Year's with Eduardo

Guy with Lucas Kirby, Pat's son, in Palermo Woods. The strap of his Nikon can be seen over his shoulder. October 198. (courtesy of Patricia Goodliffe)

Marchigianni, on his ranch there. Eduardo was an older Italian gentleman Guy befriended in 1980 in Buenos Aires. His family regaled Guy and Pat with a feast, lots of good food and wine, and lively conversations in Italian. The quiet lifestyle on the ranch was a welcomed getaway from the bustle of the city, and something Guy liked to do from time to time.

A month later Guy went with Pat to Le Tigre, a 30-minute train ride along the river, to spend the day with Oscar Deurer, the father of Lucas' godmother. Lucas, his godmother, and her children were with them at the small rancho on top of a hill. Because it was so small, Deurer jokingly named it El Pupo Ranch (the belly button). A boat service took them to the islands for swimming, and Guy watched Pat water ski. "Word got around that El Zorro was there," said Pat, "and all the neighbors came to see him."

No work and all play suited Guy. He enjoyed these jaunts with Pat and her relatives. Pat recalled a funny incident when they visited her little nephews. The boys watched *Zorro* on TV and they eagerly awaited meeting the man they saw every night on television. Children, however, don't account for time and age, so when Pat introduced Guy to the boys, they stared, thinking he didn't look the same. "That's not him," they said.

"Guy struck his fencing pose and began advancing and thrashing all over that small apartment with an imaginary sword to show them it really was him. The kids just stared in shock, and said, 'OK, well, I guess so.' They were still not quite sure."

At home, he still enjoyed his music and reading, but his favorite pastime had become his computer. Before he had left the United States in 1984, his son Steve had given him a small computer, one of the first personal computers sold, and Guy brought it back with him on the plane. While Guy spent a lot of time trying to land aircraft on navy ships, and playing computer chess, it was the word processor that fascinated him the most. He wrote letters to Steve on it and worked on his script. No one got a handwritten letter from Guy anymore. They were typed on his computer and printed. When he wanted to relax, he played chess with the computer. Guy thought it ironic that the computer took so long to make a move since they were touted to be great "brains." He jokingly called it "the stupid" to Pat to make her laugh. He would lay down and take a twenty-minute nap before the computer made its move.

Guy was enjoying the "life of Riley," doing whatever he wanted to do, a lifestyle he had always wanted. Offers came in for work, but Guy would turn them down. "I asked him," said Pat, "'What's the matter? Are you sick?,' and Guy said, 'Yes, I have a hopeless case of terminal laziness.'"

In 1985 Fernando and his wife Adriana had their first child, a little girl, Alejandra. Guy and Pat shopped together for a gift for the baby. "We brought the baby a big teddy bear because Guy said every child should have a teddy bear," said Pat.

Guy was pleased that Fernando's acting career had taken off and he was getting steady TV work. They still occasionally met in Palermo Park to keep their hand in fencing. They never completely gave up on the movie. Should the opportunity arise, they wanted to be physically prepared. But at this time Guy had no inclination to perform.

Guy's sister Valerie recalled a conversation with Guy in the mid-1980s when she called her brother for advice about investments on the stock market. "It was obvious he had no desire to go back to his acting career in Hollywood," said Valerie. "He said to me, 'You have no idea what it's like. You have to live through it to know what they can do to you. It's horrible. They destroy something in you.' He told me that the only kind of involvement he would consider now would be as a financier. He thought that was a cleaner business. He called Hollywood the 'Land of Butter Contracts.' They melt away." Valerie was happily remarried now, and preoccupied with raising her three daughters.

Guy was in a different place in his life than he was from 1973 to 1978, and for whatever reason, he was more reluctant to work. Some thought it was because Guy would not do something if the quality of the production was not good and if the pay was not good, but a few others suspected his health was not good.

Chapter 70

"I had all that. I don't need that anymore."

– Guy Williams

After Guy's one-year lease was up, he moved to a larger and nicer apartment at 1964 Ayacucho, apartment B, in Recoleta, the most elite area of the city. Resembling Paris with its French-style buildings, Recoleta is graced with large green gardens along the streets, first-class restaurants, fine specialty stores. Like Beverly Hills in Los Angeles or Fifth Avenue in New York, it is a prestigious place to live. Across the street from his apartment, at the corner of Ayacucho and Libertador, is the beautiful Alvear Hotel where he and Janice had once stayed. There was only one other apartment on the 2nd floor[311] next to his, which gave him a lot of privacy. Mahogany panels and a marble floor gave elegance to the small lobby. No one could enter the security building without being buzzed in by a tenant or by ringing for the concierge, Hugo.

For $375 a month, Guy was in a two-bedroom apartment, with one and a half bathrooms, a kitchen, a living room, a study, and a washroom with washer/dryer combination, in the most desirable neighborhood. The streets below were like Rodeo Drive in Beverly Hills, with Cartier's a few doors down. Grocery stores were near and his apartment had a private lift to conveniently bring up purchases. It was funny that the apartment had a secret closet, because Don Diego's hacienda had many.

Renting was different in Argentina in that utilities and the phone service were kept in the name of the owner of the building, but were paid by the tenant. Heat in each apartment was controlled by the building manager, not the tenant, so there was no thermostat in his apartment. "If you became too hot in the winter, you opened the window," said Pat. "Guy had an air condition unit in one of the rooms for the hot summers.

"It was a well-furnished apartment. Guy personalized it by putting pictures of Toni and Michael, and Steve and Darlene around the apartment."

Guy considered himself very lucky to get this apartment in Recoleta. He told Carlos it was like a penthouse on Fifth Avenue, but it would be five times more in New York. Guy still lived modestly, but comfortable, with the bare essentials in furniture. He had no cleaning lady, so he said he spent part of each day cleaning and cooking. "I do the best I can," was his customary saying with a shrug.[312]

427

Guy and Oscar Deurer, father of Lucas's godmother, at Oscar's ranch at riverside in Le Tigre,
Buenos Aires. January 1986. Oscar's ranch was so small, he jokingly named it
El Pupo Ranch, the belly button. (courtesy of Patricia Goodliffe)

"Guy did his own laundry and vacuumed his carpets, but always missing the corners," said Pat. "Sometimes he took his heavier clothes, like his Levi jeans and jacket, to
my apartment to wash, because my machines were bigger. I gave him a key to my
apartment to use anytime he wanted, but he would never give me a key to his place. He
read the paper, or watched TV sometimes, because I had cable."

Guy dressed well, but he had a limited wardrobe for years. He hated to shop. When it
came to meats and fine wines, Guy liked the best, but material things were no longer important to him. "Guy's clothes were very worn," noted Carlos, "nothing brand-new, everything
well used, and the explanation he gave me once was, 'Listen, Carlos. At one time in my life
I had a lot of money. I had a boat. I had beautiful cars, and I had beautiful clothes. I *had* all
that! I don't need it, and I don't care to have all that anymore. I like to be comfortable. I like
to have a good steak, a nice glass of wine. I don't need *any* more than that.'"

Guy sat in front of the TV more than he ever had, now that he could watch Cable
with none of the interruptions he could not tolerate. "When I got a VCR he liked to
rent old movies and come over to watch them, usually a classic black-and-white drama
or *film noir. Casablanca* and *A Funny Thing Happened on the Way to the Forum* were
among his favorite movies. The AFL games, soccer, and the Admiral Cup were his
favorite sports events.

"Guy preferred black-and-white Hollywood classics from the 1940s. Guy didn't
like the early tinting and colorization they were trying to do to these traditional films.
He thought those films were great *because* they were shot for black and white, and said

they would lose their drama and effect if colorized. He could do a good imitation of Humphrey Bogart, reciting his lines and sounding just like him. *Ssheet-hawt.*

"Guy often arrived at my place with strange and unusual 'presents.' He was not like anyone else. His presents could be anything from a roasted chicken to a sandwich maker. Just simple gifts, but useful. If I said I liked something, Guy would buy it for me," said Pat, "a purse, or anything. The sandwich maker was great. We loved to make those hot sandwiches when we watched TV.

"Sometimes he brought me 'gomas de pomas,'" she laughed. "Guy spoke Spanglish, his own way of speaking sometimes, and it was funny. There was a candy I liked, a little spicy gumdrop candy called 'pastillas de goma,' but Guy would call it 'gomas de pomas,' which doesn't mean anything. It's just his word for them. To this day when Lucas surprises me with some of this candy, he will call them "gomas de pomas."

A typical day in Guy's life started with a walk to the kiosk near his house to buy his *Buenos Aires Herald.* At La Biela, a sidewalk café, he had coffee and usually a croissants for breakfast. He always took his walks for miles around Buenos Aires, usually with his headset, listening to Bach and Mozart. He went to the market daily because he didn't like to buy large quantities at a time. He liked to drop into the shoe shop near his apartment to visit Vincente, the Italian shoe repairman, where he could have a conversation in Italian. For business matters or just conversation he stopped in to see Ian Stanley, at the Stockbroker Firm, or have coffee with Hugo Cortina to talk about land deals, or visit Carlos Souto. It was a lifestyle that suited him and he felt was ideal.

"In the hot summertime he used to come to my place," recalled Carlos. "There I was with a jacket and tie, and he was in short pants, with tennis shoes, and his headset on his ears. I said, 'Guy, I envy you.' But, he would wave his hand at me and say, 'Awgh, don't say that.' Sometimes he would be carrying his movie script under his arm. He was very happy in Buenos Aires and he lived quite well."

Guy' apartment at 1964 Ayacucho, with four potted plants on the balcony, as it looked in 2003, was on the 2nd floor, above Tradiciones. In the U. S. it would be called the third floor. (courtesy of whitefoxdomain.com)

Guy worked on his script and also had a storyboard book made, depicting each scene of the movie to try to attract producers.

Carlos never greeted Guy as Don Diego or Zorro, which had become a little annoying to Guy at this point in his life. Carlos didn't think of Guy as a celebrity, but a friend, and his love and admiration for him was sincere. When he talks about him, it's evident he misses him deeply.

"Oooh," he sighed, "he was such a *fine* person. It was always a pleasure to talk to Guy, because he could talk about many, many, things with a lot of knowledge. He had a very good point of view, and was very clear in his thinking. And he was always with good humor.

"He was a very grateful person. Once he spent Christmas with all my family and he was so grateful for that. My family had a good time with him. He was a very nice person. When my daughter was born [1986], he went to the clinic and brought a bunch of roses. Ah, he was very sweet.

"Guy was a good man. He wasn't envious. He wasn't selfish. He was very respectful for other people. Really, he was a good man. He loved children. Always in winter he was with a cold," laughed Carlos, "because all the kids had colds and he kissed all the kids, so they give it to him. But that never stopped him from kissing all the kids! Once I went with him to the circus with my son, and Guy went through *all* the kids. He didn't have to, but he went through all the kids, giving kisses and kisses, a thousand kisses from Guy. He never, never rejected anybody.

"He enjoyed a lot to be with the computer, writing scripts for movies, working on many things. He was a very cultured person, an intellectual. He loved to read a lot. He liked good music. He knew a lot about the economy. He loved to learn about everything."

Guy would call Pat at work if he had read something interesting in the paper he had to talk about. "He was like a little kid," she laughed. "He would get excited over something he read and call me right away to tell me about it. He was very funny sometimes.

"He called me at work or I called him, to set up what we were going to do later if one of us didn't have something else to do, or we were just too tired. But that was how we planned the next time we would see each other. Sometimes we would meet on Florida Street and walk all the way to his place or mine. We just did whatever was most convenient that day. And sometimes, since Guy had the key to my place, he would surprise me and have dinner waiting for me, which was very nice. Something simple, but delicious. Always beef, a steak. I remember seeing his cookbook that he wrote, but I never used it."

Guy enjoyed going to parties with Pat. "They were not big parties, just some friends getting together or sometimes relatives," she said. He was always happy to give an autograph to a young boy or girl.

Guy's ongoing sense of humor made it difficult to determine sometimes whether he was serious or joking. "Guy was always making up stories about his idea of God. He told me he had his own Theory about God. He said that God was Hydrogen! Hydrogen is invisible. It's powerful, and is everywhere. If you fool around with hydrogen, it is fire. You burn to death which is Hell. He went through all his logical reasoning and finally concluded after much thought that God must be Hydrogen.

"He was always practicing his ability to get people off balance, especially me. I would go for it full-speed, and after I spent hours trying to prove him wrong, I realized he was just teasing me."

By now, Guy had gotten back in shape and was keeping his weight down. "He was doing some training at the Club (gym), working out and fencing. He used to ask me to go and see him, but it was difficult for me, because it was during working hours and I couldn't go. I deeply regret not having done so."

Pat wanted Guy to get a divorce and marry her, and although he professed his love for her, he never would commit. Carlos Souto had only one thing to say to any woman who wanted to marry Guy: "Tough luck, baby!" he said. "Guy didn't want to marry Pat or *any* girl. They could just forget it. Patricia was too controlling for Guy. She wanted things done her way, and Guy was very independent. I feel sure he wanted to stay married to Janice. Guy always loved Janice."

Guy was planning a trip to the states to be with his family for the wedding of his only son, Steve, on May 10, 1986. Pat thought this was the perfect opportunity for Guy to introduce her to his family, but Guy, still keeping his two worlds separate, never so much as mentioned her name to his family.

Guy emphatically refused to take Pat to the States with him. A big argument developed between them. "Guy was used to getting his way," said Pat, "but I was the youngest in my family and used to getting my way, too. I don't think he was quite used to someone like me, because I would fight back about many things. I told Guy if he went without me, not to ever call me again."

Guy never took these threats from women seriously. When he returned from the States, he called Pat and she forgave him. "I tried," she said, laughing at herself. "It didn't work. Because as it turned out, I was not at the wedding, and I was still with him. It was impossible. *Impossible.*

"I said to him one day, 'You're impossible! Why can't you just be difficult?' And knowing it would drive me crazy, he teased and said, 'Why be difficult, when I can be *impossible?*'"

Guy (with mustache) August 1987, with Pat and her sister, Moira, outside at LaBiela, Guy's favorite neighborhood café. (courtesy of Patricia Goodliffe)

While Guy was enjoying his newfound lifestyle in South America, he never forgot his family in North America. He phoned them on a regular basis. Pat walked with him many times on weekends to put those calls through to his children, sometimes Janice. "Guy had a phone in his apartment, but he used it only to *receive* long distance calls, not to make them. Back then it was a headache to have a phone." Pat explained, "If you rented a place the price was higher if it had a phone. The phone was the landlord's. It was too complicated to make an overseas call and have it charged to your rent, and have the landlord asking questions. So, Guy used his phone only for local calls, and rather than have a hassle with the landlord complaining about the bill he would go to the phone company to place a call to the children, which he did regularly. I often went with him on many Sundays to make his call. He was always caring and thoughtful, walking to the telephone company on holidays and the children's birthdays to call them in the States.

"I was with Guy when he shopped for their Christmas gifts. He bought all of them gifts, Janice, too—fine sweaters and leather items, gloves, handbags—and sent them to the States.

"Guy often bragged about his family. He always spoke very highly of Janice. I must admit I was a little jealous when he did that, but you could tell he had great respect for her and she for him. When she took a trip to Venice, Italy with some friends from Los Angeles, she bought Guy some silk ascots there and sent them to him. You could tell he really liked that. He wore them all the time."

Chapter 71

"Now, what do we do for an encore?"

– Guy Williams

Steve and Darlene decided to tie the knot on May 10, 1986. Steve met Darlene, a pretty Japanese American, a few years earlier when they both worked at City Hall. Guy flew in for the formal affair alone, and would stay only two weeks, now that he had his own apartment in Buenos Aires to maintain.

Guy was picked up at LAX by Toni and his new son-in-law, Michael, who he met for the first time. They drove him to their new house in the Hollywood Hills, high above the hotel Chateau Marmont where Guy and Janice had stayed with the children years ago after their trip to Europe. Janice was in the back of the house when Guy arrived through the front of the house. She heard his voice and could not hold back the tears. She went into a room to composed herself, then she came out smiling to join them. She had not seen Guy in almost two years.

The wedding took place at St. James Episcopal Church on Wilshire Boulevard in Los Angeles. Janice, beautiful in a flowing pink formal gown, and Guy, handsome in his tux, walked in and took their seat side by side in front of a myriad of friends they had acquired in the past thirty-four years in Hollywood: Dennis and Gerry Weaver; Strother Martin's widow;[313] Noley Walsh Fishman and her husband, news anchorman Hal Fishman, and her son; actor Richard Mulligan and wife, Lenore; Mrs. Curt Bernhardt, wife of the director of *Damon and Pythias;* Mr. & Mrs. Arthur Silver; Mr. & Mrs. Don Burnett; Mrs. Chris (Eleanor) Dark; the Wileys and their children, who were the ring-bearer and flower girl; Councilman Gil Lindsey, who was the best man, and many more.

The reception followed at the posh Beverly Regents Hotel in Beverly Hills. Janice and Guy stood together in the receiving line, greeting old and new friends. To the new ones, Guy introduced Janice as "my wife, and mother of the groom."

Everyone sat down for dinner, and Guy and Janice were seated next to Don and Barbara Burnett. Guy was animated, his large hands moving as he spoke continually. He put his new glasses on, and kept asking Janice if they looked all right on him. They had dark heavy rims, popular at the time, and Guy referred to them as his "Cary Grants." He only wore them when he had to.

Guy danced the evening away with Janice. In the wedding video Guy and Janice are seen dancing next to Don and Barbara. They join hands and dance together, kicking in step to a kind of lively polka, laughing and switching partners. During a slow dance with Janice, Guy turns and dips her, leaning in with a fixed sexy gaze into her eyes.

All their friends found it inconceivable that these two could separate. Don Burnett found it hard to understand why Guy would leave at all. "Guy and Jan had been 'Mr. and Mrs. Perfect' to me," said Don, "the perfect couple, with the beautiful house, nice cars, and beautiful kids. Guy had it *all*."

Toni and her husband Michael were part of the entertainment line-up. Toni, in a soft blue Matron of Honor dress, took the microphone, while Michael played a special song he wrote for the newlyweds. Guy stood front and center. He loved Toni's sultry deep voice. When the song was over, he applauded wholeheartedly, his famous smile beaming. It made him happy to see that Toni and Michael had something together. He complimented Toni and encouraged her to keep up her singing.

As the bride and groom were preparing to leave, all the guests spoke to them through the video, sending love and good wishes. Guy is standing with his arm around Janice and says: "We had two wonderful kids, and now they are both married. Now what do we do for an encore?" Janice was speechless. Guy spoke of the "joy and happiness" he felt at this "union, Steve's marriage." He points to Janice saying, "I know *she's* happy. I can say this for her, their *Mother*." He looks at Janice, and says, "And she's also my *Friend*. Give me a kiss." They kiss. Camera fades out.

Michael Anderson had his first talk with his father-in-law during the dinner party the night before the wedding. He was also meeting his childhood hero. "When I was a boy, I watched *Zorro* every week," said Michael. "One time I spent the night at my cousin's house and he wanted to watch something else. I got in a fist fight with him so I could watch *Zorro*.

"He was my hero as a child, and when I met him for the first time as an adult, he did not disappoint. He was charming, intelligent, and still with that big smile. *Patented*.

"Guy told me that the role of Zorro was very important to him. It really *was* him. He was very proud of it. I asked him about *Lost in Space*, but just from the way he talked about it, I got the feeling it just wasn't the same."

Michael asked Guy if he missed working, if he was yearning to get back into acting. "I got the feeling he wasn't interested at all. At this point in his life, Guy loved to be on the computer. He was fascinated with the word processor. At the time, I didn't even know what it was! But he was very excited about using it. Guy was so intelligent."

Guy told Michael how Walt used to tap him on the shoulder until he got the accent right. He told Michael how they would sometimes ad-lib which he said was the way they got some of the funniest lines. Since Michael was a musician, Guy thought he'd appreciate one of his favorite lines. It was an ad-lib by Tony Russo, as the Zorro imposter, when he doesn't rob the musicians because he says, "they never have any money."

Guy spent most of the two weeks at Toni's house, so Michael had a chance to get to know him. "He enjoyed our place very much, and seemed very up, very happy, jovial. He was very outgoing at the reception, mixing with everyone.

"He told me he liked Argentina because of its European style. He loved the city life, the good food, steak and wines and the late night dinners. And since he liked to stay up late, he liked the fact that everything—stores and restaurants—stayed open late into the night."

Toni rented *Zorro, the Gay Blade*[314] (1981) for her dad, figuring he'd enjoy the parody of his show. "He loved it," she said. "Michael and I were behind him while he was watching and once in a while we'd see his shoulders moving up and down, so we knew he was laughing a lot. He was glad they had expanded on Zorro in *The Gay Blade*. Dad thought the gay side, amplified in the movie, was funny. He had tried to do this, but Disney wouldn't dare."

A writer from *Starlog* magazine, Mike Clark, had been waiting patiently to get an interview with Guy for a long time for his *Lost in Space* fans. There had been rumors about a *Lost in Space* movie with the original cast, and Clark wanted to ask Guy's opinion on behalf of all the fans who had been writing in about it. Steve made the arrangements and Mike Clark got a two-hour interview with Guy for his article that appeared in the January 1987 issue, No. 114, of *Starlog*, now a collector's item.

Fans wanted the *Lost in Space* reunion movie to happen, but it was not getting off the ground. Guy opined that if it was up to Irwin Allen to make the movie for TV, he would love to do it. But it was his guess that the problem was with the networks. What Guy had learned from his days in Hollywood was if the networks wanted to do something, they would do it. If the networks didn't want to do something, it would not be done.

When Clark asked Guy about his living in Argentina, Guy replied: "I am a resident of Argentina, because it's simple to move that way. I went into some land things and I'm sitting there leading a very pleasant life, as quiet or a loud as I want it to be."

When asked if he had done any TV shows or movies since *Lost in Space,* Guy said no, and added that he had no itch to be in front of the camera again.

During the interview, Guy inadvertently revealed how he felt about Buenos Aires by referring to it as "home."

Janice invited Guy to her place for dinner with the entire family and Don and Barbara, who were considered family. Janice had bought a spacious and beautiful condo in Westwood and Guy was seeing it for the first time. He was impressed, but he didn't let on to her that he was. Guy was very proud of Janice, her talent, and what she had accomplished. Early in her career he used to tease her about her job, saying all she did was move some chairs around. "Guy just didn't think I could do anything by myself," she said.

Just before Guy left for Argentina Toni and Michael gave a barbeque for him on their front patio, which offered a panoramic view of the city. Michael observed Guy and Janice as they broke away and stole a moment alone.

Near the edge of the cliff overlooking all of Hollywood, Guy and Janice looked out over the vast city of dreams, a soft sea breeze brushing their faces. Everywhere they looked there were reminders of Guy's success, his disappointments, his joys, sadness, and their life together. The city below their feet became a virtual roadmap of their life together. Buildings, studios, the beach, streets, and boulevards each had a story, a milestone in their journey from the time they arrived in Hollywood to now.

"We could see the roof of our first apartment on Harper," said Janice. "There were a lot of happy memories in that apartment."

A flood of memories rushed them as they recognized streets and landmarks. "They were very nostalgic," said Michael. "We could see them pointing and talking about what used to be here and used to be there. They talked a lot about the Garden of Allah, the Villa Capri, *the old Hollywood,* and how the neighborhood had changed.

"They were very cordial and polite to each other, always showing respect for one another."

Guy and Janice were connected by more than just their children. Their lives were woven together with the same threads. They had shared the same goals and objectives for more than thirty years.

That evening they watched a home movie Guy' mother had taken in 1955 in front of Guy and Janice's first apartment on Harper Street, almost directly below where they were now. They watched the scenery through Clare' eyes: the tiled-roof homes and neatly landscaped yards she so admired. Then as the silent Super 8 flickered in the dark, they watched Clare pan slowly above Sunset Boulevard and up into the Hollywood Hills to a distinct palm tree standing alone. Everyone was shocked when they realized it was the *same* palm tree in Toni' front yard! Clare had unwittingly made an arc from the past to the future and by doing so she became a part of the present, as though she was focusing on them through her lens.

Guy was used to staying for months at a time so the two weeks went fast. Suddenly they were all back at the airport saying goodbye again. "We had a very nice visit," said Janice. "He didn't seem particularly eager to leave."

Chapter 72

"Why are they doing this?!"

– Guy Williams

In 1987 *Zorro* made a comeback on Argentina television, this time on Channel 11. Alberto Lopez, a producer at Channel 11, and Robert Cristían, his partner, wanted to make a new *Zorro* series, and put together a stage show for kids with Guy and Fernando fencing. They told Guy about this and many other plans they had. Guy listened with interest, but he told them not to make any decisions for him, that he was the *only* one to decide what, where, when, and under what conditions, he would do anything. Everything was in the talking stages, so Guy waited to see what would develop.

The two men set about getting publicity for Guy, hoping to lure a sponsor for a new TV show and any of their other plans. Guy's phone was ringing once again. More interviews and offers for personal appearances. Several periodicals (*TV Guia*, *Gente*, and *Radiolandia*, to name a few) ran articles about Guy and *Zorro* in June and July 1987. Reporters were trying to analyze why *Zorro*, a black-and-white show from the 1950s, had remained so popular even with the competition of color and computerized special effects of the day.

Guy was asked why he thought *Zorro* was so successful after thirty years:

> It was not too violent and gory, everything was in small doses so the kids could absorb it with their hearts.[315]

And:

> I think that children's fantasies never die. Each generation has the same dreams and fantasies as the ones before them. That's the only explanation that I have found.[316]

Lopez and Christían set up a photo shoot in beautiful *Vicente Lopez Park* (named after a national hero) in Recoleta. Guy, in one of his trademark pullover sweaters, is stooping down surrendering with open arms to the little boy in a Zorro costume who had him at point. This photo accompanied an article.

Publicity shot taken in Vicente Lopez Park when the *Zorro* series came back on the air. This publicity shot was used with Cora Laso article in *La Semana*, July 7, 1987. (author's personal collection)

The Weekly, June 23, 1987 (Semanario, p. 47):

Guy Williams, "Zorro," Explains How His Success in Argentina Prevails.

In addition, he does not discount the possibility of making a new show for kids.

(Caption) *Today...without his famous mustache Guy Williams remembers old times of Zorro with affection.*

Just as his sword never falters in his great adventures, neither does his stardom. In effect, everyone is surprise that this *Zorro* show has a new found success in reruns. A surprise because it has been 30 yrs. since it was filmed at the Walt Disney Studios.

Moreover, the numbers of the ratings have flabbergasted the television managers and executives: *Zorro,* shown every day on Channel 11 at 6:30 p.m., has a rating of 39.6 points, a very high rating. No less than 4 million viewers a day. It's a real surprise almost inexplicable for a show this old and being shown in black and white.

He was logically happy about the success his character was having. "I'm really very happy, I confess, even though I can't explain why the Argentinean public loves Zorro so much. Maybe it's because he reminds us of a classic romantic struggle between good and evil in which the winner is always justice. Something which we all try to achieve in our hearts," said Williams with great sincerity.

He still has the same freshness in his smile and the same elegant posture. He admits being 62 yrs old[317] which you can only tell by some gray hair and his having abandoned his trademark mustache which gave so much personality to Diego de la Vega and Zorro.

"I'm a happy man. I love Argentina and that's why I spend so much time here. Besides, I've made enough money to live peacefully, comfortably, since the time I made the series," he tells us, and he adds an anecdote about his personal lucky star.

"The contract with Walt Disney was for 4 years, but what happened was, all the *Zorro* episodes were made in only two years. But they still continued to pay me on the terms of the 4-year contract. So think about it. I made a fortune without even working," he adds with a charming smile.

We know that his infatuation with our country certainly has its origins in financial negotiations and real estate, but Zorro has denied our reason and insists his principle reason is love for our country and affection for the public.

"Take for instance, the summers I spent in Mar del Plata where the love of children and grownups was for me an unforgettable memory."

Returning to the current success of the show Guy believes, "It is interesting in a world full of violence and children's programs equally as violent that the public feels a necessity to find a different message, where we have adventure and risks, but not violence. Maybe it's not impossible to change the content of television shows dedicated to children," he says with conviction.

Obviously, we ask him if he would like to return to television and do a program in Argentina. He smiles, thinks for a minute, and says, "Maybe. It wouldn't be a bad idea to do a show for kids, but I don't want to look ridiculous. I have to respect my years, and protect my image."

In this manner he concluded our interview showing us that winning smile Zorro made famous all over the world.

Guy is watching *Zorro* on TV in his apartment, July 1987, while being interviewed.
When he saw himself, he said he felt like he was watching his younger brother.
(author's personal collection)

The July 1987 issue of *TV Guia*, titled "El Zorro Today in Argentina – A man who continues to be the model of charm and magic on TV," noted:

> In spite of making a lot of money, he is transformed into a legend, who makes justice and the law unbeatable. Fighting for the poor, he tries to avoid violence, but only resorts to it when he has no other way to defend the truth.
>
> Guy Williams is a sensible man, very friendly, and loves our country. He has been living in a large apartment in Recoleta for about a year and a half. With his friends and his agents, Alberto Lopez and Roberto Cristían, he usually goes out to eat pizza, asada, or roasted chicken.

The reporters asked Guy about his childhood. It had been their experience that so many actors had traumatic or disturbingly unhappy childhoods, but not Guy.

> I went to the movies a lot when I was a kid. It opened around ten in the morning, and cost ten and twenty cents to get in. Then we would spend all of Saturday watching movies. At ten years old I went to military school so I could go to West Point. I had a very very happy and good childhood.

The writer points out that Guy is without his mustache and asks if he plans to do any TV shows.

> I have some proposals to do a TV show, and make some special personal appearance in the circus.[318]

A business trip sent Pat to New York for a few days in June. Guy was excited that Pat would be in his hometown and he typed a list of things for her to "try" and a list of things to "buy" as though he were making the trip vicariously through her.

Under the TRY list was:
- PIZZA WITH SAUSAGES AND MUSHROOMS
- LINGUINI WITH WHITE CLAM SAUCE (MAYBE AT SUPREME MACARONI CO. AROUND 38TH AND 9TH AVE) PASTA ALLA CARBONARA THE SAUCE IS MADE WITH BACON AND EGGS.
- SOFT SHELL CRABS – PADDY'S ? ON OR AROUND 34TH ST. IN THE MACY GIMBLES AREA.
- COLD DAY? TRY SOME CLAM CHOWDER BOSTON WHITE CREAMY, MANHATTAN DARK NO CREAM.
- BASS ALE – TRY IT ANYWAY, GREAT WITH MAINE LOBSTER
- HAYDEN PLANETARIUM AND NATURAL HISTORY MUSEUM ARE BOTH ON THE OTHER   SIDE OF THE PARK FROM THE METROPOLITAN AT 9TH ST.
- STATUE OF LIBERTY COMING FROM EUROPE IT'S AT THE ENTRANCE TO MANHATTAN AND THE HUDSON

RIVER ASK ANYONE OR BETTER STILL ASK ANY CHILD
OR MATRONLY LADY
- SUPERMARKET DIET MUNCHING
  SARAH LEE CHEESECAKE
  SUPER CHUNK SKIPPY PEANUT BUTTER
  SNICKER BARS IN THE CANDY SECTION
  THESE LAST ARE EVEN SWEET ENOUGH FOR
  ARGENTINA.
- PALM COURT TEA AT THE PLAZA

Items on the BUY list:
- A SUPPLY OF FUJI FILM SPEED 800. 24 IN EACH
- SUPPLY BEEFEATERS GIN, SCOTCH-CUTTY SHARK,
  GRANTS, BALANTINES, OR TEACHERS
- SUPPLY KRAZY GLUE
- WELLA BALSAM CONDITIONER EXTRA BODY STRENGTH
- SUPPLY OF SNICKERS BARS
- LARGE SIZE SUPER CHUNK SKIPPY PEANUT BUTTER

Not on the lists were his verbal requests for Pat to bring back packages of Semolina Pasta and to go to the Metropolitan Museum of Art. The Met was a priority on her list as Guy had told her so much about it. Since she could not share her experiences with Guy, she bought a cuddly brown teddy bear in the gift store "because Guy is like a teddy bear," she said. She named it Guyucho and held it the whole time she strolled through the museum seeking out the things Guy had asked her to see. When she returned to Buenos Aires she gave the bear to Guy.

There were rumors among journalists that Guy Williams was becoming weary being called Zorro and Don Diego and a legend and that he was tired of doing interviews. Undaunted, Cora Laso was still going to try to get an interview with the legend for a July 11 issue of *La Semana*.

While she waited for him, Laso reminisced about her childhood days watching *Zorro* every night on TV:

LAPARACE EL BRAVO ZORRO[319]
"For Disney to pick me up as Zorro, I had my physical appearance and the fencing I practiced since I was a kid."
A cup of very hot coffee with milk was on the table. There was bread with butter and sugar; uniforms starched so hard the stiff collars chaffed our neck. My fingers were swelling from using the pencil so much, but at 6 o'clock the homework was pushed aside and completely forgotten. We went to the TV. It was winter. There was the kerosene heater and some cookies in the plate on top the table. We saw the jumps and actions of *Zorro* come on the screen. He was always there. Pure black and white for a half hour every day. Twenty-seven years has passed and it's the same: the music, the same mustache, the same cape, and the same zip-zip-zip into the wood.
I can remember it all.

It's about half past noon. I'm on my third cup of coffee. I am waiting, and every time I heard the elevator, I imagine he is going to come out. Someone told me he doesn't like interviews anymore. He doesn't care about fame at all and he laughs when he hears people are measuring ratings. Someone said his show reached 27 points. Someone told me he looks the same, the only thing missing is his little mustache. I calculate he must be 63 now and I can't believe it. I imagine him rather bald, fat, and grouchy.

I look outside and the sun is going down. Soon it will be the time of day when we used to have the café and bread, butter and sugar.

Finally he shows up. I can't believe it's him. I was afraid to look. I looked the other way, then slowly I looked toward him and I can't believe my eyes, because I was imagining a grampa, and he is exactly like they said. He looked the same, but with the mustache missing. His eyes are very light. He has little wrinkles around the eyes, but they are because he laughs so much. He put aside his raincoat. He is impeccably dressed. He's a little bit chubbier than before. He has a little gray mixed with his dark hair. But, it's true. If you imagine him with the little mustache, he is the same guy. It looks like all those years never went by. He speaks perfect English, of course, some Italian mixed in with the English, and very little Spanish.

He looked around and all of a sudden he sees the tape recorder on the table. He made a cross with his index fingers and said "Back!"

I said, "Aren't you ashamed, Zorro is afraid of a tape recorder?"

"I'm not Zorro. You're wrong. That's my younger brother, Diego de la Vega. I came to excuse him, because he never showed up at this interview. He loves pictures and interviews. Not me, and I hate that I have to come and give explanations because of him. It's all his fault. He's a little (touches his head, implying a little loco). It's because of this show returning on TV. He thinks he's a legend."

"I can't believe that somebody so used to fame like you, doesn't like publicity."

"That's it. For us, his relatives, it's embarrassing, and he's a pain in the rear. This man is really a show off, never gets tired of bringing his show back on TV. His behavior is really shameful."

He likes to play this game. I speak about the other guy who obviously never showed up. I think he's doing it to hide his shyness, so I keep playing this game with him. I ask "Zorro's brother" if he ever felt jealous of his famous brother.

"Never," Guy says, "but he's really not very good company, because he spends all day talking about himself."

Then in a more serious mood, he criticizes the current Hollywood serials on TV, "with lots of destroyed cars. In California nothing seems to be more successful than excess. But in the long run, one gets tired of that."

He says he loves children: "I could never have made all those programs for them if I didn't love them."[320]

While Pat was in New York, Guy was called to meet Lopez and Cristían, who were now calling themselves Guy's managers or representatives. The meeting was under the pretense that they would be meeting a man involved in show business who might be willing to put up the money for a big outdoor Zorro show and possibly sponsor a TV show for Guy. When Guy arrived it didn't take long for him to sense something suspicious about the meeting. The man did not show, and nothing came of it, but it weighed heavy on his mind. When he got home he called Carlos.

"Guy had called me after the meeting with the two men and a strange woman," said Carlos. "He was trying to figure *why* they had brought this young woman along and made her sit next to him, and then someone wanted to take pictures of them."

When Pat returned from New York, Guy told her about the curious meeting. "Guy said it was very strange. He was sitting there and one of the two fellows, who called themselves his managers, came in with a flashy blonde, bimbo type. Guy found it curious that this woman, who had nothing to do with the deal, was there. He asked the other fellow who she was and he just said she was someone the other fellow had brought along. Guy thought there was something not quite right. They waited and waited for this show business character to show up and he never arrived. Meanwhile a photographer walked in asking if he could take a picture of Guy and the woman. He knew then that something not to his knowledge was going on, and he flatly refused to let a picture be taken."

On July 14, 1987, it all came to light. Pat and Guy were watching *Zorro* on Channel 11 when during a commercial break Guy saw a picture of himself on the cover of *Antena* magazine being flashed on the screen. A voice off camera was telling about a big scandal involving El Zorro and an ex-actress, Fabriana Rouquad from a soap opera that followed *Zorro* on the same station. She was pointing to the camera as though to Guy and claiming she was expecting Guy Williams' baby.

Guy was shocked. He could not believe what he was hearing and seeing.

"Guy was not just angry. He was *transformed!*" said Pat. "It was the first time I saw Guy lose his temper. '*WHY are they doing this?!*' he yelled. What upset him the most was that they showed these lies during *Zorro,* when all the children were watching."

Guy immediately went out and bought a copy of the July 8, 1987 issue of *Antena* magazine. On the cover was a picture of Guy smiling in his raincoat, and the headlines to sell the tabloid magazine read:

"Ex-actress of *Como La Heidra* expects a child.
Big Scandal against El Zorro
The pregnant young actress wants Guy Williams not to abandon her.

After the reader buys the paper and opens it to read the *whole* story inside, they find the headlines were not true.

At the top of his fame. The series now has about 3 million viewers. As it happens with many big stars, this actress is claiming him to possibly be the father of her child.
Great Mystery.
Guy Williams may possibly be the father of her baby. *She is not sure.*

A second article followed up on July 21 with more lies claiming they had talked to Guy Williams about this and he gave his version of the story and "denied the facts." The article continued to make degrading insinuations about an alleged, romantic affair. The entire story was totally fabricated.

Guy suspected that Lopez and Cristí had planned the whole thing as a publicity stunt when their set up with the blonde woman at the aforementioned meeting failed because Guy refused to have his picture taken with her.

"Guy was *so* angry," remembered Carlos. "He had always been very careful about his image. The whole thing was lies, all made up, just to sell magazines. Guy had never even seen the woman before. He said, 'They have no right to do this to me.' Well, they do what they want. They had nothing to put on the front page, so they paid this woman some small amount to be photographed and say she might be pregnant from Guy Williams. Actually, she didn't say *anything,* because they wrote everything themselves. They even said they had asked Guy things, but they never talked to him at all. He was really hurt by this, and he didn't know what to do."

The magazine article called the two men Guy's "managers" It quoted them as saying, if it was money the woman wanted, Guy Williams had none, and remarked on the "indigence of Guy's life and his personal surroundings."

Guy decided to hire a lawyer, Horatio Lynch from Estudio Dabinovic Law Firm in San Isidro, to try to clear his name. All he was asking was for a retraction of statements from the woman and the magazine, and he would forget the matter.

Lynch sent out a letter to the publisher, Editorial Abril, on July 22, one day after the second article. A representative of the publication called Lynch and was indignant. Not only did he refuse to retract the statement, but he was rude and threatening. He said the article had been arranged by Guy's "managers," Lopez and Cristían.

When Guy asked Lopez and Cristían outright if this was true, they emphatically denied it. "Guy never stopped suspecting they planned the whole thing," said Pat, "because they wanted him to do a big show with Fernando and they needed someone to come forward to sponsor it. They thought any publicity was good publicity to 'promote his image.' They, evidently, had no idea who they were dealing with!"

Guy, then, decided to file suit against them for defamation of character and compensation for damages that the bad publicity would cause him. Who was going to hire an actor for children, a symbol of Justice, who has been accused of romance, a baby, and abandoning his paternal duties? Not only was this damaging to his career, but to his family.

Before he proceeded, he remembered that his old friend Leon Balter had worked for Editorial Abril. Not wanting to inadvertently affect Leo, Guy called him to ask if a lawsuit against the publishers would hurt him. Leon gave Guy the green light when he told Guy he no longer worked for Editorial Abril.

"Most of the people of Argentina never believed the story in the first place," affirmed Pat. "They were used to these magazines printing trash."

Still, the words had their effect. Years later some articles would still come up with a line that Guy Williams lived destitute under poor conditions.

After the article came out an event that Guy was scheduled to do was canceled and Guy firmly believed it was due to this bad publicity.

"The litigation took *forever,*" said Pat. "It was not until April 1988 that the lawyers presented the deposition, with copies of the articles, written statements, letters, and anything else needed as proof and evidence. The magazine tried to counter sue."

In the papers prepared by the lawyers, Guy stipulated that Lopez and Cristían were *not* his managers. He had never signed anything with them or given them that title or the power to manage his career.

"At first he spent a lot of time with the lawyers at their office, then he mainly talked to them on the phone," said Pat. "Sometimes he asked me to explain to him some of the legal words."

Lopez and Cristían continued to try to produce a children's show for Guy and Fernando. When they approached Fernando about it, he was ready to do anything with Guy. But they approached Guy and he refused to do it. No matter how much Fernando tried to talk him into it, Guy would not budge. He was not happy with the way the two men operated.

"Fernando asked me to talk to Guy for him and convince him to do the show," said Pat. "I had to laugh, because no one could tell Guy what to do. Stubborn is soft compared to what he was. When his mind was made up, he was like stone. He didn't want to listen to any arguments. He will do exactly what he wants.

"I don't want that to be misunderstood. Guy was stubborn, but only in decisions about himself, for himself. In that no one could persuade him. But, if you told him you needed or wanted something, *anything*, even if it was a cup of ice cream, he would go get it for you. He was very kind and giving in that respect."

Without consulting Guy first, Lopez booked Guy on a talk show he co-produced, a South American version of the Larry King show, for a one hour interview and questions called in afterwards.

"They had it all set for Guy to appear on a TV show for an interview, but they didn't ask him beforehand," remembered Pat. "When Guy found out, they were already advertising it on TV! Well, Guy was furious. He said to them, 'No. I'm not going.'"

The people at the station were panicky. The show was already scheduled. "These people tried *everything*. They asked *me* to try to convince Guy to go. They offered to come get him with a cab, and everything they could think of. The producer's wife was a good friend of Guy's, someone he had met on a previous trip to Argentina, and cared very much for. Well, they even sent *her* over to beg Guy, thinking he would do it for her, but he continually refused. It was a matter of principle. He had asked them to always check with him first, and they hadn't. Guy's attitude at this time in his life was 'Nobody is going to handle my life.' He said, 'I'm NOT going.' And he didn't go."

After a few months, when he was no longer needed by the lawyers and his time was his own again, Guy contentedly went back to his regular daily routine. "He was quite happy with what he was doing—walking every day, going to Hugo Cortina's office, having coffee, talking, doing a little business. Guy was very intimate about his spending, so no one knew what he was investing in, but it was easy to suspect he and Hugo were buying small properties at auctions, and later selling them with a small profit. He would make his rounds, then he'd walk back home."

Chapter 73

"Take all those pictures off the wall."

– Guy Williams

Due to circulation of the French TV Guide article and the *Disney Channel Magazine* article of 1985, fan mail was beginning to find Guy in Argentina from various places around the world. A woman in New York had read the Philippe Garnier article in *Télé 7 Jours* and wrote to Guy via the *Herald Examiner*. There were others who reached him via La Fechoria, the restaurant mentioned in the article. Some tried to reach him through the American Embassy.

One day Guy was taken back when he came face to face with one such devoted fan. A young pretty French girl approached him on the street and said she was a reporter from France writing an article about him. Elise was going on twenty, but she looked more like a girlish fifteen in her ponytail and jeans. "He didn't believe me, but he was such a gentleman he agreed to meet with me," she said.

Elise lived in a city near Paris, France and had been in love with Guy Williams since 1985, when her goal in life became to meet him. For her he *was* Zorro. When she read the article in *Télé 7 Jours*, she found out that Guy was living in Recoleta, the same area where her uncle and aunt lived. Elise begged her parents to let her go. They consented on the hopes that meeting him would put an end to this childish crush which her mother called her disease. "My Pa wanted to cure me," said Elise. "He thought if he sent me to Buenos Aires I would see an old man, not the Zorro in his thirties, and I would be disappointed. Bad luck for him! I could never be disappointed. I was too fond of him."

The locals remember the curious young girl walking the streets of Recoleta everyday asking everyone if they knew Guy Williams. She became known as The French Girl. Elise went into a church and prayed that she would find him and that day the people at a newspaper kiosk told her that Guy buys his paper there every day and has breakfast right next door.

On March 9, 1988, Elise met the love of her life and hero, Zorro/Guy Williams, and their next meeting was set for March 11. As planned she met him in front of his apartment and they walked to the café. Guy ordered a beer and Elise a milkshake. She knew Guy did not believe her introduction so she immediately confessed all and they talked for six hours in Spanish and English. Guy was gracious as ever and flattered by Elise's dedication to him. But the more he listened to her and got to know her the more concerned he was about her fantasies about him.

446

Elise found her hero and love of her life at the kiosk where he bought his newspaper and had this picture taken on March 11, 1988 when Guy gave her five hours of his time to talk with her. (courtesy of Elise)

"I know I am childish. It's my big problem. I don't act like a girl of my age. I am not mature. Guy wanted to help me develop my mind. In my mind, I am a little girl. It is the reason why girls and boys were nasty and bad to me in school. When I was 17, I still didn't look at boys. I played with girls of 12. Psychologically, I was like them. The teenagers were cruel to me and called me a baby.

"I first watched *Zorro* when I was two years old. It came back on the air again in 1985, and I fell in love. I went to a boarding school far away from my parents. Girls and boys were bad to me. When I was sad, I locked my door and with my walkman I listened to my *Zorro* audio tapes in my room. They made me feel at home. I felt safe. Zorro became the most important thing in my life, and I knew I had to meet him."

Adding to her problems were traumatic sexual experiences. "After my sexual attacks, I refused to work, and closed my mind to that idea. Only Zorro could save me. He would take care of me forever. At home, I closed myself in my bedroom, where the walls are covered with pictures of Guy, or stayed in front of the TV watching my Zorro tapes. My mom was anxious for me.

"I confessed everything to Guy. He knew all about my life. Guy, for me, was my doctor and he knew it. He wanted to help me. He advised me to meet people my age, and have interest in boys, someone other than himself. But, I couldn't."

He tried to reassure her that she would get over him, but to her it seemed impossible. "He told me 'Your needs and tastes will change with time. They will be new to your *new* self.' He was so kind."

Guy didn't talk about Janice to Elise, but a reference to her once stuck in her mind. "He said to me, 'There will come the time some day, when you will find the one who will have your heart, as I found my wife.'"

From an upperclass family, Elise was bright and had a well-rounded education. She was fluent in several languages and wrote poetry. A horsewoman, she rode and competed in horse shows. Intelligent and physically mature, she was immature emotionally. Guy was baffled and intrigued by the paradox.

Guy agreed to meet Elise again before she left, to talk to her and try to shake her into reality, so she could go back to France, forget about him, and acquire other interests in her life.

Guy called Carlos and told him about Elise but he never mentioned her name. "Guy told me about the French girl. He said he thought she was very strange. And told me that she loves him. I told Guy to be careful, and he understood that. He said she was like a daughter to him, not a woman. He told me that he talked to her and gave her advice like a father would."

Guy's friends were nervous about him seeing the French girl, and kept reminding him to be careful. Pat warned Guy that his kindness and attention toward her could easily be misinterpreted by her, and just prolong her infatuation.

Guy talked to Aracelli about Elise. "I never met the French girl," she said, "but from what Guy told me she was very nice, a very sweet person. She was in love with him, but she was so young, like a daughter for him. Her parents and her doctor called Guy and thanked him for helping her by taking time to be with her. After she had the chance to meet him, the illness went away, at least for a while. They felt she was recovering. She sent letters, cassettes, and presents to Guy, every day."

This picture of Guy's apartment was taken by Elise in March 1988 while he was living there. Guy kept the large potted plant on his balcony for privacy. (courtesy of Elise)

Elise snapped this rare photo of Guy wearing his glasses he called his Cary Grants, which he used for reading. March 1988.
(courtesy of Elise)

Before Elise returned to France on March 16, 1988, Guy met with her again. They took a long walk and talked. "Guy had a lot of admirers. People would say hello to him all the time. I felt proud to be with him. He was like a Pa to me. He was very tall and very strong. I felt safe with him.

"When I went to the pub with Guy, people came up to him asking for his autograph. Someone asked if I was his granddaughter. What an honor!"

Guy felt responsible for Elise because she idolized him so much. He tried to guide Elise into other interests, things to study and do to get her mind off him. His concern made her feel closer to him. She clung to him and wanted to see him every day. In the wake of the bad publicity, the last thing Guy needed was the risk of a photographer lurking and making up stories about him and Elise.

Elise remembers Guy's primary advice. "'When you go back home,' he said, 'Take all those pictures off your wall.' He told me I was in love with a fictitious character, with an *image*. That I did not know *him* at all."

Guy gave Elise projects to do when she got back to keep her busy and distract her from him: Apply to the Sorbonne to study writing, or languages (she already could speak four); call modeling agencies to try to get modeling jobs; and *go* to her cousin's upcoming wedding and socialize, mingle, rather than stay home and feel sorry for herself.

Elise had hoped to stay in Buenos Aires into April, but her uncle disapproved of her behavior. She had come on the pretext of taking a trip with them and their daughter, but after the trip, he found out her true objective to come to Argentina—chasing after an older man. He thought it was disgraceful and arranged to send her home earlier than planned. Elise was furious with him for the implications he made against Guy, and never wanted to see him again.

She went back to France on March 16, 1988, feeling good that Guy cared about her, but angry at her uncle. She hoped Guy would come to France and visit her soon. The first two months she was home, she and Guy wrote each other twice a month, then once a month. Guy felt sure he could change Elise and he wanted to keep up with her progress. He enjoyed her letters, as she had a gift for writing interesting letters and poetry.

Chapter 74

"I'm watching a whole transition…"

– Guy Williams

Some producers wanted to do a children's show for the school winter break, and wanted Guy and Fernando for a Zorro act. Guy kept refusing, no matter how much Fernando pleaded with Guy to do it. Guy was always saying it was either that the quality was not good, or the pay was not good. Some thought maybe Guy didn't feel up to performing, physically. Regardless, Fernando would do no Zorro acts unless Guy did them with him, so Fernando turned them down too.

The producers decided to do the show anyway, and hired an actor to play Zorro. When Guy found this out, he was upset. "It bothered him that people would think the man in the costume was *him,* when it was not," said Pat. "He didn't like for anyone else to wear the costume, because he felt he was the only Zorro. He knew the audience thought of *him* when they saw the character. He called the TV station to talk to Gerardo Sofovich, a popular talk show host, to ask if he could come on his show and let the people know that it will not be him doing that show. I went with him to the station and watched them tape the show. Guy was on for an hour talking about his career and himself and during that time he explained on TV that the Zorro they were going to see on stage would *not* be the REAL Zorro. Him, GUY WILLIAMS."

This was Guy's last personal appearance on TV and to those who saw it, they remember it as a very wonderful and satisfying interview.

Politics intrigued Guy and with Argentina going through a major change, Guy felt privileged to observe this milestone in history unfolding before his eyes. When he first came to Argentina, it was under a very oppressed military government. Now Democracy was trying to get a foothold in the country under President Alfonsin. Some of the people were ready, some were not. "I'm watching a whole transition of a very sophisticated type of people moving into an area they're not familiar with, which is Democracy, and their trying to bring that same sophistication, that same way of looking at things, into this new form. Sometimes it works, sometimes it doesn't. Very interesting."[321]

Pat can never forget how Guy taught her the meaning of democracy. "One day Guy and I were grocery shopping together in the supermarket. When we got to the cashier, she asked me to open my purse so she could look inside," said Pat. "I was used to this system ever since I was a child, so I opened my purse as I had always done. It was the way of our old form of government. They told us what to do. Rather than use an expensive system like mirrors or cameras to watch shoppers in the store, *this* was their system. Guy was astonished! When we left, he said to me, 'What are you doing? They don't have the right to make you do that. Do they think you might have STOLEN something from the store!?'"

Pat had never given it a second thought. "It was Guy who taught me to realize I had rights. People here open their purses even without being told! They are so used to it. They know to do it. Everyone already knows they are suspected. This is what Guy meant when he said changes were happening. People were just beginning to realize they had rights and could not be bossed around anymore.

"Guy told me the contents of a purse was a very personal and private thing. He said I no longer had to be treated as a suspected thief, and be ordered to open it to the cashier."

A crusader of justice in real life, Guy had a plan. "Guy said to me, 'The next time they ask you to open your purse, you say, 'Why?' and if they think you might have stolen something, then you tell them to call the police, and they had better be *sure* you stole something, or you will sue them for defamation of character in front of all these people.'"

Pat trusted Guy so completely she decided she would do it. The next time she went to checkout, she braced herself. The cashier said the inevitable, "Open your purse, so I can see the contents."

"Why?" asked Pat.

The cashier was stunned. After her initial speechlessness, she said, "Well, because the sign here says I have to ask everyone to open their purse."

Pat, her heart pounding with fear, replied, "Well, then, if it's a matter of a sign, I will put a sign here on my purse saying, 'I will not open my purse at the register.'"

The cashier called her supervisor. The supervisor told Pat she had to open her purse. Pat parried with, "Why?"

The supervisor called the manager. Now the line is long and everyone is waiting and watching to see how this shocking scenario would unfold. "Of course they were all whispering that surely I had stolen something, otherwise, I would open my purse."

Everyone was staring when the Manager came. She commanded Pat to open her purse. Pat asked her why, and the manager pointed to the sign that said so. Pat told her she would make a sign for her *purse* that said, "I do not open my purse at the cashier."

The manager, dumbfounded, was supposed to accuse Pat of stealing but since she did not give the line, Pat, pumped on adrenaline, went into her dialogue. "Is it because you think I STOLE something? Because if that is the case, you had better call the police if you are accusing me of stealing. And when the police come and prove to you that I have not stolen anything, I will sue you for slander and defamation of character in front of *alllll* these people!"

With that she pushed her cart toward the door and left. Behind her she heard a round of applause and cheers from the customers.

"And *that* is how Guy taught me how to stand up for my rights."

Chapter 75

"I felt the need to see the family"

– Guy Williams

Letters from Elise came regularly. Guy liked getting them, always hoping Elise would mature, find someone to love, get married and have children. Sometime in Argentina's spring, late September-early October, Guy wrote to Elise about his concern over all the strikes and the blackouts they were having. It was because of these strikes that Elise did not get this letter and several others for three months.

"It was a difficult time in Argentina," noted Pat, "when you didn't know from day-to-day what would happen next. The strikes were so unpredictable. Guy and I used to joke about it day by day, saying we wondered who would be striking today."

Guy knew Elise wrote regularly, so when he was not getting mail from her, he walked to the post office once a month to inquire. He would be told there was no mail for him, but Guy would insist and ask them to look further. Still they said there was none.

A few offers of work came his way, but Guy refused them. He would say either the production was not up to his standards or the pay was not good. But Pat wondered if it was not more than that. He had headaches, occasional dizziness, and would stay up all night reading or on the computer, then sleep a lot during the day, and to her dismay, he was drinking more. He still ate a lot of beef, but he was strict about not having salt, which he was told would be very bad for him; he still liked his cocktails and wine.

Guy had what was called "episodes," after the stroke. He began to recognize certain sensations and would know when he was going to have one. They occurred a few times when he was with Pat. "Sometimes the symptom was dizziness, and one time he told me he had the taste of burnt rubber in the back of his throat," she said. "They were not frequent, but they worried me. He made light of it, and said, 'Probably just one of my circuits blew.' He referred to his brain as a computer."

Pat was afraid and begged him to see a doctor. He had not had a follow-up since his surgery. She had his blood pressure medicine refilled at her pharmacy, but it was the same prescription he had gotten years ago in the States. He usually took one when he thought he needed it.

Guy had his own remedies. "For a toothache he would walk it off; for a headache he would sleep it off. He took one aspirin a day to prevent a heart attack. One time his

Guy (with mustache) and Fernando continued to practice in case the right opportunity came along. Guy would not settle for anything but a first rate production for their act. He still hoped to make the movie. (author's personal collection)

toothache was so bad the whole side of his face was swollen. It had to come to that for him to finally see my dentist. He went to my dentist because he spoke English.

"When he had these episodes, his remedy was to lie down and rest until it went away. He would pull down the shades in his bedroom to dim the light, close the door to keep out the noise, and go to bed until he felt better.

"I would say to him, 'You HAVE to go to a doctor,' and he would say, 'OH no, I'll get over it.' I would get so mad and I would tear out of the house and go to my place. I begged him to see a doctor, but he flatly refused.

"I said to him, 'But if something happened to you, you won't have the kind of social thing here to go to the doctor, like you have in the States.' Guy said, 'No problem. If something happens to me, you call Steve. He will take care of everything.'

"'But Steve is in the STATES!' I said, 'What am I going to do with you *here?*'

"I was terrified about what could happen if Guy needed to be rushed to a hospital. I wanted him to get a medical plan. Things have changed here for the better now, but then there was a Public Ambulance Service, that took you to the public hospitals that may not be well equipped. Compared to what you get in private services, they were not good. Our services were different from his in the United States.

"At that time we didn't have paramedics. That was just something you saw on TV. I told him they would drop him off in some public hospital and they were terrible. To understand what it was like then, you had to live in Argentina. But he wouldn't listen."

Guy did not like to talk about doctors, hospitals, or dying. He tried to avoid it. "He used to just joke and say he was immortal. When he did talk about it, he said he wanted his ashes to be thrown to the sea."

On October 3, 1988, Guy renewed his passport. For whatever reason, Guy wanted to make a trip to the United States, to California, and see his family. When he renewed his passport, he didn't want to have his picture taken again. He liked the old one taken ten years earlier and asked if he could be allowed to use the same one. They honored his request.

Guy's family was curious as to what was bringing Guy back to the States. There was no wedding that they knew of, no family occasion. Maybe a business trip?

Guy told Janice it was not a business trip. "I just felt the need to see the family," he said.

Guy stayed with Toni and with Steve and spent a lot of time with Janice. They talked about a lot of things, but one thing usually recurred. "Guy said he regretted that he didn't keep the family in Europe," said Janice. "He thought it would have been better for the children: better schools, better lifestyle, and better for the family. He dwelled on it. Thought about it a lot. Argentina was a substitute for the lifestyle in Italy. He was very Old World in his thinking."

It was October 1988 and all of Los Angeles was rooting for the Dodgers in the World Series. Steve had four VIP tickets, for himself, Darlene, and his mother and dad. The four sat in the dugout of Dodgers Stadium and had a blast watching the Dodgers win the pendant that year.

It was during this visit that Steve and Darlene took Guy with them to visit one of Steve's old school friends and his wife, who had moved into a new condo downtown on Bunker Hill.

"The last time my dad was here, he went with us to see them, and after dinner we went for a walk. My buddy pointed to a brand-new street sign that had just been named, and said, 'I'll give a dollar to the first person that can pronounce that name.' And I looked at it and it was a long Polish name: General Thaddeus Kosciusko, which I now know, because when he saw it, my dad orated on who he was for fifteen minutes. Dad said, 'Oh! Thaddeus Kosciusko! He led the Poles in blah blah blah…,' and he knew the years and dates, *and* who his *brother* was! My friend was just, like—amazed! He had just wanted someone to pronounce it," laughed Steve. "But *that's* what Dad was like. We would try to stump him with stuff like that, obscure things, and he could give you the refinement of it. He was really a self-read intellect, one of those minds that you just don't run into often. He could retain everything.

"He loved books and always pushed me to read. I thought reading was more of a chore you had to do in school when you took a course, but he said "Reading lets you actually communicate or get in touch with the person who wrote that book and you look at things through another person's eyes." So he had a different appreciation for reading than most. It was his biggest entertainment. He was always reading. If it wasn't a script, it was a book. He loved reading. Mom reads a lot too."

Steve pointed to a set of encyclopedias on the shelf in his mother's house. "That's maybe a tenth of the library he had, and I swear, he would get a new encyclopedia off the shelf and sit down at the long dining room table at Hillside and he would start at A and go page by page. He would literally read the entire encyclopedia from front to back. And he could quote you anything he had read. Dad was a walking encyclopedia."

Guy was pleased with Steve's new business ventures and his success in real estate. One night Steve and Darlene had friends over to their house for a small party and Guy enjoyed stimulating conversations with Councilman Gil Lindsey about politics, as he had done in the past, but with a few noticeable changes to his family. For one thing, he no longer sounded like the staunch liberal he used to be, but rather like a conservative. This really amused his family. Recalling that time, Janice said, "Steve and I feel sure if Guy had lived longer he would be a *Republican!*" she laughed.

Steve made another observation about his dad during this visit with family and old friends. "I noticed the last time Dad was here that he had really mellowed out a lot. I remembered he used to have a tendency to get worked up about something when it wasn't the way it should be. And the last time he has out here his attitude was like, 'Wehh, so what,' type of thing. He was on blood pressure medicine so I thought maybe that was part of it too, but he did seem to have a whole different attitude. He seemed more content with things, more resigned, more at rest with things, and less confrontational. He didn't get upset about stuff like he used to."

Rather than make these observations a cause to worry about his dad, Steve thought it was good for his dad's health to be more relaxed, more resigned, and he told his dad what he saw and how he felt about it. "We talked about it," he said, "and he seemed to be realizing life's too short, so why worry about it. I think toward the end he was shifting gears. I think he missed being back here, being with the family. I got that sense from a couple of people I spoke to. I think he was restricted financially and couldn't come back for that reason, rather than anything else. I think if he had the means he would have done it."

Steve and Janice took Guy to the airport at the end of his two-week stay. "We took him to the airport and found there was a delay for about an hour, so he stayed with Steve and me until it was time to go," said Janice. "He seemed happy that we had some extra time together."

"I had just gotten a new video camera," said Steve, "so I brought it along to tape him. I was watching him through the lens as he walked away to the gate to board the plane. At one point he fumbled a bit with his luggage, stopped and made some adjustments. Then as he was walking away I got this eerie feeling that this would be the last time I would see him. As the plane started to back up, the red light in my camera came on, which means the battery is dying. Then as it was leaving, the picture went black. I got this strange feeling of premonition. I told myself it was silly to feel that way, and I tried not to dwell on it."

Chapter 76

"Like Zorro—I want justice"

– Guy Williams

This time when Guy returned to Argentina, he seemed to have left his heart in Los Angeles. He talked to Pat at great lengths about his family, bragging about everyone and showing off pictures and gifts they had given him. "It was obvious that he had enjoyed himself," recalled Pat. "I have to admit I was a little jealous, because he kept showing me pictures of Janice and him together. He talked about everyone, but he bragged a lot about Janice. He bragged about how great she was doing and how beautiful her condo was and the progress she had made on her own. He was very proud of her. I had the deep inner feeling that he was somewhat regretful of their breaking up.

"He never talked about his relationship with Janice to me. Guy was very private and very careful about what he said. But whenever he spoke about her, it was always with tenderness and respect. He cared very much for Janice. They had a terrific relationship as far as I know. They were close.

"He said he had just found out after all these years that all the time she went sailing with him, she suffered from sea sickness. That seemed to really impress him.

"Guy bragged about Toni's singing voice. Sometimes he'd hear someone on the radio and tell me that was how Toni sang.

"Janice kept sending him things and for Christmas Guy would always send sweaters and things for the whole family."

For Christmas 1988, Toni, Steve, and Janice made an audio tape for Guy on which they sang Christmas songs to him, and sent Christmas greetings with their love and good humor. They mailed it to him, and waited. They wanted it to be a surprise, but after a considerable amount of time for him to receive it, they decided to ask if he got the tape. Guy explained the complications with the mail strikes. It was still going on in December. He told them he would go to the post office to inquire about it.

"Guy was really looking forward to that tape," said Pat. "We were having a terrible strike at the time. I went with him to the main to translate. It's hard for Americans to understand how everything can stop here, but the mail was terrible. Guy raised hell at the post office because they said they had nothing there for him. He was furious because he knew his family had sent it. He tried *everything*, even his, 'I am Zorro' number. And, 'Everybody will know you took personal things from Zorro's

456

mail!' But it did no good. They said they did not have it. Sadly, he never did get the tape."

On January 14, 1989, Guy turned sixty-five, and he became eligible for his pension. He took his time going to the American Embassy to fill out the papers, but after a couple of months passed he finally complied.

"Guy was looking forward to receiving his first check because it would be a sizable amount, considering the retroactive months. He was making all sorts of plans. I was thinking of retiring and we were talking about doing some traveling. There were so many places in Europe he wanted me to see. He said when he got his first check we would celebrate with a romantic dinner at a wonderful restaurant."

Pat and Guy's relationship had had its ups and downs. She broke up with Guy a few times because he was not going to marry her, but Pat had reconciled herself to the conditions, and at this time they were getting along better than ever. "We were at a very good period, at an easy and happy stage in our relationship, probably better than ever," she said.

The lawsuit, still in litigation, seemed near an end and Guy was hopeful for a sizable settlement. Having lost some unwanted weight, he was feeling good and looking fit. He had kept his mustache for a year. He was also practicing his fencing with Fernando on occasion to keep his wrist loose. He and Fernando still talked about the movie, exchanging ideas, rewriting, and hoping one day they could film it.

The mail strike that had begun in October ended after December. Elise received several letters from Guy at once, some dated a couple of months back and one relatively current, saying the army had taken control and stopped the strike. Elise wrote to Guy to tell him she would be in Buenos Aires again for the summer, but she arrived before Guy ever received the letter.

It came as a shock in February 1989, when Guy opened his door, and there stood Elise. Pat had just left his apartment, so he thought it was Pat returning for something she had forgotten.

"He had not received my letter, so he was surprised to see me," said Elise. "The first year he was really happy to see me. The second year in '89 he was surprised and upset with me."

Guy left the door wide open the whole time they talked to avoid any gossip. She had presents for him and he signed things for her that she brought from home, then they went out for a walk.

This time Elise had come to get a job in Buenos Aires so she could live near Guy and see him any time. For months before she left Paris, she was begging her parents to let her live in Buenos Aires with Guy as her guardian. She promised her mother she would go to the French school in Buenos Aires if only she could live there. Her mother, anxious about her only daughter's emotional state, wrote to Guy to explain the situation, and to ask his opinion.

Guy wrote back to Elise's mother telling her that Elise would be better off staying in France and starting a life for herself; that there was nothing more he could do for her if she came back; and that he had a life of his own and could not accommodate her, or be responsible for her. With that said, Guy did not expect to see Elise, but her parents sent Elise to Buenos Aires anyway. "My parents told me afterwards that Guy had answered them and the answer was no, he couldn't, he had a personal life. But my parents could

Elise took this picture of Guy in March 1989 by the set of encyclopedias that came with his furnished apartment. When he saw the books, he took the apartment. (courtesy of Elise)

not tell me. They sent me there for Guy to tell me himself, because they knew I would not believe them and they were frightened of a suicide. They figured if I heard it from Guy himself, then I would believe it, and would come home."

Elise's mother secured lodging for her with a French family as a live-in babysitter for their little girl. They lived in Buenos Aires, several miles from Recoleta. The first month she was there, she could not ask for time off to go see Guy. After that, she was taking off to go to Recoleta to seek him out once a week.

During her weekly meetings with Guy, they met at Ital Park, an amusement park, the zoo, and a public park to talk. Elise told Guy she could not take the pictures off her wall. Guy saw so much potential in this lovely girl, he wanted so badly for her to have a full and normal life instead of dreaming of him all the time.

"I felt sad because I knew Guy was bored with me. It was not like the first time when he called me Bella, and Sweetie, and was cheerful. He was kind, but he seemed irritated with me. I admit I was a bit clinging. The second time in '89 I went to see Guy very often. Sometimes I would sit on the floor outside until he came, or sit in the lobby until he opened the door for me. I forced him gently to open the door. I had such a pitiful face, he didn't dare turn me away. He was usually angry at me, but he let me enter just to please me. He always left the door wide open, each time, I guess so no one could make up stories about him and a young girl.

"Guy wanted me to go home, explaining to me he has a life with Pat. He told me I made a bad choice coming back, that Buenos Aires was not the place for me. He wanted me to go to college, find a boy, get married, and have kids. Guy explained to me there were different kinds of love and different kinds of associations among people who care for one another. He told me he loved me from afar. He explained that for him I was a 'writing association.' He liked getting my letters and writing to me. He called our relationship 'Heartfelt friendship.'

He tried to make me promise I would stop loving him, but I could not oblige him that."

In an effort to please Guy and show him she had grown up, Elise tried to have a relationship with a boy named Daniel, who she met at Ital Park. The romance failed from the start, but they remained friends.

By March she was trying to see Guy every day, and the French couple decided to replace her. Elise told Guy she would go back home, but before her flight left, she could not bear to say goodbye in person. The day before she left, she watched Guy from a distance, as he bought his paper at the kiosk where they had met. "He looked so quiet and so handsome," she said. "If I had known it would be the last time I would see him, I'd have gone to him and given a big hug.

"The last time I saw Guy was in March 1989. Easter was in March of that year, and I sent him a bunch of yellow roses for Easter by my friend Daniel.

"Before I left I sent Guy three potted plants in addition to the yellow roses on Sunday, by Daniel, as my way of saying Adios.

"I did not dare bother him again. I was ashamed for the many times I had. I said goodbye by phone at the Buenos Aires airport. My heart was broken. I cried my eyes out and took my plane. I knew I would not come back.

"Later, Daniel told me Guy had said he wanted to say goodbye to me. How sad. I went to bother him when he didn't want to see me and when he wanted to see me to say goodbye, I didn't come by, afraid to annoy him again."

Elise called him when she got home to let him know she arrived safely. He made her laugh, teasing her about all the flowers. "I expect to see you pop out from behind one of them at any moment," he said playfully. "He was always joking, and always very sweet to me," she said. "But he was frustrated with me. He said he wished he could just shake me, and make me wake up.

"I tried to get into college, and I tried to socialize with others my age. I called about modeling, but they wanted me to be willing to take off my clothes, and I could not do that. I found that I could not take down the pictures and I could not stop my devotion to Guy.

"Guy was more than a friend to me. Our relationship was one of a daughter to her Pa. My love was platonic. He cared for me about anything. I was not afraid of talking about personal problems, because he didn't laugh at me. He was like my confessor. I trusted only Him. He was a gentleman, and I felt protected with him. He was really Someone. For me, he was and still is Zorro himself!"

About a week into April Pat and Guy went to a large family party for Pat's mother's 80th birthday. Guy looked sharp in a vest sweater Pat had given him and enjoyed a lively conversation with Pat's brother, the doctor, who flew in from the United States for the occasion. His face was animated and his hands were going constantly as he spoke.

A few weeks later on April 21, 1989 Guy, very willingly, gave an interview that Aracelli set up for him to express his views and feelings about the hurtful lies and allegations in the scandal sheet, and why he took action against it. At 4 p.m., journalist Silvia Rojos took her seat at the elegant Petit Colon coffeehouse (at Lavalle and Libertad), named for its proximity to the famous Colon Opera house, and waited. She ordered tea and went over the questions she would ask Guy Williams about his pending lawsuit. She looked up and saw this athletic figure walking in. She waved to him, and as he looked at her, she was thinking that he looked more like fifty than sixty-five. His weight appeared only a little more than when he rode the faithful horse, Tornado, in the TV series. She found him to be in a good mood, and with an excellent sense of humor. A few minutes later they were joined by Aracelli, who would help translate, and Carolina Mulder, the photographer.

Guy told how startled and outraged he had been when he learned of the accusations while watching TV, and turned the matter over to his lawyers.

> "I would not have chosen to take this path, but I had no alternative. This false charge has noticeably done damage to my public image and my livelihood, because it has damaged me publicly. I have never seen or had any relationship whatsoever with that young lady (Fabiana). Therefore, the matter has caused harm in my personal life as well as professional life."

Horace Lynch, the actor's lawyer, was the one who explained the indemnity he is seeking for the damage caused by the young model's charges: "We are seeking 310,500 australes as of the date the charge of paternity was made, that is, July 1987; we ask also for interest on that amount which accrues to the date of payment. Since the dollar was worth a little over two australes at that time, the sum amounts to some 141,000 dollars. My client wanted to reach an agreement with the defendant, but had no success. He asked for 50,000 dollars or there about (less than half of what we are asking now) but they refused to pay it and preferred to go to trial. Of course, the constant devaluations of the austral have affected the sum of the damages sought in this case, but sooner or later my client will recover them."

When Guy was asked if he considers the amount he is seeking as "economic reparations" to be excessive, he answered without hesitation.

"The harm this has done to me is considerable. My career, my good name, my image as Zorro, have all been dragged through the mud. This whole thing is one big cock-and-bull story made up by that young lady,

Guy was angry over the false accusations made about him in the tabloids in July 87 and spoke out in an interview on April 12, 1989. He was hopeful that a sizable settlement would soon take place.

The reporter and photographer went outside the cafe to take these pictures of Guy for the interview, April 12, 1989. They are the last known photos taken of Guy.

whom I've never met personally. The public who is so faithful to me and who admires me is made up mostly of little children and teenagers, and I cannot allow that kind of trash to be said of me. It has also affected my financial affairs."

In what sense?

"Look, when I worked here in 1978, in the Segura Bros' circus, I was paid 10% of the take and earned $100,000, during the winter vacation period. When this supposedly pregnant young lady's accusation was published, I was in discussions with several impresarios-TV, circus, etc. Among them were the Segura Bros, who had discussed the proposal that I would earn 50% of the box office—but in the end, nothing came of this deal, because the scandal caused by this article would diminish the public's inter-

Standing by subway entrance.

Playfully pointing to the camera was one of Guy's signature moves he often made when being
photographed. (photos courtesy of Aracelli Lisazo)

est. I have seen a definite diminishing of job offers, which has eaten into a
large portion of my income. That's the rationale for my suit for moral and
financial damages."

*When asked if he might return to acting, perhaps on TV doing personal
shows (projects of his own choosing), he replied:*

"My current work is in the courts, because—like Zorro—I want justice. As far as performing goes, I have no plans to do so at present. I have
business matters to attend to, and this case. The rest of my time I use to
enjoy and take advantage of the city that I have loved since the day I first
arrived here many years ago."[322]

During the two-hour animated discussions Guy downed a Gancia and three

Camparis while the women drank cocktails, and enjoyed several orders of tapas.

When the waiter added up the bill and announced that the tab had hit 319 australes, Williams allowed himself a small joke. "Is your paper planning to pay for all this?" he inquired with a straight face. "We're paying for just one cup of coffee," the reporter responded. "Well, then, we're going to have to wash dishes," he shot back. When the laughter subsided, the actor took charge of the check, consoling himself by saying, "OK, let's just let that *other* newspaper pay when I win my lawsuit."

After the interview, they went outside to take photographs of Guy. When they were done, Guy got in the car with the three women and rode to the edge of the Recoleta district. He asked to be dropped off at the supermarket. From there he would walk home. He kissed each one of them, got out of the car, waved and said, "bye-bye." It was beyond their wildest imagination that this would be the last time they would see him, that those would be the last words they would hear him say.

Chapter 77

"I had a terrible sense of doom about him"
                                    – Toni Williams

Toni recalled the last conversation she had with her dad when he made one of his regular phone calls home in early April. "He seemed more sentimental than usual. He said, 'When are you going to write to me.' That wasn't like him."

A few days later, Toni bolted from a deep sleep. "In my dream I was Dad, and my head was aching with a sharp pain. I had a terrible sense of doom about him. It was so strong I woke my husband to tell him about it. I felt I needed to write him right away."

Toni's sense of urgency was frightening. She wanted to say everything she ever wanted to tell her father. "Each day and night I wrote, and everywhere I went for days, I was composing this long letter to him in my head day and night. I was so afraid I couldn't get it to him in time. That's how strong this premonition was."

When Toni saw her mother, she told her she wouldn't be surprised if they received some bad news from Argentina soon about her dad.

Toni told her father things she had always wanted to say but hadn't, and things she had already said, but said again: how much she loved him, how much he meant to her, how she cared about him, what a wonderful father he was. They had talked about Christianity last time she saw him, and it worried Toni when he told her she was better off not trying to figure out such things as God and life after death. Toni had sent him a book about Christianity that had inspired her, and she hoped he had read it.

Her letter was pages long and took longer than she had intended to write it. "I didn't want to waste time by mailing it, so I faxed it to him at a place where he went almost daily for business transactions."

Guy used to go to the office of Ian Stanley, a broker for a company like Merrill Lynch, almost daily. He could use the phone there to call his children, and of late, for his business with the lawyers, he would use a new gadget called a fax machine, something nobody had yet in their homes, and many people did not even know about. When Guy told people his daughter had one of these little machines on which she could send letters, they laughed and didn't believe him. "They could not imagine such a thing," said Pat. "Guy was so proud of Toni and Steve for having these new pieces of modern technology."

Toni prayed for her dad to pick up the letter soon. For five long anxious days she waited to hear. Finally a telegram:

Wednesday, April 19, 1989. *"Fax received Thursday. Couldn't get it until Monday. Lawyers and courts business. Will write later."*

Toni thanked God for that message. It would be their last correspondence.

Carlos saw Guy after he had received Toni's letter and noted that Guy looked very happy. "Guy told me he was a happy man and that this was a happy time in his life," said Carlos. "He said that things were going so good for him right now, and he mentioned getting a nice long letter from Toni."

Guy and Toni had spoken some harsh words at times. At one time he was so angry with her he tore up a favorite picture of the two of them, only to regret it terribly later. He had long forgiven her and now he knew she had forgiven him. The peace he felt in their relationship was welcomed and satisfying. The lawsuit was to end soon and he was counting on a decent settlement. That, plus his pension, would give him more freedom to do whatever he wanted to do.

On the evening of Wednesday, April 26, Pat wanted to call Guy, but her phone was out of order. "With the government we had in those days, the worst thing that could happen to you is that your line went dead, because it could take ages to be fixed. It could be out for days and days. Today it only takes one day to get it fixed."

She called Guy from work the next day, on Thursday, the 27th, and they planned to meet at her place that evening to spend some time together before Lucas came home Friday evening from school for the weekend. After a late dinner, Guy complained of a headache. He laid down to sleep it off and slept at her place until the morning.

"In the morning Guy left early. I had thought he might want to stay and read the paper, or just goof off after I went to work, but he said he would leave when I leave. He may not have been feeling well, but at the time, I couldn't tell. We left the apartment at the same time. We said goodbye, and that Friday, April 28, was the last time I saw him."

Lucas came home Friday and was home for a three-day weekend, because Monday, May 1, was Labor Day. "I phoned Guy every day from the office, but this was a busy weekend for me with Lucas home, and my phone was not working. It was not until Sunday that I was able to go downstairs to my neighbor's house to use her phone to call Guy. It was about 2:00 p.m. on Sunday, April 30, and he answered. We talked about making plans for the week. I said, 'OK, tomorrow is Monday. Lucas will be going back to school. I'll call you tomorrow, to see what will happen.' This was how we made our day-to-day plans to know when we would see each other, and know what we were doing."

Pat was supposed to be off for Labor Day, because the banks are closed on that holiday. On this particular Labor Day, however, Argentina's economy was in deep trouble. The bottom was falling out of the stock market. Banks went bankrupt. Pat had to go to work. Pat knew Guy thought she was home with a broken phone. She called him from work to let him know she had to go to work.

"I called Guy on Monday from work, and he did not answer, but that was not strange because many times he was out of the house. We didn't have answering machines then, so I tried again later. He didn't answer, but I didn't worry, really, because it was not unusual. I just thought, 'OK, he's out walking.' He used to always be walking around."

On Tuesday all banks continued to be closed because they had declared *falliono bankado*—

bankruptcy. "We had the hyperinflation going on," said Pat. "The exchange money market went crazy. So even though the banks were closed, and there were no bank activities to the public, we had to work."

Pat still thought that Guy would think she was home and would not call her at her office. She wanted to let him know how he could get in touch with her, so she called again on Tuesday from work.

"I got no answer. I started to get a little nervous, but it was not unusual to not hear from him. He knew my home phone was out of order and he didn't know I was at work.

"On Wednesday I began to worry so I went to his place. He did not answer the bell, and I didn't have a key. Guy had a key to my place, but he never gave me a key to his place. I rang for the concierge, and his wife buzzed me into the lobby. Normally, if Guy was not in, Hugo, the concierge would let me in, but this time Hugo was not around. I asked his wife anyway for the key, and she said she was not sure where the key was or which one it was. I knew I wasn't going to get any help there, so I turned to leave. As I left the lobby, I was thinking, 'How *strange*.' I looked up at his windows and the bedroom shades were down, which he did when he wanted to rest or had an 'episode.' But the living room shade, a very big heavy shade, nearly the length of the whole living room, was down. He usually kept this shade just lowered enough to keep curious glances from the street out of the scene. I had never known him to put this shade all the way down unless he was leaving Buenos Aires. That was when I felt some relief. I remembered that our friend Eduardo Marchigianni in Cordoba was planning to come to Buenos Aires for the Labor Day weekend, and he had invited Guy and me to go back with him to Cordoba. I couldn't go because of work but Guy had talked about possibly going to spend a few days. So, I thought, 'Well, that's it. He went to Cordoba, and he couldn't call me at home to tell me because the phone was not working. And I didn't get a call from him at work because he thought I was not at the office. He couldn't even send me a *telegram*, because the main was on strike!'"

"On Thursday, May 4, the banks were open again, and I didn't hear from Guy. I started to go again to his place, but I told myself nothing has happened. I didn't want to panic, because Guy didn't like for me to call him every time I didn't hear from him. He used to get mad at me when I worried about him.

"On Friday my phone was working again. I told myself, 'He's in Cordoba, and he is going to call me today at work or tomorrow at home. I will hear some news. I could not believe he had not called, but I would not let myself think the worse. Besides, I thought if something had happened to him I would have heard by now."

Lucas came home Friday evening on May 5. His 17th birthday was Thursday, May 11, and since he would be at school, Pat planned to take him out Saturday for an early celebration. "I took him to the movies and a MacDonalds pig-out. That sort of program, you know, and when I got home, my phone was ringing. It was my brother, Ralphie.

"'Are you alone,' he said.

"'No, Lucas is with me here.'

"He said, 'Well I have something to tell you, but I don't want you to be there alone. Put Lucas on the phone.'

"'*What happened?!!*' I said.

"'Give me Lucas,' he said.

"'*Is it Mommy, Pappy?*' And he said, 'No, it's Guy.'

"And then, you know, I didn't need to hear anything else. I immediately knew what happened, because that explained the last few days."

Chapter 78

"Murió Guy Williams, El Zorro"[323]
– *Clarin,* Buenos Aires, Lunes May 8, 1989. p. 24

It was an extremely cold day for fall in Buenos Aires when on Saturday, May 6, the police answered a call at 1964 Ayacucho. Hugo, the concierge, had gone to check on Guy after his neighbor told him she sensed something was wrong. She had not heard or seen Guy in days and there was an eerie stillness around his place. Hugo took the master key upstairs and when Guy didn't answer his door, Hugo took the key from his pocket. When he slid the key into the keyhole, he pushed Guy's key out the other side. He heard Guy's key hit the floor on the inside. That's when he called the police.

Hugo entered the apartment with the police and they found Guy's body lying on the floor of the bedroom between the bed and the closet. He had one arm in his pajamas and a slipper on one foot. His head was facing the door of the bedroom. The bed covers were pulled down, as though it had been slept in. He was clean-shaven, but for his mustache. There was no sign of a struggle or foul play.

At 9:00 p.m. the police filled out their report. The building was taped off. Guards were placed outside at the front entrance, and no one was allowed in the apartment. A thorough search and investigation had to take place.

The coroner concluded that Guy had been dead five or six days. His clean-shaven face was no clue as to the time of day he died, because Guy shaved anytime he was going out. He could have slept late, and shaved late, which he had been prone to do lately.

Some believed Guy was probably feeling bad and was going to the phone in the next room. The dial on the phone by his bed was broken, so he had to use the one in the den to make calls. They think he was getting up and did not have time to put on his top and slippers.

Guy's next door neighbor knew Pat's brother, Ralphie, because he was a friend of her son's. She called Ralphie, and he called Pat while the police were still there.

Florencia, Pat's cousin, took her to the police station right away to answer questions. Since she was considered closest to Guy at the time of his death, she was the one who signed all the official papers to proceed.

"I had to tell the police and the coroner the last time I talked to Guy. It was terrible, really. It was *so* terrible. The police would not let anyone in the apartment after they investigated and removed the body. It was off limits to anyone, except Guy's immediate family or someone designated by them to go in to collect Guy's effects.

"Some of my things were in Guy's apartment, and I wanted to get a sweater I had given him to keep as a memento, but they would not let me in. I told them where Guy's address book was and they gave it to me so I could call Steve."

Pat went to her cousin Florencia house that night to spend the night. Now she had to bear the bad news to Steve in California. She knew he would have no idea who she was. "I can't remember all the conversation," said Pat. "I was still in a state of shock. I remember Steve's wife, Darlene, answered. I think I gave my name and just said I was a close friend. She told me Steve was out of town, but she could contact him, and let him know what happened."

Pat never did talk to Steve, and he never did know *who* it was who called. "I had gone to the desert with some friends where I fly my sail plane," said Steve. "It's a little town called Valyermo, southeast of Palmdale, nestled against the hills. I had a little trailer there that I stayed in on the field. I was riding my bike at night for exercise when Darlene contacted my friend. He came out on the runway. I saw him coming toward me with a flashlight and I wondered what he was doing. He told me quickly. They say that's the best way, so he flat out said, 'Darlene called. Your dad passed away.'"

Steve went home right away. Darlene had already called Toni and they went to Toni's house to spend the night together, dreading the morning when they had to tell their mother.

When morning came, Toni didn't think she could handle it. "I didn't want to go," she said, "but they decided we should all go together, so the four of us went to mom's place."

Janice buzzed them into the building. As soon as she saw them coming down the hall, she knew. "No!" she shouted, and shut the door.

"Steve went in alone and told her," said Toni. "My knees buckled when I heard my mother. Then we all went in. We called Art and his wife and Don and Barbara and they all came over and fixed pasta."

Aracelli heard the terrible news on TV. She called Carlos and then Fernando. "I got a call from Aracelli very early in the morning," remembered Carlos, " she asked me if I had heard any news about Guy lately. I said, 'No, what happened?' She began saying that no one had seen him for days and he had not answered his phone for days. I told her I would be in his neighborhood today and would call on him. And that's when she told me, 'Guy passed away, and they found him in the apartment.'"

Fernando can never forget that shocking call that came in the middle of the night. "One night, actually, very early in the morning, the telephone rang, and it was Aracelli. She told me 'Guy has died.' I was so shocked. So sad. I had lost my father, and now I had lost Guy, my second father. She told me Guy was in the morgue and someone close to him had to identify the body. The morgue was walking distance from my house, in the next block, so I said, 'OK, I will go.'"

Steve called the only person he and his mother knew well enough in Argentina who could speak English, Carlos Souto. Steve knew it was impossible to make the trip to Argentina in time for his dad's funeral. "Dad had been clear in his life that he wanted to have his ashes scattered over the Pacific Ocean, and we had confidence in Carlos to handle those details for us and take inventory of Dad's possessions."

"I told Steve that by all accounts Guy died instantly," said Carlos. "A blood vessel exploded in his head."

"I understand it was very quick when he went," said Steve, "which is the way he said he hoped it would be. I remember him saying, 'When I go, I wanna just...(snaps fingers). That's it! Then, just put my ashes in the ocean.' He got his wish."

Pat and Carlos met Fernando at the morgue on Sunday, May 7. Pat had to be there to sign the papers. "I wanted to go in and see him," said Pat, "but the doctor would not let me. I peeked from the door, though, and I saw a tuft of his hair."

Carlos tried to comfort Fernando. "I went into the room with Fernando and stood a few steps behind him as he viewed the body. Poor Fernando," he said, his voice dropping. "It was terrible for him. I embraced him, and we went out."

Guy's death certificate states that the body was identified by Patricia Goodliffe, but it was actually Fernando Lupiz who identified him, simply because the coroner wanted to spare Pat.

Due to the circumstances under which Guy died, "muerte dudosa," doubtful death, there had to be an investigation. Permission to cremate the body could not be given by the judge until the investigation was over. The long wait was disconcerting for those who knew Guy wanted to be cremated. "He told me he wanted his ashes in the sea and in the sky," said Pat. "He said, 'I want to disappear. I don't want to be left in a box.'"

Carlos explained. "In my country or any country when a person dies alone in their own home, and is not found for several days, it's mandatory by law to have an autopsy done and an investigation. This is to determine whether the person died of natural causes or whether they were murdered, etc. The autopsy report said there were no drugs or chemicals found in his body, no sign of struggle or foul play, nothing. From all signs and evidence, the coroner concluded that Guy died of natural causes, from a massive brain hemorrhage."

On a cold and windy Sunday all of Buenos Aires got the word. They listened and watched as grim-faced reporters gave the shocking and sad news about their beloved hero. Two reporters commented at the end of their report: "His Z has made a mark in our hearts forever, and we will never forget him." And, "Only Guy left; Diego de la Vega surely is immortal."

Pat went to the Casa Lazaro Costa, 2842 O'Higgins in Belgrano, and selected a beautiful tapered casket of polished ebony with gold handles. While she prepared for the "velatorio" that Sunday evening, newspapers were printing their stories for the morning editions. TV reporters surrounded the entrance of Guy's apartment building, waiting to get an interview with the concierge, his daughter, and anyone who knew Guy or had seen him lately.

Shock and dismay hung over a gray Buenos Aires. In front of 1964 Ayacucho, the tall plant on Guy's balcony whipped furiously in the chilling winds. Somber voices reviewed the history of Guy's life and his career as they expressed the grief of losing someone Argentina loved and were proud to have among them. Newspapers and newscasters were calling it a "mysterious death."

"The reason the media wrote that it was something mysterious was because he was dead for 5-6 days," said Aracelli, "and the media was trying to create a story linked to the lawsuit he was involved in. But his door was locked from the inside, so no one had access to his place. They found nothing fishy, no evidence or proof of anything, such as murder."

By Sunday evening the news of Guy's untimely death had been broadcast around the world. In Los Angeles, Guy's friend and anchorman for KTLA News, Hal Fishman, gave an emotional tribute to Guy when he announced his sudden death. Fans and friends in the United States could not have been more shocked and saddened.

Close friends in Argentina who learned of the funeral arrangements through word of mouth, filed inside the funeral parlor Sunday evening. They touched Guy's casket as they said goodbye. They made the sign of the cross, some knelt and prayed. Pat, Aracelli, Fernando, Johanna Fonseca, a former Miss Argentina who had dated Guy for a few months, Leon Balter, and relatives of those who loved Guy, were among those who were able to pay their respects on such a short notice. Eduardo Marchigianni was already on a bus to Buenos Aires to attend the funeral in the morning. Reporters from TV stations came into the visitation room to interview a grieving Patricia, who answered the best she could between her tears. Finally when asked to describe Guy Williams, the man, she thought for a moment, and replied, "The best way to describe him is simply, '*Guy Williams*.' He was unique. He was not an imitation of anyone. He was one-of-a-kind."

Fernando had one day to make Guy's funeral the best it could be. "It was my duty to bury him with honor, because Guy was like family to me," he said. "I wanted him to be buried in the Actor's Pantheon, a special place for actors in my country, until he could be cremated. It was not easy, because Guy was not an Argentinean. I had to make

Those closest to Guy gathered around his coffin. Eduardo Marchigianni, Fernando, Pat's cousin, Florencia, behind Pat with her head down, a relative of Pat's, Carlos Souto with mustache and sunglasses, Aracelli Lisazo. (courtesy of Aracelli Lisazo)

Guy's funeral procession to Chacarita cemetery on Argentina television.
(Author's personal collection)

a little noise. I called the media, and talked to lots of people to pull strings, until finally they agreed to let me put Guy temporarily in the Actor's Pantheon.

"I called the American Embassy and they gave me a big American flag to put over the coffin. They sent two representatives from the Embassy, so he would have a dignified funeral."

Monday, May 8, 1989 was the day Guy's death made headlines in all the major papers around the world. For months countless newspapers and magazines in Argentina went on and on with headlined stories about Guy and his "mysterious" death. Just a few of these articles were:

Pallbearers going into the chapel: clockwise starting front center: a representative from the American Embassy; Lucas Kirby, son of Patricia Goodliffe; Ricardo Segura; Nino Segura from the circus; Guillermo Buganem, Aracelli's husband, (she married in September 1984); and Hugo Cortina, Guy's business associate. Carlos Souto in dark glasses can be seen behind Nino Segura.

"Murió Guy Williams, Intérprete de El Zorro" – *La Nacion* – May 8, 1989
"Se Nos Fue El Zorro, héroe de toda una generación, Lloran Tornado" *El Cronista Joven* – 5-10-89 p. 8.
"La Misteriosa Muerte De El Zorro, Adios A Guy Williams, La única Derrota De El Zorro" – *Randiolandia* – May 11, 1989 No. 3165
"Murio Guy Williams, El Zorro," Confuso Deceso en departamento del la Recoleta
"Fueron inhumados los Restos de Guy Williams, Ultima morada de El Zorro," May 9, 1989 – *La Voz Del Interior*, p. 4C.
"Desde Ayer, Hay una 'Z' En El Cielo," *Cronica*
"La Triste Muerte De El Zorro" – *La Semana*, May 11, 1989
"El Zorro Nos Dejo una marca en El Corazon"
"El Zorro Quiso Morir en Argentina"
"La Inesperada Muerte De Guy Williams" – *Ahora*, #293, 18 May, 1989
"Lo Lloran Los Niños Del Mundo" – *TV Guia,* May 17, 1989
"La Vez Que Le Hizo Una *Z* a la Muerte"
"Fue Ultima Voluntad de Guy Williams" – *Cronica* – September 1, 1989,

Invitations to the funeral were printed in the Monday morning Buenos Aries newspapers, listed in separate boxes:

from Janice Williams, her children, Steve and Darlene Catalano, Toni C.W. de Anderson and Michael Anderson;
from Patricia Goodliffe and son;
from Norah Barber Jones (Pat's cousin, whom Guy knew);
from Aracelli and Fernando;
from Florencia and Alberto Urruti.

A request that donations be made to the Children's Hospital, in lieu of flowers, accompanied the invitations. By the time most people read it, the funeral was in progress or was over.

Had there been more time to plan and announce Guy's funeral, there would have been a larger attendance. However, on Monday morning, around sixty of Guy's closest friends and acquaintances, business associates and high profile celebrities turned out to honor him and say goodbye.

The procession from the funeral home to Chacarita Cemetery came to a stop outside the small chapel at the Actor's Pantheon. Grieving men, women, and children who had never met Guy Williams but loved him and would not be attending the service, gathered outside the chapel to say goodbye. They placed bouquets on top of the black hearse, until it was covered with flowers when it came to a stop.

TV reporters stood by to ask celebrities for comments. Zulma Faiad and Mirtha Le Grand were among the many legendary figures there. "He was a very nice man, a real gentleman," said Le Grand. "He had a wonderful sense of humor. He made everybody happy, especially the children." In the years after Guy had been on Le Grand's TV show for the first time, her career began to decline because of governmental changes. Some shunned her and would not be on her show, but Guy remained loyal to her.

Actor Federico Luppi, who used to have coffee with Guy occasionally, said he was a wonderful man who he always enjoyed talking to.

Leon Balter said, "He was an incredible human being and a really nice personal friend."

"I had a little funeral held at the cemetery," said Pat, "in what looks like a small chapel, with an altar and some pews. A priest said some farewell words. Even though Guy was a 'hydrogen' believer," she smiled, "he was baptized as Catholic, and as I'm also Catholic, I wanted it that way. After the ceremony, you go downstairs to the resting place."

Pallbearers were Lucas Kirby, son of Patricia Goodliffe; Guillermo Buganem, Aracelli's husband (she married him in September 1984); Hugo Cortina, Guy's business associate; an official from the American Embassy; Nino Segura, from the circus, and Ricardo, his son.

Guy was laid to rest, temporarily, in Chacarita, in crypt Number 278 with his name on a gold plaque and a vase on each side filled with yellow and white mums.

Friends gathered afterwards at Carlo Souto's house.

In Los Angeles, Guy's family and friends found it hard to come to grips with the shocking news. Janice made arrangements for a memorial service on Saturday, May 13, at St. Victor's Church where their children had gone to school, and where 18 years ago, almost to the date, Guy had been a pallbearer for Don Burnett's ex-wife, Gia.

Mayor Tom Bradley declared May 13, 1989 in Memory of Guy Williams Day. The family asked that donations be made to the Motion Picture and Television Fund, 23388 Mulholland Drive, Woodland Hills, CA 91361, in lieu of flowers.

"Amazing Grace" was sung at the intimate service and Guy's closest living friends Don Burnett and Arthur Silver gave the eulogies. There were tears and laughter as

The crypt (No. 278) at Chacarita where Guy was laid to rest for almost four months before the court granted his wish to be cremated. May 1989. (Courtesy of Patricia Goodliffe)

the two men told stories about Guy, his humor and his charming, lovable personality. Among the many in attendance with the immediate family were Guy's sister, Valerie; June Lockhart; the Ricardo Montalbans; Robert Foster; Noley Walsh Fishman and husband, Hal Fishman; Bob May of *Lost in Space;* Marge Silver; and Barbara Anderson.

Janice received hundreds of sympathy cards, many of them finding her through others such as June Lockhart. Some were from people of the golden era of *Zorro.* Edie Debney, wife of Lew Debney the publicist from Disney during the *Zorro* years, recalled happy memories with sweet and endearing sentiment about Guy.

Those who attended received a memorial card with Guy's picture on one side and a poem on the other. The poem was found by Guy's family by strange coincidence. They were going through Guy's things when they found his Book of Poetry lying on the table as he had left it. They opened it to a page that was bookmarked and found this poem. "He must have seen himself described here. *We* certainly did," said Janice. "Absolutely."

"My dad was not self-centered," said Toni. "He was not insecure. He didn't keep a journal, no chronology of his career, or pictures of himself on the wall. Just couldn't be bothered. Didn't care what people thought or said about him. Didn't dwell on what had happened. He moved on to the next thing. Looking to the future."

> A HAPPY LIFE
> How happy is he born and taught
> That serveth not another's will;
> Whose armor is his honest thought,
> And simple truth his utmost skill!
>
> Whose passions not his masters are
> Whose soul is still prepared for death,
> Not tied unto the world with care
> Of public fame or private breath;
>
> Who envies none that chance doth raise,
> Or vice; who never understood
> How deepest wounds are given by praise;
> Nor rules of state, but rules of good;
>
> Who hath his life from rumors freed,
> Whose conscience is his strong retreat;
> Whose state can neither flatterers feed,
> Nor ruin make accusers great;
>
> Who God doth late and early pray
> More of his grace than gifts to lend;
> And entertains the harmless day
> With a well-chosen book or friend;

This man is freed from servile bands
Of hope to rise, or fear to fall;
Lord of himself, though not of lands;
And, having nothing, yet hath all.

– SIR HENRY WOTTON

Everyone gathered at June's house afterwards.

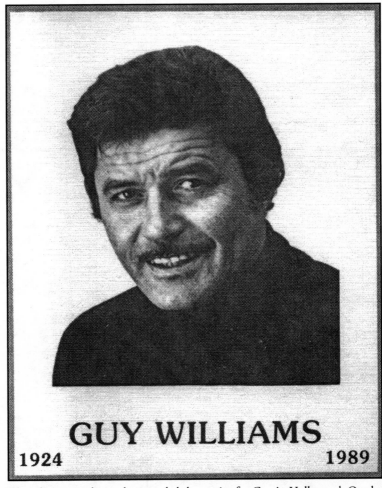

Memorial card given to those who attended the service for Guy in Hollywood. On the back is the poem, *A Happy Life* by Sir Henry Wotten. (courtesy of Kathy Gregory)

Chapter 79

"...in the middle of the silence of death...
...a silver fox crossing the road."
    – *Ambito Financiero*, May 9, 1989, an excerpt from Guy's script

In the script Guy wrote for his movie, he had Zorro killed near the end. It was Guy's way of saying he was ready to relinquish the role to Fernando, who plays his son in the movie. Guy loved the character and was grateful for all it brought to him, but he was ready to turn the spotlight on Fernando as the next Zorro. He had taught him everything he knew about the character, and now Guy was ready to retire, to enjoy life, and just be himself, Guy Williams, not Zorro or Diego. Those close to him never called him that, and forewarned others they introduced to Guy *not to call him Don Diego* or *Zorro*. Guy indicates in his script, however, that he does intend to keep the *spirit* of Zorro around, haunting and helping those in need.

Ambito Financiero (Segunda Seccion) (No. 7) Tuesday, May 9, 1989
"Guy Williams Leaves Behind a Script Which Was Never Filmed"
    Guy Williams not only had his last applause and his death in Argentina but he also had his last dream of performing in front of the camera with a black cape blowing in the wind. We know this because the script from his ambitious project of 1979 is preserved at the Museum of Cinema.
    The script was written by Williams himself. He was thinking of a co-production between Italy and Argentina, like *Los crapulas* with Lando Buzzanca, and the successful *Barbara* with Rafaella Carra.
    The movie was going to be called *Zorro, Dead or Alive*, or, better still, *Zorro, Twenty Years Later*. Somewhat like *Robin and Marion* from Richard Lester, an ironic tale about the legend of Robin Hood. In this case, Don Diego de la Vega twenty years after his famous adventures lives a peaceful life on his Rancho with his wife and son. Arriving by boat, Fernando, the son of Don Diego, has been going to school at the same college his father went to. His mother died when he was a young boy. Soon after, old enemies begin to reemerge, an ambitious governor, a dishonest colonel with abusive soldiers, high taxes. And Zorro must reemerge and fight. Then in the story,

his son discovers his father's secret identity and also discovers his inheritance (as Zorro), his destiny. During the last battle without his mask Zorro kills his adversary, but he is badly wounded and Don Diego dies. During the silence of his death, in the middle of the silence of death we hear the far off sound of waves of the ocean hitting the shore. Instead of seeing the famous image Zorro on Tornado we see a silver fox crossing the road.

This article says that Guy had found a producer, Ranato Collovati, by 1981, but:

...after several setbacks, right when it was about to take off, it was killed by the dollar.[324]

Guy's family had nothing tangible or visible for closure, only word, which made the reality of Guy's death harder to accept. Then, something very odd happened. On the morning of Guy's funeral in Argentina, Steve and Toni were with Janice at her house. They were having breakfast when the phone rang. "I was talking to someone on the phone, telling them what had happened to Guy and I kept hearing this funny noise in the house. Someone on the phone was asking the specifics about Guy's death, and while I was talking I kept thinking, '*What* is that *sound?*' When I hung up, I followed it and found that it was coming from a wall cabinet above our heads. I reached up and there was an old Rolodex of mine stored up there, and it was *spinning*! It was something Guy had given to me, during that time when he was staying with me in Santa Monica when he was going back and forth to Argentina. We were shopping and I saw this Rolodex somewhere, and thought it was really neat. I said I thought it was something I could really use for my business. Well, he went out and bought one for me. It was battery operated and when I moved here I hadn't used it. I had stored it in the wall of cabinets up high. I hadn't touched it for several years. My first impulse was to switch it off, but the kids wouldn't let me. They said, 'No. Don't touch it. Let's see what happens.' We set it out on the table and it ran for 24 hours until it eventually stopped." Janice had never believed in spirits moving things or communicating, but after this, she said, "It made a believer out of me."

Other stories told to Janice reinforced her belief that Guy was around them. June Lockhart, who does believe in ghosts, was in a theater in Cincinnati, on Sunday, May 7, 1989, starring in *Steel Magnolias*. Between the matinee and the evening show on the last day of the run of the play, everyone had gone home except June. She was the last one in the theater, sitting at her makeup mirror. "There was a mirror in front of me and a mirror to the right of me," she said. "As I looked into the mirror in front of me, my peripheral vision saw an image in the side mirror of a tall man with a single-breasted overcoat and a white scarf with a long fringe. I looked at the side mirror and no one was there. I turned again to the front mirror to put on my make up and I could see it again in my side vision. I turned again and no one was there. I thought of my father,[325] who was deceased, because the coat looked like his, but the man was too tall to be my father." June, at this point, did not know Guy had died.

"I knew some theatres had their ghosts, so I walked out of this old green room, toward the stage to see if anyone else was in the theatre. NO one. Later, before the last performance that night, I asked the stage manager if this theatre was haunted. He said no. So, I forgot about it.

"The next day I went to Washington, D.C. and it was there I heard the news of Guy's death. Later, after the memorial service I asked Jan if Guy had a coat like that, and a long white fringed scarf. She said, 'Yes.' Steve added that they still have that scarf! Well, I thought, that was really nice of the ol' boy to stop by and say goodbye."

Pat was tormented by her memories of the week before Guy's body was found. "I felt so *guilty*. I kept asking myself, 'How could I be so stupid?' Then there were all the *ifs*: *'If* only I had done this,' and, 'Why didn't I…' Or, 'I should have…,' that kind of thing, but at the time it was not so simple. I had thought of all the logical reasons why he could not get in touch with me. I was trying to think positive thoughts."

Pat had exhausted all her efforts to talk Guy into going to a doctor and take better care of himself. He would not do it. Guy would not have wanted Pat to blame herself for anything. When Gia Scala died, her best friend, and Guy's friend, William Ramage, was blaming himself for her death, because he was not with her, and possibly could have saved her. Guy said to Bill that no one should blame themselves for someone's death, because it was just meant to be.

"I kept thinking about those shades pulled down at Guy's apartment, wondering why they were down, even the large heavy one," said Pat. "My theory is that he had definitely had one of those episodes, and was not feeling well. I believe he had pulled the shade down to shut out the light and the noise. His apartment was very noisy. It sounded like the buses would pass right through his bedroom. The street was directly below his window."

Pat took a month off to go to Caracas to visit her sisters. When she returned, she went to therapy for months to reconcile herself of the guilt. She often had dreams about Guy that were so real she expected him to be there when she woke up.

Shortly after Guy died, Aracelli was hospitalized with hepatitis, which she said was brought on by the shock of Guy's death. "When I was lying in the hospital, I thought about the French girl," she said, "wondering how she was taking this. I knew how much she loved Guy, and that made me worry about her. But I never heard about her again."

Carlos, too, thought about the French girl. "One thing that got my attention was after he died she didn't write a word. She didn't appear anymore. She disappeared totally. She saw him two months before he died."

In France, Elise's parents hid the newspapers from her so she could not read the news of Guy's death for fear of what she might do. A month later she found out.

"I learned of Guy's death when I read it in a Disney magazine for kids, June 3, 1989. My parents had known, but they stopped me from hearing of it by hiding the newspapers. They also hid a letter I had sent to Guy that came back, stamped with the word *Fallecio* on it. Deceased in Spanish.

"After I heard he died, I remembered something. When I met Guy the very first time, as we said goodbye to each other, waving from the sidewalk, to one another, a funeral coach separated us. It passed on the street between us. Guy watched it and so did I, and I made a sad face to him. He went to his apartment and I went to my uncle's. It was a sign of fate.

"Soon after I heard he died, Guy sent me a message from Heaven to tell me he was in peace. A dove, a sign of peace, came to my window to sleep every night for a month."

Elise went into a deep depression. Her parents sent her to a clinic where she received counseling and occupational therapy for six months. She has not married as of this writing and remains devoted to Guy's memory.

The women from *Ahora* who had conducted the interview with Guy at the Colon Coffee house only ten days before he died, were haunted by the fact that when their article, "Like the Good Zorro, He Wants Justice," came out on May 3, Guy was not alive to see it, and nobody knew.

> "I am inconsolable. I still can't believe Guy is dead," confesses Aracelli Lisazo, through tears.
>
> "We remained good friends. He would call me frequently, just to talk about things, and the last time we talked he promised he would call me on May 1, which is my birthday. But he didn't call. I suppose it's because he had died by then."[326]

Aracelli believes Guy died on her birthday. She was in Los Toldos, her hometown, at the time, and he usually called her every year on her birthday, but this time she did not hear from him.

Pat thinks Guy died either late Sunday, April 30, some time after she spoke to him around 2:00 p.m., or possibly Monday morning, because he never answered again.

Fernando had seen Guy a few weeks before he died. Having realized it had been some time since he and Guy had gotten together, he told him he was going out of town, but when he returned he wanted to get together with Guy for dinner. Sadly, he did not call him in time. Fernando is still struggling to accept Guy's premature death, thinking that maybe the stress brought on from the scandal sheet contributed to it. "Guy was very upset to see the word 'scandal' linked to his name in headlines on the front page," said Fernando. "He was very straight, very old-fashioned, and that hurt him very much."

The reporter from *Ahora*, who had done Guy's last interview, and the photographer, who had taken the last photos of Guy, wrote a tribute to Guy in the May 18, 1989. They stated that it was so hard to believe this man, who looked so healthy and fit, was no longer with them. He was happy and seemed at a good time in his life.

The article titled "El Zorro Nos Dejo Una Marca En El Corazon, La Inesperada Muerte De Guy Williams," stated this tribute recited by Aracelli after the burial on May 8:

> Guy was an idol, a beautiful idol to millions of children the world over, but he was also a great man with a fascinating personality. He had a great sense of humor all the time; a very Yankee mind set, self discipline, responsibility, a ramrod straight approach to life. With regard to his work, he was a perfectionist, on top of every detail.
>
> He was also a very cultivated man, passionate about literature. In Argentine literature he read Borges in English, and he had a fondness for Dostoyevsky, although he regretted not being able to read him in the original language as he believed one should. He loved to recite verses from the Divine Comedy.
>
> In spite of his fame, his success, he was a man who loved to listen, to get to know others. Social status meant nothing to him.
>
> He was simple, and straightforward his whole life - for 30 years he

wore the same watch, an omega, "because it runs perfectly." It was not his custom to discuss money matters; he was very closemouthed about it. He never spoke about his own finances and although he wasn't much on giving presents, he always gave when someone asked for a loan or a favor.

She recalled Guy's great wit. "Guy asked me once if I knew how Yassir Arafat got his name. He said, when he was a baby his mama would rock him and sing, 'Yaa-suh, That's my baa-by.'" She laughed. "Guy was so funny that way, but he would say, 'I'm not funny, I'm witty.' That was his favorite word."

Chapter 80

"Ashes to the Ocean and the Sky"

– Carlos Souto

Months went by before the investigation of Guy's death was finalized. Those who had personal belongings in Guy's apartment, Fernando, Pat, Aracelli, could not retrieve them, as no one was allowed in Guy's apartment except his immediate family, until the investigation was over.

Everyone, from close friends to the general public, hoped Guy's children would come to Argentina to finalize his affairs. But neither were able to come. Decisions had to be made to the best of Carlos' ability.

"Steve asked me to oversee the things of his father here," tells Carlos. "By the time I was allowed into the apartment, after all the investigation, many of Guy's things were missing: his Nikon camera, his binoculars, a small Sony walkman, his practice sword (Fernando's), and his .38 caliber gun, which he kept in a drawer. All of his clothes and shoes were well worn, but he had some jewelry."

The jewelry Carlos found consisted of a pair of expensive cufflinks Janice had given Guy after they were married (fortunately, they were still on a dress shirt in his closet or they might have been missing too); his watches, an omega with a black leather band, and an omega he wore for dress with a stretch band, which he was wearing when he died.

"Carlos reported to us that there was really little of value there," said Steve. "Apparently, many things had disappeared once the police had gained access. We arranged for certain items to be given to certain parties there, and some minor personal effects to be sent home to us."

Lucas Kirby, Pat's son, to this day, holds resentment and hostility toward the Buenos Aires police for the disappearance of many of Guy's things.

Pat was not made aware that Carlos had entered the apartment so she was not given the opportunity to retrieve her things.

Finally, Judge César Quiroga gave permission for Guy's body to be cremated. Pat signed the permitto cremeate, and she and Carlos began making arrangements to carry out Guy's last wish. All attention was toward Toni and Steve. Would they come to Buenos Aires for the final farewell?

"At first there was the possibility that Steve might come," said Carlos, "and I said to him, 'You just call me, and I will pick you up at the airport. You have a room to stay at my house. I will take you to the cemetery where you father is buried, and, if you want,

Fernando went to Chacarita to have Guy's body exhumed to grant his
last wish that he be cremated.

I will make a memorial at my house. With good friends. Not to make a funeral, not
something sad, but to make a reunion, to remember what a good person he was, to be
something full of love to Guy.' Steve said 'I will call you and tell you.' Well, later he
called and said he could not come. He asked me to please send him the ashes.

"After that, I went to the funeral home, and I told them that I had to incinerate the
body, and send it back to the United States. I had to choose the little box for the ashes,
and that was a very sad thing for me to do," his voice somber, as though it was yesterday.
"The funeral home, which is a very important place in Buenos Aires, took care of everything through the Embassy and the cemetery, whatever had to be done."

"I wish I could have gone," said Steve. "I was curious about it. I wanted to go down
there to resolve things, but I was so busy up here.

"I had an office at City Hall at this time, as a political and land use consultant (a.k.a.
lobbyist) in the City of Los Angeles," reflected Steve. "I worked primarily in getting large
high-rise development projects through various local government processes. Most of my
projects were in downtown Los Angeles and other urban center areas like Warner Center,
Hollywood and so forth. I just couldn't see getting away. Not only did I have several
pending projects in L.A. that I was juggling, but also the cost of the trip was a concern. It
was so expensive. It's a long way. I couldn't afford it. So Carlo helped us. We had an
attorney here working with an attorney down there."

Pat in particular was most disappointed. "I was expecting Steve to come for the
cremation," she said, "so I was disappointed to hear he couldn't manage to come. He
didn't even know of me, but for me, it was as if I had known him for a very long time. I
wanted to tell him how many hours Guy spent telling me about him, and how proud
he was of him. I had hoped we could go to the apartment together, and I would have

been able to get back my personal belongings. They were lost. I have no idea what happened to them. All I have is an old tee shirt Guy used to like to wear when he was at my place. But I don't need those things, really. I have my memories."

Pat cherishes a ring Guy gave her. It was lost in 1999, and miraculously found about a year later.

Guy's last request was carried out at the end of August. For their final farewell, Pat, Fernando, and Aracelli went to La Chacarita to witness and conduct the removal of Guy's coffin from its crypt to be transported to the crematory. A panel truck was waiting, the coffin was placed inside and ready to go, but before the doors were closed, Pat jumped inside the truck for one last moment with Guy. "I knew this was the last time I would ever be this close to Guy, so I got into the back of the truck to say my last goodbye, alone." When she was finished the threesome clung to each other as the doors closed and they watched the truck go out of sight.

Cremaron Restos De El Zorro
Crónica – September 1, 1989
Fue Ultima Voluntad de Guy Williams
The legendary "El Zorro," the unmatched creation of artist, Guy Williams, loved by children all over the world, once again was recalled from his legend world, when this morning his remains were cremated at La Chacarita Cemetery.

Bidding their last farewell, Pat, Fernando, and Aracelli watch the truck carrying Guy's body to the crematory as it goes out of sight. (courtesy of Aracelli Lisazo)

This is how his last wish was fulfilled, for which Miss Patricia Goodliffe was granted the authorization of the deceased actor's kids, who are living in the North Country.

In a bright morning, *Cronica* joined the others at the ceremony steps. From now on, El Zorro's ashes are waiting to be sent to the United States, to his beloved Los Angeles, that saw him arrive years ago and rise to achieve universal fame, together with his horse "Tornado," his invincible sword, and the unique Sergeant Garcia.

In California, the last step of his wishes will be accomplished when his ashes will be spread over the Pacific waters and the mountains, where his adventures took him riding for the imaginations of grown ups and kids, throughout the plains where his enemies awaited him, and whom he defeated, confirming our faith in Justice and good will.

When that happens, when his ashes are taken by the wind over the ocean waters and the Californian mountain tops, the image of the charming "Don Diego de la Vega" character with which Guy Williams protected El Zorro's identity, will be appearing in the horizon.

Ms. Goodliffe told *Cronica* that in order to complete the incineration a judicial order which she enforced, was necessary. Previously, Guy Williams' kids, who live in the United States, respectfully agreed and will be the ones to carry out the last part of their father's wish.[327]

A friend of Steve's was flying to Argentina to visit his family and would pick up the ashes and personal effects for Steve. Carlos said, "I gave Steve's friend the ashes, all the papers about the lawsuit, Guy's jewelry, and I took him to see the clothes. Guy's clothes were well worn so he did not take the clothes."

Guy did not like to shop. He had a limited wardrobe, but what he bought was made to last. He was comfortable with what he had, and felt he didn't need more. Guy never gave up his Luteral leather jacket—the one that matched Janice's. Even when the leather on the elbows had frayed and Pat teased him calling it in Spanish "the worn-out upholstery" and "the old sofa," he still wore it.

"Well," said Carlos, "this fellow went back with the ashes, Guy's jewelry, and just a few of Guy's things. That's all. When the lawsuit was final, I collected the small amount, not much, just a few thousand or so, and sent that to Steve."

The magazine had claimed bankruptcy and hardly paid at all.

In Malibu, California, Janice stood on the beach in front of their friend's house where Guy had often visited. Her eyes were searching the sky. The small plane came into view. Moments later, Steve released his father's ashes and the gentle winds took them to the mountain tops and the calm blue waters of the Pacific Ocean he so loved. The waves kissed the shore and quietly crawled toward Janice's feet. Finally there was closure.

A few days later, Carlos got a call from Steve. "He told me they threw the ashes to the ocean and the sky from a small plane. I think it was a really beautiful thing to do."

Epilogue

"He was a good man."

— Janice Williams and friends

Don Diamond recalled how he just missed getting in touch with his old friend after more than twenty-five years. Regrettably, it was not meant to be. "I went to Argentina in 1988 and before I left the United States, I tried to locate Guy's ex-wife, a very lovely lady, and I couldn't find her," said Don. "So, I get in touch with SAG and they say they don't have an address. I get down there, I go to the American consulate in Buenos Aires. They can't give it to me. They know it, but they can't give it to me. I come back home, and I'm talking on my ham radio set with some Argentines talking about Guy Williams, when two guys interrupt. They work for a TV station there and they are going to send me his address. Then, within days, I read in the paper that he died."

Those two would have had a wonderful time reminiscing. "I used to sail with him and his family. I had a tiny sail boat, not big like Guy's. Guy was a good friend. A very educated man."

Don Burnett couldn't expound enough on Guy's contribution to television as the best Zorro ever. "It's amazing to see those *Zorro* shows on television. They were running some on the Disney Channel when we were in New Mexico and we saw them. Jiminy Crickets! He was really terrific! Nobody could do that show now, and there's nobody I know of who could do what he did at that time. I mean nobody had that *flair*. No other young actor was driving around town in a brand-new fire engine red Maserati at that time. He was a cut from the old Errol Flynn kind of guy. That *flair about life* is what shows on the screen and makes the series so good. I saw *Zorro* recently—it still holds up, because it's honest. Guy is honest in it."

Don Burnett retired and became a full-time artist, like his father who was a professional illustrator and painter. His landscape and seascape paintings are found in galleries in Santa Fe, New Mexico and Carmel, CA. He remains a part of Guy's family.

Leon Balter reminisced about his wonderful days with Guy. After Guy's first two visits to Argentina, Guy and Leon had established themselves as eating buddies, and got together to feast every chance they had. "We started a 'pilgrimage' through many restaurants of Buenos Aires, between 1974 through 1978 whenever they came to visit.

"Between 1978 and 1982, I was contracted by Editorial Abril as the U.S. West Coast correspondent for their 23 magazines, and I made my headquarters in Northridge, CA. I met with Guy on a couple of opportunities. We visited him at his residence in Marina del Rey, where Betty and I were invited for a dinner. Janice made a great dinner for us. I interviewed Guy for the Argentinean magazines. He called me to come to his place in Marina del Rey, to try something. That 'something' was a big complete provolone cheese, that was 'cured' with whiskey. Guy, as usual, did a good job!

"After I returned to Buenos Aires, in 1982, we kept in touch very often by phone. My residence was close to Guy's apartment. He loved to walk many city blocks. I also liked to do the same, so every Saturday afternoon, as a ritual, Guy walked from his residence, Recoleta sector, through my sector, and continued his walk to the telephone company, to phone Janice, and sometimes other persons (probably his children and a producer of Disney Studios who was a very good friend of his.)

"Among many topics, we liked to talk about was U.S. politics. He never liked Ronald Reagan. He laughed about Reagan becoming a U.S. president. Guy was a stubborn democrat, in the same way I was a stubborn republican! But, we had a good relationship. Guy always called me 'Kiddo.' We liked each other as friends. We were very honest with each other. It wasn't any material interest, just friendship."

Interviewed after Guy's death in May 1989, June said, "Guy was a dear, dear man. A delight! Guy was the funniest man. He was lusty and bright. He was a great chess player, and he was a brilliant musicologist, too. We had such a neat time working together. He was just a GRAND colleague. We enjoyed each other's company so much."[328]

In the early 1990s collector shows sprang up all over the nation. Most popular were the *Star Trek* conventions, but others carried a Sci-Fi or Classic TV theme. The cast of *Lost in Space* was invited to many of these.

At a *Lost in Space* convention in 1992 in New Jersey, June spoke to a crowd and remembered Guy. "After the memorial service, the *Lost in Space* family, Billy, Angela, Marta, their husbands and wives, took the Williams family out for a dinner. We had known the Williams children as we were doing the show. It was kind of neat, because we all got to sit around and talk about how much we loved 'Guido,' which is what we called him on the set." Having never heard of anyone ever doing this before, June felt the occasion may be unprecedented in Hollywood.

Co-star Mark Goddard tipped his hat to Guy on a PBS TV show produced by Perry Corvese in Boston in 1995: "I'd like to say that Guy's memory will live with the cast of *Lost in Space* for as long as we're around. He was a very special person and he'll be missed deeply. He had a wonderful family and he was a wonderful man. He contributed greatly to our entertainment, not only in *Lost in Space*, but also in *Zorro* and in *Bonanza*, and other epics that he did as an actor. You're missed, Guy. June, Marta, Billy, Angela, Jonathan and Bobby May and myself, we send you our love."[329]

On the same tribute show to Guy Williams, Bill Mumy said: "Guy Williams was a close friend of mine for several years. One of the biggest inspirations in my life. He inspired me to get into acting in his role as Zorro. He was a great gentlemen, a noble man, a funny man, and he'll be sorely missed."

At StarCon, July 1997, in Pasadena, CA, they sat at long tables signing autographs and sometimes on a panel answering questions from the fans. Someone in the audience always asked a question about the handsome father, John Robinson, and the cast loved to remember Guy:

"When did Guy Williams die?" someone asked.

June replied, "He died in April 1989."[330]

Bobby May, interjected: "Too SOON! I gotta say this. I really felt this way about Guy Williams. Guy Williams was the class act of our show. He was a friend to everybody and he gives us class."

June: "He was a good man."

Francine York, Queen Nolani in episode #54, "The Colonists": "He was nice to work with. And he was *beautiful*. I mean, he *looked* like a movie star!"[331]

Marta: "And he was a gentleman. He was really Something. And we miss him. We got together after he passed away and had a special dinner with his wife and son and daughter in memory of Guy."

Someone in the audience asked June Lockhart if she thought Guy would like doing these public appearances with them. June answered, "Oh, he'd love this. He would be right here having a great time."

At another convention, Jonathan Harris, who always had good things to say about Guy, said: "He was a wonderful, wonderful man. Delightful to work with."

One memorable event took place in Beverly Hills, commemorating the launch date of the fictional Jupiter II. In the first episode of *Lost in Space,* the Robinson family was launched into space on the Jupiter II on October 16, 1997, a date randomly picked. When that date finally rolled around, thirty-two years later, Kevin Burns of 20th Century-Fox, arranged a gala reunion for the cast of *Lost in Space* and invited guests at the Museum of Television and Radio in Beverly Hills.

Members of the cast pulled up in limousines, which readily drew a crowd on the street and in the lobby. One excited couple from England had heard of the event and flew in to see the cast in person.

The lobby displayed a six-foot model of the Jupiter II, and the actual robot from the show, refurbished by Kevin Burns, a fan and executive at 20th Century.

There was a special screening of the *Lost in Space* pilot that never aired on television, followed by comments and discussions by the cast, and Shelia Allen, wife of Irwin who had passed away in 1991 at age 75.

Guy's sudden death didn't allow his children a final word with him. Each one pondered what they would tell him if they could see him one more time. Steve said, "To this day I think about things he said to me, and I tell myself, 'You know, he's right about that.' Or, 'So *that's* why he said that.' If I could see him again, I would tell him that he was *right*. But then, I wouldn't have to tell him, because he would have known it," he laughed.

"I would tell him," said Toni, "that as an adult, I appreciate the things he gave us and did for us like the music and the things that he introduced us to, things that you just take for granted and you just don't think about. You don't think to thank people. He taught us so much culture and awareness of what is out there in the world and he really worked hard to do that."

Reflecting on Guy and his career, Janice brought to mind something that only a person living with Guy throughout his career would know. "He had a LOT of disappointments in his career. People don't think of that, because they see him as being famous for Zorro, but he had a lot of disappointments," she said. Janice understands that many of Guy's actions, decisions, and behavior later in his life evolved from those disappointments. She understands how he liked the attention and rejuvenation Argentina gave him. She reiterates what so many others say, "He was a good man."

In 1998 the *Lost in Space* movie was realized, but with an all-new cast and a more modern world. June Lockhart played Will's teacher, Marta Kristan and Angela Cartwright played reporters who ask questions at a press conference with the Robinsons.

That same year, 1998, *The Mask of Zorro* opened in movie theaters, starring Anthony Hopkins as an aging Zorro. With a basic storyline that closely resembled Guy's script, the movie starred Antonio Banderas, as the man El Zorro trains to take over his duties.

As fate would have it, the only two TV shows Guy had starred in were not only made into movies, but were released in the *same* year, and *both* were nominated for Academy Awards for best costumes in the same year. Those costumes were on display at FIDM (Fashion Institute of Design and Merchandising) in Los Angeles before the winners were announced. Moreover, the mannequins were facing each other across the aisle in the showroom. If Guy could have been there, he could have stood in one spot and seen *Zorro* to the right of him and *Lost in Space* to the left of him. He would have liked those odds. It was a remarkable piece of serendipity for any Guy Williams fan.

The year 2000 saw the beginning of ongoing efforts, and achievements, to honor Guy Williams with plaques, monuments, a postage stamp, charity contributions and anything that could get his name and memory to the public. Undaunted fans have achieved several goals aspired for Guy in the last few years.

On May 20, 2000, due to the effort of devoted fans, Guy was given a place on the Bronx Walk of Fame. On the Grand Concourse, a street sign that bears his name, was the first ever to be awarded posthumously to a famous celebrity born in the Bronx.

Sonny Hudson (alias Johnny Guitar/Johnny Inzillo), who once had a crush on Guy's sister, attended with his daughter, Gabriella, who was in a Zorro costume. They met Steve/Guy Williams, Jr. for the first time.

In 1995 Janice had a dream. Guy was carrying a small boy and walked toward Janice and said, "This is for Toni." A few months later Toni was pregnant and had a beautiful, bright baby boy. She named him after her father Armand. Nicknamed Nando for a character "Nando Hamilton" who stole the show in *It Started in Naples*, Nando was born on April 28, 1996, exactly seven years to the date that Guy was last seen.

In time, Pat Goodliffe met Toni on a trip to the United States. She brought with her a gift for little Nando, something that had belonged to Guy. It was Guyucho, the little bear she had bought at the New York Met for Guy. Guyucho had lived at Guy's house until one day near the end of 1988 when Pat had an argument with Guy, she took the bear back. Had she not done so, it would have been lost with all his other items when he died. Now, it was all she had of Guy to give to his grandson.

On August 2, 2001 came the crowning jewel. Guy got a star on the Hollywood Walk of Fame,[332] something his fans had wanted for years. Due to their persistence, and

Guy's star on The Hollywood Walk of Fame at 7080 Hollywood Blvd at La Brea Ave.
(photo by Mary Spooner; courtesy of Mary Spooner)

the help of Guy's family and friends, Guy's star on Hollywood Boulevard was achieved. Fans flew in from all corners of the United States including Hawaii, and other countries around the world: Italy, France, Spain, Belgium, Holland, Australia, and Argentina.

Johnny Grant, the honorary mayor of Hollywood, proclaimed August 2, 2001 *Guy Williams Day*. His was the 2,183[rd] star on the internationally famous sidewalk. Those who knew Guy said he would have *loved* it.

A reception followed at the Hollywood Roosevelt Hotel, hosted by Guy's family, for hundreds of fans and actors who worked with Guy. All had come together to celebrate Guy's life and achievements. Sentimental comments and anecdotes were given about Guy by some members of the cast of *Zorro* and *Lost in Space,* as well as fans.[333]

With a thick head of white hair and a big smile, Melone Tanzini, who had sold Guy the souvenir newspaper on Olvera street in 1957, came to the celebration with an armful of copies of the paper, which pleased fans who bought them.

On October 25, 2002 a bench in Central Park, near the Columbus Statue, was acquired by fans and dedicated to Guy Williams. A plaque on the bench reads:

OUT OF THE NIGHT CAME MAGIC
Guy Williams (1924-1989)
THE FRIENDS OF ZORRO AND JOHN ROBINSON
SALUTE THE PARK GUY AND JANICE LOVED

Janice and Steve flew to New York for the dedication along with several fans from coast-to-coast. A play about Zorro was in Queens at the time, and the actor who played Zorro dropped by in costume for photo ops.

On August 2, 2003, another tribute took place at the Mission San Luis Rey in Oceanside, California, the location for several *Zorro* episodes in 1957, and a beautiful retreat. Fans donated a bench in the garden next to the chapel and dedicated it to Guy.

This plaque, dedicated to Guy Williams by his fans, is under a bench at the Mission San Luis Rey near the chapel where several *Zorro* episodes were filmed in Oceanside, CA..
(courtesy of Jill Panvini)

A sentimental plaque was installed, with an inscription that reads:
In Loving Memory of Guy Williams
The One and Only "Zorro"
1924-1989
You carved a "Z" in our heats and changed our lives forever.
Your friends salute you!
August 2, 2003

Located only a few feet from the bell tower where Guy had filmed several scenes, it serves to honor and keep the memory alive of a man who brought joy to many generations and continues to do so. Janice, Steve, Toni, and Nando attended, along with fans who came from all over the United States. Elise flew in from France for this and for the Star ceremony, when she met Guy's family for the first time.

Fans contributed in Guy's name to the Families of Freedom Scholarship Fund Project for the children whose parents died in the World Trade Center and the Pentagon on 9/11. They bought limited editions of commemorative items bearing Guy's image and signature, and the monies went to the Fund.

Fans continue to think of ways to immortalize Guy and do good for others in his name. Several tributes are in the works. Most recent was a large sum of money given to the Shriners in Guy's name toward a Children's hospital.

The accolades about Guy have never stopped. William Ramage said, "I loved Guy. Anyone who knew Guy loved him. He was a sweet and generous man. He sat next to me at Gia's funeral and got me through the day. He was a tower of strength for me."

In Argentina's *TV Guia*, May 17, 1989, in an article titled "Lo Lloran los Niños del Mundo,"[334] Fernando gave tribute:

"Fue un Ser Maravilloso"

He was a wonderful human being. One of the things which struck me was his quality of warmth and kindness. Always ready to offer his willing hand to anyone who needed help, Guy well knew how to harvest the loyalty and affection of everyone who surrounded him.

It seems an exaggeration, but Diego de la Vega's personality was made flesh in Williams. Like El Zorro, he couldn't stand injustice and on some occasions even seemed ingenuous. He was a wonderful man and I feel this death of his to be most lamentable because he was a great man who nevertheless never tried to hide that little kid that we all carry around inside us. I want to remember him that way, always happy, always with a good disposition, and showing everybody the never-ending project of the script that would immortalize him in his adventurous life in the movie.

Here he made friends and turned his life around. ... he met Patricia Goodliffe, with whom he maintained a tender relationship for some time. A short time after his death it was stated that he had been living in poverty. Other people however, affirm that Guy was well off and that he lived on the money he made from stocks he kept on the New York Stock Exchange. It was also said that he owned land in Mendoza. What was written in the police report matters very little to those who affectionately remember that paladin of justice. Only death could vanquish his glorious blade.[335]

Years later Fernando kept his promise to Guy by taking over the role of El Zorro to the best of his ability, using everything he had learned from the master. He achieved this goal by putting on a first-class stage production of Zorro that Guy would have been proud of. Produced by the brilliant Alejandro Romay, and directed by the renown Claudio Hochman, two of Argentina's most important talents, it was spectacular in special effects and outstanding fencing. The show was completely choreographed by Fernando, who plays Zorro and also had a hand in the production and lyrics. Complete with a full orchestra, it opened in June 2000 to a roaring success on Corrientes Avenue, the Broadway of Buenos Aires. Although the storyline was a new version, it followed the basic story of the TV show. In one scene, Fernando fences with two swords, dazzling the audience with a fantastic display of sword fighting. Since the success of his ongoing play and his TV show, on which Guy's Zorro episodes are shown, Fernando is greeted on the streets as El Zorro, keeping Guy's memory alive.

Fernando had fulfilled a prophesy made by a reporter in 1978 when he and Guy had been interviewed numerous times during their circus acts. The reporter said, "Who knows, perhaps we have here the Zorro of 2000!" Fernando thought nothing of it, after all Guy Williams, the man sitting at his side was Zorro, and 2000 was too far away to even think about.

On opening night, after a standing ovation, Fernando took center stage and addressed the audience. He announced that the show was dedicated to one man, Guy Williams, his friend and mentor. With his sword raised and his eyes to the heavens, he said, "Guy, this is for you." There was not a dry eye in the house.

That same year, his own FL Productions took the show to Mar del Plata and each year since then. As of this writing, the show continues to be sold out for each performance in Buenos Aires, and Mar del Plata. Guy continues to be Fernando's inspiration. His acting career on TV and in movies continues to be active.

This sensitive graphite drawing made by Kathy Nance in 1999 is just one example of the talent many discovered they had when they were first inspired to draw Guy's face. It's another way he touched so many people. (courtesy of Kathy Nance. www.kathynance.com.)

In 1992 Aracelli was nearly killed in an auto accident on a lonely dark road outside Buenos Aires. Carlos remembered. "She hit a horse in the middle of the night with her little car," said Carlos. "The hoof of the horse came through the window and hit her in the face. I went to the hospital to see her and I really was shocked, because all of her face was black. It was terrible, terrible. The back of her seat broke and that is what saved her. It was a miracle. God didn't want her to die. She had to have surgery on her face. It was a terrible time for her."

Aracelli has no scars on her face, but the accident changed her looks. "I had a lot of plastic surgery. One side of my face looks chubbier than the other, but almost everyone has something chubbier than the other. I have some difficulty chewing and swallowing, but, in general, I'm OK. I had 19 fractures in my face," she said, "I had my accident at night on January 10, 1992, my father's birthday, and I was in a coma. And on January 14, Guy's birthday, I came out of my coma."

After she recovered, she traveled a lot and was in plays mostly for children. For the past few years she has lived in Mexico City, and helps her famous actor brother, Saul Lisazo, in his popular restaurant, Piantao. Childless, she spends a lot of time playing with her little niece and nephew.

Patricia Goodliffe continues to work for the bank, and never married. She is devoted to Guy's memory and protects his image. TV and radio stations contact her from time to time to talk about Guy when they have retrospective shows on Zorro. Her son, Lucas Kirby, is a successful professional photographer in Mexico City, who says he owes the beginning of his interest and inspiration to Guy and his Nikon, when he taught young Lucas how to use it.

With Argentina in such poor economic state, Carlos Souto moved to Costa Rica where he could make a living and support his family. He loves to talk about his old friend, and hopes his memory will live forever. "As long as we talk about him, he is alive," he said.

For Janice Williams, Guy was and is the love of her life. Family and friends will tell you that for Guy she was the love of his life, as well. Today she finds fulfillment in her grandson, Nando, who is "a chip off the old block." She continues to work and feels Guy's presence with her every day.

Guy Williams lives in the hearts and minds of each generation who sees his work. His delightful portrayal of Zorro continues to be seen on TV all over the globe, in videos and DVDs, as well as his stoic John Robinson of *Lost in Space,* leaving a lasting impression. But in the minds and hearts of most, he *is* El Zorro—the *only* Zorro. He is the good guy, the one who comes to the rescue of the meek and the poor. He is *The A-Team* rolled up in one. He is the rogue, the romantic, the playful, the caring. In the annals of television history, he represents the quintessential hero of the ages, and all without being from another planet or morphing into a creature, but with spiritual or supernatural guidance. He was Real. And most of that portrayal WAS Guy Williams.

As long as there is television he will be among us, smiling that broad smile that is only his, entertaining the world.

Anna Maria (Jolene Brand), in episode 42, asks him, "Will I ever see your face?" In his words, as Zorro, Guy replies, "You have only to look about you."[336]

Guy Williams as Zorro.

Author's Note

This book is a tribute to Guy Williams, a unique talent and individual. It was written to celebrate Guy's life, and to give insight into his personality so people who didn't get the chance to meet him could get to know him.

To know and love Guy's work is to love him. When a man is constantly described as good, humorous, kind, wonderful, sensitive, gentle, loving, and always a gentleman, you know he is loved no matter what his human imperfections. It takes a special person with a bright light within to do that, and Guy Williams was that kind of special human being. They don't come around too often.

Ashley, a 12-year-old *Zorro* fan, who posted to my internet Guest list, so eloquently reminds us:

"When I watch *Zorro*, I always remember that it is not the man behind the mask who makes Zorro, it's the heart of the man that makes Zorro."

Z

Guy Williams:
Film, TV, and Personal Appearances

<u>MOTION PICTURES:</u> (With release dates, if known)

The March of Time – Vol. 11, No. 9 – "The Returning Veteran" 1946 (Short)

The March of Time – Vol.16 No. 1A "Mid-Century Half-Way To Where?" 1946**
    (Short) (Guy in short clip from Vol. 11 No. 9,   "The Returning Veteran")

The Beginning or the End – Feb. 19, 1947

Bonzo Goes to College – Sept. 1952

Back at the Front – Oct. 15, 1952

The Mississippi Gambler – Jan. 29, 1953

Take Me to Town – May 1953

House Party – 1953 (Short)

All I Desire – June 1953

The Man From the Alamo – July 1953

The Golden Blade – Aug. 12, 1953

Seven Angry Men – March 27, 1955

Sincerely Yours – Nov. 1, 1955

The Last Frontier – Dec. 7, 1955 (released as *Savage Wilderness*)

I Was a Teenage Werewolf – June 19, 1957

Zorro, the Avenger – 1959 (released overseas)

The Sign of Zorro – June 11, 1960

The Prince and the Pauper – March 11, 1962 (three parts for television)

Damon and Pythias – June 1962

Captain Sindbad – June 19, 1963

Roger and Me – Sept. 27, 1989 (clip of Guy as Zorro in a parade in Flint, Michigan
    1958 for the 50th anniversary of General Motors)

<u>STAGE PLAYS:</u>

Kenley Players at Lakewood (PA) Summer Theater – *Pal Joey* – Summer 1950

Kenley Players at Lakewood (PA) Summer Theater – *Fledermaus* – June 11-16,1951

Kenley Players at Lakewood (PA) Summer Theater – *Rain* – July 16-21, 1951

LIVE APPEARANCES:

7-Up luncheon, NY, mid-April 1958

Zorro, Disneyland, April 26-27, 1958 (first appearance)

Zorro, John Tracy Clinic for the Deaf Children, Saturday Bazaar, Anaheim, CA, May 24, 1958

Zorro, Disneyland, May 30-June 1, 1958

Zorro, Junior Rose Festival Parade, Grand Marshal, Portland, Oregon, June 13, 1958

Zorro, Grand Floral Parade, Portland, Oregon, June 14, 1958

Zorro, International 7-Up Convention, St Louis, Missouri, Oct. 10-11, 1958

Zorro, Disneyland, Nov. 27-30, 1958

Zorro, 50th Anniversary of General Motors, Flint, Michigan, 1958

Zorro, Rose Bowl Parade, Pasadena, California, Jan. 1, 1959

Zorro, Terrace Gardens, Lagoon, Kaysville, Utah, June 17, 1959

Zorro, Baseball Game, Dodgers (3) vs Pirates (0), Forbes Field, Pittsburgh, Pennsylvania, July 15, 1959

Zorro, Disneyland, Nov. 26-29, 1959

Zorro, Plaza Theater, *Sign of Zorro* Premiere, El Paso, Texas, June 11, 1960

Zorro, Disneyland, Nov. 11-13, 1960

TELEVISION

Studio One – "The Paris Feeling" – Dec. 31, 1951 (sponsored by Westinghouse)

Hey, Mulligan! (a.k.a. *The Mickey Rooney Show*) – "The Average Man" – Feb. 25, 1955

Four Star Playhouse – "Trudy" – May 26, 1955

The Lone Ranger – "Six-Gun Artist" – June 23, 1955

Damon Runyon Theater – "Big Shoulders" – June 25, 1955

Cameo Theatre – "Bending of the Bough" – July 17, 1955

Highway Patrol –
    "Plane Crash" – Feb. 20, 1956
    "Runaway Boy" – May 28, 1956
    "Harbor Story" – March 12, 1957
    "Officer's Wife" – April 8, 1957

DuPont Cavalcade Theater – "Decision for a Hero" – Feb. 7, 1957

State Trooper – "No Fancy Cowboys" – March 17, 1957

Pepsi Commercial (during intermission of Rodgers and Hammerstein's *Cinderella* starring Julie Andrews) – March 31, 1957

Code 3 – "Bail Out" – May 18, 1957

Men of Annapolis –
> "Sea Wall" – Oct. 24, 1957
> "Crucial Moment" – Nov. 21, 1957

Disneyland's 4th Anniversary Show – Sept. 15, 1957 (Walt Introduces El Zorro to the Mousketeers)

Sgt. Preston of the Yukon – "Generous Hobo" – Jan. 2, 1958 (but filmed before *Zorro*)

Zorro – Oct 10, 1957- July 2, 1959

Walt Disney Presents – *Zorro*
> "El Bandido" – Oct. 30, 1960
> "Adios El Cuchillo" – Nov. 6, 1960
> "The Postponed Wedding" – Jan. 1, 1961
> "Auld Acquaintance" – April 2, 1961

Here's Hollywood (1961)** 15-min. segment. Jack Linkletter visits Guy and family at his house.

Bonanza –
> "Return to Honor" – March 22, 1964
> "The Roper" – April 5, 1964
> "The Companeros" – April 19, 1964
> "The Pressure Game" – May 10, 1964
> "Triangle" – May 17, 1964

Lost in Space – Sept. 15, 1965 – March 6, 1968

You Don't Say – March 7-11, 1966 (with June Lockhart)

Password – June 19-23, 1967 (with Irene Ryan)

Dream Girl of '67 – April 3-7, 1967 (with Shari Lewis, David Hedison and Noel Harrison)

The Woody Woodbury Show – 1968

The Jerry Lewis Telethon – Sept. 2-3, 1973

The Wonderful World of Disney, 25th Anniversary, NBC, Sept. 13, 1978 (Guy in a clip as Zorro)

Family Feud – April 15, 1983 – (with *Lost in Space* castmates: June Lockhart, Marta Kristen, Angela Cartwright, Bob May)

Good Morning America – Sept. 8, 1983 (with Adam West, Van Williams, Kirby Grant)

(Cable) *David Halverstam's The Fifties – Vol.3*, "Let's Play House," a documentary for the History Channel, Nov. 30, 1997 (Guy in clip from *March of Time*, Vol. 11 No. 9, "The Returning Veteran")

Endnotes

1. JOHNSTON MCCULLEY' *Curse of Capistrano* had sold 1,200,000 copies since 1919. *The Mark of Zorro* (1924) sold 95,000 copies that year. Fairbanks brought the character to life on the silent silver screen in 1920.

2. *New York Times*, January 14, 1924, first section, p 17.

3. PMA closed in 1968 and fell victim to the wrecking ball. Only the administration building still stands with the old oak.

4. It is believed that Joseph had more than three sons, but they are not known to this author.

5. *Sunday News*, Los Angeles, *Tuning In on TV*, "'Z'Man Guy Williams leaves his mark as star of TV's Zorro", by May Okon, p. 4, August 2, 1959.

6. *TV Guia*, July 1987, "El Zorro Hoy en Argentina"

7. Ken Mayer interview. WBZ radio talk show, September 1983, Boston, MA.

8. From a recording of Guy at his home.

9. *Movie Stars Parade, TV Close-Ups*, "Four Faces of Love" September 1958

10. Racetrack in Queens before it was replaced by Aqueduct.

11. *Télé 7 Jours*, French TV Guide, October 1986. "After Thirty Years, We Found Zorro!"

12. *New York Times*, "*Mark on Zorro*", April 11, 1958 by Harriet Van Horne.

13. Doug Warren quit acting and became a successful writer of novels, screen plays, and celebrity biographies.

14. *Life* magazine, September 2, 1946.

15. *Life* magazine, July 15, 1946.

16. *The MGM Story, The Complete History of Fifty Roaring Years*, by John Douglas Eames, Crown Publishers, Inc, New York.

17. *Télé 7 Jours*, Part II by Philippe Garnier. "After Thirty Years, We Found Zorro!"

18. deDienes became famous for being the first to photograph Marilyn Monroe.

19. *TV/Radio Mirror*, April 1967, "They Took Pictures of us falling in love!", by Bob Lucas, p 28.

20. *Picture Life* magazine, September 1959, "In Love with a Wonderful Guy," by Janice Williams as told to Maurine Myers Reminih.

21. The Crocketts moved to Long Beach, California. Guy and Janice visited them in the late 1960s, then eventually lost contact with them.

22. *TV Picture Life* magazine, September 1959, "In Love with a Wonderful Guy," by Janice Williams as told to Maurine Myers Reminih.

23. Popular star of *Hawaii Five-O*, CBS, 1968-80.

24. Sci-Fi/Horror, 1951, aka *The Thing from Another World* stars Kenneth Tobey and a young James Arness (*Gunsmoke*).

25. Télé 7 Jours, Oct. 5-11 1985 by Philippe Garnier. "After Thirty Years, We Found Zorro!"

26. CBS in now at that location.

27. Become a household word after winning Tony Awards for Broadway's *Sweet Charity* and *Cabaret*.

28. On TV from October 1950-December 1951, CBS.

29. The 1932 movie version starred Joan Crawford

30. Coincidently, Bob Kane created Batman, which was inspired by McCulley's Zorro.

31. Later become Universal Studios.

32. The *Studio One* anthologies received an Emmy award in February 1952 for Best Dramatic Show on television.

33. Fairbanks' ranch in Rancho Santa Fe was called Rancho El Zorro.

34. Discovered Barbara Stanwyck.

35. Guy was 6'2 ½" but Hollywood rounds off.

36. Released January 29, 1953.

37. *TV Guide*, April 26-May 2, 1958, "Zorro Foils His Rivals".

38. Ronald Reagan was in *Bedtime for Bonzo*, but not in *Bonzo Goes To College*.

39. Story from June Lockhart, paraphrased as Guy told it to her.

40. *Movie Stars Parade TV Close Ups,* September 1958, Vol. 18, No. 10.

41. Russ's wife, Kaye, died in 1980, and he remarried.

42. Russell Johnson is best known as the professor on the ever-running *Gilligan's Island* in the 1960s.

43. *Télé Sete Jours*, Part I, October 1985. "After Thirty Years, We Found Zorro!"

44. Gave Rock Hudson his start.

45. The Estelle Harman Actors Workshop, Inc., founded 1957, Catalogue 1983-84, Vol. X No. 3, 522 N. LaBrea, Los Angeles, CA 90036.

46. *Gunsmoke* first aired in September 1955 and lasted twenty years. In 1959 Dennis Weaver won his first Emmy for Best Supporting Actor in *Gunsmoke* (CBS). He left the show in 1964.

47. Ninety-seven shows are listed to his credit as director/writer on imdb website on the Internet.

48. Major movie star and pin-up girl of the 1940s.

49. On the air Saturday nights on CBS from April 1955 to-June 30, 1956

50. Janice Williams thinks Guy may have played a small role on *a Alfred Hitchcock Presents*, but Guy kept no written records of the shows he was in, so it is not certain.

51. Aired May 18, 1957.

52. *TV's Top Stars, 1961,* produced by Editors of *TV Radio Mirror Magazine*. p. 55; "Guy Williams, Hero of the Kindergarten Set".

53. This commercial can be seen in the Museum of Radio and Television in New York and Beverly Hills on the video tape of Julie Andrew's *Cinderella*, 1957.

54. http://www.geocities.com/TelevisionCity/Stage/2950/Military/MenOfAnnapolis.htm

55. Complete Encyclopedia of Television from 1947 to 1976

56. As a democrat.

57. Fairbanks' *Mark of Zorro* was a silent film in 1920, and Tyrone Power made the first Zorro film with sound in 1940.

58. Out of Sight, but Not out of Mind", from radio interview with Ken Mayer, *TV Collectors*, July - August 1989.

59. Bob Thomas, *Walt Disney, An American Original*; 1st edition, (New York: Simon and Schuster), p. 242.

60. Robert Anderson of *Trail Dust* Magazine (at Beverly Garland Hollywood Collector's Show)

61. Out of Sight, but Not out of Mind", from radio interview with Ken Mayer, *TV Collectors*, July - August 1989.

62. *Starlog* #114, January 1987, "Guy Williams, Relaxed, Retired, and 'Lost in Space'", interview with Mike Clark in May 1986.

63. "What I like about Zorro," by Guy Williams; *Zorro Newsletter* 1958

64. *The Philadelphia Inquirer, TV Programs and Personalities*, Week of Jan. 5, 1958, "Zip-Zip-Zip Stands for Small Fry Idol".

65. *The Philadelphia Inquirer, TV Programs and Personalities*, Week of Jan. 5, 1958, "Zip-Zip-Zip Stands for Small Fry Idol".

66. The drug store where actors liked to hang out and meet, made famous by tales of Lana Turner being discovered there.

67. Popular Italian restaurant on Sunset Boulevard across from Schwab's Drug Store, no longer exists.

68. Episodes #11 "Double Trouble For Zorro" and # 12 "Luckiest Swordsman Alive", and #70, "An Affair of Honor", because of his skill with a sword.

69. Leonard Maltin's *Movie and Video Guide*, 1998 Edition; A Signet Book, Published by Penguin Group; New York, NY, 10014.

70. *TV Life*, "Has Zorro Fouled-up Guy Williams?", July 12, 1958.

71. This famous mantra of maestros is recited in *Saramouche* by actor John Dehner.

72. *Télé Sete Jours*, Octorber 1985, by Philippe Garnier. "After Thirty Years, We Found Zorro!"

73. Curtis, Sandra, *Zorro Unmasked, The Official History*, 1998, Hyperion NY, p 131.

74. *TV Radio Mirror* Magazine, January 1958.

75. Vicente Gomez' movie credits at this time included the beautiful guitar music in *Blood and Sand* starring Tyrone Power in 1941.

76. Bill Lee was another singer for Diego.

77. *Zorro Unmasked, The Official History*, by Sandra Curtis, 1998, Hyperion, NY.

78. *The Philadelphia Inquirer*, Jan 5, 1958, *TV Programs and Personalities* "Zip Zip Zip Stands for Small Fry Idol" by Harry Harris.

79. "Fred Cavens...impressive". from Section of *The Philadelphia Inquirer*, Week of Jan. 5, 1958; *TV Programs and Personalities* "Zip-Zip-Zip Stands for Small Fry Idol" by Harry Harris.

80. Ken Mayer interview. WBZ radio talk show, September 1983, Boston, MA.

81. *Zorro Television Companion: A Critical Appreciation*, (galleys) by Gerry Dooley, McFarland, 2005.

82. *The Wonderful World of Disney Television, A Complete History*, by Bill Cotter: Disney Enterprises, Inc., Hyperion, New York, 1997, First Edition, p. 202

83. In 1992 Disney hired Color Imagining to make a colorized version of all the black and white episodes.

84. *"Zorro Unmasked,"* an interview by Stephen Kahn, for *Calling All Girls*, 1958, p. 45.

85. Mike Clark's interview for *Starlog* #114, January 1987 issue. "Guy Williams, Relaxed, Retired, and 'Lost in Space.'"

86. Mike Clark's interview for *Starlog* #114, January 1987 issue. "Guy Williams, Relaxed, Retired, and 'Lost in Space.'"

87. *TV Guide*, April 26 - May 2, 1958 edition, "Zorro Foiled His Rivals".

88. Don Diamond is also fondly remembered in two other long-running TV series, as "El Toro" on *The Adventures of Kit Carson* (1951-55) and "Crazy Cat" on *F - Troop* (1965-67).

89. "Out of sight, Out of Mind" an interview with Ken Mayer in *The TV Collector*, July-August 1989, p. 21

90. Guy had a birth mark, usually hereditary, called poliosos, which is a patch of white due to lack of pigment, not related to Guy's cause of death. His son, Steve has one on top of his head.

91. "Zorro Unmasked", An interview by Stephen Kahn for magazine *Calling All Girls, 1958. p. 44*

92. Actors were paid extra for stunts.

93. *Starlog* #114, interview with Mike Clark, January 1987 issue."Guy Williams, Relaxed, Retired, and 'Lost in Space.'"

94. *Starlog* #114, interview with Mike Clark, January 1987 issue."Guy Williams, Relaxed, Retired, and 'Lost in Space.'"

95. From a personal letter from the Walt Disney Archives in Burbank, CA, June 20, 1989, by Paula M. Sigman.

96. Ken Mayer interview. WBZ radio talk show, September 1983, Boston, MA.

97. "Has Zorro Fouled-Up Guy Williams" by Jack Holland, *TV Life*, July 12, 1958, p 5

98. "Out of Sight but not Out of Mind", T*he TV Collector* July-August, 1989, p 21

99. From interview on *Good Morning America*, Sept 8, 1983.

100. Michael Forest is best remembered for his role as "Apollo" in *Star Trek*. He was in *Castaway* (2001) starring Tom Hanks.

101. Episode #4, at Mission San Luis Rey in Oceanside.

102. *North County Times*, July 31, 1957, "Old Mission"

103. *Longview Daily News*, December 27, 1958 "Guy Williams Stars on TV as Zorro, Don Diego", by Erskine Johnson.

104. *Zorro Unmasked*, an interview by Stephen Kahn, for *Calling All Girls*, 1958, p. 45.

105. *TV Programs and Personalities*, Week of January 5, 1958, Section of *The Philadelphia Inquirer*, "Zip, Zip, Zip Stands for Small Fry Idol"

106. A *Zorro 7-Up Newsletter*, September 1957.

107. *Starlog* #114, January 1987 issue, Mike Clark interview. "Guy Williams, Relaxed, Retired, and 'Lost in Space.'"

108. *Starlog* #114, January 1987 issue, Mike Clark interview. "Guy Williams, Relaxed, Retired, and 'Lost in Space.'"

109. "Zorro Unmasked", an interview by Stephan Kahn for *Calling All Girls*, 1958, p. 46.

110. "Out of Sight But Not out of Mind", *TV Collector*, July-August 1989, transcript from radio interview by Ken Mayer, Boston Radio, 1983.

111. A second unit director for Clint Eastwood since early 1970s, and sometime Director

112. Used in *Mississippi Gambler* as well as earlier movies.

113. "Mark on Zorro" by Harriet Van Horne, April 11, 1958; *New York Times*.

114. Corky Randall staged a scene very similar to this for Antonio Banderas' double in *The Mask of Zorro*, 1997.

115. Diamond Decorator

116. Episode 16 - shot late Sept. 57- Aired January 23, 1958

117. Disney newsletter in the Disney Archives.

118. Buddy Van Horn is an honored inductee in the Hollywood Stuntmen's Hall of Fame. On May 19, 2002 at the World Stunt Awards, he received The Taurus Honorary Award for his lifetime achievements in stunts on television and in movies.

119. Screen Actor's Guild, the actor's union.

120. Tony Russel played Zorro in Spain for Italian Production, *Giuramento di Zorro* (*The Oath of Zorro*) aka *El Zorro Cabalgo Otra Vez* (*The Fox Rides Again*). He was famous in Europe for gladiator-type movies. In the 1970s he made the dinner theater circuit touring the country in plays.

121. *Daily Variety*, Friday, January 2, 1959.

122. This episode aired May 28, 1959, the day before John F. Kennedy's birthday.

123. This is not the same Bob Stevenson who was Guy's friend from *Men of Annapolis*.

124. Mike Clark interview of May 1986 for *Starlog* #114, January 1987."Guy Williams, Relaxed, Retired, and 'Lost in Space.'"

125. *TV Guide Fall Preview* , Sept. 14-20, 1957

126. *Hollywood Reporter*, Thursday, Oct 24, 1957, Trendex Ratings.

127. *Hollywood Reporter*, October 14, 1957

128. *TV Programs and Personalities*, Week of January 5, 1958, Section of *The Philadelphia Inquirer*, "Zip-Zip-Zip Stands for Small Fry Idol"

129. *Sunday News, Tuning in on TV,* "Z Man Guy Williams leaves his mark as star of TV's Zorro" by May Okon, Aug. 2, 1959. p 4.

130. *The Anaheim Bulletin*, May 29, 1958, Thursday

131. *The Anaheim Bulletin*, p. 8, Wednesday, May 28, 1958.

132. No longer there. A stage was set up were Rancho Del Zolalo restaurant is today.

133. August 13, 1958, cover photo of Anne Frank.

134. *Zorro Unmasked, The Official History*, by S. R. Curtis, Introduction, p 2. Hyperion, New York, 1998. First edition.

135. *The Wonderful World of Disney Television, A Complete History,* by Bill Cotter. Hyperion, NY, 1997 .

136. *Anaheim Bulletin*, Thursday , May 22, 1958

137. 1958, directed by Lewis R. Foster. Aired on TV in two parts as *Comancho.*

138. Britt was the bachelor of the cast, until he married Diane in 1958.

139. *Zorro Unmasked, The Official History*, by Sandra Curtis, 1998, Hyperion NY

140. *TV Radio Life*, January 4, 1958, "Will Zorro Be Another Davy Crockett Smash ", p. 5.

141. *Liberty*, Canada's Young Family Magazine, June 1959. "How I *Zorro*ed To TV Fame"

142. Interview with Mike Clark in May 1986 for *Starlog* #114, January 1987 issue. "Guy Williams, Relaxed, Retired, and 'Lost in Space.'"

143. Footage shown on the Biography of Zorro on A& E network.

144. *The Wonderful World of Disney Television, A Complete History*, by Bill Cotter: Disney Enterprises, Inc., Hyperion, New York, 1997, First Edition.

145. *TV Picture Life* magazine, September 1959

146. In 1959, Kendall-White Agency, 8923 Sunset Blvd.

147. *Movie Stars Parade Magazine*, September 1958, "Four Faces of Love", features four different celebrities.

148. *Movie Stars TV Close-ups*, September 1958, "*Four Faces of Love*" .

149. *TV Life*, "Has Zorro Fouled Up Guy Williams?" by Jack Holland, p. 4. July 12, 1958.

150. Four Faces of Love", *Movie Stars Parade*, September 1958

151. *Movie Stars Parade* Magazine, September 1958, "Four Faces of Love"

152. Canada's *Liberty* magazine, June 1959, "How I 'Zorroed to TV Fame" .p. 44, by Guy Williams as told to Bob Willet.

153. Fleitz Landing was renamed Cabrillo Way Landing in 1998.

154. Guy bought the Oceana in 1958 while he was living on Harper St. He moved his family to Hillside Drive in 1959.

155. *TV Guide* " Zorro Foiled his Rivals" April 26- May 2 1958, edition.

156. *The Star Weekly Magazine*, May 24, 1958

157. *Zorro Television Companion: A Critical Appreciation,* by Gerry Dooley, McFarland, 2005.

158. *A Dream is A Wish Your Heart Makes, My Story*, by Annette Funicello with Patricia Romanowski, Hyperion, New York, 1994.

159. *Zorro Television Companion: A Critical Appreciation,* by Gerry Dooley, McFarland, 2005.

160. Aired January 8, 1958

161. Wife of actor Joseph Cotten.

162. Disney Archives

163. Name after Tubersio Vasquez, an outlaw, who hid in these rocks in the 1800s, believed by some to be the inspiration for McCulley's fictitious El Zorro.

164. Call sheets in the Walt Disney Archives.

165. *Daily Variety*, November 25, 1958.

166. Jonathan Harris would later work with Guy on *Lost In Space*.

167. *New York Journal-American*, Sat. May 16, 1959, "Rescues 'Zorro' Can't Make"

168. *Daily Variety*, "Just for Variety" Tuesday, December 23, 1958.

169. *The Wonderful World of Disney Television, A Complete History*, by Bill Cotter, 1997 Disney Enterprises, Inc., Hyperion, New York, First Edition, p. 63.

170. Disney Archives, Production Notes

171. *The Wonderful World of Disney Television, A Complete History*, by Bill Cotter, 1997 Disney Enterprises, Inc., Hyperion, New York, First Edition

172. Canada's young family magazine: *Liberty*, June1959.

173. *Movie Stars TV Close Ups*, April 1959.

174. *Daily Variety*, Monday, June 1, 1959 ("Who's Where")

175. *The Wonderful World of Disney Television, A Complete History*, by Bill Cotter: Disney Enterprises, Inc., Hyperion, New York, 1997, First Edition

176. *New York Journal-American*, Sat. May 16, 1959, "Rescues 'Zorro' Can't Make"

177. "Best Foods May Get ABC Bounce," *New York Post* (circa Summer 1959)

178. *The Wonderful World of Disney Television, A Complete History*, by Bill Cotter: Disney Enterprises, Inc., Hyperion, New York, 1997, First Edition, p. 203

179. Bill Anderson passed away in 1998.

180. *Daily Variety*, June 18, 1959 ("Who's Where")

181. Mike Clark's interview in May 1986 for *Starlog* #114, January 1987 issue. "Guy Williams, Relaxed, Retired, and 'Lost in Space.'"

182. Walt planned to make a movie out of the series of episodes Cesar Romero was in.

183. *Daily Variety*; Wednesday, Feb. 3, 1960, "Out of the Tube"

184. Peggy and Gene Sheldon separated in 1968.

185. *Captain Sindbad* press release, 1963.

186. Guy was referring to his desire to get out of the contract and move on with his career, now that *Zorro* was canceled.

187. Ultimately only four were filmed.

188. They are not related.

189. RCA was the parent company of NBC.

190. *Beating The Odds, The Untold Story behind the Rise of ABC*, by Leonard H. Goldenson with Marvin J. Wolf

191. *The Wonderful World of Disney Television, A Complete History*, by Bill Cotter: Disney Enterprises, Inc., Hyperion, New York, 1997, First Edition, pp. 66 and 203

192. *The Charlotte News*, July 9, 1966.

193. *The Disney Films*, by Leonard Maltin, third printing, Crown Publisher; NY. 1973.

194. "When Guy Hisses the Villain—He Means It" by Michael Fessier, *TV Guide*, September 24, 1966, p. 26.

195. Bridget Boland also wrote the screenplay for *Damon and Pythias*.

196. Balsam lived there for many years and died in the hotel in 1996

197. The movie that would be shot next in Germany in which Lawrence was also cast.

198. A popular Steve McQueen film shot in Germany around this time.

199. Best known for her performance in *The Guns of Navarone* with Gregory Peck.

200. Dell had a childhood career, playing in the TV series *Arny* with Hersel Bernardi, and in *Tammy Tell Me True* with young Bill Mumy.

201. An article by May Mann in a movie magazine during *Lost in Space*, titled unknown.

202. Later to be in *Lost in Space* with Guy.

203. Born April 22, 1899, died April 16 1984.

204. All Haskin's quotes from *The Director's Guild of American Oral History*, Byron Haskin, Interviewed by Joe Adamson. The Scarecrow Press, Inc. Metuchen, N.J. & London 1984, p. 246.

205. Zavitts and Byron Haskin had worked together on *His Majesty O'Keefe*.

206. The actors were finished filming, but Haskin stayed to finish the special effects.

207. Pedro Armendáriz died shortly after this movie was made on June 18, 1963, by suicide. His son, Pedro Armendáriz, Jr. was in *The Mask Of Zorro* in 1998.

208. Mike Clark's interview for *Starlog* #114, January 1987 issue. "Guy Williams, Relaxed, Retired, and 'Lost in Space.'"

209. Called *Il Tiranno di Siracusa*.

210. A large company that makes sound systems and was the first to make VCR machines in the early 1950s for studios, then in 1977 produced VHS/VCR machines for home use.

211. Aired September 12, 1959 - January 16, 1973, NBC.

212. *Bonanza, A Viewer's Guide to the TV Legend* by David R. Greenland. Foreword by David Dortort, creator and producer, R&G Productions, Hillside, IL. 1997.p. 66

213. Guy was in five shows: # 159 - "*Return To Honor*" on March 22, 1964; # 161 - "*The Roper*" on April 5, 1964; # 163, "*Los Campaneros*" on April 19, 1964; # 166 "*The Pressure Game*" on May 10, 1964; and #167, "*The Triangle*", on May 17, 1964.

214. Guy was back at Disney's Golden Oaks Ranch in Placerita, CA to film some scenes from this episode.

215. Ken Mayer interview. WBZ radio talk show, September 1983, Boston, MA.

216. A rare statement about making *Bonanza* to Mike Clark for *Starlog*, issue 114, January 1987. "Guy Williams, Relaxed, Retired, and 'Lost in Space.'"

217. Later called the Jupiter II.

218. Panel discussion at the *Lost in Space* Reunion, October 16, 1997, the Museum of Radio and Television, Beverly Hills, CA.

219. *Lost in Space Forever* by Joel Eisner & Barry Magen; Windsong Publishing, Inc., Staunton, VA 1992, Forward by June Lockhart

220. Star Con panel discussion, July 1997, Pasadena, CA

221. *Lost in Space Forever*, by Joel Eisner & Barry Magen, Wingsong Publishing, , Inc., Staunton, VA, 1992, p. 45

222. *Lost in Space Forever*, by Joel Eisner & Barry Magen' Wingsong Publishing, Inc., Staunton, VA 1992. p. 63

223. *Lost in Space Forever*, by Joel Eisner & Barry Magen' Wingsong Publishing, Inc., Staunton, VA 1992.

224. Copies are sold in video at collectors shows.

225. He was also the announcer for *Zorro* for Disney.

226. His and June's hours.

227. Interview with Mike Clark for *Starlog* magazine, January 1987 issue #114. "Guy Williams, Relaxed, Retired, and 'Lost in Space.'"

228. *Lost in Space Forever*, by Joel Eisner & Barry Magen' Wingsong Publishing, Inc., Staunton, VA 1992.

229. *Lost in Space Forever* by Joel Eisner & Barry Magen Wingsong Publishing, Inc. Staunton, VA 1992.

230. *TV Guide*, Sept 24, 1966, "When Guy Hisses the Villain—He Means it" by Michael Fessier, Jr.

231. *Starlog* #114, January 1987, "Guy Williams, Relaxed, Retired, and 'Lost in Space.'"

232. *Lost In Space 25th Anniversary Tribute* book by James Van Hise, 1990, Pioneer book, Las Vegas, NV.

233. *Lost In Space Forever* by Joel Eisner & Barry Magen, Wingsong Publishing, Inc. Staunton, VA 1992.

234. *Lost in Space Forever,* by Joel Eisner and Barry Magen, Windsong Publishing, Inc., Staunton, VA, 1992.

235. *TV Guide,* September 24, 1966 "When Guy Hisses the Villian He Means It" by Mike Fessier, Jr. p. 24

236. Mike Clark's Interview for *Starlog* #114, January 1987. "Guy Williams, Relaxed, Retired, and 'Lost in Space.'"

237. *Lost in Space Forever"* Joel Eisner & Barry Magen; Windsong Publishing, Inc.: Staunton, VA 1992

238. an abbreviated name for Pacific Coast Highway 1.

239. Sometime during the run of *Lost In Space* June Lockhart and Guy made a guest appearance on the daytime version of a TV show called *You Don't Say.* with host Tom Kennedy.

240. *Los Angeles Times,* March 5, 1967, "Camera Angles", "He's an earthbound spaceman", by Aleene MacMinn.

241. *Lost in Space Forever* by Joel Eisner and Barry Magen, Windsong Publishing, Inc.: Staunton, VA 1992, with forward by June Lockhart

242. Wright King played Dr. Galen in *Planet of the Apes.*

243. *Lost In Space 25th Anniversary Tribute Book,* by James Van Hise, 1990, Las Vegas

244. Blatey wrote *A Shot in the Dark* (1963), co wrote *The Great Bank Robbery* (1969) with Blake Edwards, then after a string of comedies he wrote the box office smash *The Exorcist* (1973).

245. April 1967 *TV Radio Mirror,* "Guy Williams and his beautiful Janice had a Truly 'Model' Courtship'!"

246. *Lost in Space Bonus,* "Guy Williams: Oh, For the life of A Sailor! ", magazine article

247. Ken Mayer interview. WBZ radio talk show, September 1983, Boston, MA.

248. made of almonds, various other nuts, citron candies, raisons, honey, and wheat flour then poured onto rice paper to set.

249. The long stays in Europe, his illness in Germany, and his birthday coming late in the year, delayed Steve's graduation.

250. Bob Stevenson gave up acting and held office as a city councilman of Los Angeles.

251. Star of TV show *Ironside,* which Don Burnett's second wife, Barbara Anderson was on from 1967-1971.

252. Janice was beginning to get into Interior Decorating.

253. Interview in *Revista Canal TV,* Número 770, April 7-13, 1973.

254. From Artículo del diario La Razón del Domingo 1 de April 1973: *LA LLEGADA DEL ZORRO - (Zorro Has Arrived)*

255. In 1979 he won the Silver Medal in Individual Foil in the Pan American Games, after coming in fourth in 1975 in the same division.

256. Small guitarlike instrument.

257. Specially treated leather that is pleated in different patterns to make belts, reins, whips, etc.

258. *Revista* (magazine) Canal TV, Número 771, del 14 al 20 de Abril de 1973

259. August 3, 1973, p. 3.

260. *National Inquirer,* December 30, 1973, "Forgotten In America, Guy (Zorro) Williams Is Making his Mark as a Hero in Argentina"

261. From *Revista* Canal TV número 785, Del 21 al 27 de julio de 1973.

262. Buenos Aires, *Clarin,* p. 9, Saturday, July 14, 1973.

263. Owned by Jerry Lewis, no longer there.

264. *Alpha Control* official magazine of LISA, by Glenn Ware.

265. Norman Foster started out in New York, then moved to Hollywood, then made movies in Mexico in the 1940's, then came back to Hollywood.

266. From Mike Clark interview for *Starlog #114*, January 1987. "Guy Williams, Relaxed, Retired, and 'Lost in Space.'"

267. A racetrack for bicycle racing, located in Palermo Woods.

268. *TV Guia*, January 15, 1975. "Guy Williams: 'Vine Para Quedarme'"/"I Came to Stay"

269. Not enough investors believed in it, and the money was never acquired.

270. *La Nacion*, January 15, 1975.

271. Fernando Lupiz and Britt Lomond, Monastario of the TV series, coincidentally, have the *same* birthday, April 12, 1953 and April 12, 1925, respectively. In Argentina, the name is spelled Monasterio.

272. A large outdoor arena for rodeos and livestock shows.

273. Videla and Massera were indicted twenty eight years later in March 2004 for baby theft.

274. Loretta Young was in love with Clark Gable in the 1930s when they made several movies together.

275. Don Petrie is the son of multi-award winning director/producer Dan Petrie and Dorothea Petrie, also a producer.

276. Buenos Aires' *Radiolandia 2000*, Sept 16, 1977.

277. A beautiful upscale city north of Buenos Aires with many boat clubs along the coast where Guy liked to go sailing.

278. *Radiolandia 2000*, Dec. 30, 1977

279. His manager

280. A public relations man for the circus.

281. Janice did not arrived in Argentina in January as the Argentina article had quoted Guy as saying.

282. Holy Week in Tandíl brings hundreds of people from neighboring cities and countries to see the reenactment of the Stations of the Cross. This was an advantage for the circus.

283. "¡ME QUEDO EN LA ARGENTINA!" pp. 14 & 15 *TV Guia* March 1978

284. *Daily Popular*, -No. 4, Thurs. May 11, 1978, "¡El ZORRO-ATRAPADO EN LA ARGENTINA! Con su carino, nuestros pibes lograraon lo imposible"

285. A large exposition with exhibits, including cattle, and attractions similar to a County Fair.

286. *ANTENA*, magazine, 12-26-78

287. Revista *ANTENA*, 12-26-78, "The Wife of Zorro Goes Home Alone"

288. A book by Diego Curubeto, published in Argentina in 1993, about Guy and other Hollywood celebrities who had visited Argentina.

289. *Corrientes*, Viernes 4 de Mayo de 1979, "El 12, el "Zorro" en el Club Córdoba.

290. In 1999, Steve began using his Screen Actor's Guild name, Guy Williams, Jr.

291. TV's news anchorman, who married Guy's friend, Noley, after her first husband, Bill Walsh of Disney Studios died in January 1975.

292. Well known local hillbilly type in a cowboy hat who advertises his used car lot to hillbilly music and at that time used live elephants, tigers, and other animals for attention.

293. cardio vascular accident.

294. *TV Guia*, Buenos Aires, 1982

295. Starlog #114, Jan. 1987, interview by Mike Clark. "Guy Williams, Relaxed, Retired, and 'Lost in Space.'"

296. *Starlog #114*, January 1987 "Guy Williams, Relaxed, Retired, and 'Lost in Space.'" an interview by Mike Clark, conducted in May 1986.

297. *Starlog*, January 1987 "Guy Williams, Relaxed, Retired, and 'Lost in Space.'" an interview by Mike Clark, conducted in May 1986.

298. *Starlog #114*, January 1987, p. 22; "Guy Williams. Relaxed, Retired & "Lost in Space"

299. "Out of Sight But Not Out of Mind" in *The TV Collector*, July-August 1989

300. They later moved to Corrientes Av. and San Martin Street under the name of Puente Bros.

301. Not the same Juan Carlos who played outside of Channel 13.

302. They did not have VCRs yet to tape TV shows.

303. Guy's last agent, Lew Deuser.

304. Part I, "After Thirty Years, We Found Zorro!", *Télé 7 Jours*, Oct. 5-11, 1985

305. Mike Clark interview, May 1986, for *Starlog* #114, Jan. 1987, "Guy Williams, Relaxed, Retired, and 'Lost in Space'".

306. Part I, "*Télé 7 Jours*, Oct. 5-11, 1985."After Thirty Years, We Found Zorro!"

307. Guy was referring to Anthony (Tony) Russo, but said Anthony Caruso, instead, who was also on the show.

308. Garnier did not know that these were Pat's spare glasses, which Guy was using until he got his own.

309. Part II, "After Thirty Years, We Found Zorro", by Philippe Garnier, October 1985 issue for *Tele 7 Jours*, France.

310. This would be late December until sometime in March, with two to three weeks off in July, (winter), plus holidays.

311. In the United States it would be called the third floor. A business is on the first floor or ground level.

312. "El Zorro Left A Mark on Our Hearts", *Ahora* magazine, May 18, 1989, #293.

313. Strother Martin died August 1, 1980

314. 1981, starring George Hamilton , comedy spoof.

315. "The Strange Phenomenon Still Alive", *Radiolandia 2000*, 1987

316. "El Zorro Hoy en Argentina" (Zorro today in Argentina). *TV Guia*, July 1987

317. He was 63.

318. "El Zorro Hoy en Argentina". July 1987, *TV Guia*

319. "The Brave Zorro Appears", *La Semana*, July 11, 1987.

320. *LA SEMANA*, "Laparece El Bravo Zorro" by Cora Laso, July 11, 1987

321. Interview with Mike Clark for *Starlog* #114, January 1987, "Guy Williams, Relaxed, Retired, and 'Lost in Space'".

322. "El Zorro Left A Mark on Our Hearts", *Ahora* magazine, May 18, 1989, #293.

323. Guy Williams, El Zorro, Has Died

324. The bottom of Argentina's economy dropped out.

325. June father was actor, Gene Lockhart.

326. *Radiolandia 2000*, May 11, 1989, "La Misteriosa Muerte de El Zorro" ("The Mysterious Death of El Zorro")

327. Aracelli and Fernando stayed for statements to the press after Pat had left.

328. *Daily News*, New York, May 17, 1989

329. *Perry's Time Machine Special*, a tribute to Guy Williams, produced and directed by Perry Corvese, 1995; P/F Productions.

330. Actual date unknown.

331. Star Con, July 1997, Pasadena , CA. Panel included Dick Tufeld, Bob May, Angela Cartwright, Marta Kristin, and June Lockhart.

332. Guy's star is centrally located at 7080 Hollywood Blvd at La Brea, only about a mile from where he lived in the Hollywood Hills.

333. Pictures from this ceremony can be found on several Guy Williams websites.

334. "the children of the world cry"

335. *TV Guia*, May 17, 1989;"Lo Lloran los Niños del Mundo"

336. Episode # 42 -"Amnesty for Zorro"

Index

Printed in the United States
88607LV00003B/1-18/A

9 781593 930165